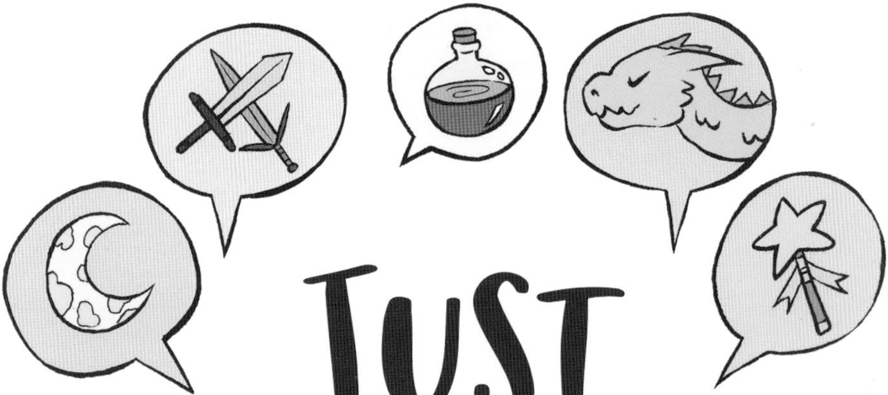

# JUST PRETEND

# JUST
# PRETEND

## TORI SHARP

**L B**

Little, Brown and Company

New York  Boston

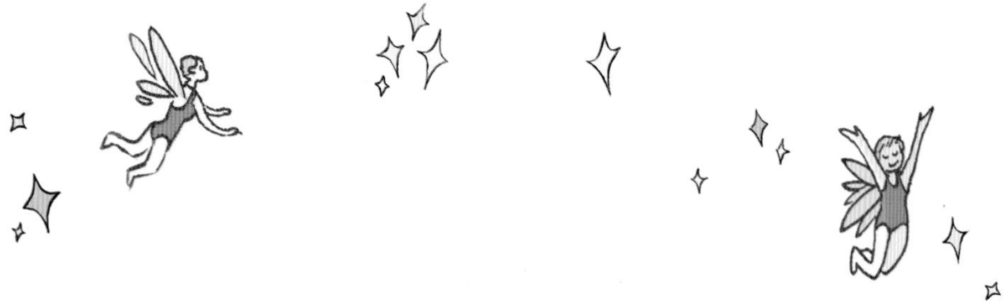

ABOUT THIS BOOK

This book was edited by Andrea Colvin and designed by Angelie Yap under the art direction of Sasha Illingworth. The production was supervised by Bernadette Flinn, and the production editor was Lindsay Walter-Greaney. The text was set in Anime Ace 2.0 BB, and the display type is Chin Up Buttercup Cutecaps.

 • Little, Brown and Company • Hachette Book Group • 1290 Avenue of the Americas, New York, NY 10104 • Visit us at LBYR.com • First Edition: May 2021 • Little, Brown and Company is a division of Hachette Book Group, Inc. • The Little, Brown name and logo are trademarks of Hachette Book Group, Inc. • The publisher is not responsible for websites (or their content) that are not owned by the publisher. • Library of Congress Cataloging-in-Publication Data • Names: Sharp, Tori, author, illustrator. • Title: Just pretend / Tori Sharp. • Description: First edition. | New York : Little, Brown and Company, 2021. | Summary: "Tori makes up stories all of the time, so she has never lived in just one world. Those stories might just save her when her world seems to crumble"—Provided by publisher. • Identifiers: LCCN 2020022102 (print) | LCCN 2020022103 (ebook) | ISBN 9780316538893 (hardcover) | ISBN 9780316538855 (paperback) | ISBN 9780316538862 (ebook) | ISBN 9780316538879 (ebook other) • Subjects: LCSH: Sharp, Tori—Childhood and youth—Juvenile literature. | Illustrators—United States—Biography—Juvenile literature. | Authors, American—21st century—Biography—Juvenile literature. | Graphic novels—Authorship—Juvenile literature. | Children of divorced parents—United States—Biography—Juvenile literature. | Graphic novels. • Classification: LCC PN6727.S488 Z46 2021 (print) | LCC PN6727.S488 (ebook) | DDC 741.5/973 [B]—dc23 • LC record available at https://lccn.loc.gov/2020022102 • LC ebook record available at https://lccn.loc.gov/2020022103 • ISBNs: 978-0-316-53889-3 (hardcover), 978-0-316-53885-5 (pbk.), 978-0-316-53886-2 (ebook), 978-0-316-59211-6 (ebook), 978-0-316-59212-3 (ebook) • PRINTED IN CHINA • APS • Hardcover: 10 9 8 7 6 5 4 3 2 1 • Paperback: 10 9 8 7 6 5 4 3 2 1

FOR TAYLOR.
I CAN'T IMAGINE A BETTER BFF.

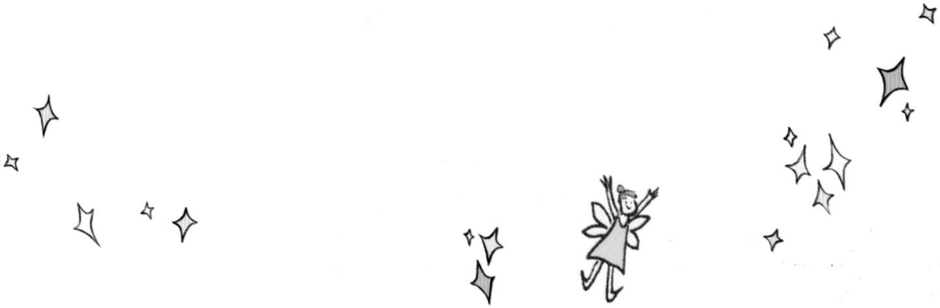

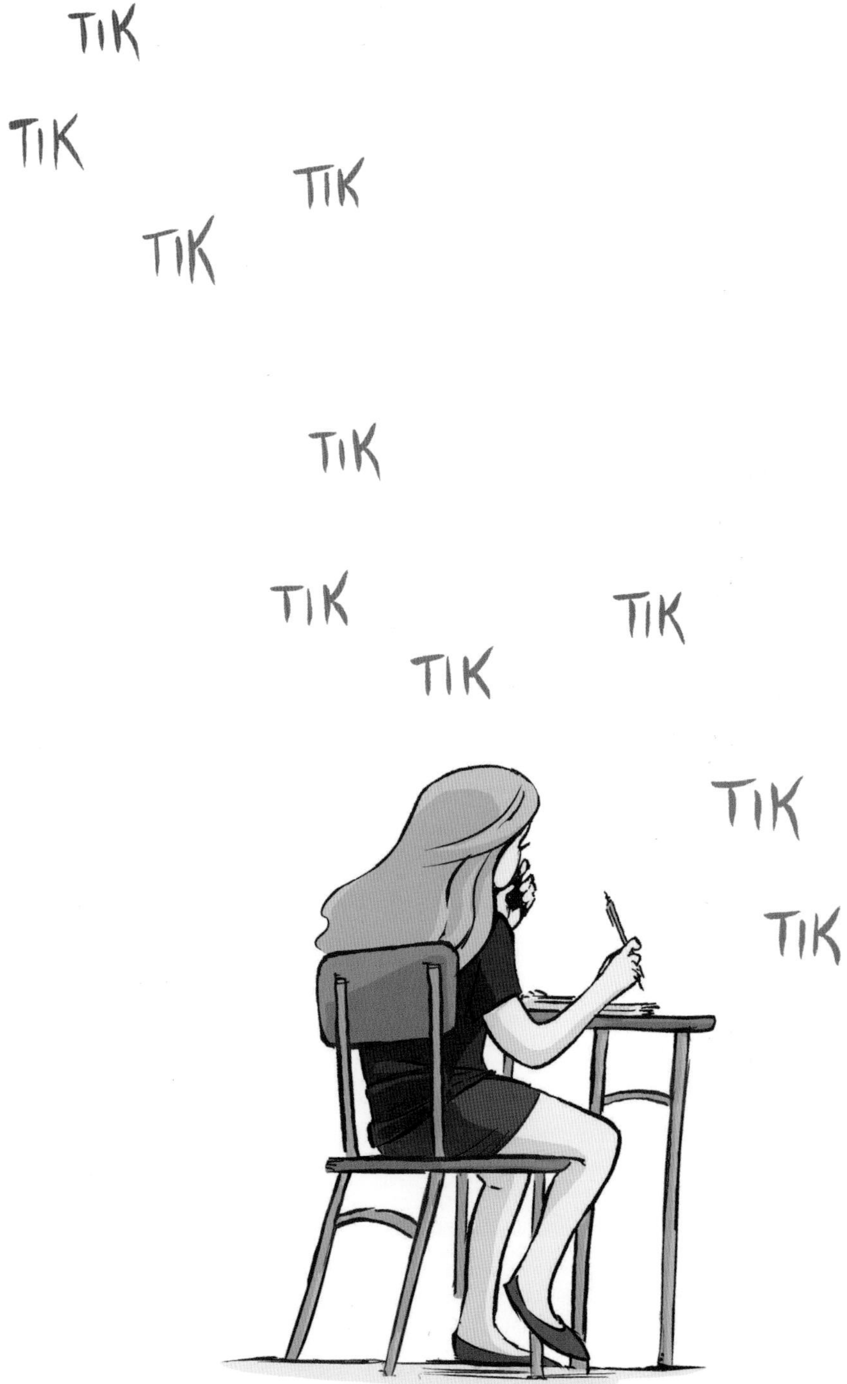

TIK
TIK
TIK
TIK
TIK
TIK
TIK
TIK
TIK
TIK

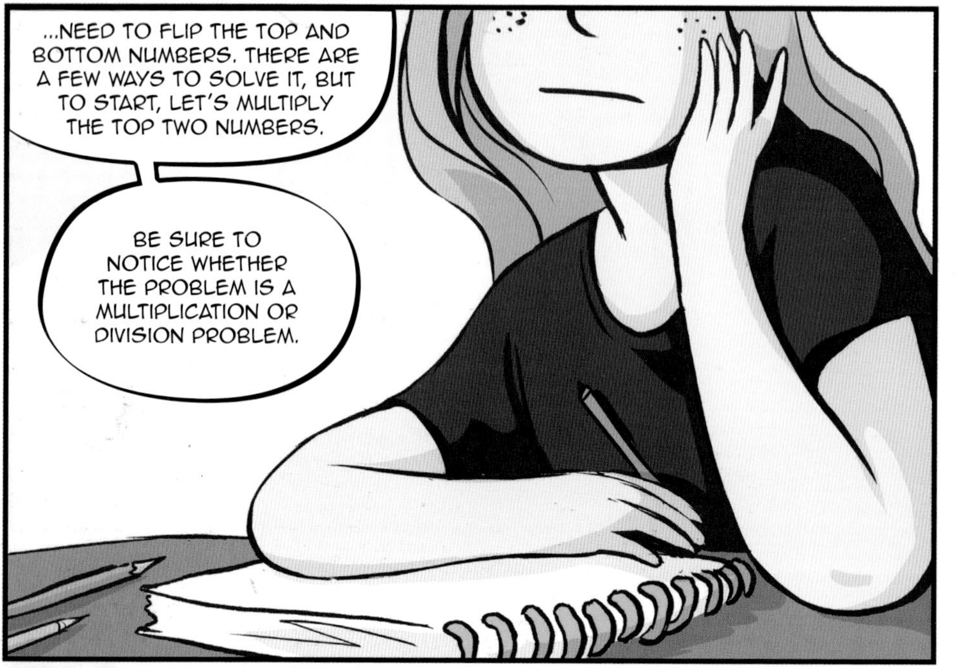
...NEED TO FLIP THE TOP AND BOTTOM NUMBERS. THERE ARE A FEW WAYS TO SOLVE IT, BUT TO START, LET'S MULTIPLY THE TOP TWO NUMBERS.
BE SURE TO NOTICE WHETHER THE PROBLEM IS A MULTIPLICATION OR DIVISION PROBLEM.

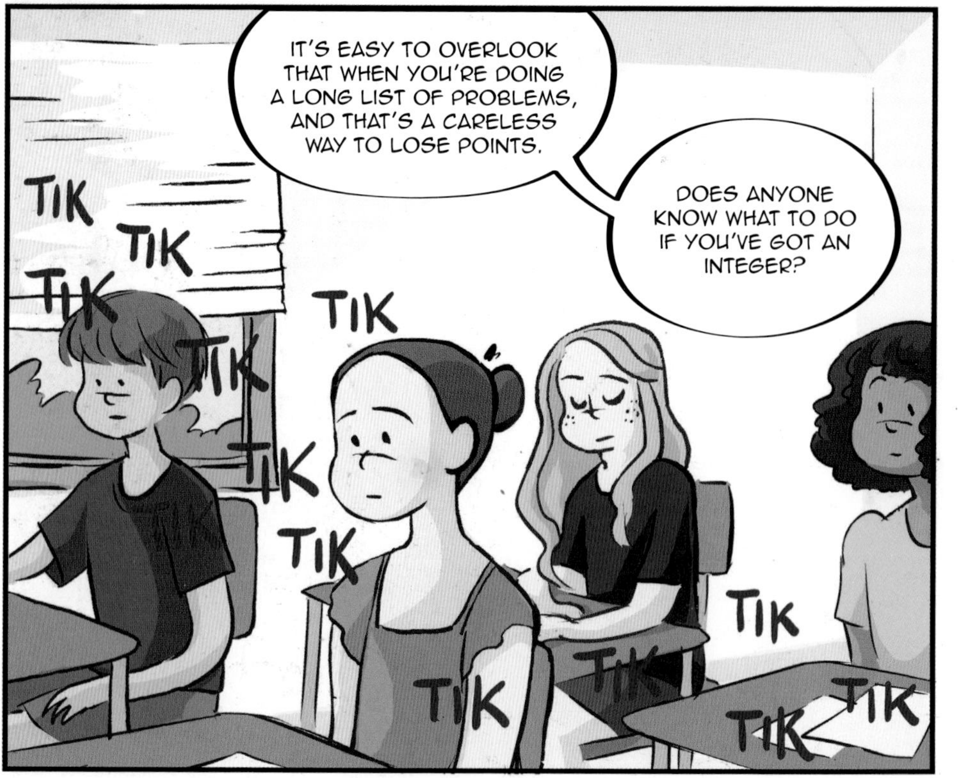
IT'S EASY TO OVERLOOK THAT WHEN YOU'RE DOING A LONG LIST OF PROBLEMS, AND THAT'S A CARELESS WAY TO LOSE POINTS.
DOES ANYONE KNOW WHAT TO DO IF YOU'VE GOT AN INTEGER?
TIK TIK TIK TIK TIK TIK TIK TIK TIK TIK TIK TIK

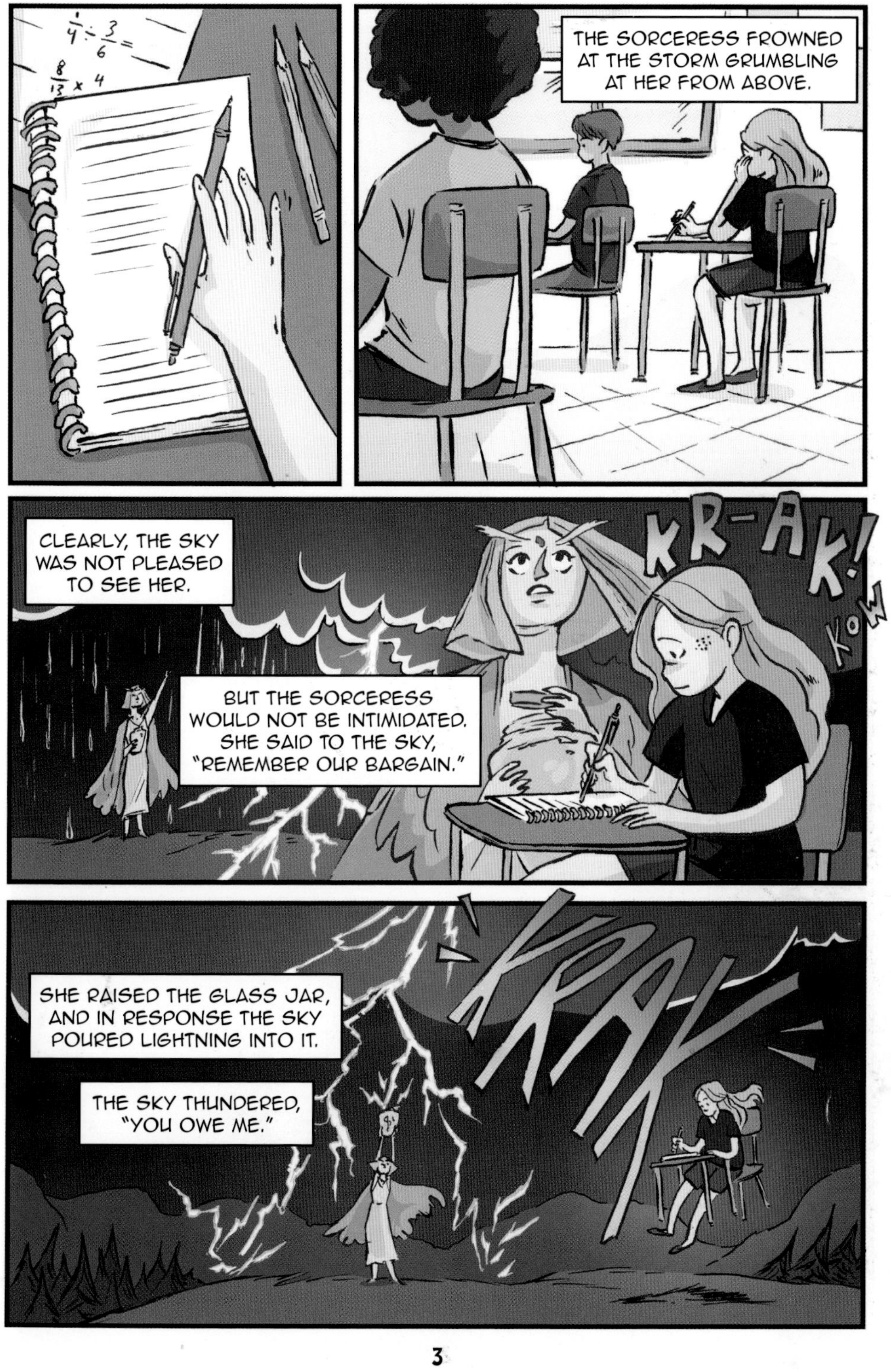
1/4 ÷ 3/6 =
8/13 x 4
THE SORCERESS FROWNED AT THE STORM GRUMBLING AT HER FROM ABOVE.
CLEARLY, THE SKY WAS NOT PLEASED TO SEE HER.
KR-AK!
KOW
BUT THE SORCERESS WOULD NOT BE INTIMIDATED. SHE SAID TO THE SKY, "REMEMBER OUR BARGAIN."
KRAK
SHE RAISED THE GLASS JAR, AND IN RESPONSE THE SKY POURED LIGHTNING INTO IT.
THE SKY THUNDERED, "YOU OWE ME."

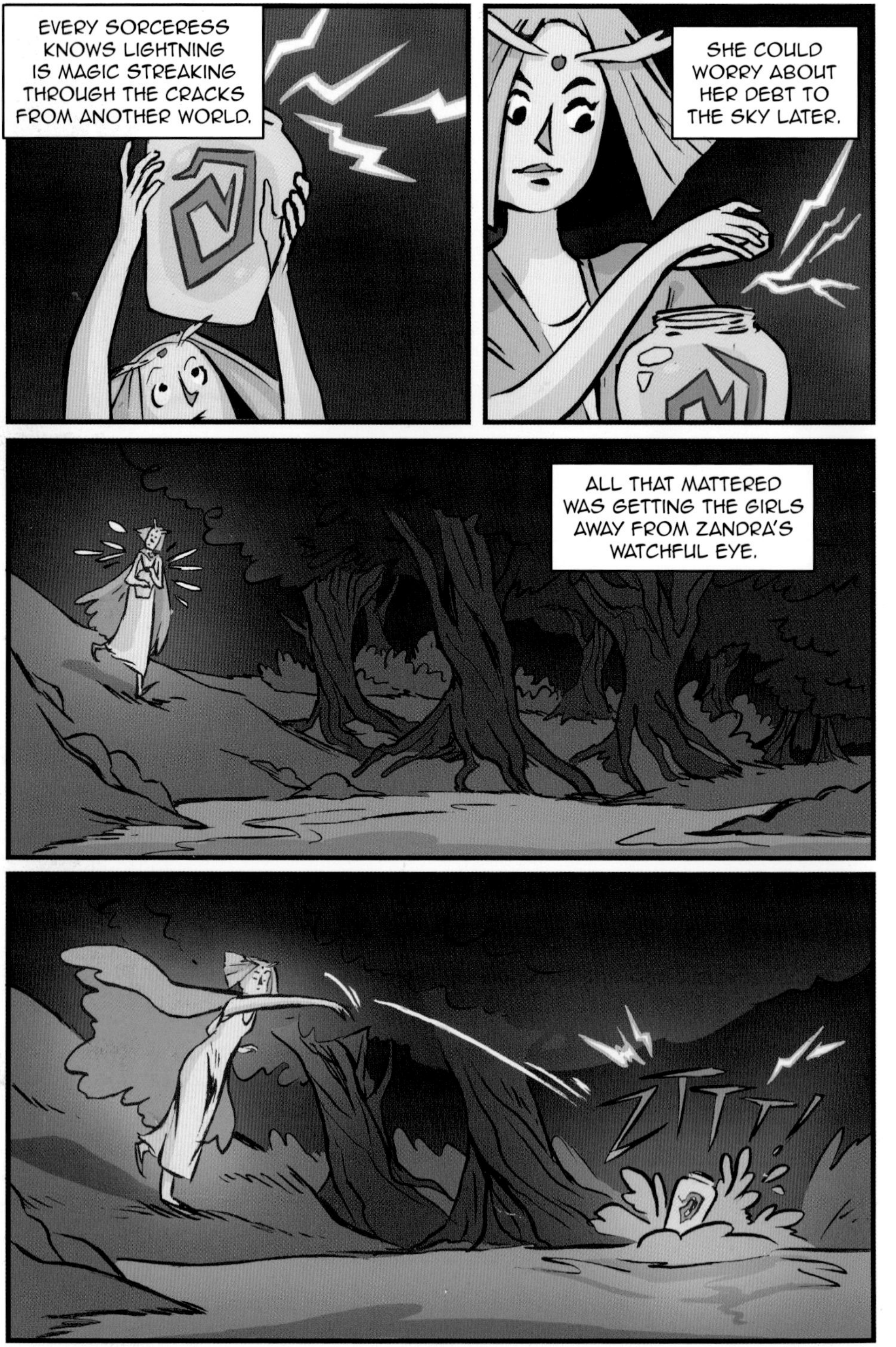
EVERY SORCERESS KNOWS LIGHTNING IS MAGIC STREAKING THROUGH THE CRACKS FROM ANOTHER WORLD.
SHE COULD WORRY ABOUT HER DEBT TO THE SKY LATER.
ALL THAT MATTERED WAS GETTING THE GIRLS AWAY FROM ZANDRA'S WATCHFUL EYE.
ZTTT!

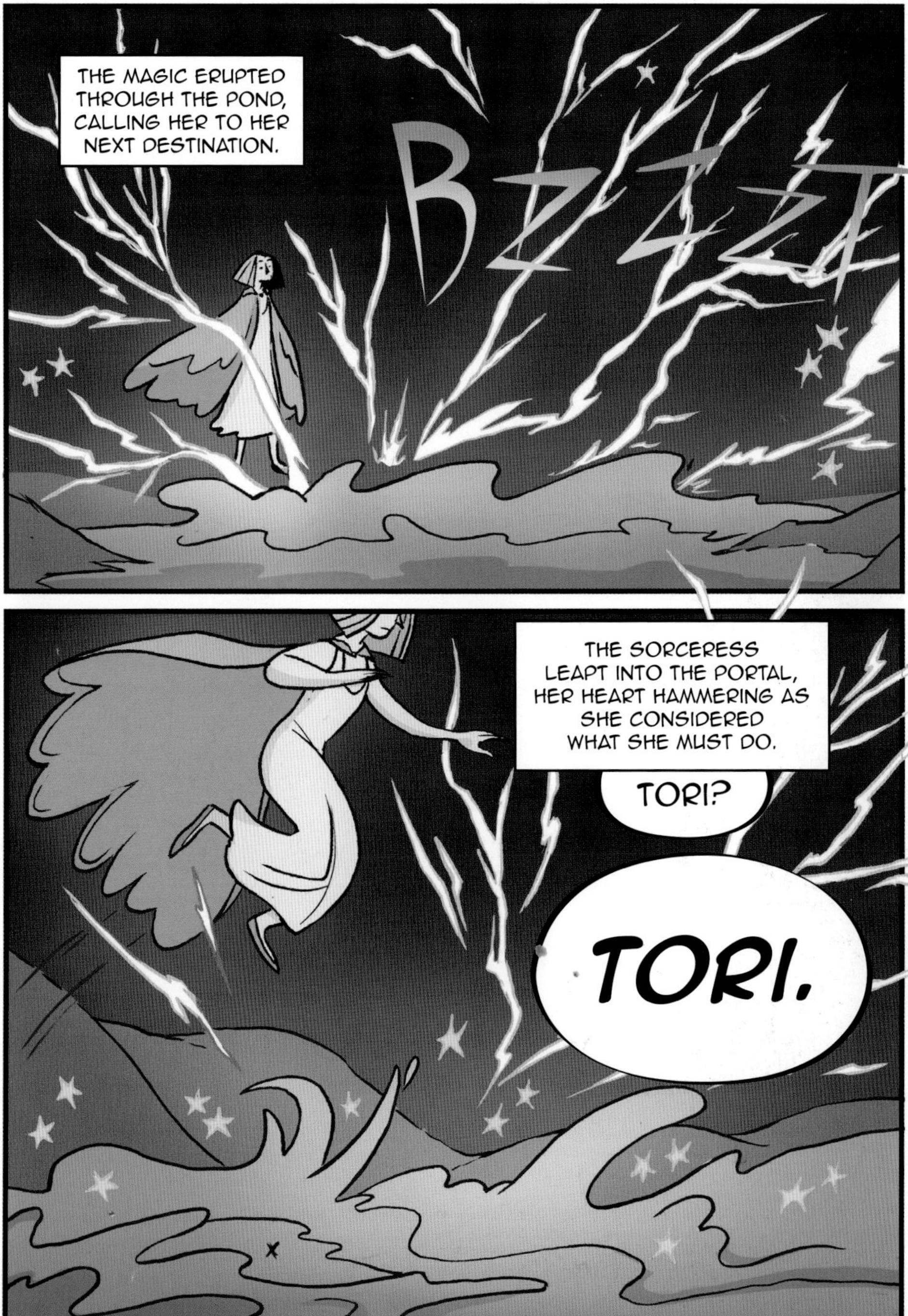
THE MAGIC ERUPTED THROUGH THE POND, CALLING HER TO HER NEXT DESTINATION.
BZZZT
THE SORCERESS LEAPT INTO THE PORTAL, HER HEART HAMMERING AS SHE CONSIDERED WHAT SHE MUST DO.
TORI?
TORI.

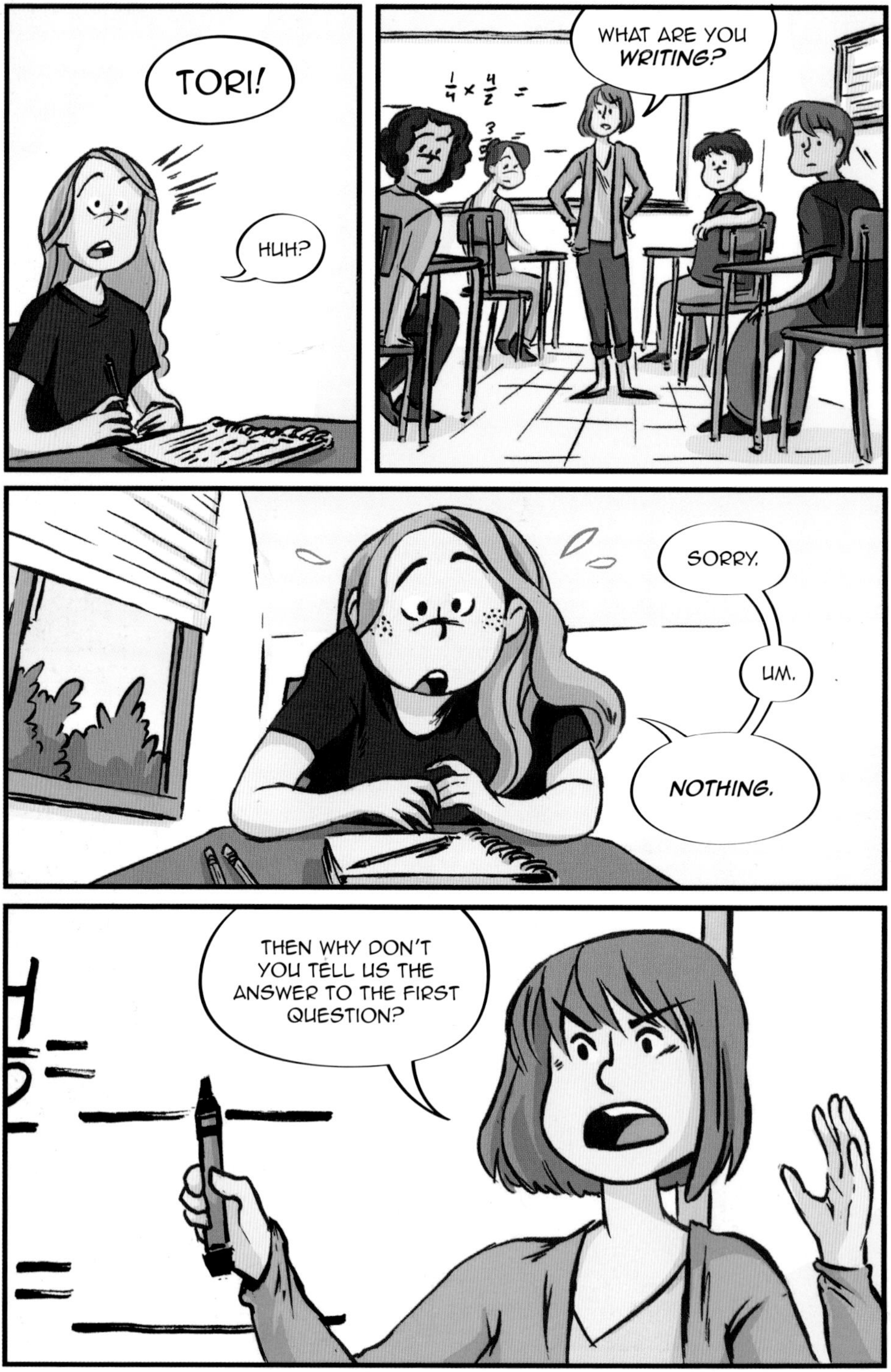
TORI!
HUH?
WHAT ARE YOU WRITING?
SORRY.
UM.
NOTHING.
THEN WHY DON'T YOU TELL US THE ANSWER TO THE FIRST QUESTION?

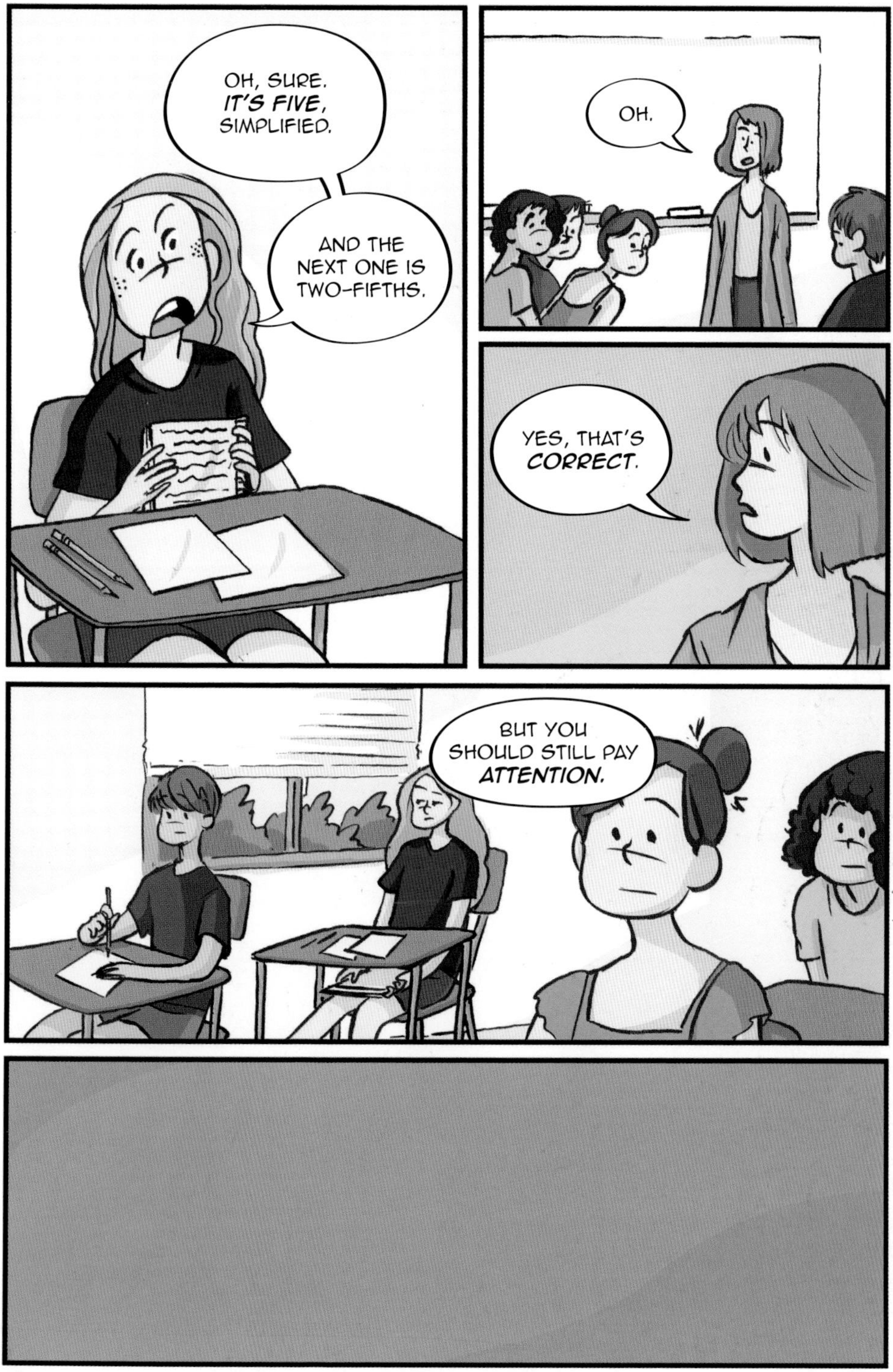
OH, SURE. IT'S FIVE, SIMPLIFIED.
AND THE NEXT ONE IS TWO-FIFTHS.
OH.
YES, THAT'S CORRECT.
BUT YOU SHOULD STILL PAY ATTENTION.

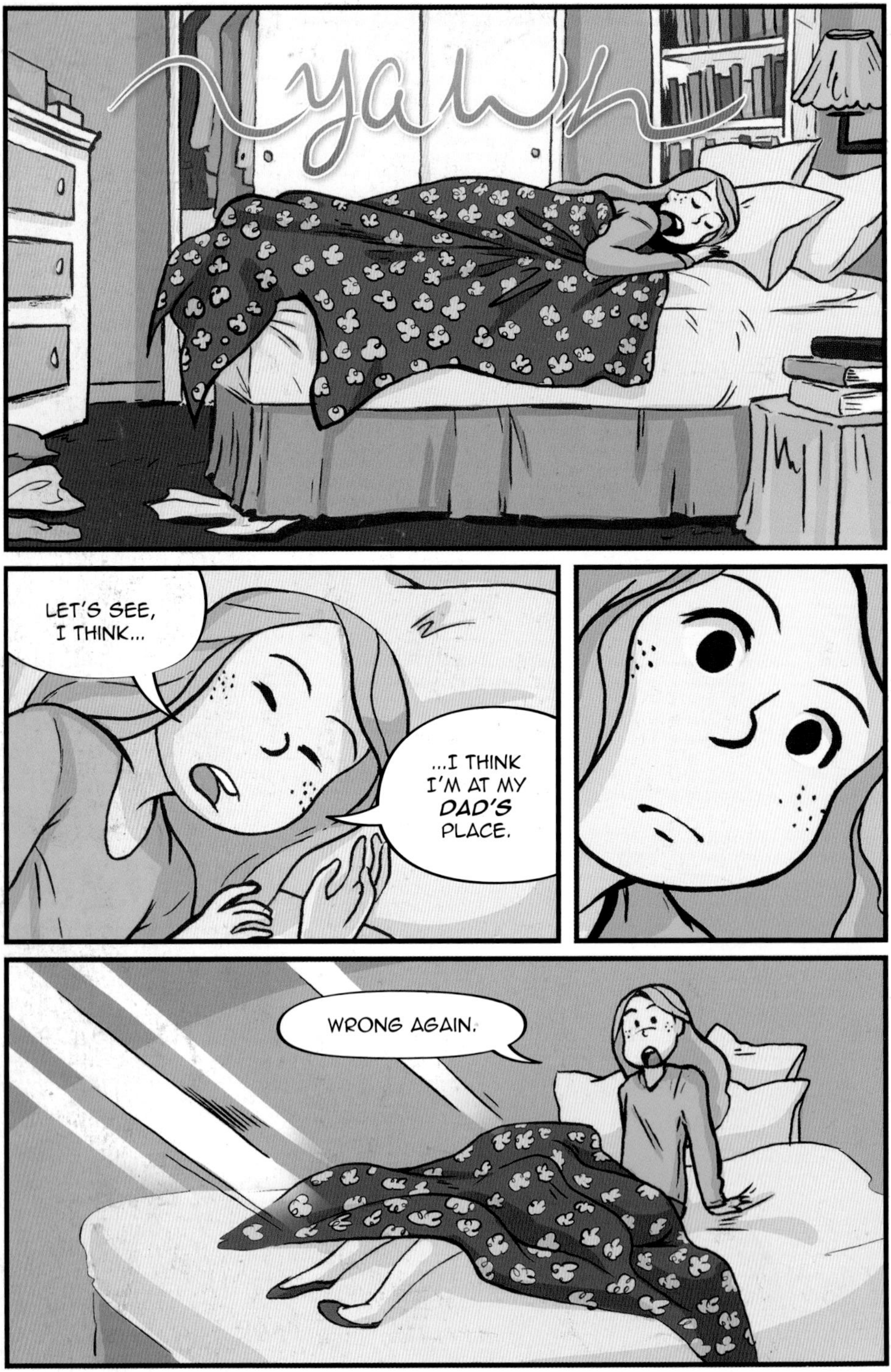
yawn
LET'S SEE, I THINK...
...I THINK I'M AT MY DAD'S PLACE.
WRONG AGAIN.

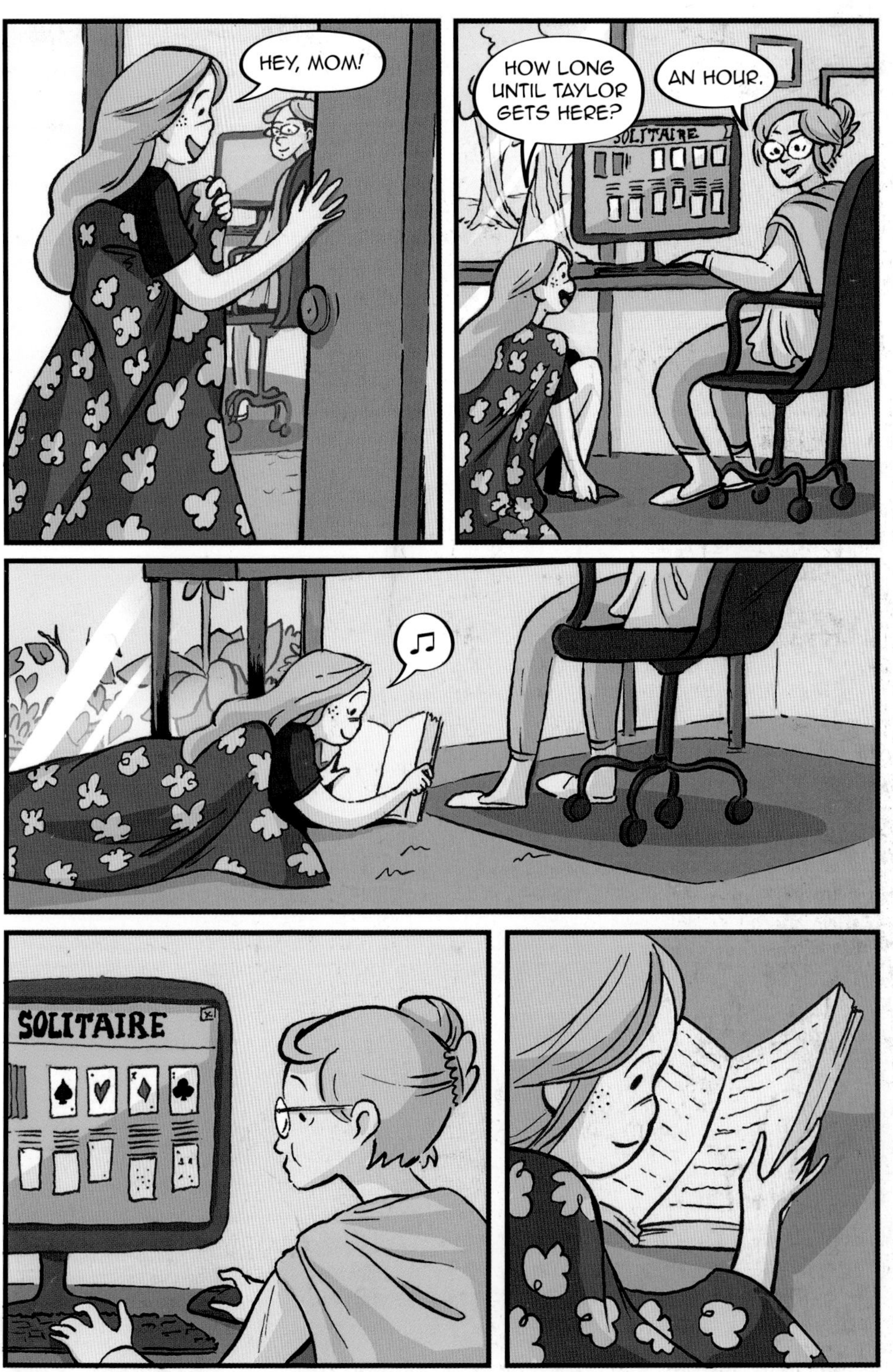
HEY, MOM!
HOW LONG UNTIL TAYLOR GETS HERE?
AN HOUR.
SOLITAIRE
♫
SOLITAIRE

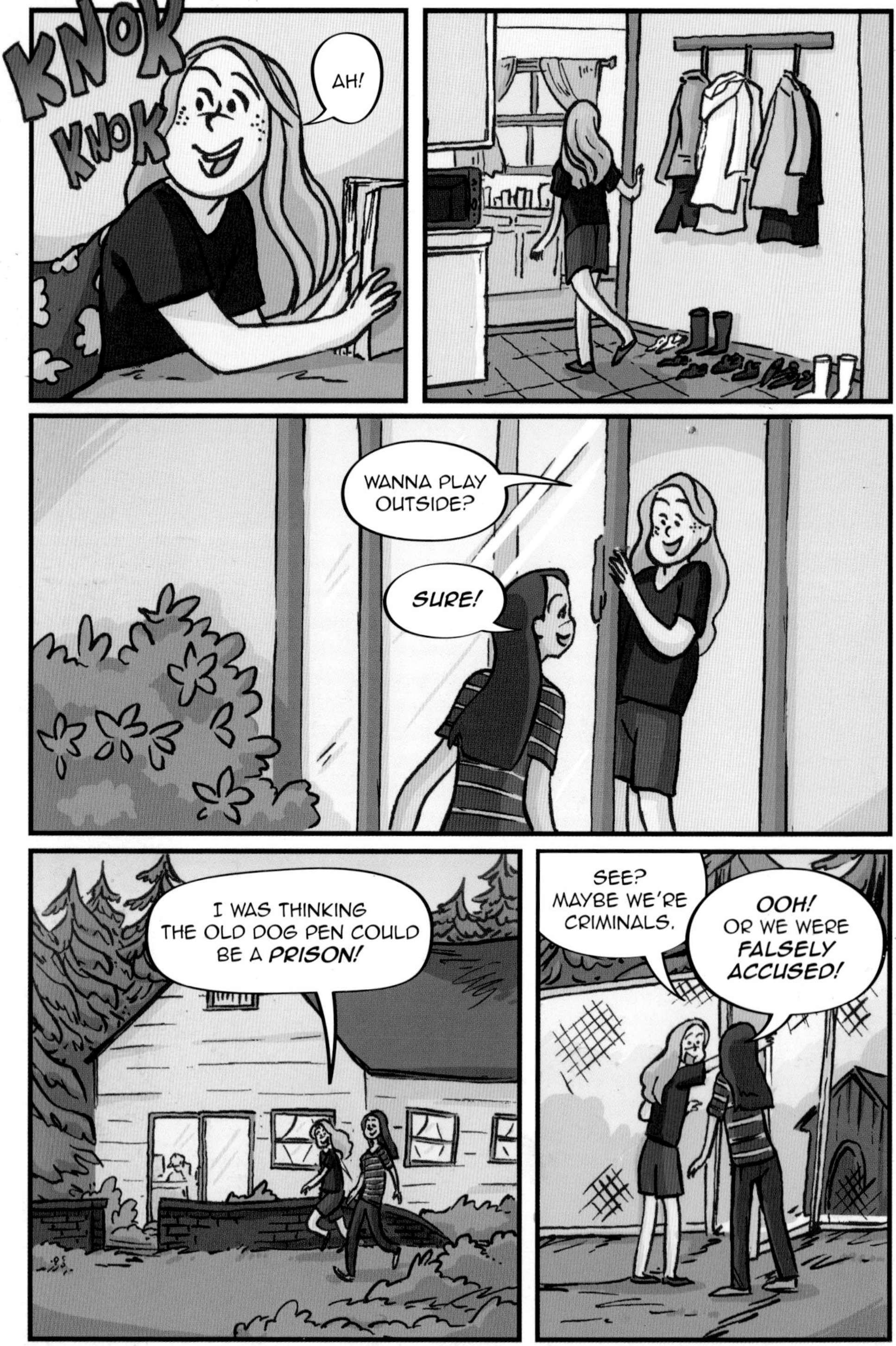
KNOK KNOK
AH!
WANNA PLAY OUTSIDE?
SURE!
I WAS THINKING THE OLD DOG PEN COULD BE A PRISON!
SEE? MAYBE WE'RE CRIMINALS.
OOH! OR WE WERE FALSELY ACCUSED!

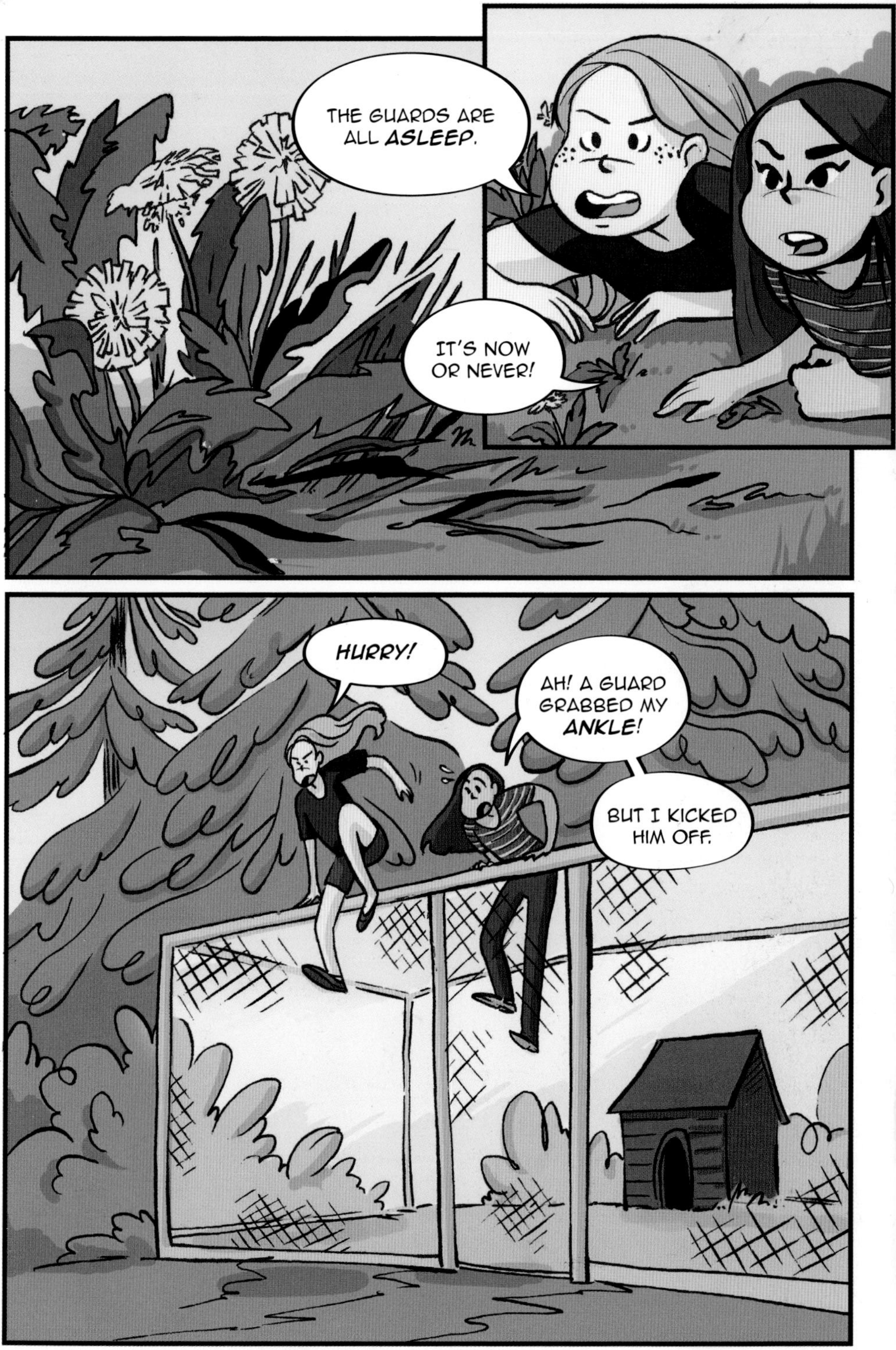
THE GUARDS ARE ALL ASLEEP.
IT'S NOW OR NEVER!
HURRY!
AH! A GUARD GRABBED MY ANKLE!
BUT I KICKED HIM OFF.

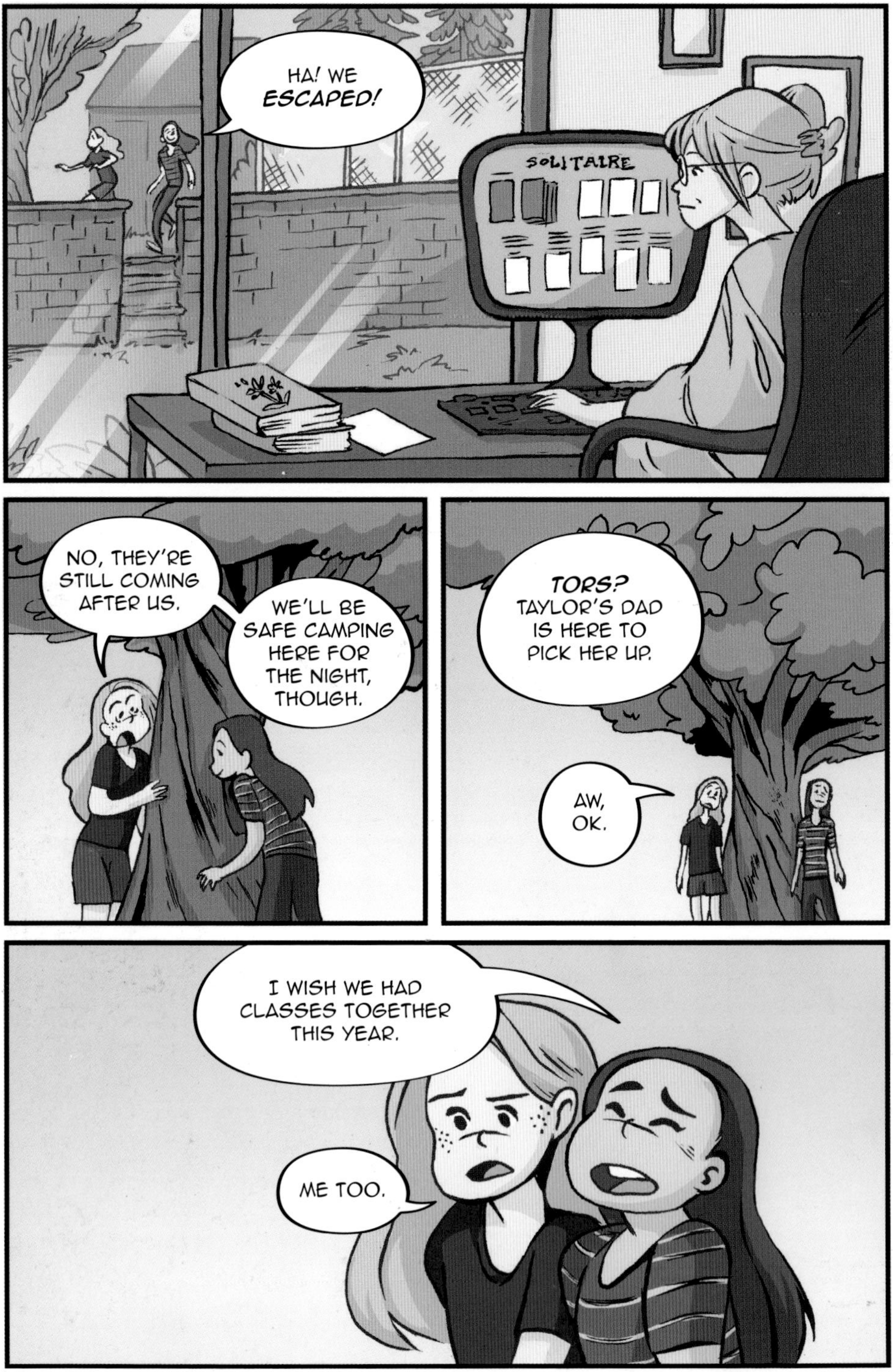
HA! WE ESCAPED!
SOLITAIRE
NO, THEY'RE STILL COMING AFTER US.
WE'LL BE SAFE CAMPING HERE FOR THE NIGHT, THOUGH.
TORS? TAYLOR'S DAD IS HERE TO PICK HER UP.
AW, OK.
I WISH WE HAD CLASSES TOGETHER THIS YEAR.
ME TOO.

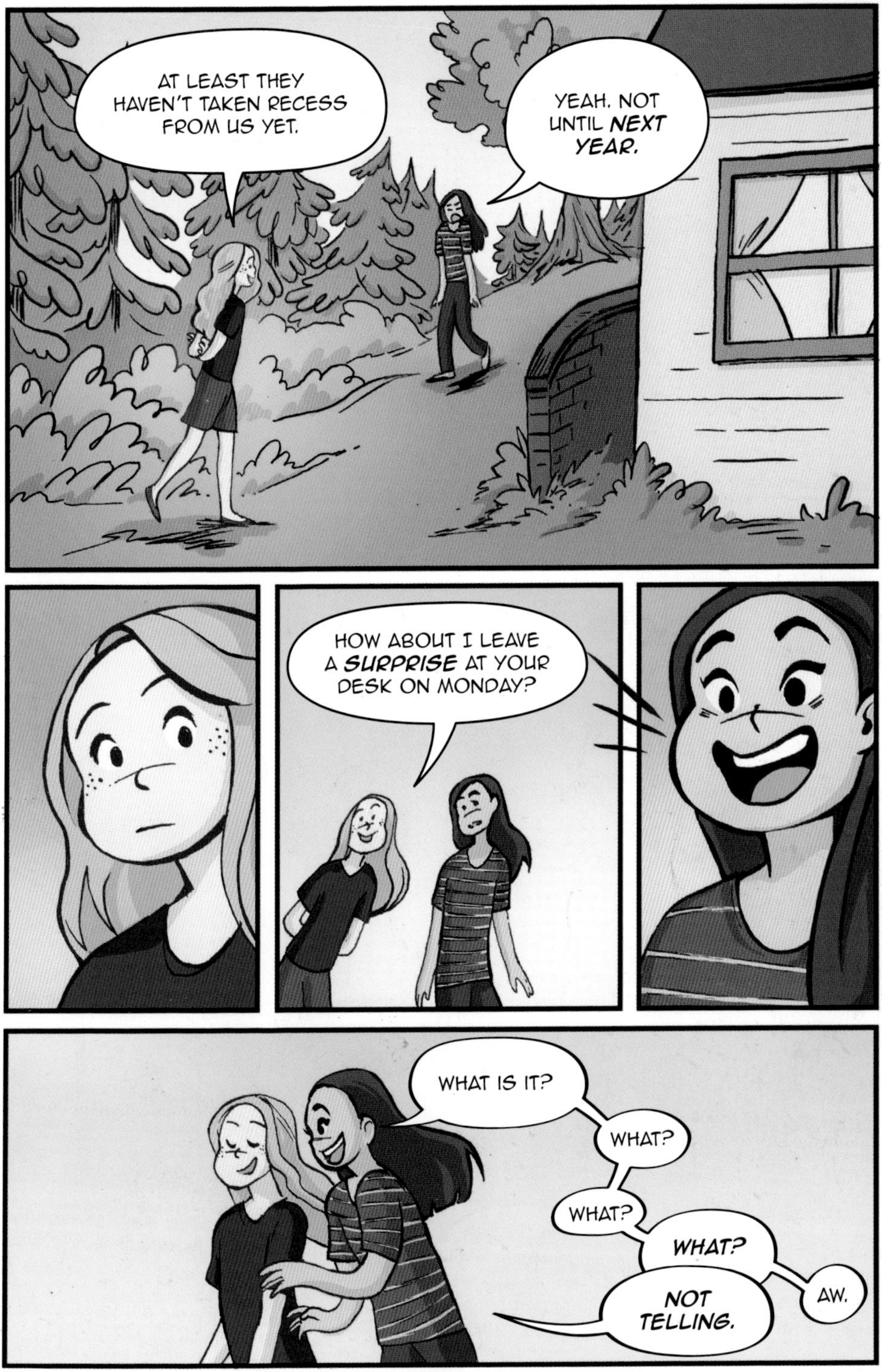
AT LEAST THEY HAVEN'T TAKEN RECESS FROM US YET.
YEAH. NOT UNTIL ***NEXT YEAR.***
HOW ABOUT I LEAVE A ***SURPRISE*** AT YOUR DESK ON MONDAY?
WHAT IS IT?
WHAT?
WHAT?
***WHAT?***
***NOT TELLING.***
AW.

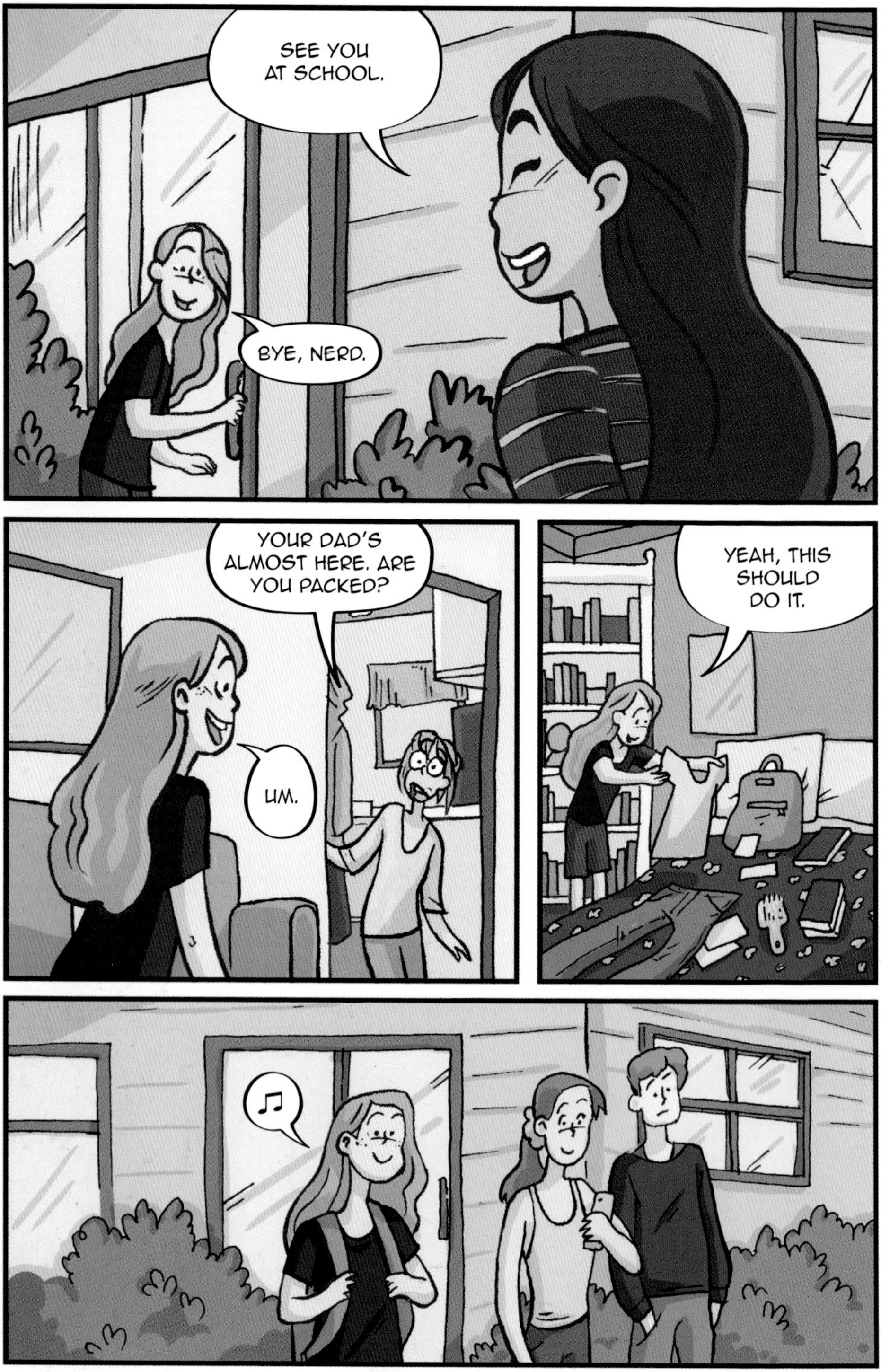
SEE YOU AT SCHOOL.
BYE, NERD.
YOUR DAD'S ALMOST HERE. ARE YOU PACKED?
UM.
YEAH, THIS SHOULD DO IT.
♫

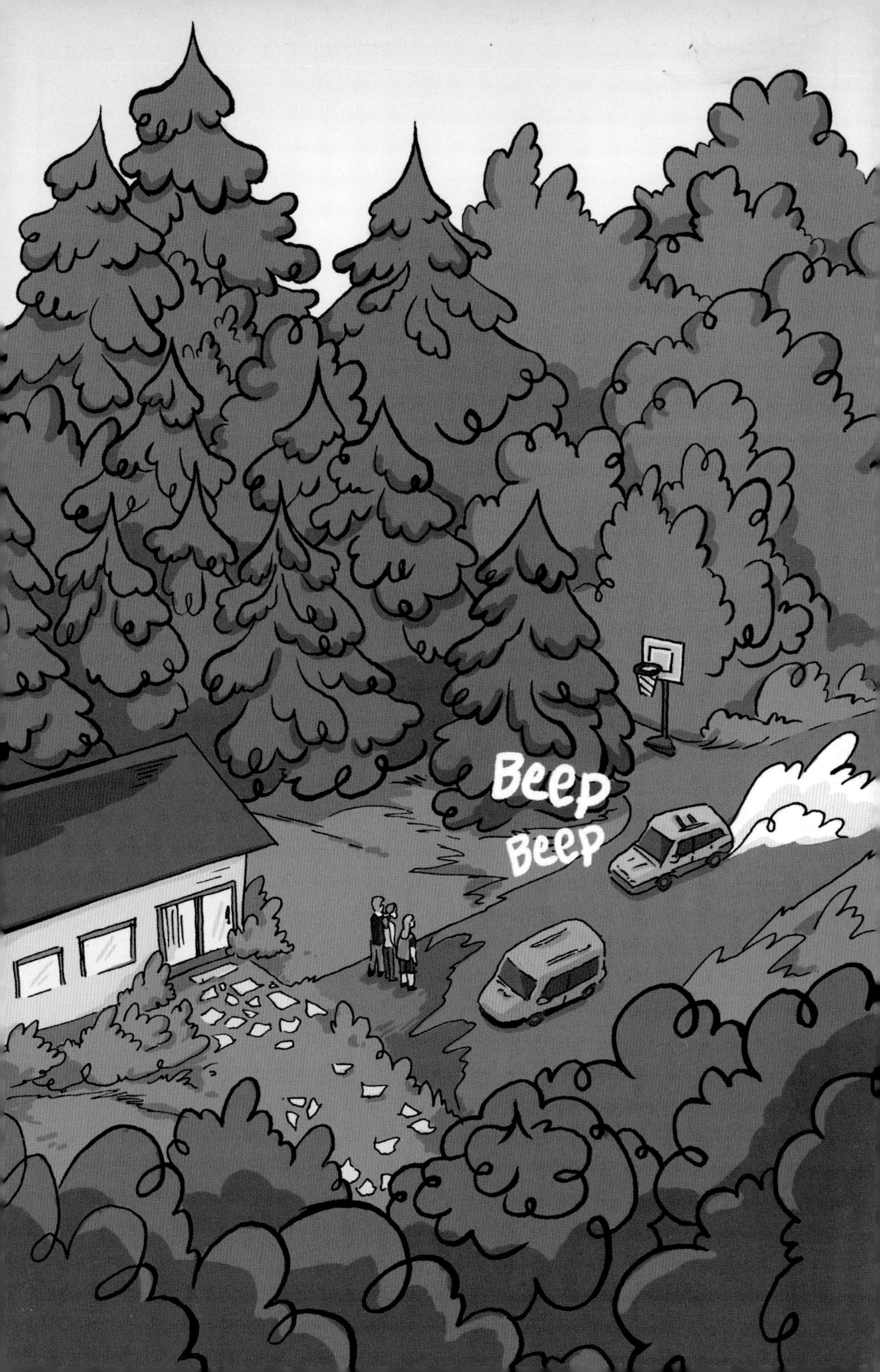
Beep
Beep

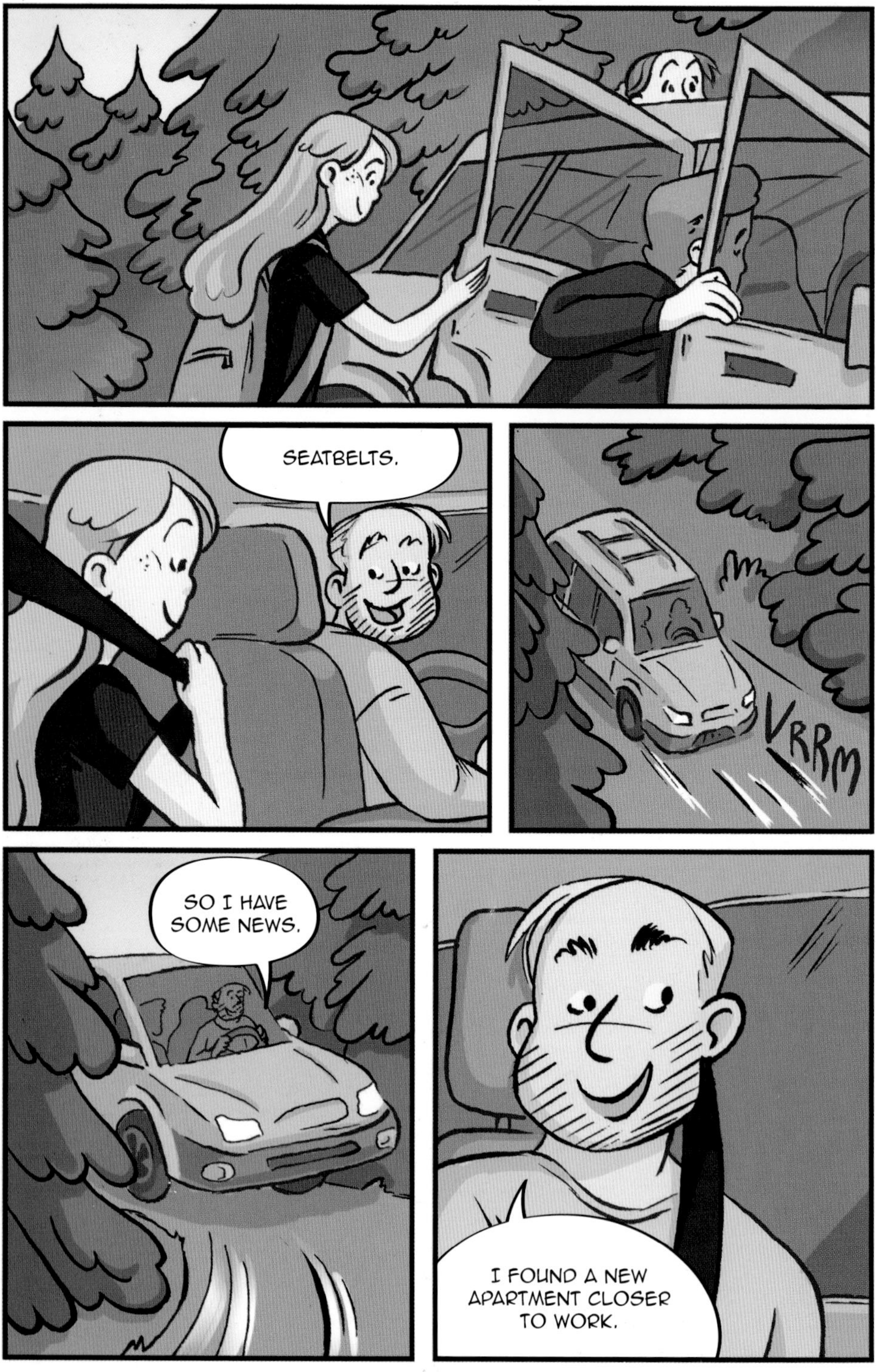
SEATBELTS.
VRRM
SO I HAVE SOME NEWS.
I FOUND A NEW APARTMENT CLOSER TO WORK.

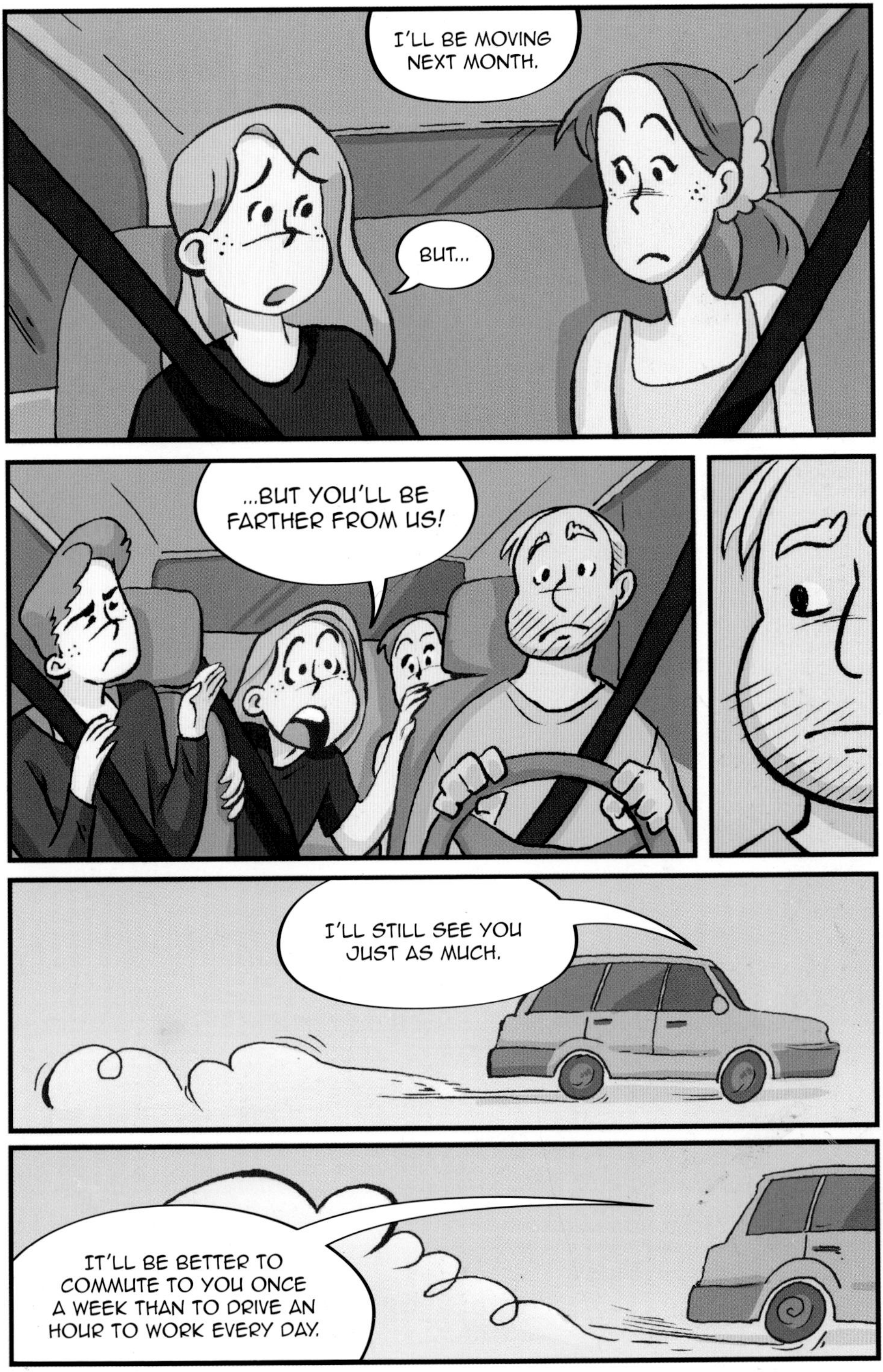
I'LL BE MOVING NEXT MONTH.
BUT...
...BUT YOU'LL BE FARTHER FROM US!
I'LL STILL SEE YOU JUST AS MUCH.
IT'LL BE BETTER TO COMMUTE TO YOU ONCE A WEEK THAN TO DRIVE AN HOUR TO WORK EVERY DAY.

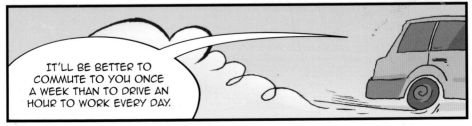

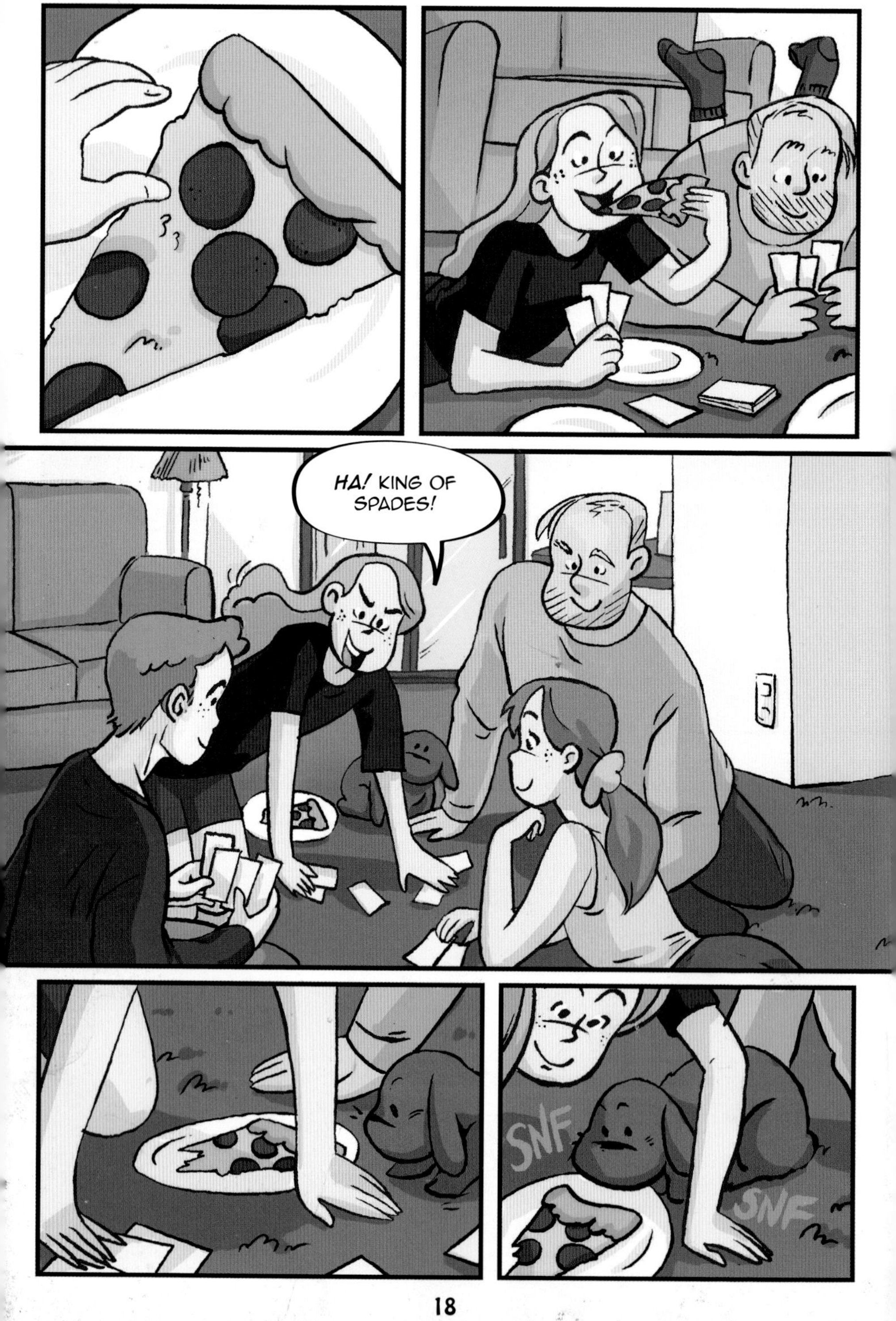
HA! KING OF SPADES!
SNF
SNF

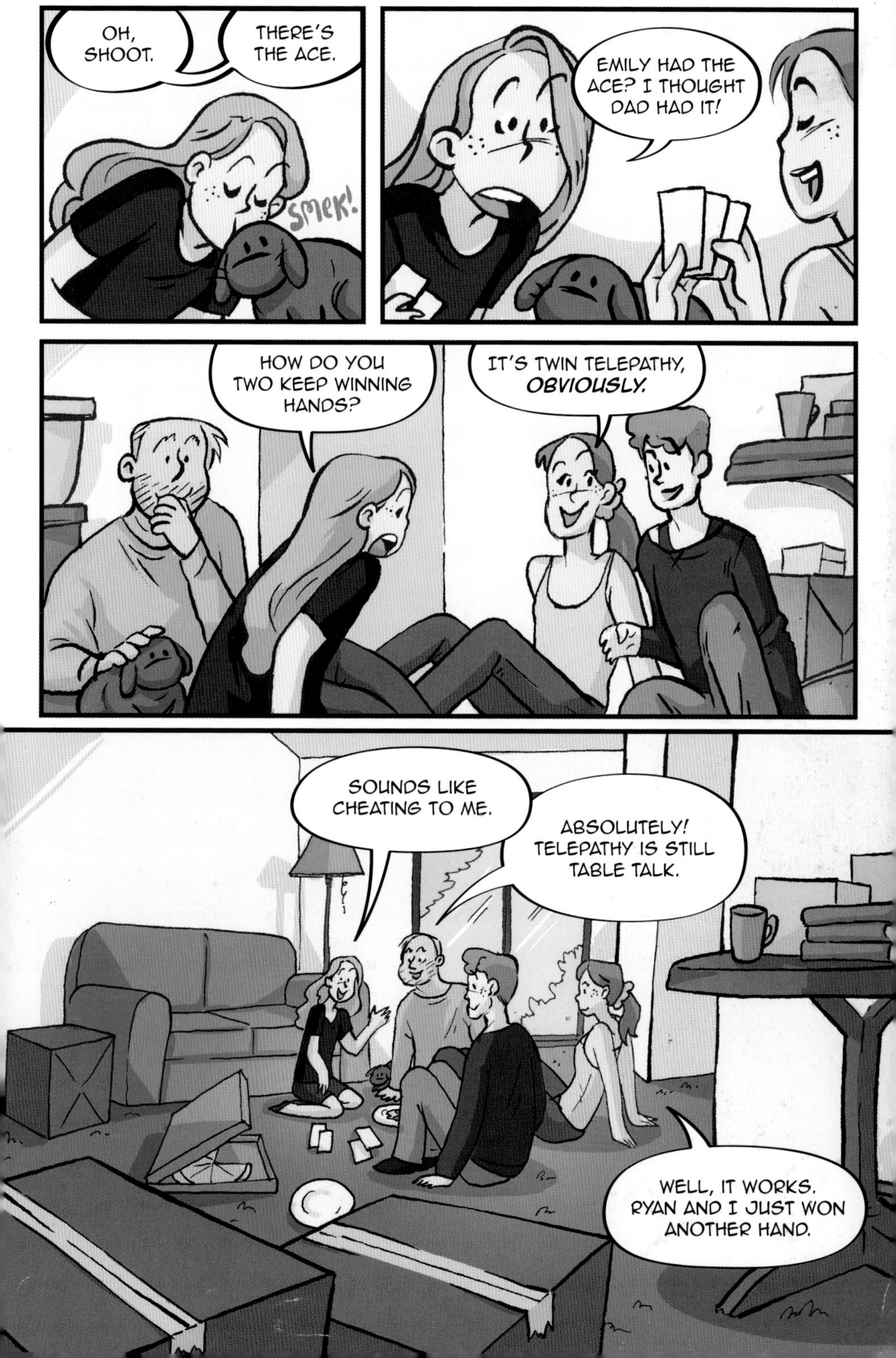
OH, SHOOT.
THERE'S THE ACE.
SMEK!
EMILY HAD THE ACE? I THOUGHT DAD HAD IT!
HOW DO YOU TWO KEEP WINNING HANDS?
IT'S TWIN TELEPATHY, *OBVIOUSLY.*
SOUNDS LIKE CHEATING TO ME.
ABSOLUTELY! TELEPATHY IS STILL TABLE TALK.
WELL, IT WORKS. RYAN AND I JUST WON ANOTHER HAND.

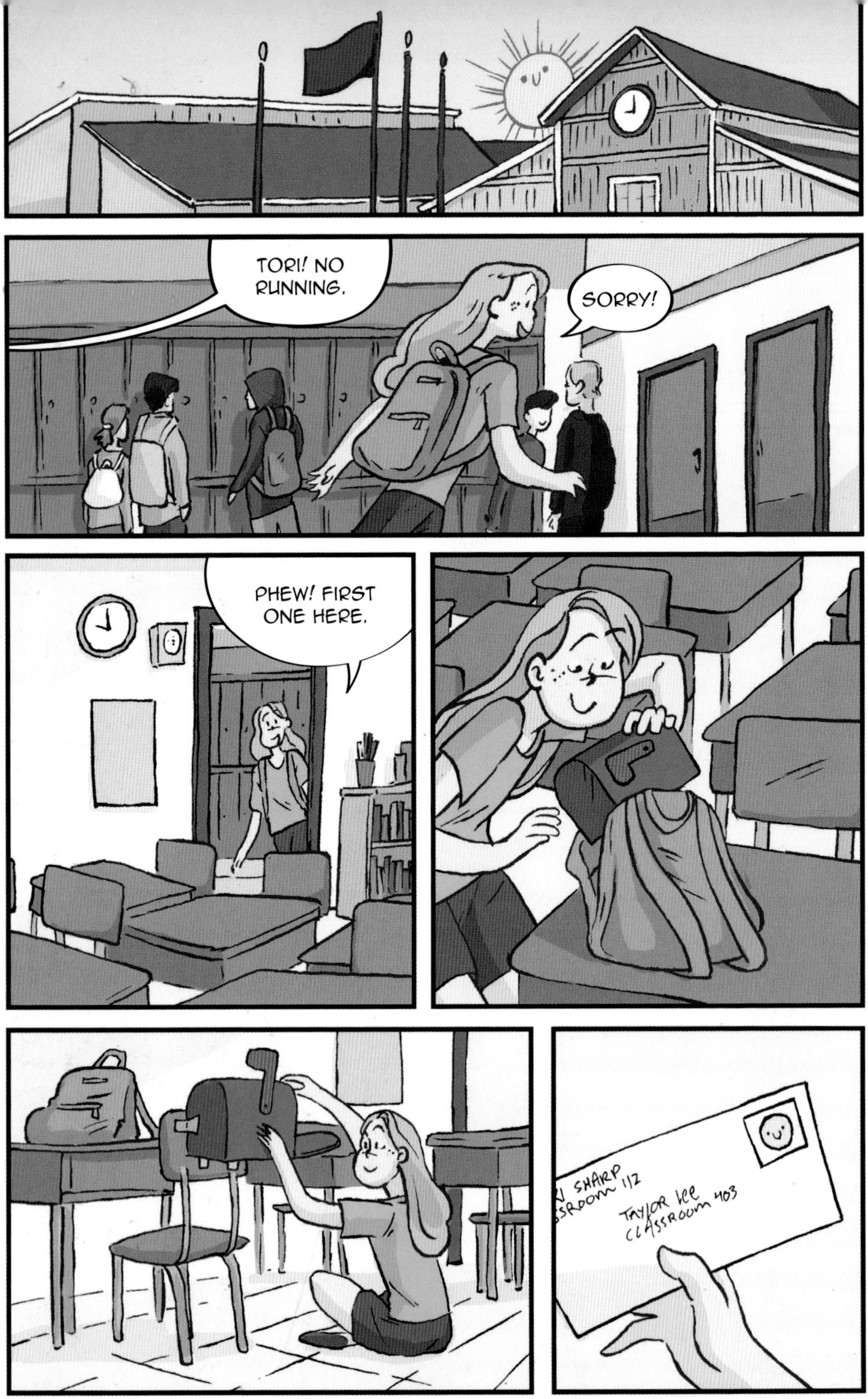
TORI! NO RUNNING.
SORRY!
PHEW! FIRST ONE HERE.
TAYLOR LEE
CLASSROOM 403

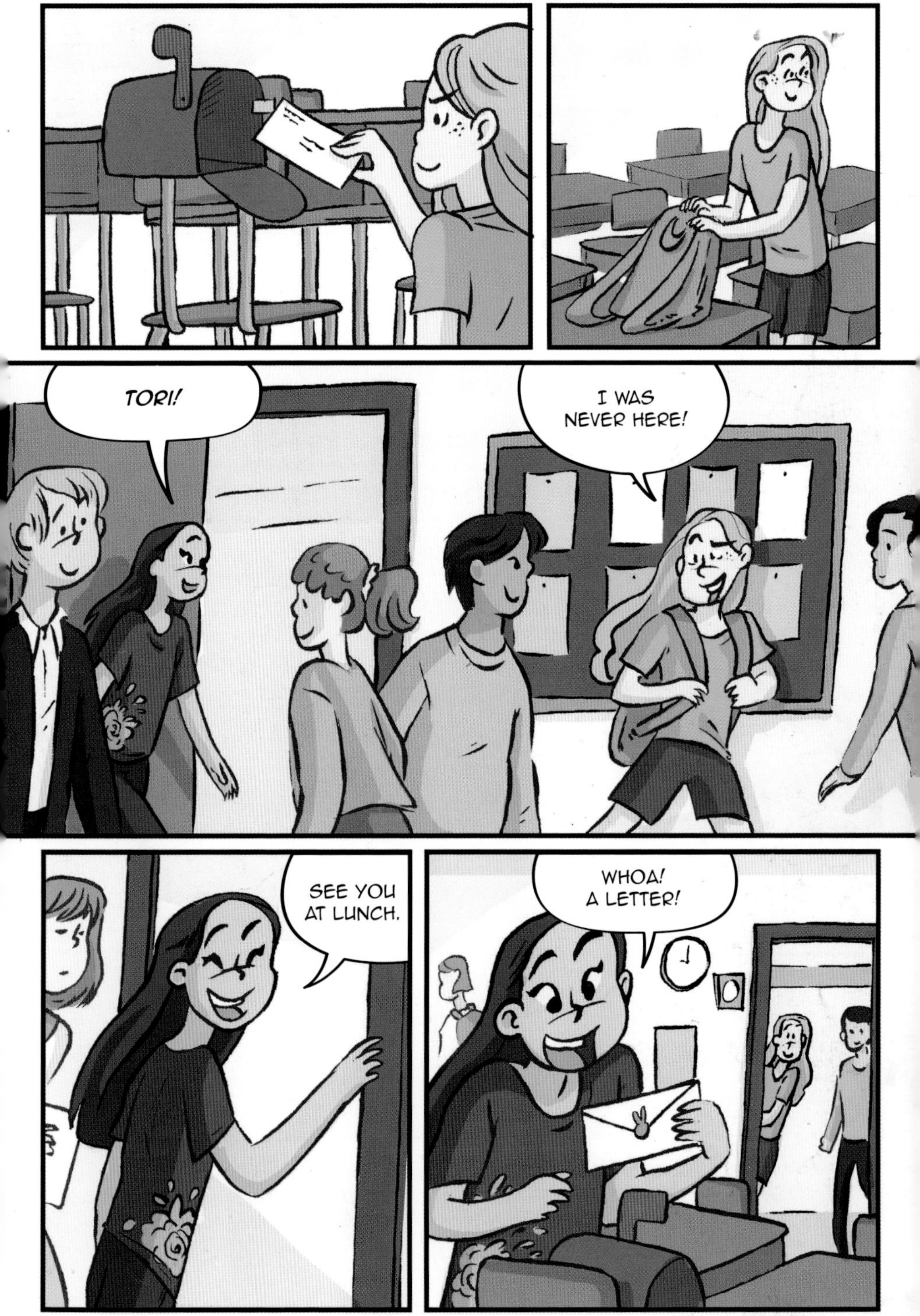
TORI!
I WAS NEVER HERE!
SEE YOU AT LUNCH.
WHOA! A LETTER!

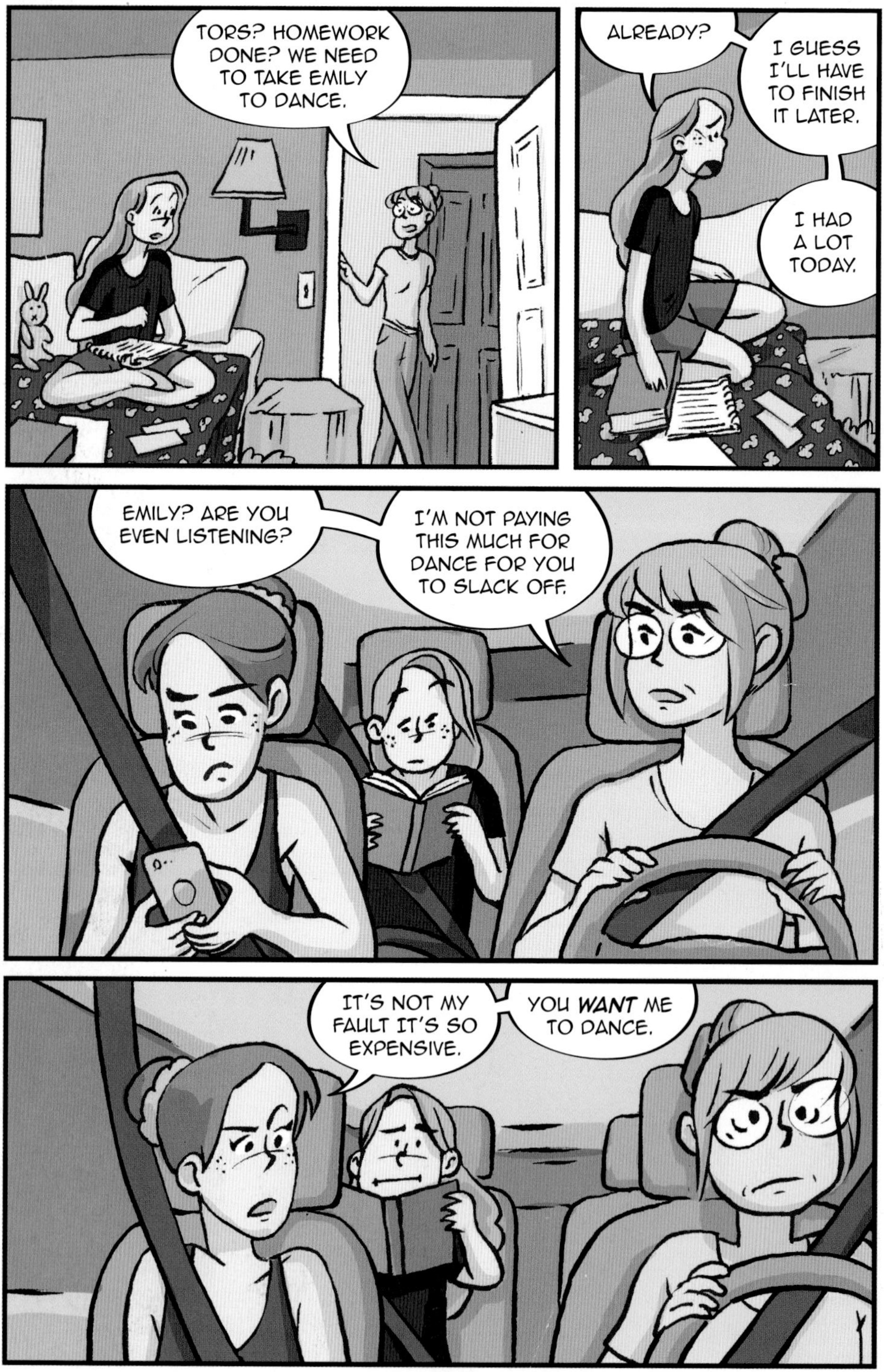
TORS? HOMEWORK DONE? WE NEED TO TAKE EMILY TO DANCE.
ALREADY?
I GUESS I'LL HAVE TO FINISH IT LATER.
I HAD A LOT TODAY.
EMILY? ARE YOU EVEN LISTENING?
I'M NOT PAYING THIS MUCH FOR DANCE FOR YOU TO SLACK OFF.
IT'S NOT MY FAULT IT'S SO EXPENSIVE.
YOU *WANT* ME TO DANCE.

ALL I'M SAYING IS, ONE MONTH UNTIL NATIONALS. PRACTICE HARD. YOU COULD GET A SCHOLARSHIP.

MOM, I *KNOW.* STOP THE MICRO-MANAGING.

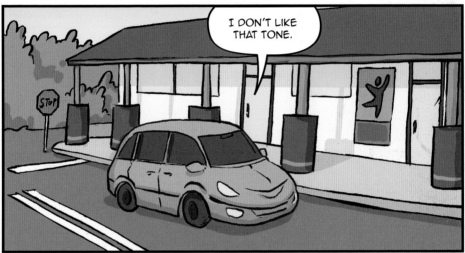

I DON'T LIKE THAT TONE.

BYE.

LET'S GO TO THE MALL.

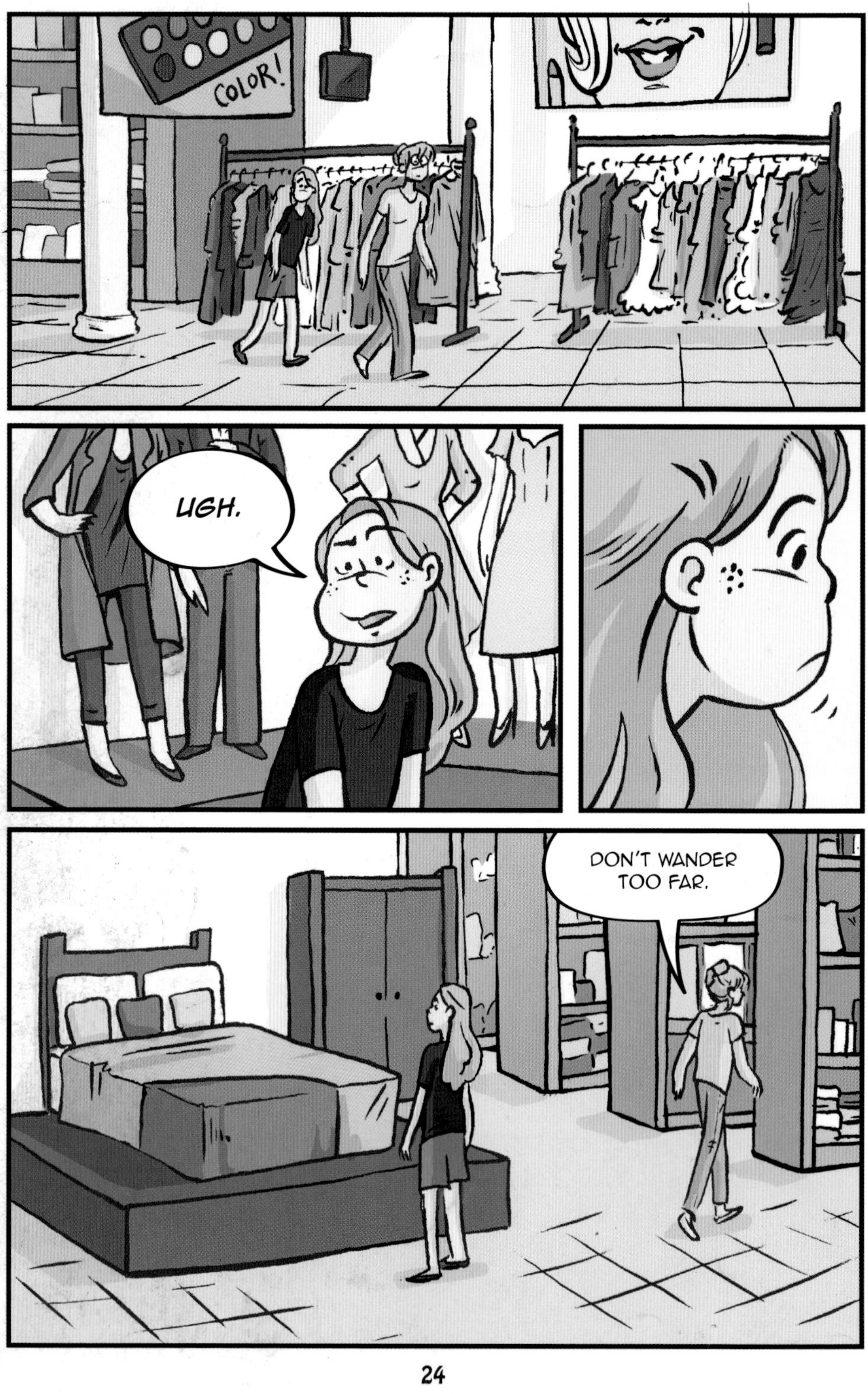
COLOR!
UGH.
DON'T WANDER TOO FAR.

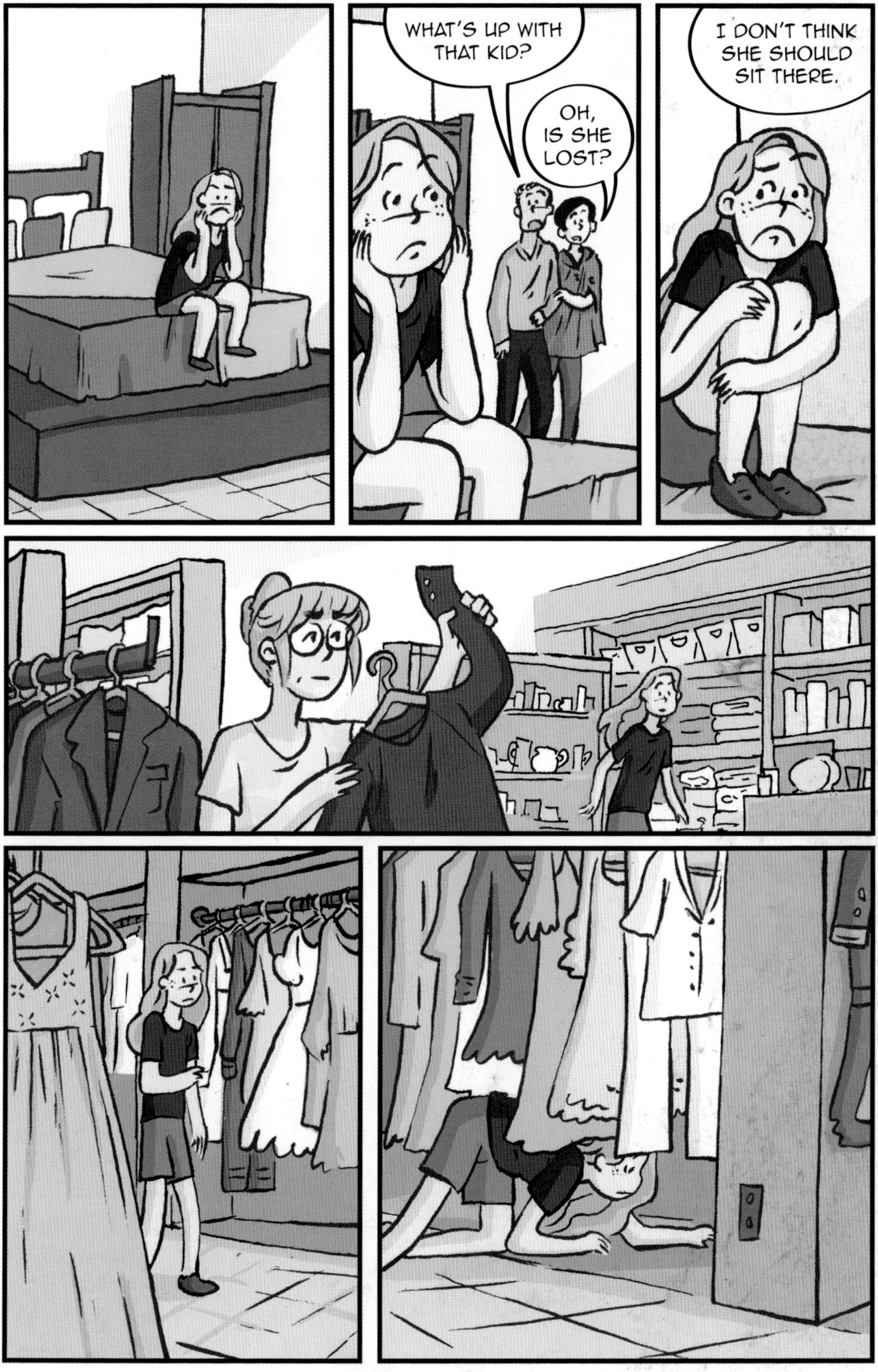
WHAT'S UP WITH THAT KID?
OH, IS SHE LOST?
I DON'T THINK SHE SHOULD SIT THERE.

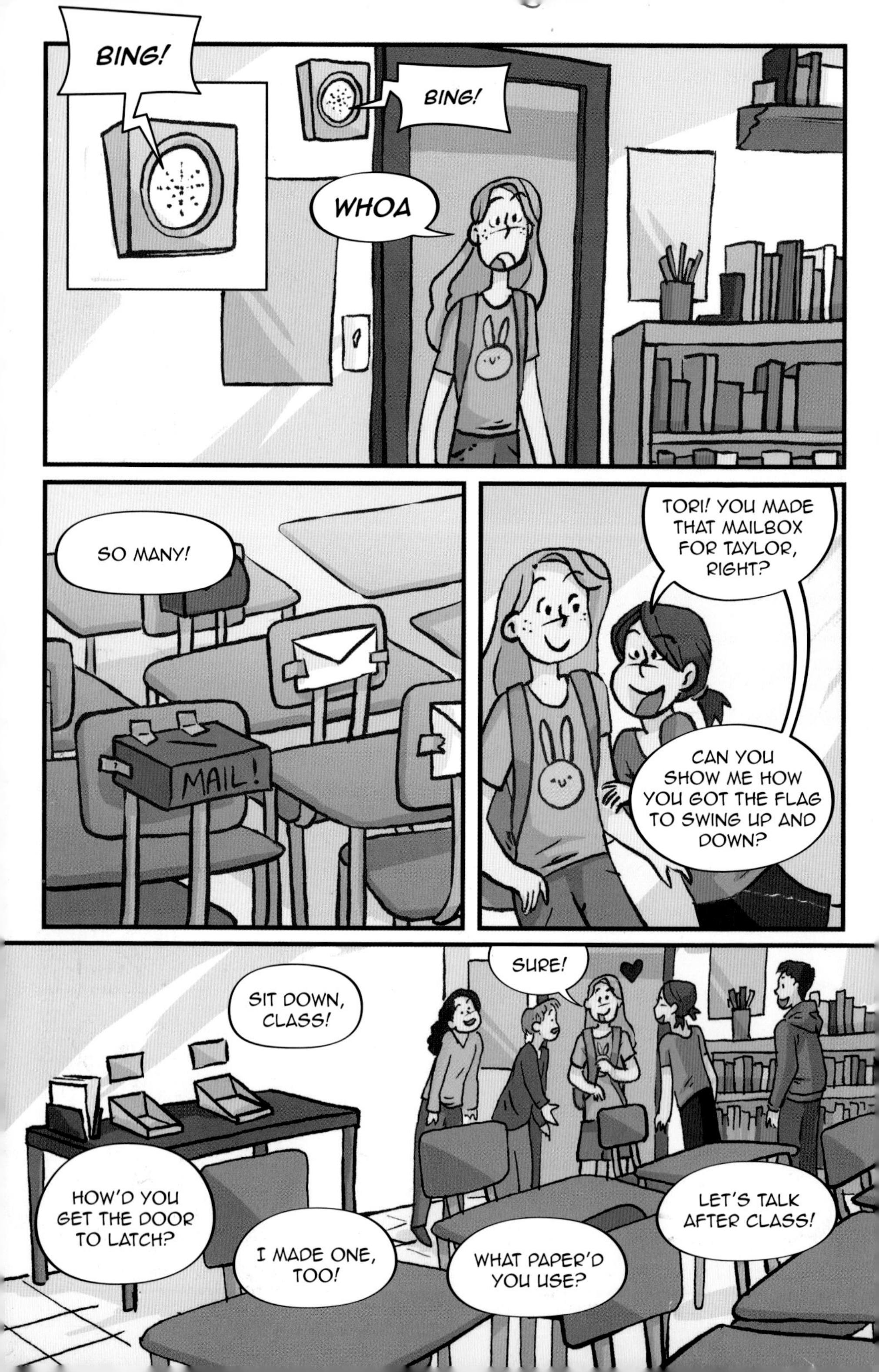
BING!
BING!
WHOA
SO MANY!
MAIL!
TORI! YOU MADE THAT MAILBOX FOR TAYLOR, RIGHT?
CAN YOU SHOW ME HOW YOU GOT THE FLAG TO SWING UP AND DOWN?
SURE!
SIT DOWN, CLASS!
HOW'D YOU GET THE DOOR TO LATCH?
I MADE ONE, TOO!
WHAT PAPER'D YOU USE?
LET'S TALK AFTER CLASS!

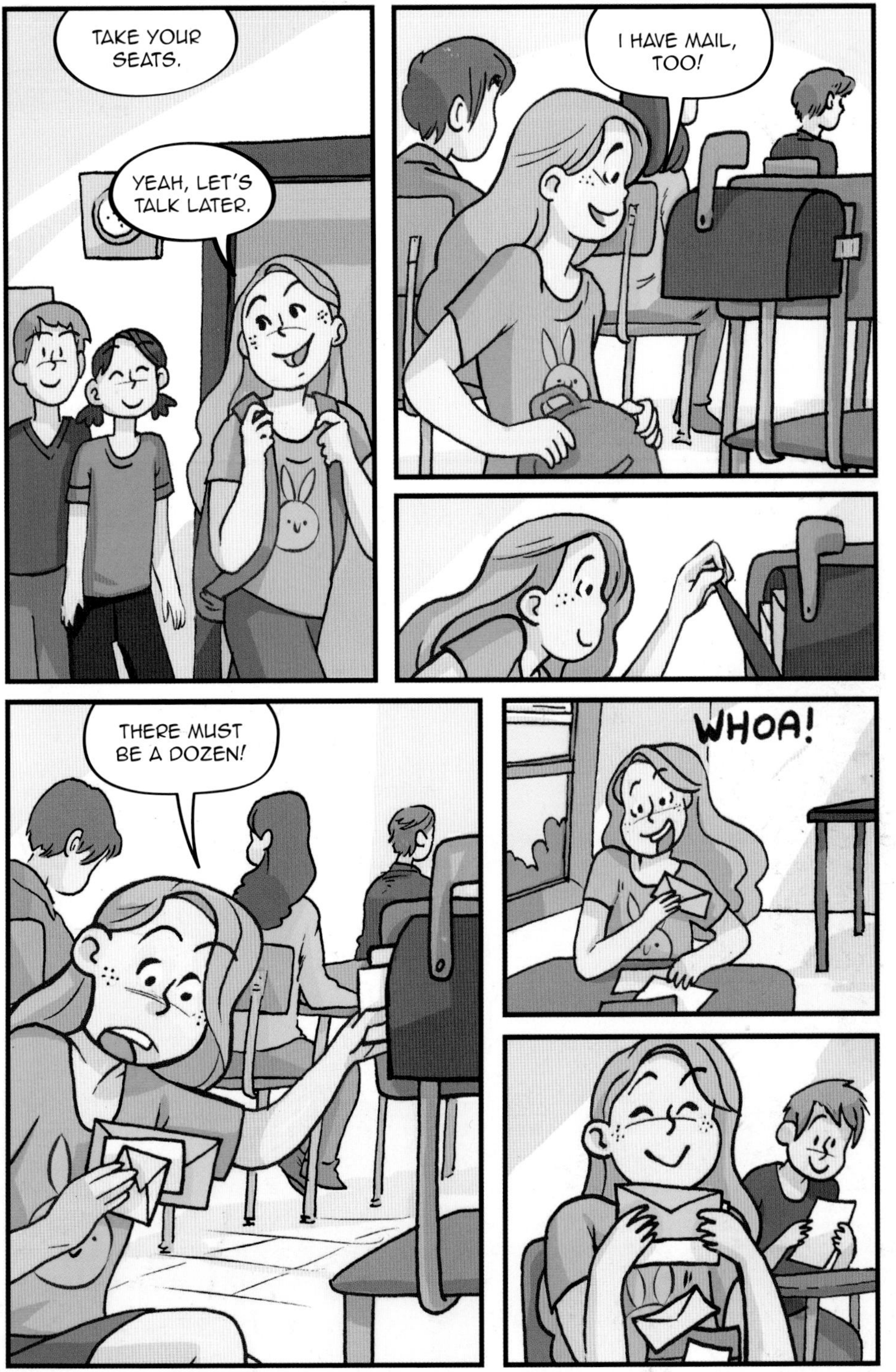
TAKE YOUR SEATS.
YEAH, LET'S TALK LATER.
I HAVE MAIL, TOO!
THERE MUST BE A DOZEN!
WHOA!

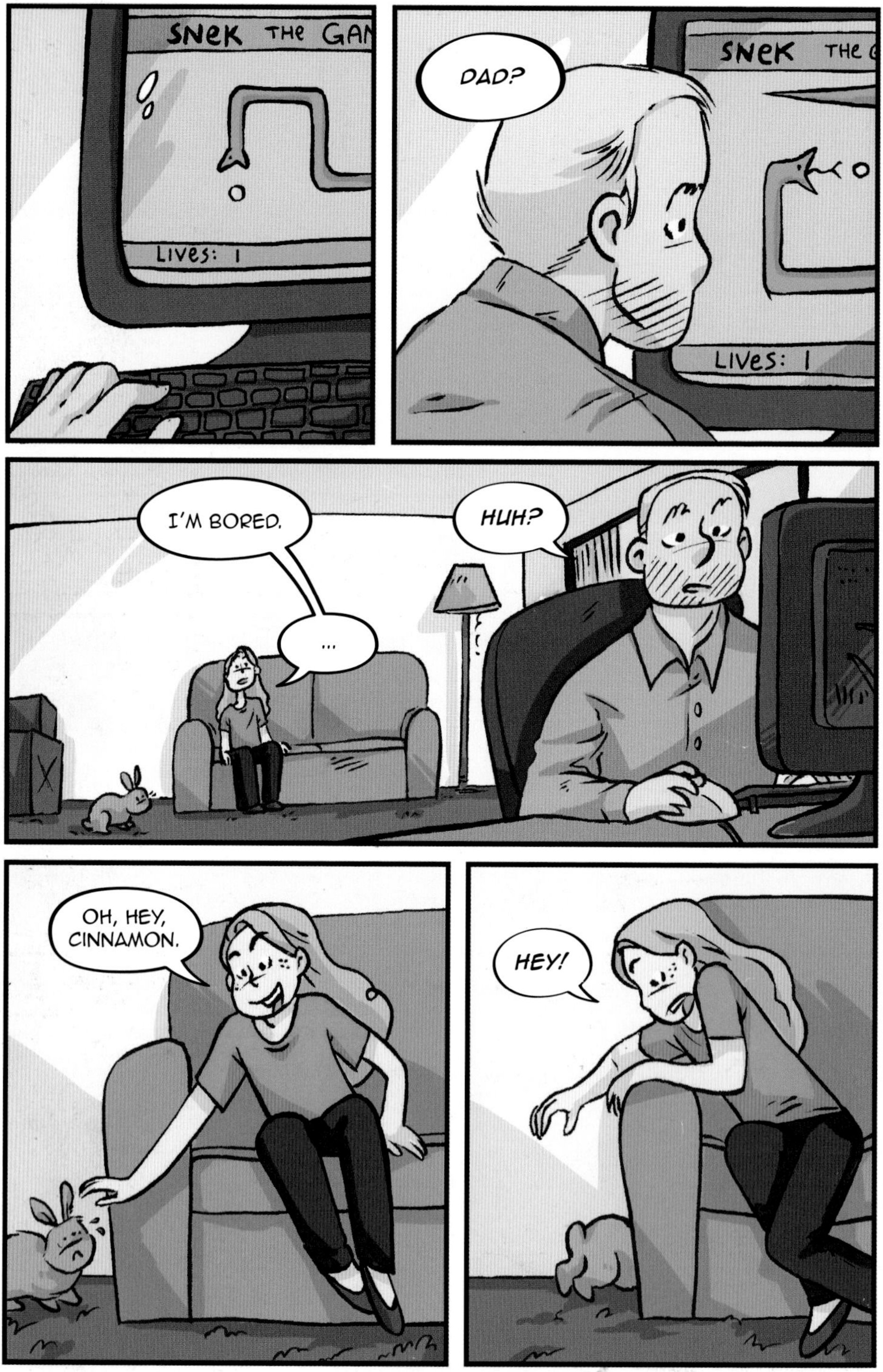
SNEK THE GAM
LIVES: 1
SNEK THE
DAD?
LIVES: 1
I'M BORED.
HUH?
...
OH, HEY, CINNAMON.
HEY!

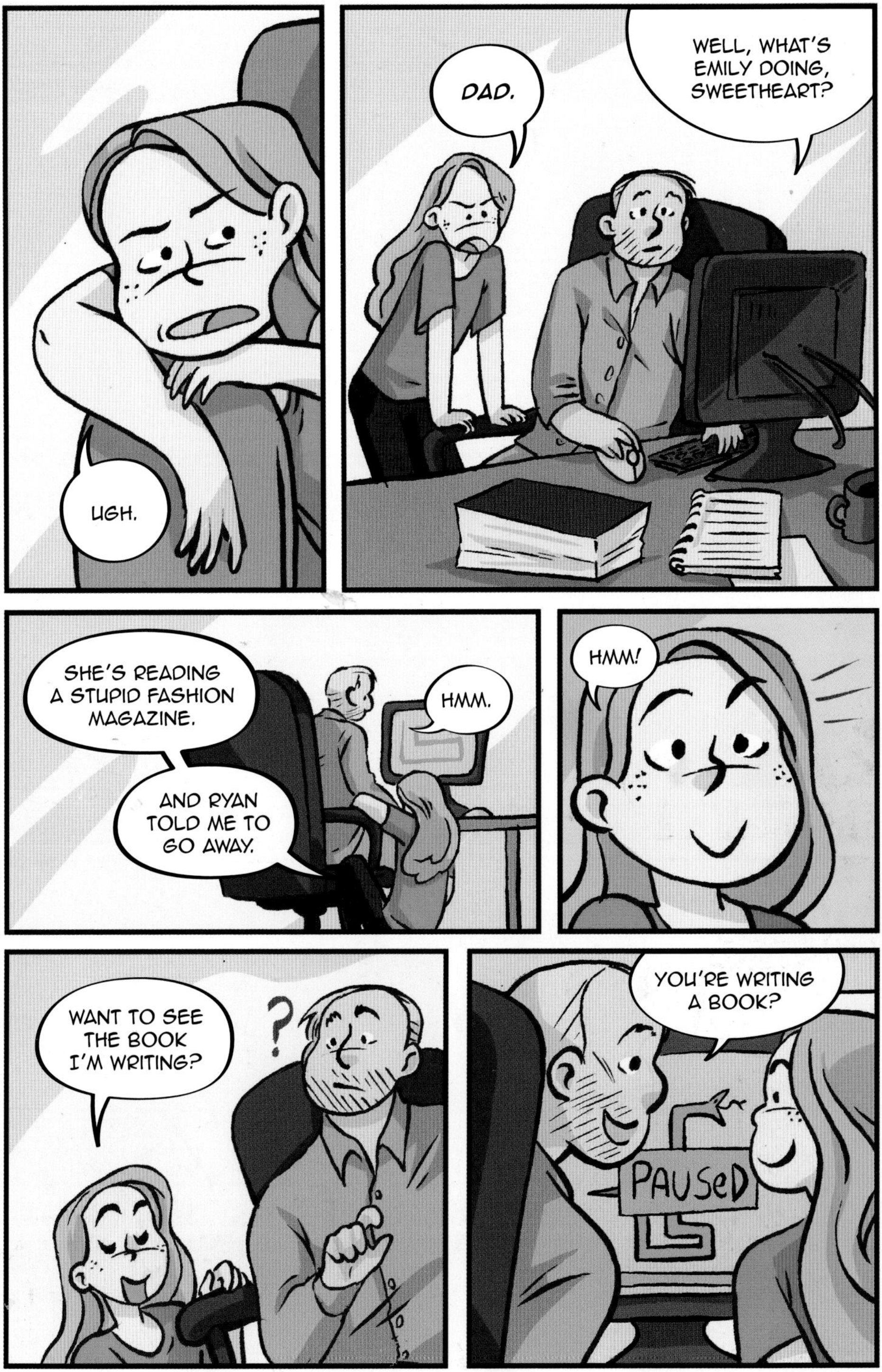
UGH.
DAD.
WELL, WHAT'S EMILY DOING, SWEETHEART?
SHE'S READING A STUPID FASHION MAGAZINE.
HMM.
AND RYAN TOLD ME TO GO AWAY.
HMM!
WANT TO SEE THE BOOK I'M WRITING?
?
YOU'RE WRITING A BOOK?
PAUSED

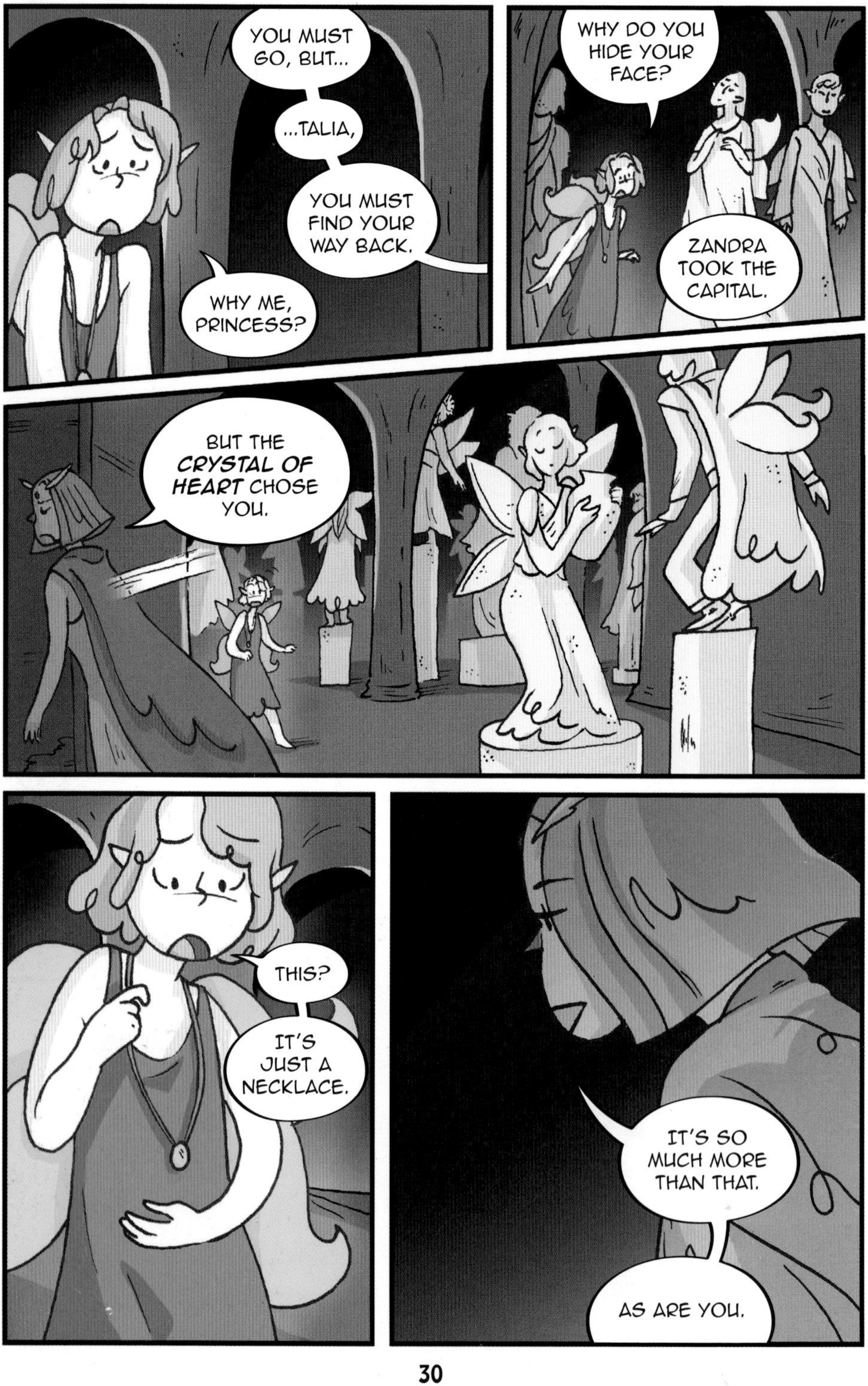
YOU MUST GO, BUT...
...TALIA,
YOU MUST FIND YOUR WAY BACK.
WHY ME, PRINCESS?
WHY DO YOU HIDE YOUR FACE?
ZANDRA TOOK THE CAPITAL.
BUT THE CRYSTAL OF HEART CHOSE YOU.
THIS?
IT'S JUST A NECKLACE.
IT'S SO MUCH MORE THAN THAT.
AS ARE YOU.

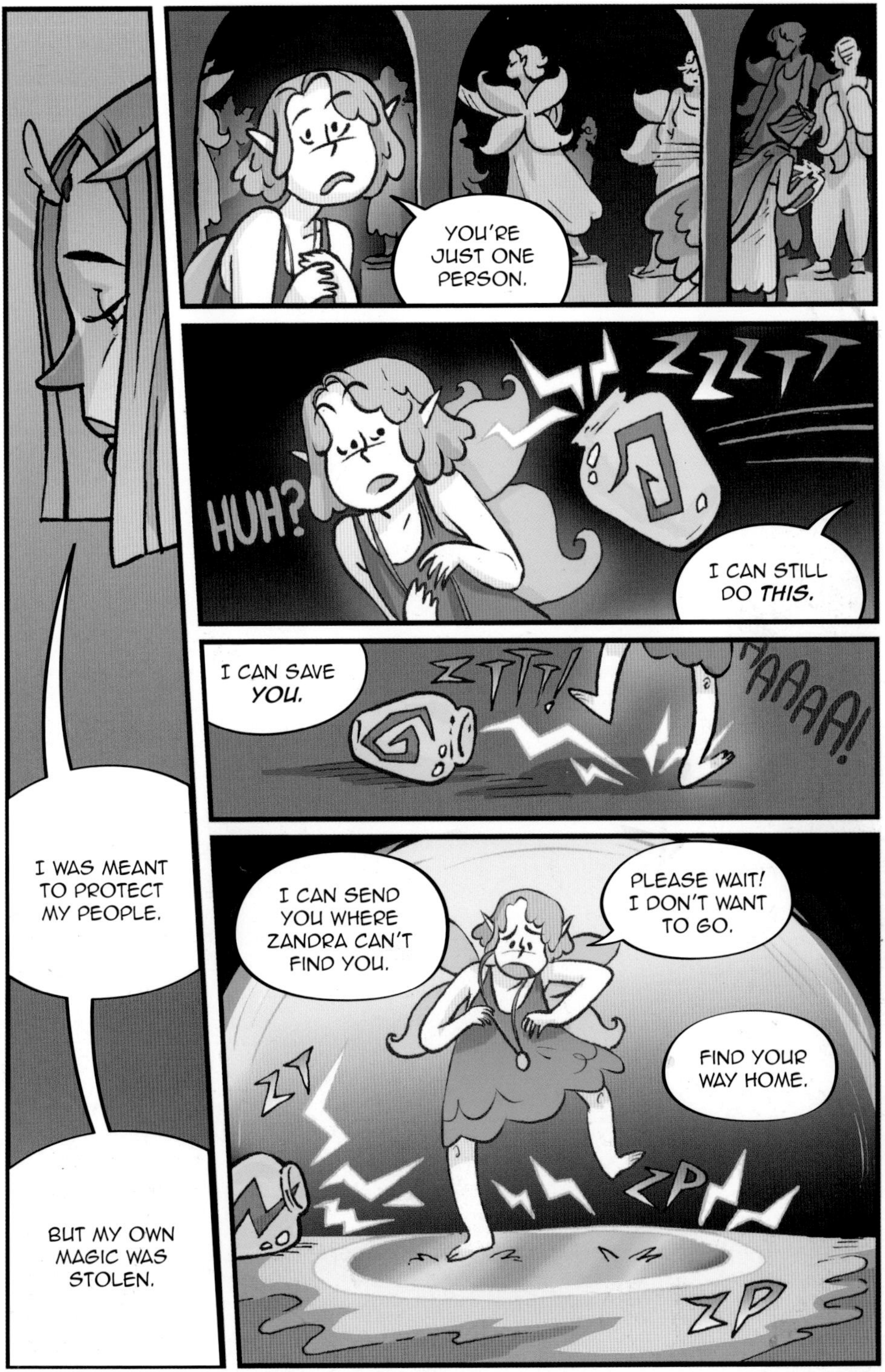
YOU'RE JUST ONE PERSON.
HUH?
ZZZTT
I CAN STILL DO *THIS.*
I CAN SAVE *YOU.*
ZTTT!
AAAAA!
I WAS MEANT TO PROTECT MY PEOPLE.
BUT MY OWN MAGIC WAS STOLEN.
I CAN SEND YOU WHERE ZANDRA CAN'T FIND YOU.
PLEASE WAIT! I DON'T WANT TO GO.
FIND YOUR WAY HOME.
ZT
ZP
ZP

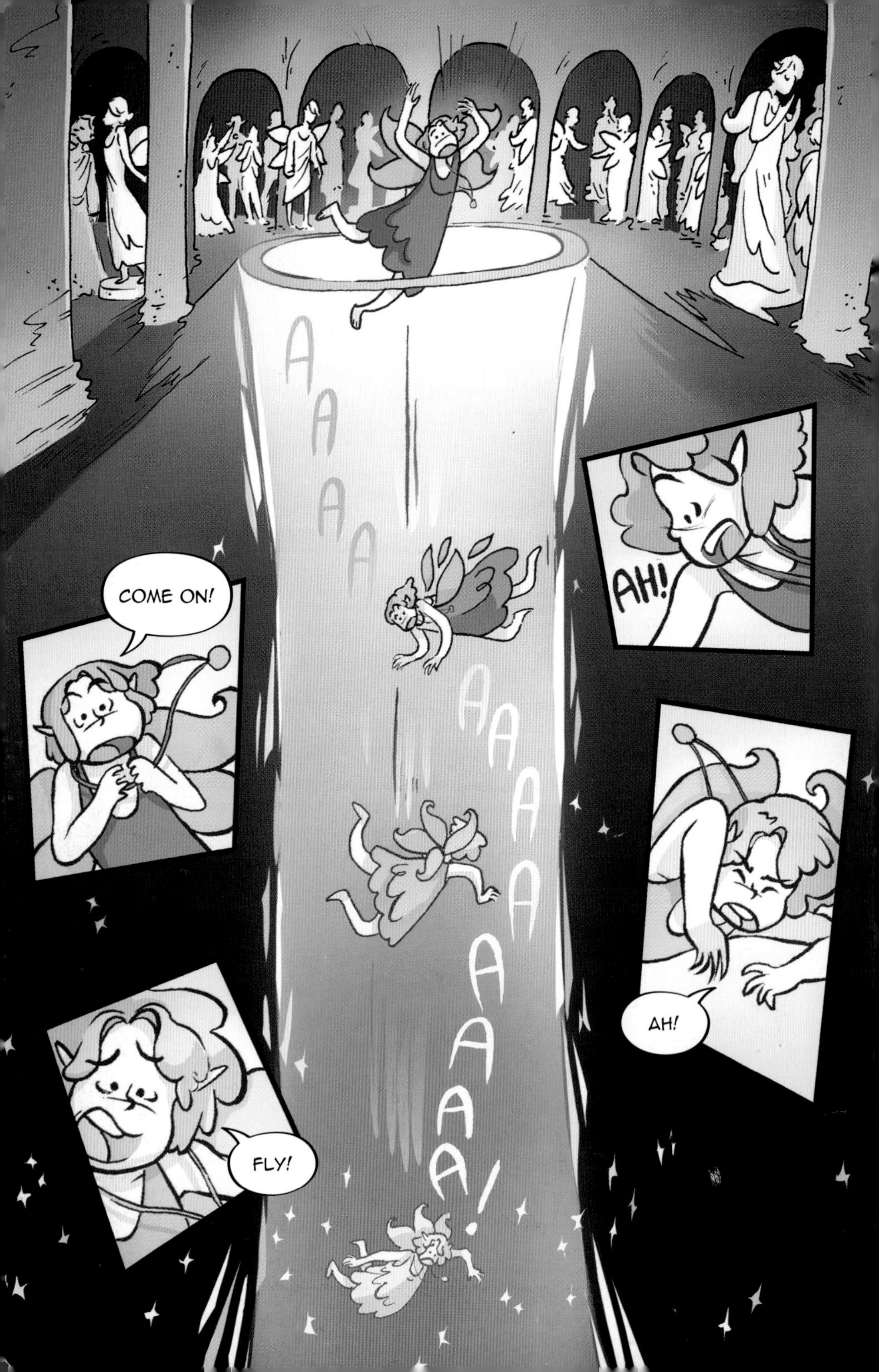
AAAAA
AH!
COME ON!
AAAAAAAAAA!
AH!
FLY!

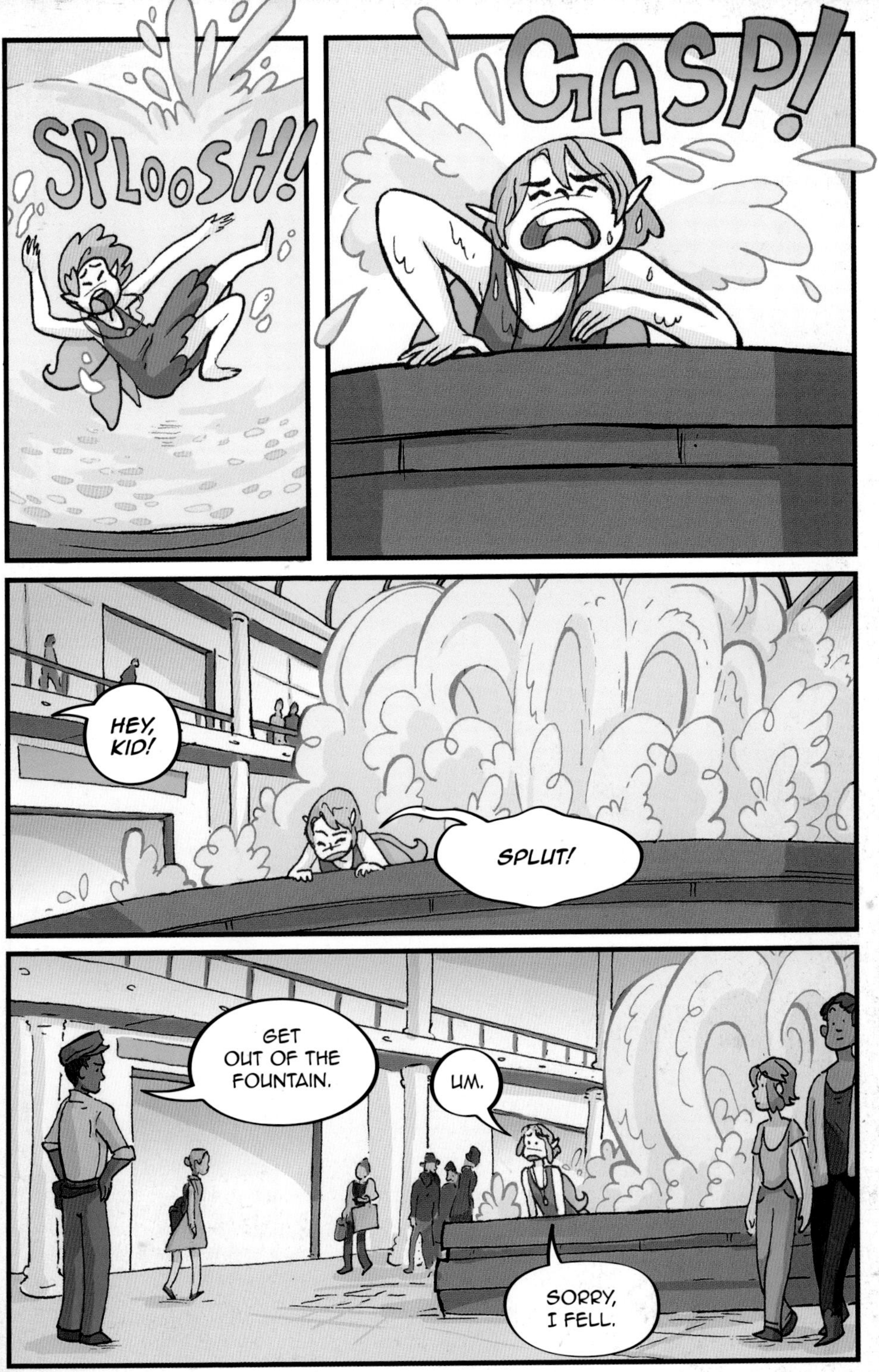
SPLOOSH!
GASP!
HEY, KID!
SPLUT!
GET OUT OF THE FOUNTAIN.
UM.
SORRY, I FELL.

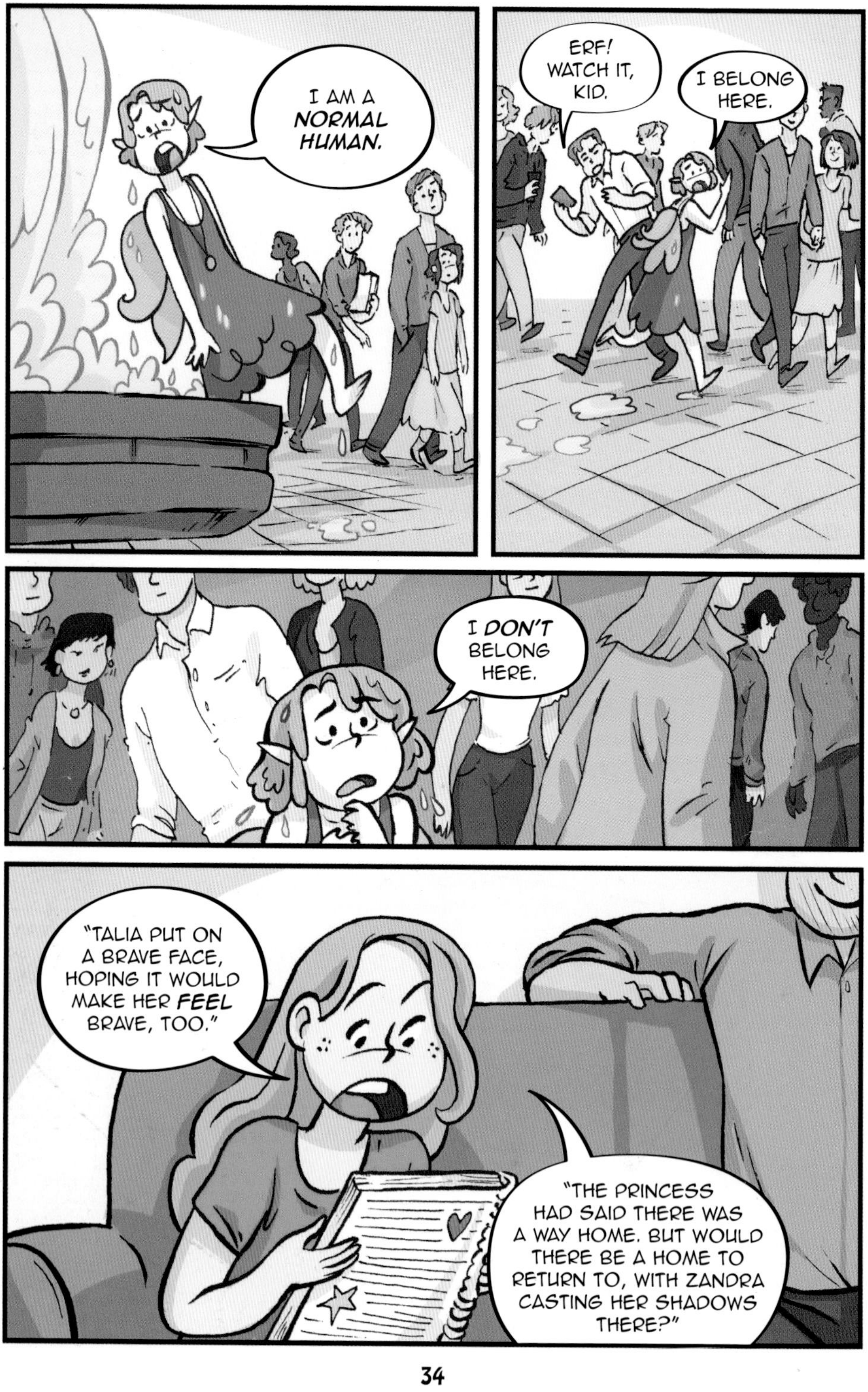
I AM A *NORMAL HUMAN.*
ERF! WATCH IT, KID.
I BELONG HERE.
I *DON'T* BELONG HERE.
"TALIA PUT ON A BRAVE FACE, HOPING IT WOULD MAKE HER *FEEL* BRAVE, TOO."
"THE PRINCESS HAD SAID THERE WAS A WAY HOME. BUT WOULD THERE BE A HOME TO RETURN TO, WITH ZANDRA CASTING HER SHADOWS THERE?"

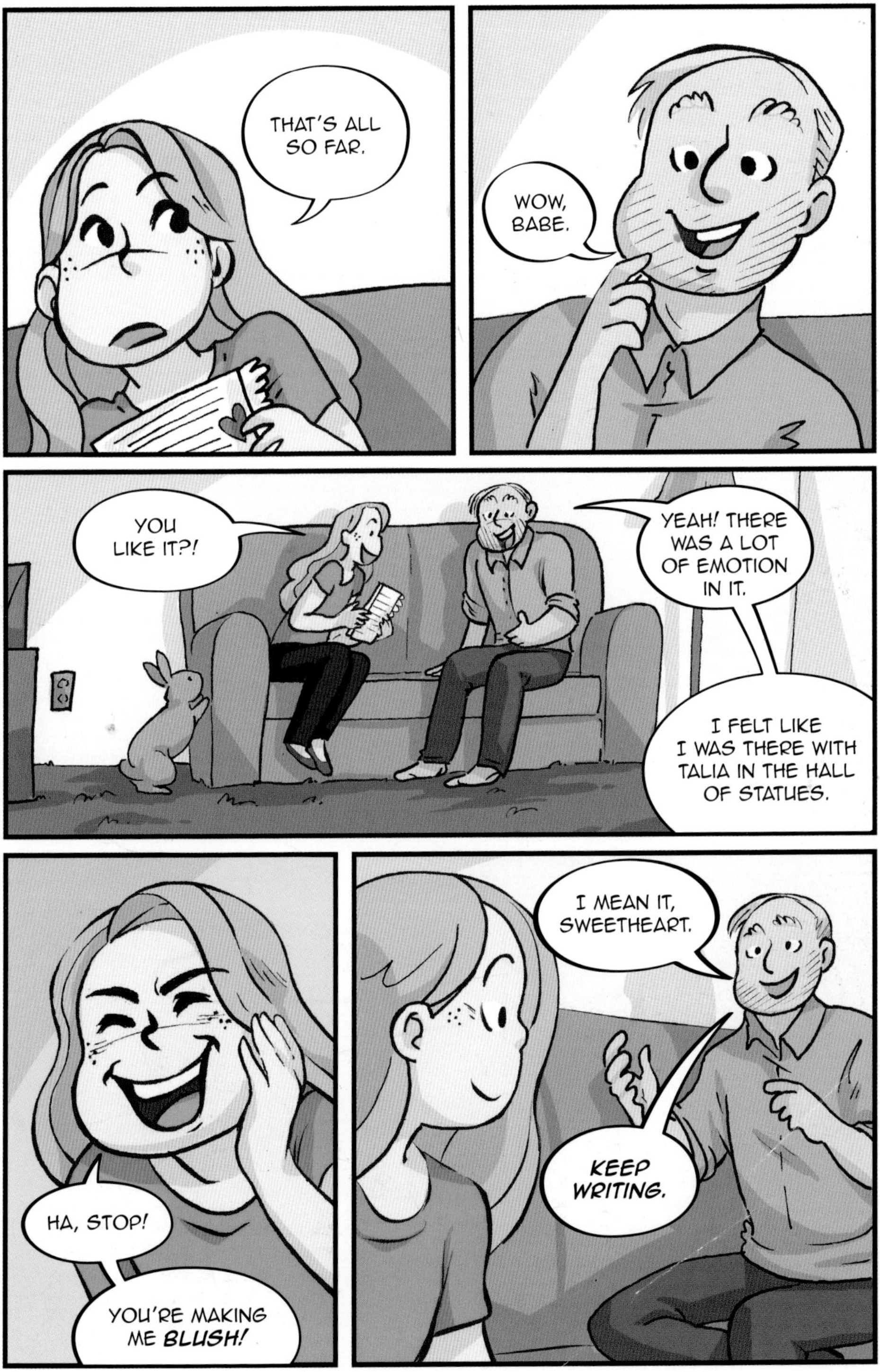
THAT'S ALL SO FAR.
WOW, BABE.
YOU LIKE IT?!
YEAH! THERE WAS A LOT OF EMOTION IN IT.
I FELT LIKE I WAS THERE WITH TALIA IN THE HALL OF STATUES.
HA, STOP!
YOU'RE MAKING ME *BLUSH!*
I MEAN IT, SWEETHEART.
*KEEP WRITING.*

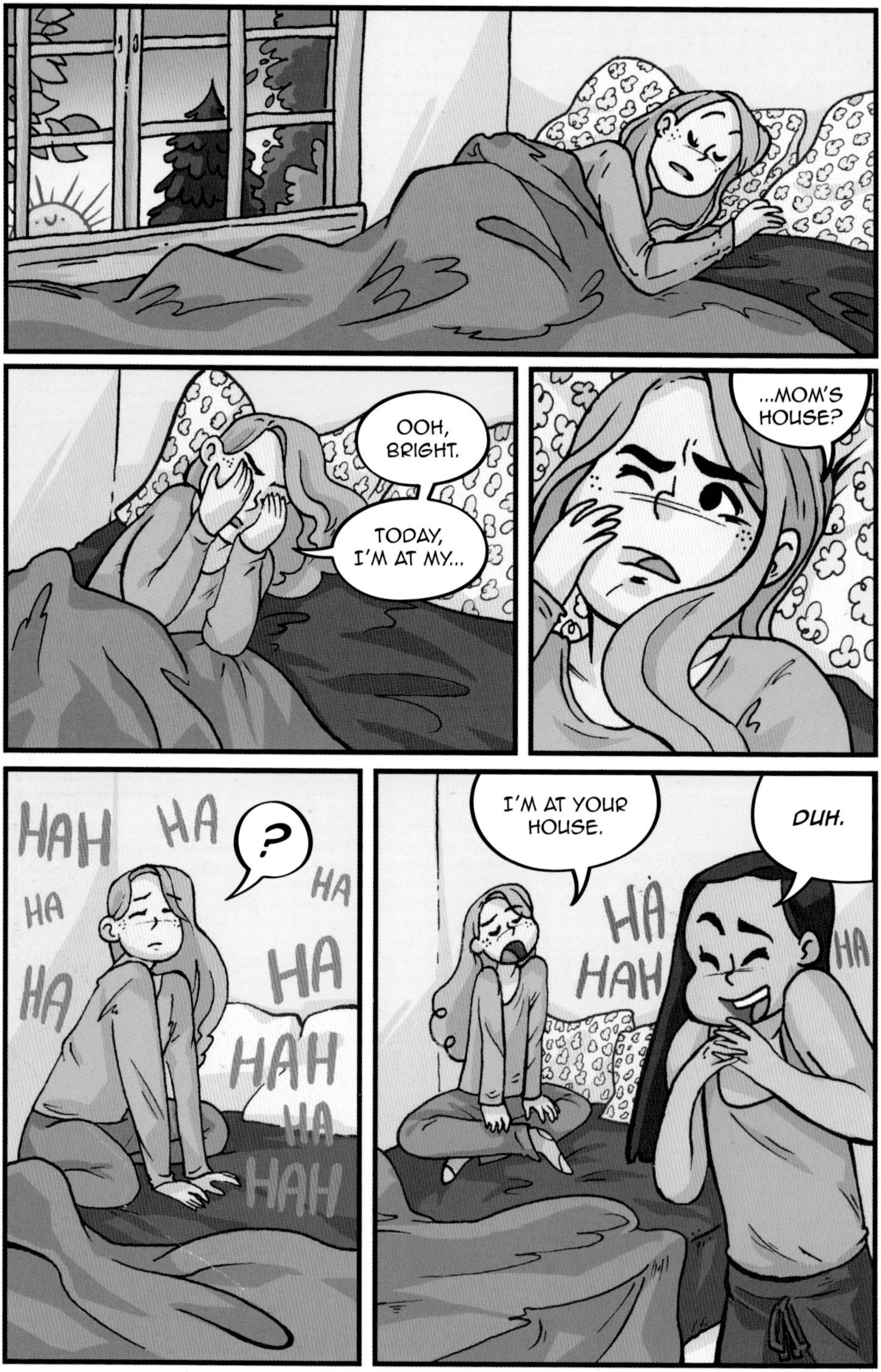

OOH, BRIGHT.
TODAY, I'M AT MY...
...MOM'S HOUSE?
HAH HA
?
HA
HA
HA
HA
HAH
HA
HAH
I'M AT YOUR HOUSE.
DUH.
HA
HAH
HA

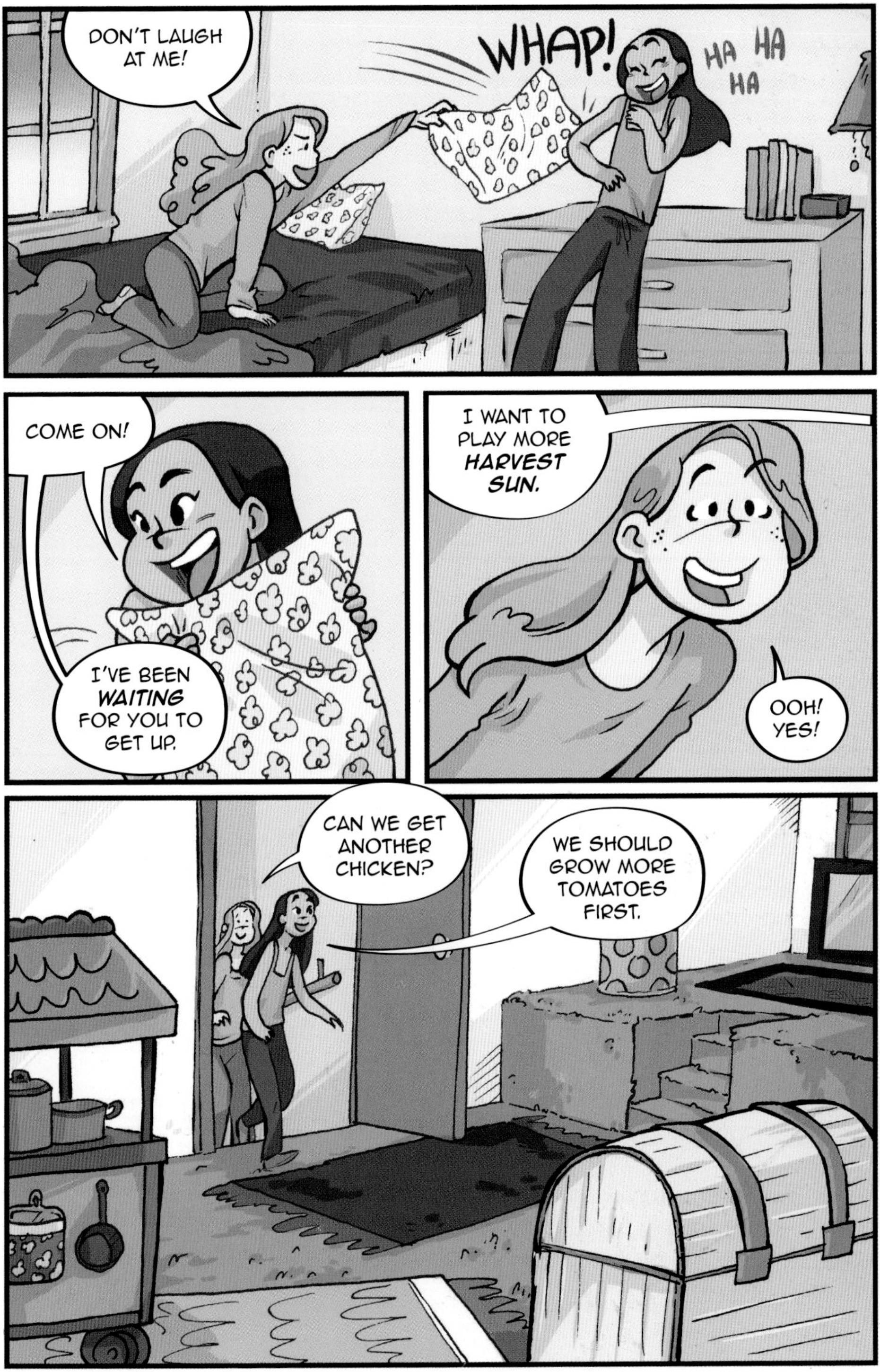
DON'T LAUGH AT ME!
WHAP!
HA HA HA
COME ON!
I'VE BEEN *WAITING* FOR YOU TO GET UP.
I WANT TO PLAY MORE ***HARVEST SUN.***
OOH! YES!
CAN WE GET ANOTHER CHICKEN?
WE SHOULD GROW MORE TOMATOES FIRST.

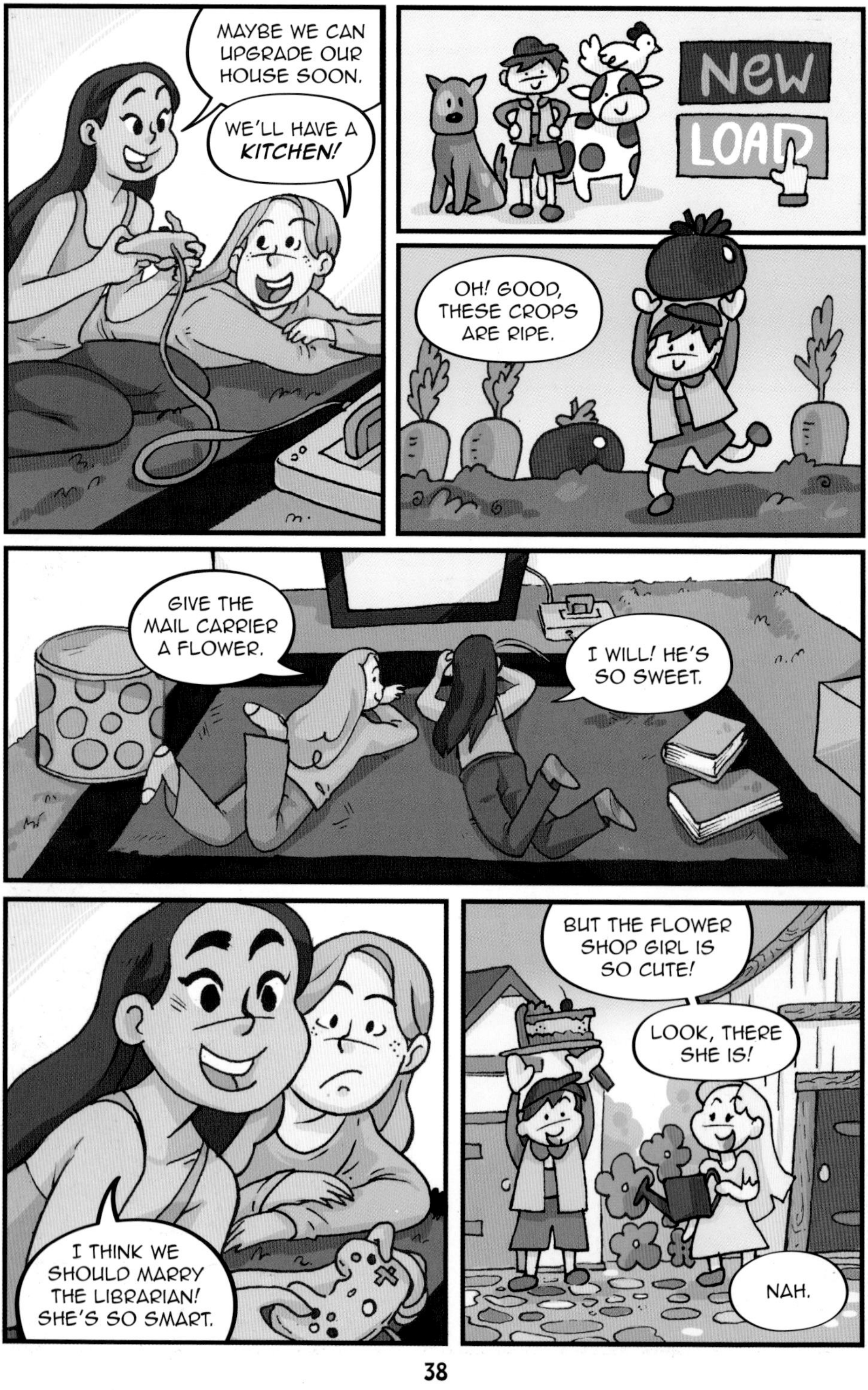
MAYBE WE CAN UPGRADE OUR HOUSE SOON.
WE'LL HAVE A *KITCHEN!*
New
LOAD
OH! GOOD, THESE CROPS ARE RIPE.
GIVE THE MAIL CARRIER A FLOWER.
I WILL! HE'S SO SWEET.
I THINK WE SHOULD MARRY THE LIBRARIAN! SHE'S SO SMART.
BUT THE FLOWER SHOP GIRL IS SO CUTE!
LOOK, THERE SHE IS!
NAH.

I'LL GET MY OWN COPY OF *HARVEST SUN* AND MARRY POPPY.

OH!

THIS IS WHAT IT FEELS LIKE!

WHAT?

THE MAILBOXES!

CUTE!

YOU'RE RIGHT!

IT MAKES OUR CLASSES QUAINT.

LIKE WE'RE ALL NEIGHBORS.

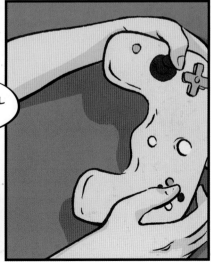

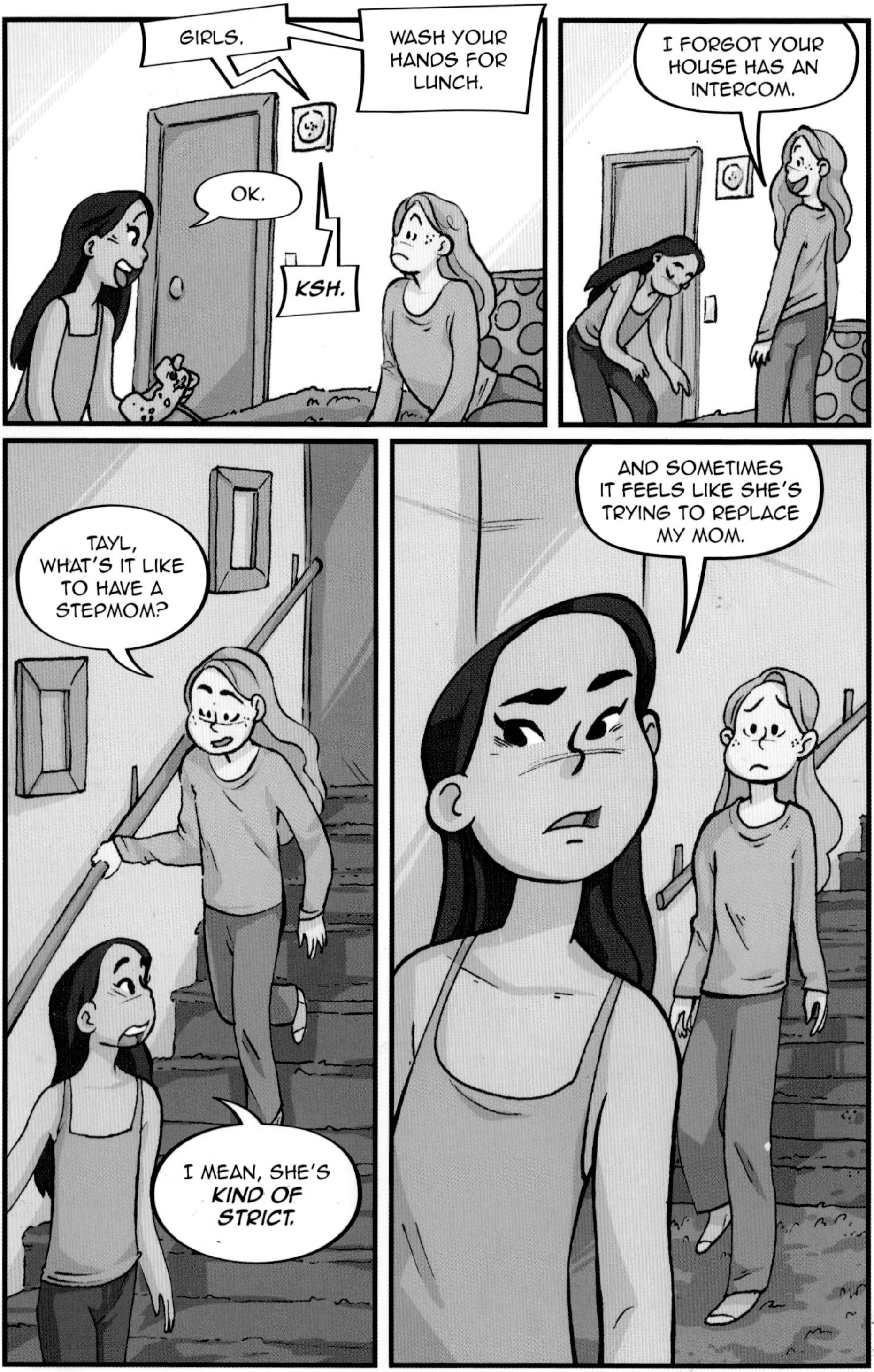
GIRLS.
WASH YOUR HANDS FOR LUNCH.
OK.
KSH.
I FORGOT YOUR HOUSE HAS AN INTERCOM.
TAYL, WHAT'S IT LIKE TO HAVE A STEPMOM?
I MEAN, SHE'S *KIND OF STRICT.*
AND SOMETIMES IT FEELS LIKE SHE'S TRYING TO REPLACE MY MOM.

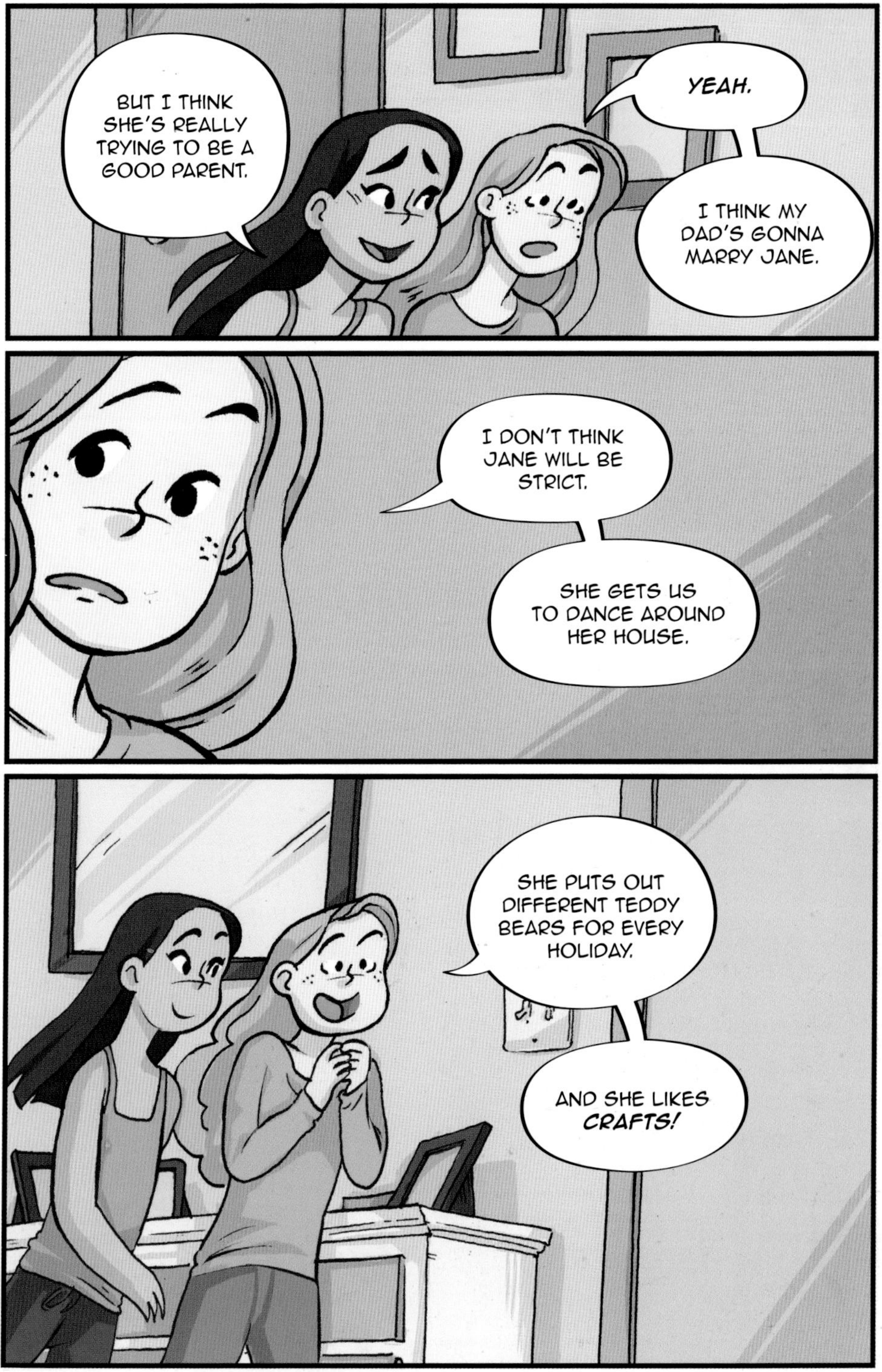
BUT I THINK SHE'S REALLY TRYING TO BE A GOOD PARENT.
*YEAH.*
I THINK MY DAD'S GONNA MARRY JANE.
I DON'T THINK JANE WILL BE STRICT.
SHE GETS US TO DANCE AROUND HER HOUSE.
SHE PUTS OUT DIFFERENT TEDDY BEARS FOR EVERY HOLIDAY.
AND SHE LIKES *CRAFTS!*

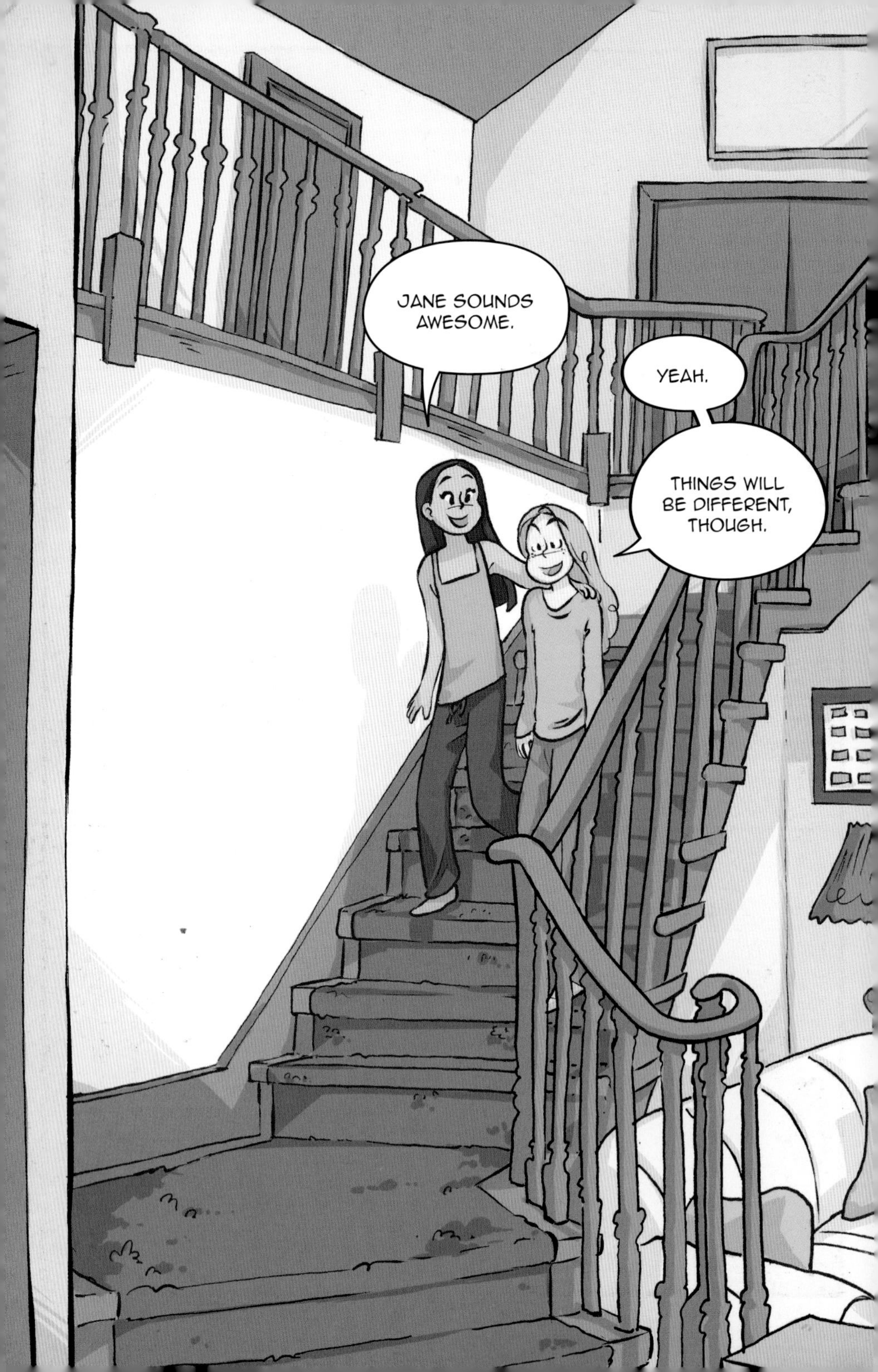
JANE SOUNDS AWESOME.
YEAH.
THINGS WILL BE DIFFERENT, THOUGH.

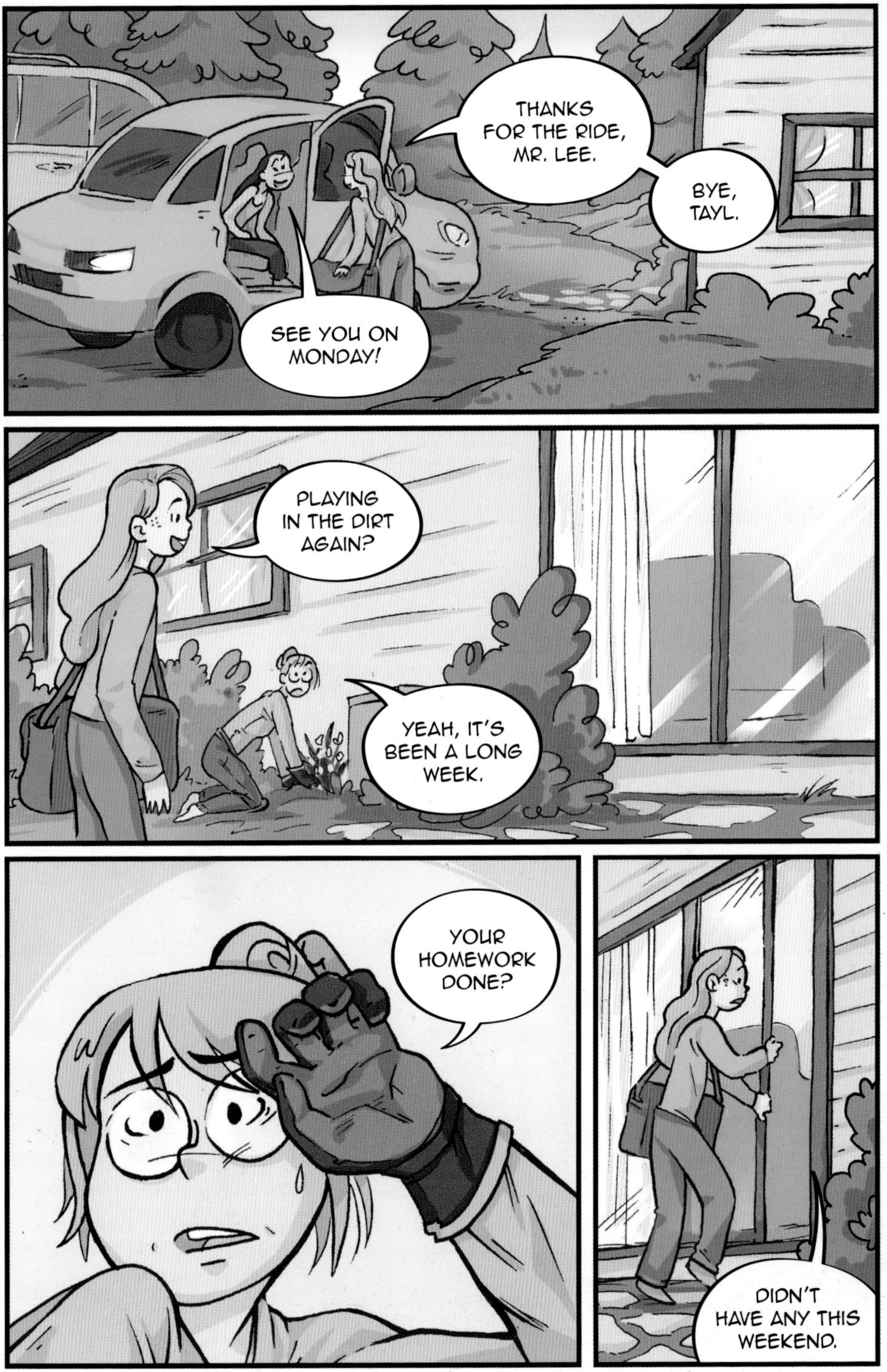
THANKS FOR THE RIDE, MR. LEE.
BYE, TAYL.
SEE YOU ON MONDAY!
PLAYING IN THE DIRT AGAIN?
YEAH, IT'S BEEN A LONG WEEK.
YOUR HOMEWORK DONE?
DIDN'T HAVE ANY THIS WEEKEND.

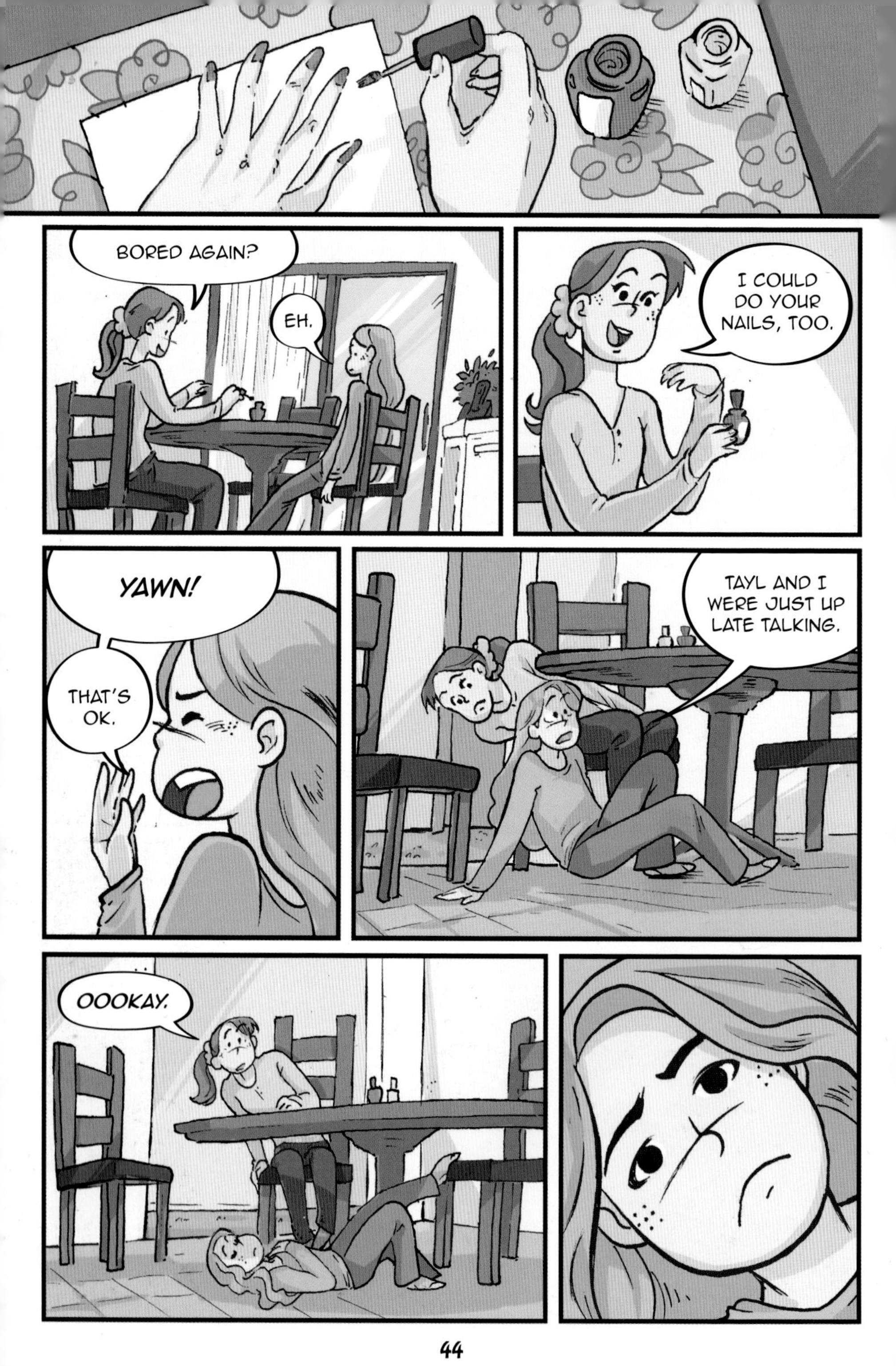
BORED AGAIN?
EH.
I COULD DO YOUR NAILS, TOO.
YAWN!
THAT'S OK.
TAYL AND I WERE JUST UP LATE TALKING.
OOOKAY.

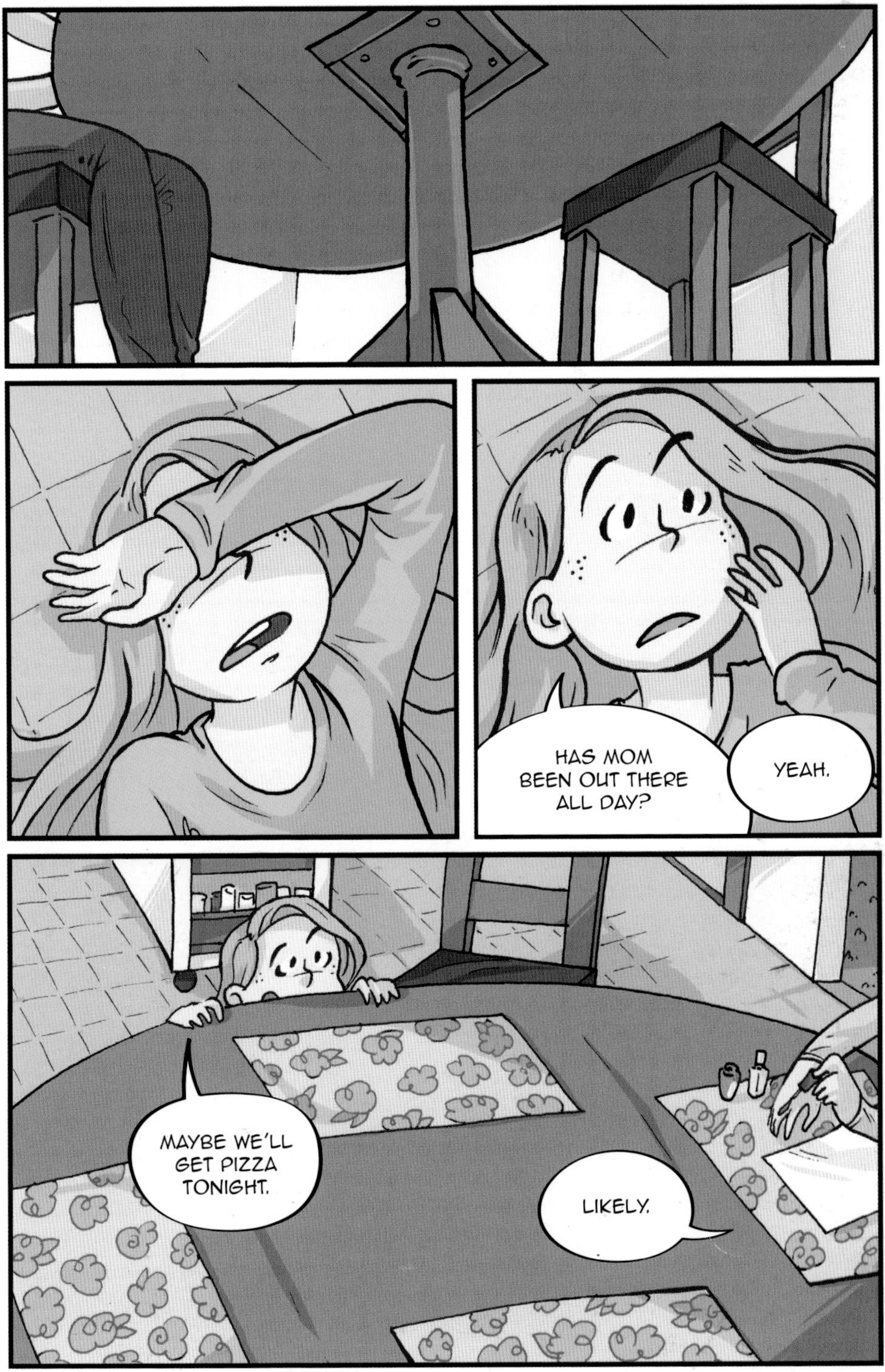
HAS MOM BEEN OUT THERE ALL DAY?
YEAH.
MAYBE WE'LL GET PIZZA TONIGHT.
LIKELY.

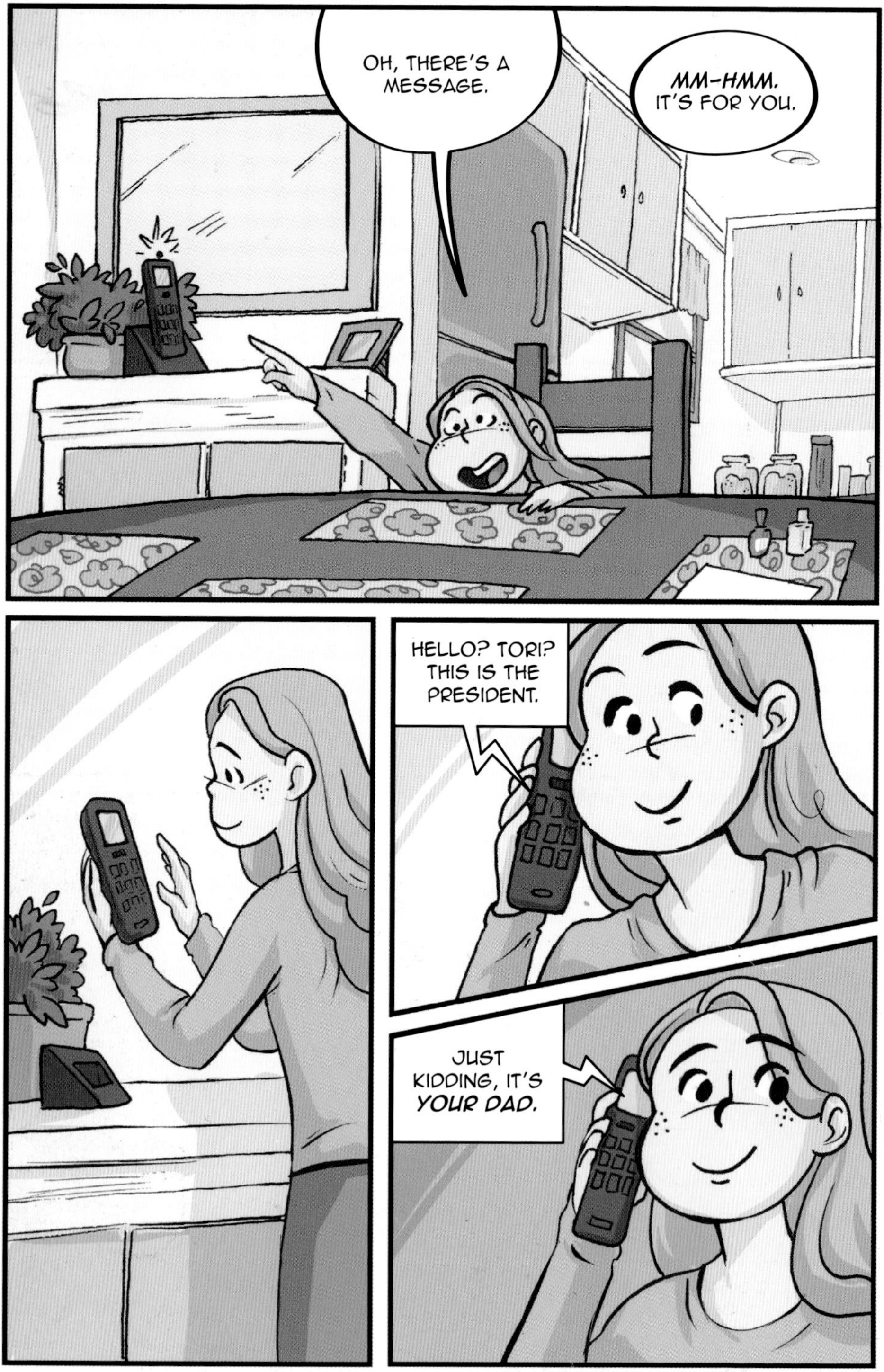
OH, THERE'S A MESSAGE.
*MM-HMM.* IT'S FOR YOU.
HELLO? TORI? THIS IS THE PRESIDENT.
JUST KIDDING, IT'S ***YOUR DAD.***

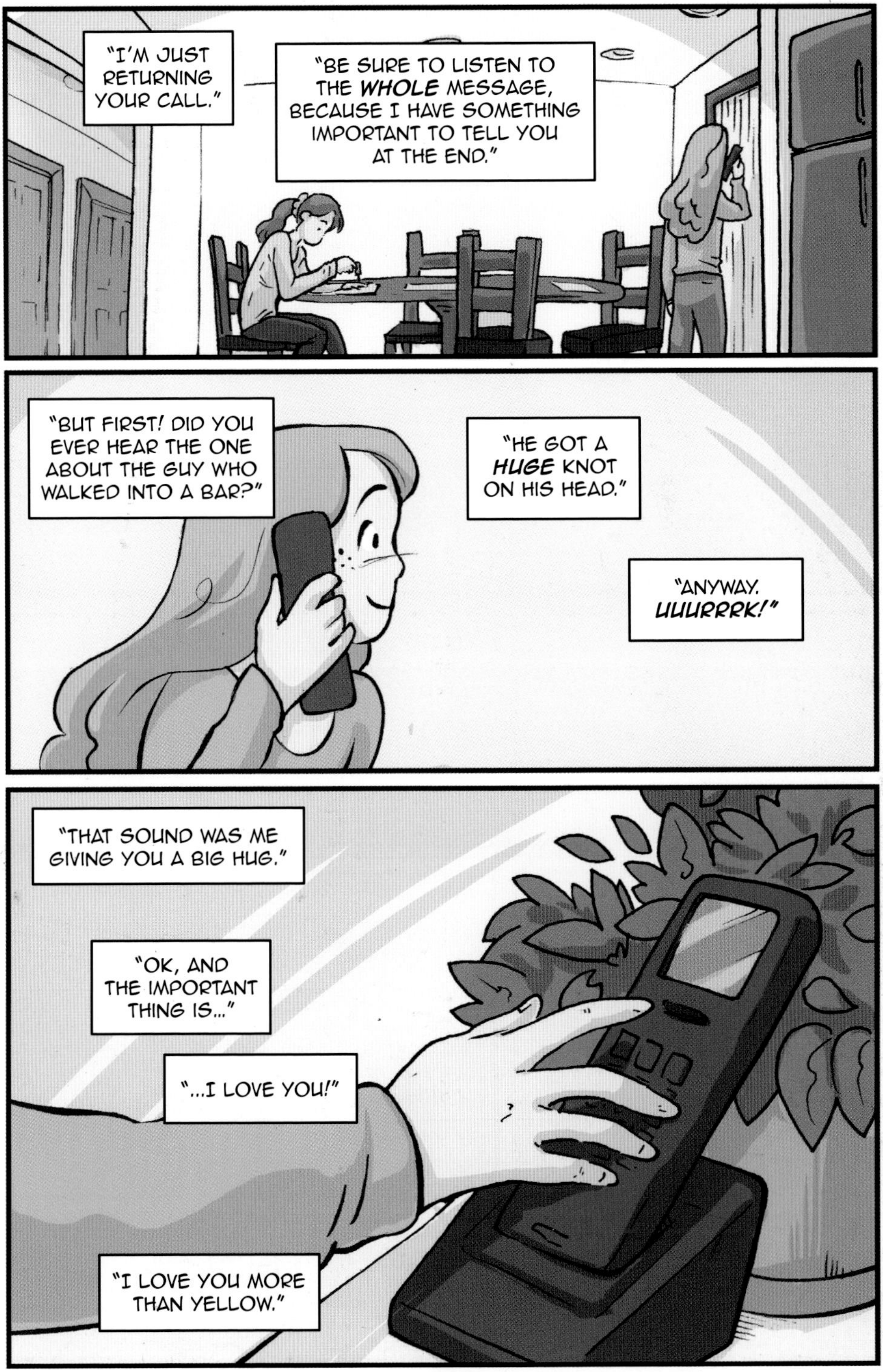
"I'M JUST RETURNING YOUR CALL."
"BE SURE TO LISTEN TO THE WHOLE MESSAGE, BECAUSE I HAVE SOMETHING IMPORTANT TO TELL YOU AT THE END."
"BUT FIRST! DID YOU EVER HEAR THE ONE ABOUT THE GUY WHO WALKED INTO A BAR?"
"HE GOT A HUGE KNOT ON HIS HEAD."
"ANYWAY. UUURRRK!"
"THAT SOUND WAS ME GIVING YOU A BIG HUG."
"OK, AND THE IMPORTANT THING IS..."
"...I LOVE YOU!"
"I LOVE YOU MORE THAN YELLOW."

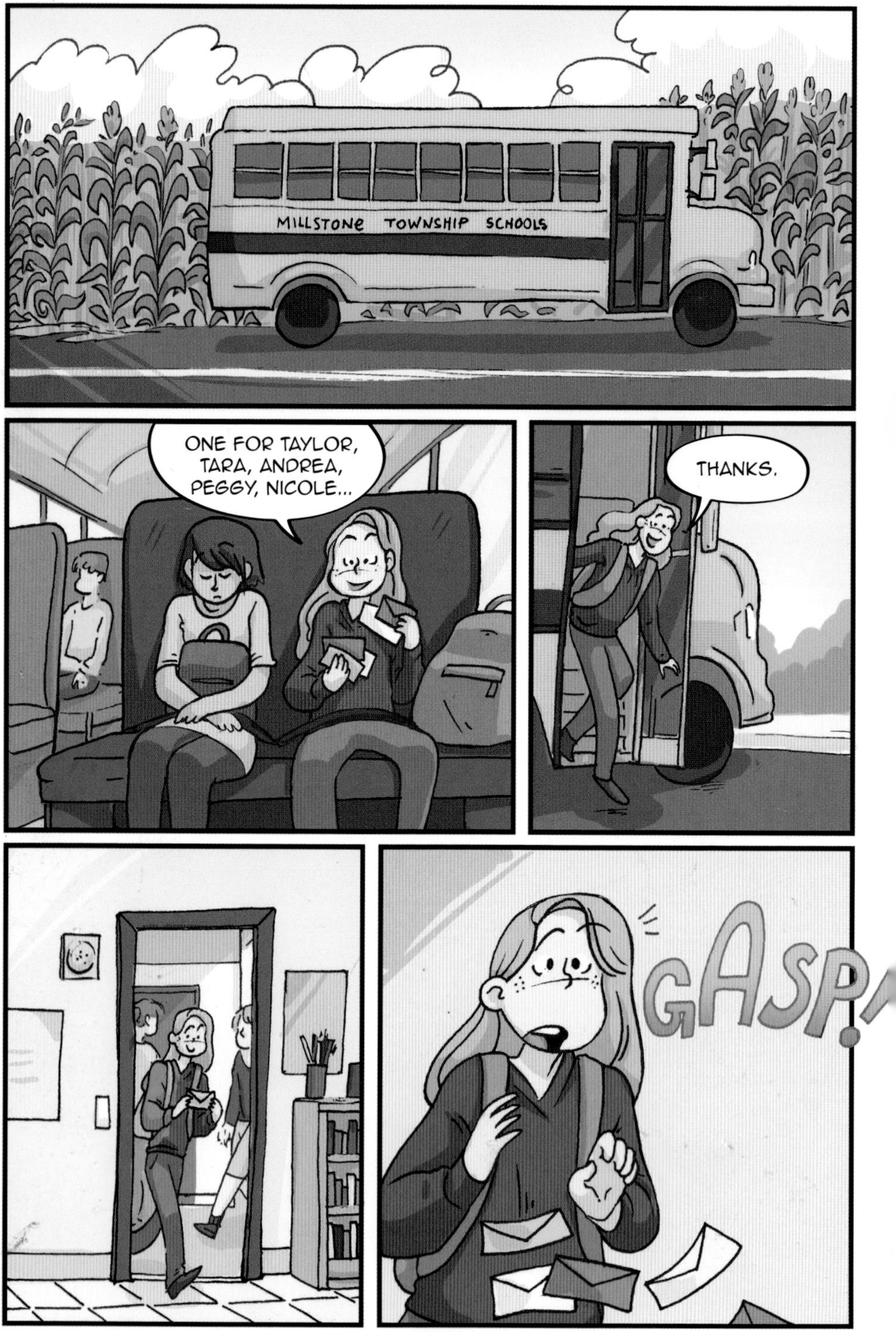
MILLSTONE TOWNSHIP SCHOOLS
ONE FOR TAYLOR, TARA, ANDREA, PEGGY, NICOLE...
THANKS.
GASP!

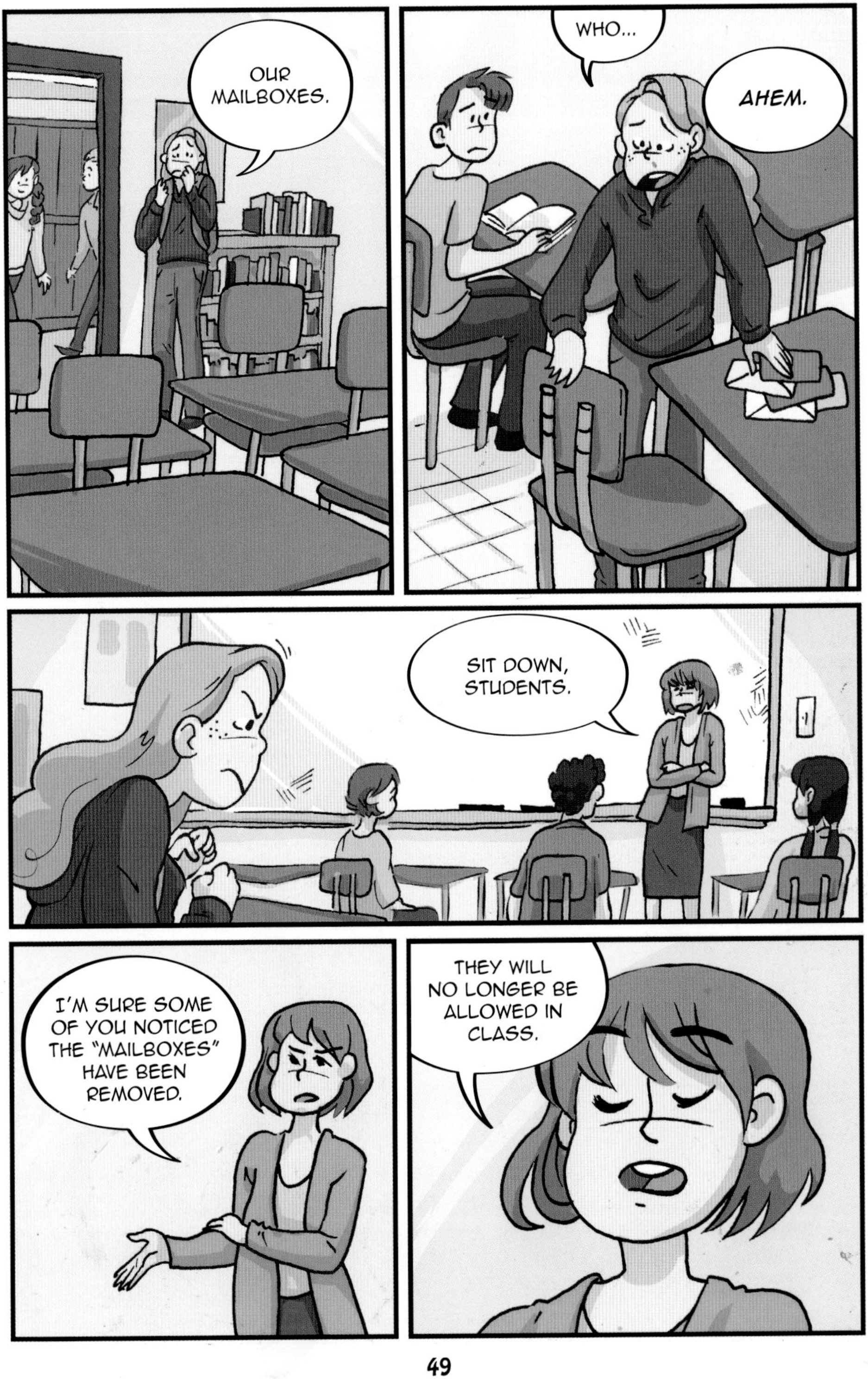
OUR MAILBOXES.
WHO...
AHEM.
SIT DOWN, STUDENTS.
I'M SURE SOME OF YOU NOTICED THE "MAILBOXES" HAVE BEEN REMOVED.
THEY WILL NO LONGER BE ALLOWED IN CLASS.

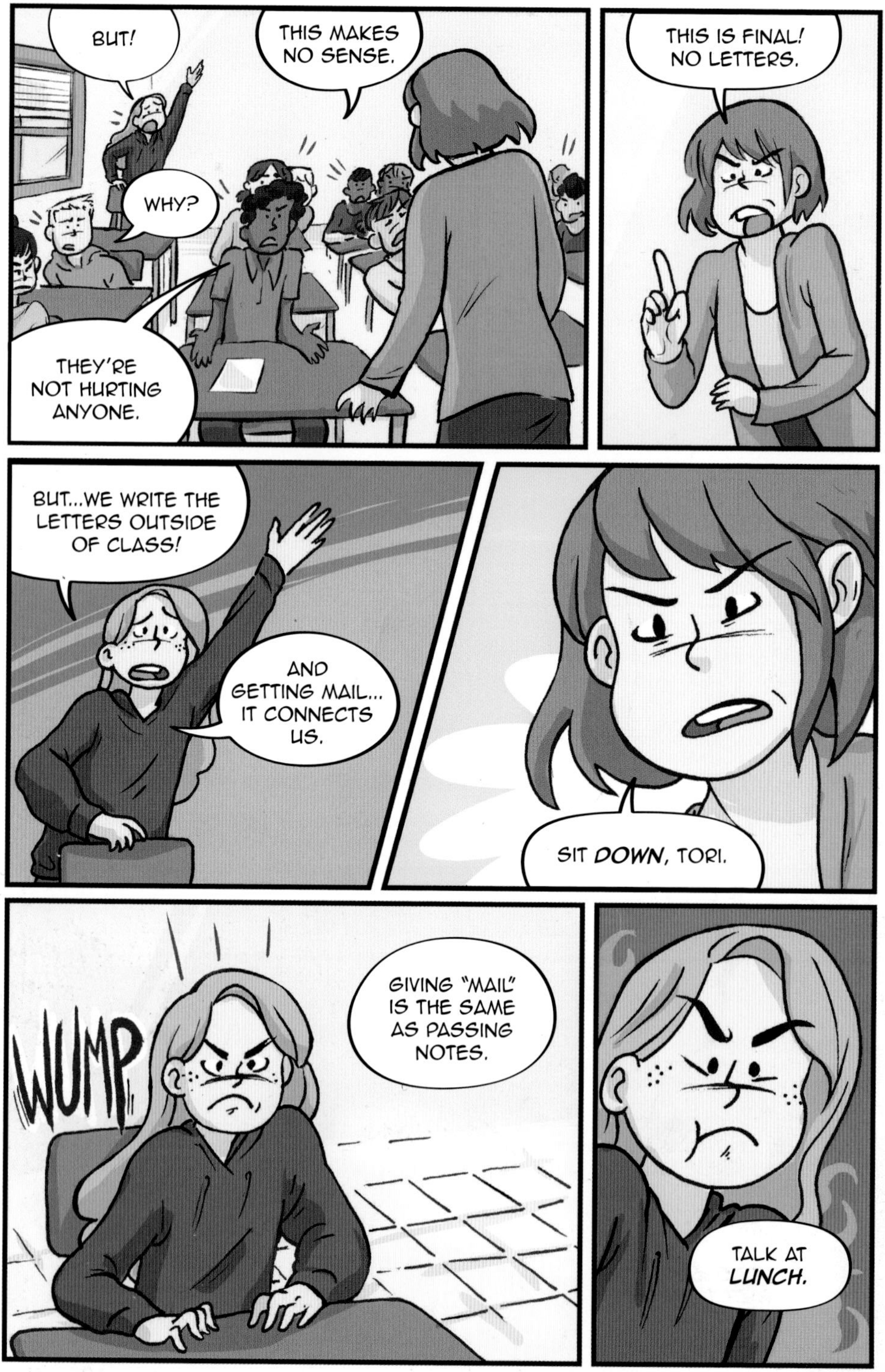
BUT!
THIS MAKES NO SENSE.
WHY?
THEY'RE NOT HURTING ANYONE.
THIS IS FINAL! NO LETTERS.
BUT...WE WRITE THE LETTERS OUTSIDE OF CLASS!
AND GETTING MAIL... IT CONNECTS US.
SIT *DOWN*, TORI.
WUMP
GIVING "MAIL" IS THE SAME AS PASSING NOTES.
TALK AT *LUNCH.*

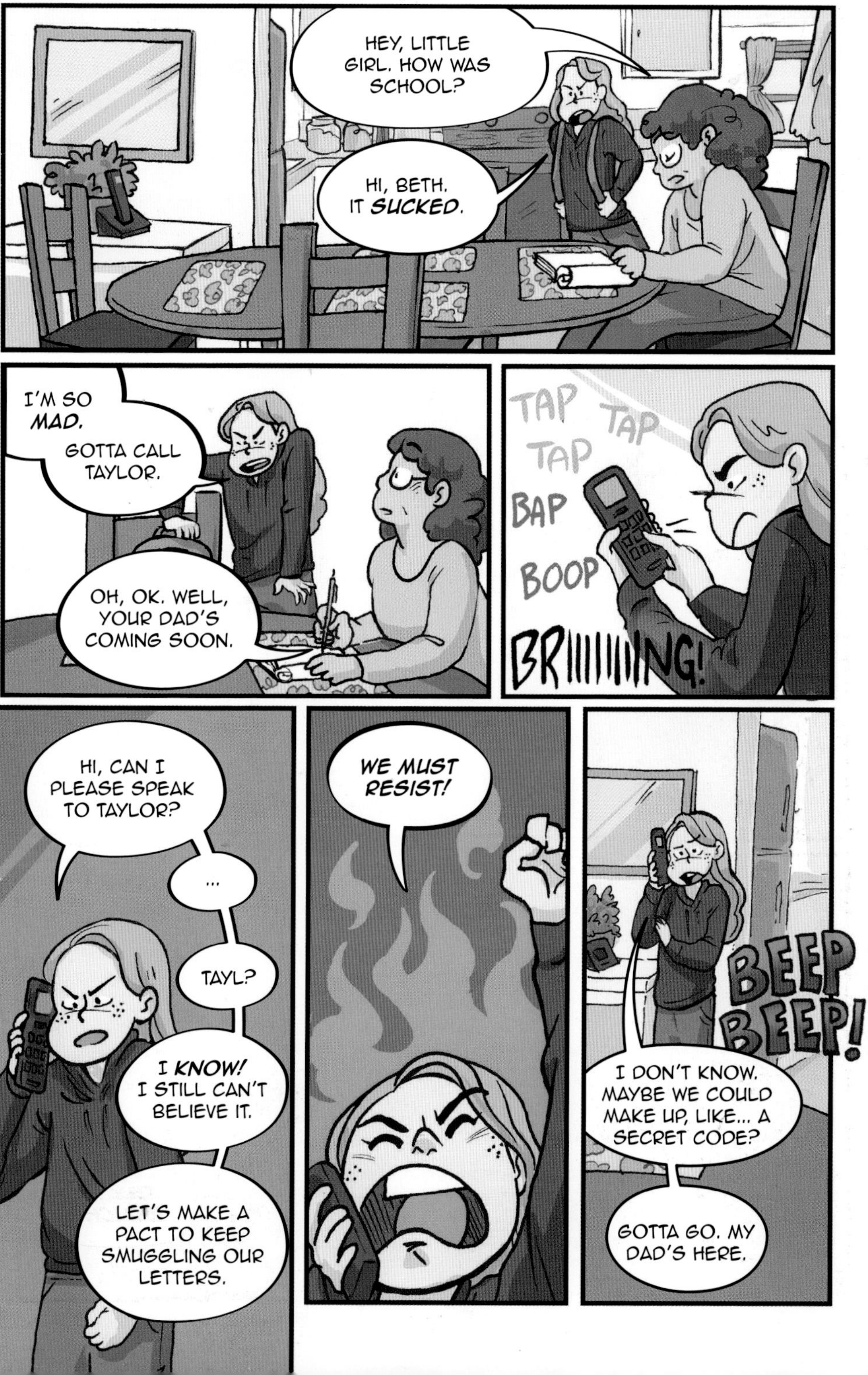
HEY, LITTLE GIRL. HOW WAS SCHOOL?
HI, BETH. IT SUCKED.
I'M SO MAD.
GOTTA CALL TAYLOR.
OH, OK. WELL, YOUR DAD'S COMING SOON.
TAP
TAP
TAP
BAP
BOOP
BRIIIIIIIING!
HI, CAN I PLEASE SPEAK TO TAYLOR?
...
TAYL?
I KNOW! I STILL CAN'T BELIEVE IT.
LET'S MAKE A PACT TO KEEP SMUGGLING OUR LETTERS.
WE MUST RESIST!
BEEP BEEP!
I DON'T KNOW. MAYBE WE COULD MAKE UP, LIKE... A SECRET CODE?
GOTTA GO. MY DAD'S HERE.

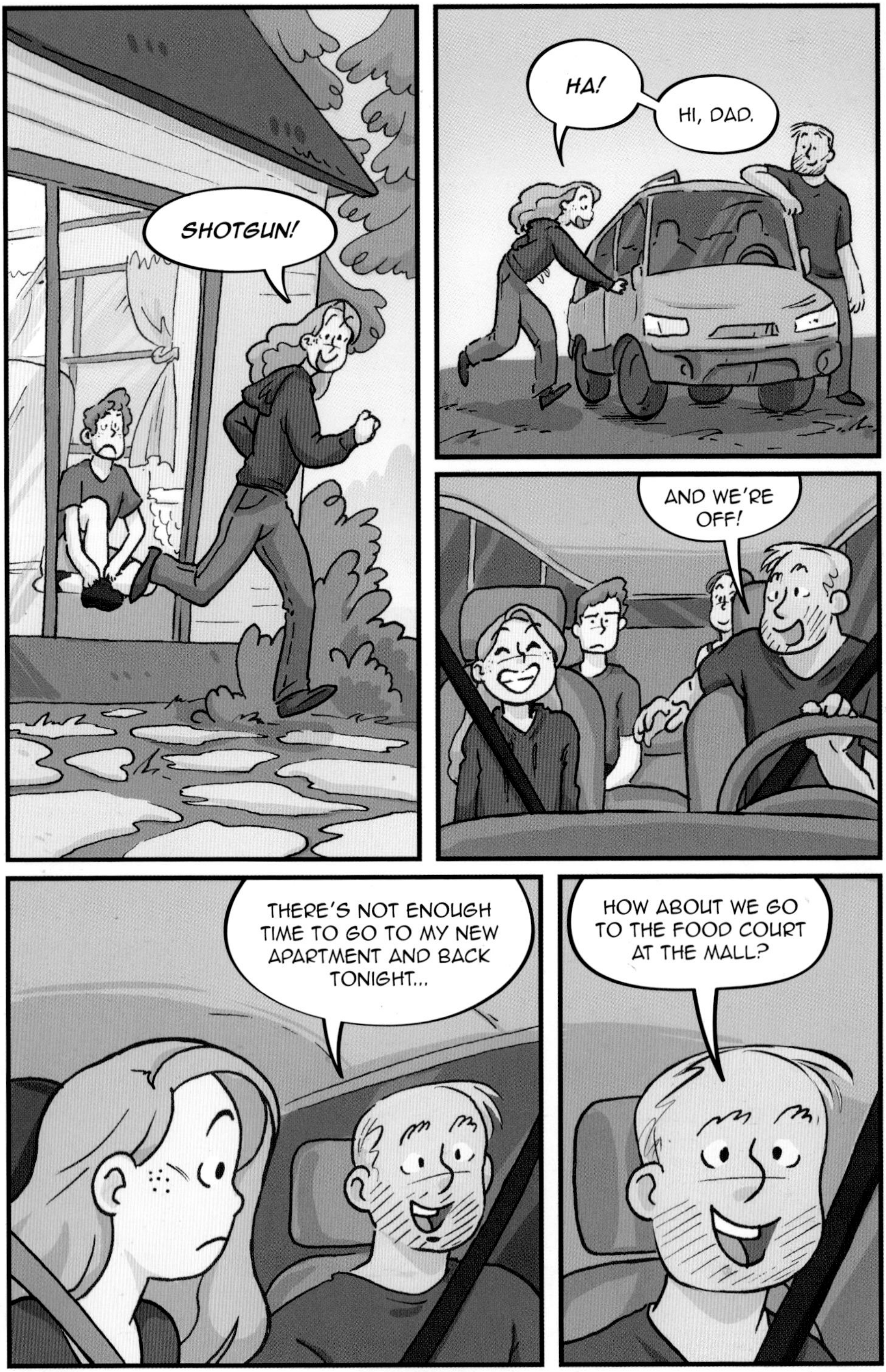
SHOTGUN!
HA!
HI, DAD.
AND WE'RE OFF!
THERE'S NOT ENOUGH TIME TO GO TO MY NEW APARTMENT AND BACK TONIGHT...
HOW ABOUT WE GO TO THE FOOD COURT AT THE MALL?

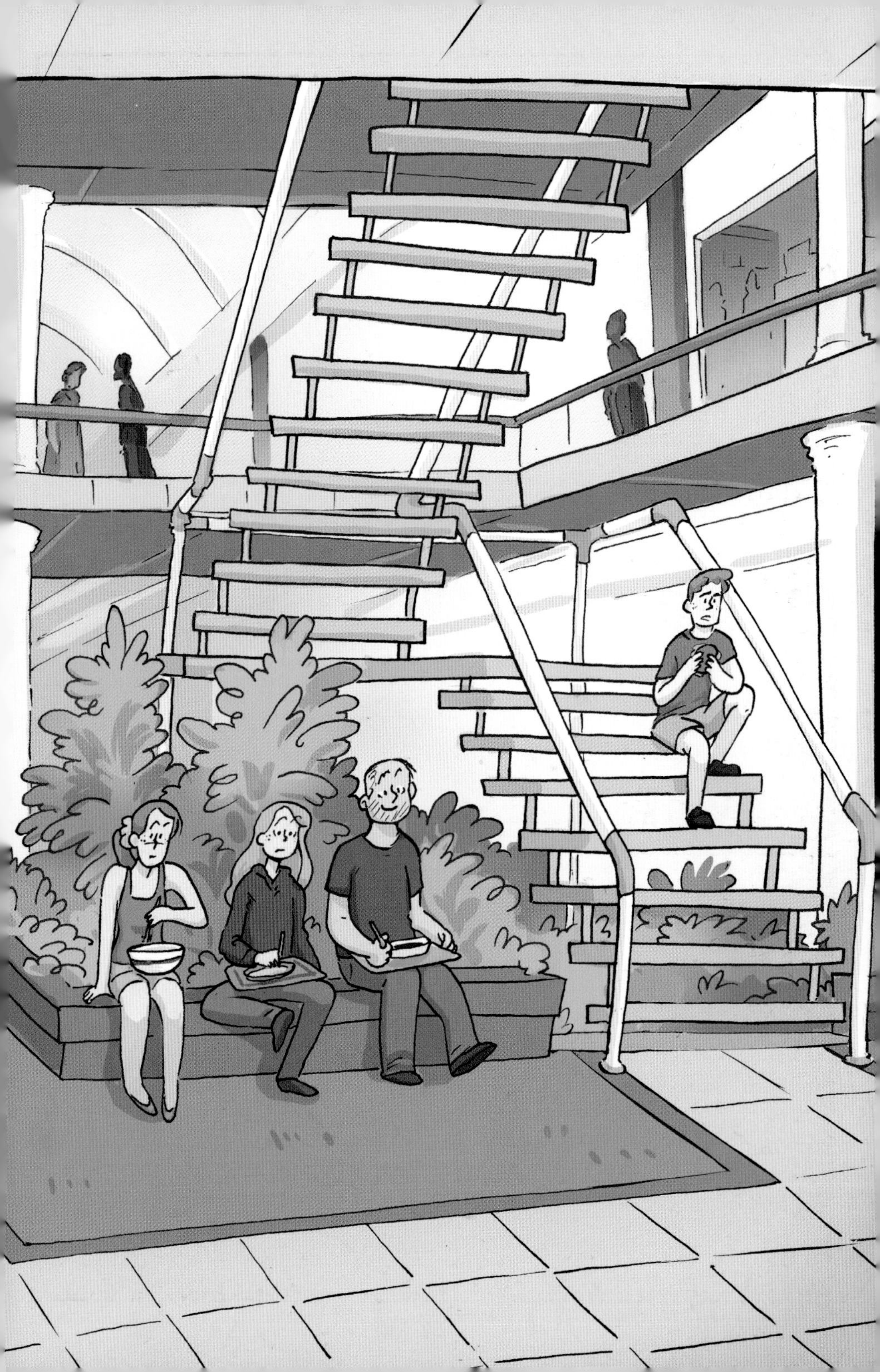

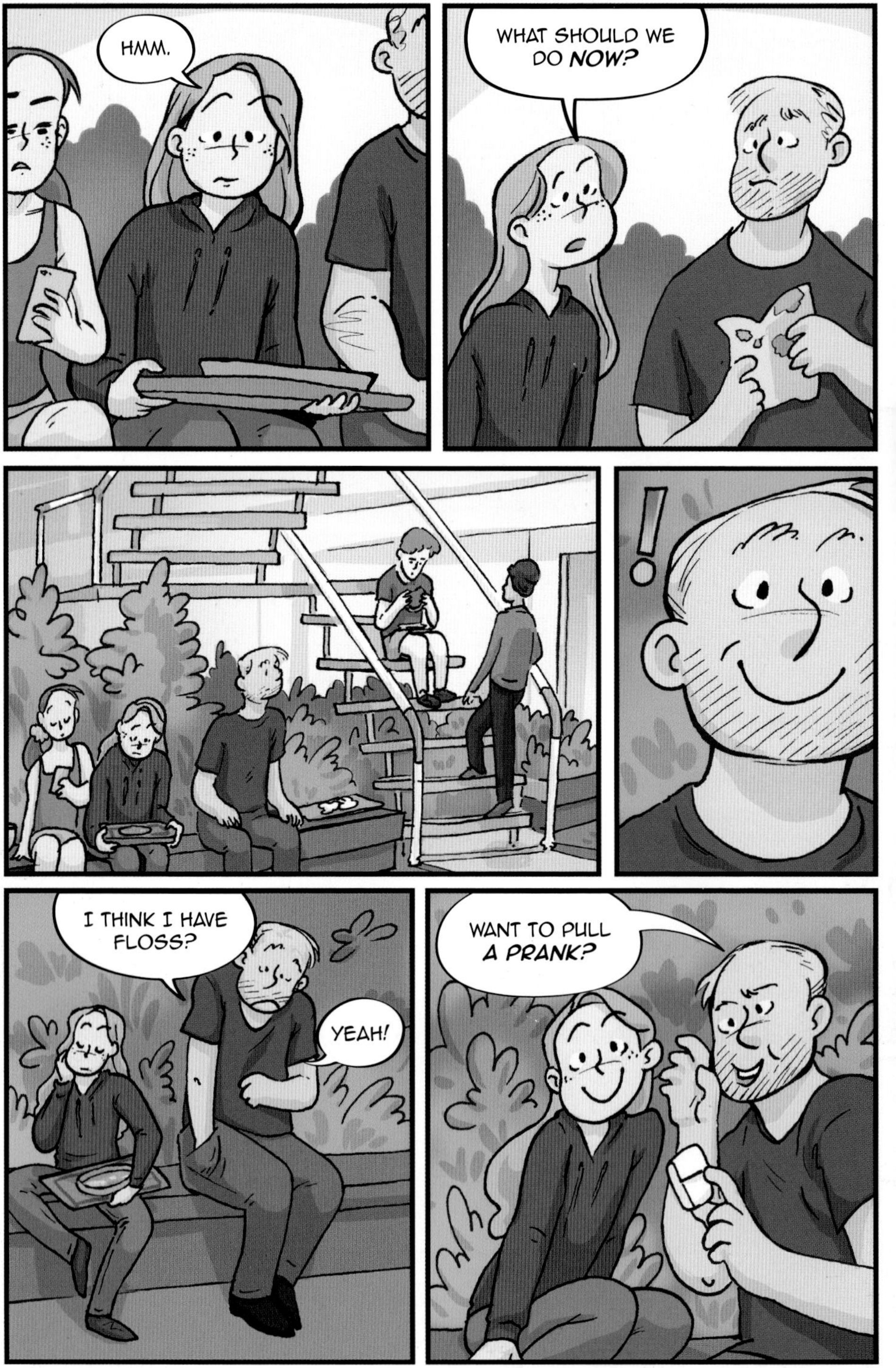
HMM.
WHAT SHOULD WE DO *NOW?*
!
I THINK I HAVE FLOSS?
YEAH!
WANT TO PULL *A PRANK?*

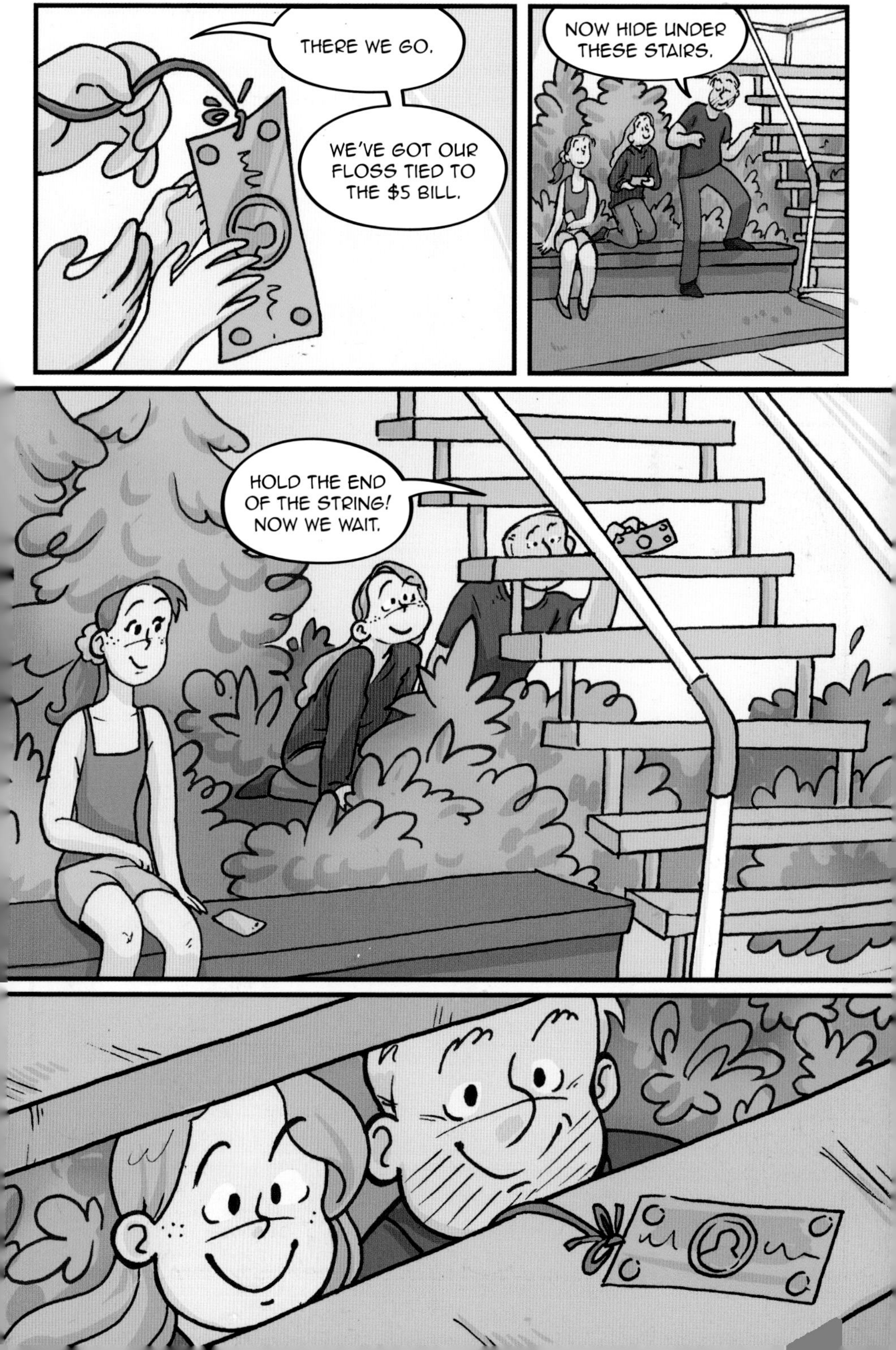
THERE WE GO.
WE'VE GOT OUR FLOSS TIED TO THE $5 BILL.
NOW HIDE UNDER THESE STAIRS.
HOLD THE END OF THE STRING! NOW WE WAIT.

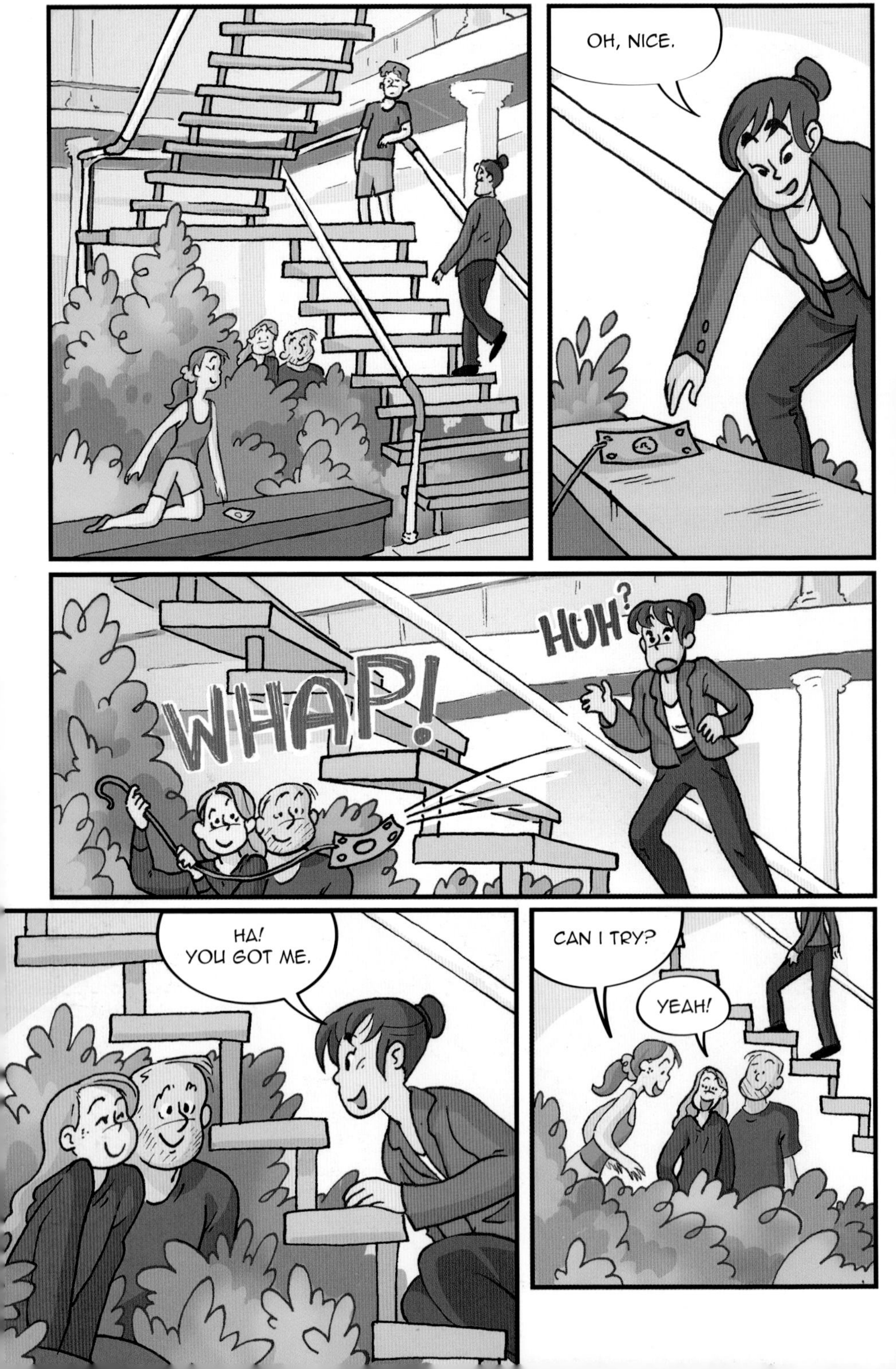
OH, NICE.
WHAP!
HUH?
HA!
YOU GOT ME.
CAN I TRY?
YEAH!

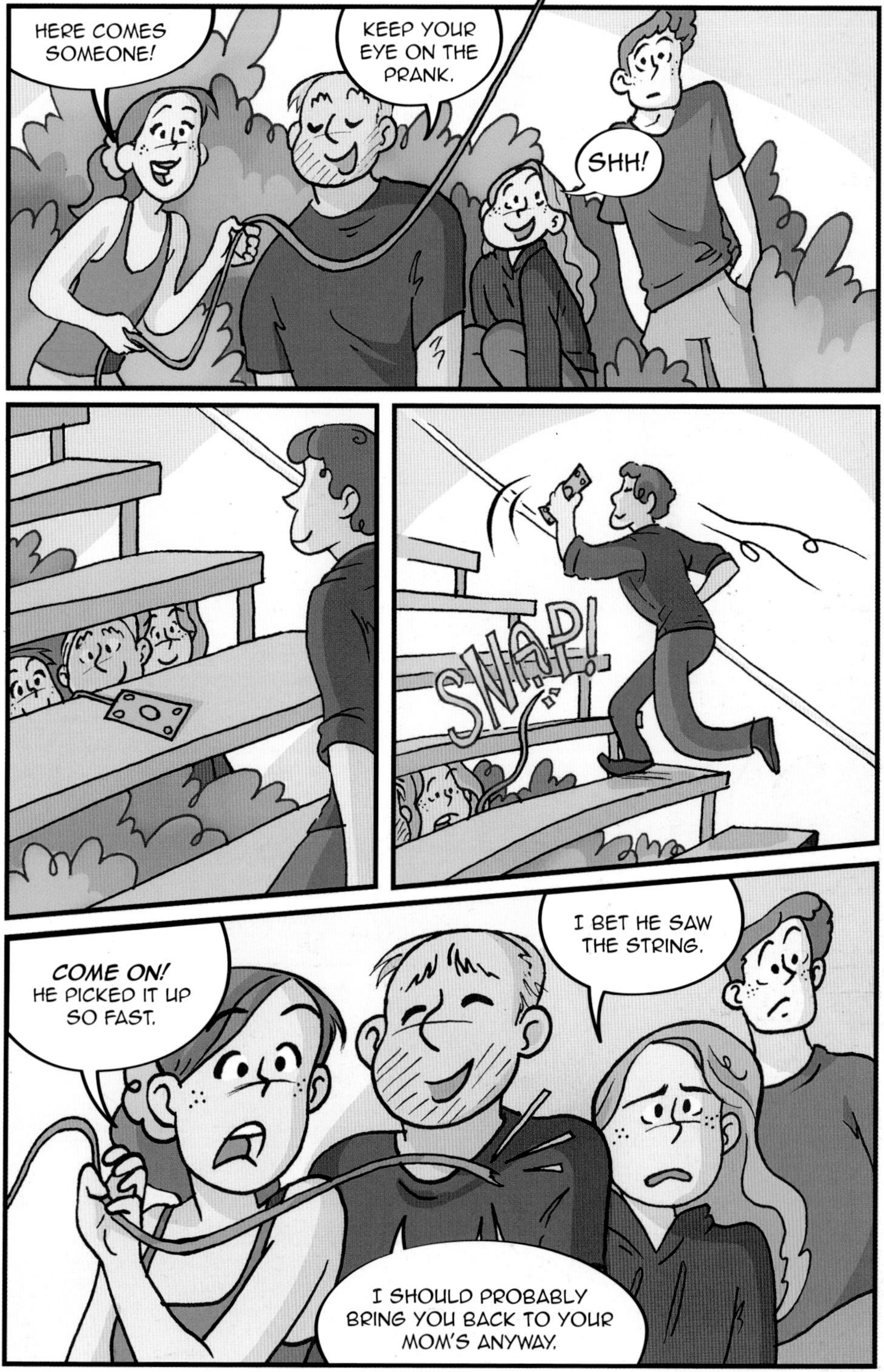

HERE COMES SOMEONE!
KEEP YOUR EYE ON THE PRANK.
SHH!
SNAP!
*COME ON!* HE PICKED IT UP SO FAST.
I BET HE SAW THE STRING.
I SHOULD PROBABLY BRING YOU BACK TO YOUR MOM'S ANYWAY.

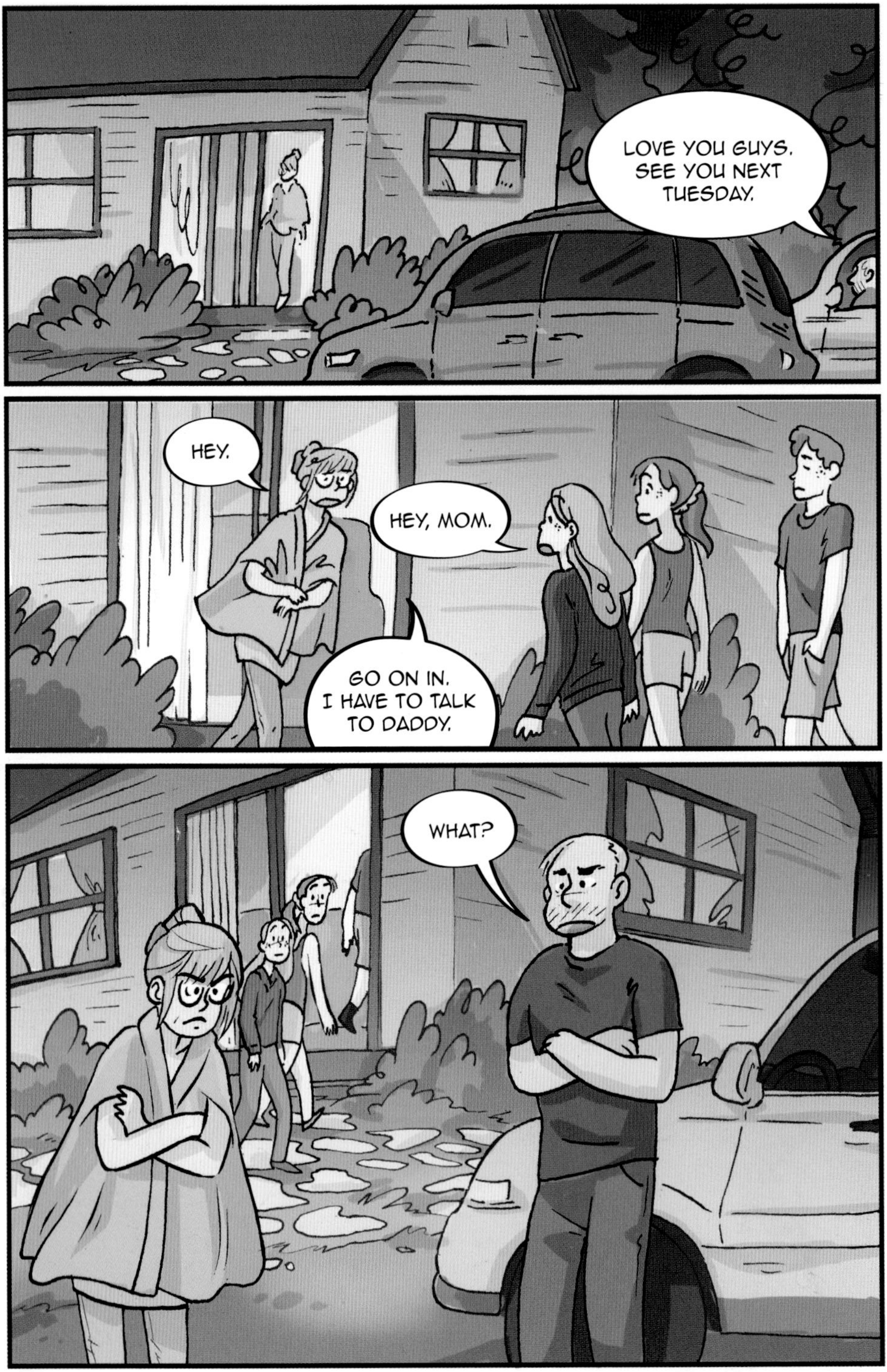
LOVE YOU GUYS. SEE YOU NEXT TUESDAY.
HEY.
HEY, MOM.
GO ON IN. I HAVE TO TALK TO DADDY.
WHAT?

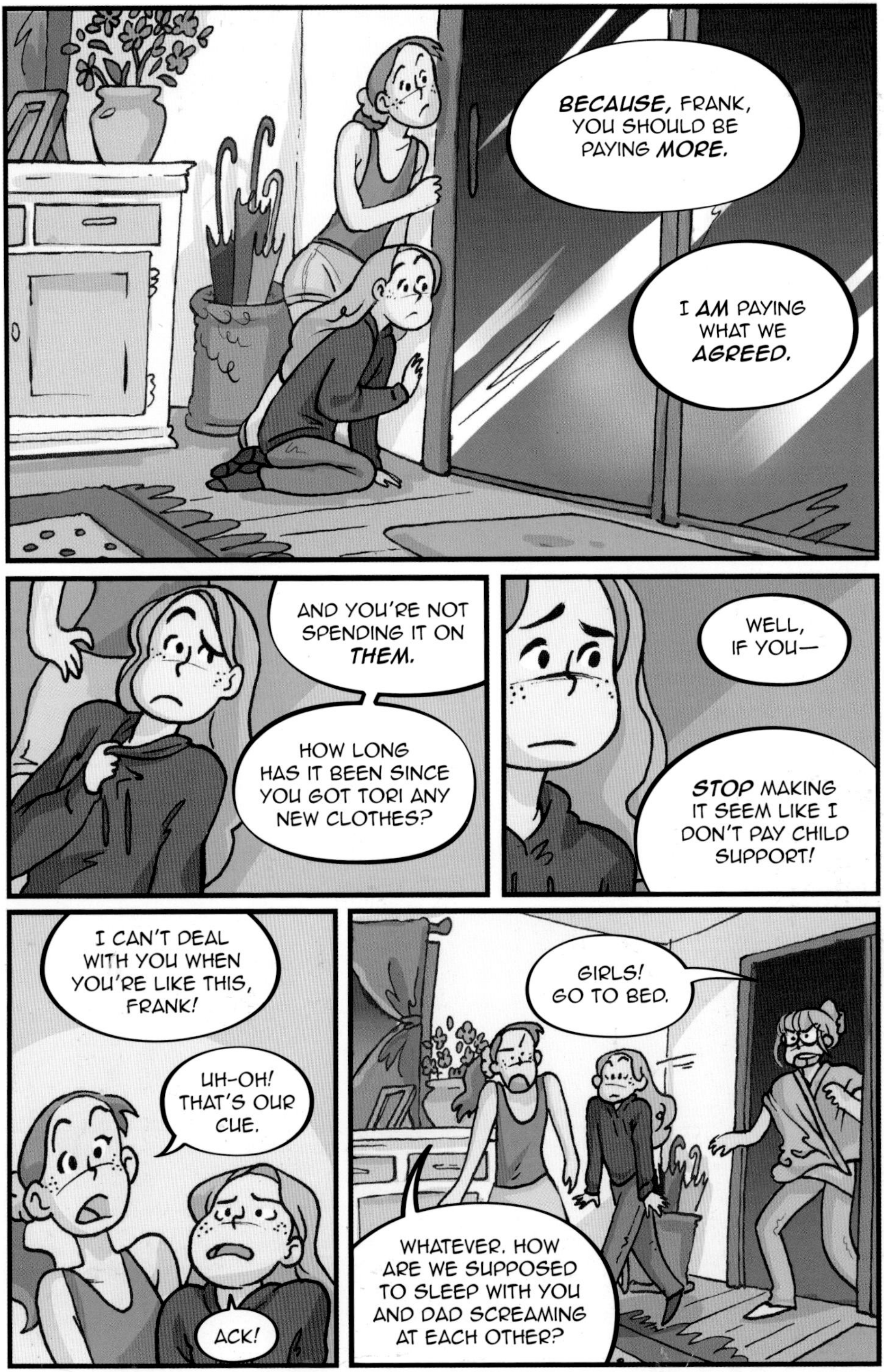
BECAUSE, FRANK, YOU SHOULD BE PAYING MORE.
I AM PAYING WHAT WE AGREED.
AND YOU'RE NOT SPENDING IT ON THEM.
HOW LONG HAS IT BEEN SINCE YOU GOT TORI ANY NEW CLOTHES?
WELL, IF YOU—
STOP MAKING IT SEEM LIKE I DON'T PAY CHILD SUPPORT!
I CAN'T DEAL WITH YOU WHEN YOU'RE LIKE THIS, FRANK!
UH-OH! THAT'S OUR CUE.
ACK!
GIRLS! GO TO BED.
WHATEVER. HOW ARE WE SUPPOSED TO SLEEP WITH YOU AND DAD SCREAMING AT EACH OTHER?

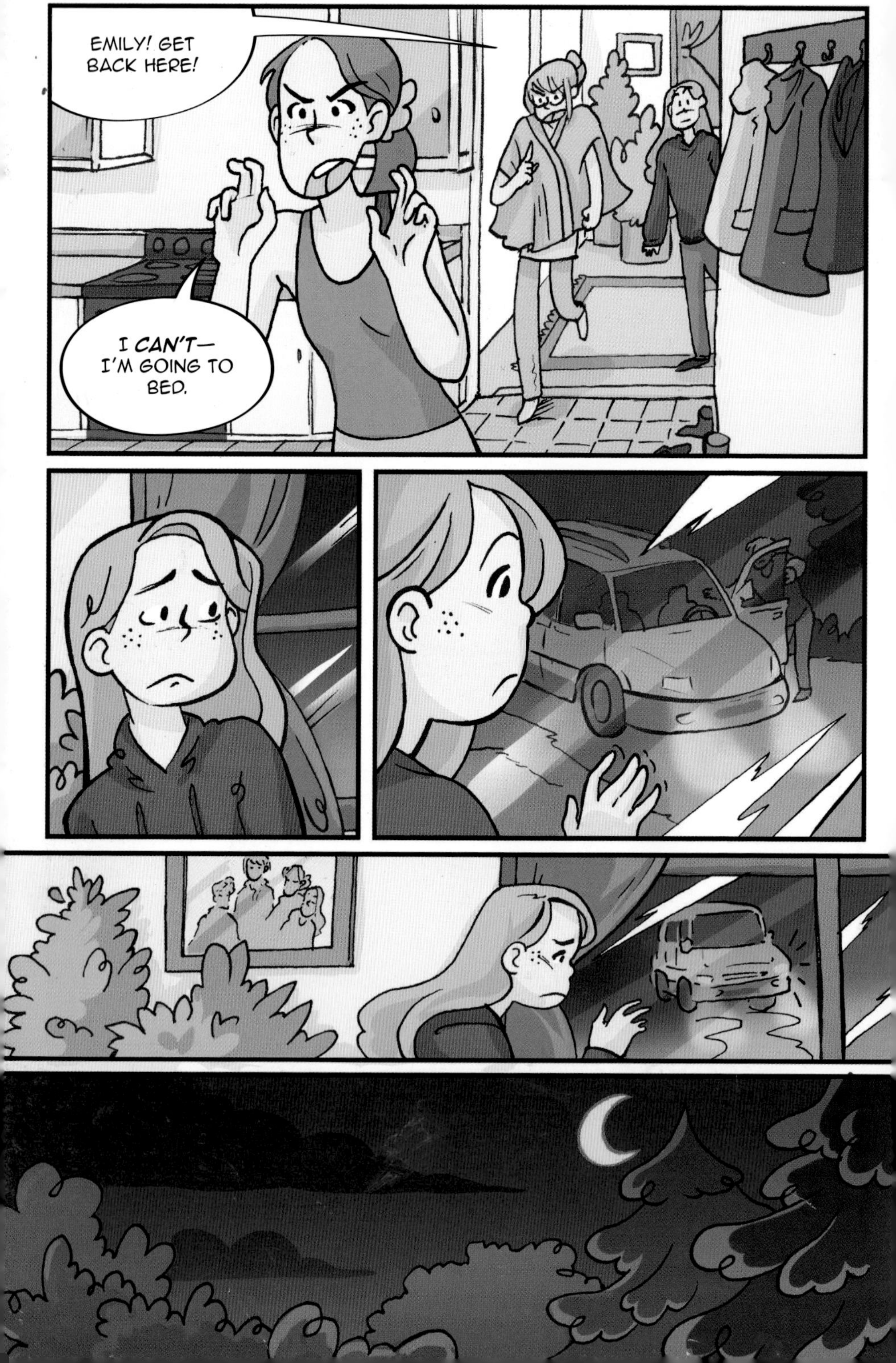
EMILY! GET BACK HERE!
I CAN'T—I'M GOING TO BED.

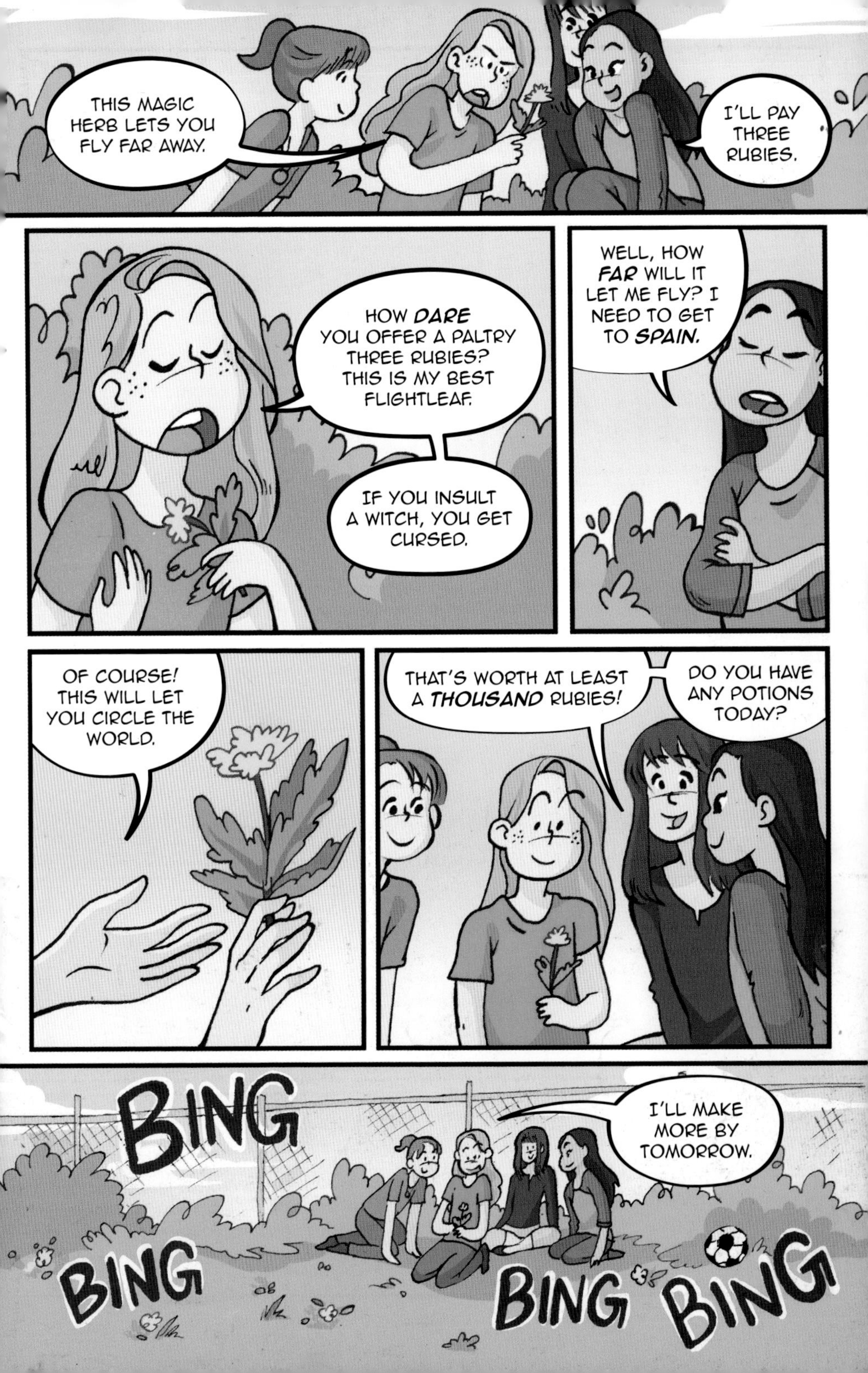
THIS MAGIC HERB LETS YOU FLY FAR AWAY.
I'LL PAY THREE RUBIES.
HOW DARE YOU OFFER A PALTRY THREE RUBIES? THIS IS MY BEST FLIGHTLEAF.
IF YOU INSULT A WITCH, YOU GET CURSED.
WELL, HOW FAR WILL IT LET ME FLY? I NEED TO GET TO SPAIN.
OF COURSE! THIS WILL LET YOU CIRCLE THE WORLD.
THAT'S WORTH AT LEAST A THOUSAND RUBIES!
DO YOU HAVE ANY POTIONS TODAY?
BING
I'LL MAKE MORE BY TOMORROW.
BING
BING
BING

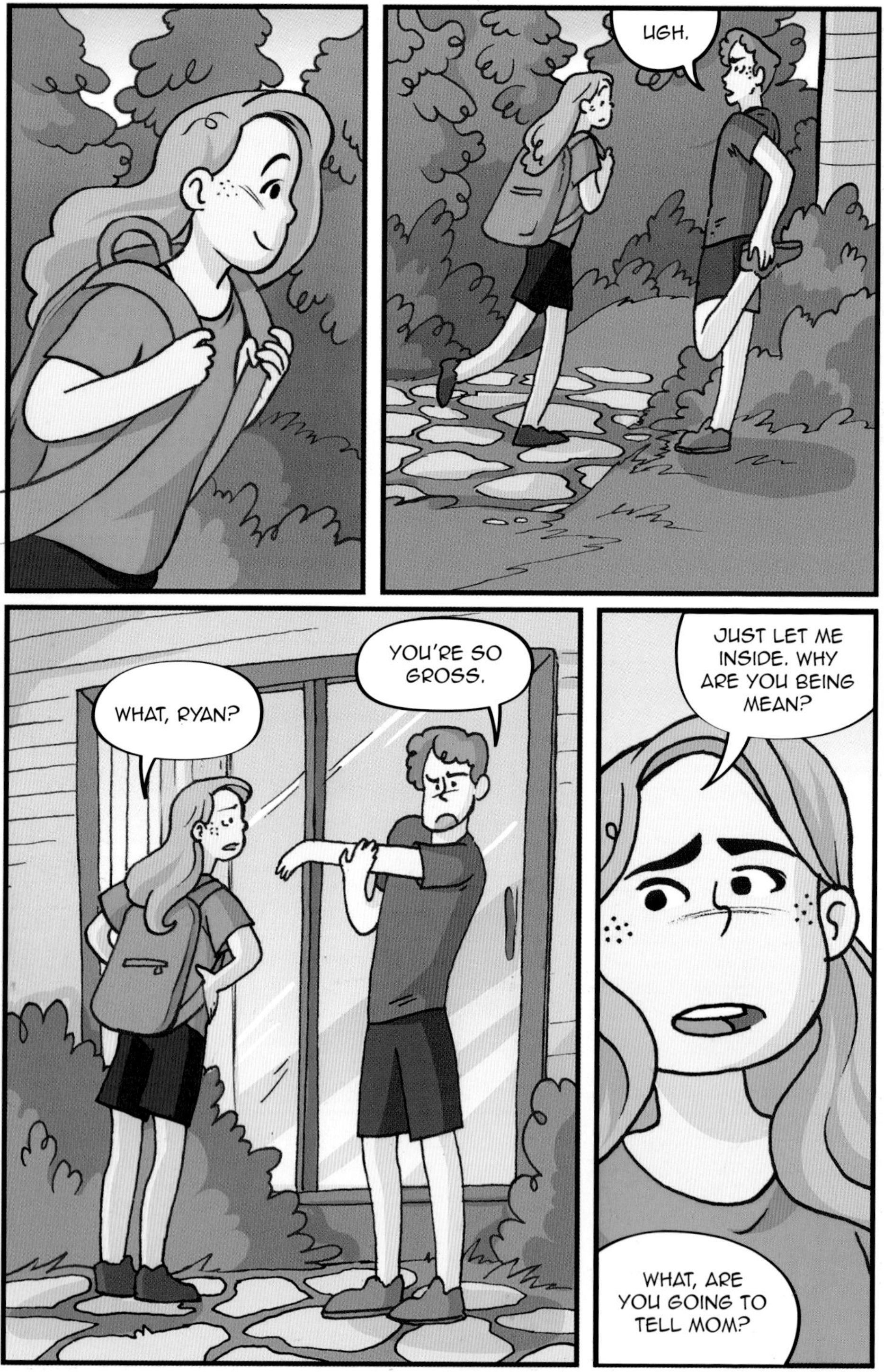
UGH.
WHAT, RYAN?
YOU'RE SO GROSS.
JUST LET ME INSIDE. WHY ARE YOU BEING MEAN?
WHAT, ARE YOU GOING TO TELL MOM?

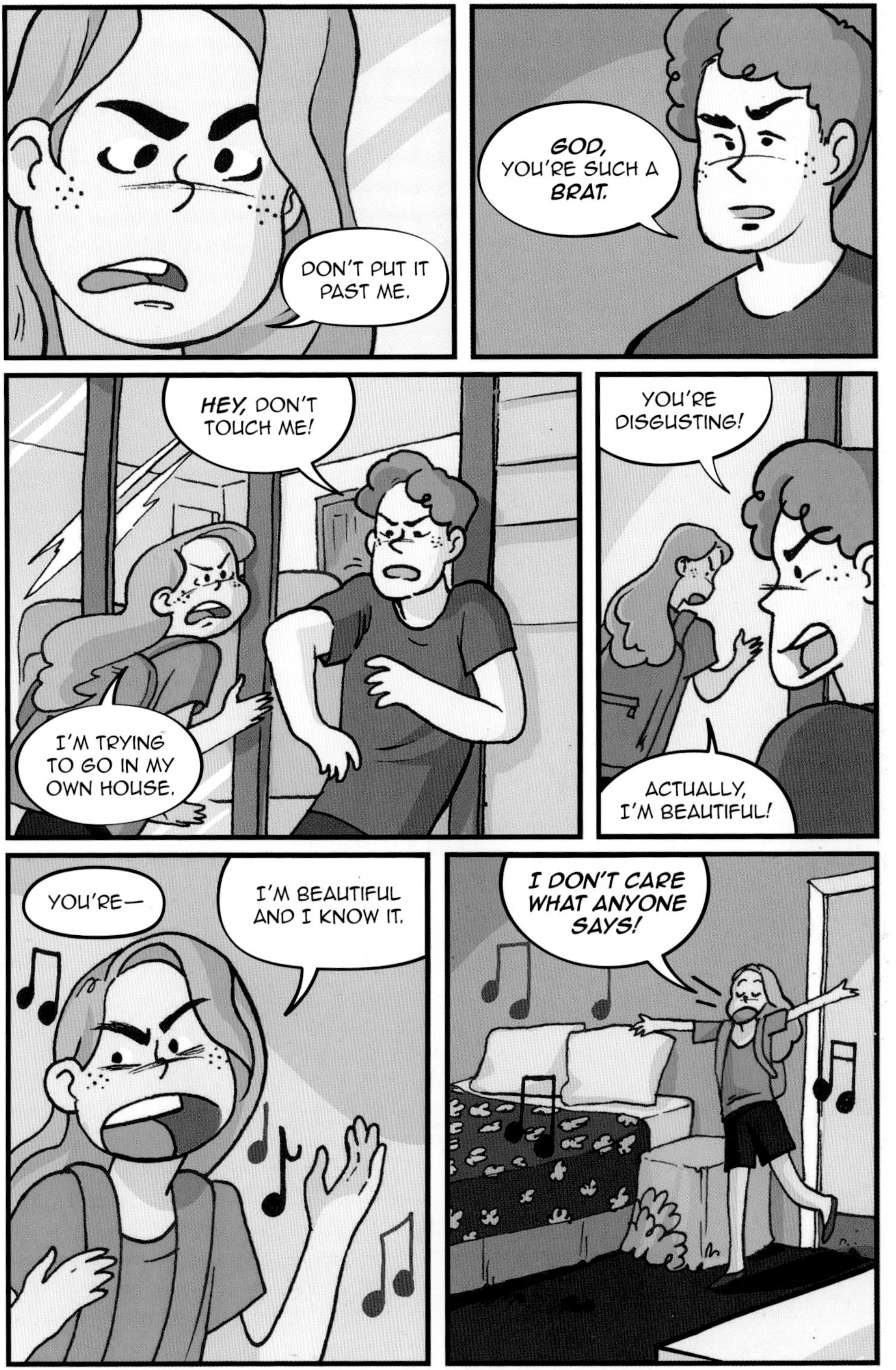
DON'T PUT IT PAST ME.
GOD, YOU'RE SUCH A BRAT.
HEY, DON'T TOUCH ME!
I'M TRYING TO GO IN MY OWN HOUSE.
YOU'RE DISGUSTING!
ACTUALLY, I'M BEAUTIFUL!
YOU'RE—
I'M BEAUTIFUL AND I KNOW IT.
I DON'T CARE WHAT ANYONE SAYS!

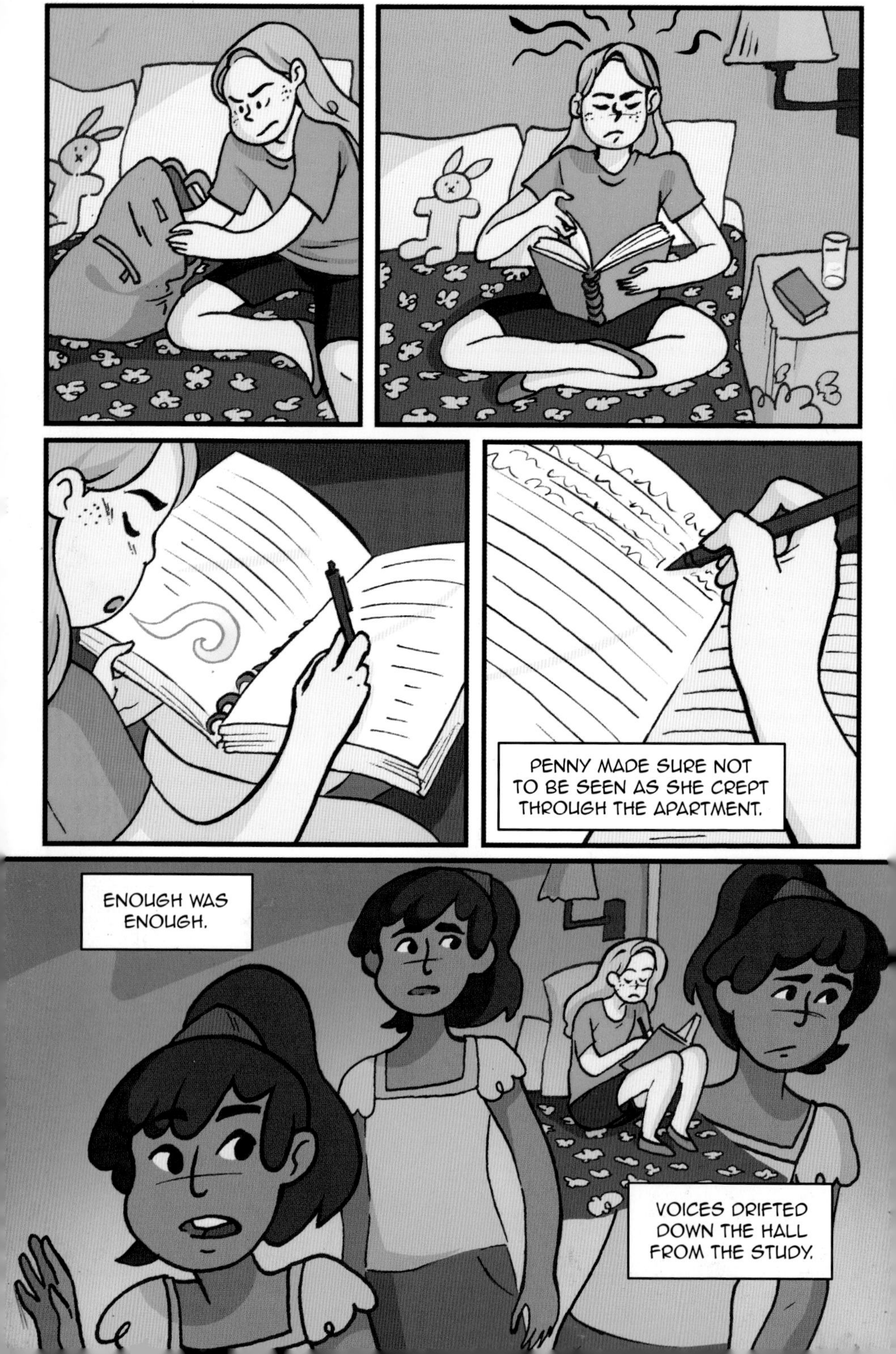
PENNY MADE SURE NOT TO BE SEEN AS SHE CREPT THROUGH THE APARTMENT.
ENOUGH WAS ENOUGH.
VOICES DRIFTED DOWN THE HALL FROM THE STUDY.

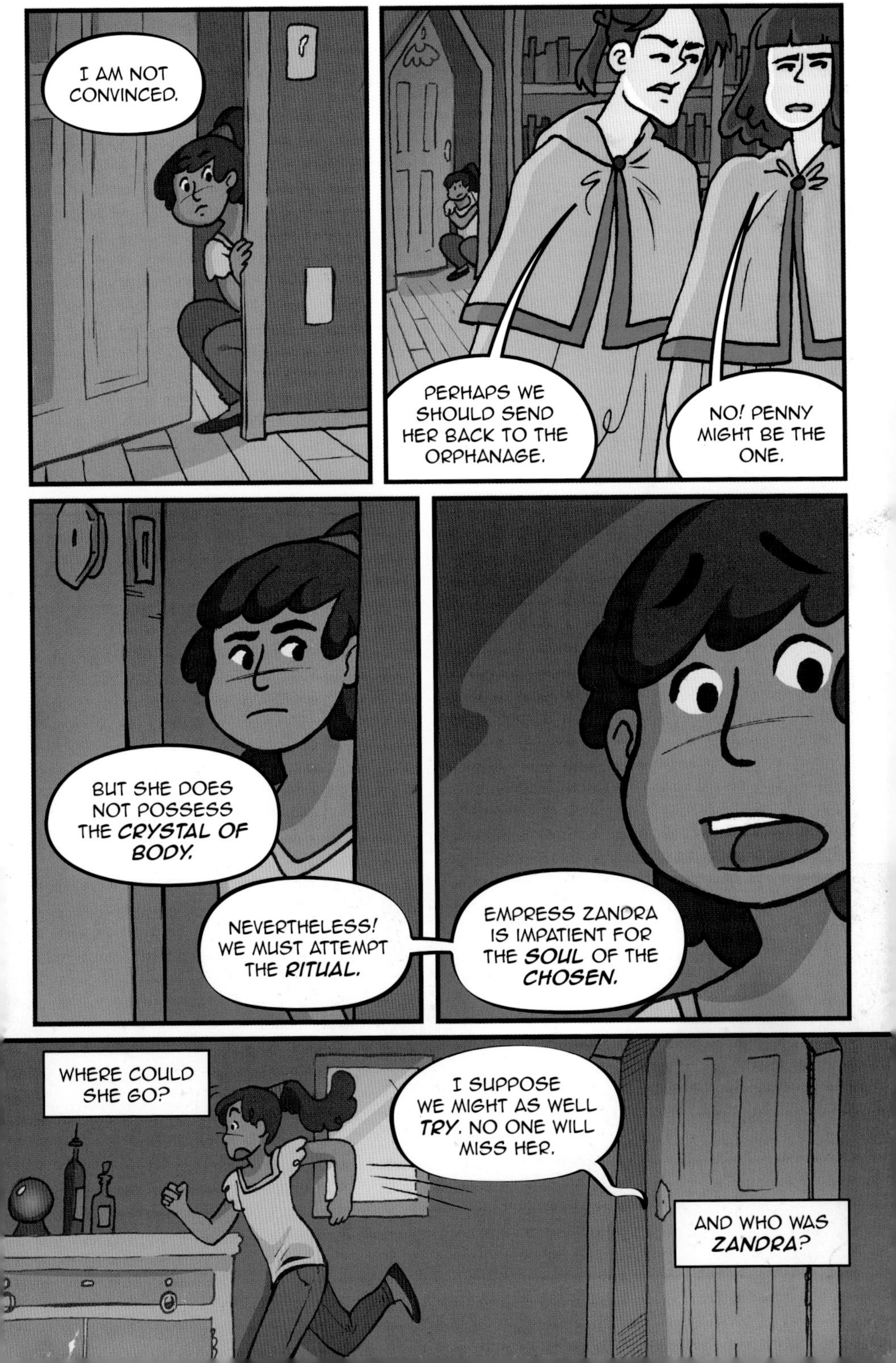
I AM NOT CONVINCED.
PERHAPS WE SHOULD SEND HER BACK TO THE ORPHANAGE.
NO! PENNY MIGHT BE THE ONE.
BUT SHE DOES NOT POSSESS THE CRYSTAL OF BODY.
NEVERTHELESS! WE MUST ATTEMPT THE RITUAL.
EMPRESS ZANDRA IS IMPATIENT FOR THE SOUL OF THE CHOSEN.
WHERE COULD SHE GO?
I SUPPOSE WE MIGHT AS WELL TRY. NO ONE WILL MISS HER.
AND WHO WAS ZANDRA?

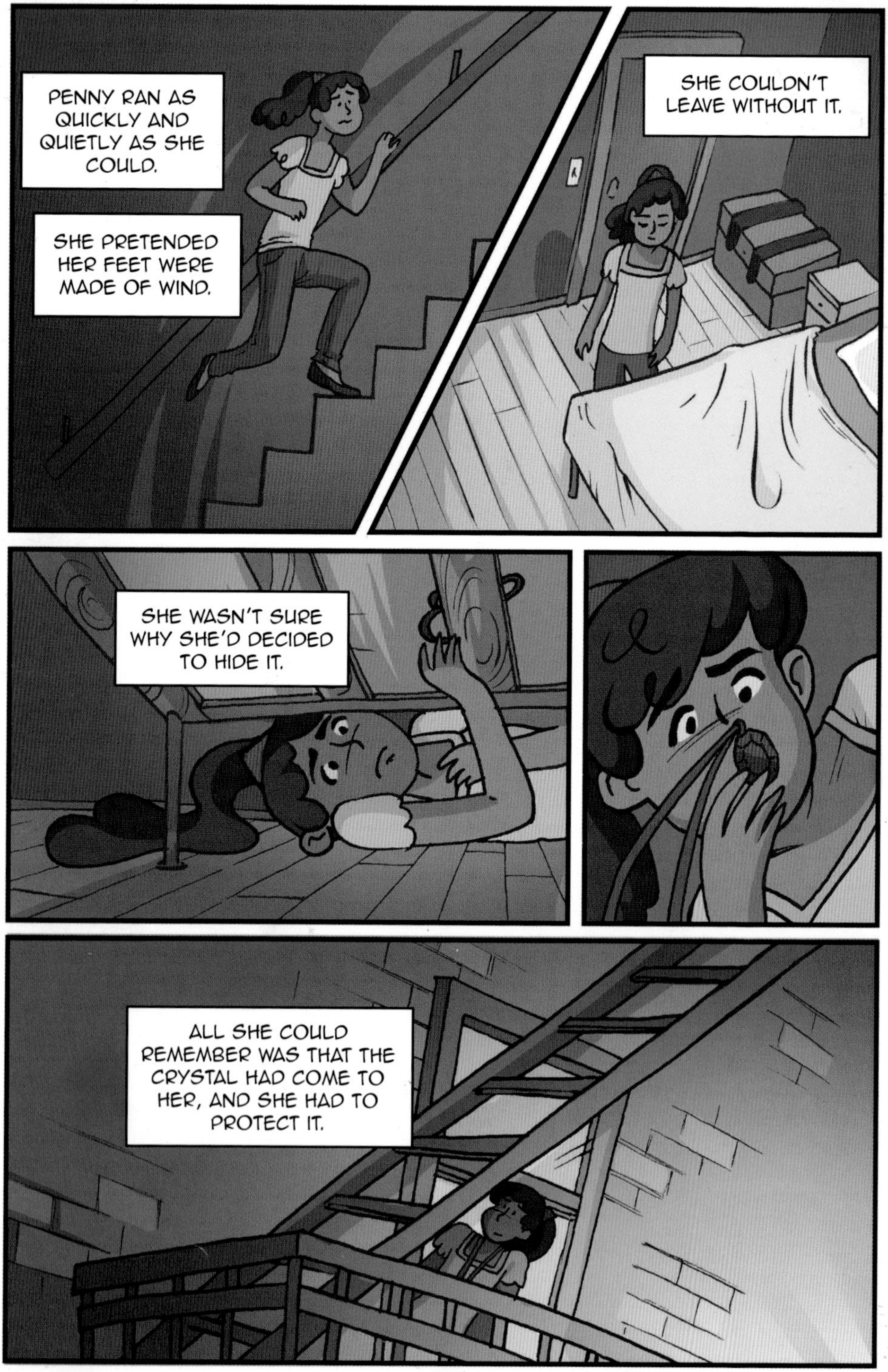
PENNY RAN AS QUICKLY AND QUIETLY AS SHE COULD.
SHE PRETENDED HER FEET WERE MADE OF WIND.
SHE COULDN'T LEAVE WITHOUT IT.
SHE WASN'T SURE WHY SHE'D DECIDED TO HIDE IT.
ALL SHE COULD REMEMBER WAS THAT THE CRYSTAL HAD COME TO HER, AND SHE HAD TO PROTECT IT.

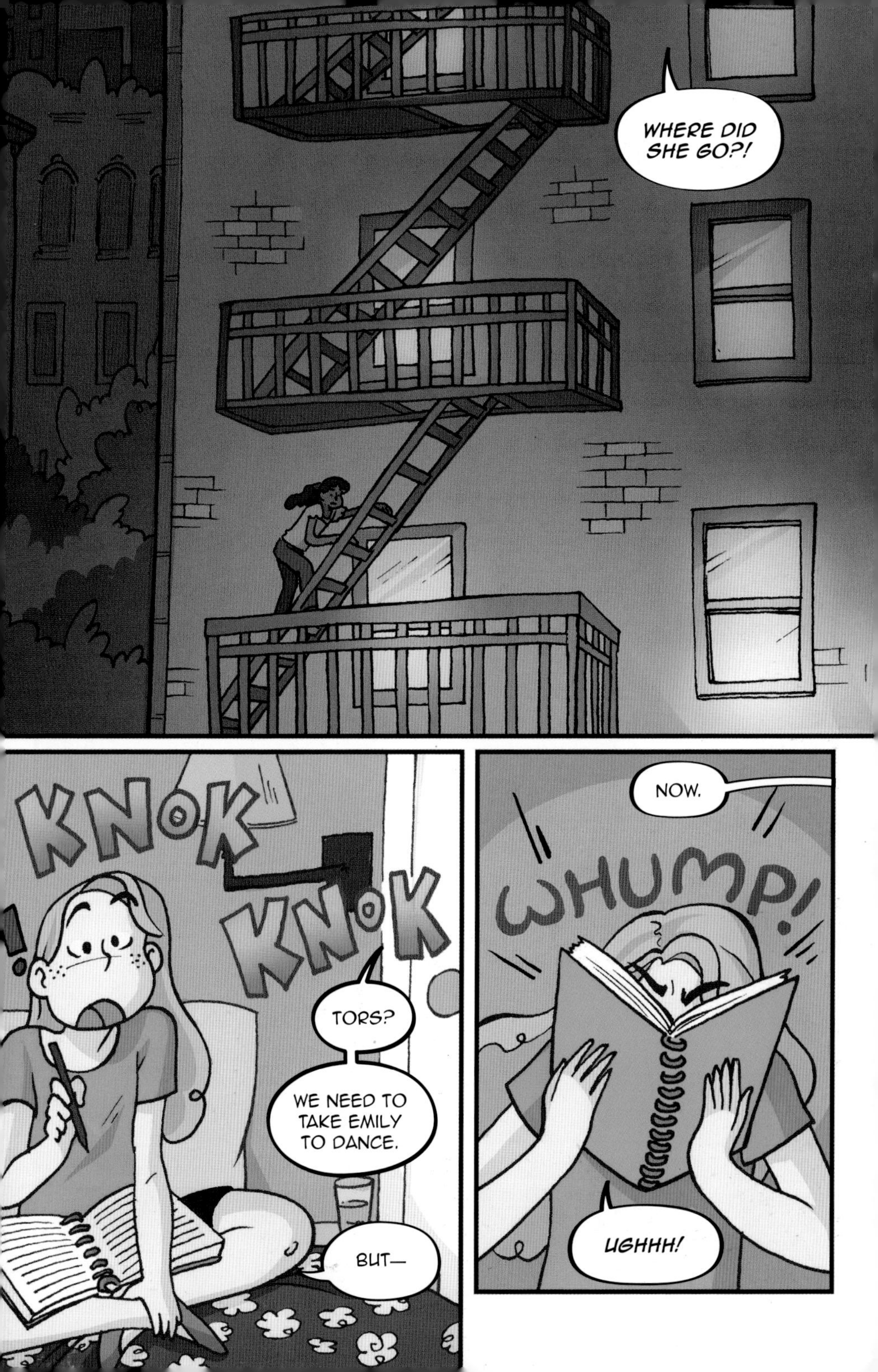
WHERE DID SHE GO?!
KNOK
KNOK
TORS?
WE NEED TO TAKE EMILY TO DANCE.
BUT—
NOW.
WHUMP!
UGHHH!

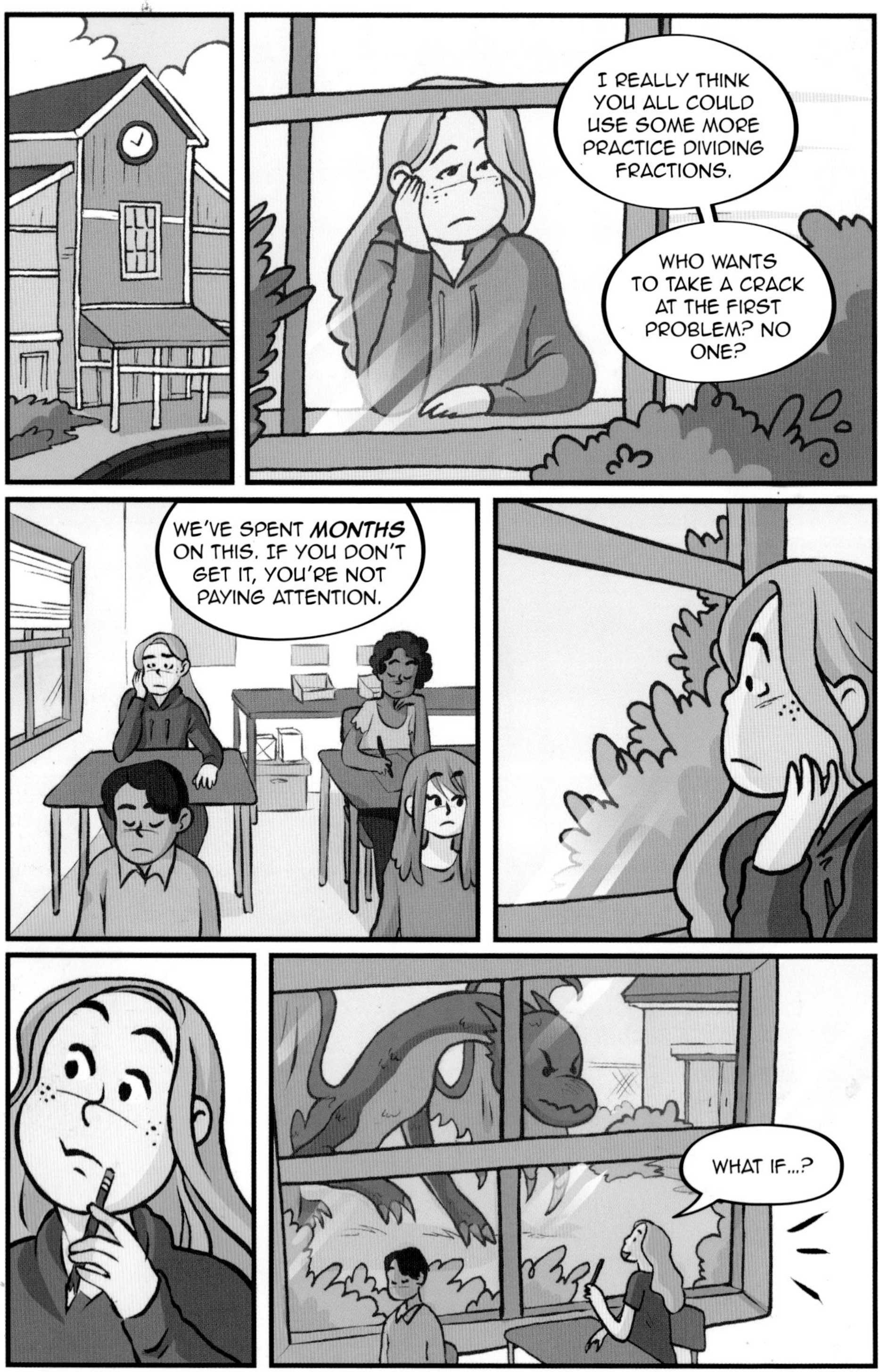
I REALLY THINK YOU ALL COULD USE SOME MORE PRACTICE DIVIDING FRACTIONS.
WHO WANTS TO TAKE A CRACK AT THE FIRST PROBLEM? NO ONE?
WE'VE SPENT *MONTHS* ON THIS. IF YOU DON'T GET IT, YOU'RE NOT PAYING ATTENTION.
WHAT IF...?

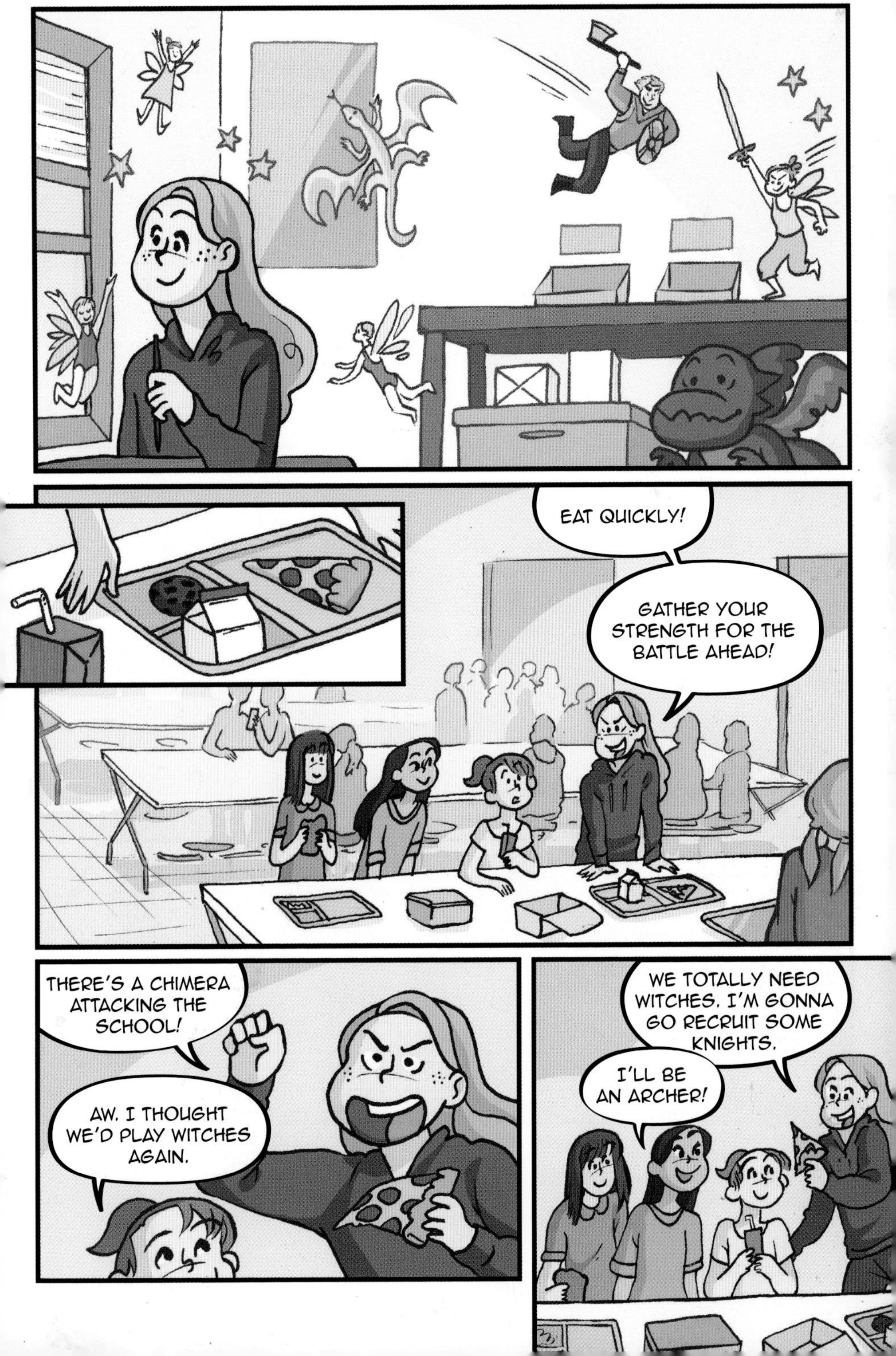
EAT QUICKLY!
GATHER YOUR STRENGTH FOR THE BATTLE AHEAD!
THERE'S A CHIMERA ATTACKING THE SCHOOL!
AW. I THOUGHT WE'D PLAY WITCHES AGAIN.
WE TOTALLY NEED WITCHES. I'M GONNA GO RECRUIT SOME KNIGHTS.
I'LL BE AN ARCHER!

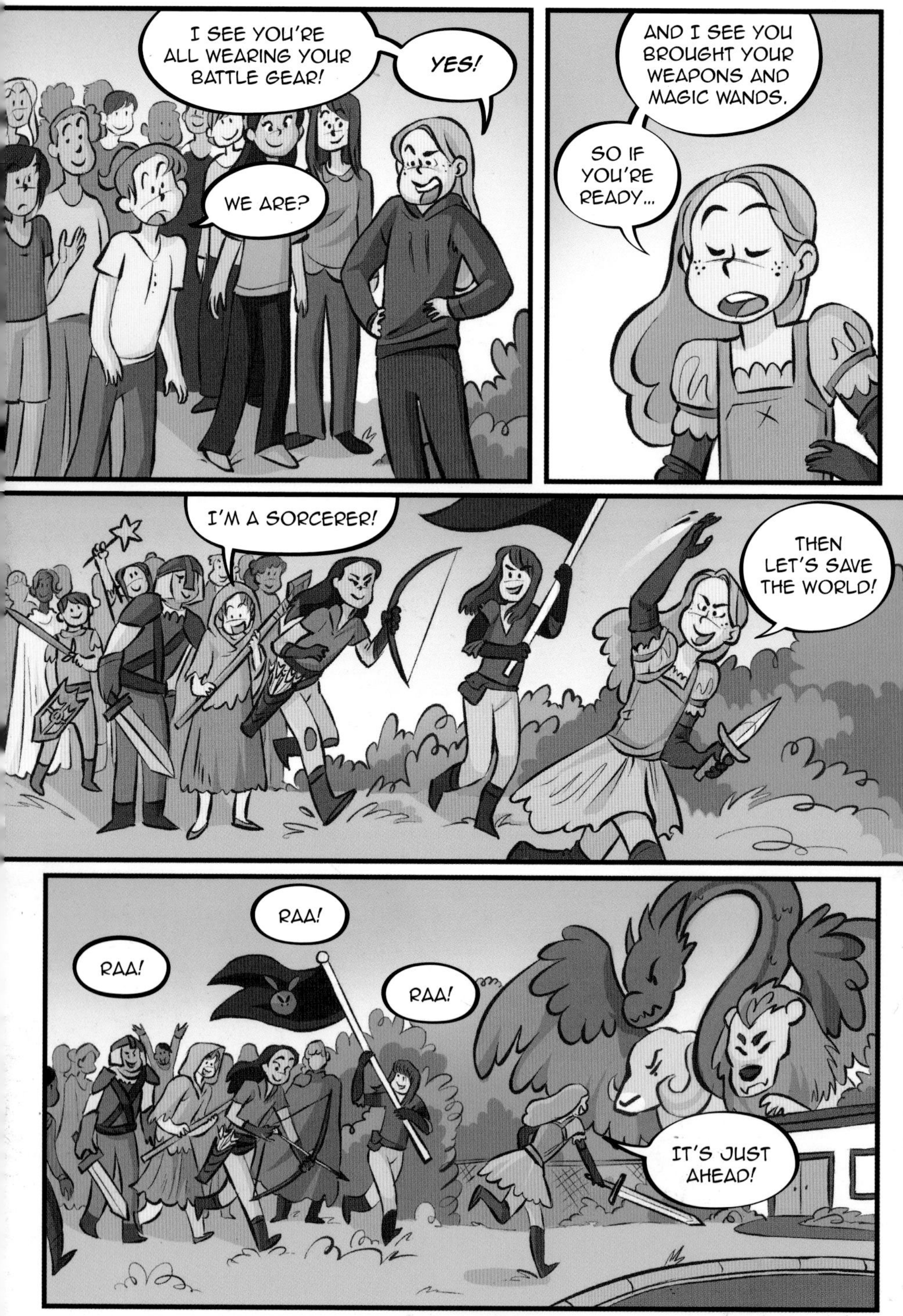
I SEE YOU'RE ALL WEARING YOUR BATTLE GEAR!
YES!
WE ARE?
AND I SEE YOU BROUGHT YOUR WEAPONS AND MAGIC WANDS.
SO IF YOU'RE READY...
I'M A SORCERER!
THEN LET'S SAVE THE WORLD!
RAA!
RAA!
RAA!
IT'S JUST AHEAD!

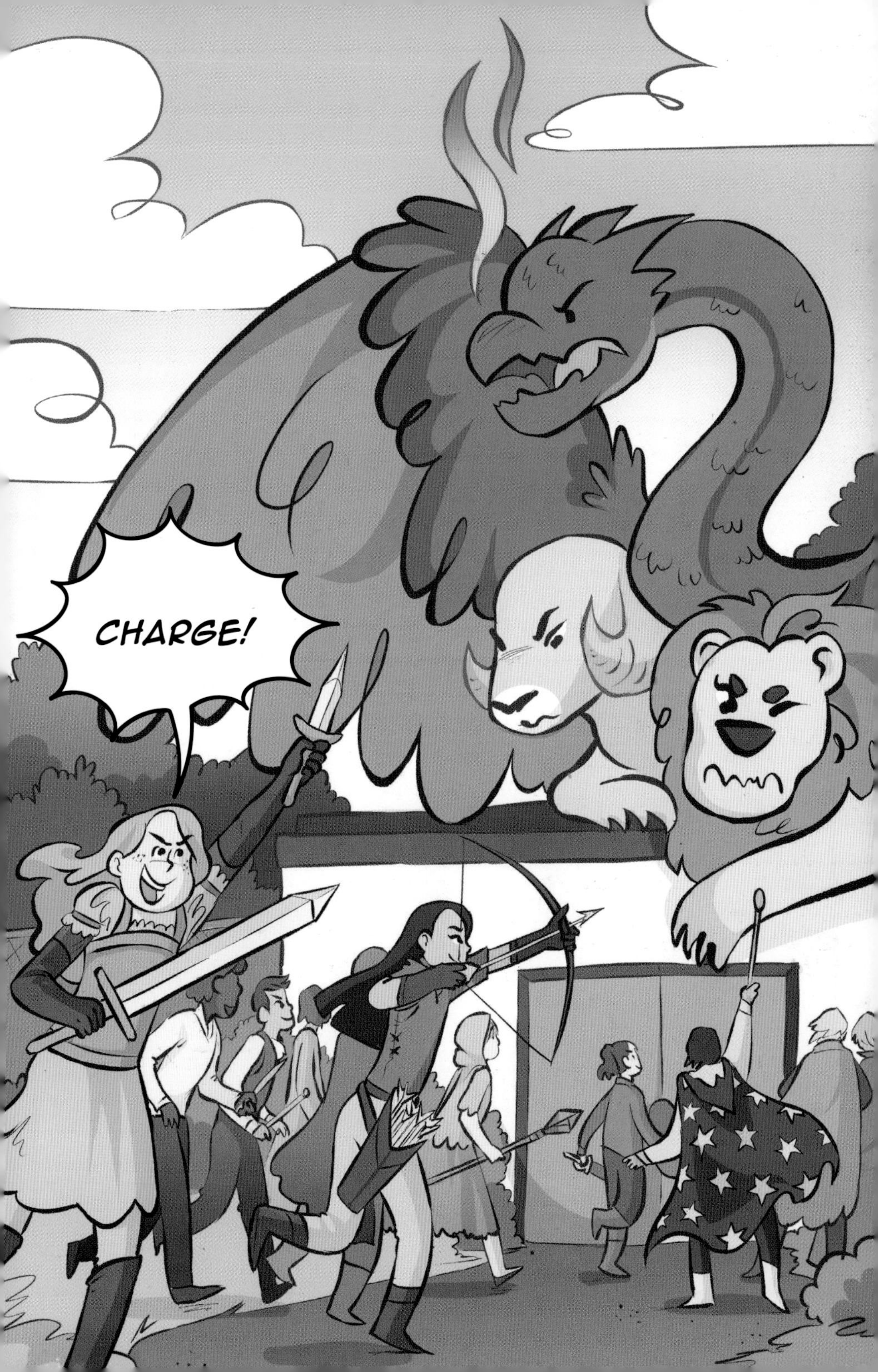
CHARGE!

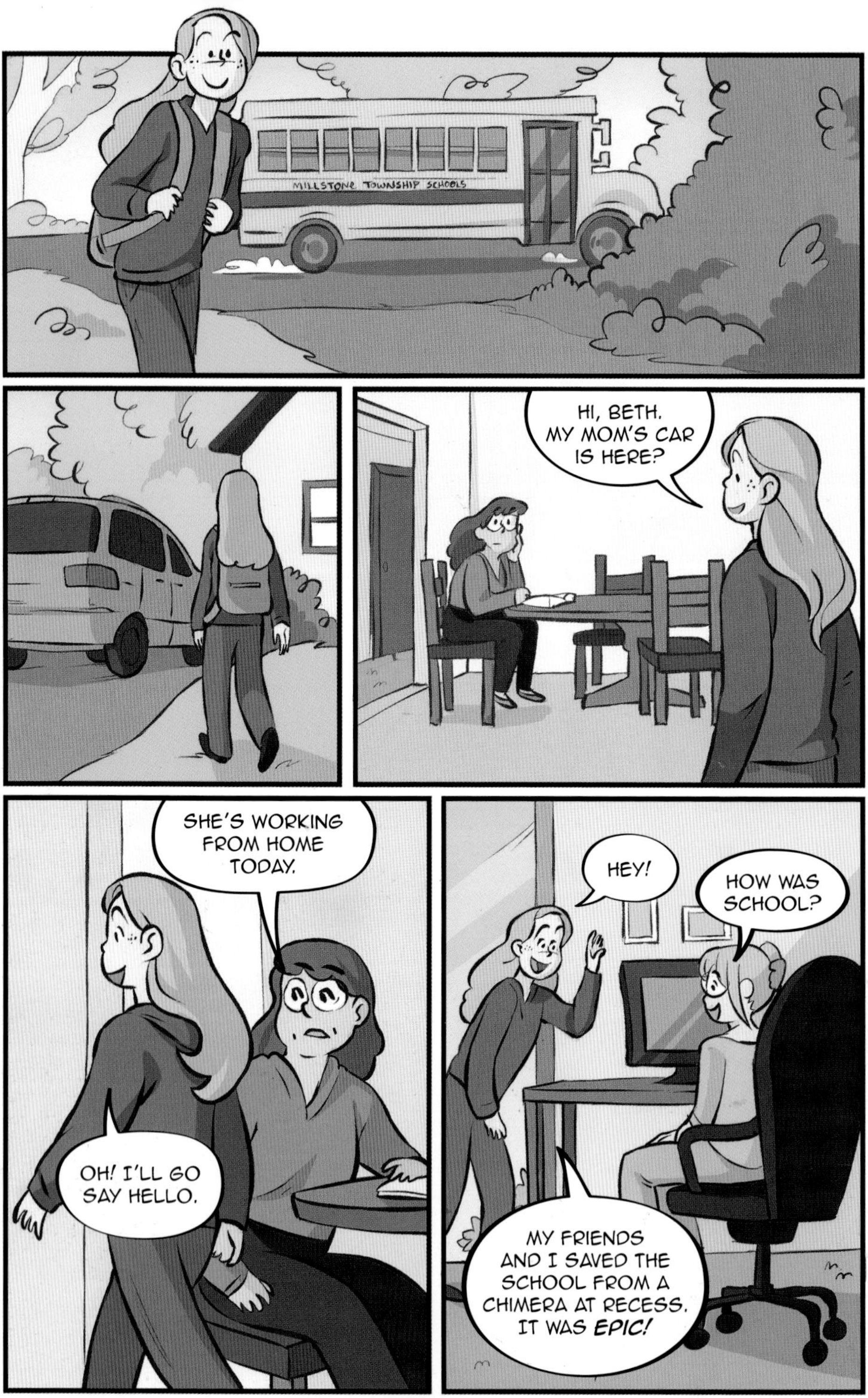
MILLSTONE TOWNSHIP SCHOOLS
HI, BETH. MY MOM'S CAR IS HERE?
SHE'S WORKING FROM HOME TODAY.
OH! I'LL GO SAY HELLO.
HEY!
HOW WAS SCHOOL?
MY FRIENDS AND I SAVED THE SCHOOL FROM A CHIMERA AT RECESS. IT WAS *EPIC!*

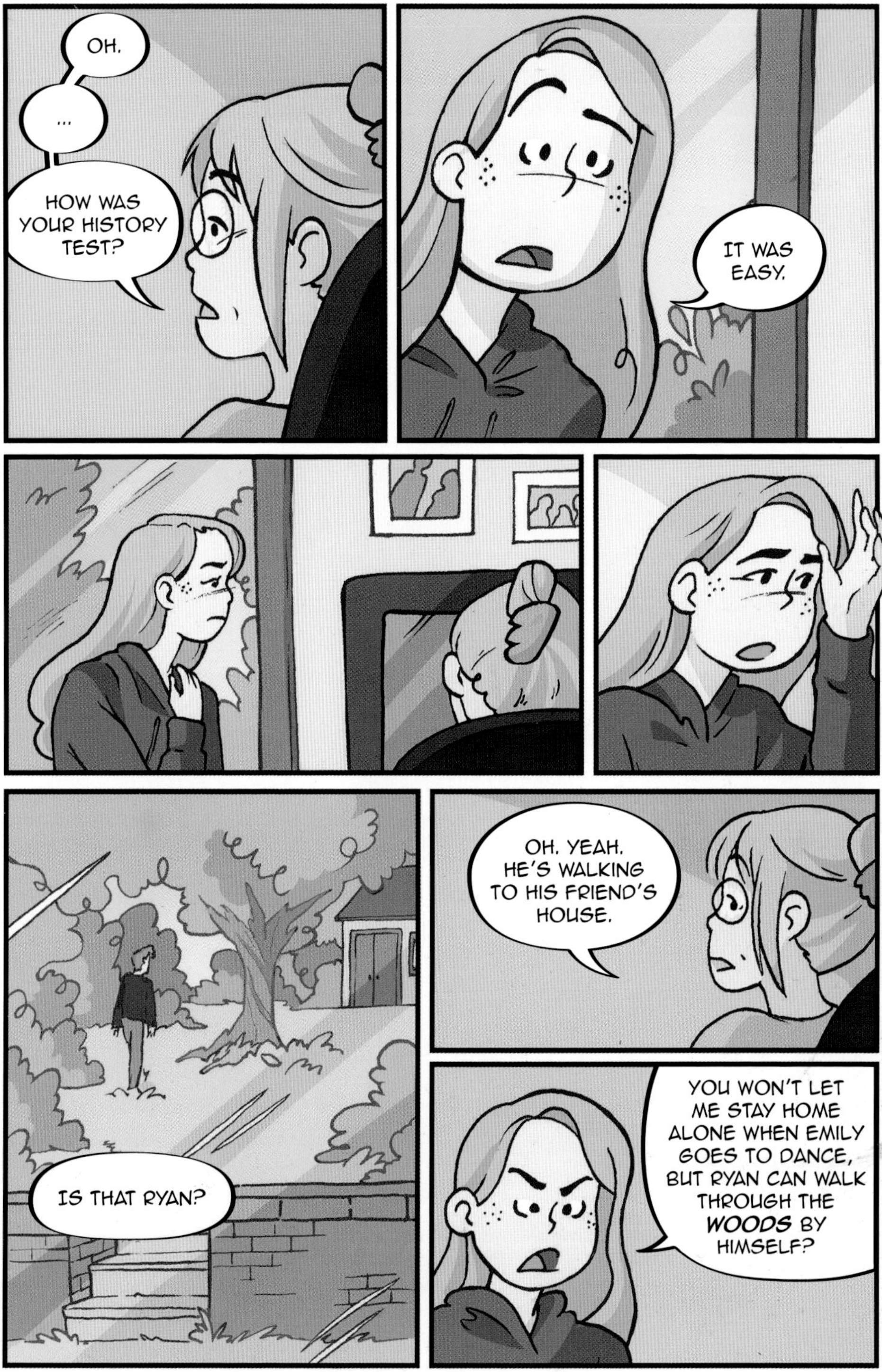
OH.
...
HOW WAS YOUR HISTORY TEST?
IT WAS EASY.
IS THAT RYAN?
OH. YEAH. HE'S WALKING TO HIS FRIEND'S HOUSE.
YOU WON'T LET ME STAY HOME ALONE WHEN EMILY GOES TO DANCE, BUT RYAN CAN WALK THROUGH THE *WOODS* BY HIMSELF?

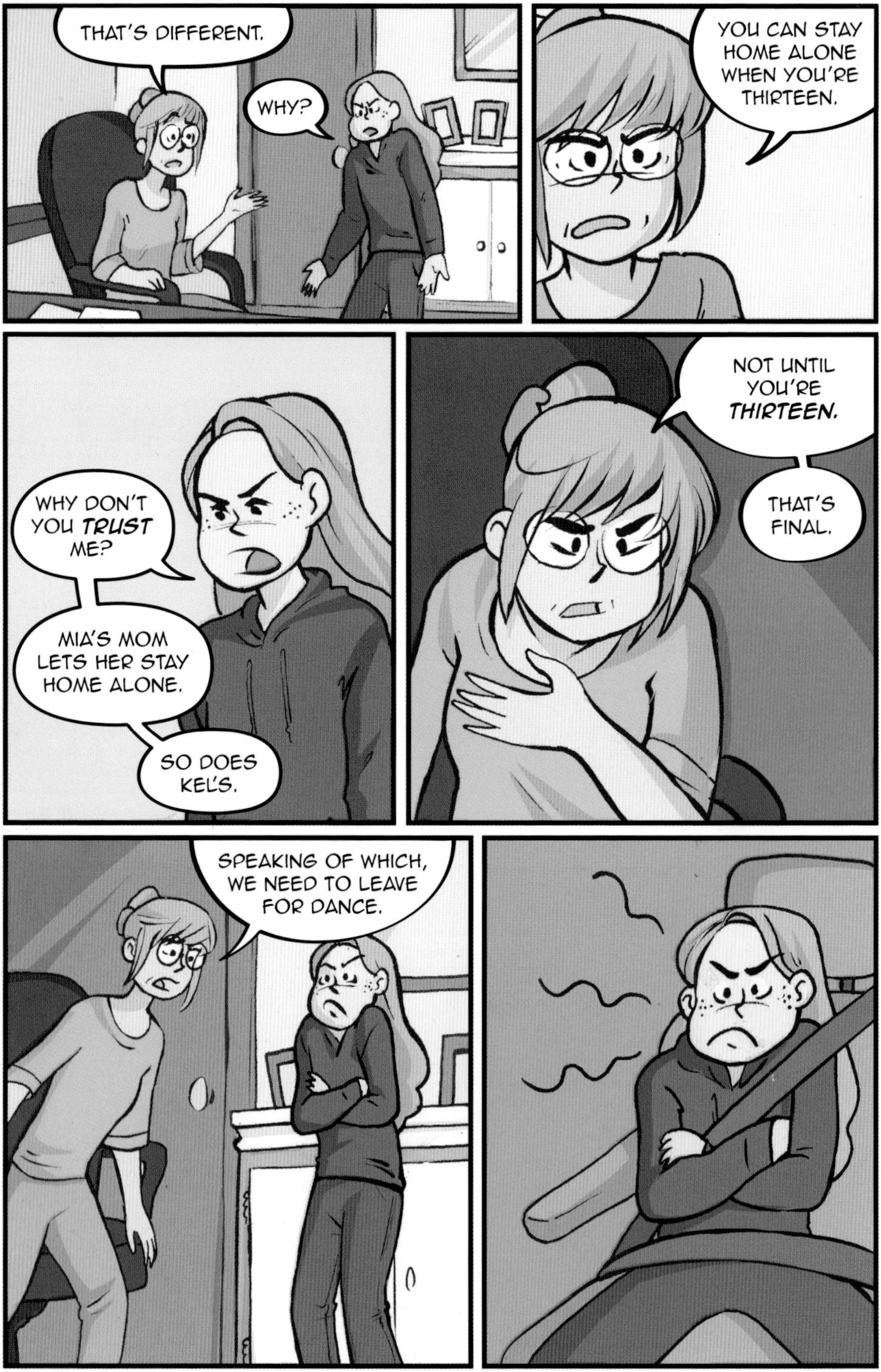
THAT'S DIFFERENT.
WHY?
YOU CAN STAY HOME ALONE WHEN YOU'RE THIRTEEN.
WHY DON'T YOU *TRUST* ME?
MIA'S MOM LETS HER STAY HOME ALONE.
SO DOES KEL'S.
NOT UNTIL YOU'RE ***THIRTEEN.***
THAT'S FINAL.
SPEAKING OF WHICH, WE NEED TO LEAVE FOR DANCE.

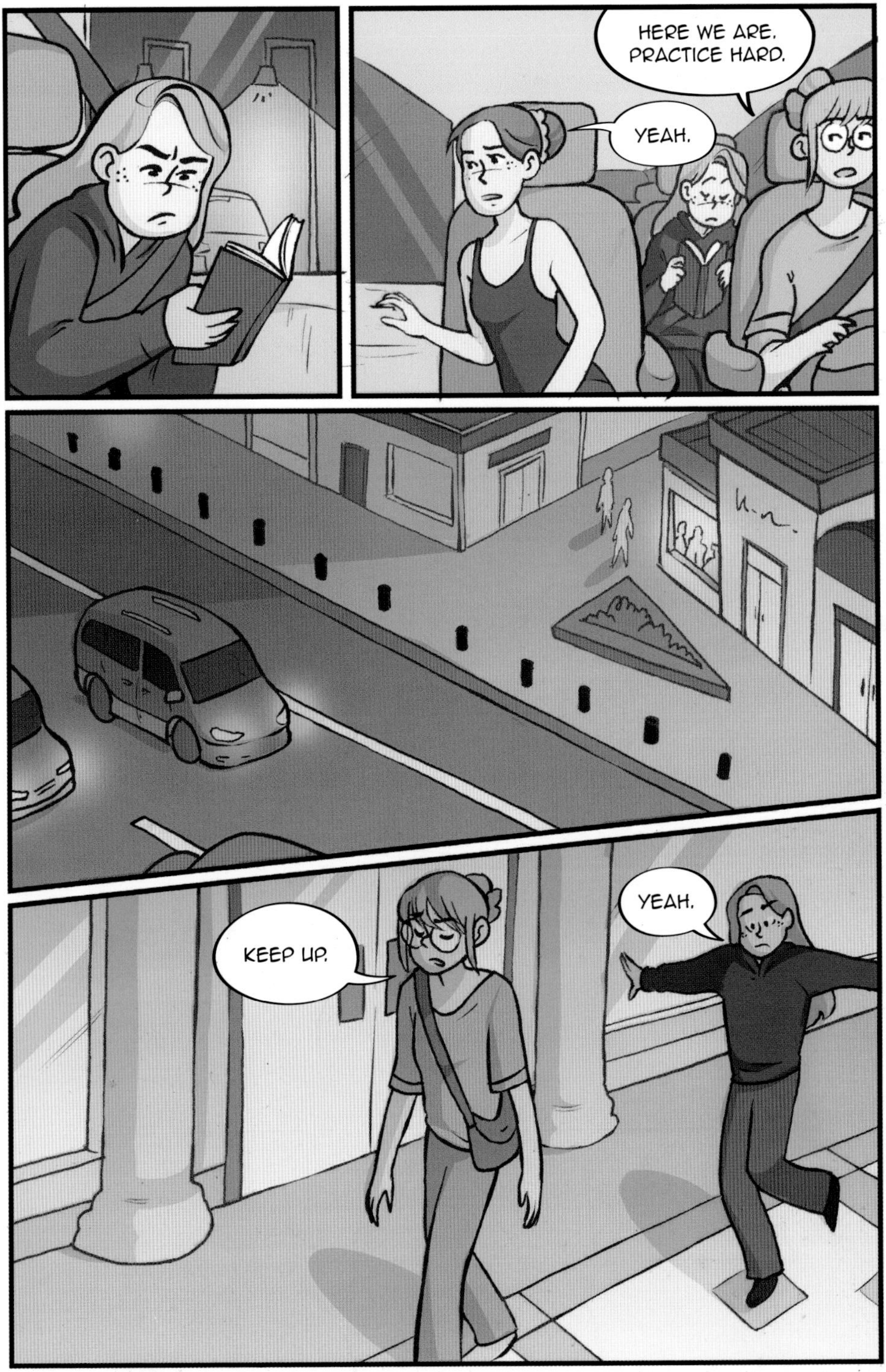
HERE WE ARE. PRACTICE HARD.
YEAH.
KEEP UP.
YEAH.

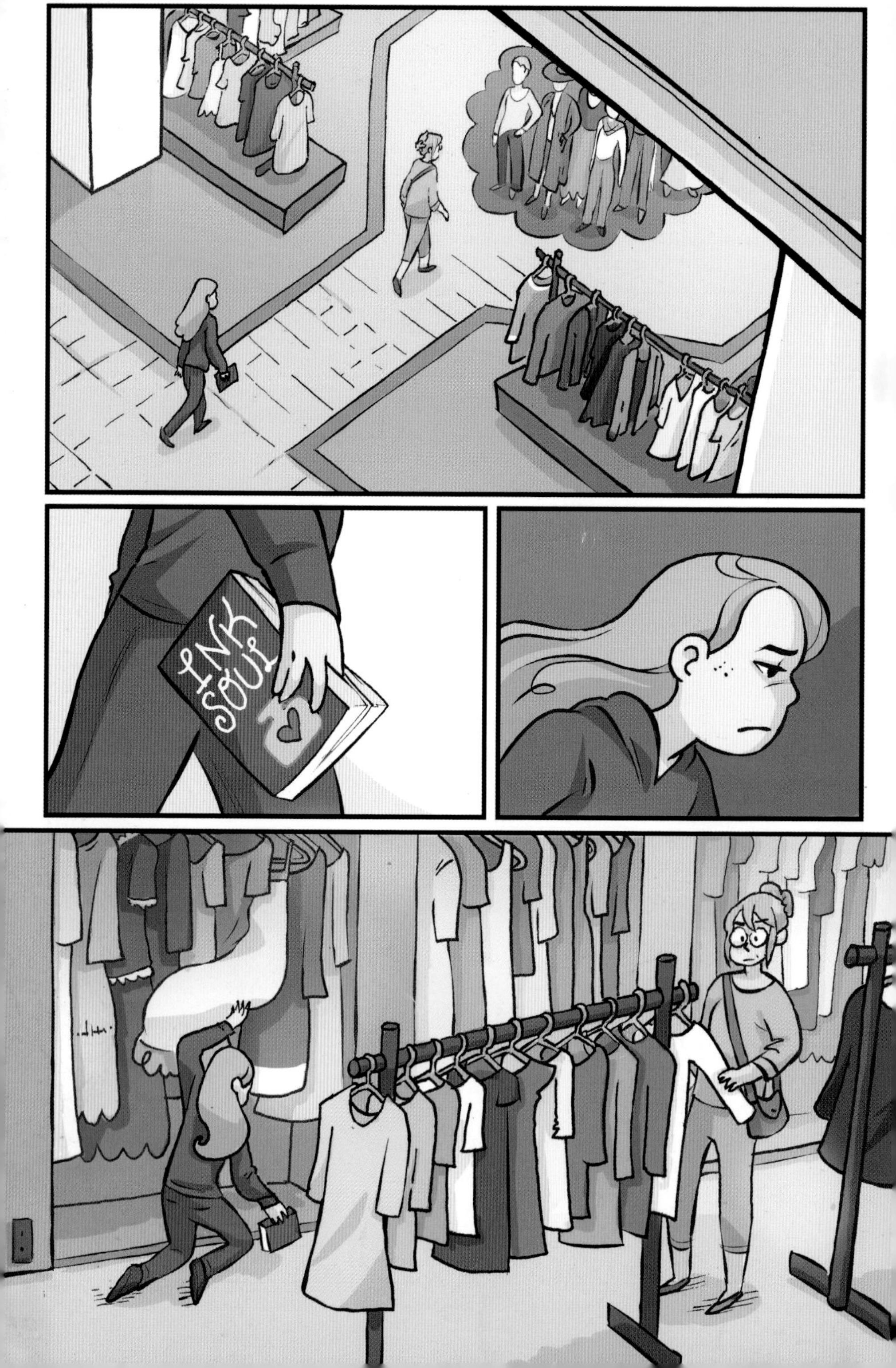
INK
SOUL

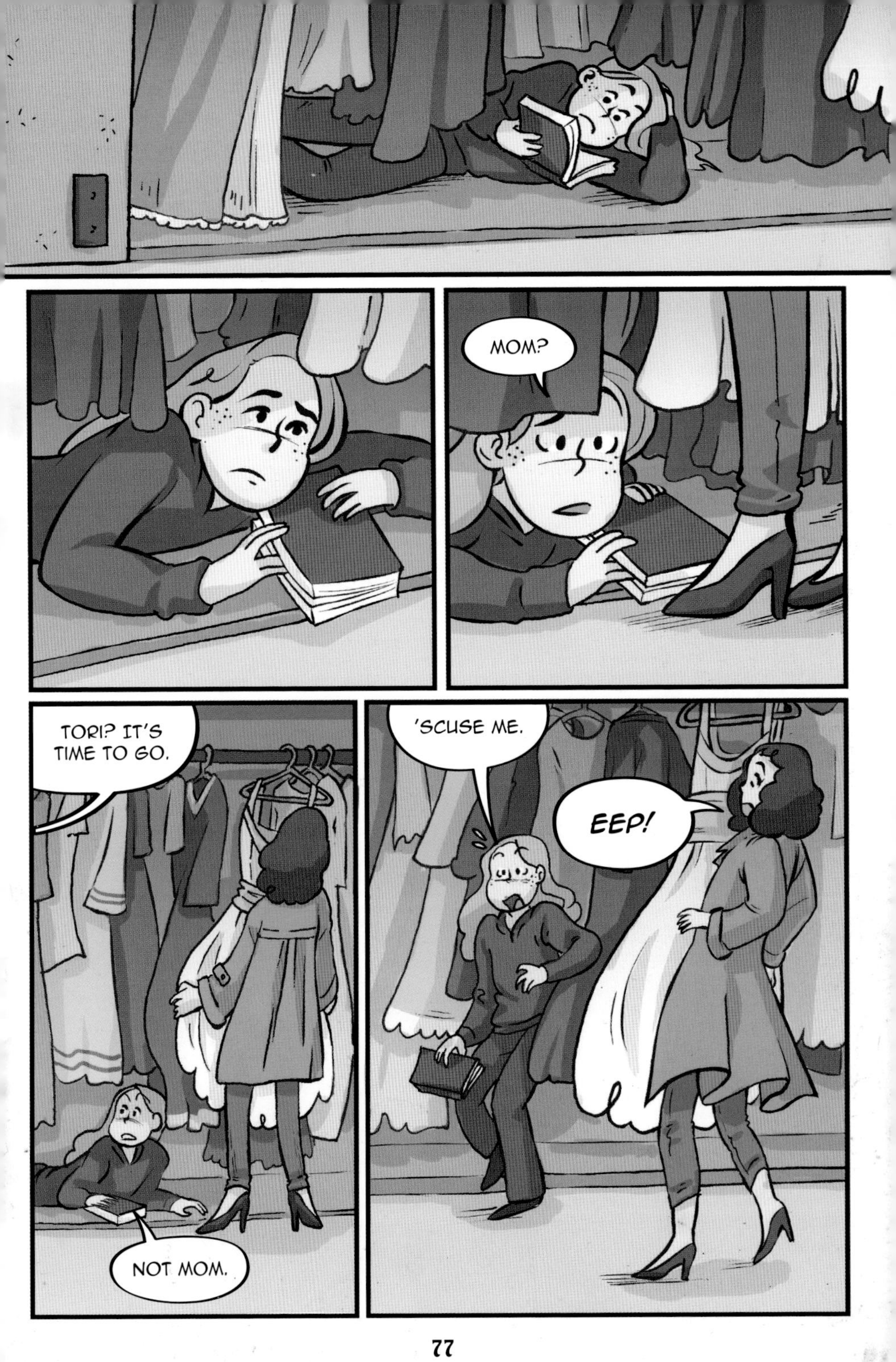
MOM?
TORI? IT'S TIME TO GO.
NOT MOM.
'SCUSE ME.
EEP!

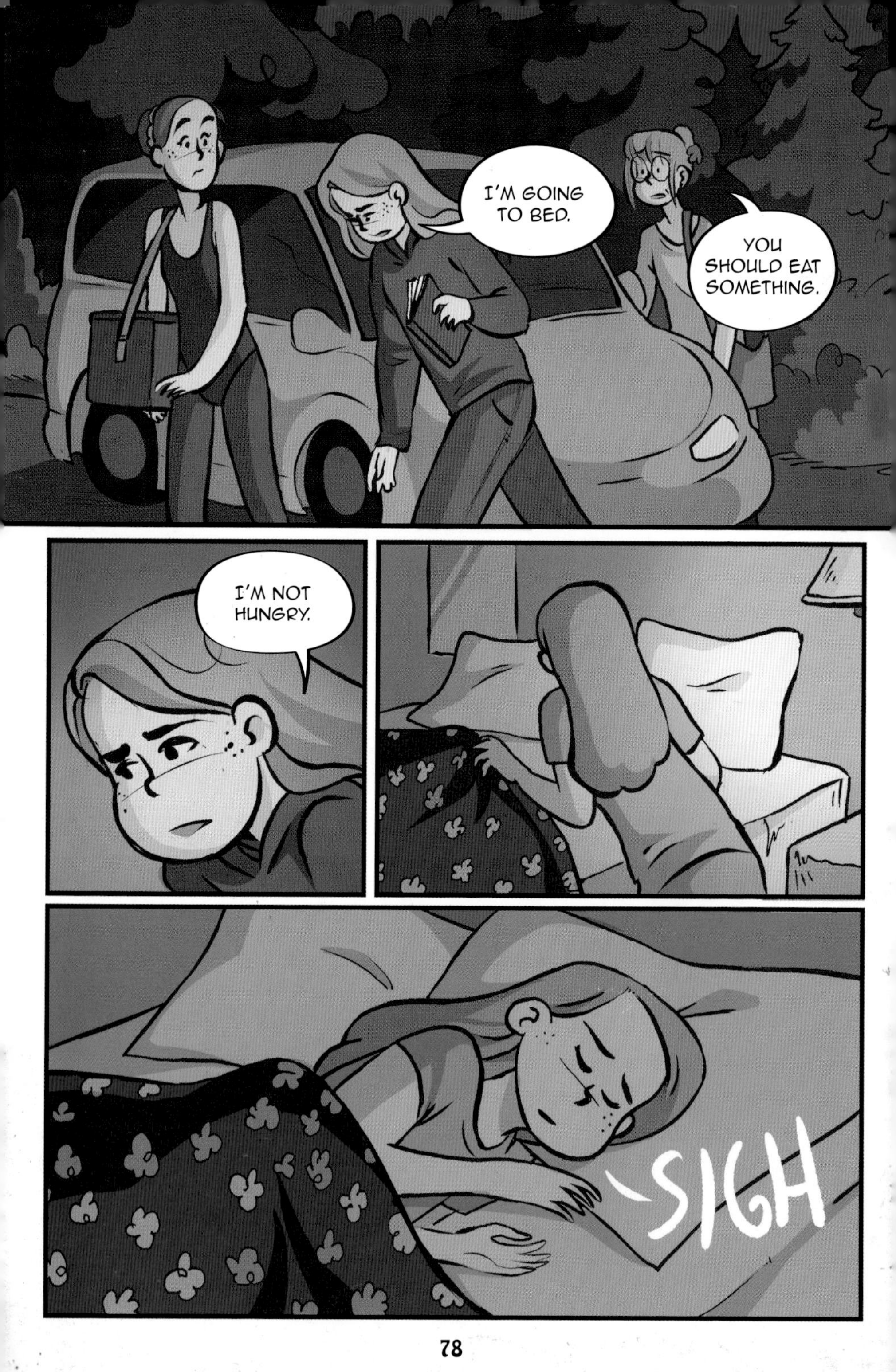
I'M GOING TO BED.
YOU SHOULD EAT SOMETHING.
I'M NOT HUNGRY.
SIGH

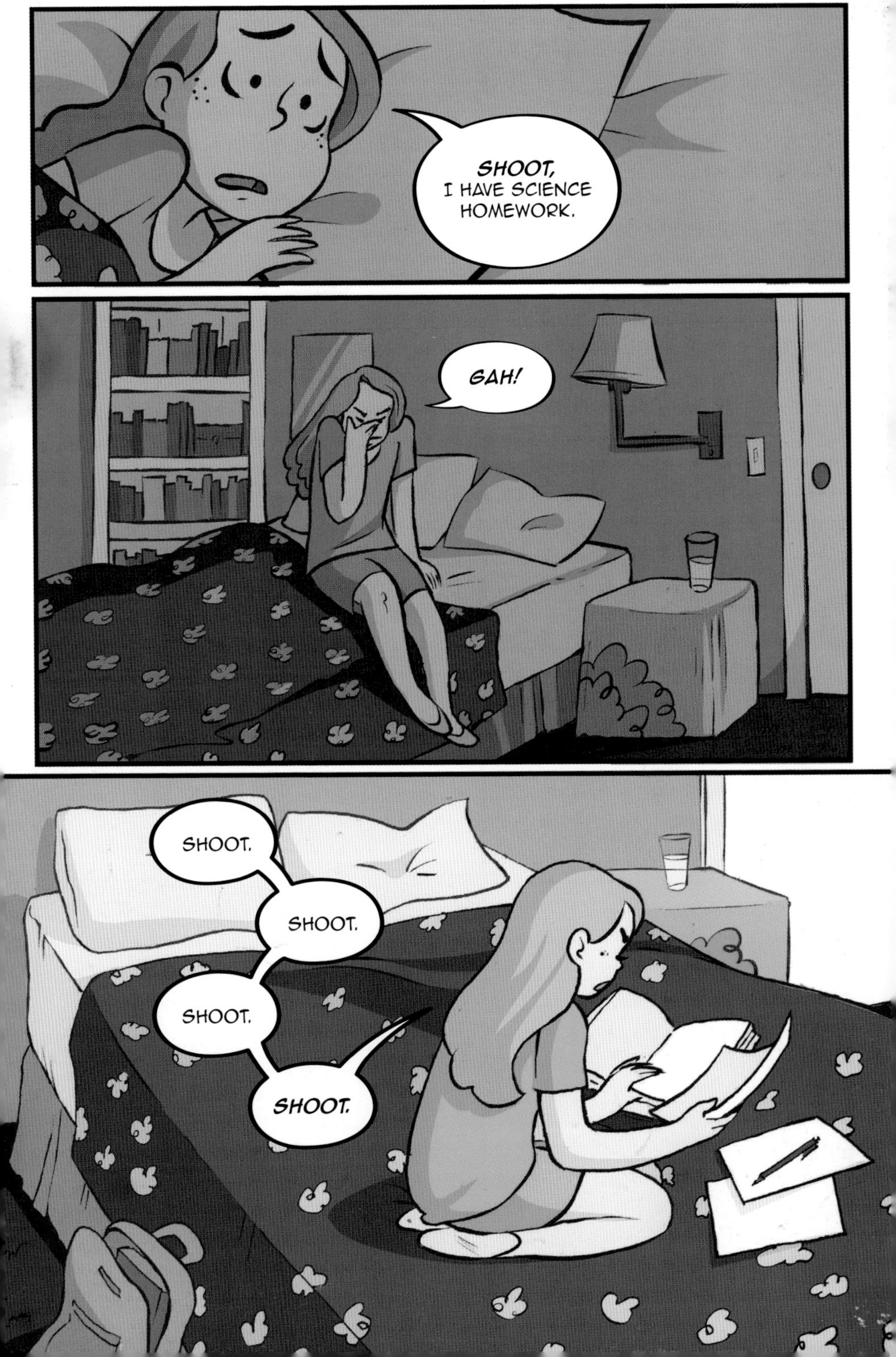
SHOOT,
I HAVE SCIENCE HOMEWORK.
GAH!
SHOOT.
SHOOT.
SHOOT.
SHOOT.

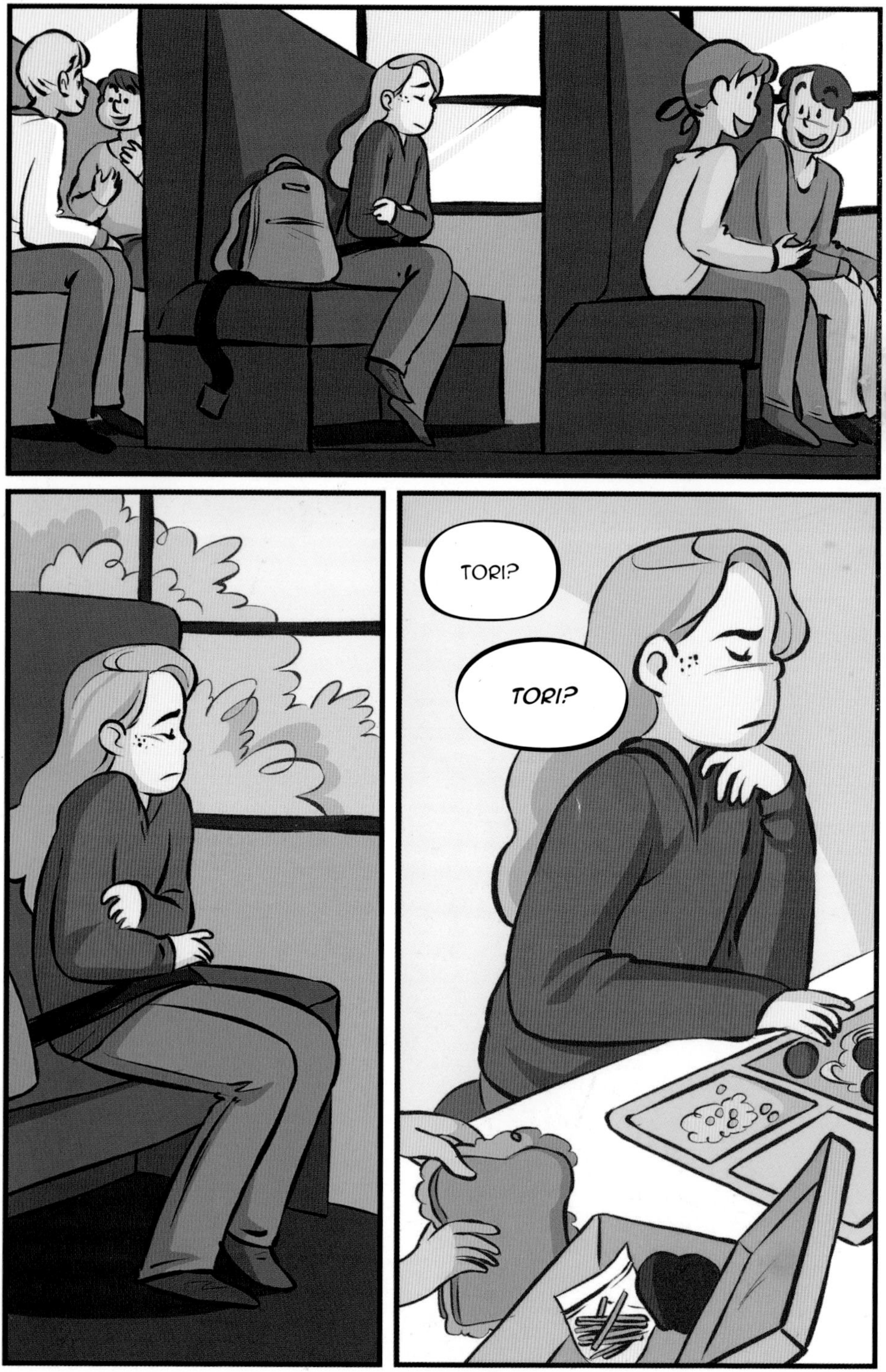
TORI?
TORI?

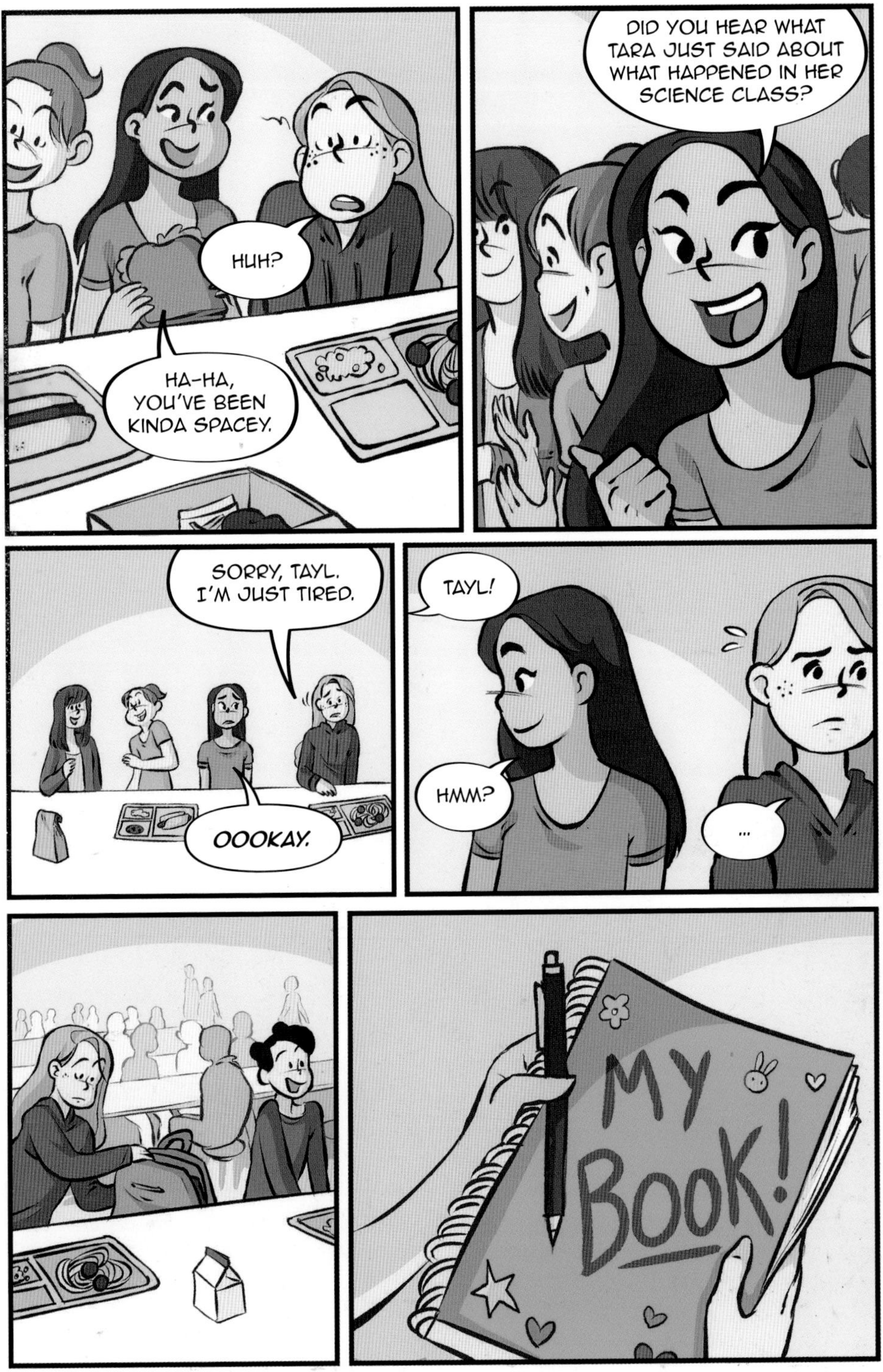
HUH?
HA-HA, YOU'VE BEEN KINDA SPACEY.
DID YOU HEAR WHAT TARA JUST SAID ABOUT WHAT HAPPENED IN HER SCIENCE CLASS?
SORRY, TAYL. I'M JUST TIRED.
OOOKAY.
TAYL!
HMM?
...
MY BOOK!

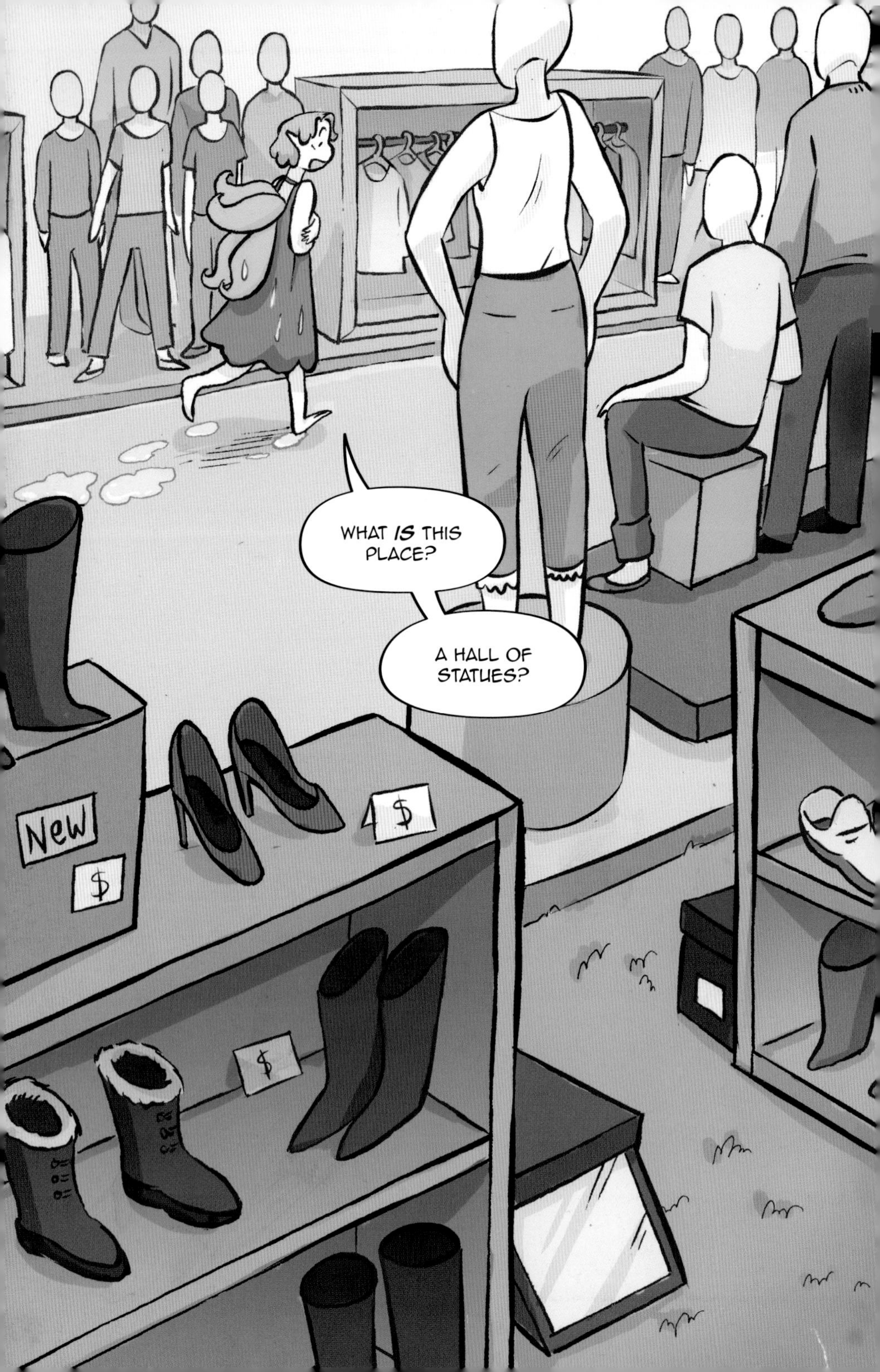
WHAT IS THIS PLACE?
A HALL OF STATUES?
New
$
$
$

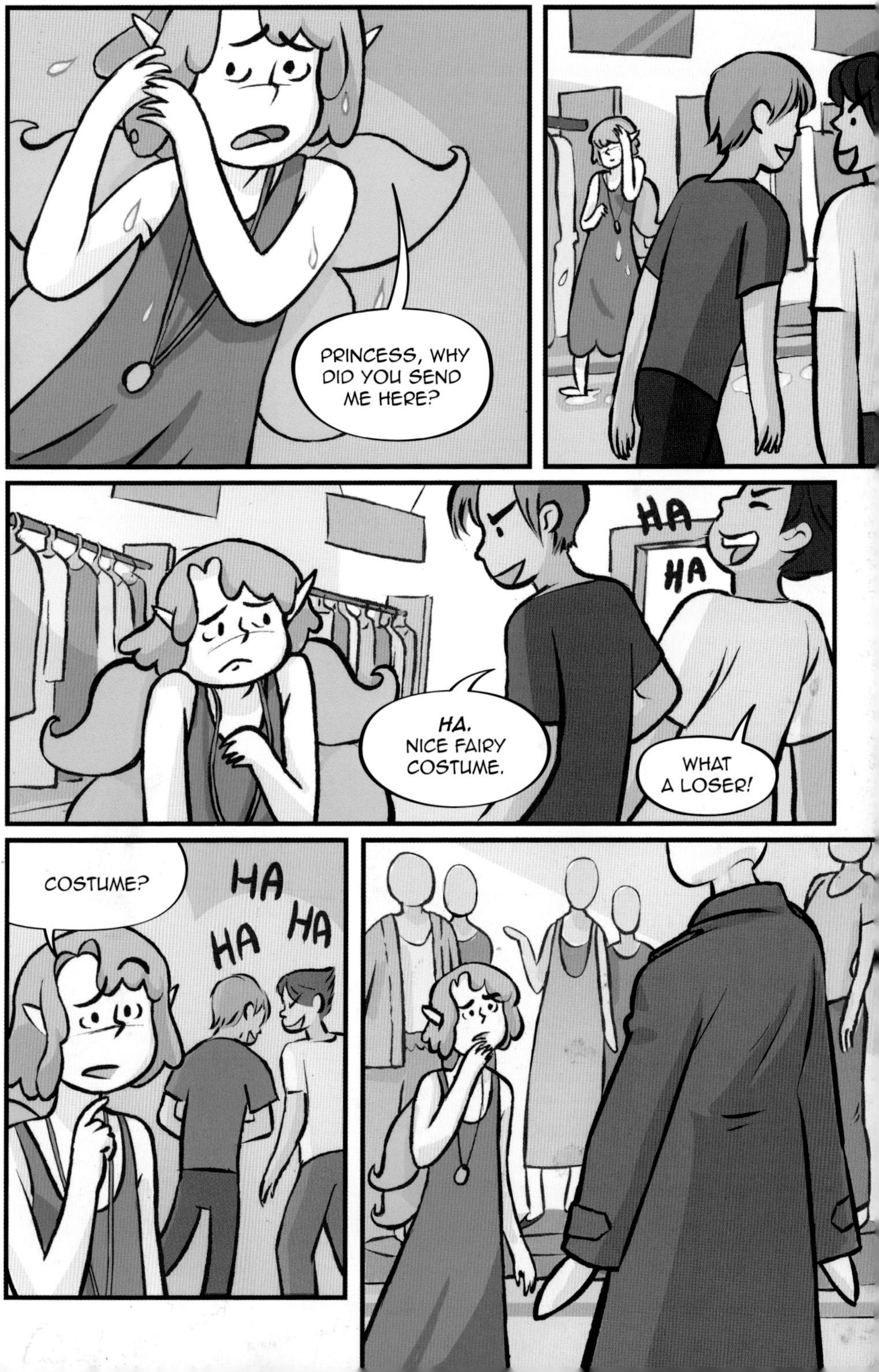
PRINCESS, WHY DID YOU SEND ME HERE?
HA HA
HA. NICE FAIRY COSTUME.
WHAT A LOSER!
COSTUME?
HA HA HA

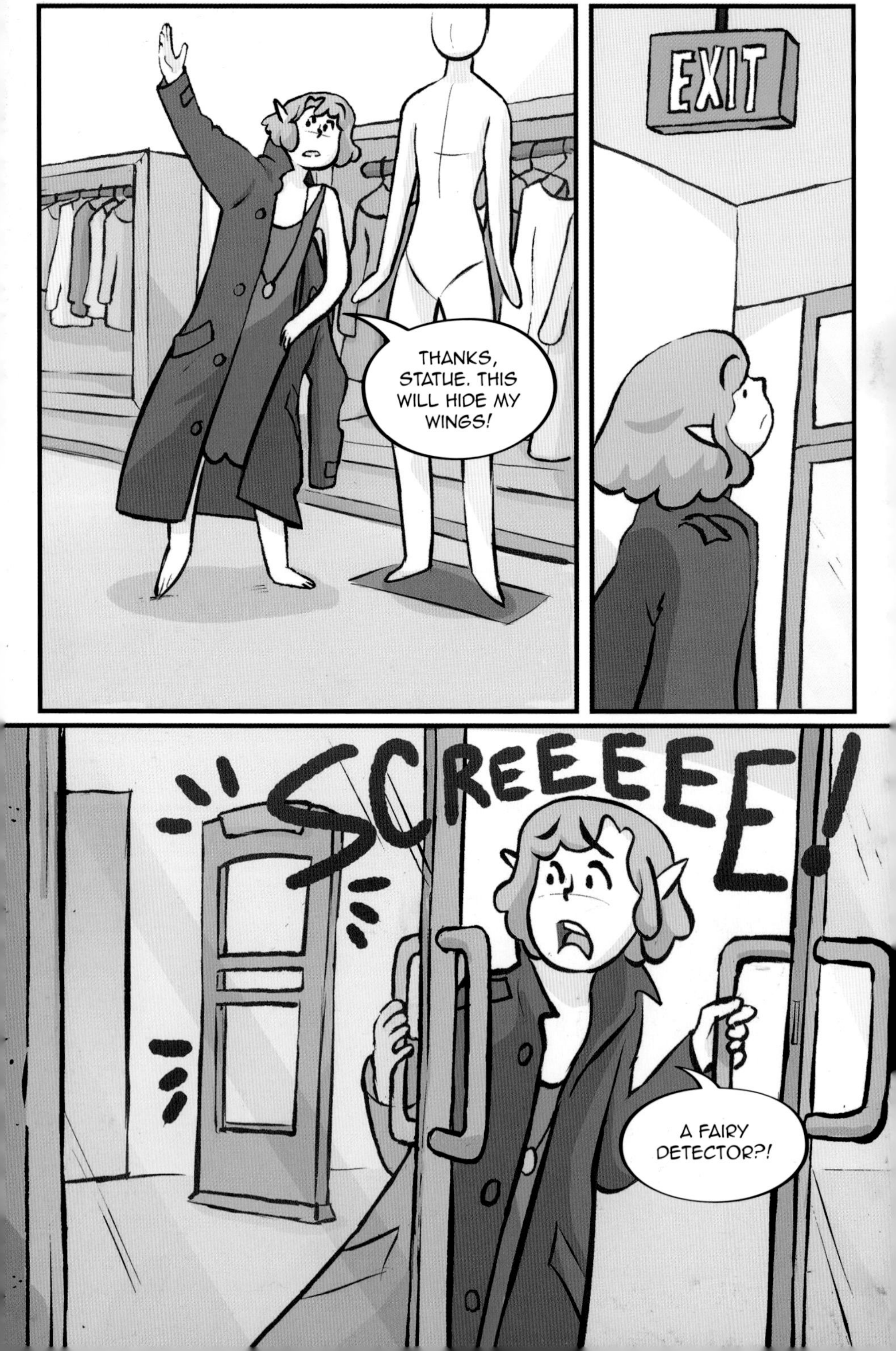
THANKS, STATUE. THIS WILL HIDE MY WINGS!
EXIT
SCREEEEEE!
A FAIRY DETECTOR?!

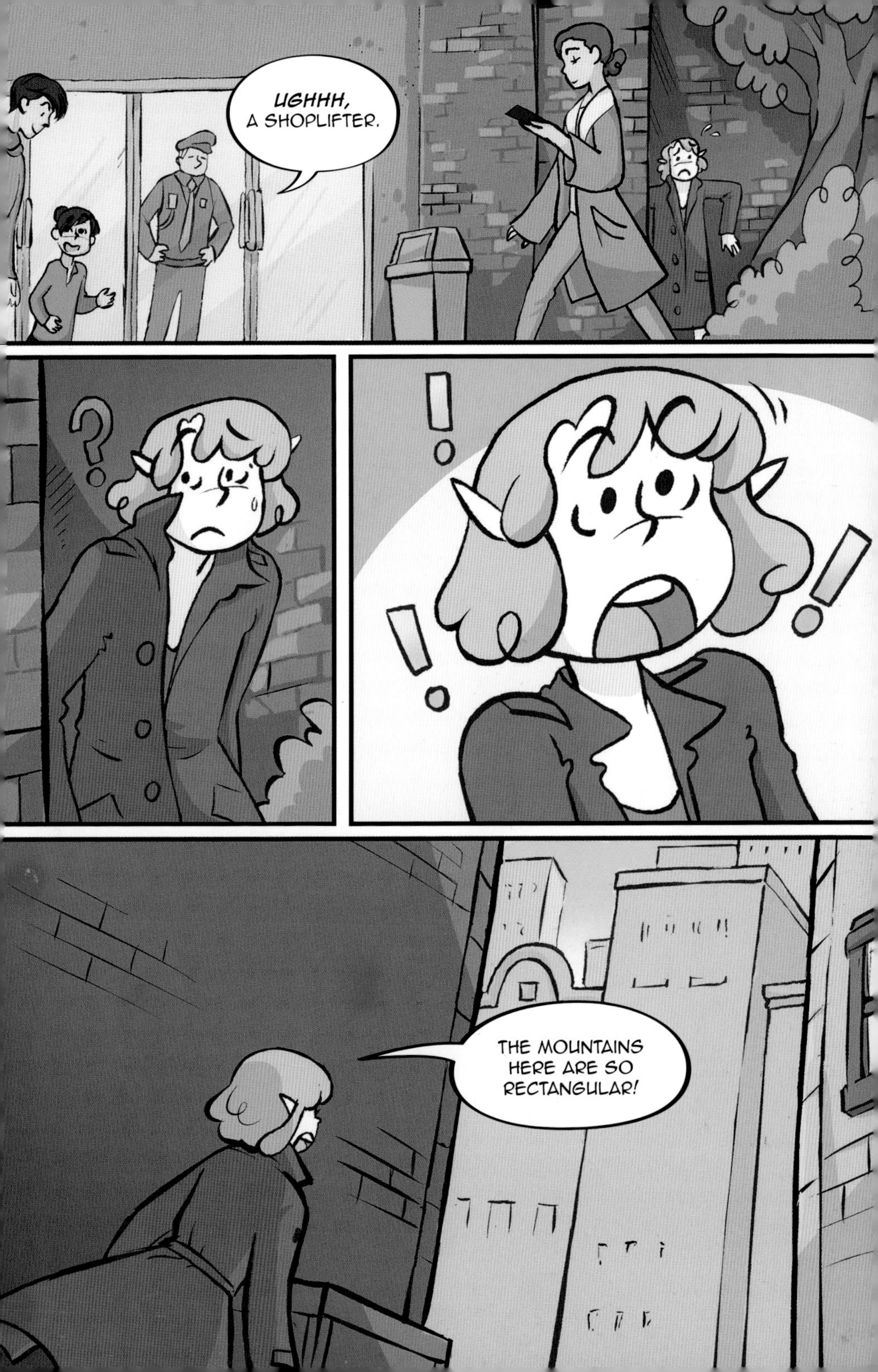
UGHHH,
A SHOPLIFTER.
!
!
!
THE MOUNTAINS
HERE ARE SO
RECTANGULAR!

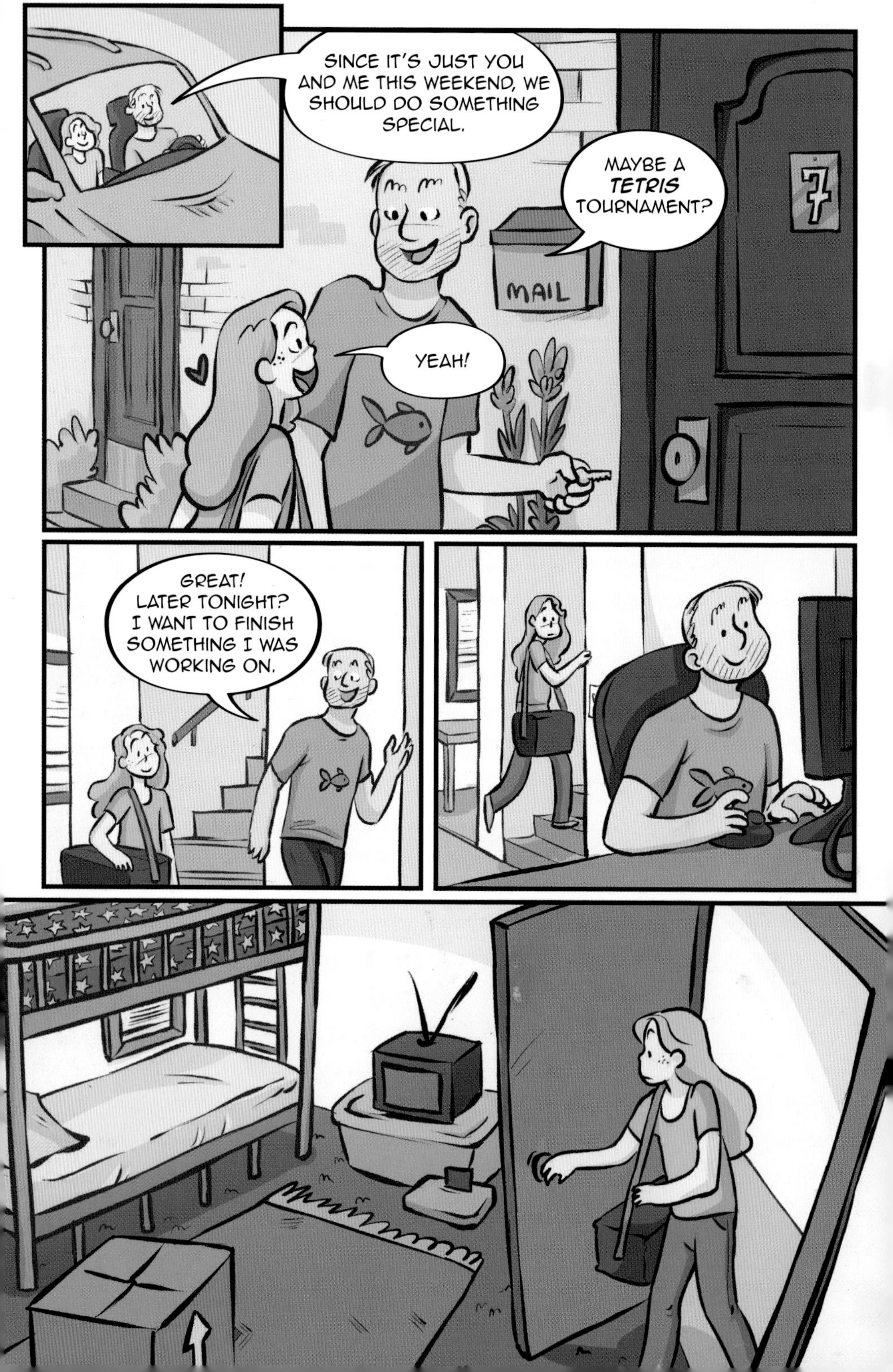
SINCE IT'S JUST YOU AND ME THIS WEEKEND, WE SHOULD DO SOMETHING SPECIAL.
MAYBE A TETRIS TOURNAMENT?
MAIL
7
YEAH!
GREAT! LATER TONIGHT? I WANT TO FINISH SOMETHING I WAS WORKING ON.

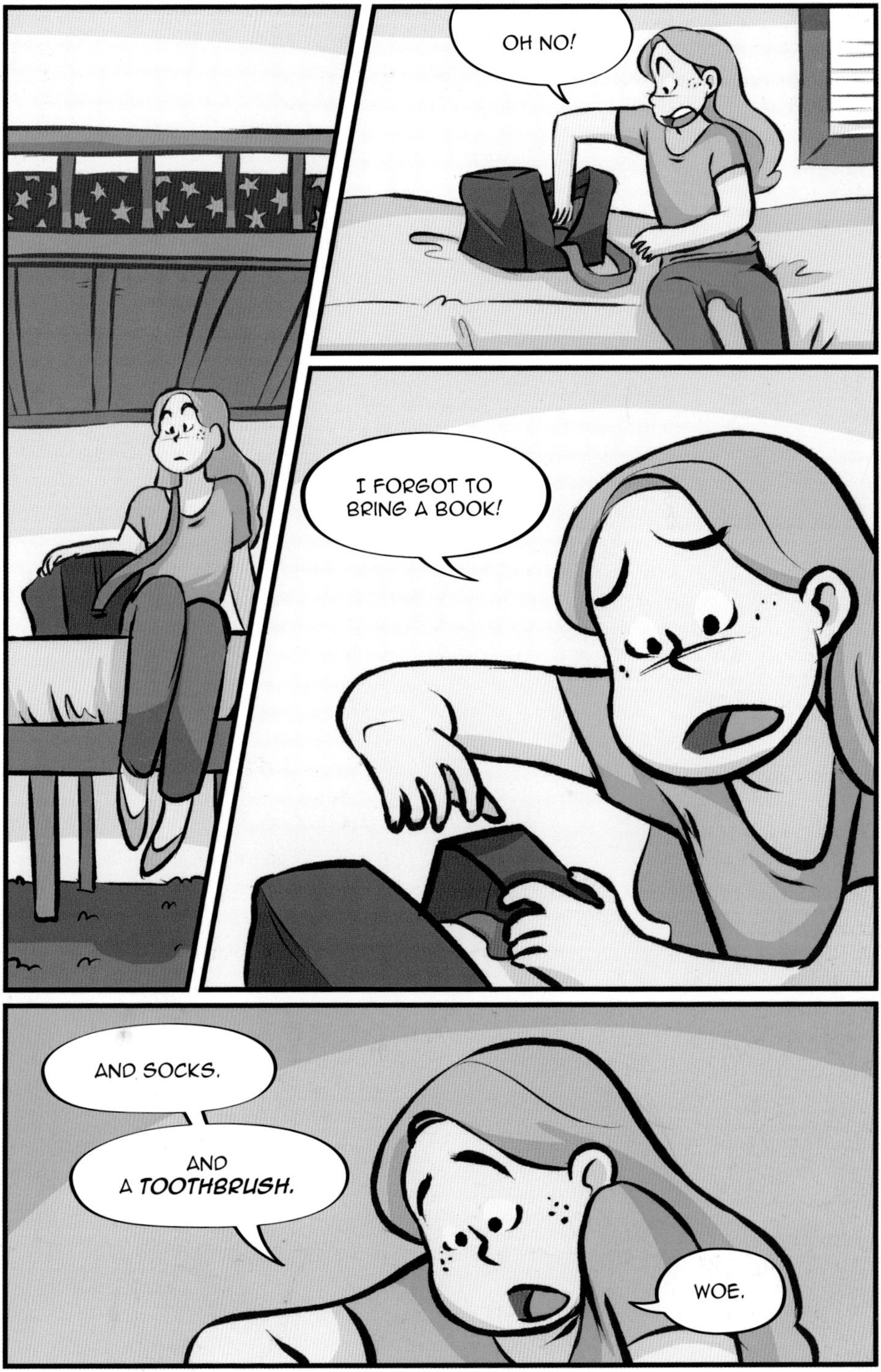
OH NO!
I FORGOT TO BRING A BOOK!
AND SOCKS.
AND A TOOTHBRUSH.
WOE.

DAAANG IT.

I COULD DRAW?

NAH.

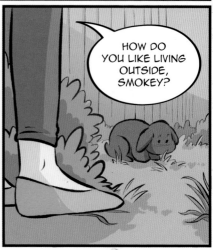

HOW DO YOU LIKE LIVING OUTSIDE, SMOKEY?

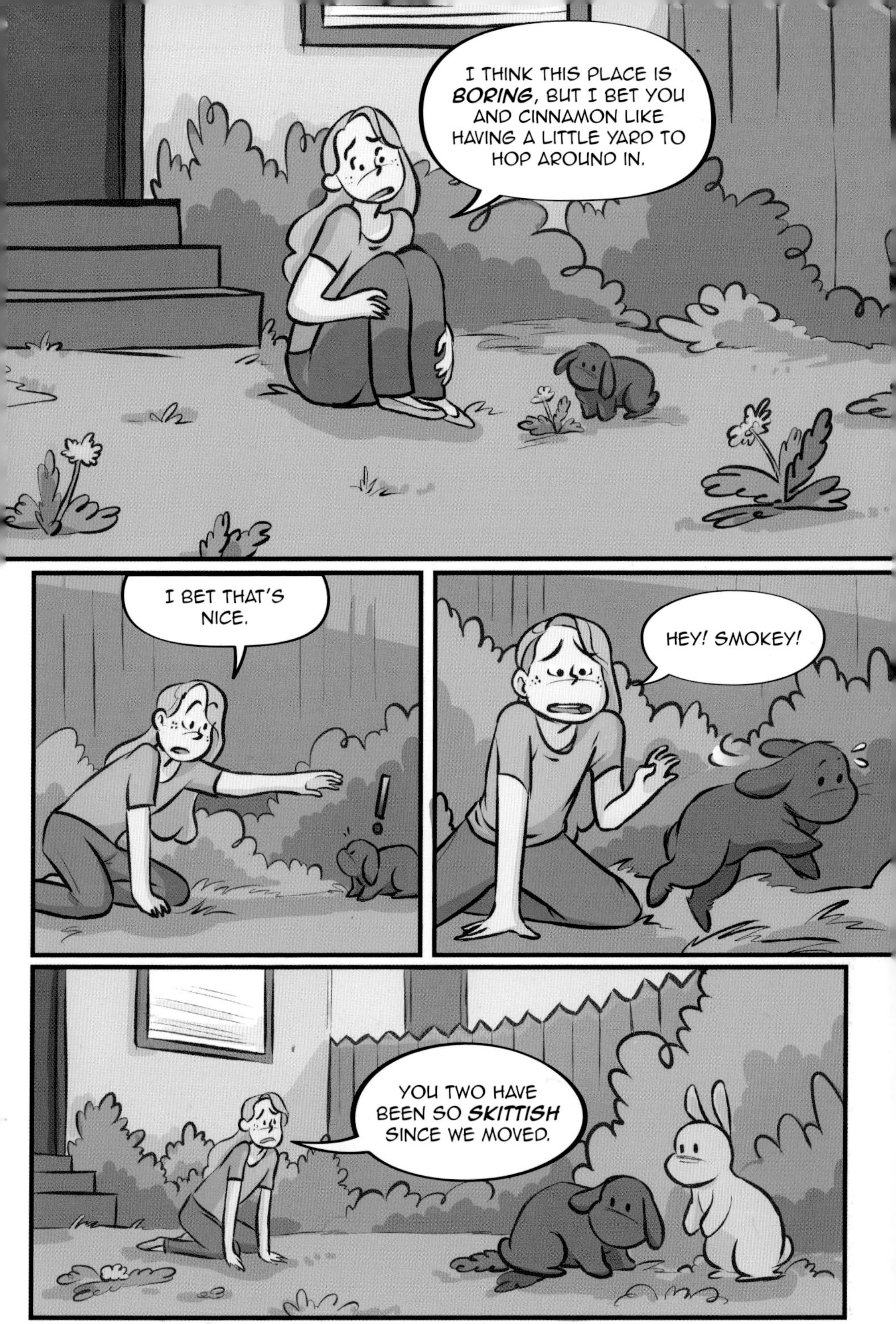
I THINK THIS PLACE IS BORING, BUT I BET YOU AND CINNAMON LIKE HAVING A LITTLE YARD TO HOP AROUND IN.
I BET THAT'S NICE.
!
HEY! SMOKEY!
YOU TWO HAVE BEEN SO SKITTISH SINCE WE MOVED.

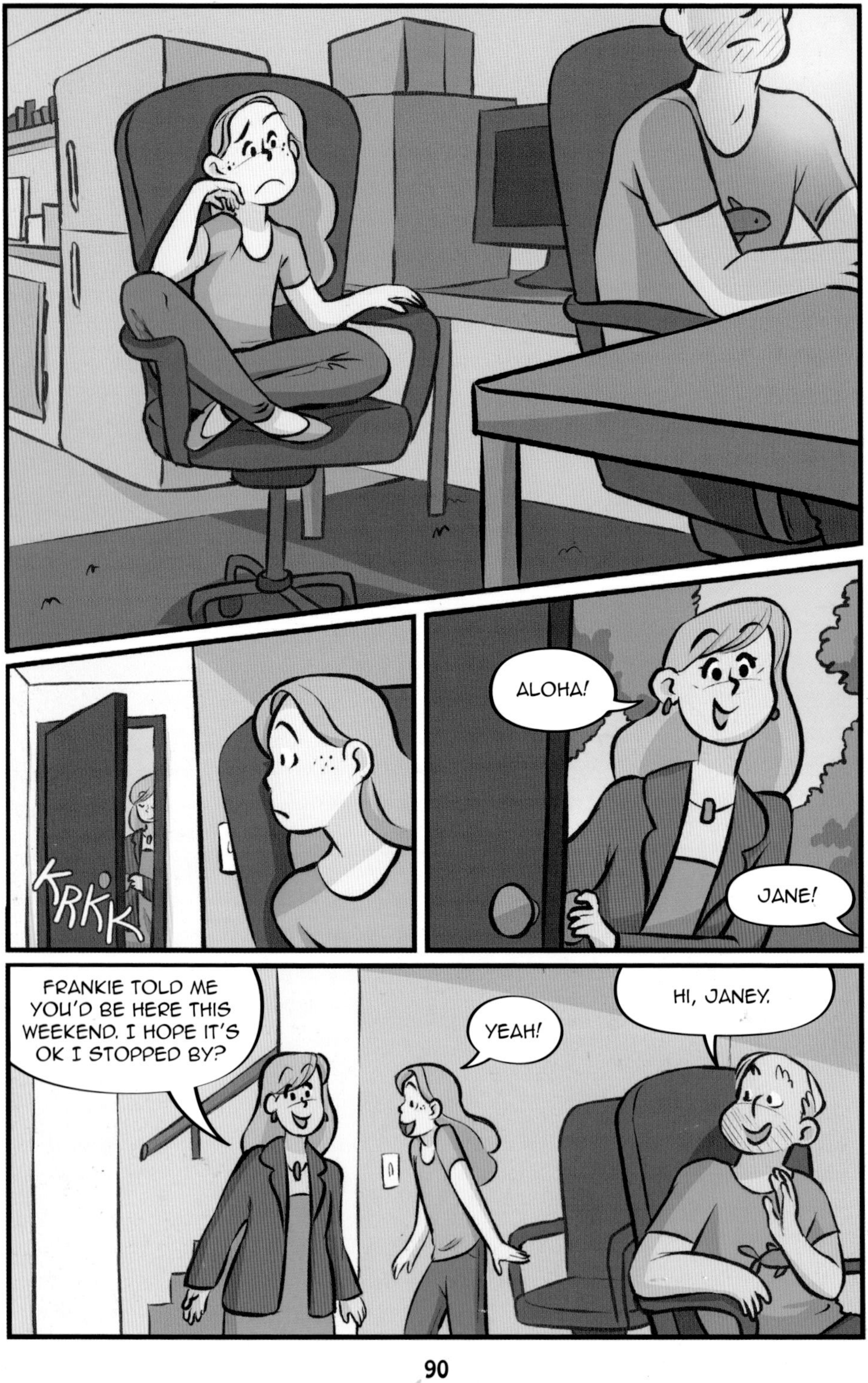
KRKK
ALOHA!
JANE!
FRANKIE TOLD ME YOU'D BE HERE THIS WEEKEND. I HOPE IT'S OK I STOPPED BY?
YEAH!
HI, JANEY.

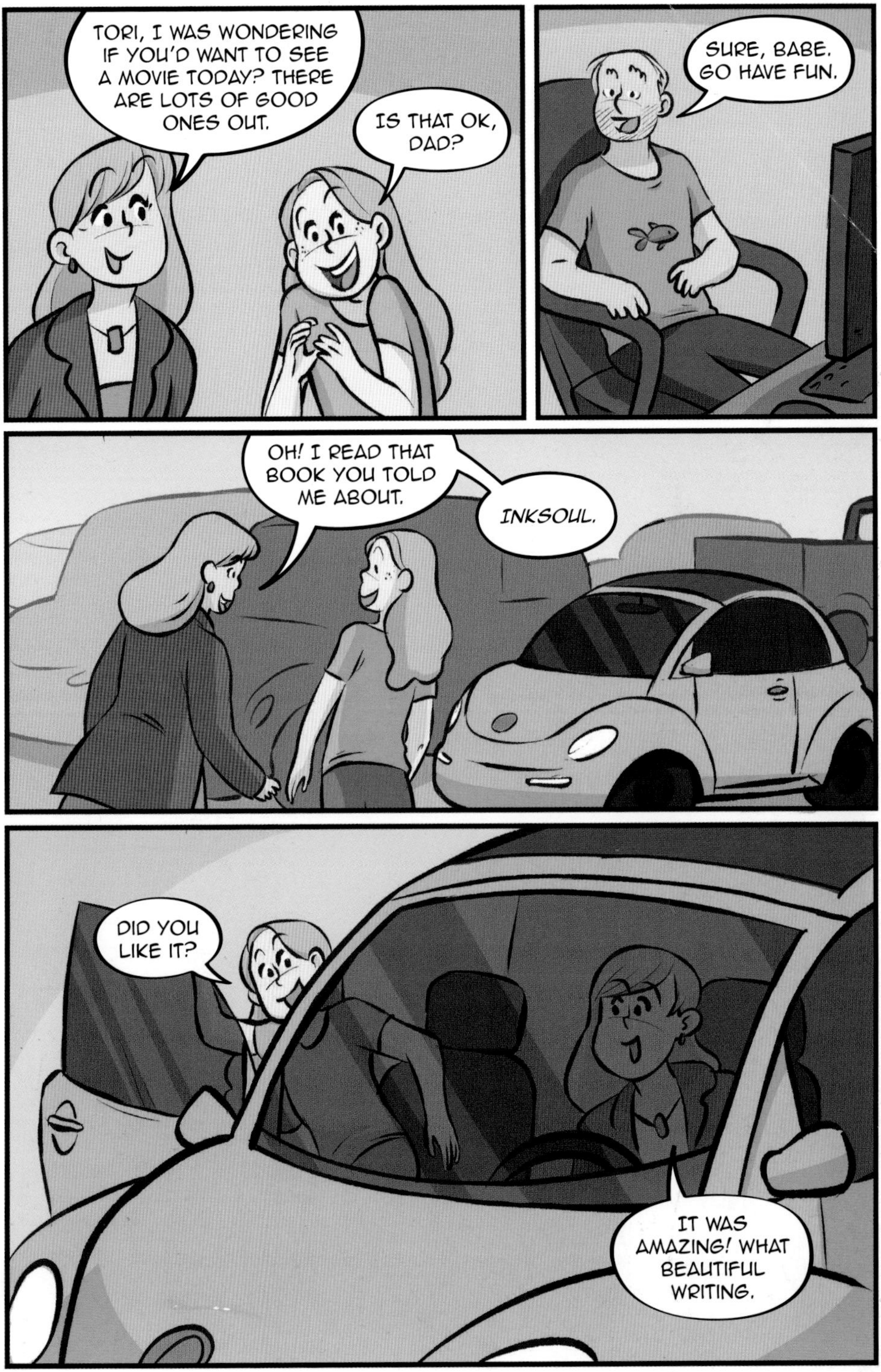
TORI, I WAS WONDERING IF YOU'D WANT TO SEE A MOVIE TODAY? THERE ARE LOTS OF GOOD ONES OUT.
IS THAT OK, DAD?
SURE, BABE. GO HAVE FUN.
OH! I READ THAT BOOK YOU TOLD ME ABOUT.
INKSOUL.
DID YOU LIKE IT?
IT WAS AMAZING! WHAT BEAUTIFUL WRITING.

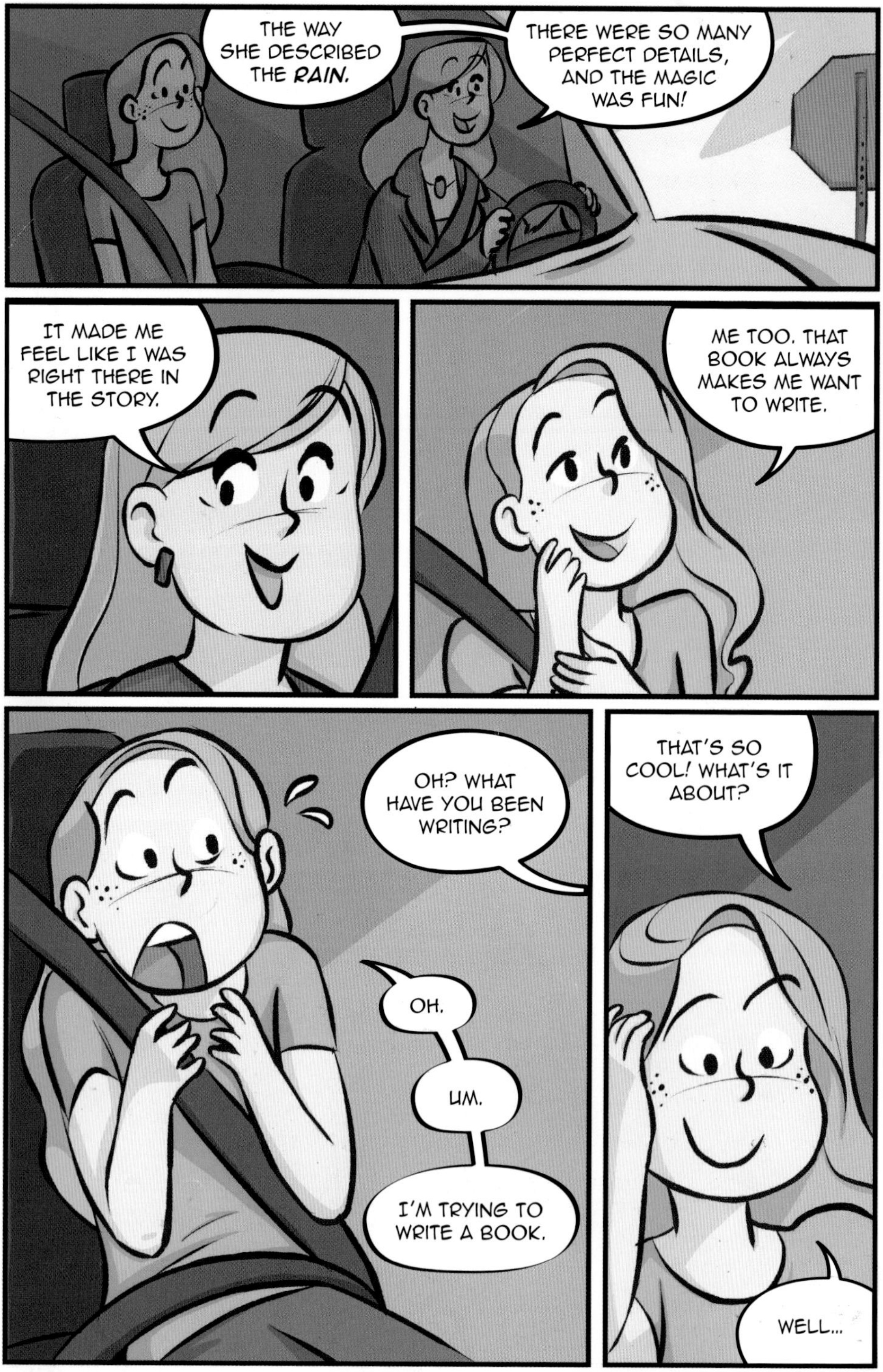
THE WAY SHE DESCRIBED THE *RAIN.*
THERE WERE SO MANY PERFECT DETAILS, AND THE MAGIC WAS FUN!
IT MADE ME FEEL LIKE I WAS RIGHT THERE IN THE STORY.
ME TOO. THAT BOOK ALWAYS MAKES ME WANT TO WRITE.
OH? WHAT HAVE YOU BEEN WRITING?
OH.
UM.
I'M TRYING TO WRITE A BOOK.
THAT'S SO COOL! WHAT'S IT ABOUT?
WELL...

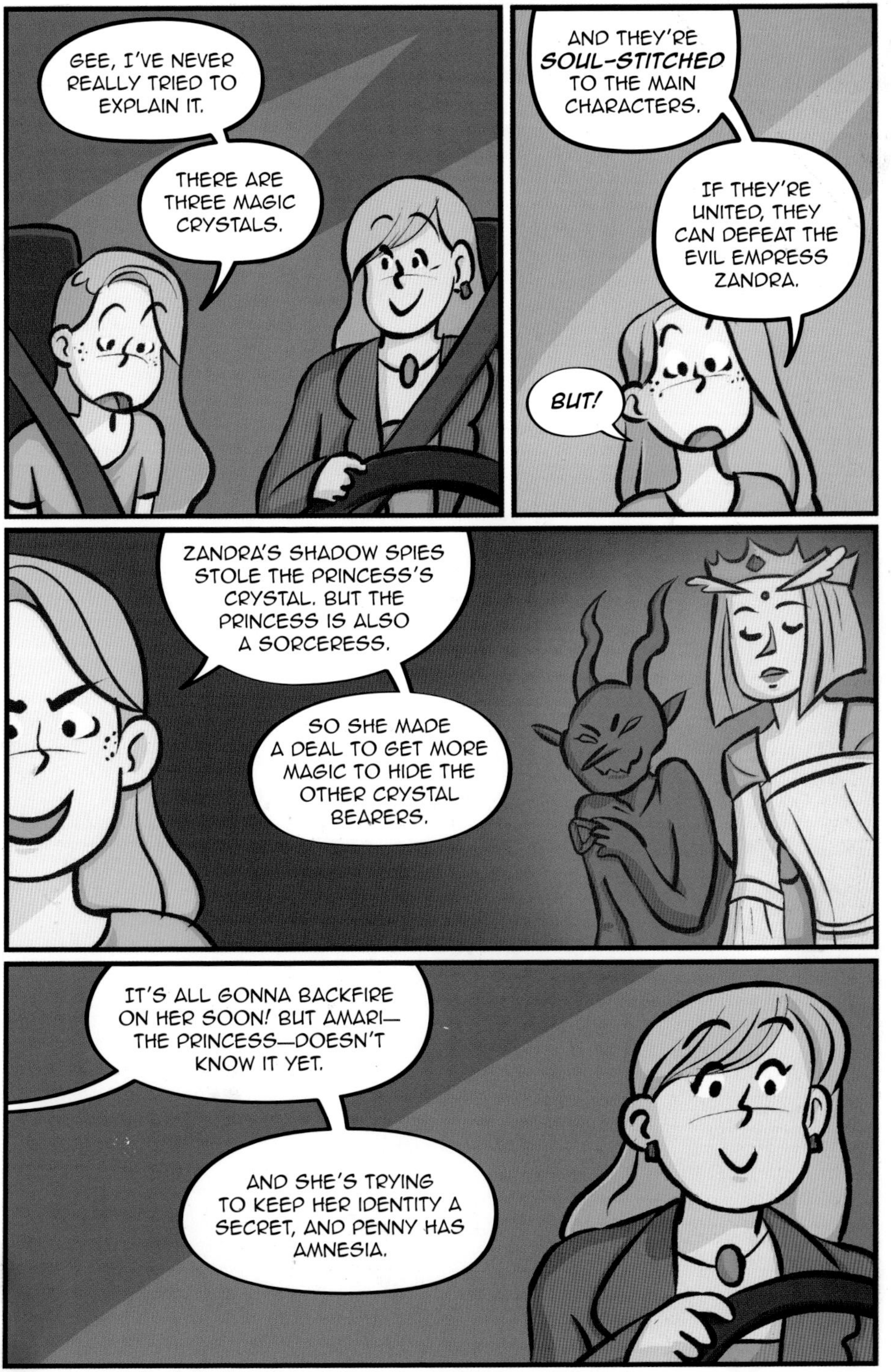
GEE, I'VE NEVER REALLY TRIED TO EXPLAIN IT.
THERE ARE THREE MAGIC CRYSTALS.
AND THEY'RE *SOUL-STITCHED* TO THE MAIN CHARACTERS.
IF THEY'RE UNITED, THEY CAN DEFEAT THE EVIL EMPRESS ZANDRA.
*BUT!*
ZANDRA'S SHADOW SPIES STOLE THE PRINCESS'S CRYSTAL. BUT THE PRINCESS IS ALSO A SORCERESS.
SO SHE MADE A DEAL TO GET MORE MAGIC TO HIDE THE OTHER CRYSTAL BEARERS.
IT'S ALL GONNA BACKFIRE ON HER SOON! BUT AMARI—THE PRINCESS—DOESN'T KNOW IT YET.
AND SHE'S TRYING TO KEEP HER IDENTITY A SECRET, AND PENNY HAS AMNESIA.

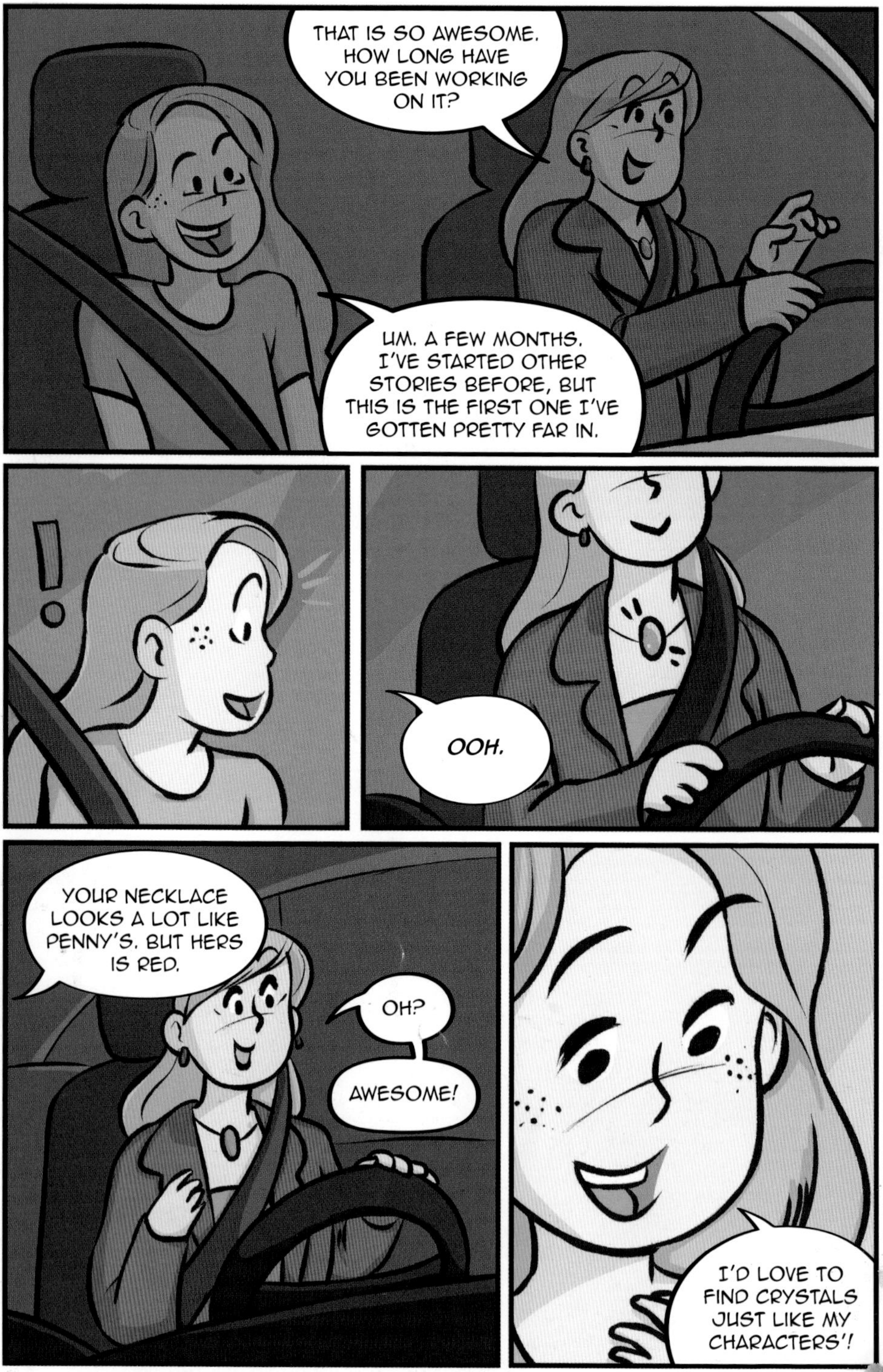
THAT IS SO AWESOME. HOW LONG HAVE YOU BEEN WORKING ON IT?
UM. A FEW MONTHS. I'VE STARTED OTHER STORIES BEFORE, BUT THIS IS THE FIRST ONE I'VE GOTTEN PRETTY FAR IN.
!
OOH.
YOUR NECKLACE LOOKS A LOT LIKE PENNY'S. BUT HERS IS RED.
OH?
AWESOME!
I'D LOVE TO FIND CRYSTALS JUST LIKE MY CHARACTERS'!

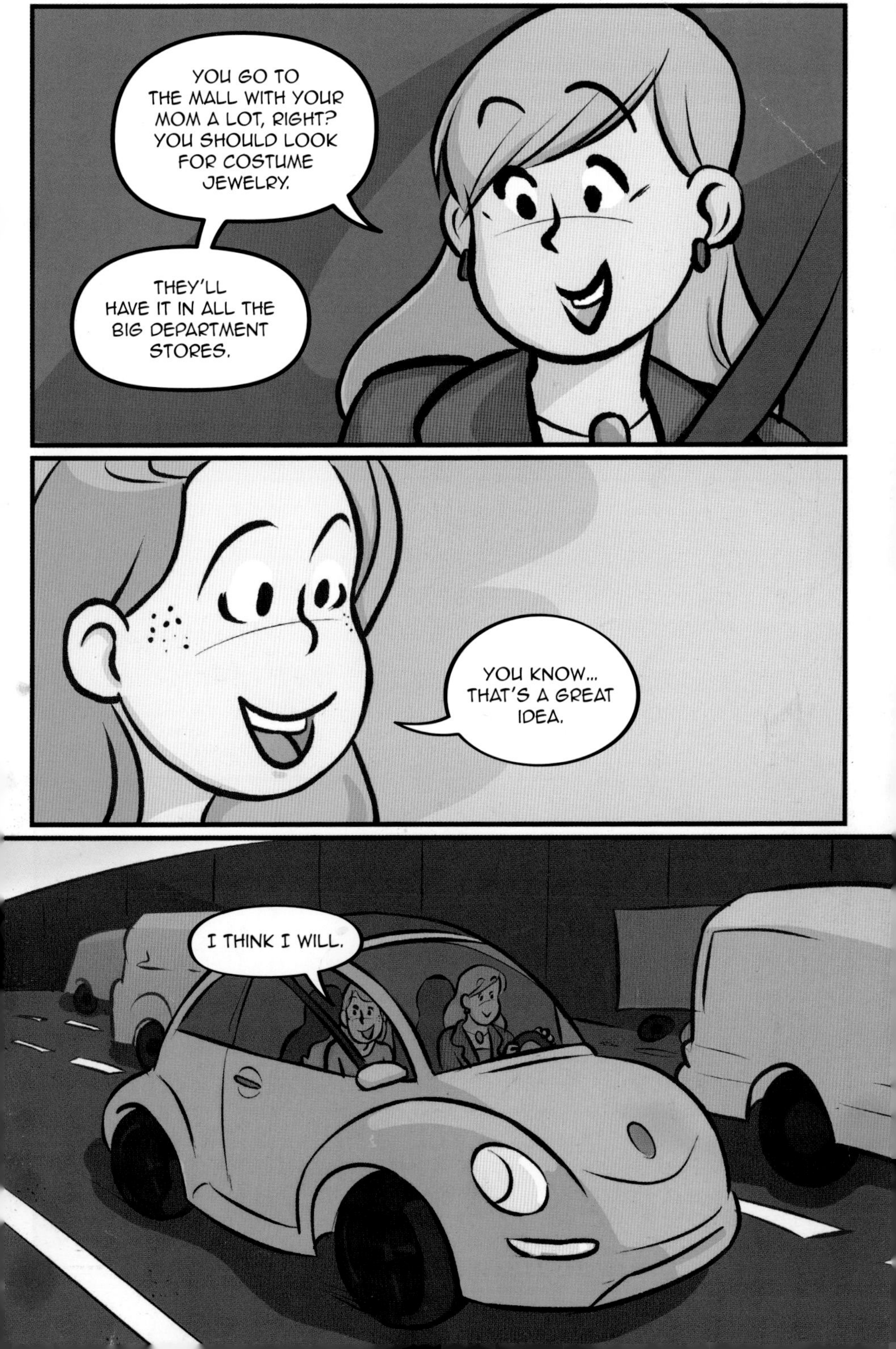
YOU GO TO THE MALL WITH YOUR MOM A LOT, RIGHT? YOU SHOULD LOOK FOR COSTUME JEWELRY.
THEY'LL HAVE IT IN ALL THE BIG DEPARTMENT STORES.
YOU KNOW... THAT'S A GREAT IDEA.
I THINK I WILL.

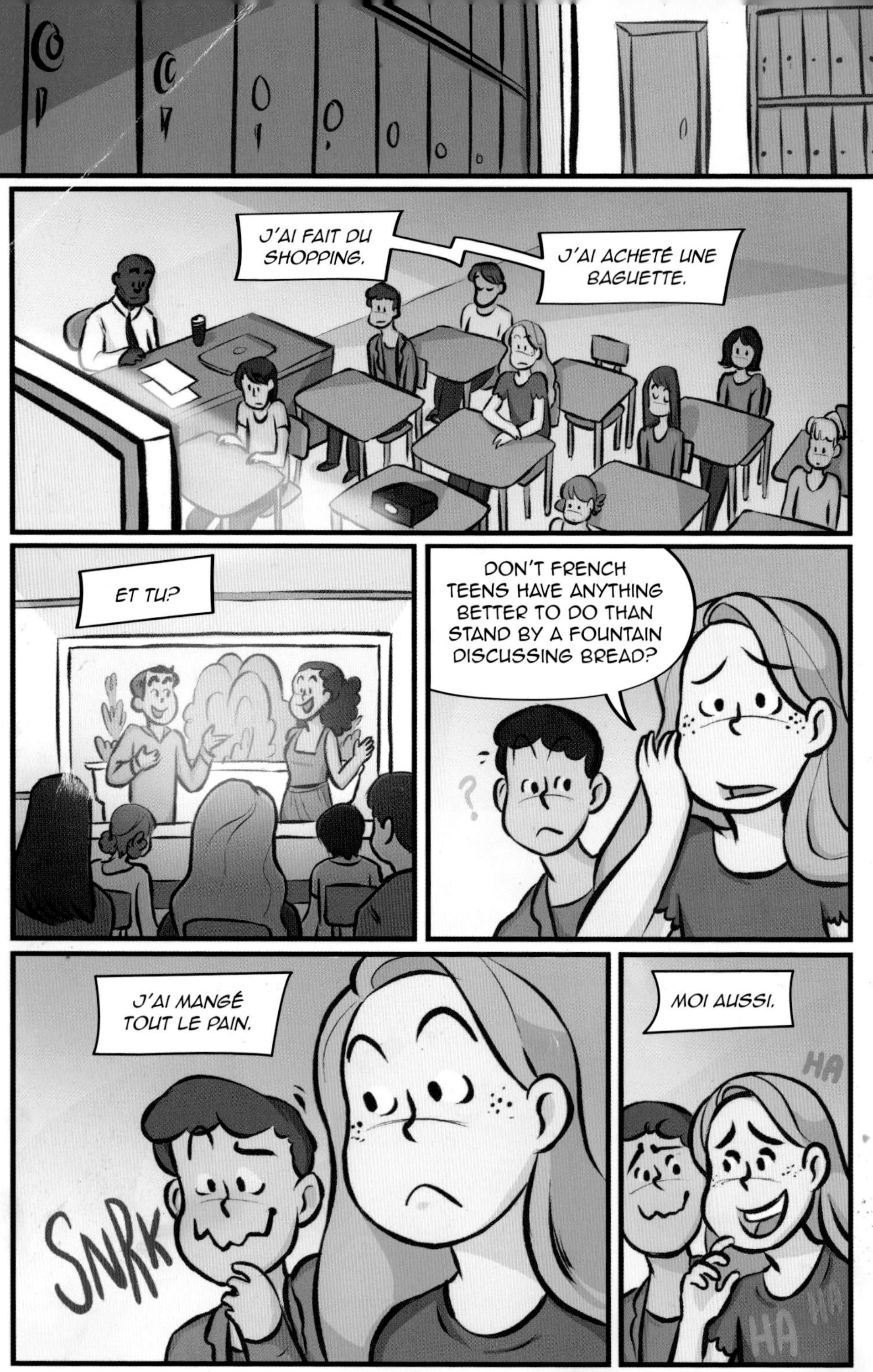

J'AI FAIT DU SHOPPING.
J'AI ACHETÉ UNE BAGUETTE.
ET TU?
DON'T FRENCH TEENS HAVE ANYTHING BETTER TO DO THAN STAND BY A FOUNTAIN DISCUSSING BREAD?
J'AI MANGÉ TOUT LE PAIN.
SNRK
MOI AUSSI.
HA
HA HA HA

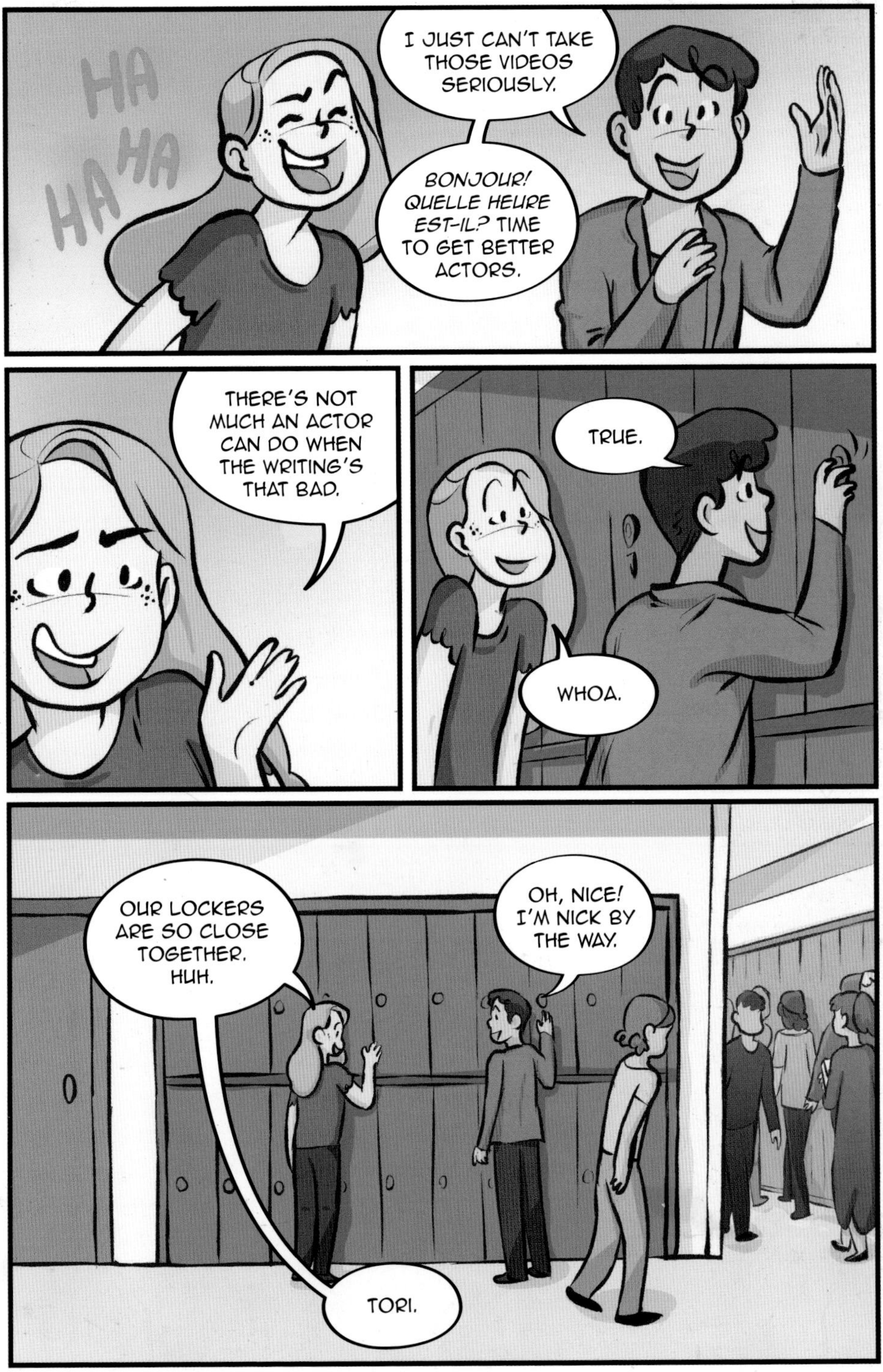
HA HA HA HA
I JUST CAN'T TAKE THOSE VIDEOS SERIOUSLY.
BONJOUR! QUELLE HEURE EST-IL? TIME TO GET BETTER ACTORS.
THERE'S NOT MUCH AN ACTOR CAN DO WHEN THE WRITING'S THAT BAD.
TRUE.
WHOA.
OUR LOCKERS ARE SO CLOSE TOGETHER. HUH.
OH, NICE! I'M NICK BY THE WAY.
TORI.

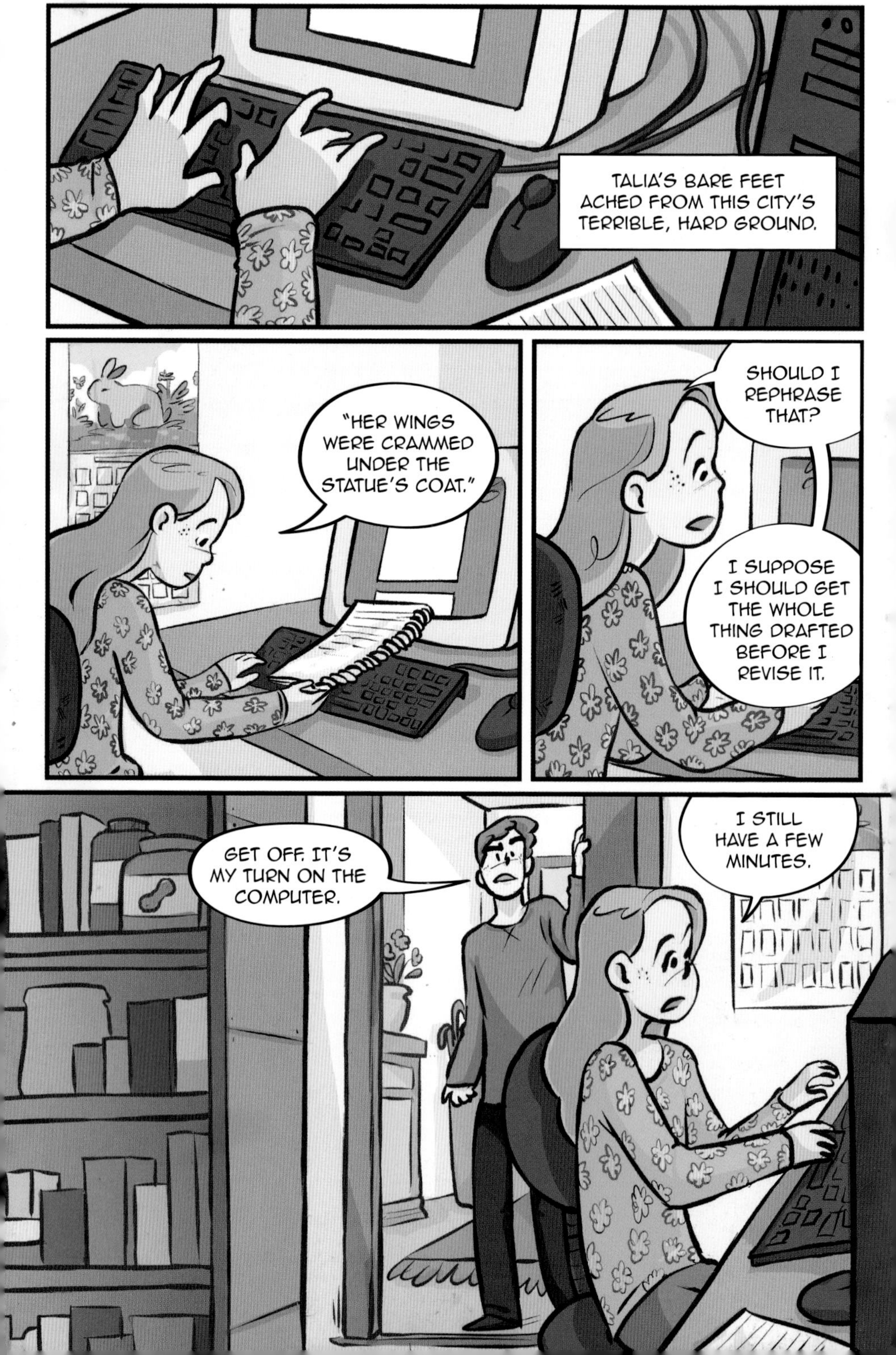
TALIA'S BARE FEET ACHED FROM THIS CITY'S TERRIBLE, HARD GROUND.
"HER WINGS WERE CRAMMED UNDER THE STATUE'S COAT."
SHOULD I REPHRASE THAT?
I SUPPOSE I SHOULD GET THE WHOLE THING DRAFTED BEFORE I REVISE IT.
GET OFF. IT'S MY TURN ON THE COMPUTER.
I STILL HAVE A FEW MINUTES.

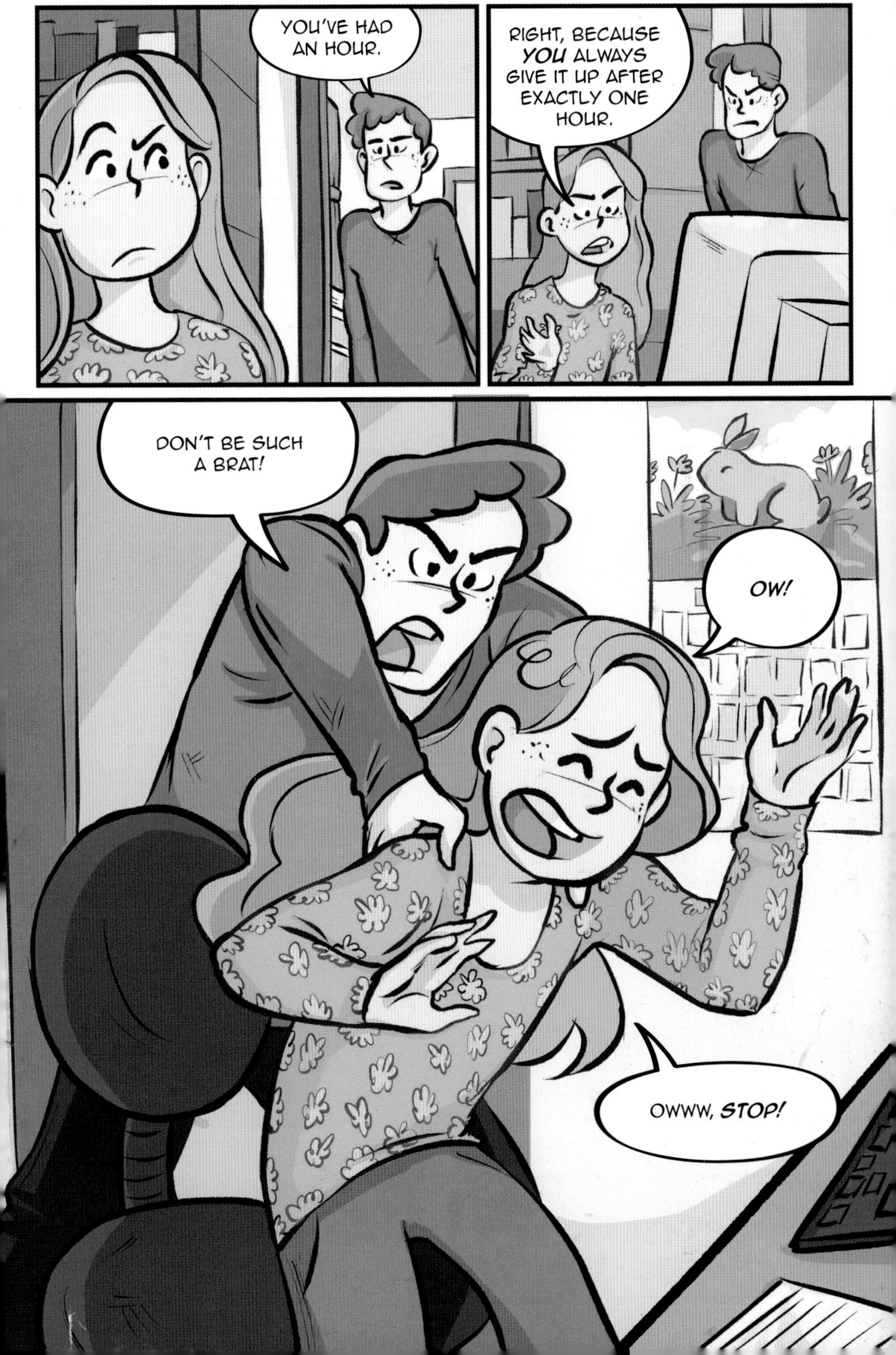
YOU'VE HAD AN HOUR.
RIGHT, BECAUSE *YOU* ALWAYS GIVE IT UP AFTER EXACTLY ONE HOUR.
DON'T BE SUCH A BRAT!
*OW!*
OWWW, *STOP!*

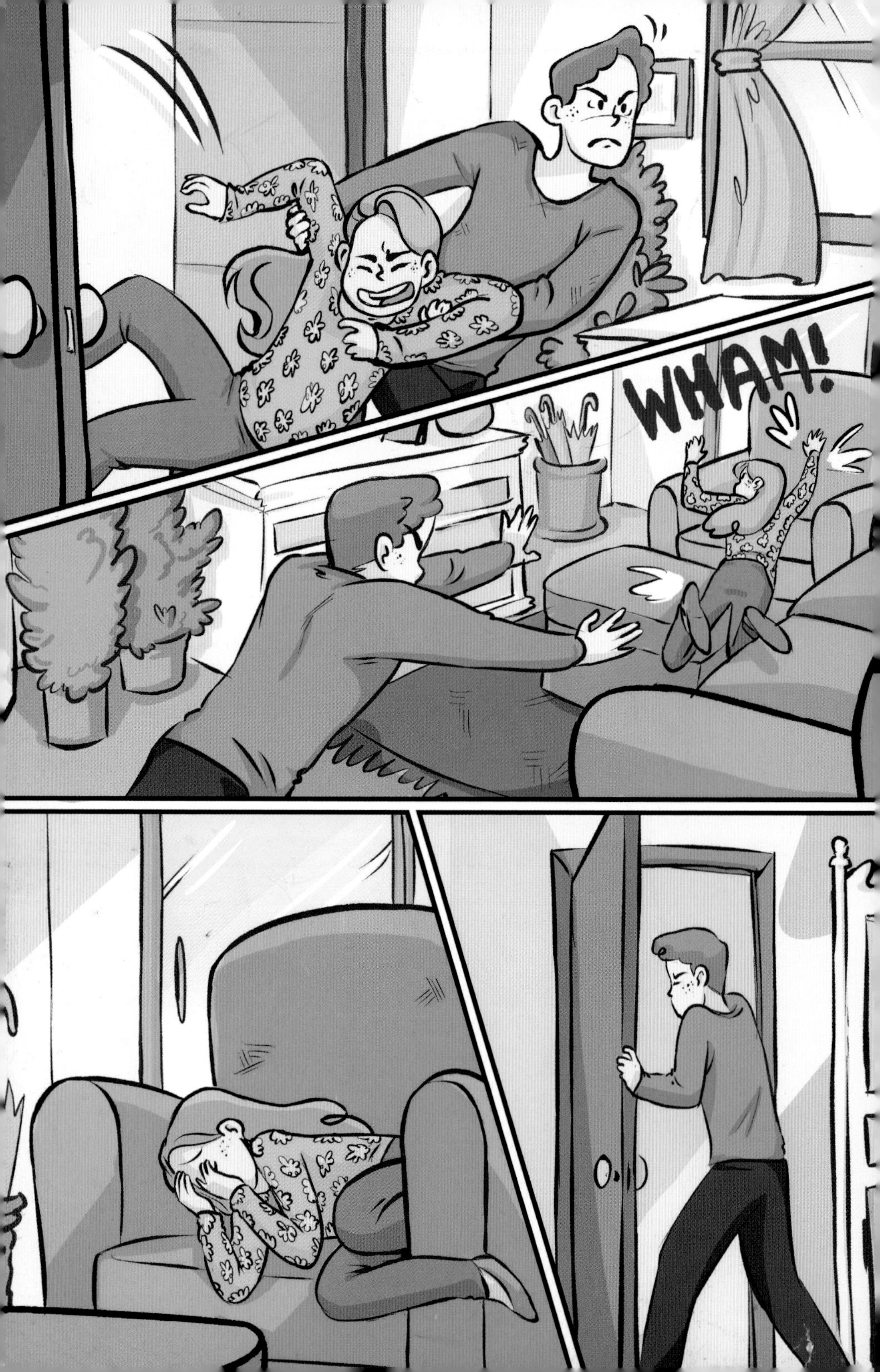
WHAM!

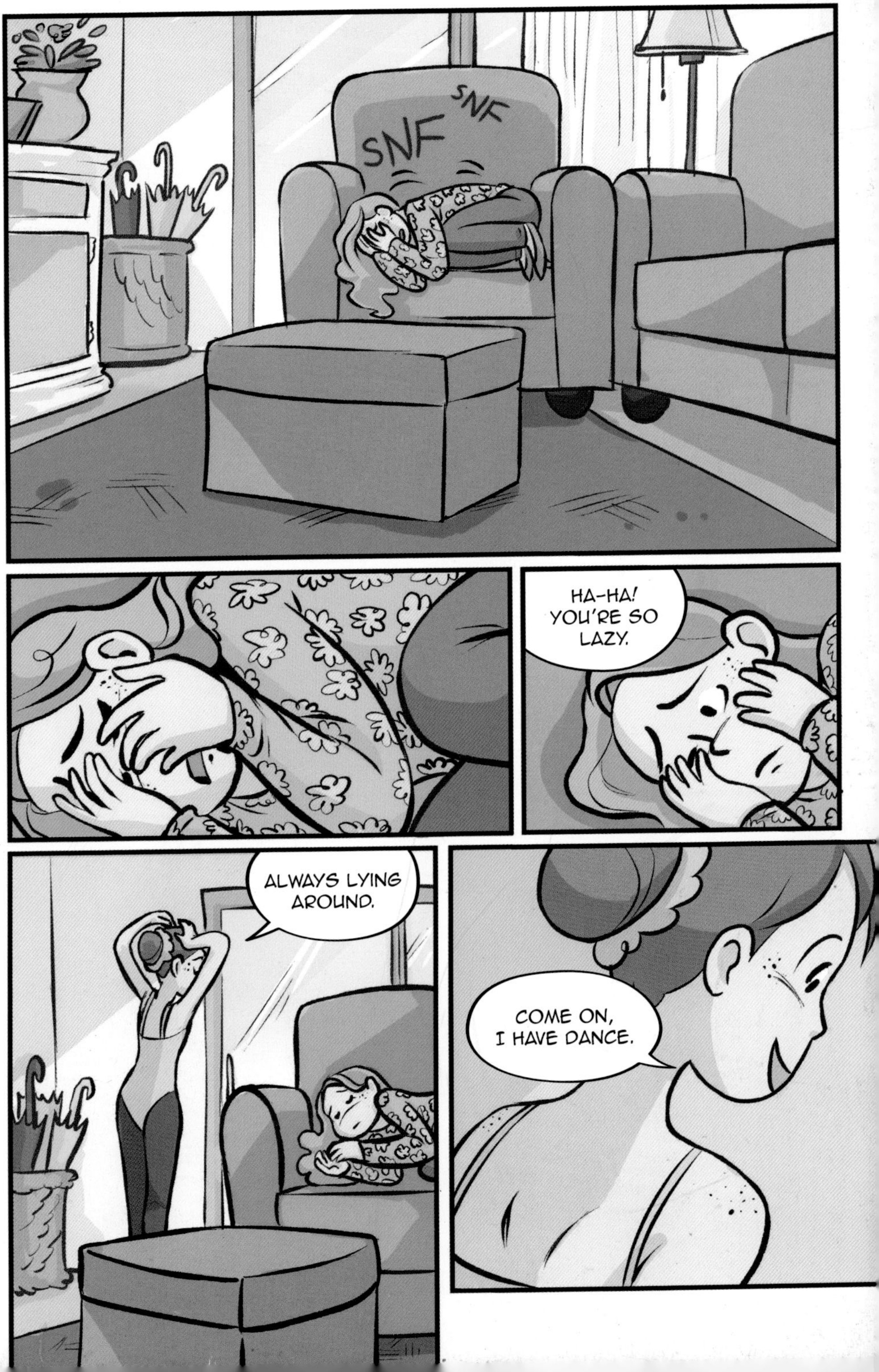
SNF
SNF
HA-HA! YOU'RE SO LAZY.
ALWAYS LYING AROUND.
COME ON, I HAVE DANCE.

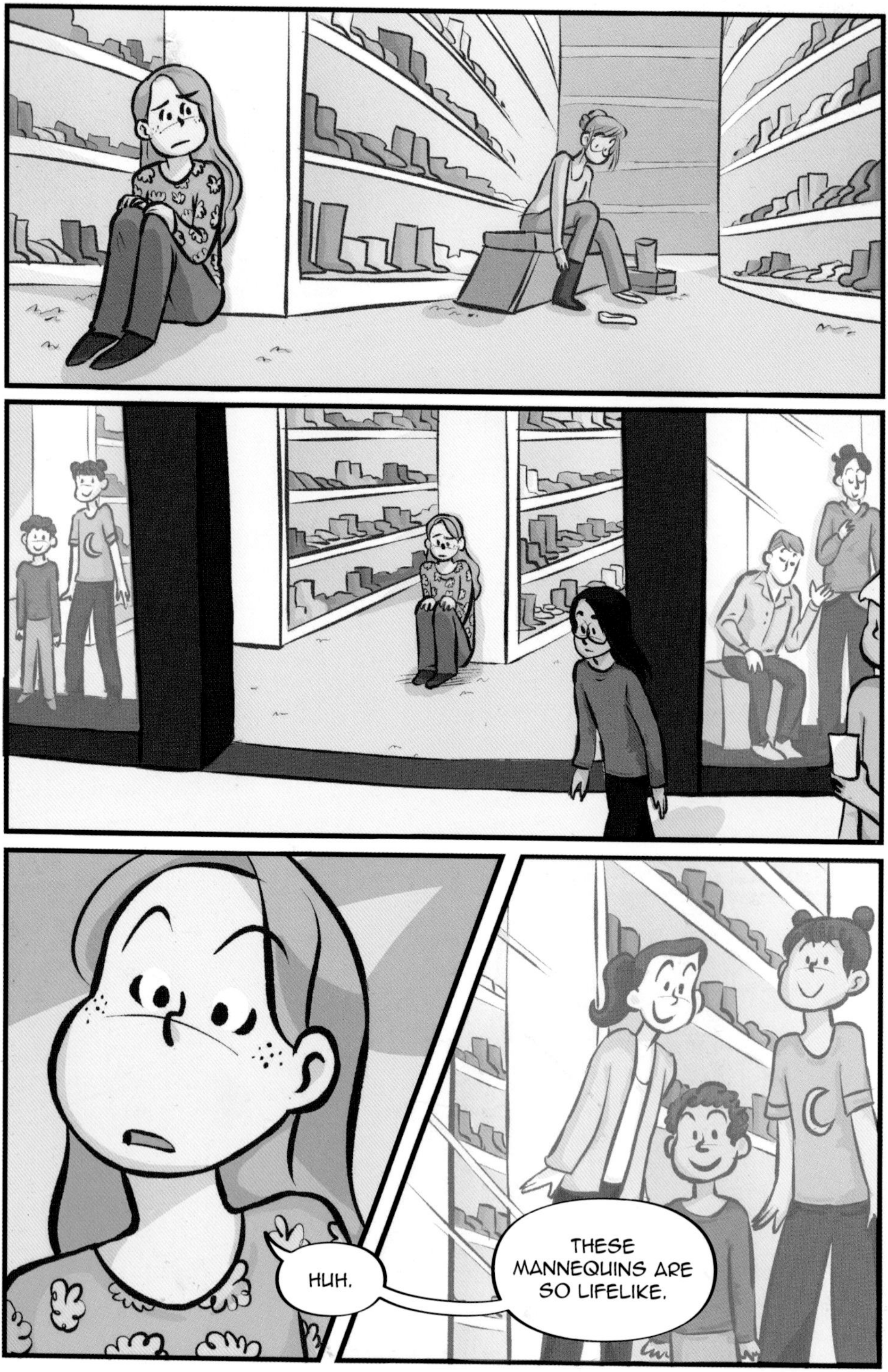
HUH.
THESE MANNEQUINS ARE SO LIFELIKE.

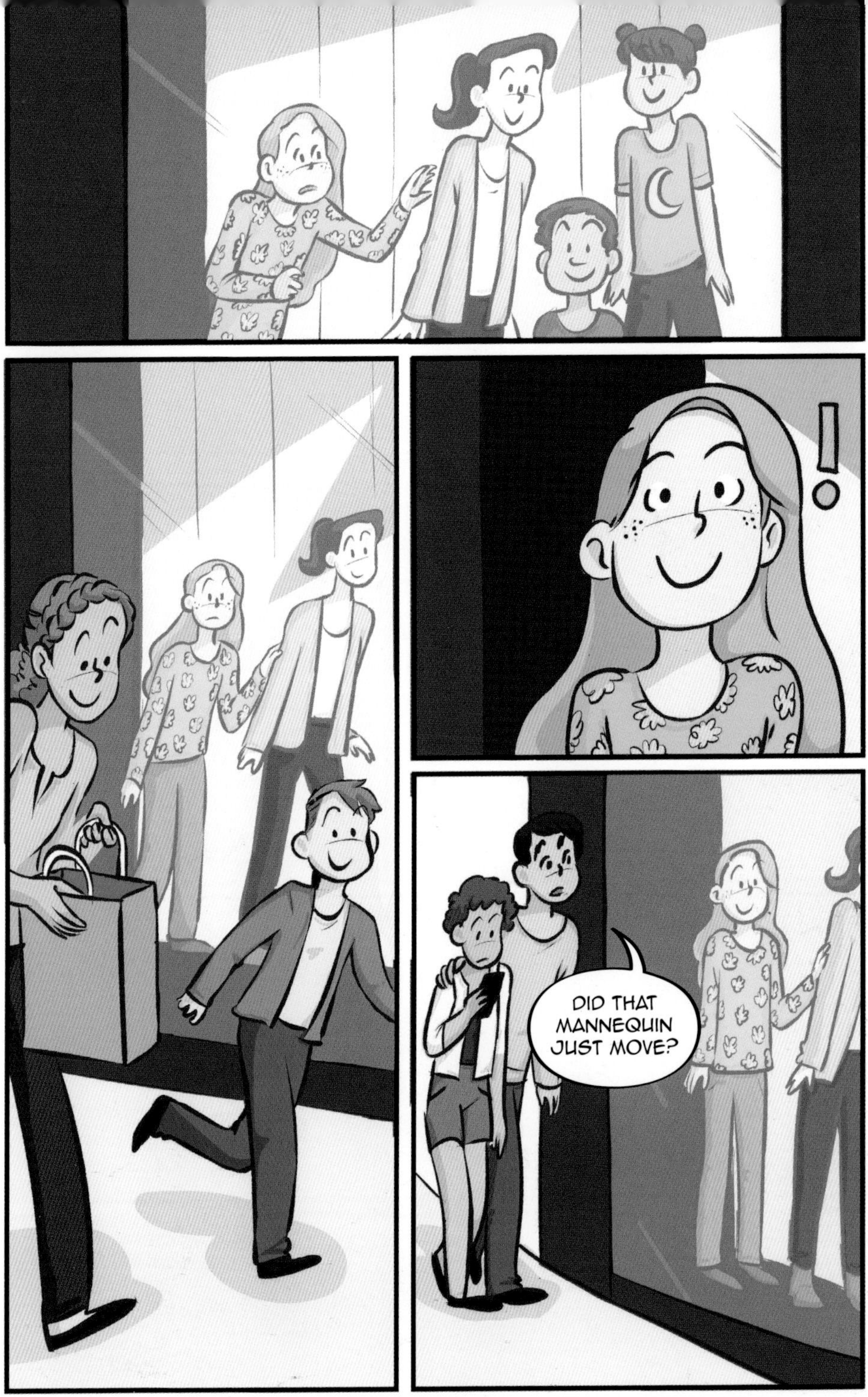
!
DID THAT MANNEQUIN JUST MOVE?

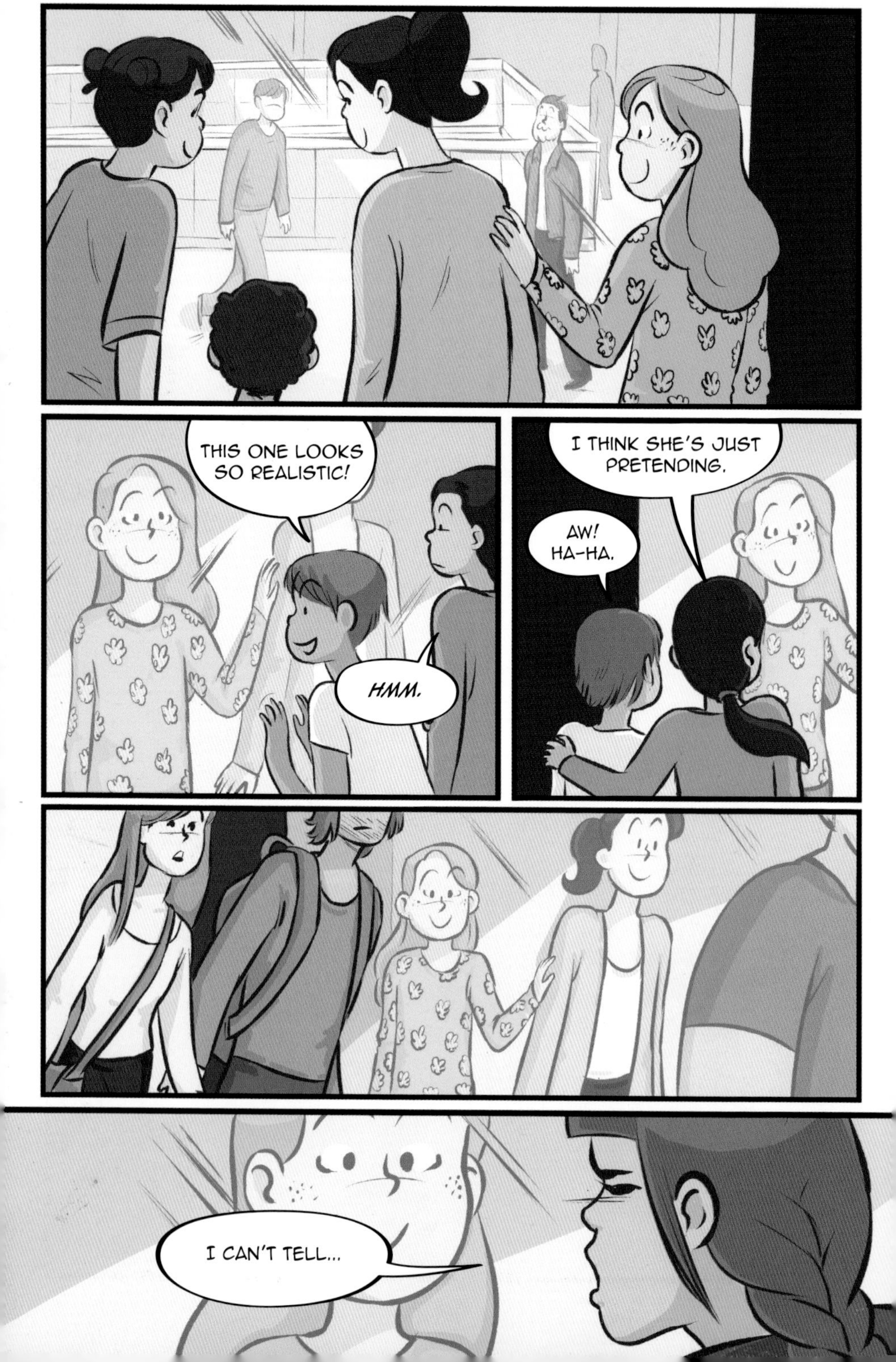
THIS ONE LOOKS SO REALISTIC!
HMM.
I THINK SHE'S JUST PRETENDING.
AW! HA-HA.
I CAN'T TELL...

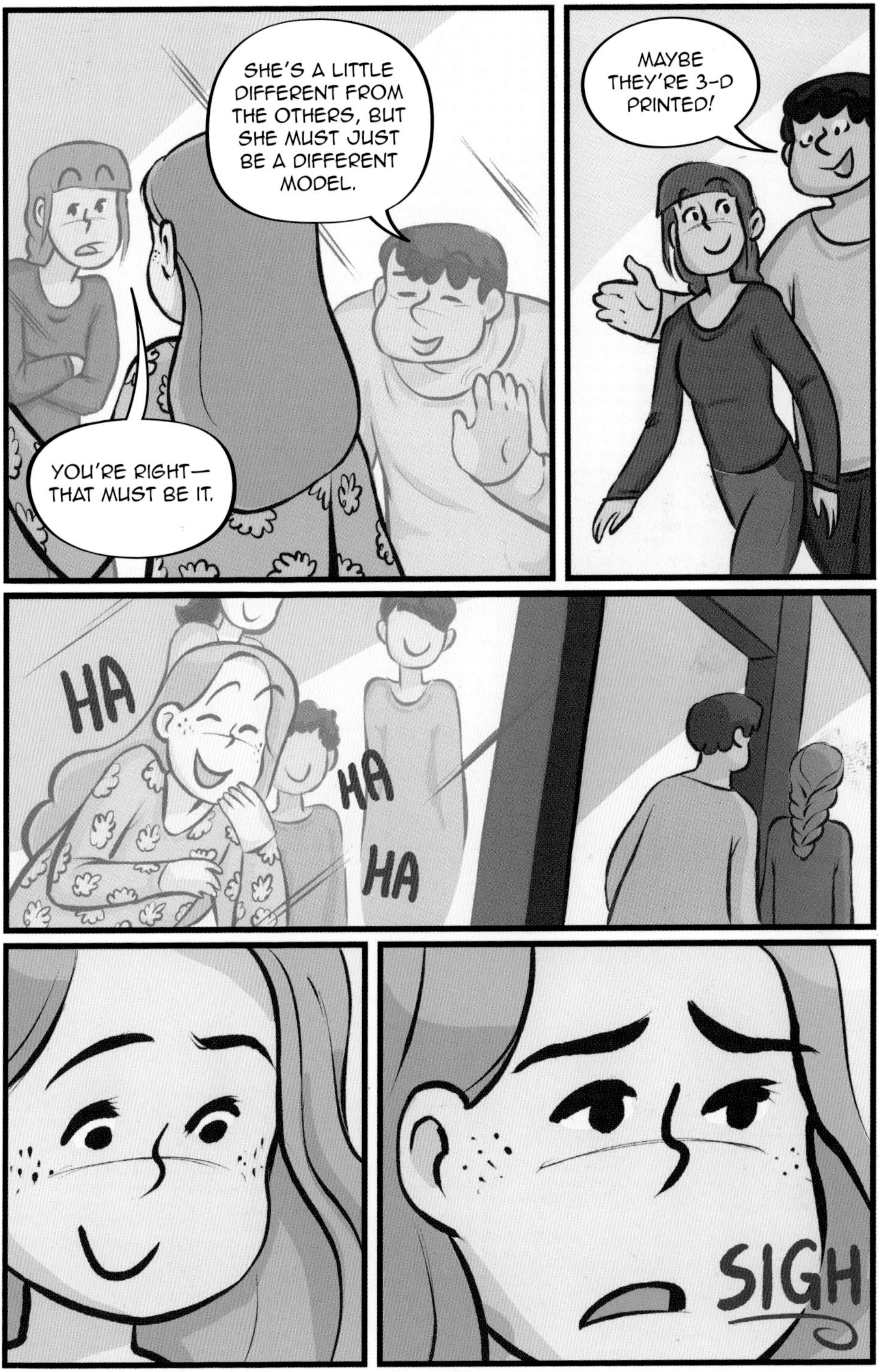
SHE'S A LITTLE DIFFERENT FROM THE OTHERS, BUT SHE MUST JUST BE A DIFFERENT MODEL.
YOU'RE RIGHT— THAT MUST BE IT.
MAYBE THEY'RE 3-D PRINTED!
HA
HA
HA
SIGH

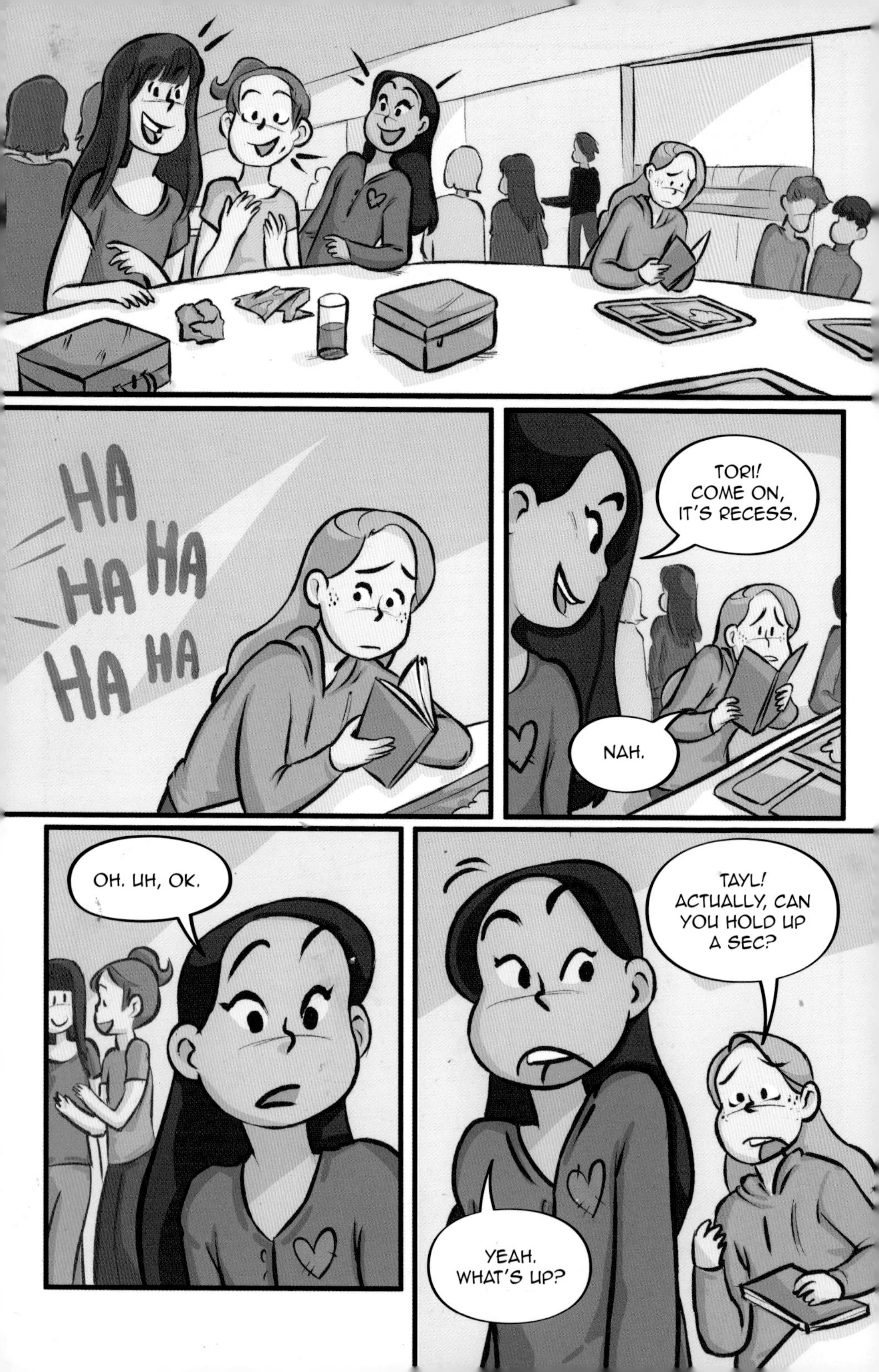

HA HA HA HA HA
TORI! COME ON, IT'S RECESS.
NAH.
OH. UH, OK.
TAYL! ACTUALLY, CAN YOU HOLD UP A SEC?
YEAH. WHAT'S UP?

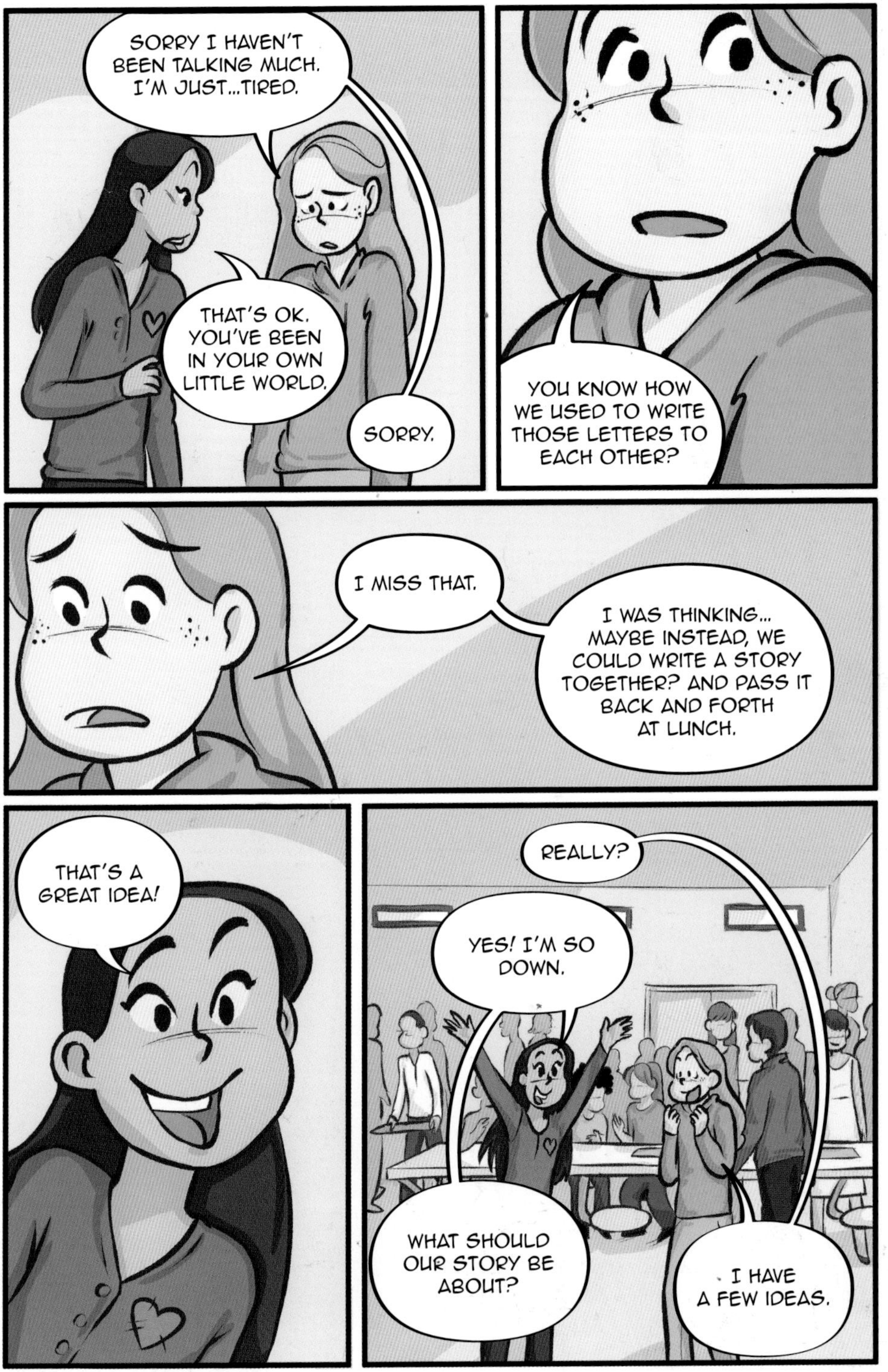
SORRY I HAVEN'T BEEN TALKING MUCH. I'M JUST...TIRED.
THAT'S OK. YOU'VE BEEN IN YOUR OWN LITTLE WORLD.
SORRY.
YOU KNOW HOW WE USED TO WRITE THOSE LETTERS TO EACH OTHER?
I MISS THAT.
I WAS THINKING... MAYBE INSTEAD, WE COULD WRITE A STORY TOGETHER? AND PASS IT BACK AND FORTH AT LUNCH.
THAT'S A GREAT IDEA!
REALLY?
YES! I'M SO DOWN.
WHAT SHOULD OUR STORY BE ABOUT?
I HAVE A FEW IDEAS.

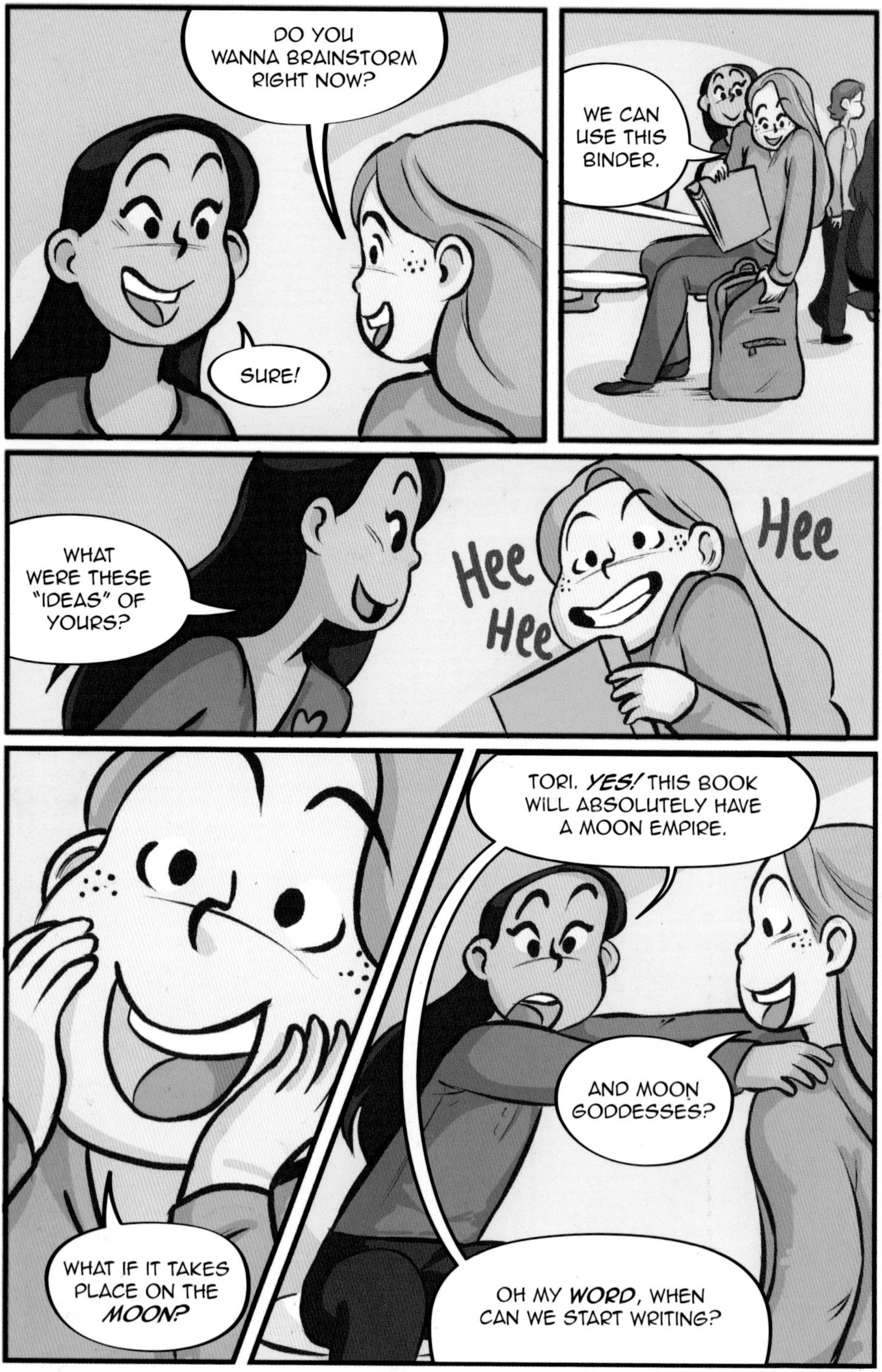
DO YOU WANNA BRAINSTORM RIGHT NOW?
SURE!
WE CAN USE THIS BINDER.
WHAT WERE THESE "IDEAS" OF YOURS?
Hee Hee
Hee
WHAT IF IT TAKES PLACE ON THE *MOON?*
TORI. *YES!* THIS BOOK WILL ABSOLUTELY HAVE A MOON EMPIRE.
AND MOON GODDESSES?
OH MY *WORD*, WHEN CAN WE START WRITING?

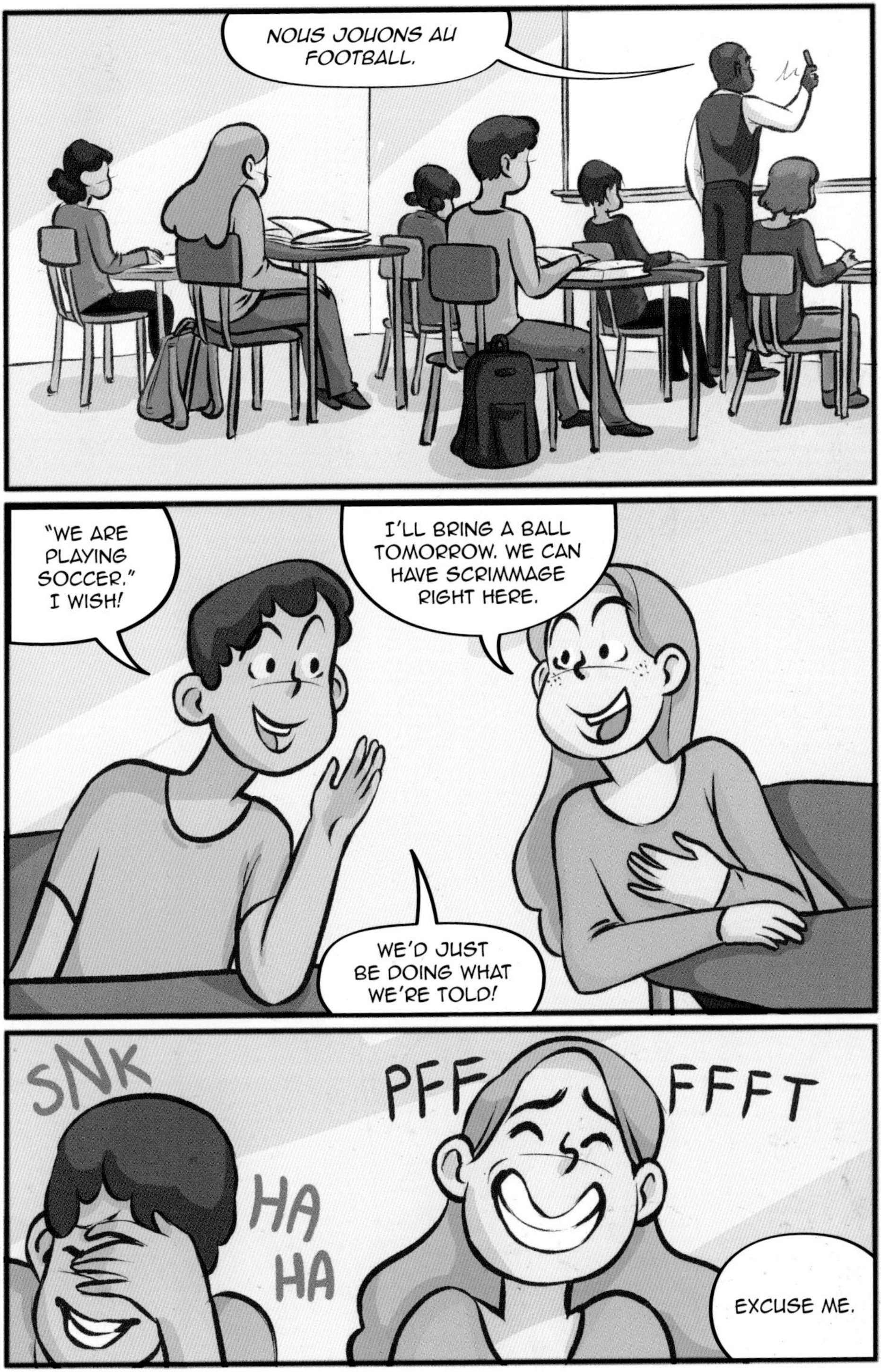
NOUS JOUONS AU FOOTBALL.
"WE ARE PLAYING SOCCER." I WISH!
I'LL BRING A BALL TOMORROW. WE CAN HAVE SCRIMMAGE RIGHT HERE.
WE'D JUST BE DOING WHAT WE'RE TOLD!
SNK
HA HA
PFF FFFT
EXCUSE ME.

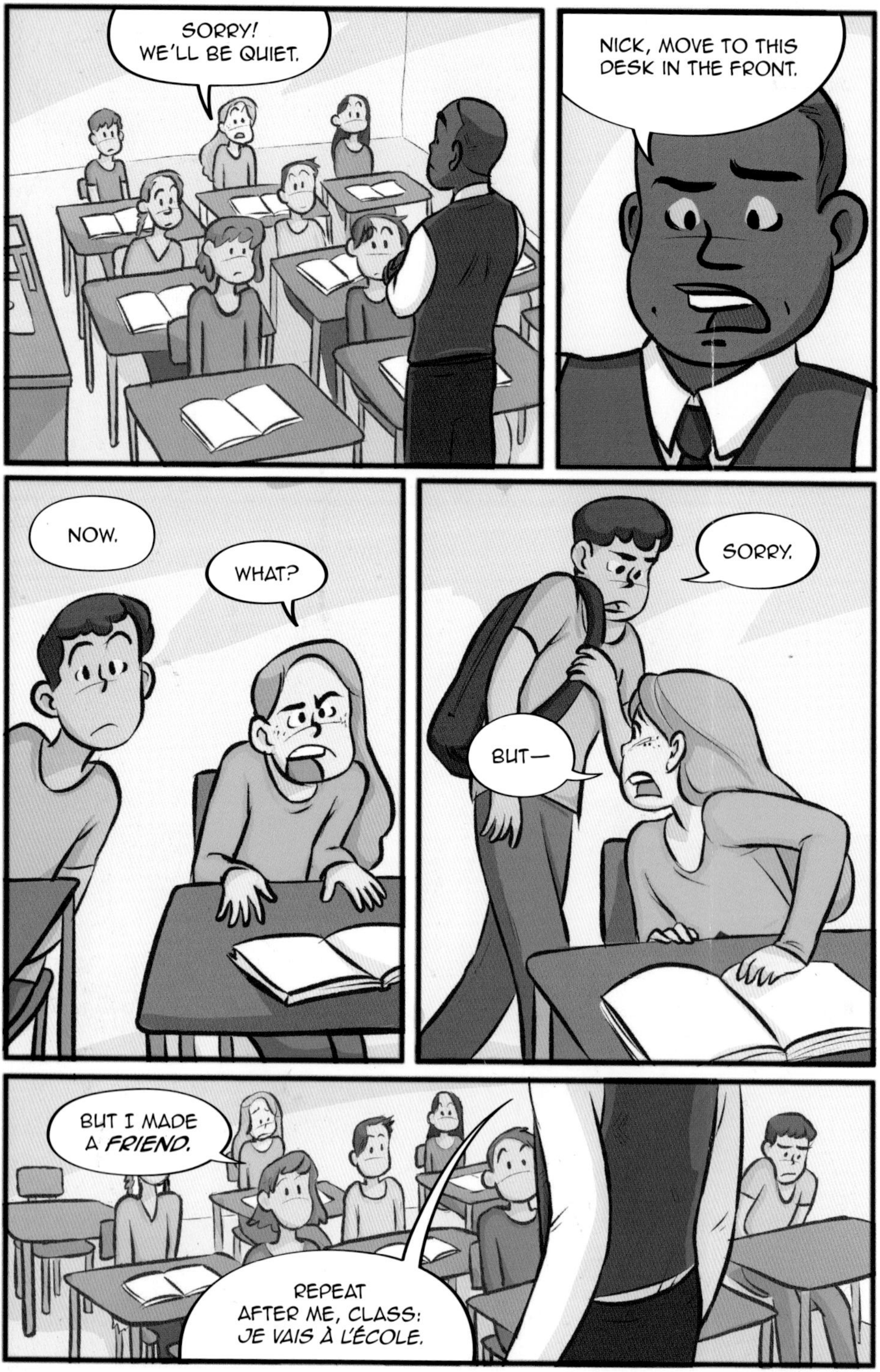
SORRY! WE'LL BE QUIET.
NICK, MOVE TO THIS DESK IN THE FRONT.
NOW.
WHAT?
SORRY.
BUT—
BUT I MADE A *FRIEND.*
REPEAT AFTER ME, CLASS: *JE VAIS À L'ÉCOLE.*

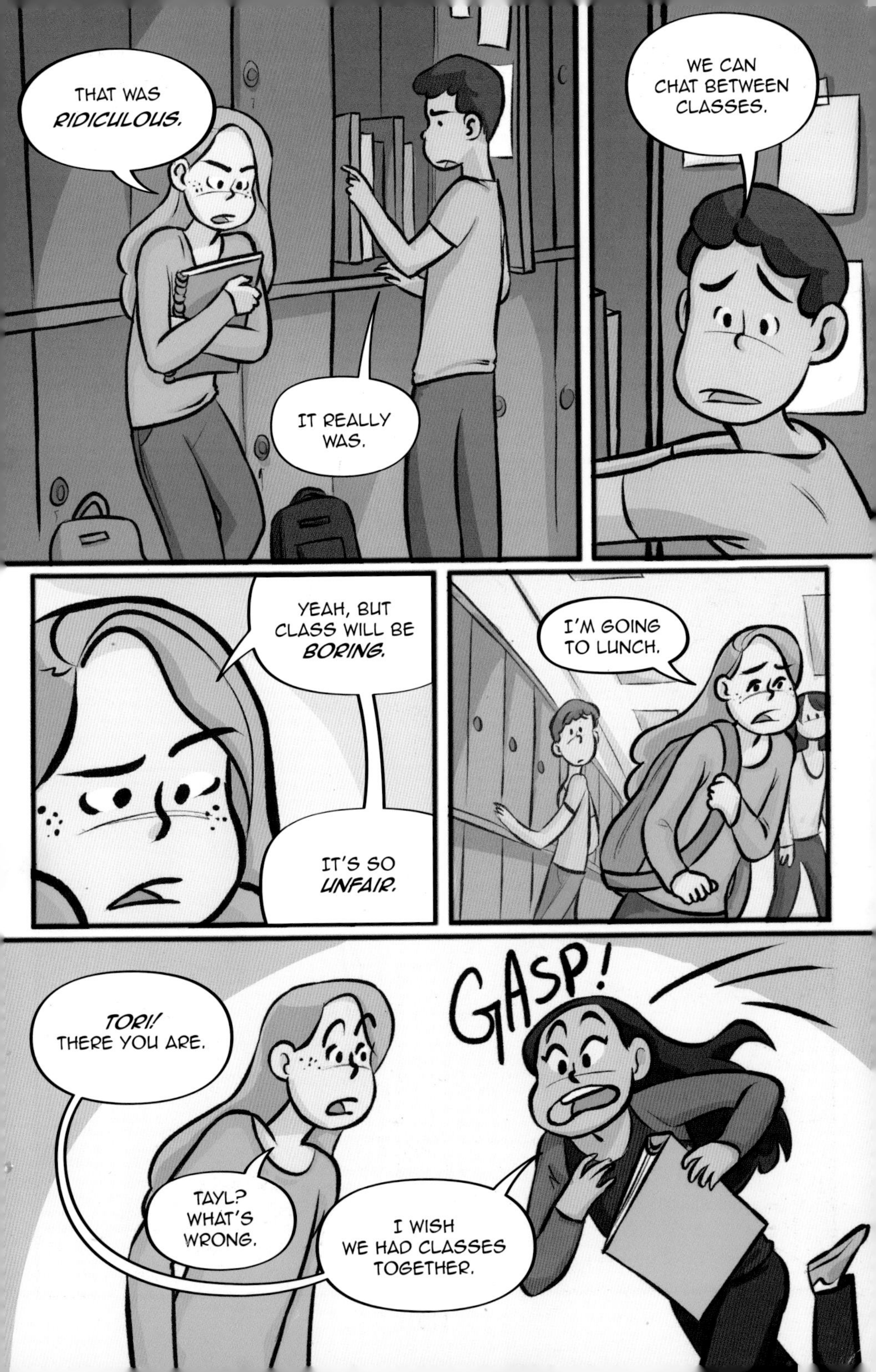
THAT WAS RIDICULOUS.
IT REALLY WAS.
WE CAN CHAT BETWEEN CLASSES.
YEAH, BUT CLASS WILL BE BORING.
IT'S SO UNFAIR.
I'M GOING TO LUNCH.
GASP!
TORI! THERE YOU ARE.
TAYL? WHAT'S WRONG.
I WISH WE HAD CLASSES TOGETHER.

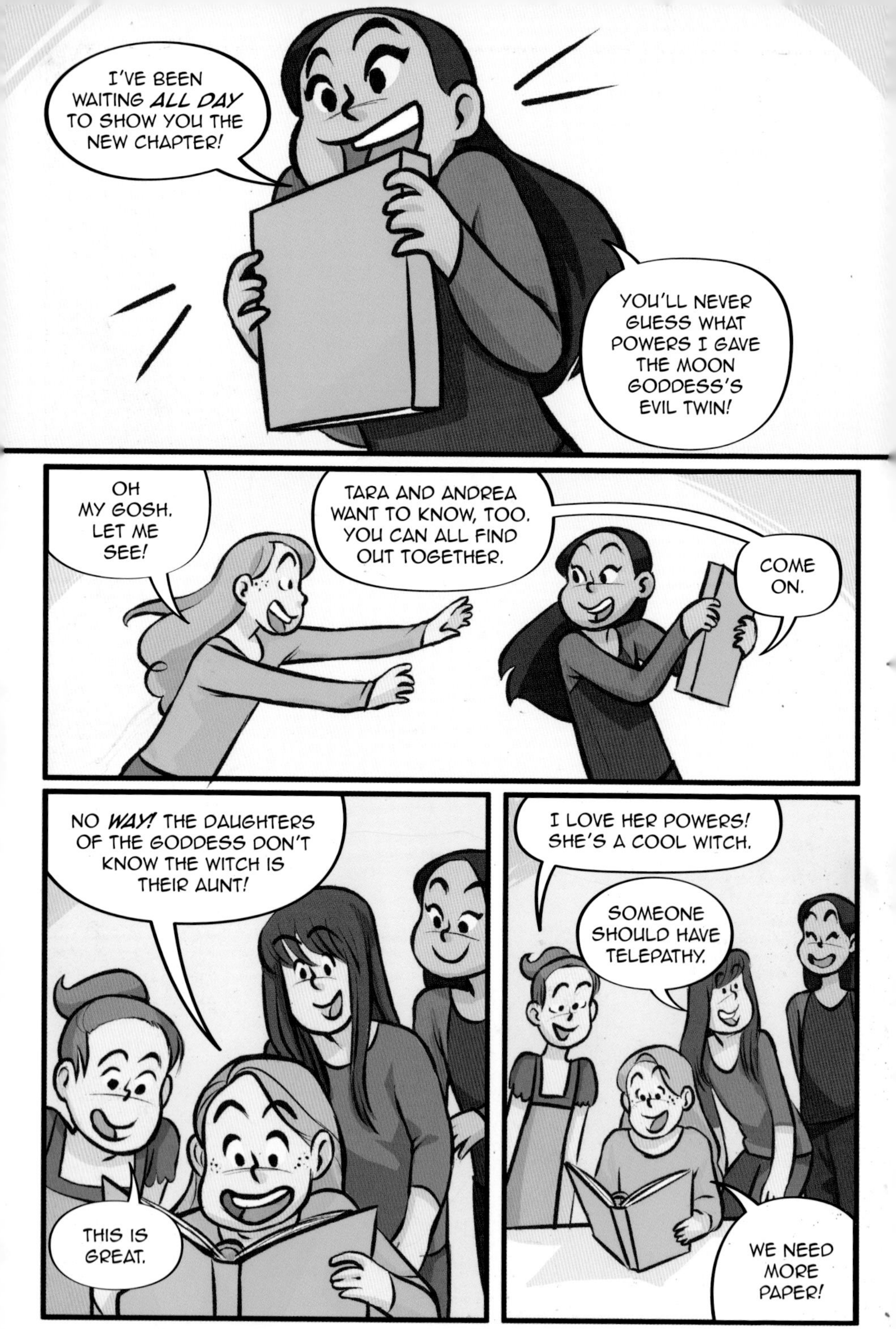
I'VE BEEN WAITING ALL DAY TO SHOW YOU THE NEW CHAPTER!
YOU'LL NEVER GUESS WHAT POWERS I GAVE THE MOON GODDESS'S EVIL TWIN!
OH MY GOSH. LET ME SEE!
TARA AND ANDREA WANT TO KNOW, TOO. YOU CAN ALL FIND OUT TOGETHER.
COME ON.
NO WAY! THE DAUGHTERS OF THE GODDESS DON'T KNOW THE WITCH IS THEIR AUNT!
THIS IS GREAT.
I LOVE HER POWERS! SHE'S A COOL WITCH.
SOMEONE SHOULD HAVE TELEPATHY.
WE NEED MORE PAPER!

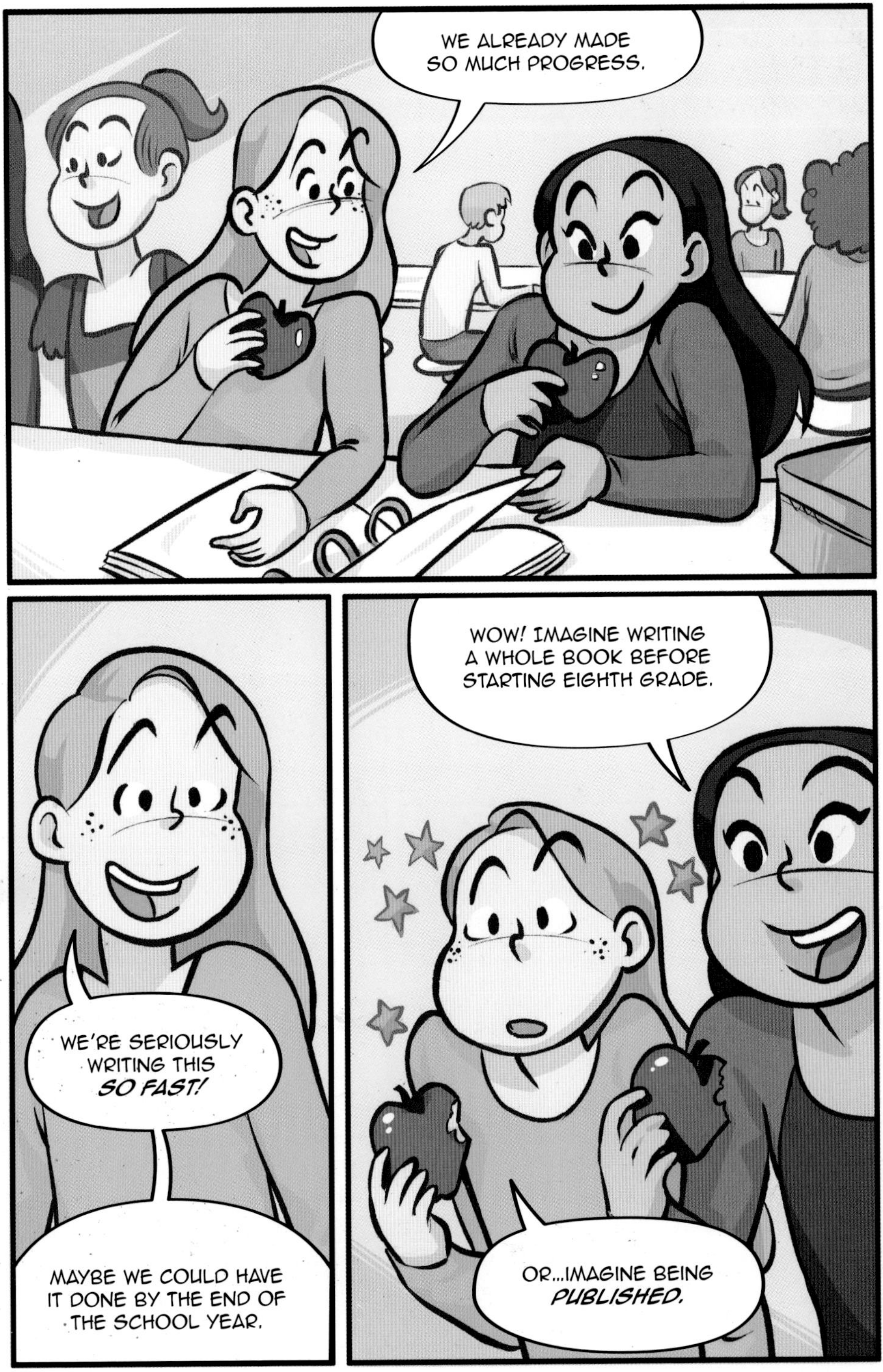
WE ALREADY MADE SO MUCH PROGRESS.
WE'RE SERIOUSLY WRITING THIS *SO FAST!*
MAYBE WE COULD HAVE IT DONE BY THE END OF THE SCHOOL YEAR.
WOW! IMAGINE WRITING A WHOLE BOOK BEFORE STARTING EIGHTH GRADE.
OR...IMAGINE BEING *PUBLISHED.*

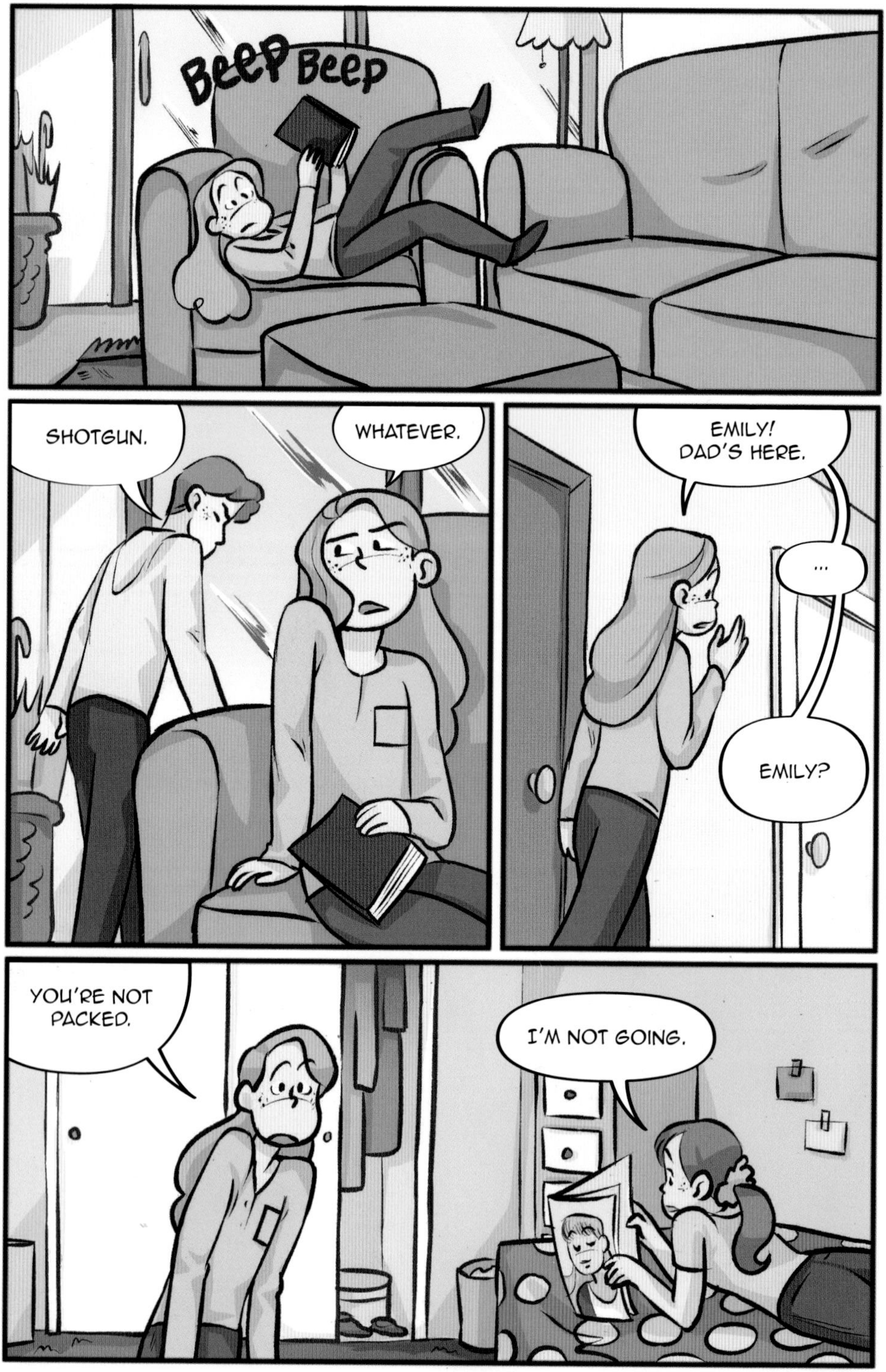
BEEP BEEP
SHOTGUN.
WHATEVER.
EMILY! DAD'S HERE.
...
EMILY?
YOU'RE NOT PACKED.
I'M NOT GOING.

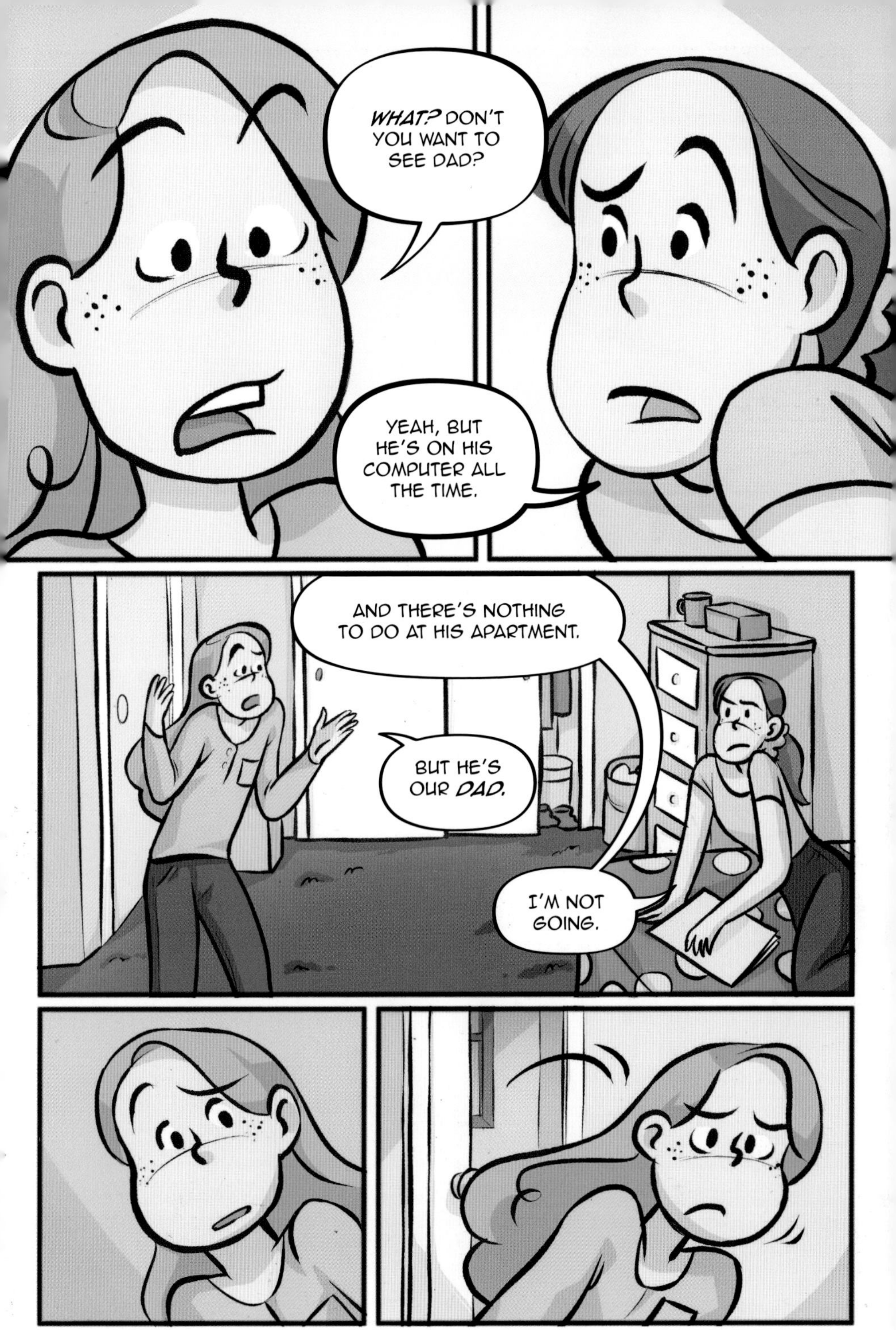

*WHAT?* DON'T YOU WANT TO SEE DAD?
YEAH, BUT HE'S ON HIS COMPUTER ALL THE TIME.
AND THERE'S NOTHING TO DO AT HIS APARTMENT.
BUT HE'S OUR *DAD.*
I'M NOT GOING.

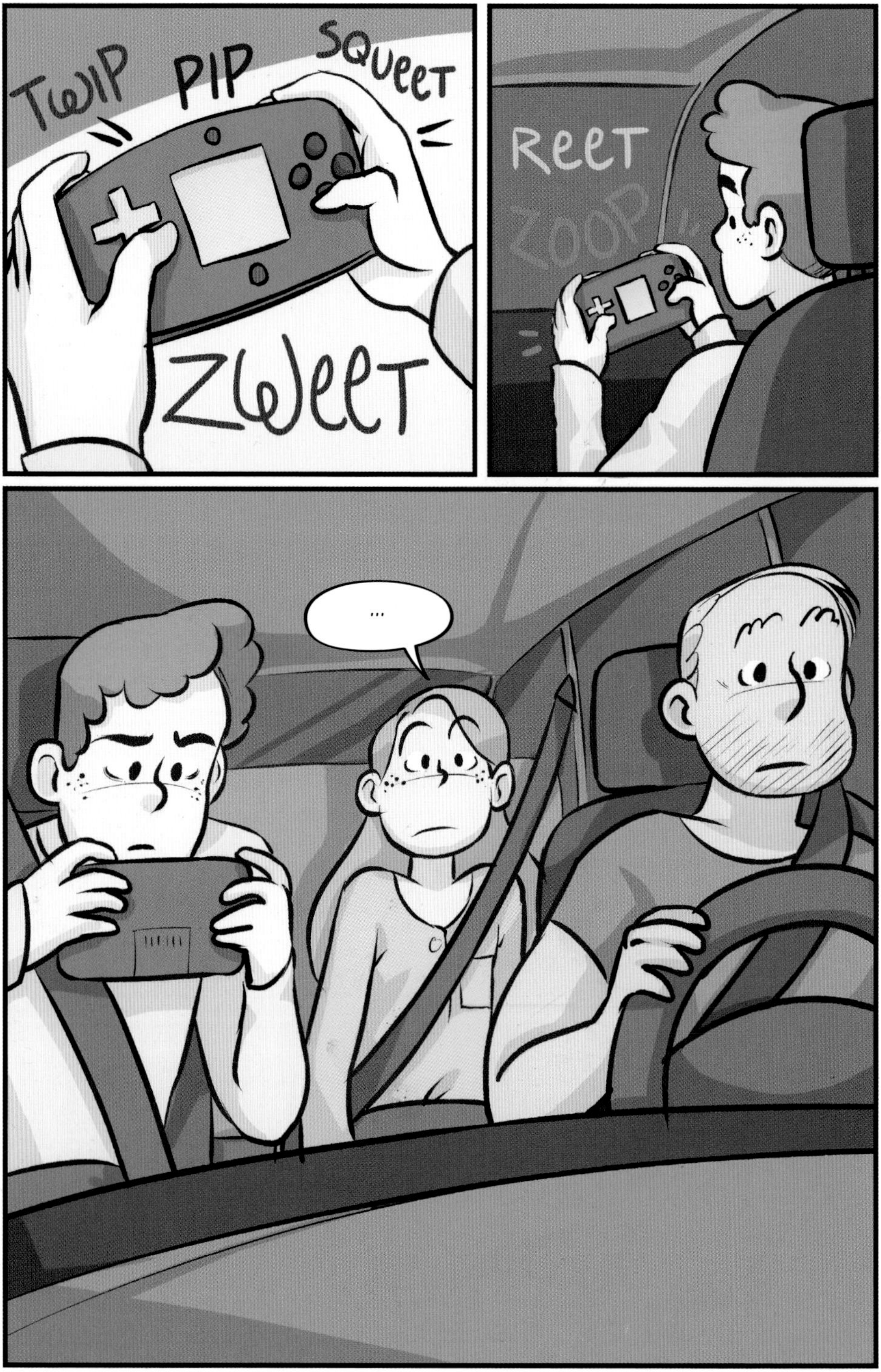
TWIP
PIP
SQUEET
ZWEET
REET
ZOOP
...

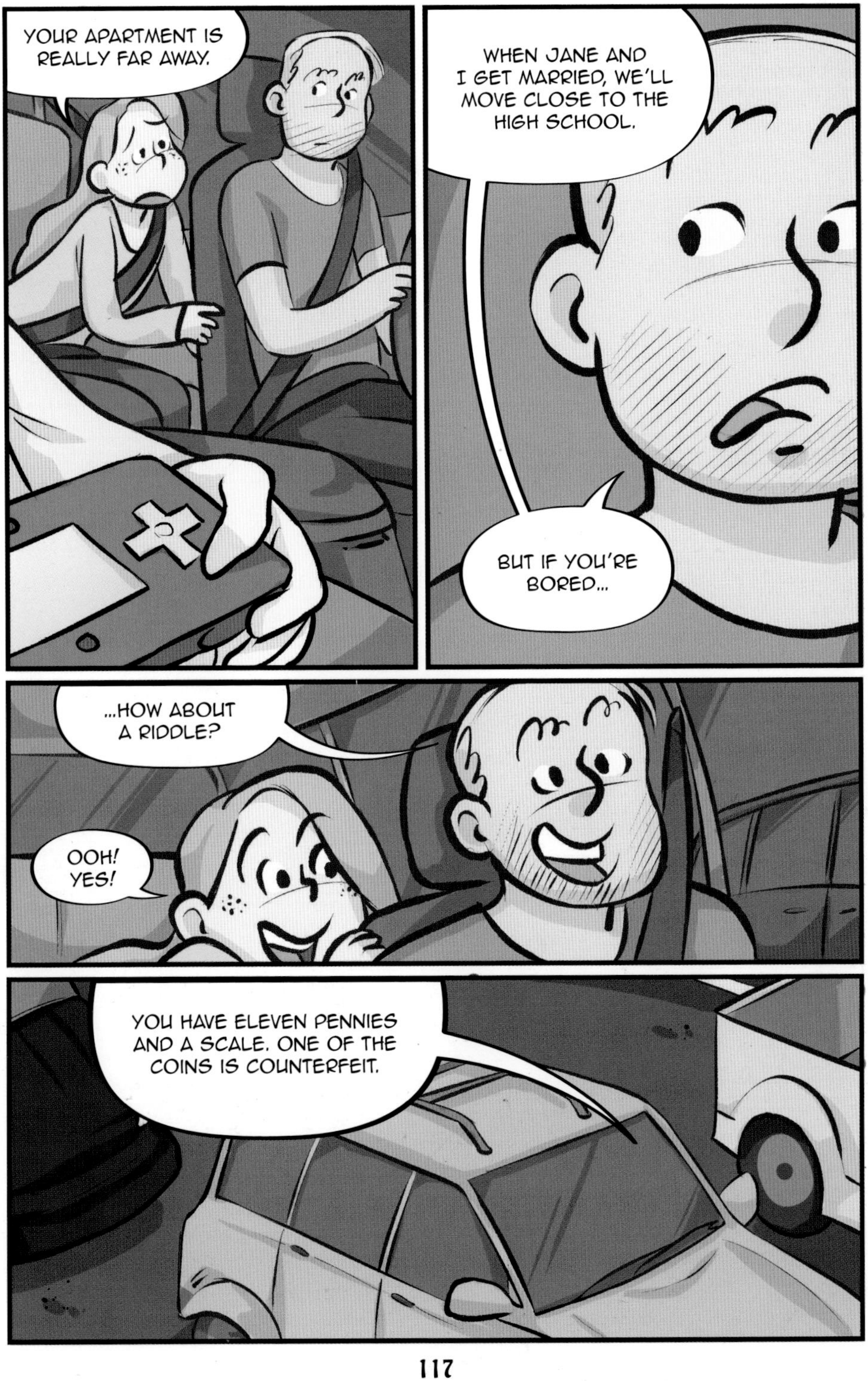
YOUR APARTMENT IS REALLY FAR AWAY.
WHEN JANE AND I GET MARRIED, WE'LL MOVE CLOSE TO THE HIGH SCHOOL.
BUT IF YOU'RE BORED...
...HOW ABOUT A RIDDLE?
OOH! YES!
YOU HAVE ELEVEN PENNIES AND A SCALE. ONE OF THE COINS IS COUNTERFEIT.

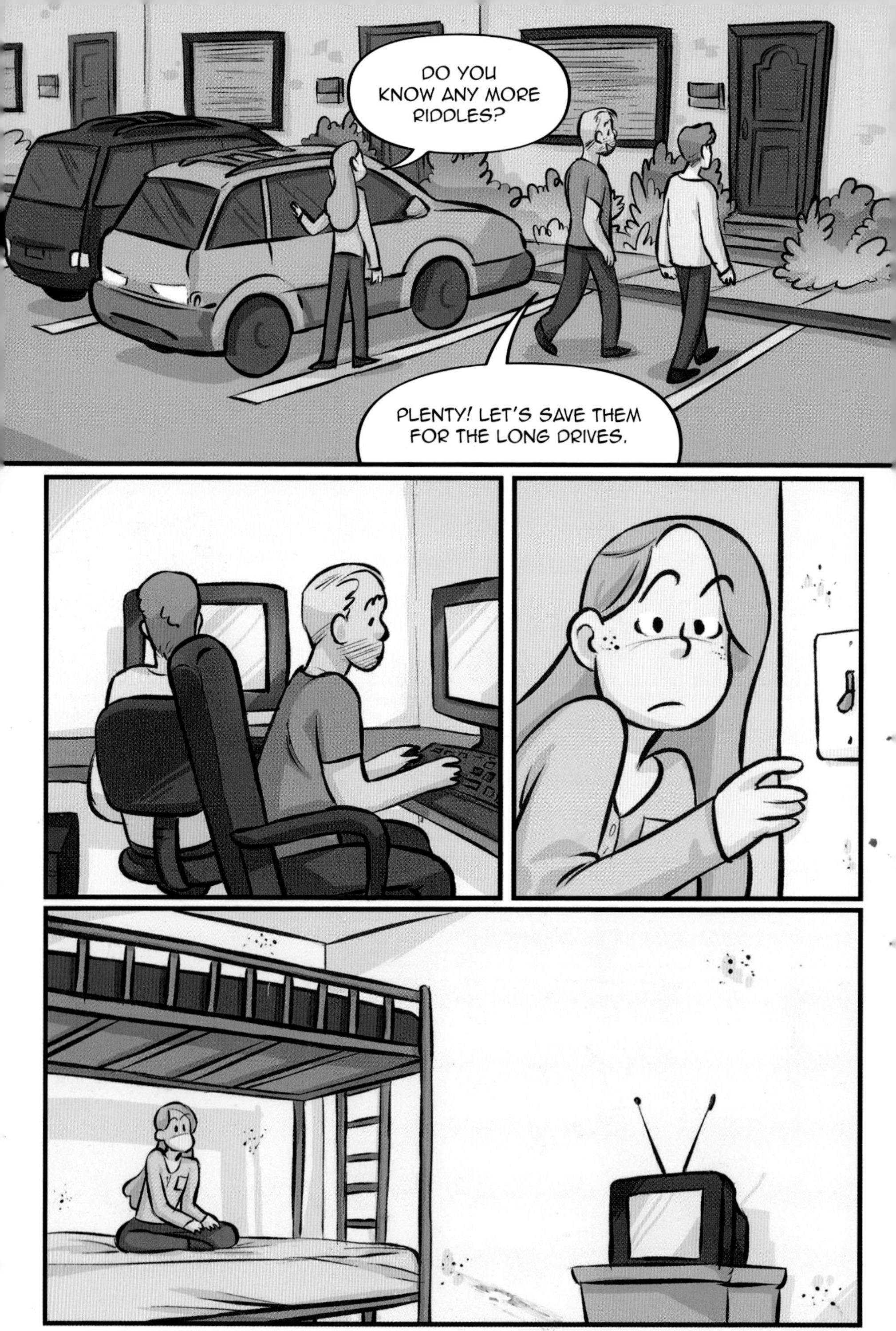
DO YOU KNOW ANY MORE RIDDLES?
PLENTY! LET'S SAVE THEM FOR THE LONG DRIVES.

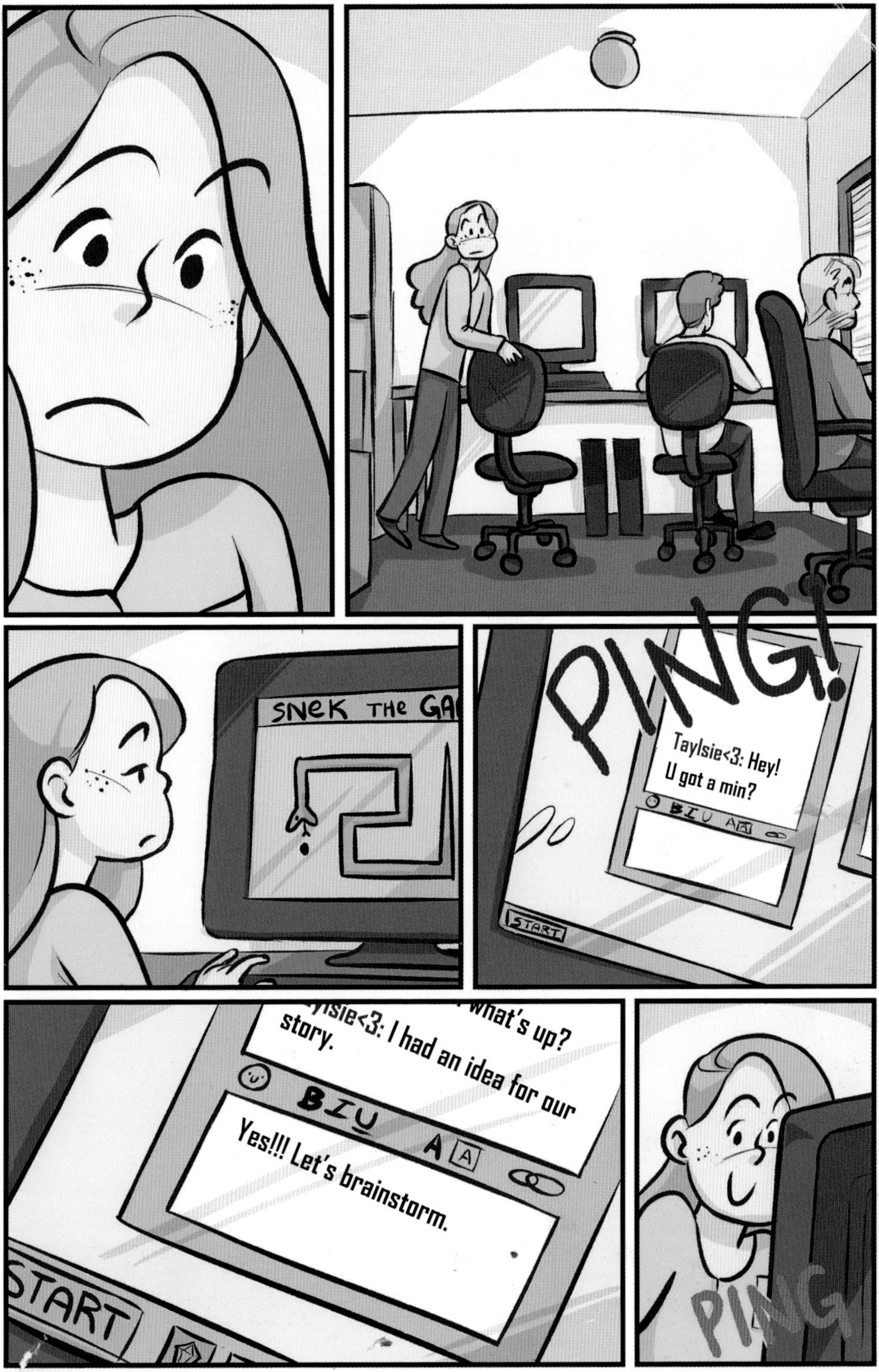
SNEK THE GA
PING!
Taylsie<3: Hey!
U got a min?
START
what's up?
ylsie<3: I had an idea for our story.
Yes!!! Let's brainstorm.
START
PING

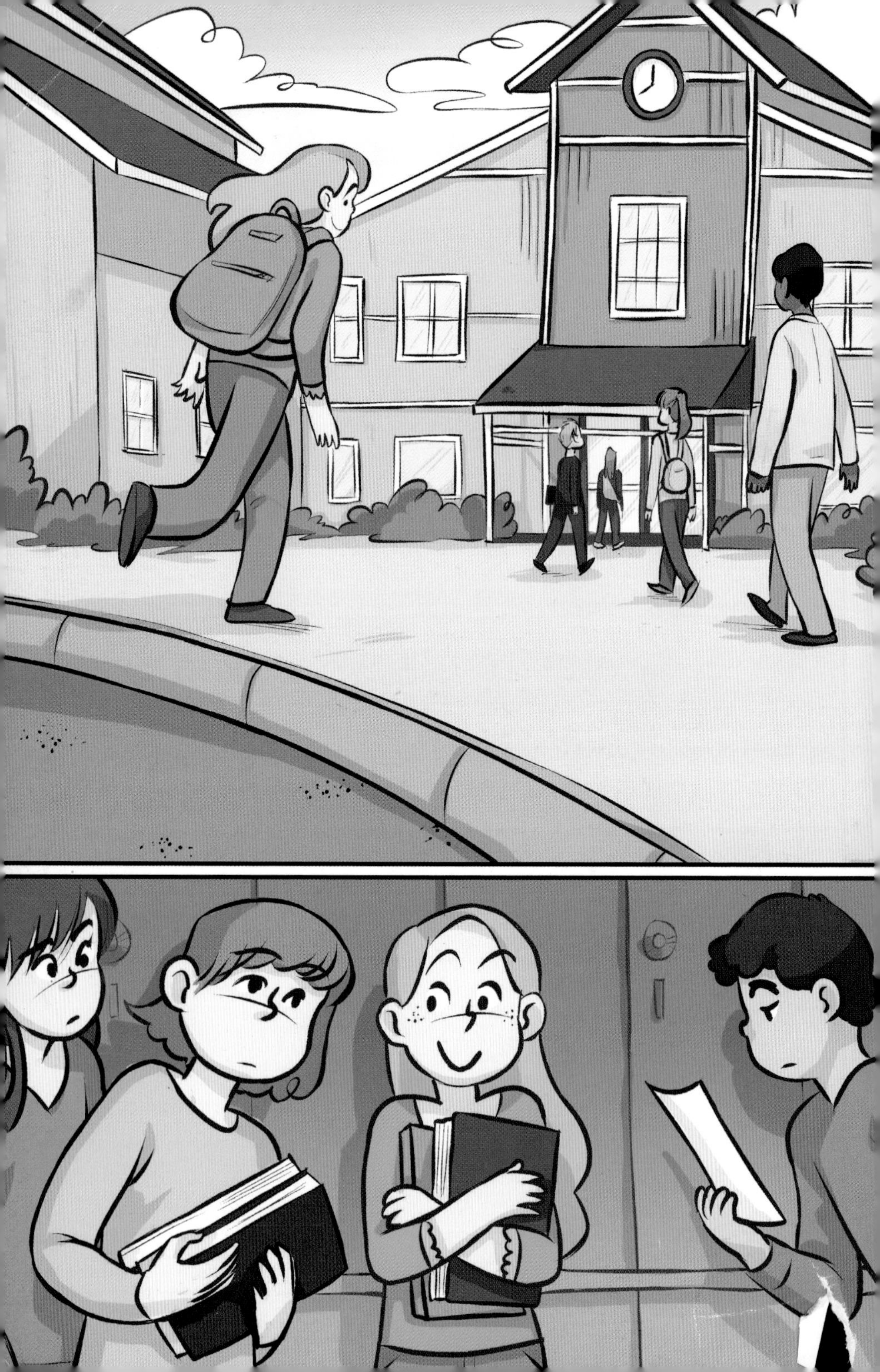

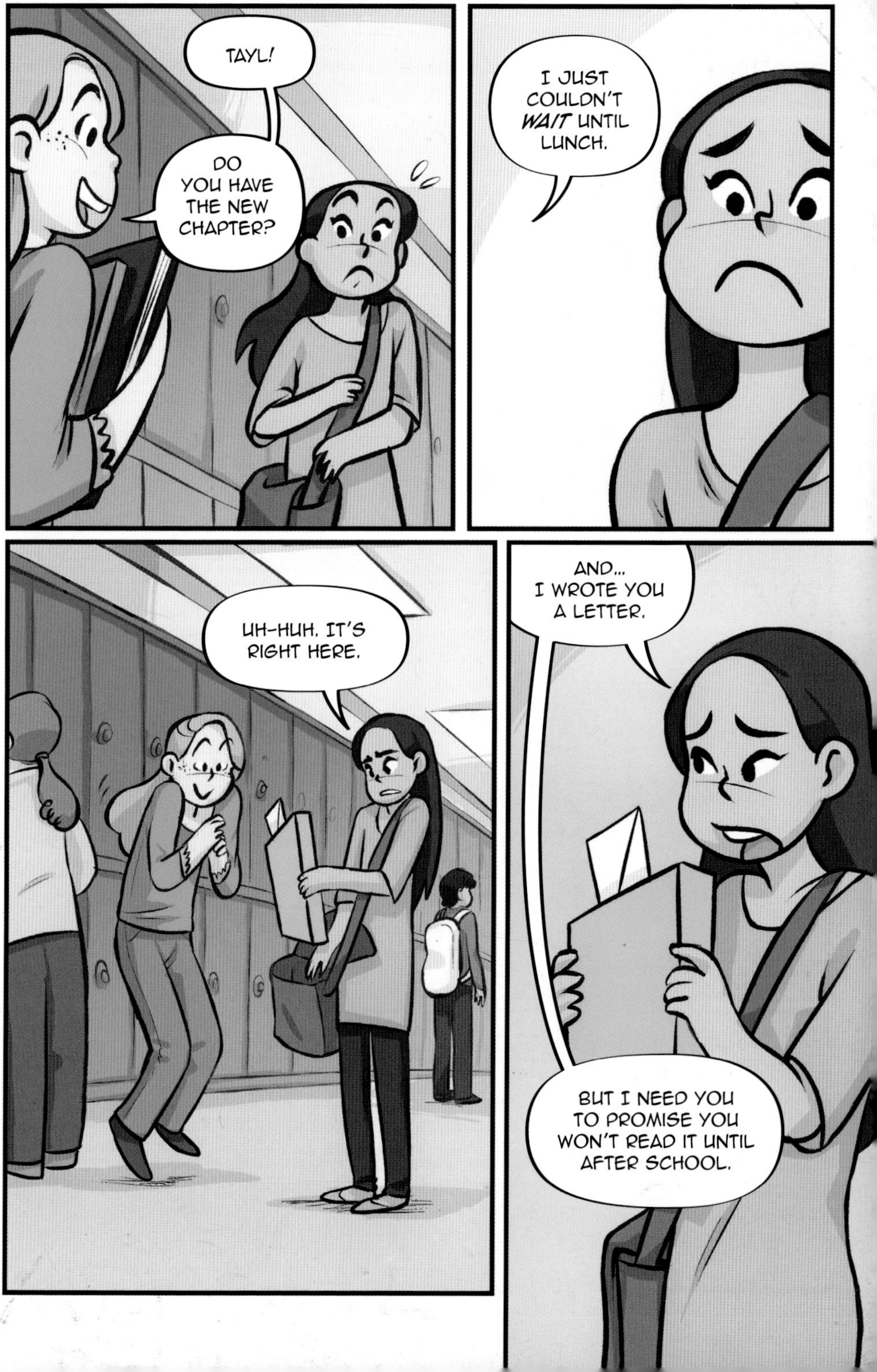
TAYL!
DO YOU HAVE THE NEW CHAPTER?
I JUST COULDN'T *WAIT* UNTIL LUNCH.
UH-HUH. IT'S RIGHT HERE.
AND... I WROTE YOU A LETTER.
BUT I NEED YOU TO PROMISE YOU WON'T READ IT UNTIL AFTER SCHOOL.

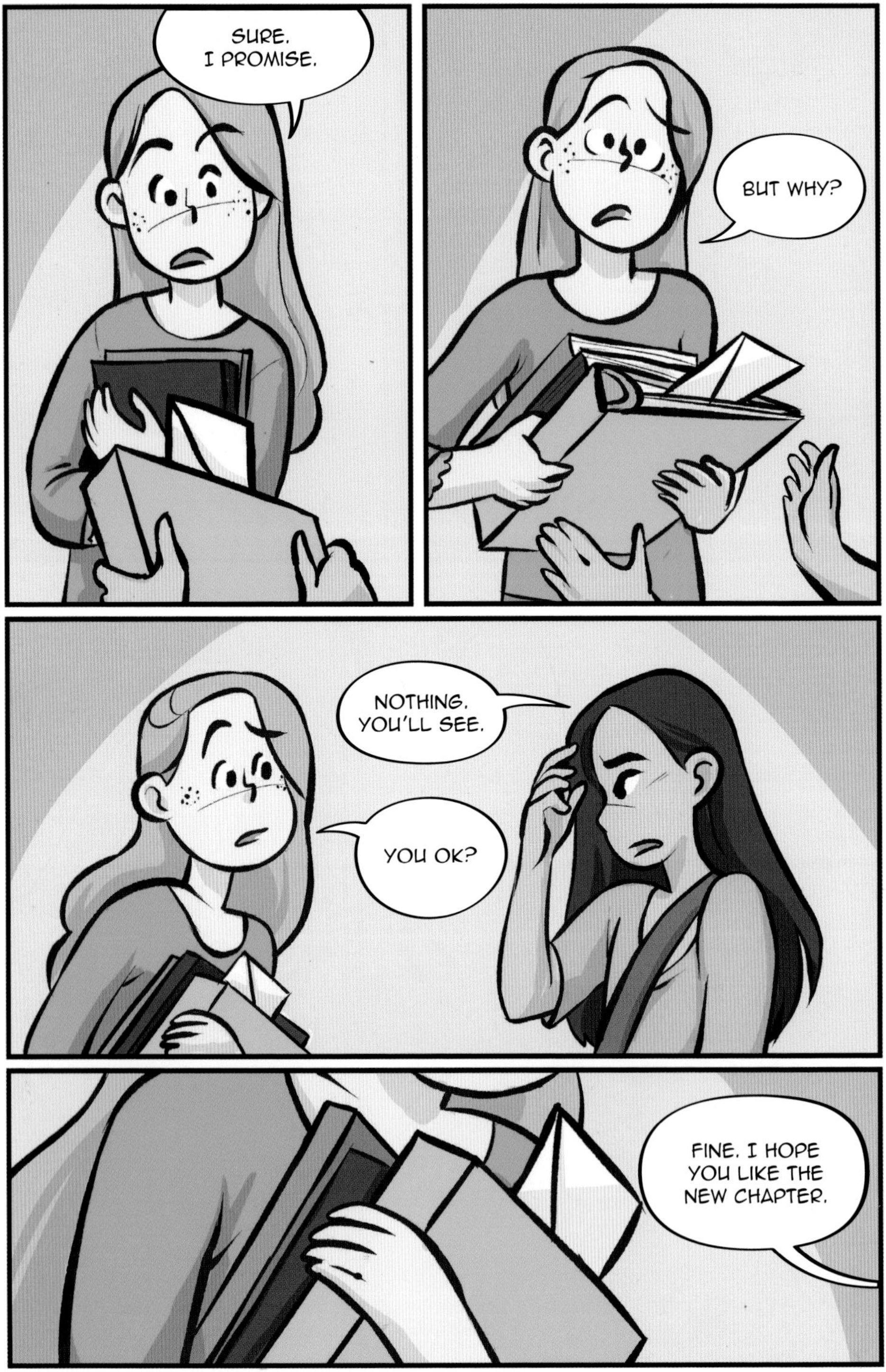
SURE. I PROMISE.
BUT WHY?
NOTHING. YOU'LL SEE.
YOU OK?
FINE. I HOPE YOU LIKE THE NEW CHAPTER.

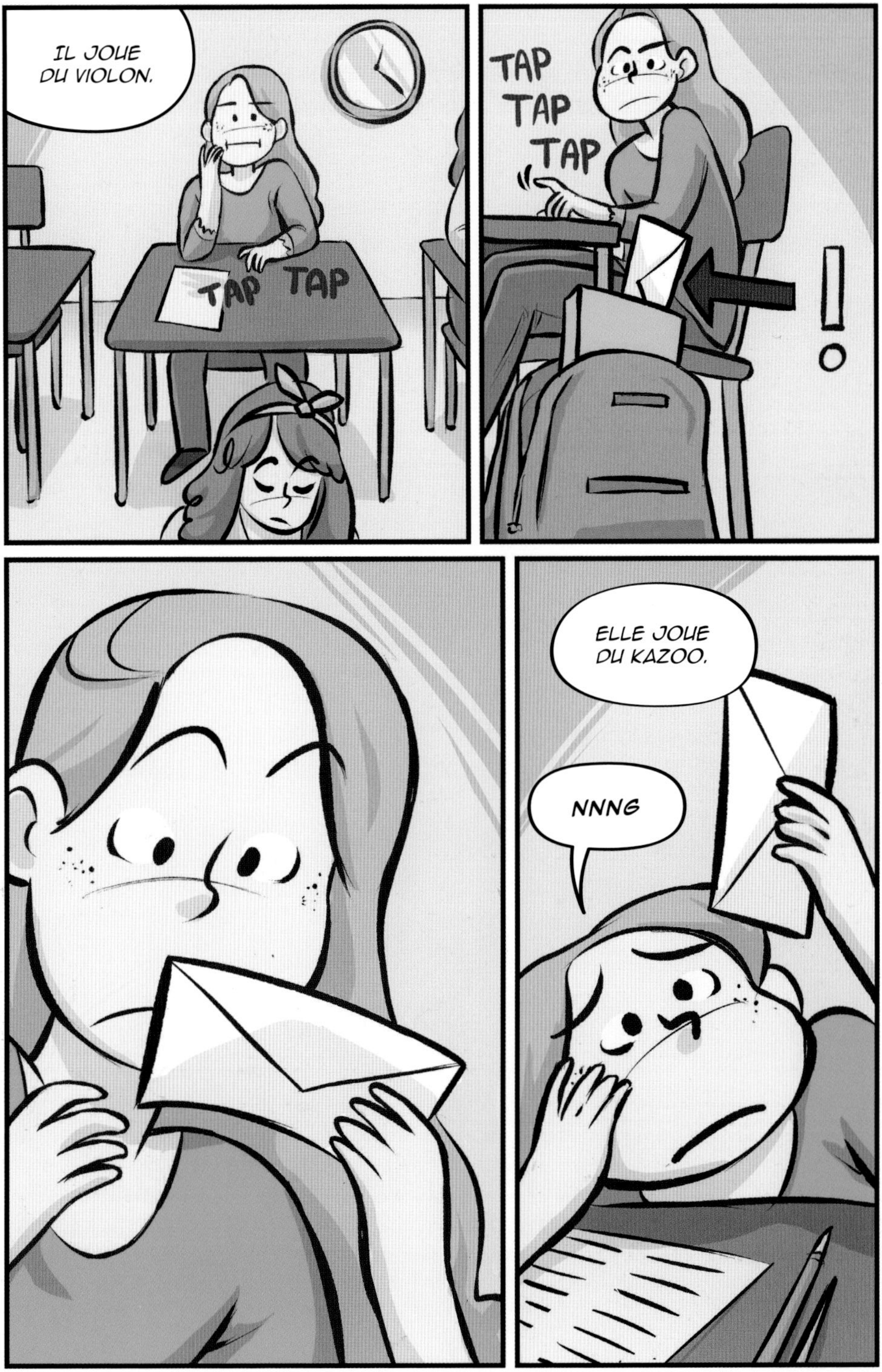
IL JOUE DU VIOLON.
TAP TAP
TAP
TAP
TAP
!
ELLE JOUE DU KAZOO.
NNNG

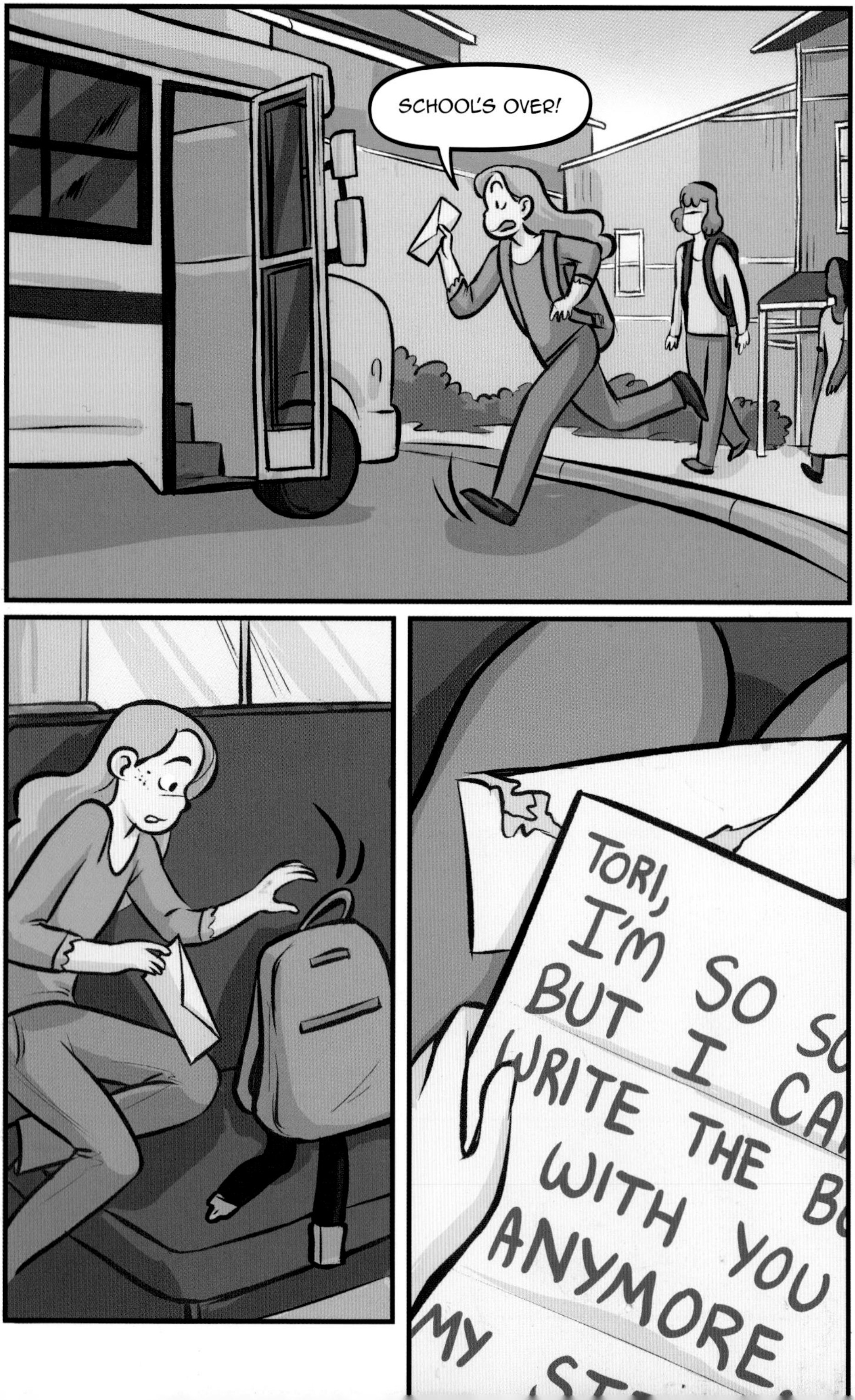
SCHOOL'S OVER!
TORI,
I'M SO SO
BUT I CA
WRITE THE B
WITH YOU
ANYMORE.
MY

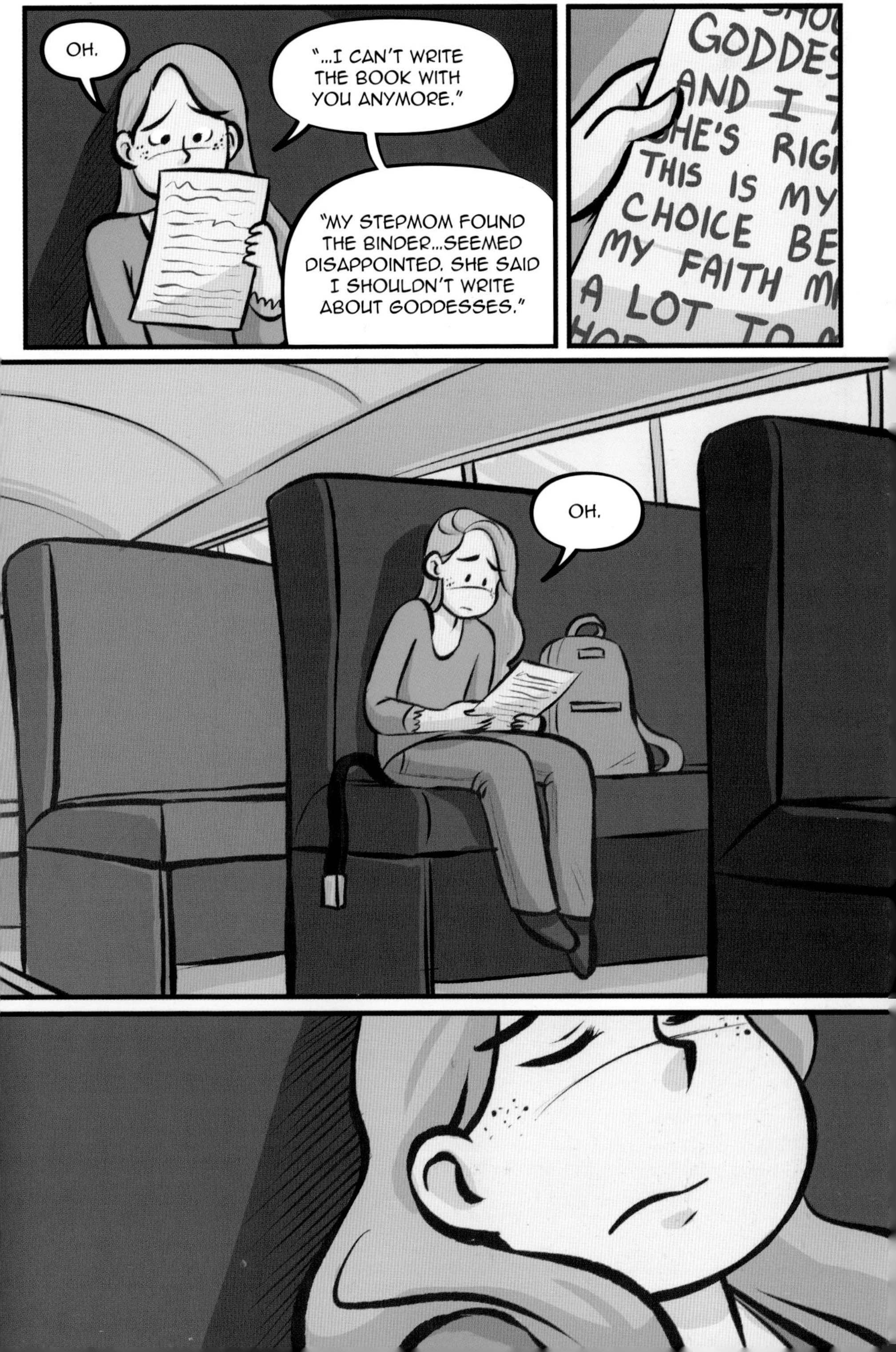
OH.
"...I CAN'T WRITE THE BOOK WITH YOU ANYMORE."
"MY STEPMOM FOUND THE BINDER...SEEMED DISAPPOINTED. SHE SAID I SHOULDN'T WRITE ABOUT GODDESSES."
GODDES
AND I
SHE'S RIG
THIS IS MY
CHOICE BE
MY FAITH
A LOT TO
OH.

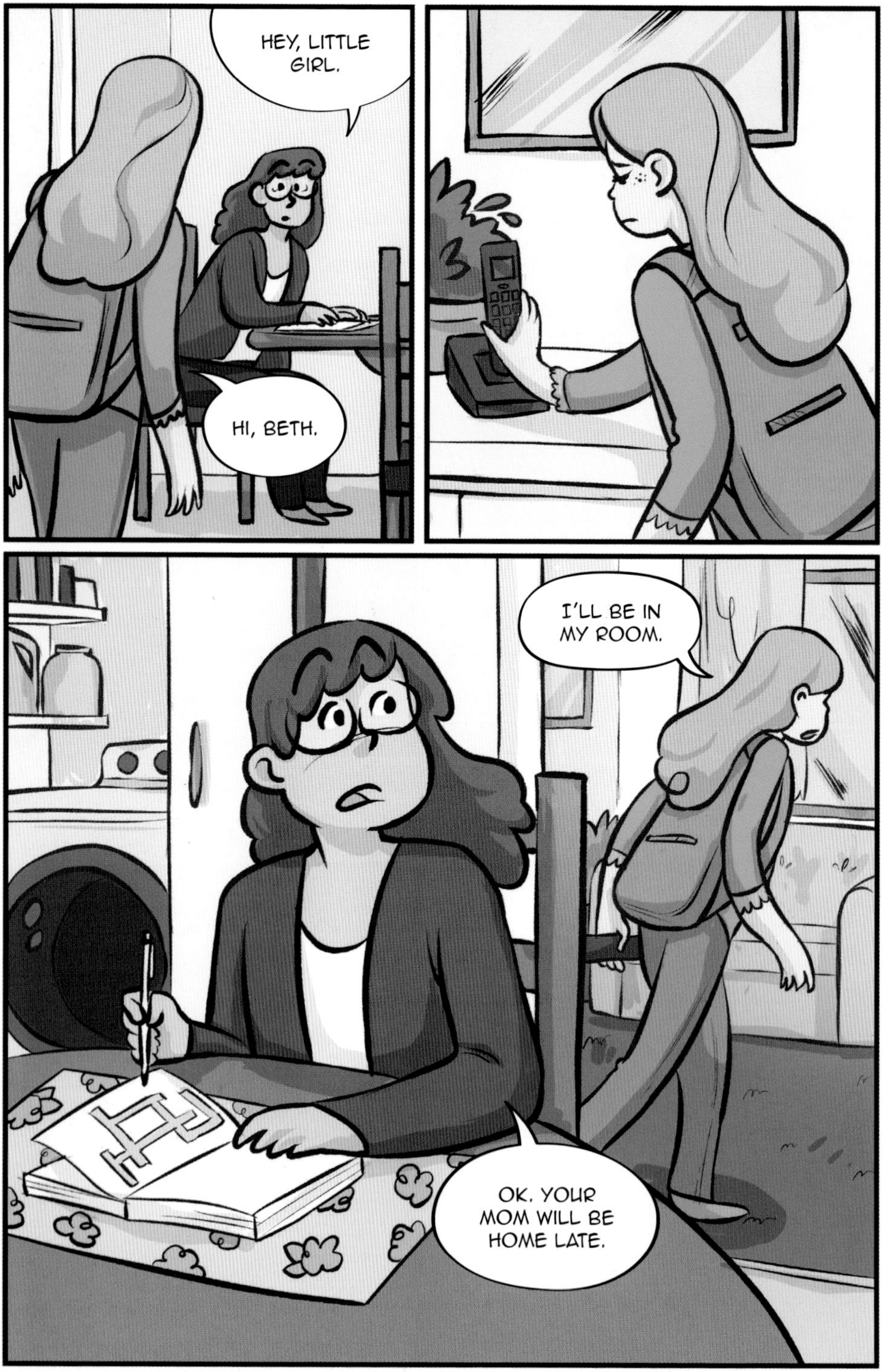
HEY, LITTLE GIRL.
HI, BETH.
I'LL BE IN MY ROOM.
OK. YOUR MOM WILL BE HOME LATE.

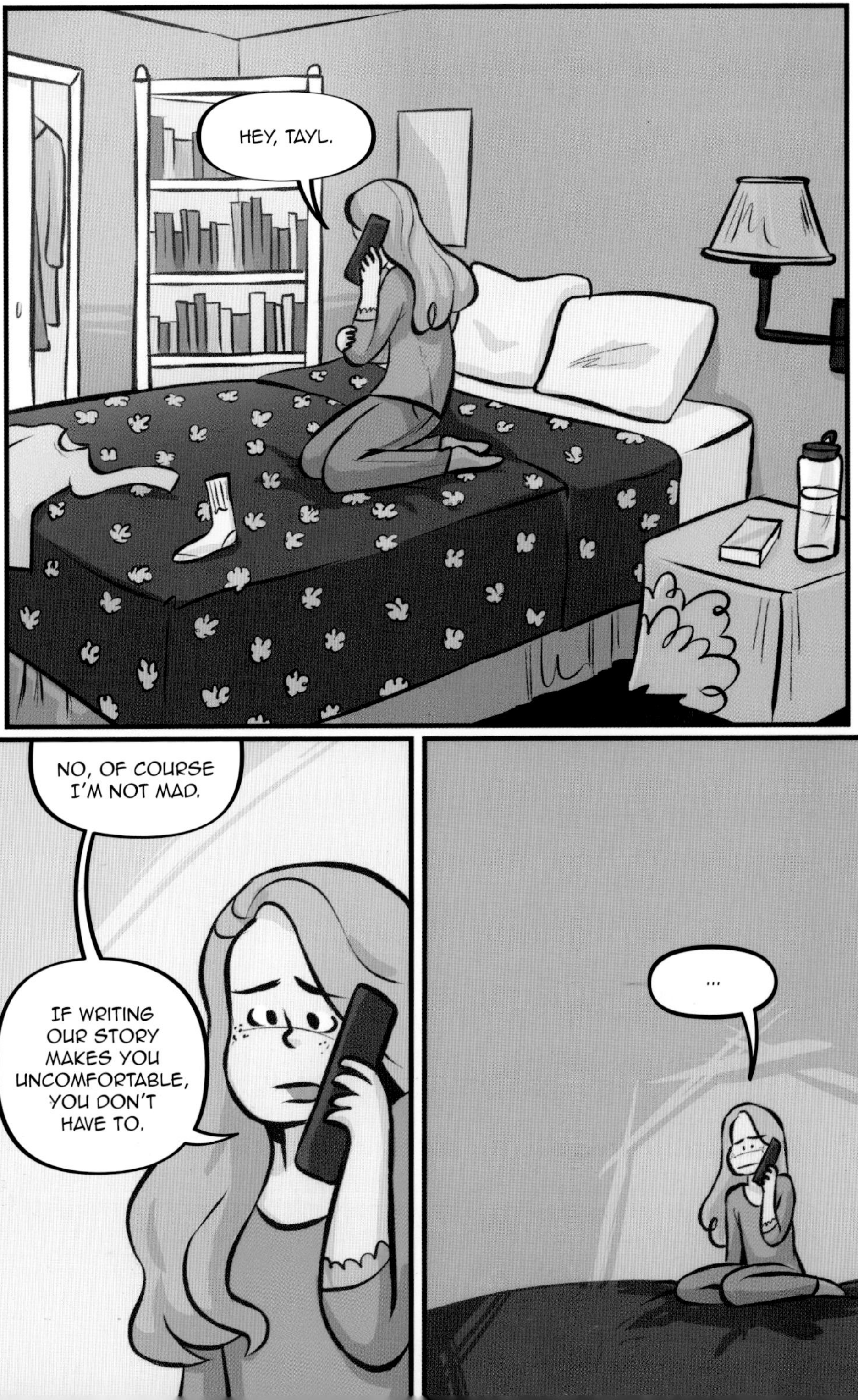
HEY, TAYL.
NO, OF COURSE I'M NOT MAD.
IF WRITING OUR STORY MAKES YOU UNCOMFORTABLE, YOU DON'T HAVE TO.
...

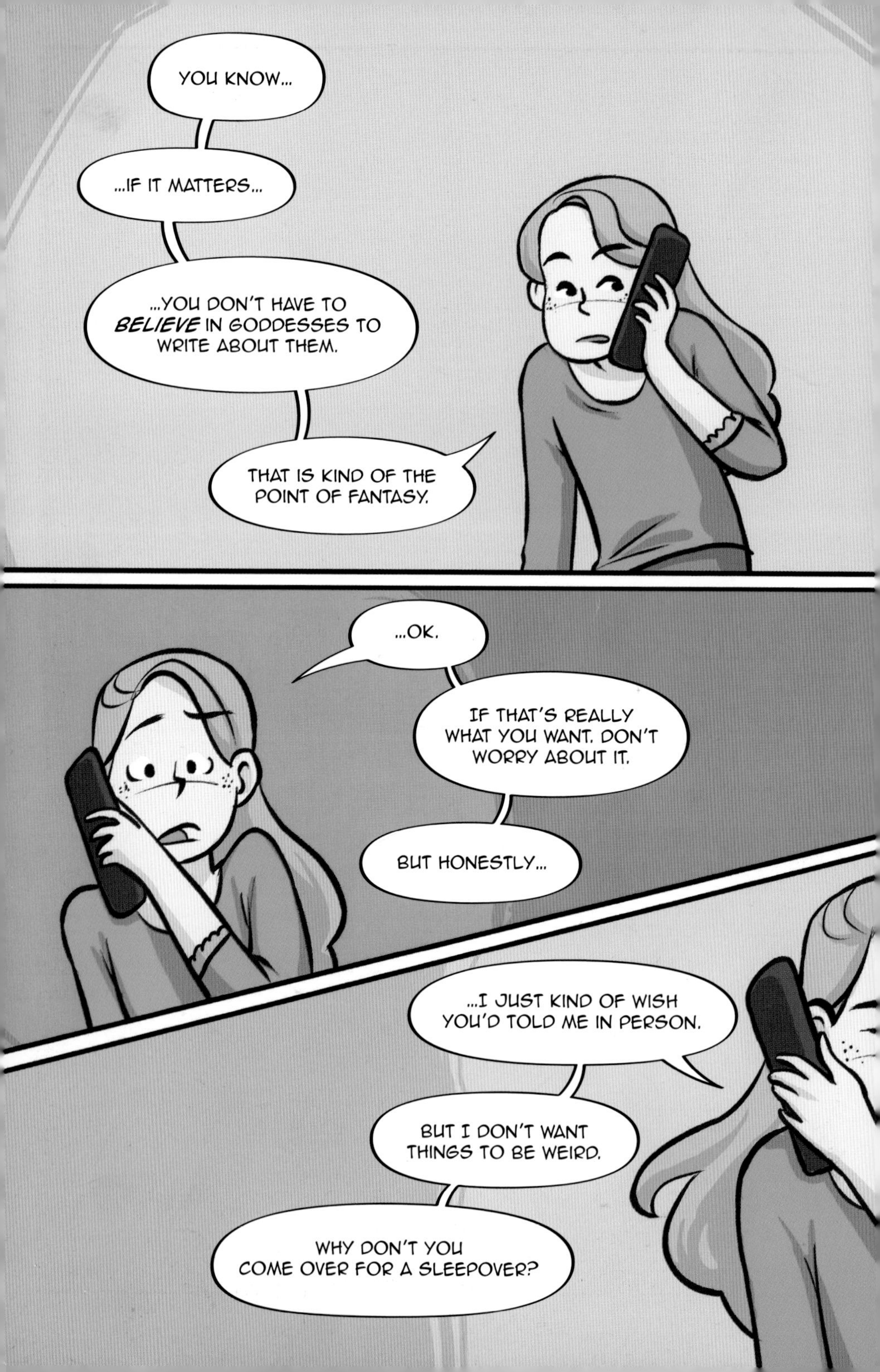
YOU KNOW...
...IF IT MATTERS...
...YOU DON'T HAVE TO *BELIEVE* IN GODDESSES TO WRITE ABOUT THEM.
THAT IS KIND OF THE POINT OF FANTASY.
...OK.
IF THAT'S REALLY WHAT YOU WANT. DON'T WORRY ABOUT IT.
BUT HONESTLY...
...I JUST KIND OF WISH YOU'D TOLD ME IN PERSON.
BUT I DON'T WANT THINGS TO BE WEIRD.
WHY DON'T YOU COME OVER FOR A SLEEPOVER?

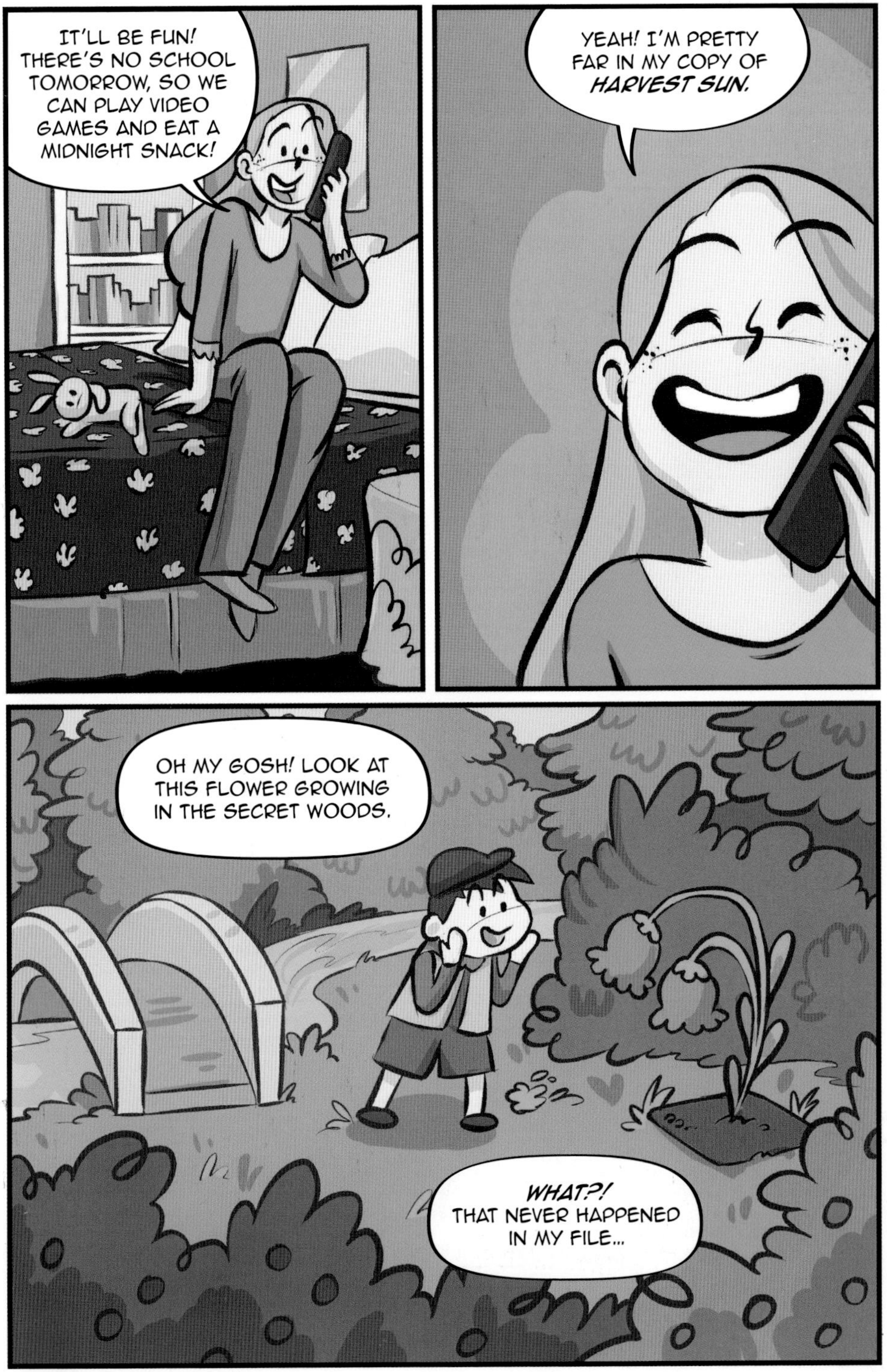
IT'LL BE FUN! THERE'S NO SCHOOL TOMORROW, SO WE CAN PLAY VIDEO GAMES AND EAT A MIDNIGHT SNACK!
YEAH! I'M PRETTY FAR IN MY COPY OF *HARVEST SUN.*
OH MY GOSH! LOOK AT THIS FLOWER GROWING IN THE SECRET WOODS.
*WHAT?!* THAT NEVER HAPPENED IN MY FILE...

I WONDER IF IT DOES ANYTHING.

PFF, I THINK IT'S JUST A FLOWER.

BUT THERE ARE *TONS* OF COOL, SECRET, MAGICAL THINGS IN THIS GAME.

REALLY? I'VE ONLY SEEN A COUPLE.

LIKE THE LITTLE HARVEST GNOMES WHO HELP ON THE FARM.

WELL, *SURE*, BUT THERE'S SO MUCH MORE THAN THAT! LIKE...

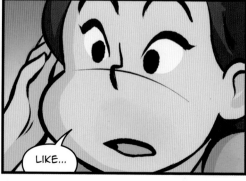

LIKE...

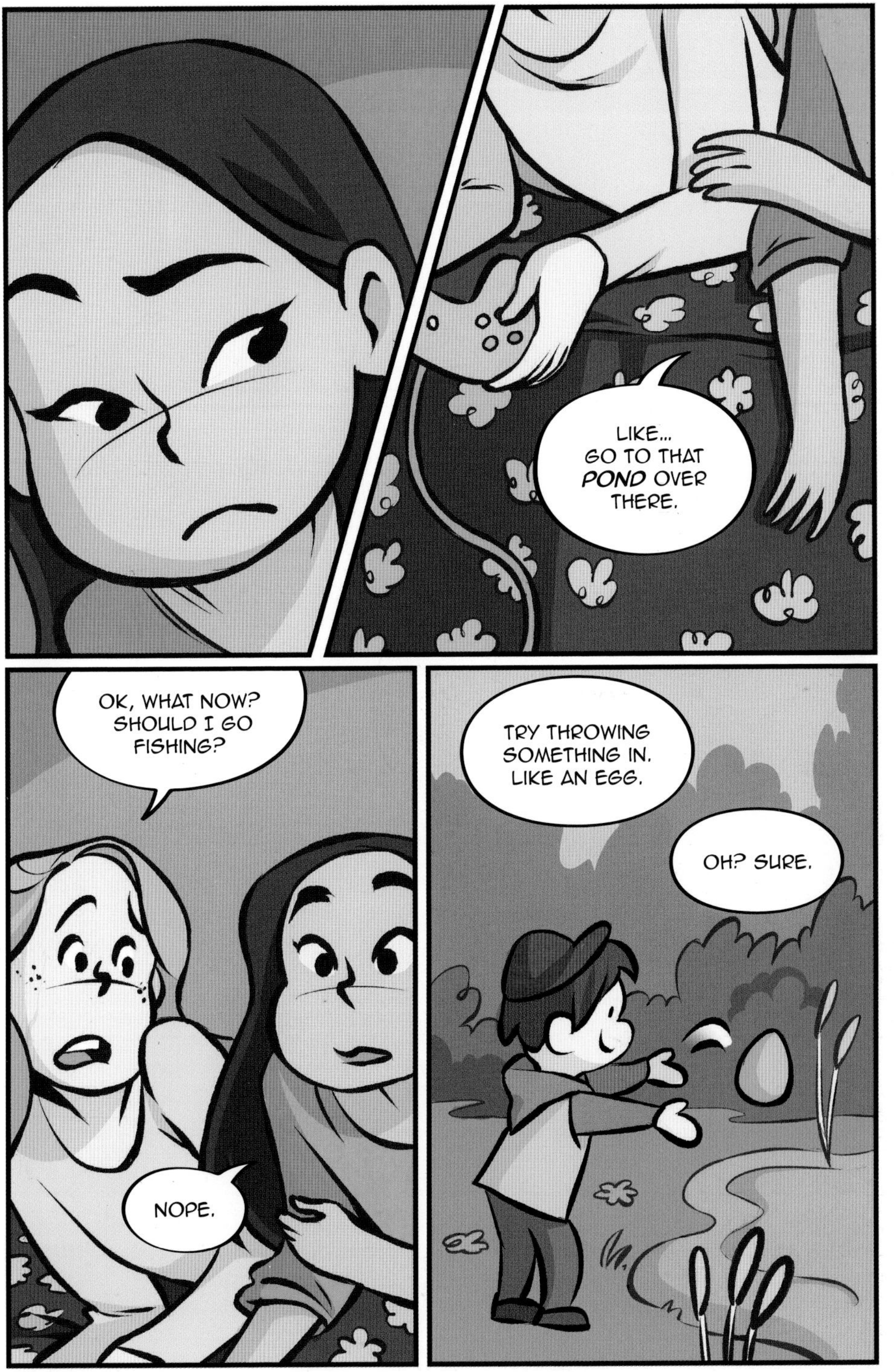
LIKE... GO TO THAT *POND* OVER THERE.
OK, WHAT NOW? SHOULD I GO FISHING?
NOPE.
TRY THROWING SOMETHING IN. LIKE AN EGG.
OH? SURE.

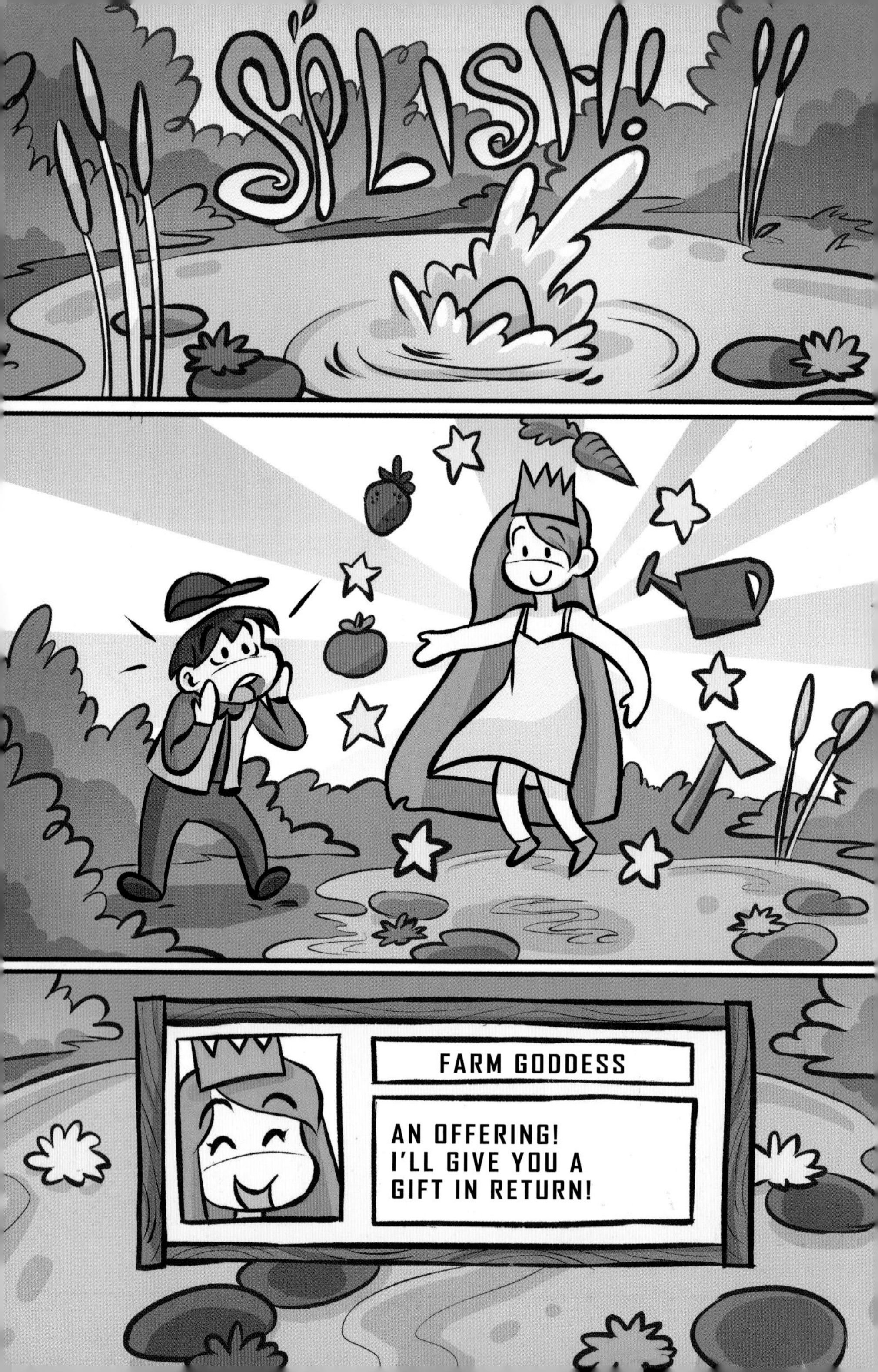
SPLASH!
FARM GODDESS
AN OFFERING!
I'LL GIVE YOU A
GIFT IN RETURN!

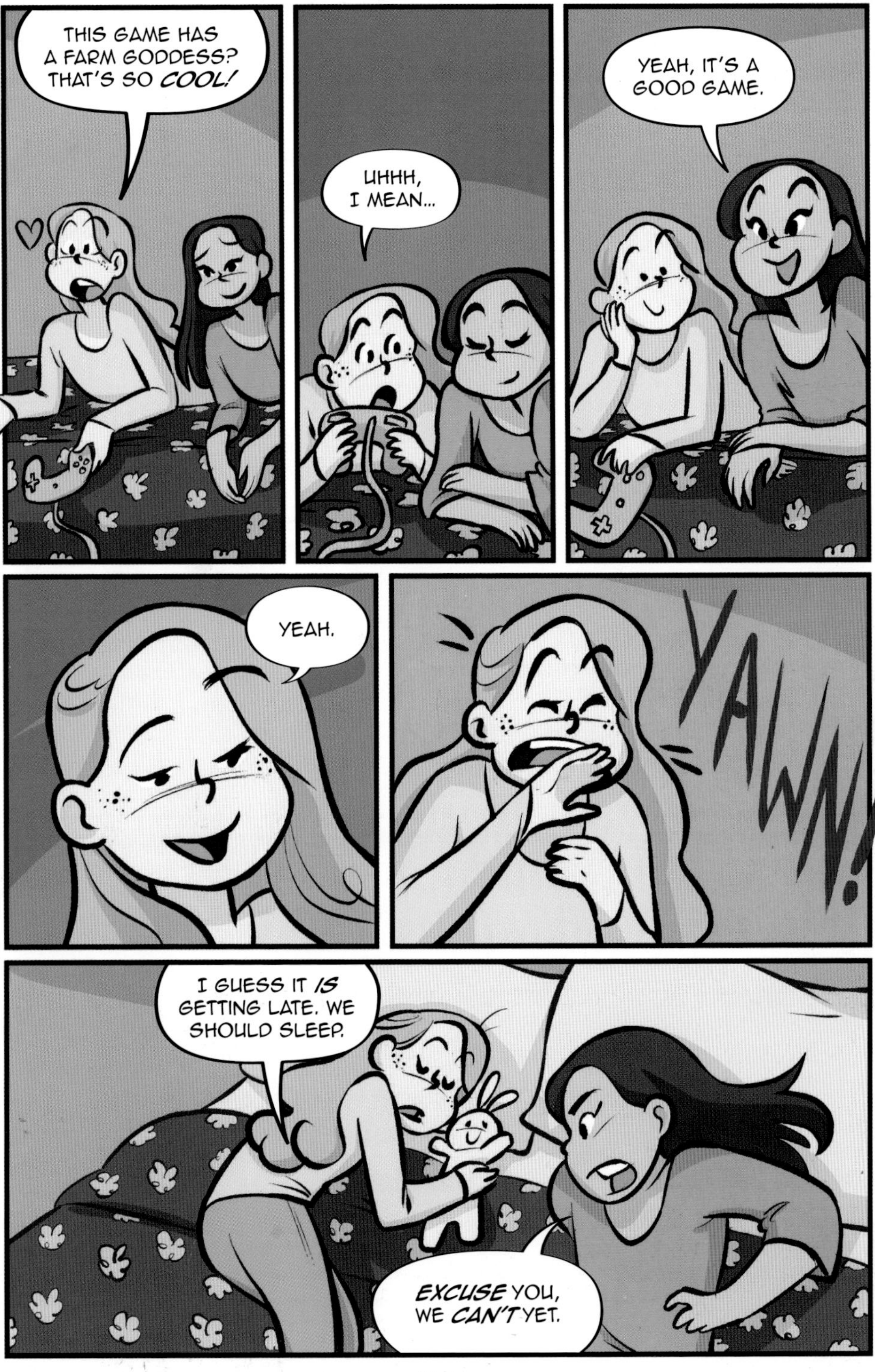
THIS GAME HAS A FARM GODDESS? THAT'S SO *COOL!*
UHHH, I MEAN...
YEAH, IT'S A GOOD GAME.
YEAH.
YAWN!
I GUESS IT *IS* GETTING LATE. WE SHOULD SLEEP.
*EXCUSE* YOU, WE *CAN'T* YET.

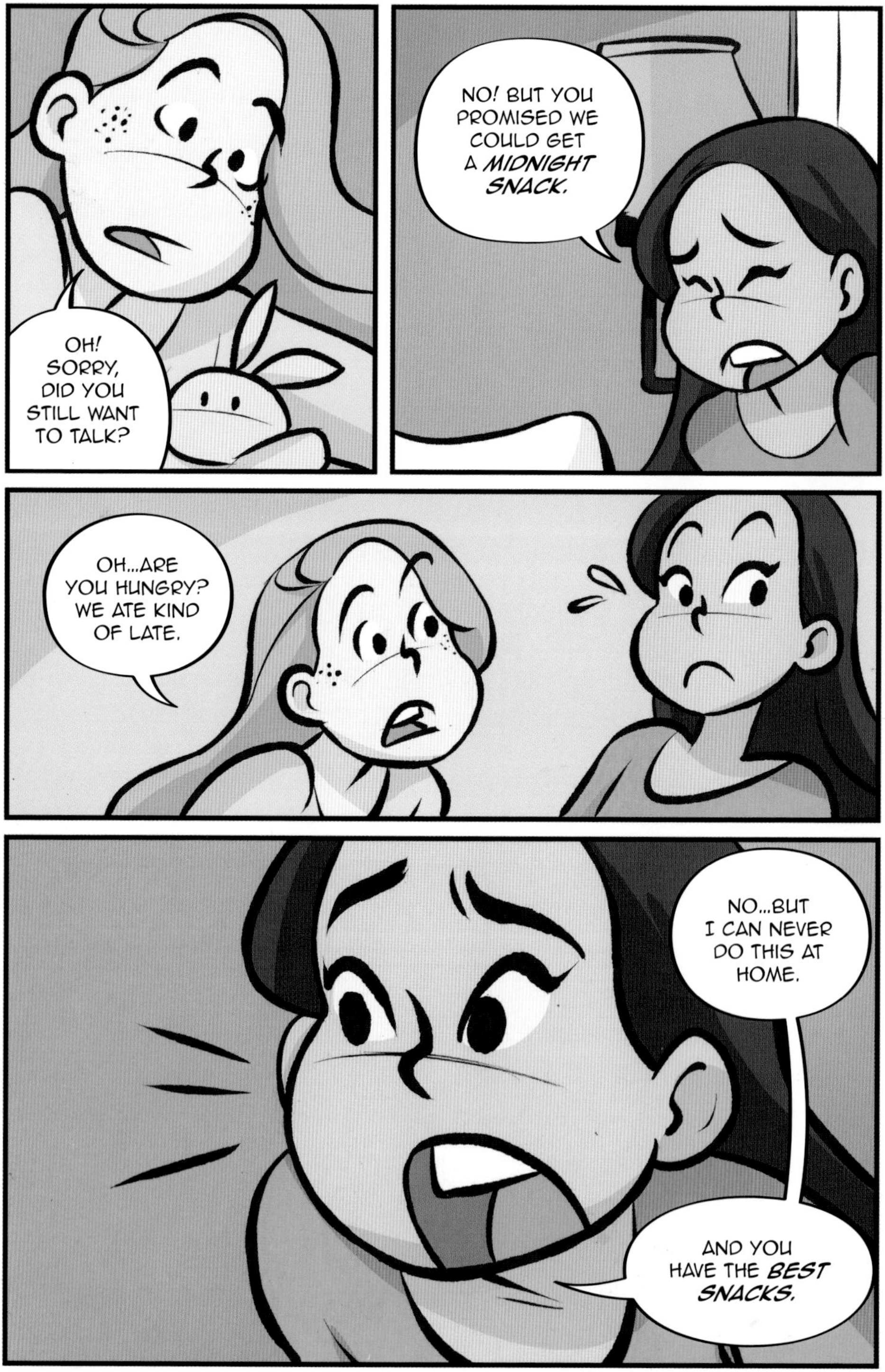
OH! SORRY, DID YOU STILL WANT TO TALK?
NO! BUT YOU PROMISED WE COULD GET A *MIDNIGHT SNACK.*
OH...ARE YOU HUNGRY? WE ATE KIND OF LATE.
NO...BUT I CAN NEVER DO THIS AT HOME.
AND YOU HAVE THE *BEST SNACKS.*

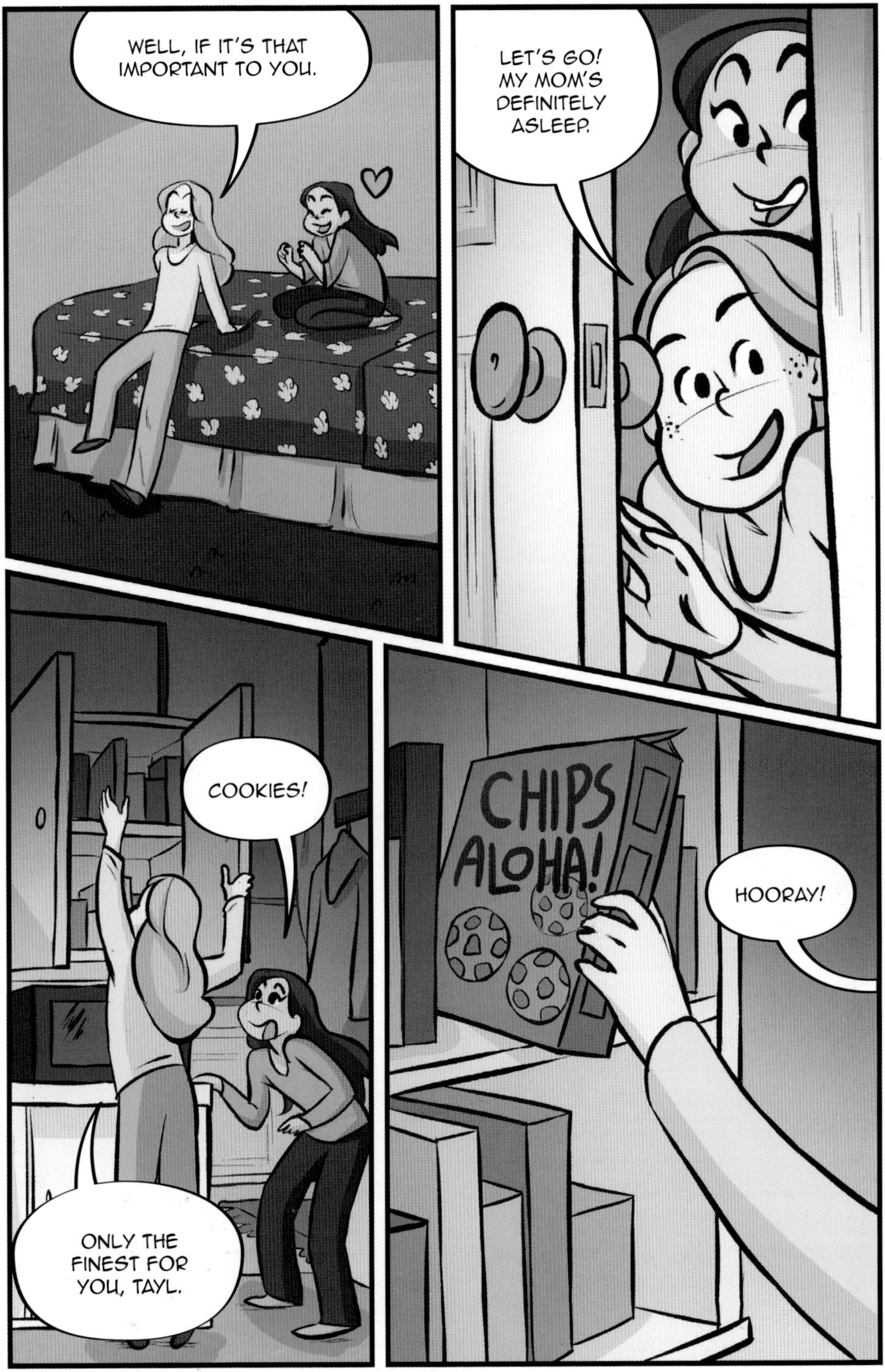
WELL, IF IT'S THAT IMPORTANT TO YOU.
LET'S GO! MY MOM'S DEFINITELY ASLEEP.
COOKIES!
ONLY THE FINEST FOR YOU, TAYL.
CHIPS ALOHA!
HOORAY!

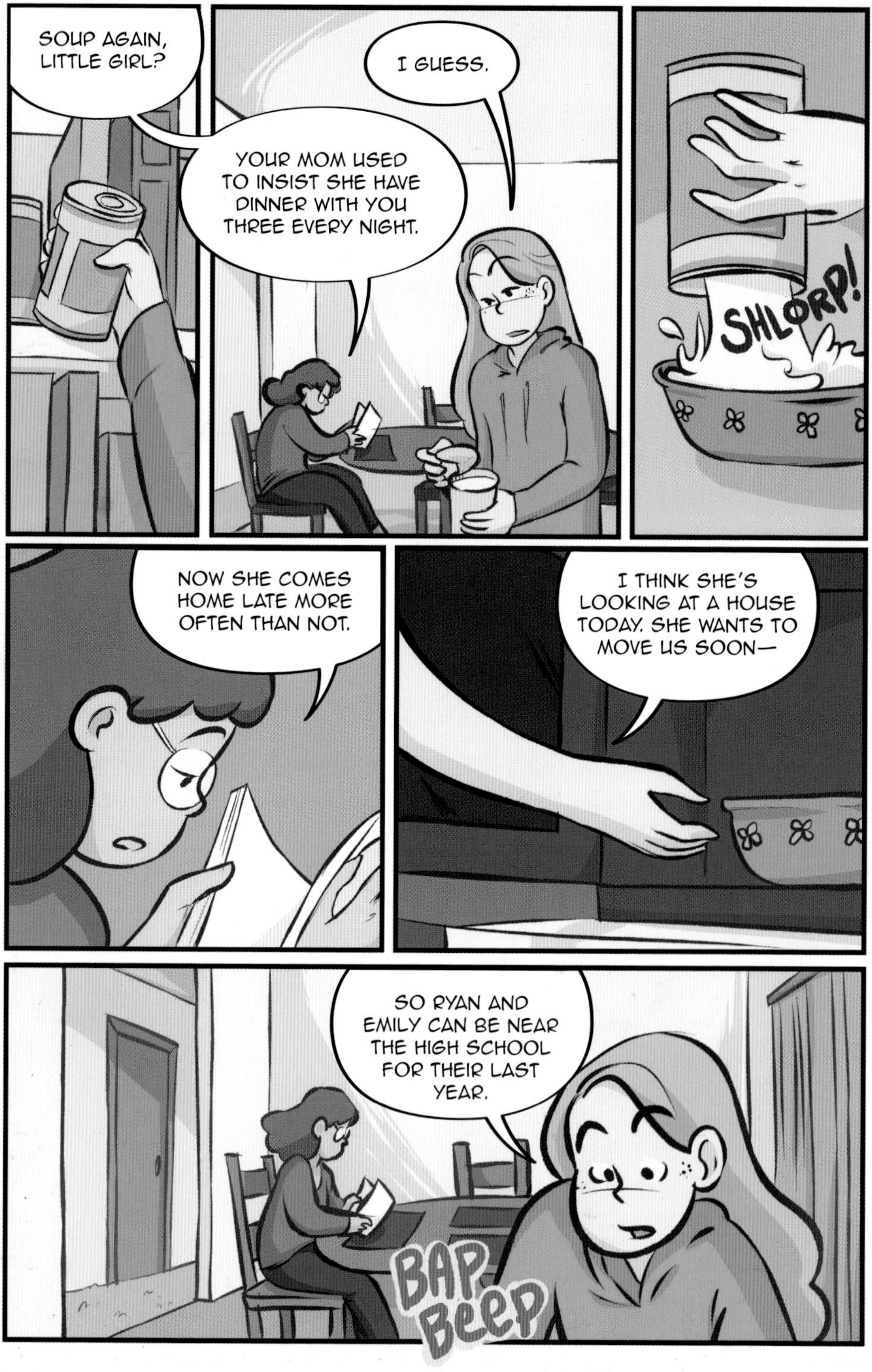
SOUP AGAIN, LITTLE GIRL?
YOUR MOM USED TO INSIST SHE HAVE DINNER WITH YOU THREE EVERY NIGHT.
I GUESS.
SHLORP!
NOW SHE COMES HOME LATE MORE OFTEN THAN NOT.
I THINK SHE'S LOOKING AT A HOUSE TODAY. SHE WANTS TO MOVE US SOON—
SO RYAN AND EMILY CAN BE NEAR THE HIGH SCHOOL FOR THEIR LAST YEAR.
BAP Beep

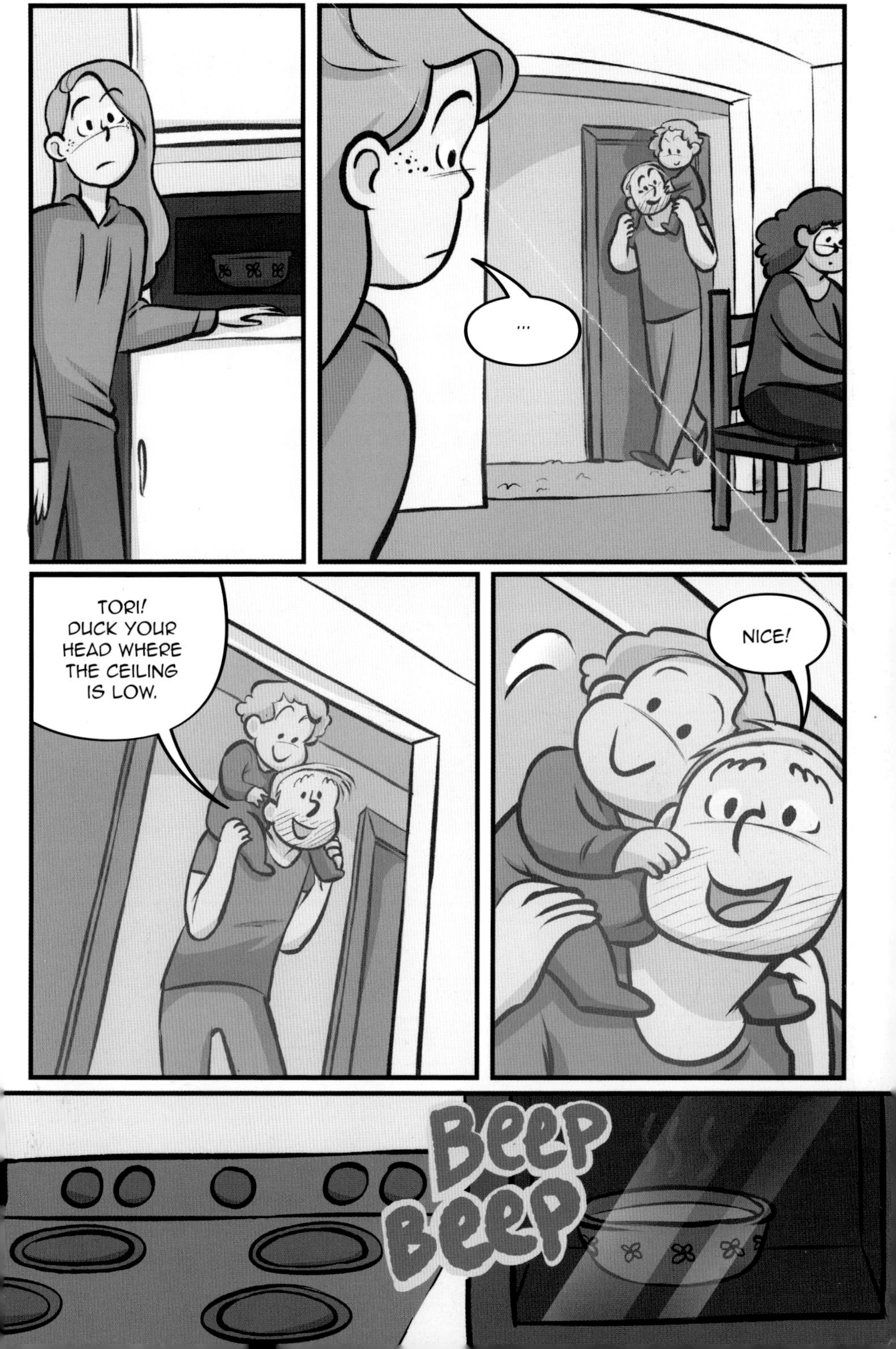
...
TORI! DUCK YOUR HEAD WHERE THE CEILING IS LOW.
NICE!
Beep Beep

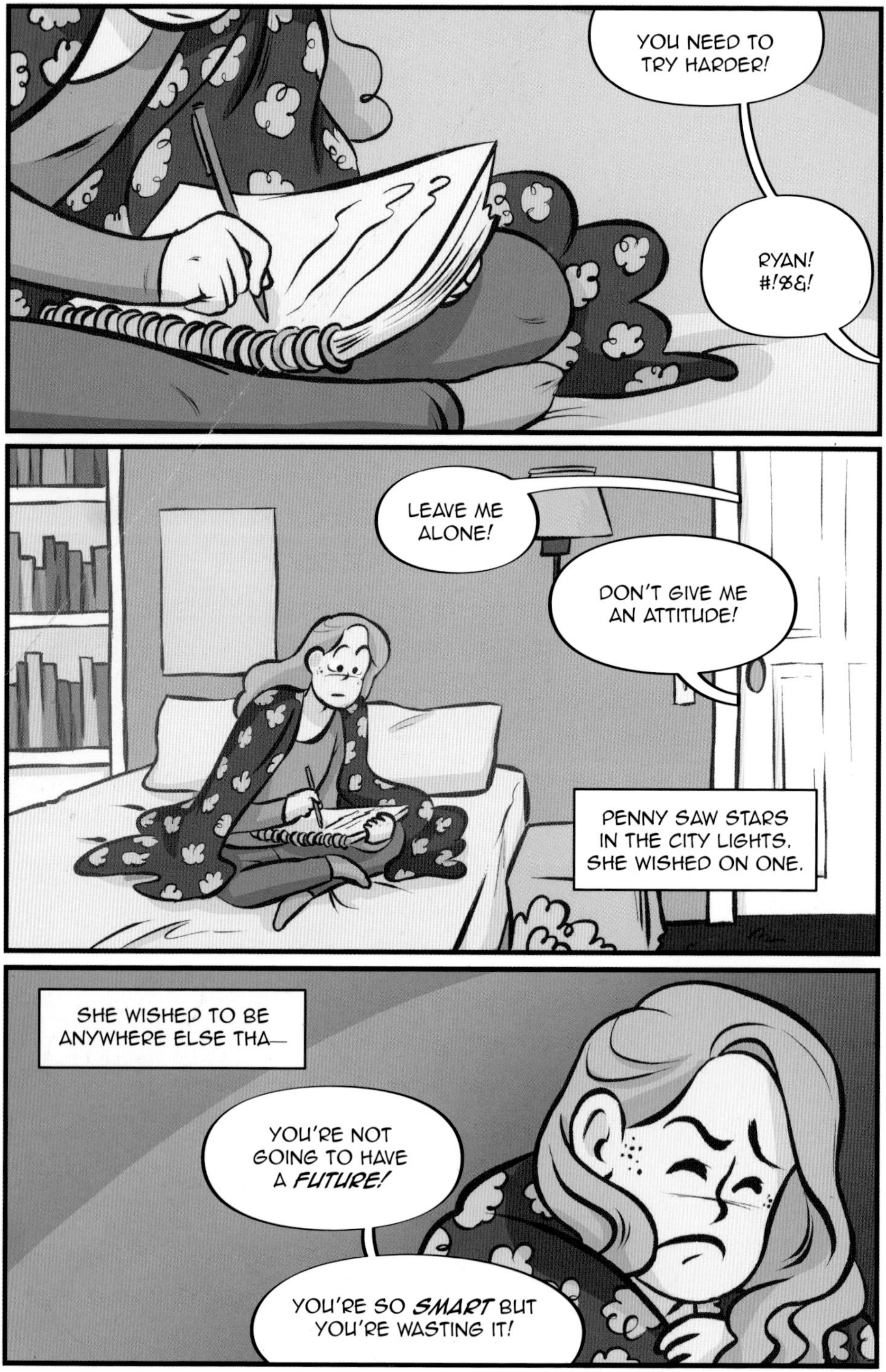

YOU NEED TO TRY HARDER!
RYAN! #!%&!
LEAVE ME ALONE!
DON'T GIVE ME AN ATTITUDE!
PENNY SAW STARS IN THE CITY LIGHTS. SHE WISHED ON ONE.
SHE WISHED TO BE ANYWHERE ELSE THA—
YOU'RE NOT GOING TO HAVE A *FUTURE!*
YOU'RE SO *SMART* BUT YOU'RE WASTING IT!

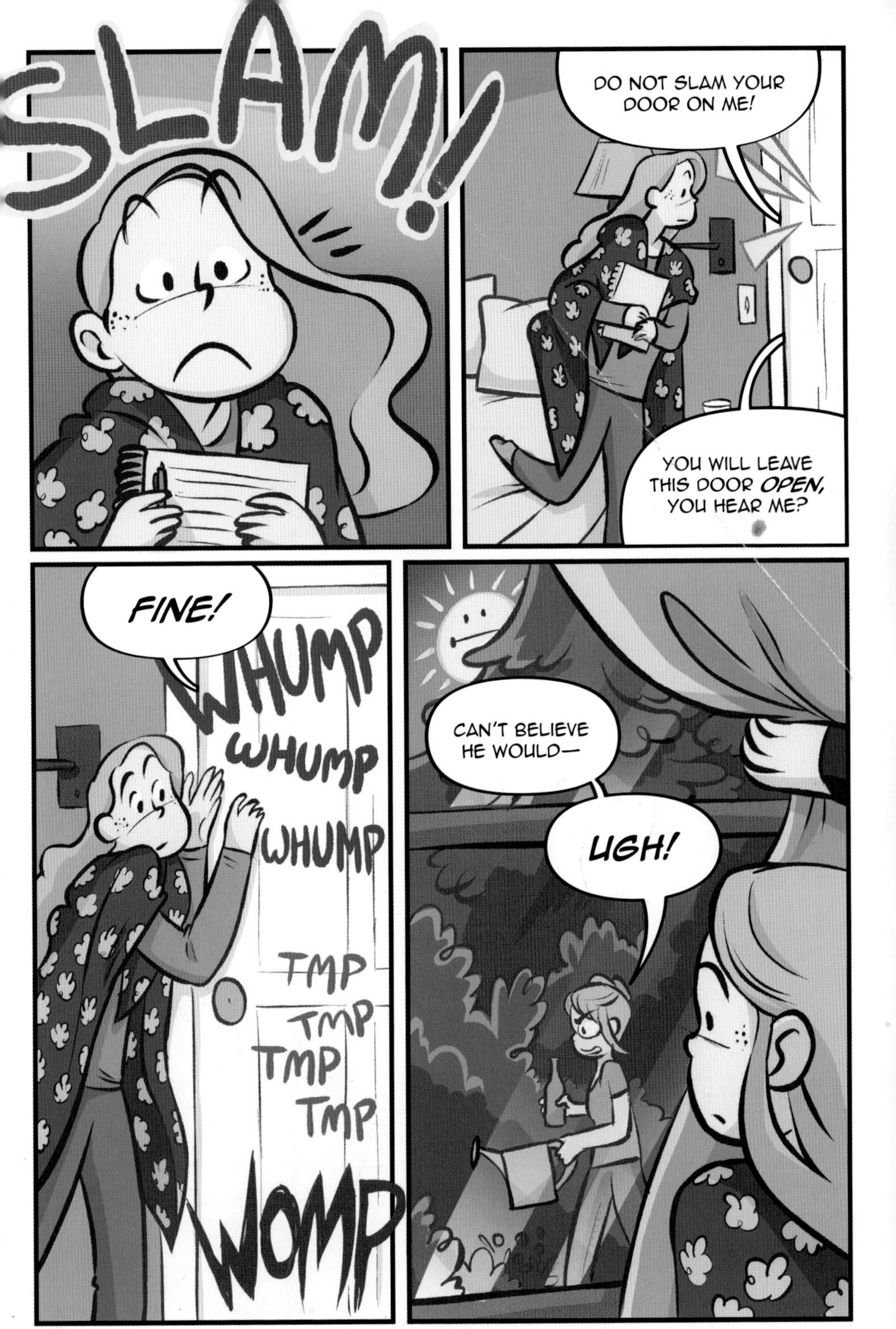
SLAM!!
DO NOT SLAM YOUR DOOR ON ME!
YOU WILL LEAVE THIS DOOR *OPEN*, YOU HEAR ME?
*FINE!*
WHUMP
WHUMP
WHUMP
TMP
TMP
TMP
TMP
WOMP
CAN'T BELIEVE HE WOULD—
*UGH!*

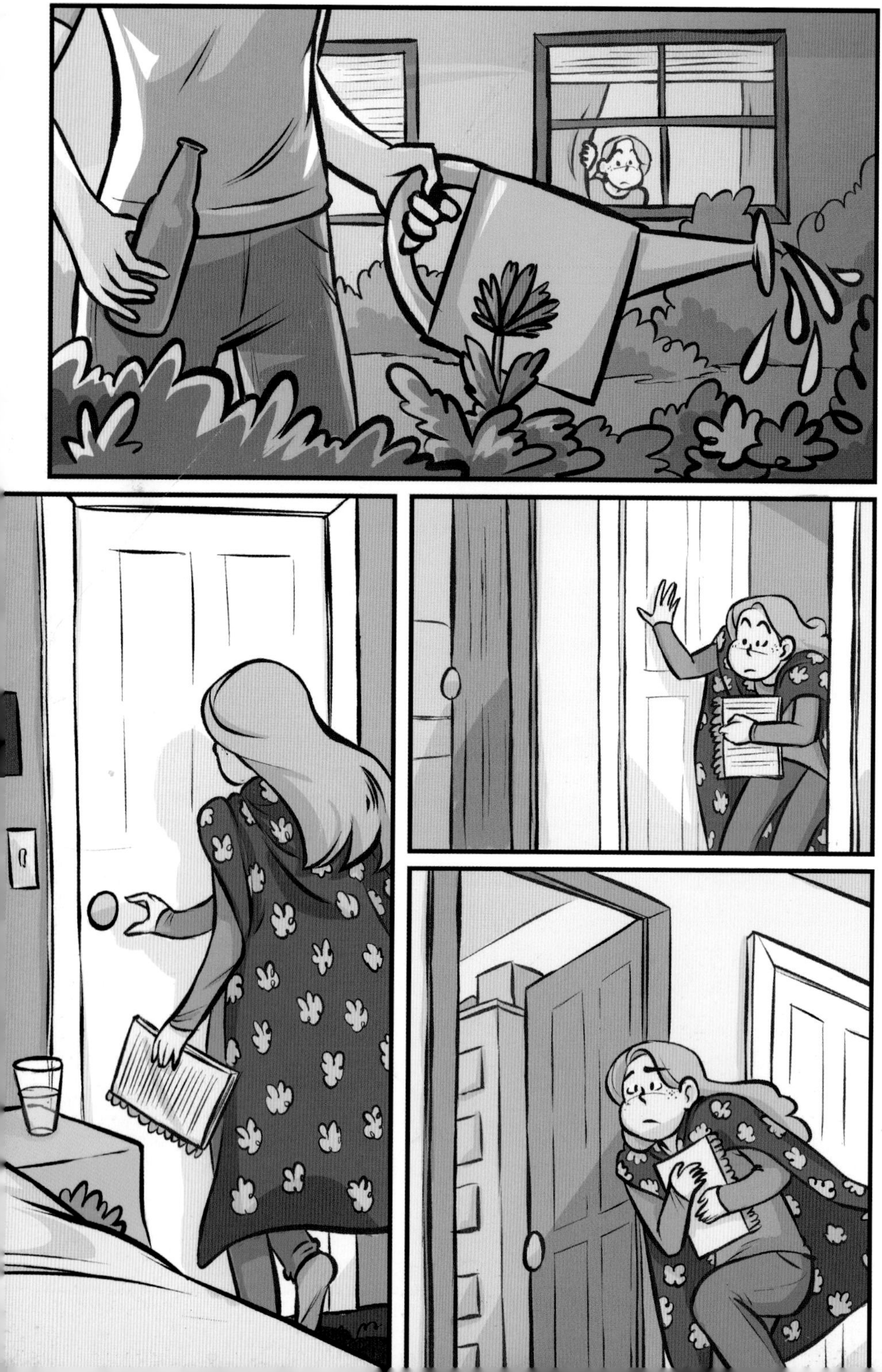

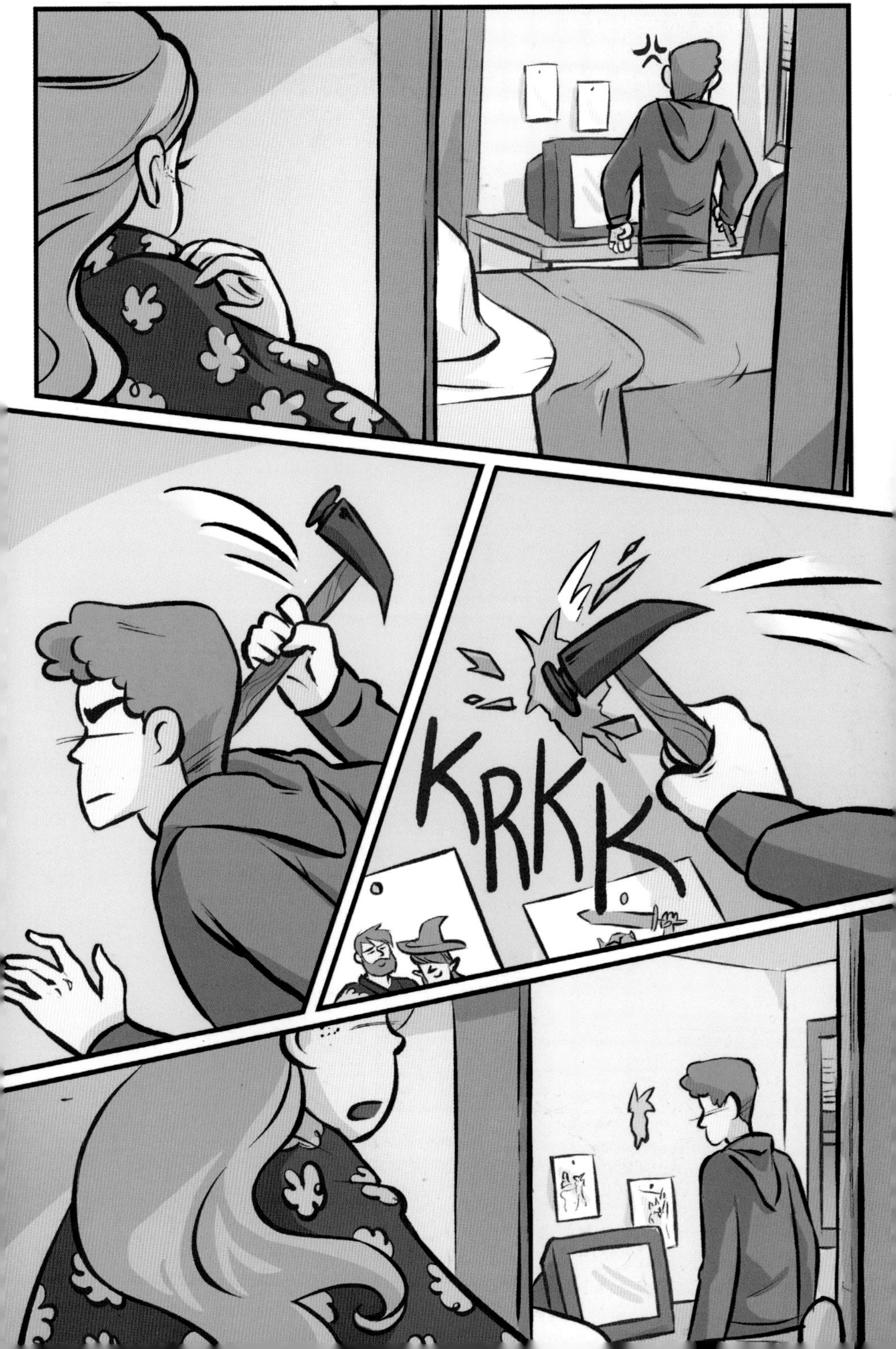
KRKK

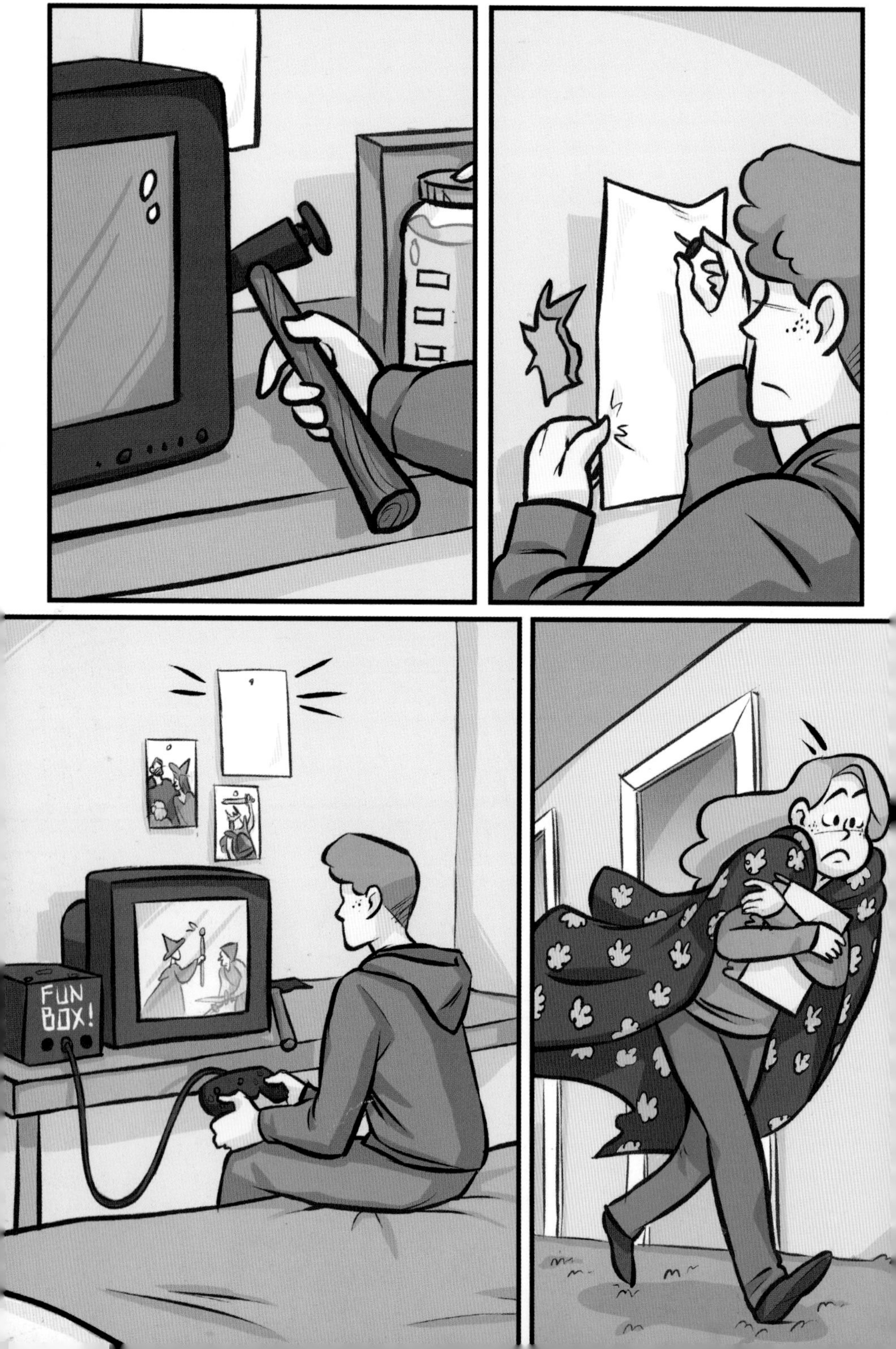
FUN
BOX!

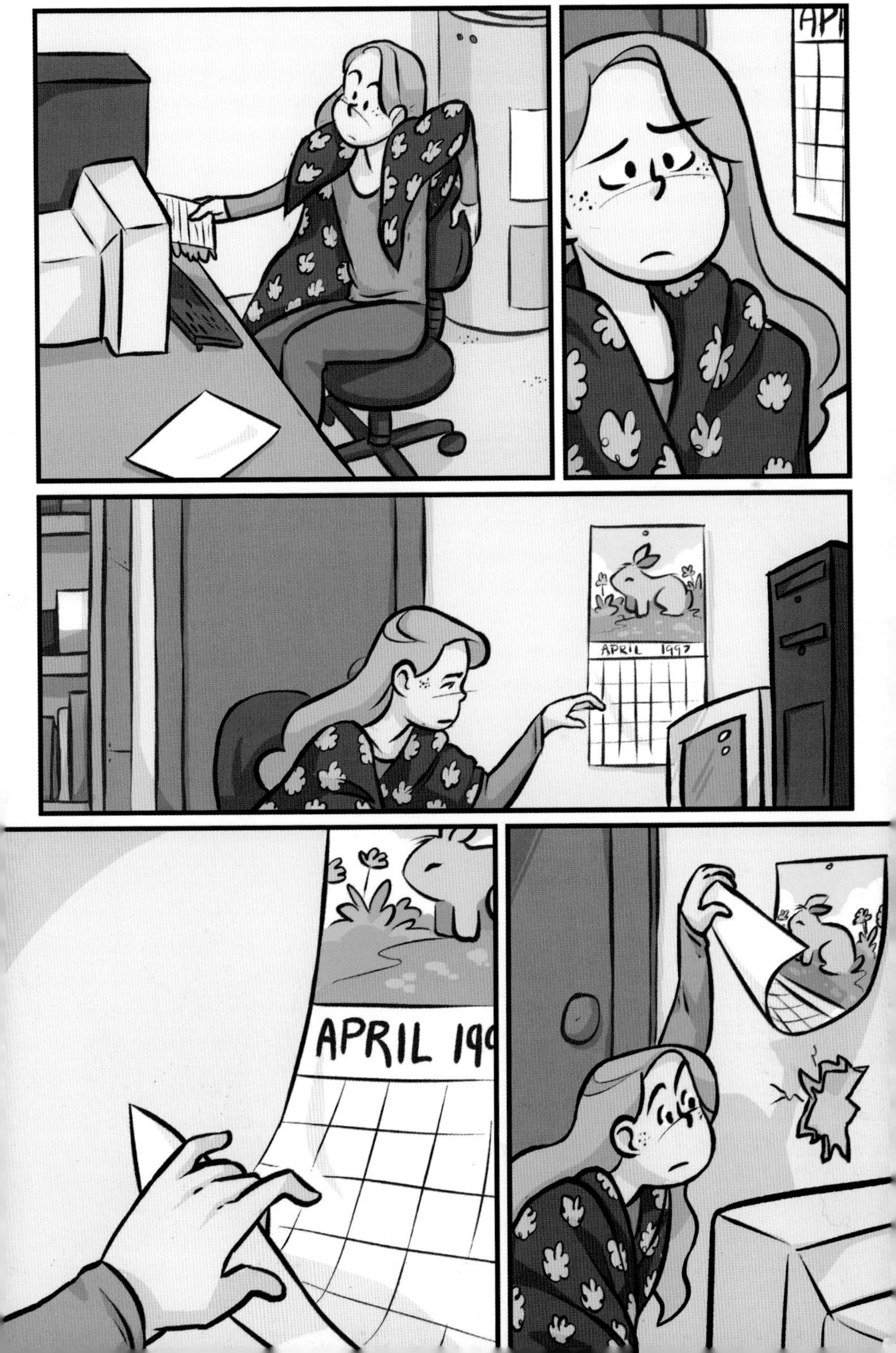
APRIL 1997
APRIL 199

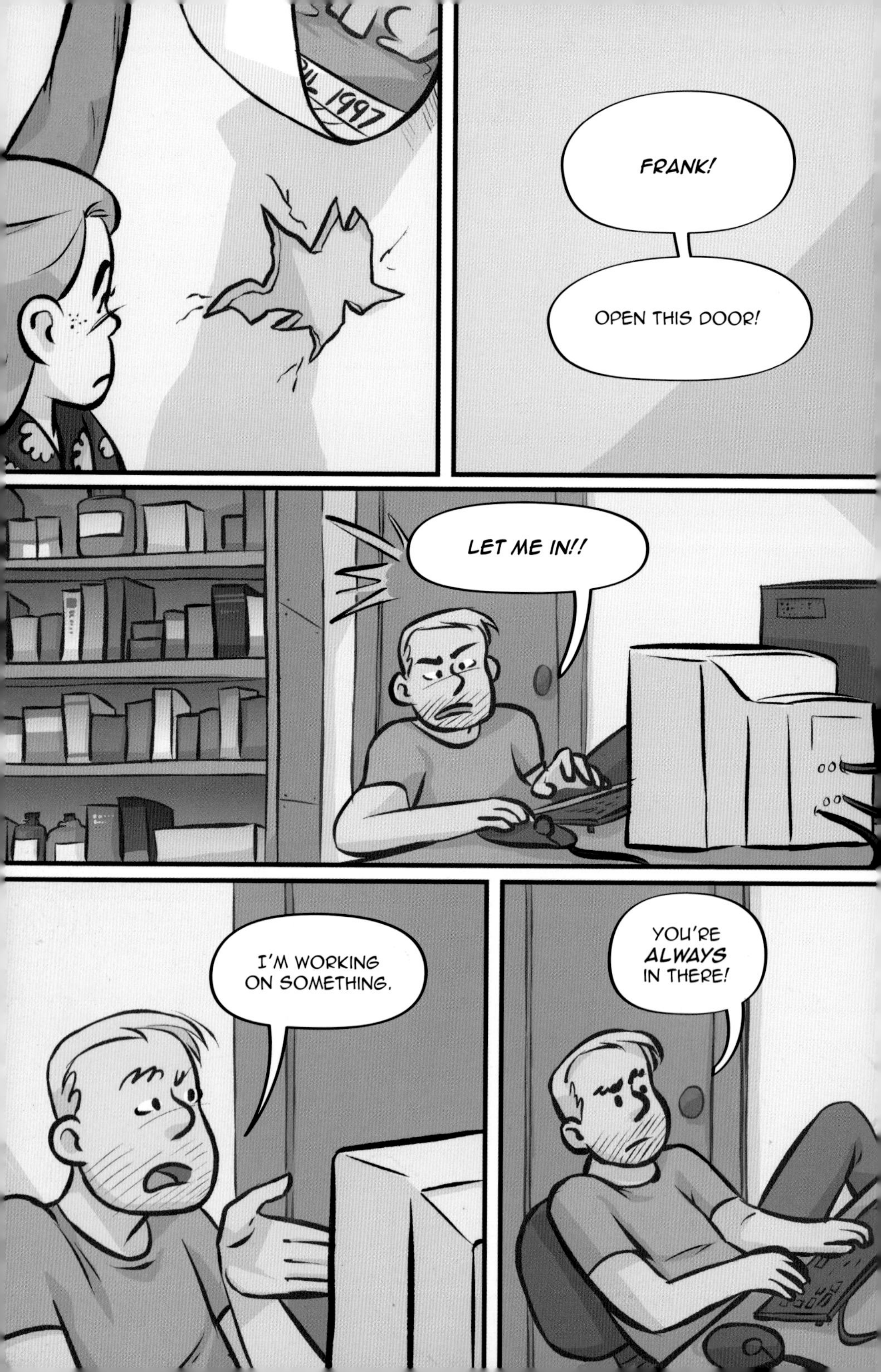
1997
FRANK!
OPEN THIS DOOR!
LET ME IN!!
I'M WORKING ON SOMETHING.
YOU'RE ALWAYS IN THERE!

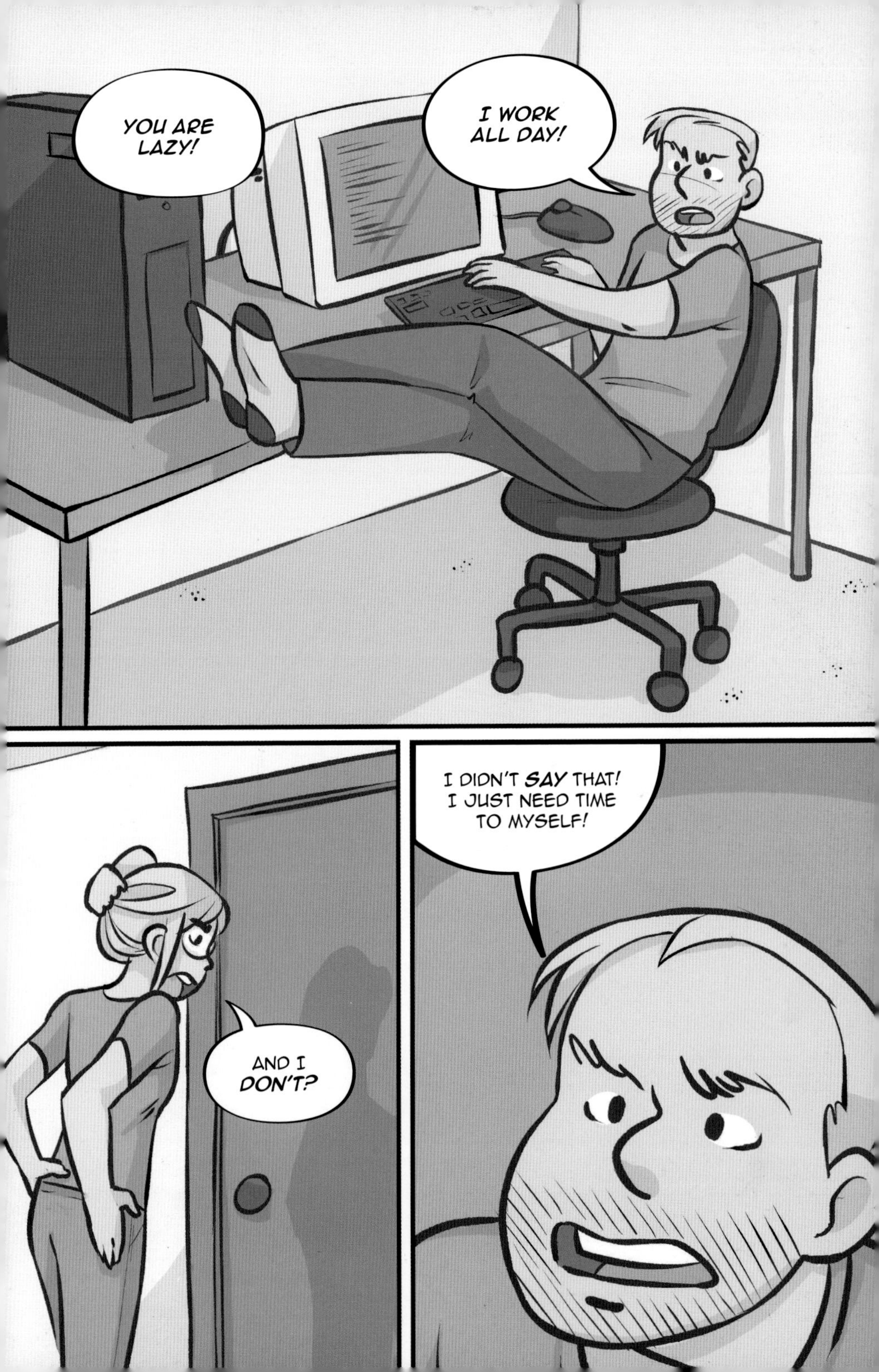
YOU ARE LAZY!
I WORK ALL DAY!
AND I DON'T?
I DIDN'T SAY THAT! I JUST NEED TIME TO MYSELF!

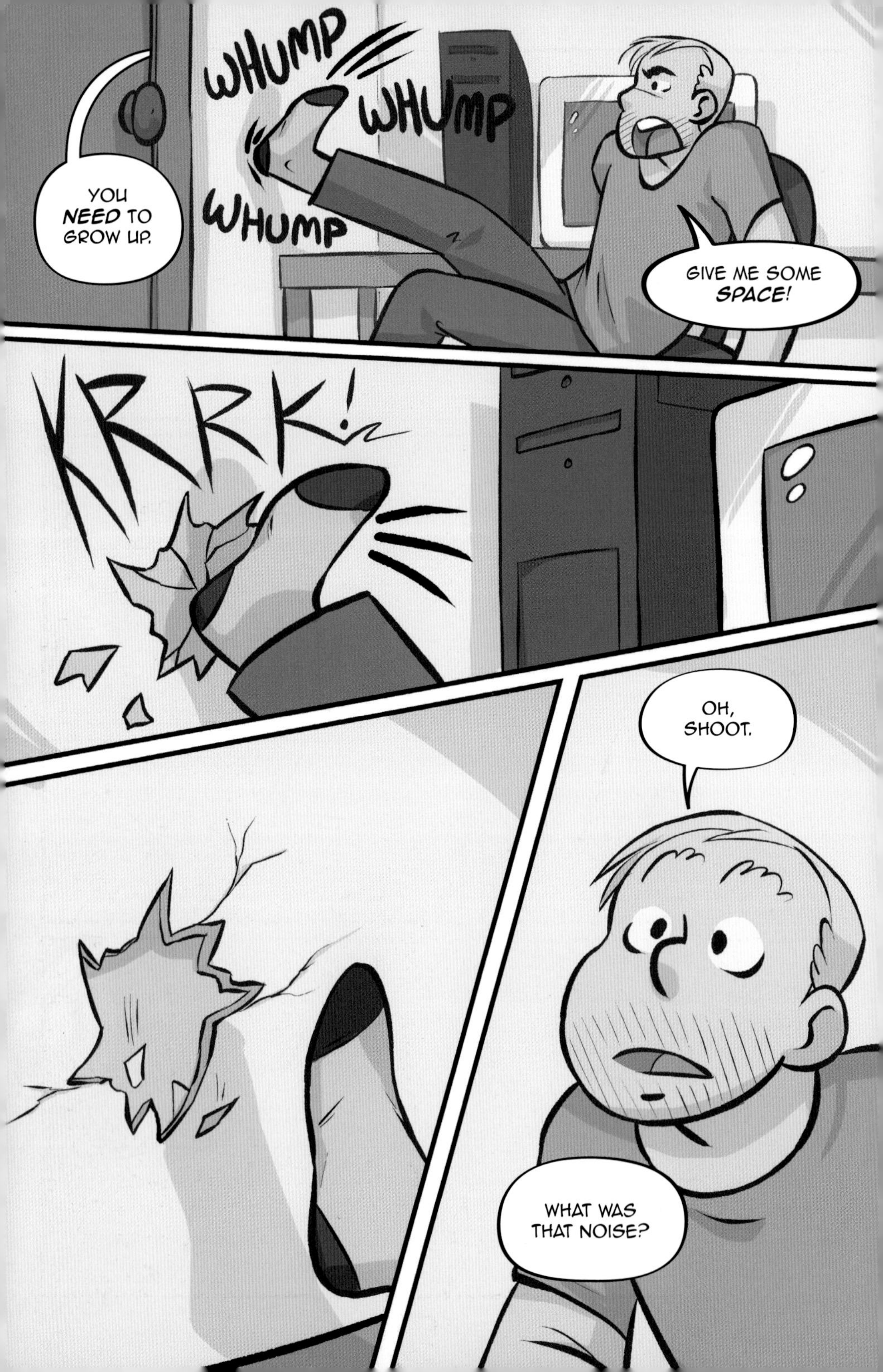

WHUMP
WHUMP
WHUMP
YOU NEED TO GROW UP.
GIVE ME SOME SPACE!
KRRK!
OH, SHOOT.
WHAT WAS THAT NOISE?

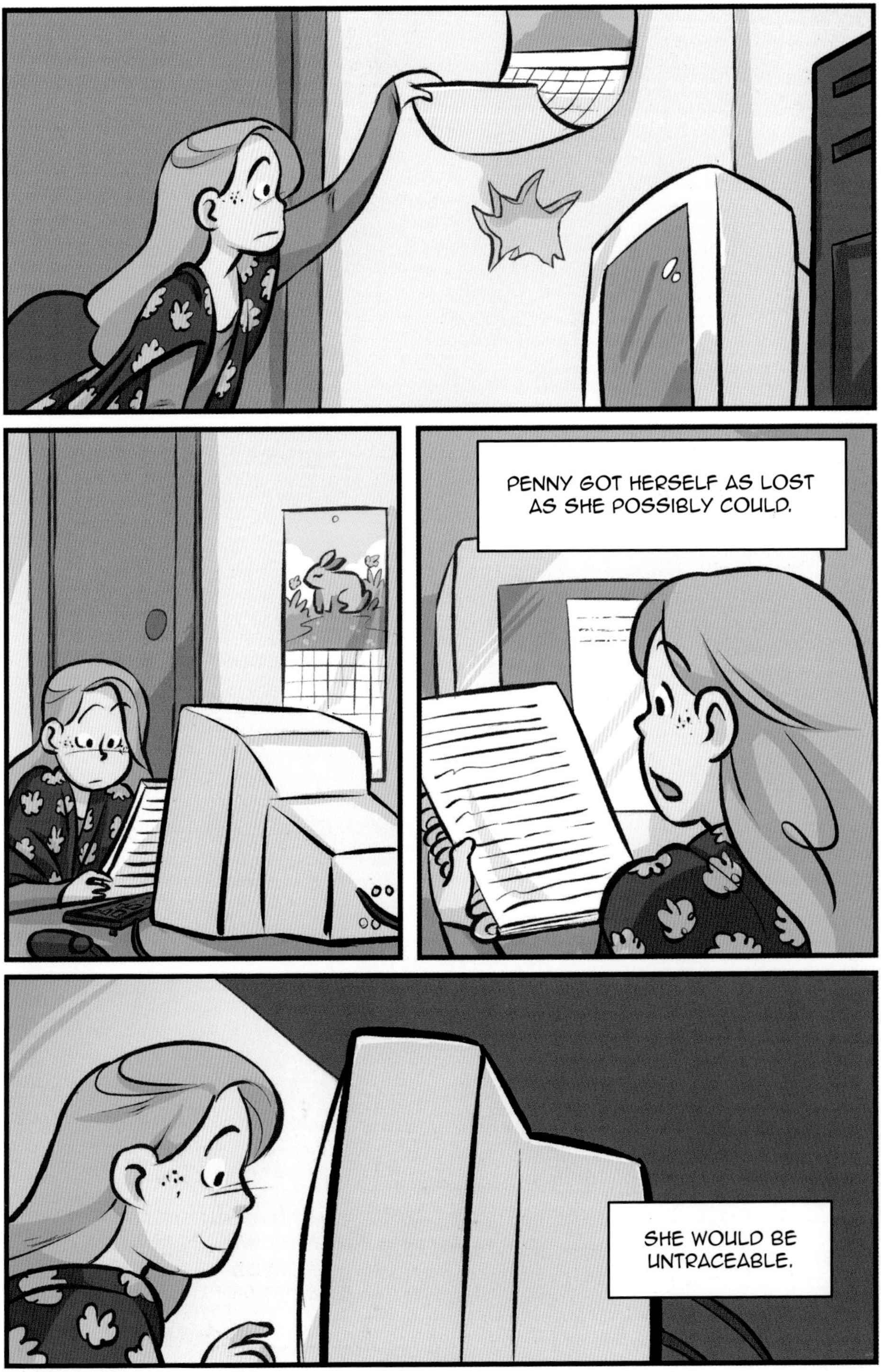

PENNY GOT HERSELF AS LOST AS SHE POSSIBLY COULD.
SHE WOULD BE UNTRACEABLE.

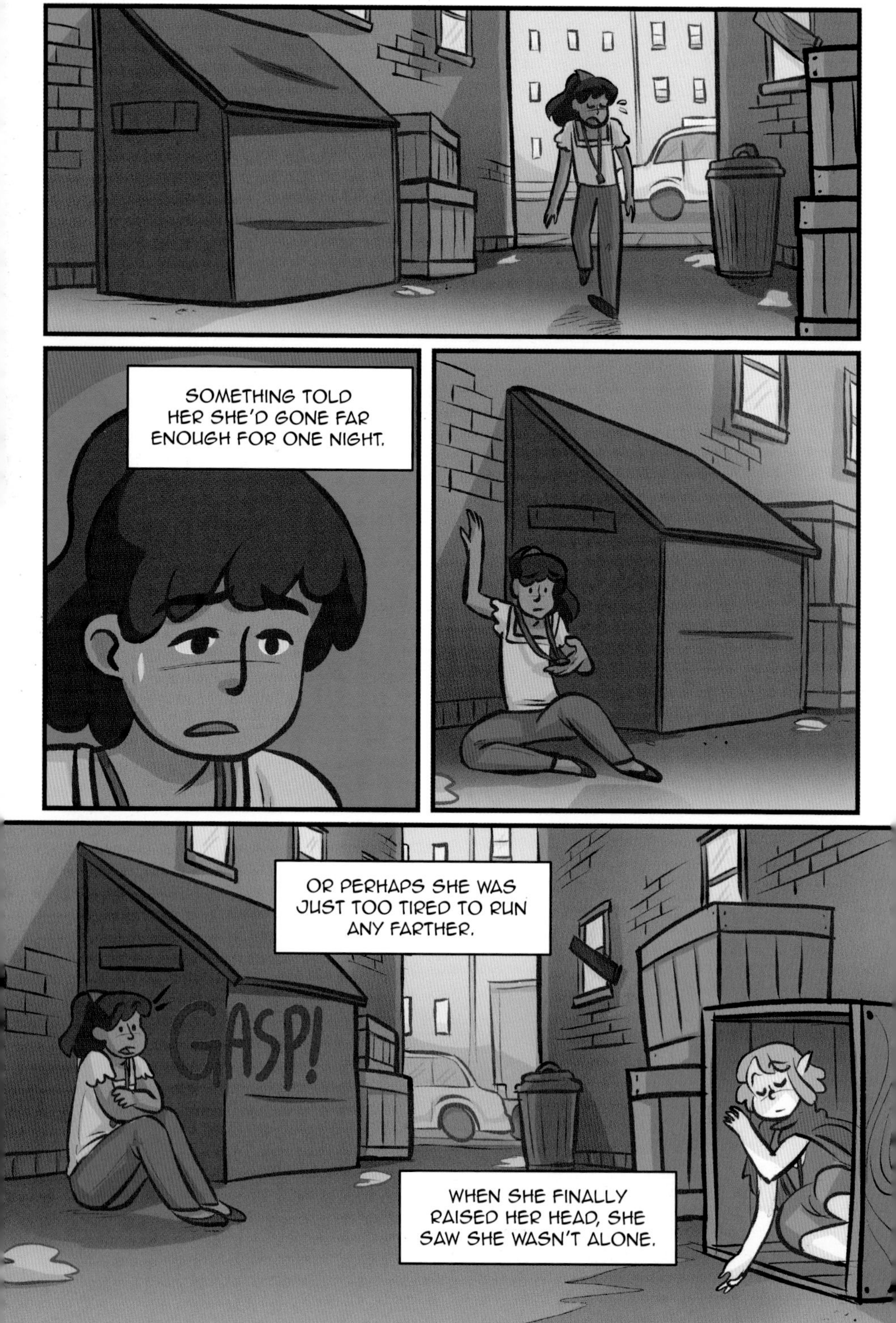

SOMETHING TOLD HER SHE'D GONE FAR ENOUGH FOR ONE NIGHT.
OR PERHAPS SHE WAS JUST TOO TIRED TO RUN ANY FARTHER.
GASP!
WHEN SHE FINALLY RAISED HER HEAD, SHE SAW SHE WASN'T ALONE.

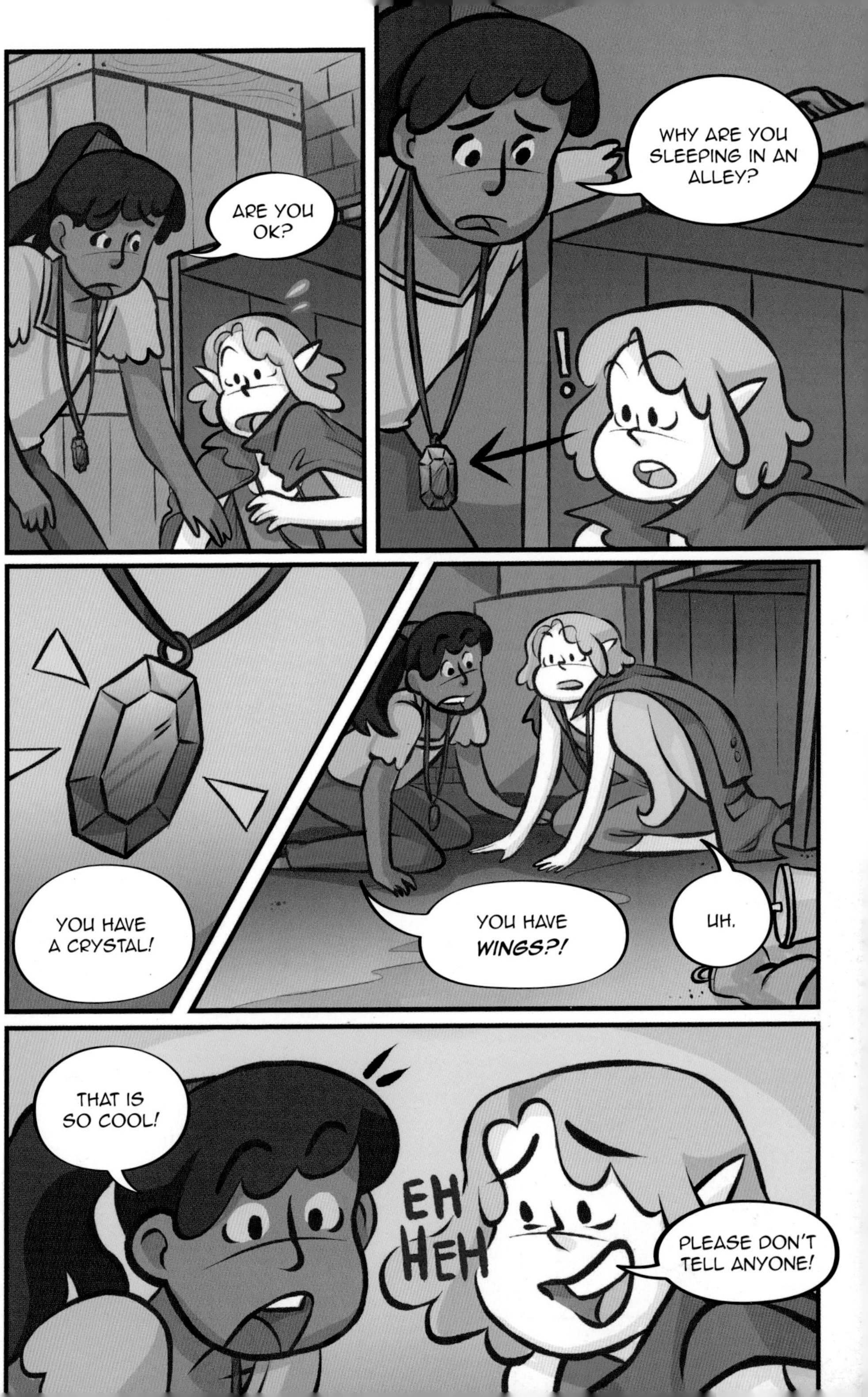
ARE YOU OK?
WHY ARE YOU SLEEPING IN AN ALLEY?
!
YOU HAVE A CRYSTAL!
YOU HAVE *WINGS?!*
UH.
THAT IS SO COOL!
EH HEH
PLEASE DON'T TELL ANYONE!

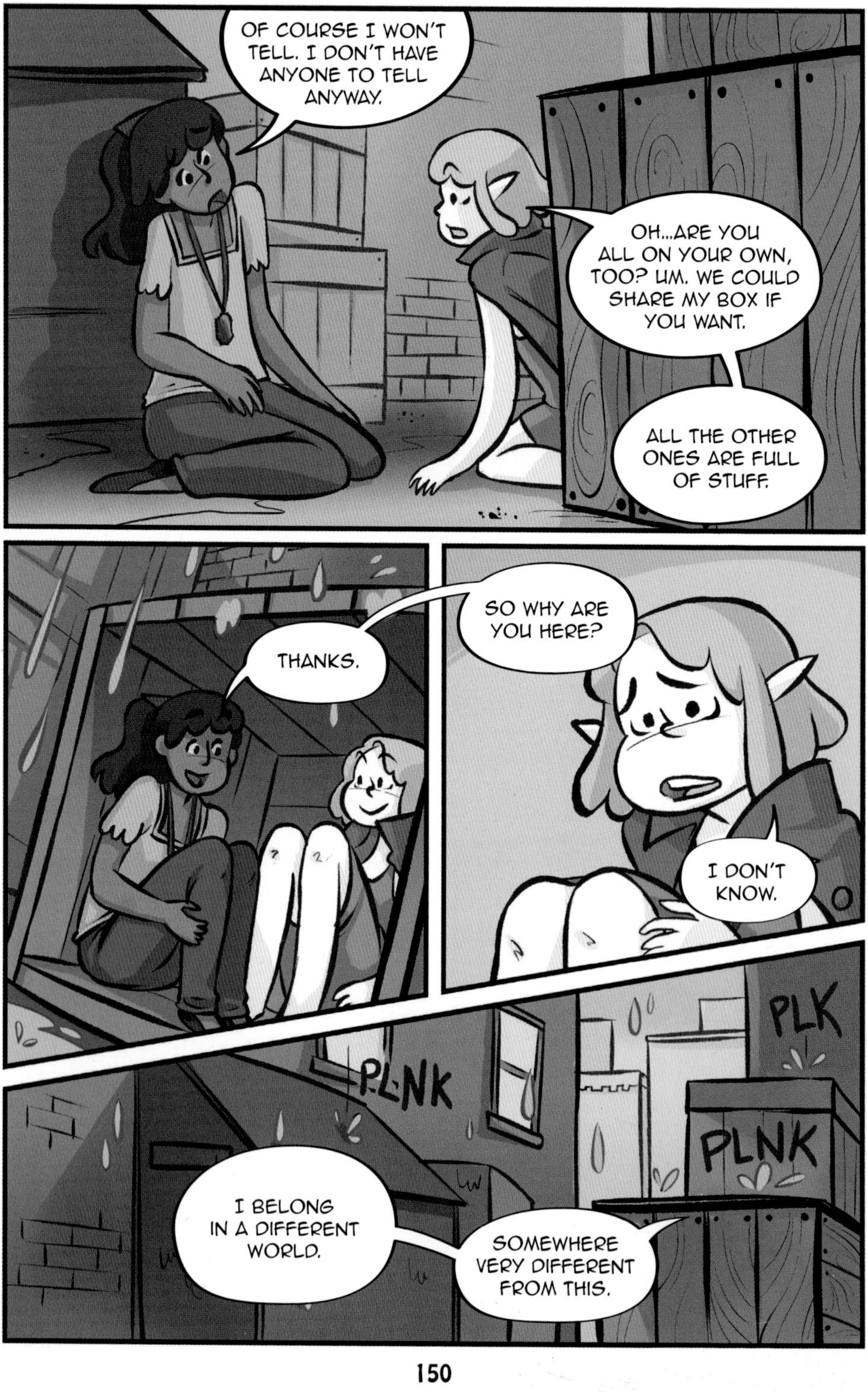
OF COURSE I WON'T TELL. I DON'T HAVE ANYONE TO TELL ANYWAY.
OH...ARE YOU ALL ON YOUR OWN, TOO? UM. WE COULD SHARE MY BOX IF YOU WANT.
ALL THE OTHER ONES ARE FULL OF STUFF.
THANKS.
SO WHY ARE YOU HERE?
I DON'T KNOW.
PLK
PLNK
PLNK
I BELONG IN A DIFFERENT WORLD.
SOMEWHERE VERY DIFFERENT FROM THIS.

YOU'RE FROM ANOTHER WORLD?

YES! AND I THINK WE WERE SUPPOSED TO FIND EACH OTHER!

I HAVE A CRYSTAL, TOO.

WHEN SHE SENT ME HERE, THE PRINCESS SAID THE CRYSTALS ARE IMPORTANT.

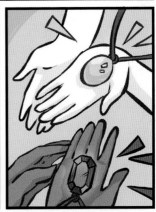

I FEEL LIKE I'M SUPPOSED TO PROTECT IT.

THE AMULETS MUST HAVE BROUGHT US TOGETHER FOR A REASON.

THEN LET'S PROMISE TO LOOK OUT FOR EACH OTHER.

NO MATTER WHAT.

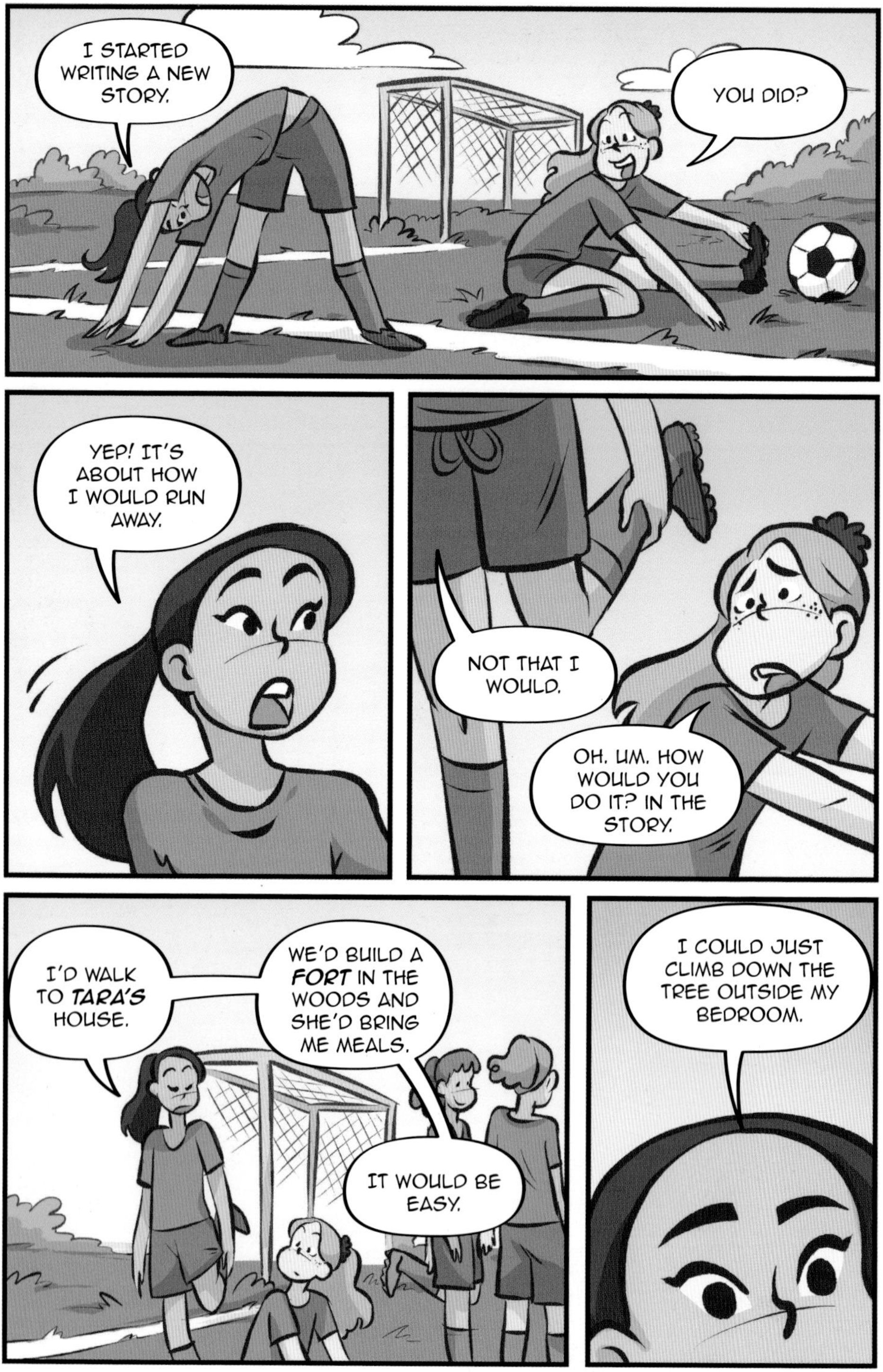
I STARTED WRITING A NEW STORY.
YOU DID?
YEP! IT'S ABOUT HOW I WOULD RUN AWAY.
NOT THAT I WOULD.
OH. UM. HOW WOULD YOU DO IT? IN THE STORY.
I'D WALK TO **TARA'S** HOUSE.
WE'D BUILD A **FORT** IN THE WOODS AND SHE'D BRING ME MEALS.
IT WOULD BE EASY.
I COULD JUST CLIMB DOWN THE TREE OUTSIDE MY BEDROOM.

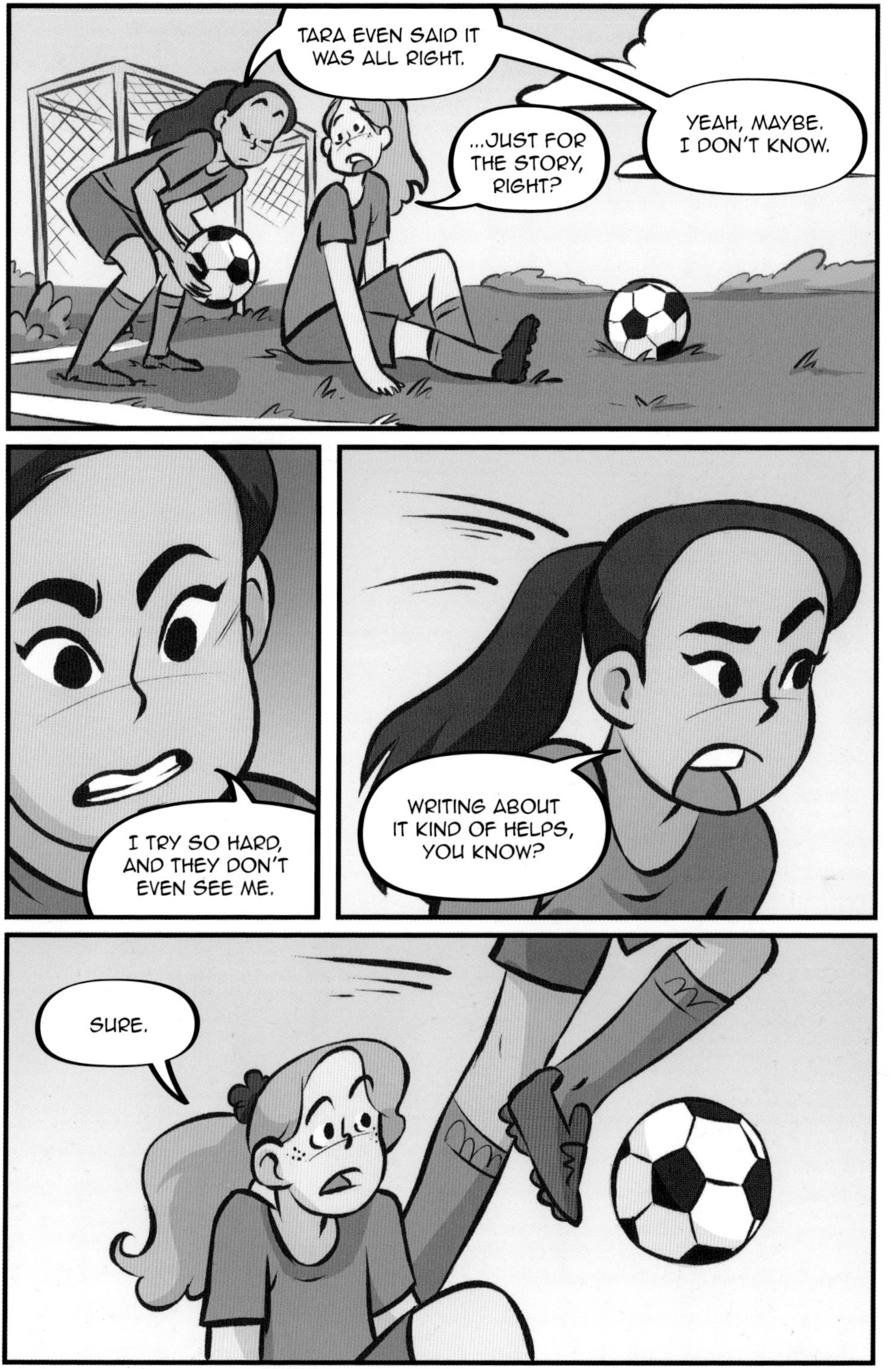
TARA EVEN SAID IT WAS ALL RIGHT.
...JUST FOR THE STORY, RIGHT?
YEAH, MAYBE. I DON'T KNOW.
I TRY SO HARD, AND THEY DON'T EVEN SEE ME.
WRITING ABOUT IT KIND OF HELPS, YOU KNOW?
SURE.

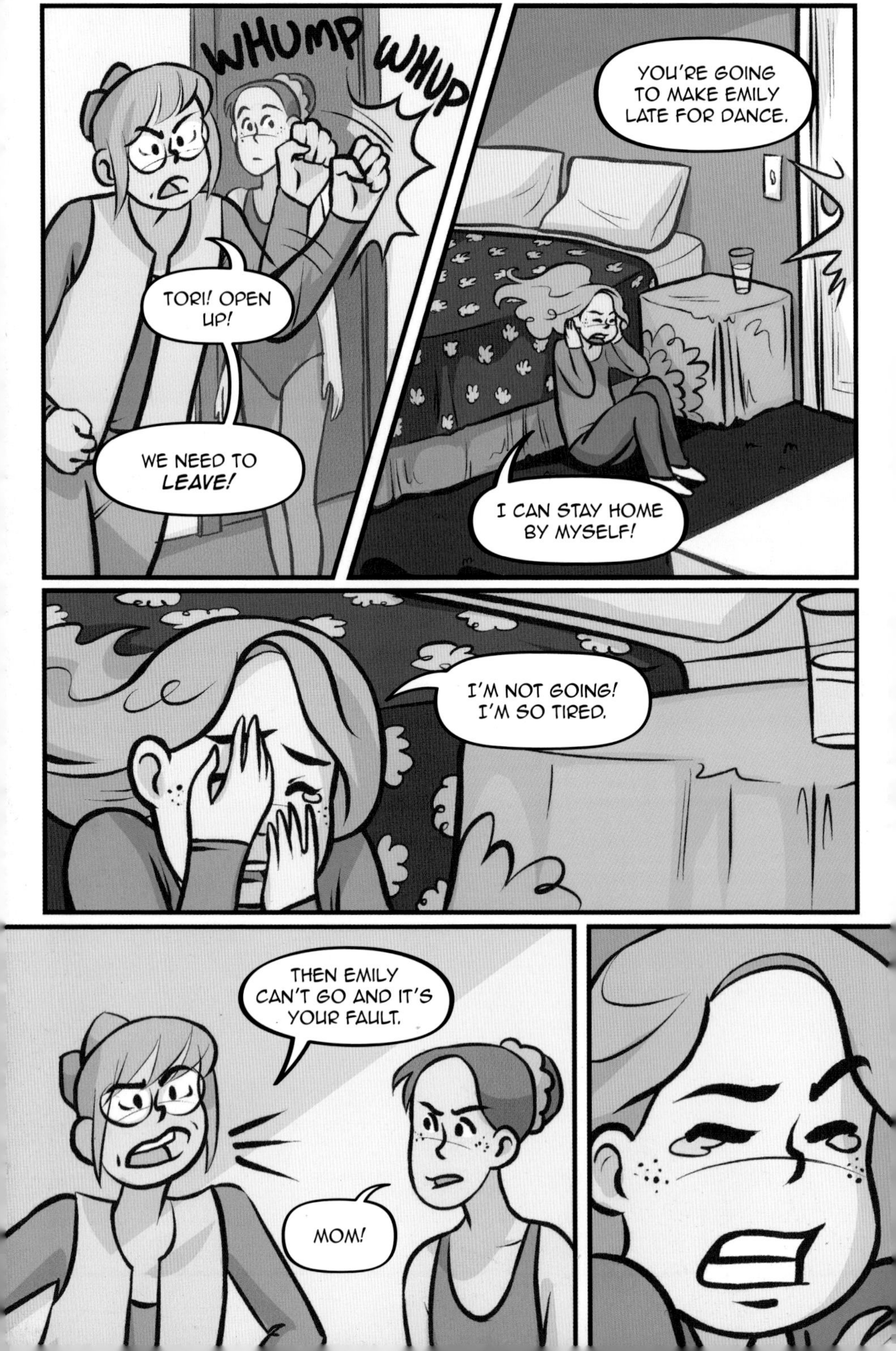
WHUMP
WHUP
TORI! OPEN UP!
WE NEED TO LEAVE!
YOU'RE GOING TO MAKE EMILY LATE FOR DANCE.
I CAN STAY HOME BY MYSELF!
I'M NOT GOING! I'M SO TIRED.
THEN EMILY CAN'T GO AND IT'S YOUR FAULT.
MOM!

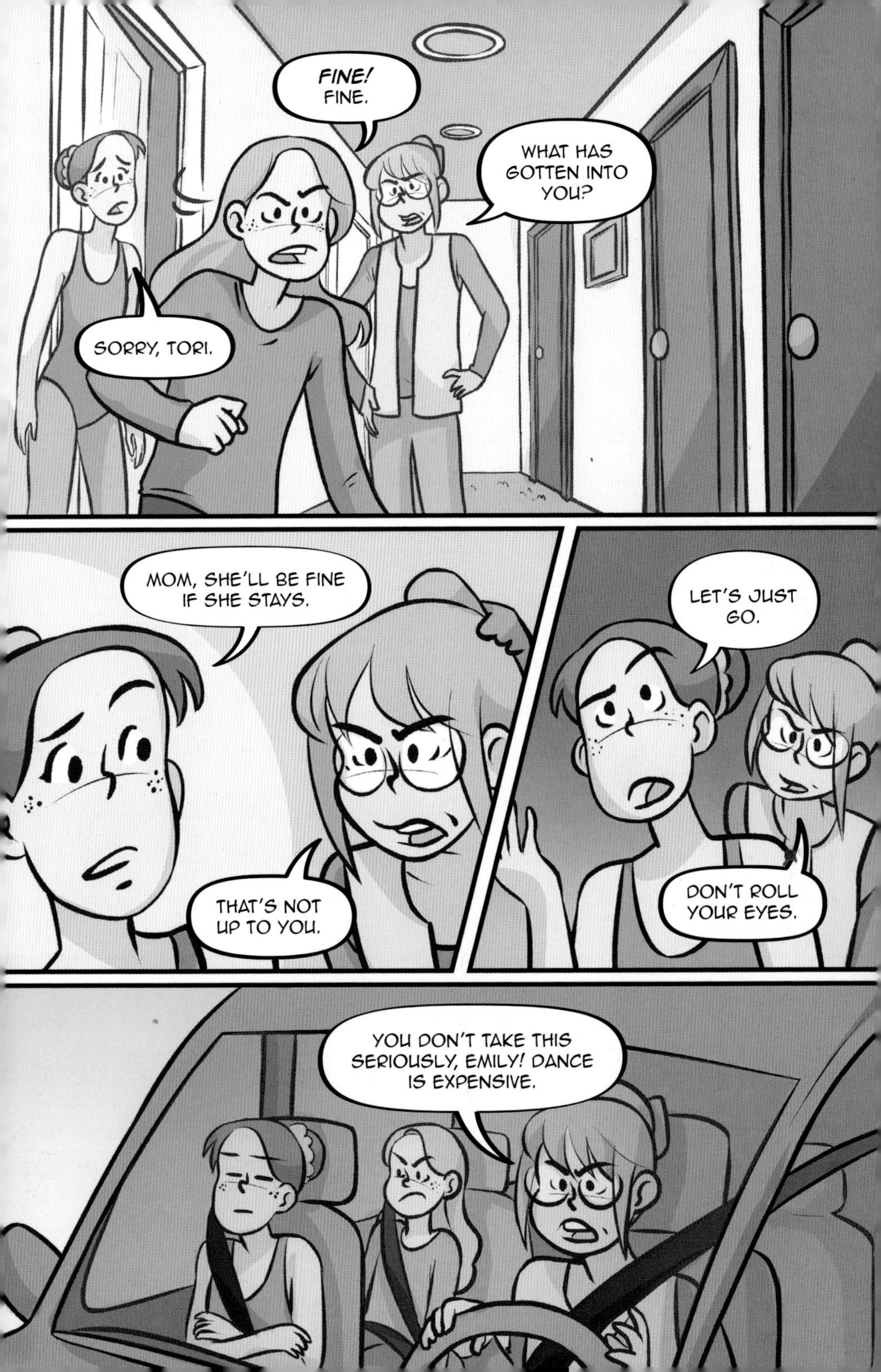
FINE! FINE.
WHAT HAS GOTTEN INTO YOU?
SORRY, TORI.
MOM, SHE'LL BE FINE IF SHE STAYS.
THAT'S NOT UP TO YOU.
LET'S JUST GO.
DON'T ROLL YOUR EYES.
YOU DON'T TAKE THIS SERIOUSLY, EMILY! DANCE IS EXPENSIVE.

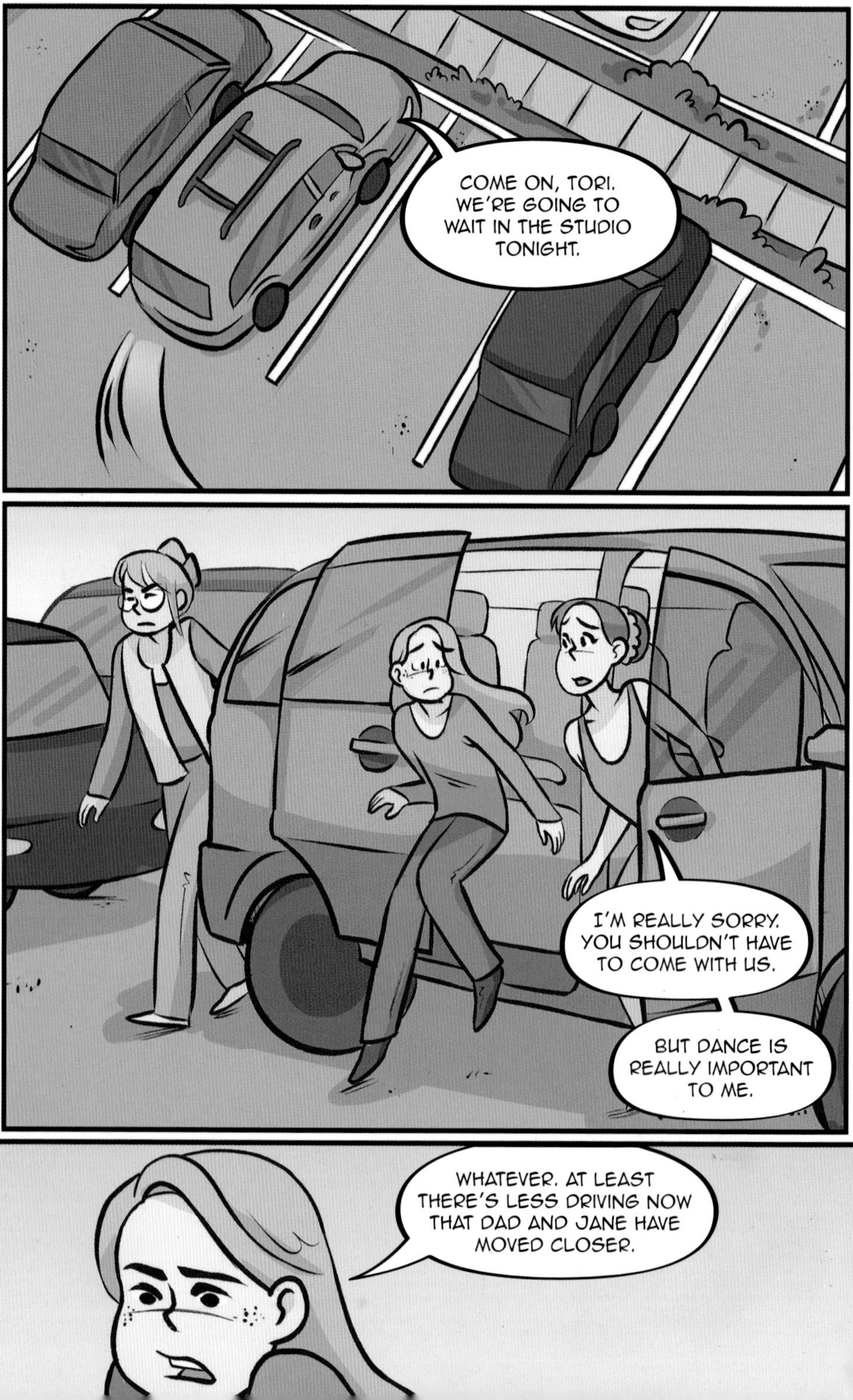
COME ON, TORI.
WE'RE GOING TO
WAIT IN THE STUDIO
TONIGHT.
I'M REALLY SORRY.
YOU SHOULDN'T HAVE
TO COME WITH US.
BUT DANCE IS
REALLY IMPORTANT
TO ME.
WHATEVER. AT LEAST
THERE'S LESS DRIVING NOW
THAT DAD AND JANE HAVE
MOVED CLOSER.

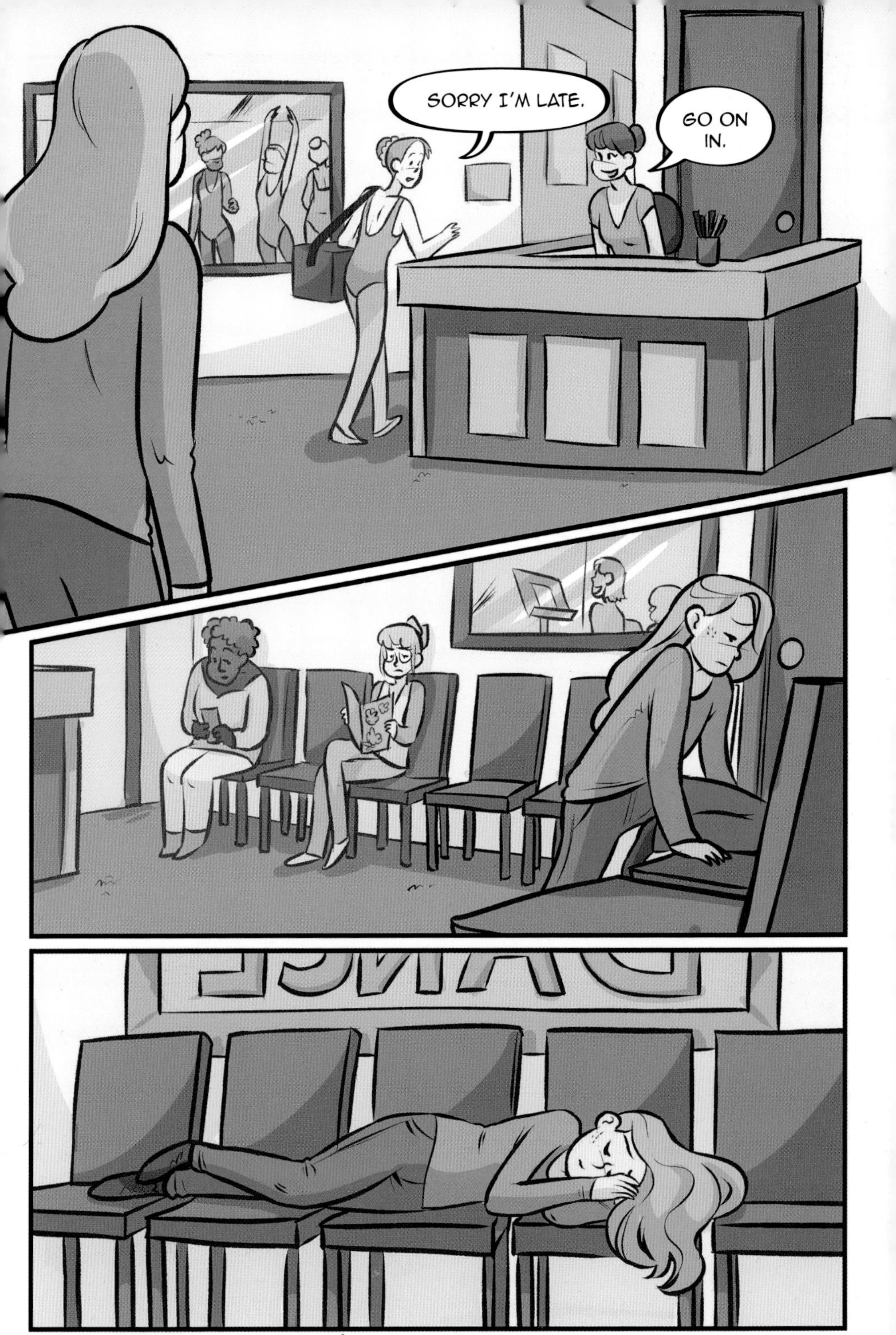
SORRY I'M LATE.
GO ON IN.

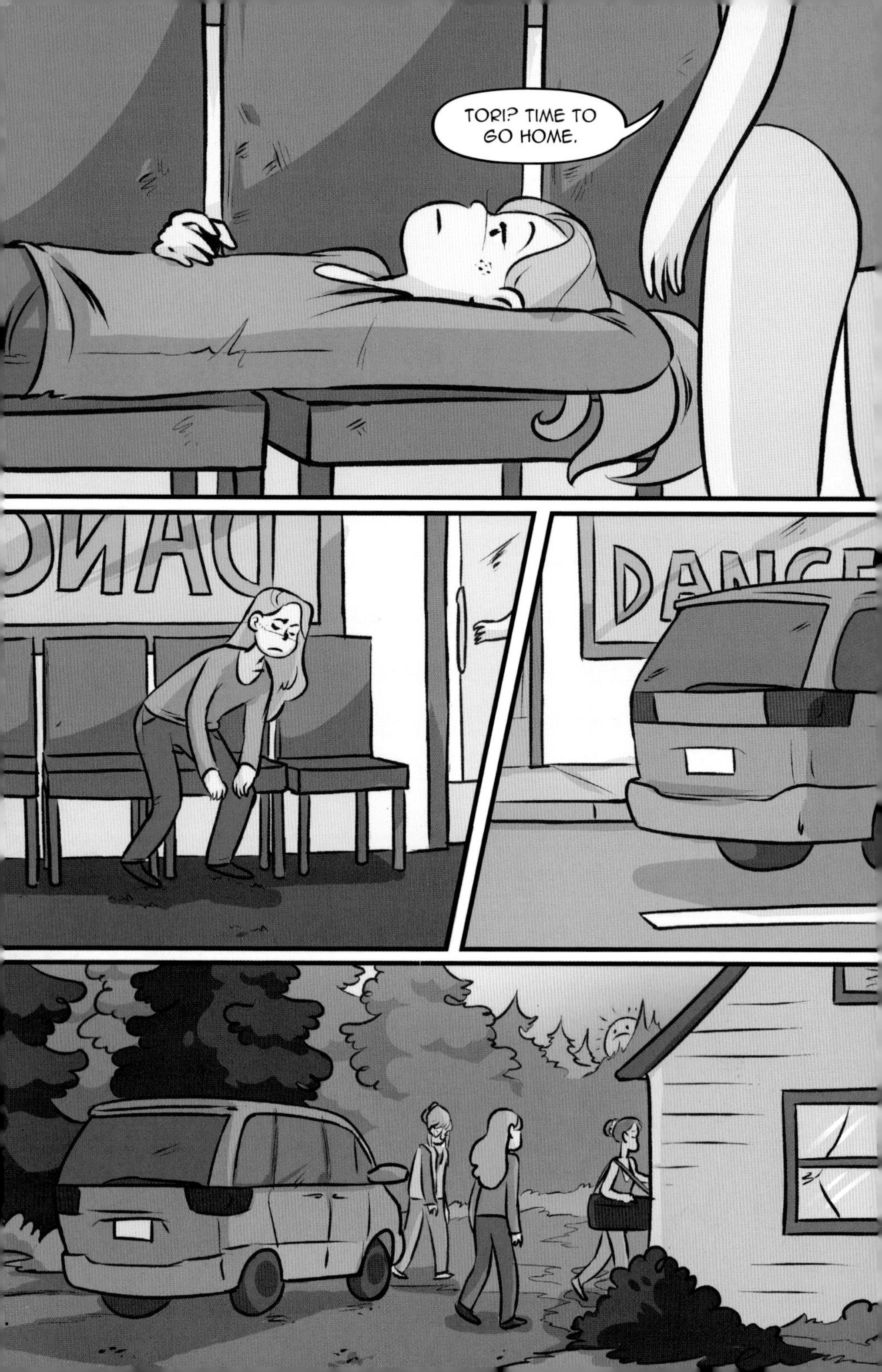
TORI? TIME TO GO HOME.

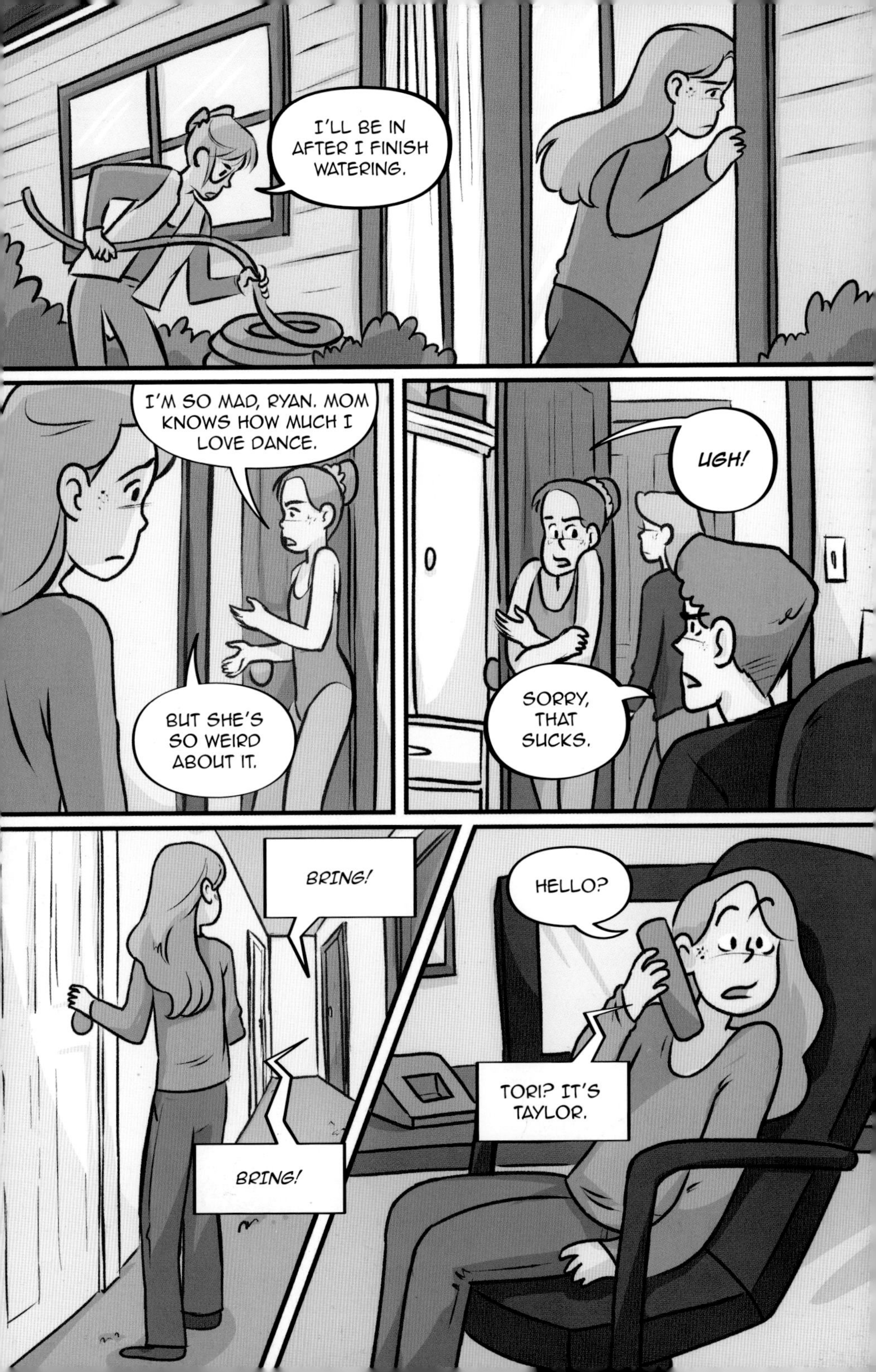
I'LL BE IN AFTER I FINISH WATERING.
I'M SO MAD, RYAN. MOM KNOWS HOW MUCH I LOVE DANCE.
BUT SHE'S SO WEIRD ABOUT IT.
UGH!
SORRY, THAT SUCKS.
BRING!
BRING!
HELLO?
TORI? IT'S TAYLOR.

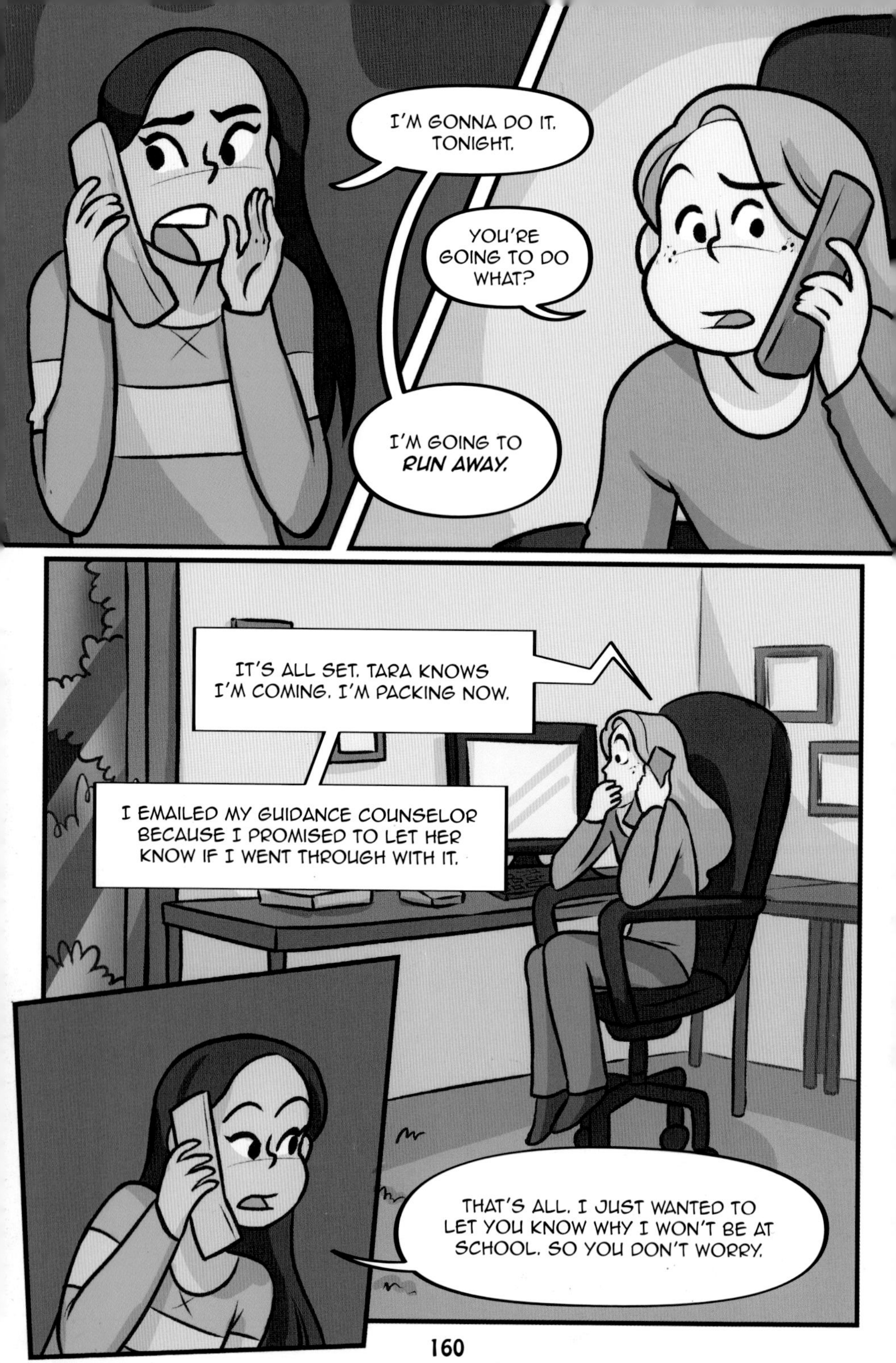
I'M GONNA DO IT. TONIGHT.
YOU'RE GOING TO DO WHAT?
I'M GOING TO *RUN AWAY.*
IT'S ALL SET. TARA KNOWS I'M COMING. I'M PACKING NOW.
I EMAILED MY GUIDANCE COUNSELOR BECAUSE I PROMISED TO LET HER KNOW IF I WENT THROUGH WITH IT.
THAT'S ALL. I JUST WANTED TO LET YOU KNOW WHY I WON'T BE AT SCHOOL. SO YOU DON'T WORRY.

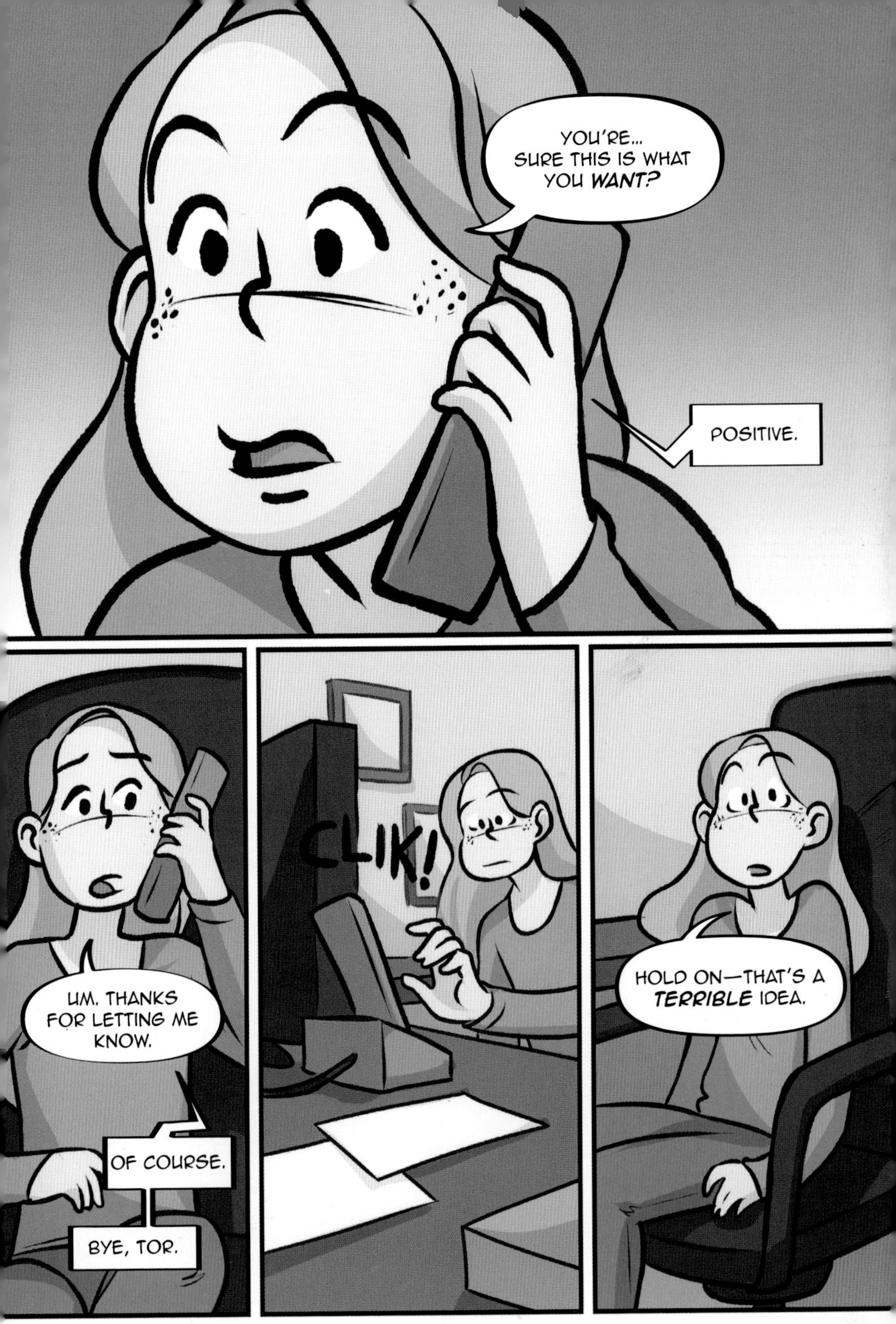
YOU'RE... SURE THIS IS WHAT YOU *WANT?*
POSITIVE.
UM. THANKS FOR LETTING ME KNOW.
OF COURSE.
BYE, TOR.
CLIK!
HOLD ON—THAT'S A *TERRIBLE* IDEA.

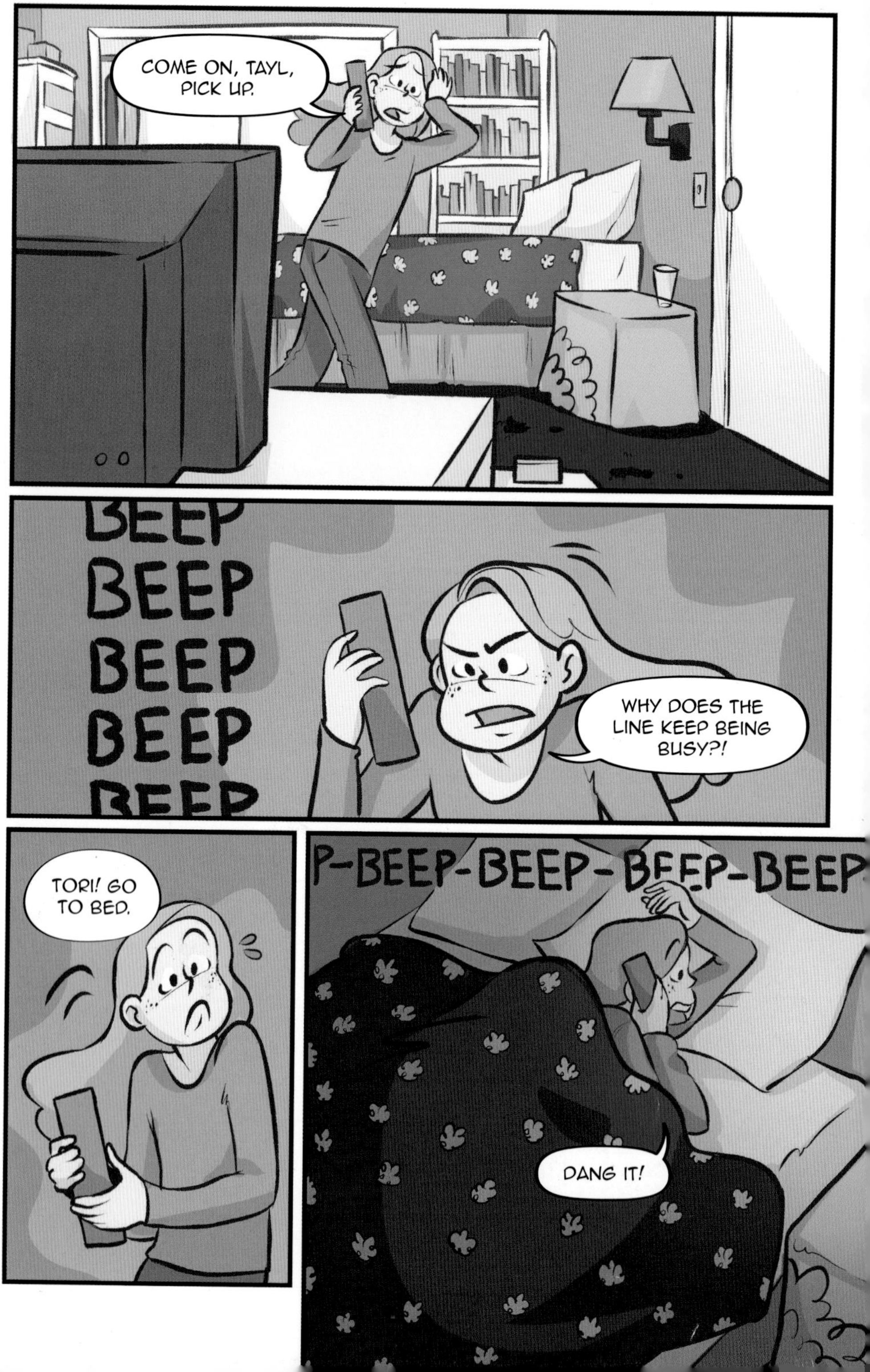
COME ON, TAYL, PICK UP.
BEEP
BEEP
BEEP
BEEP
BEEP
WHY DOES THE LINE KEEP BEING BUSY?!
TORI! GO TO BED.
P-BEEP-BEEP-BEEP-BEEP
DANG IT!

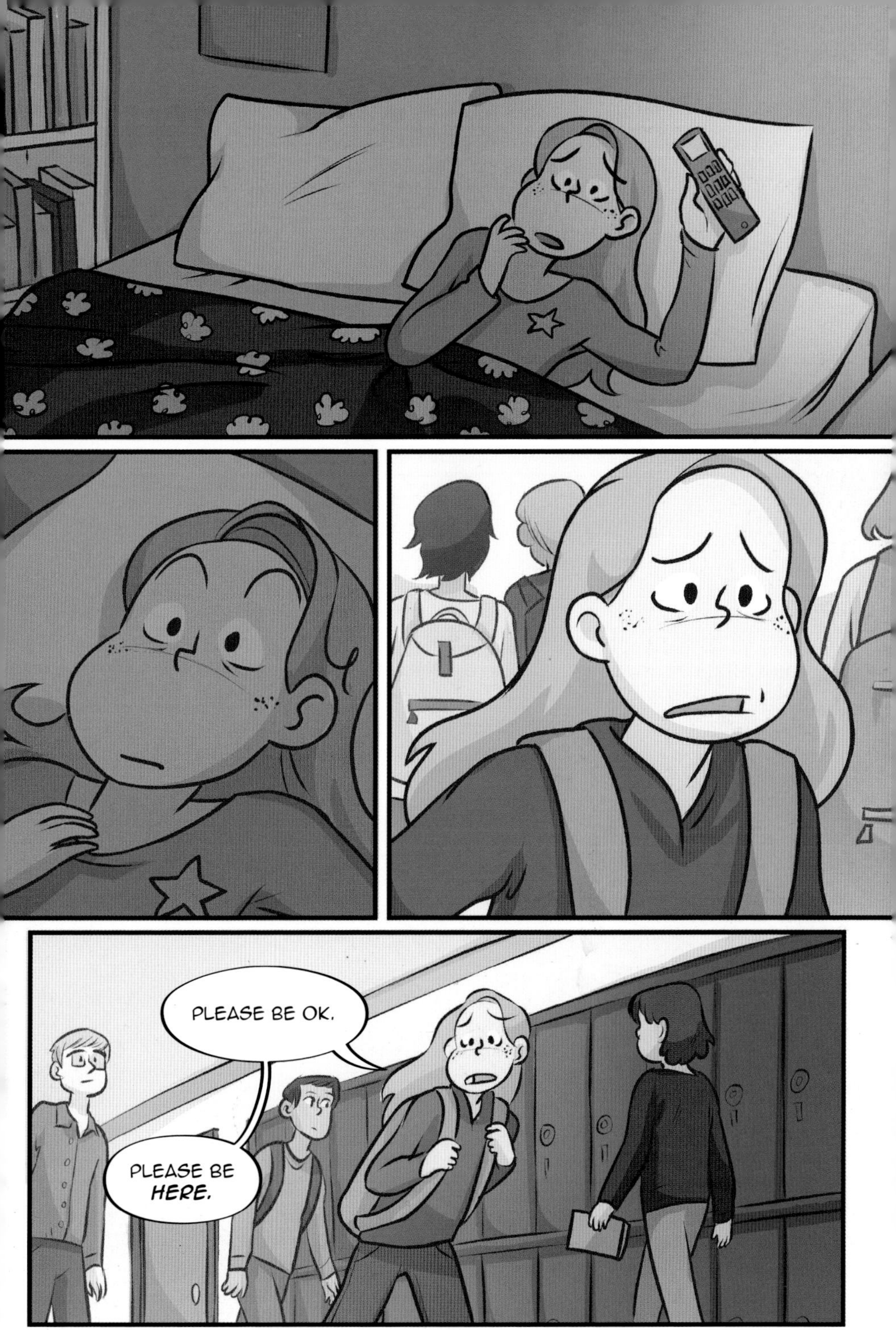
PLEASE BE OK.
PLEASE BE HERE.

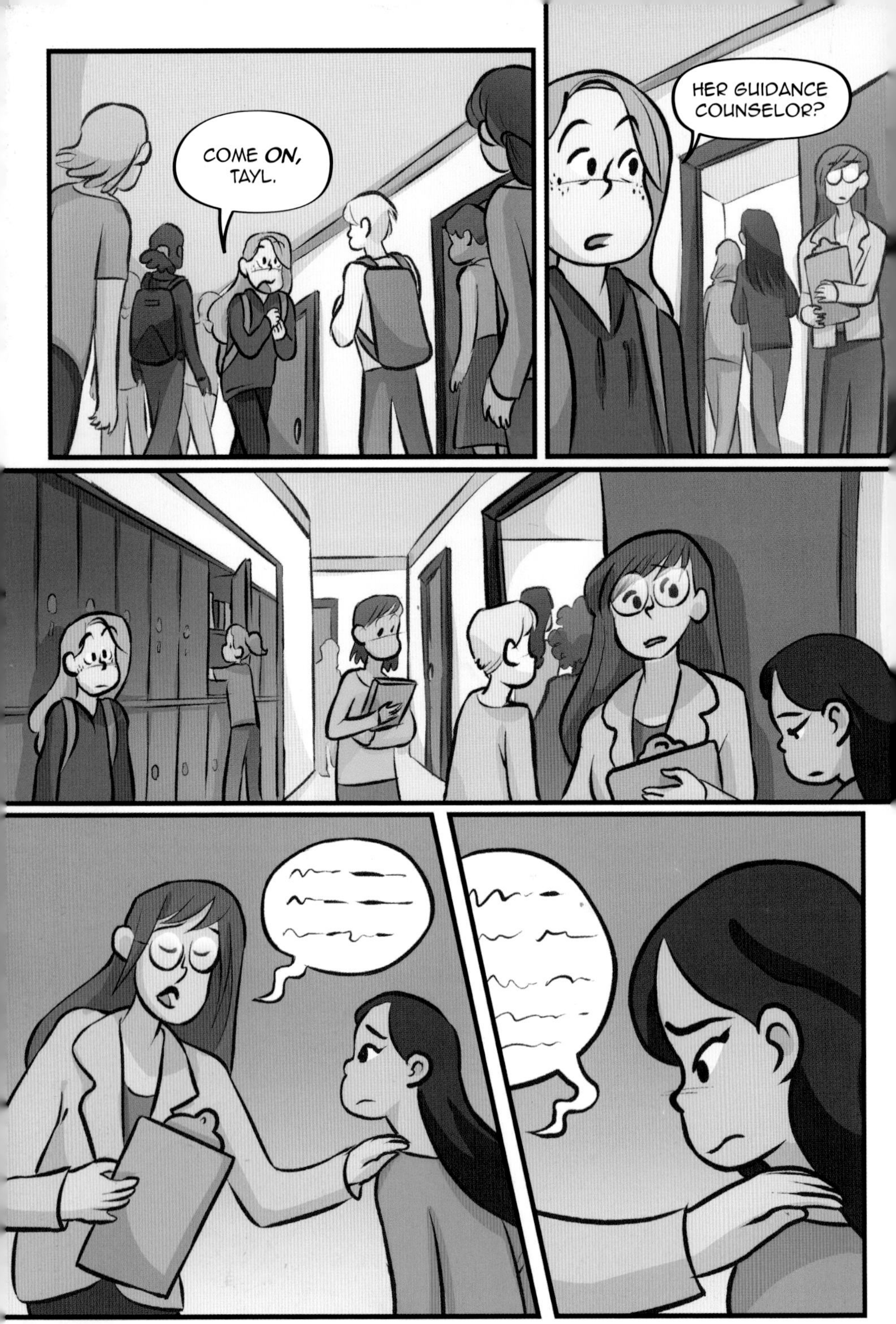
COME ON, TAYL.
HER GUIDANCE COUNSELOR?

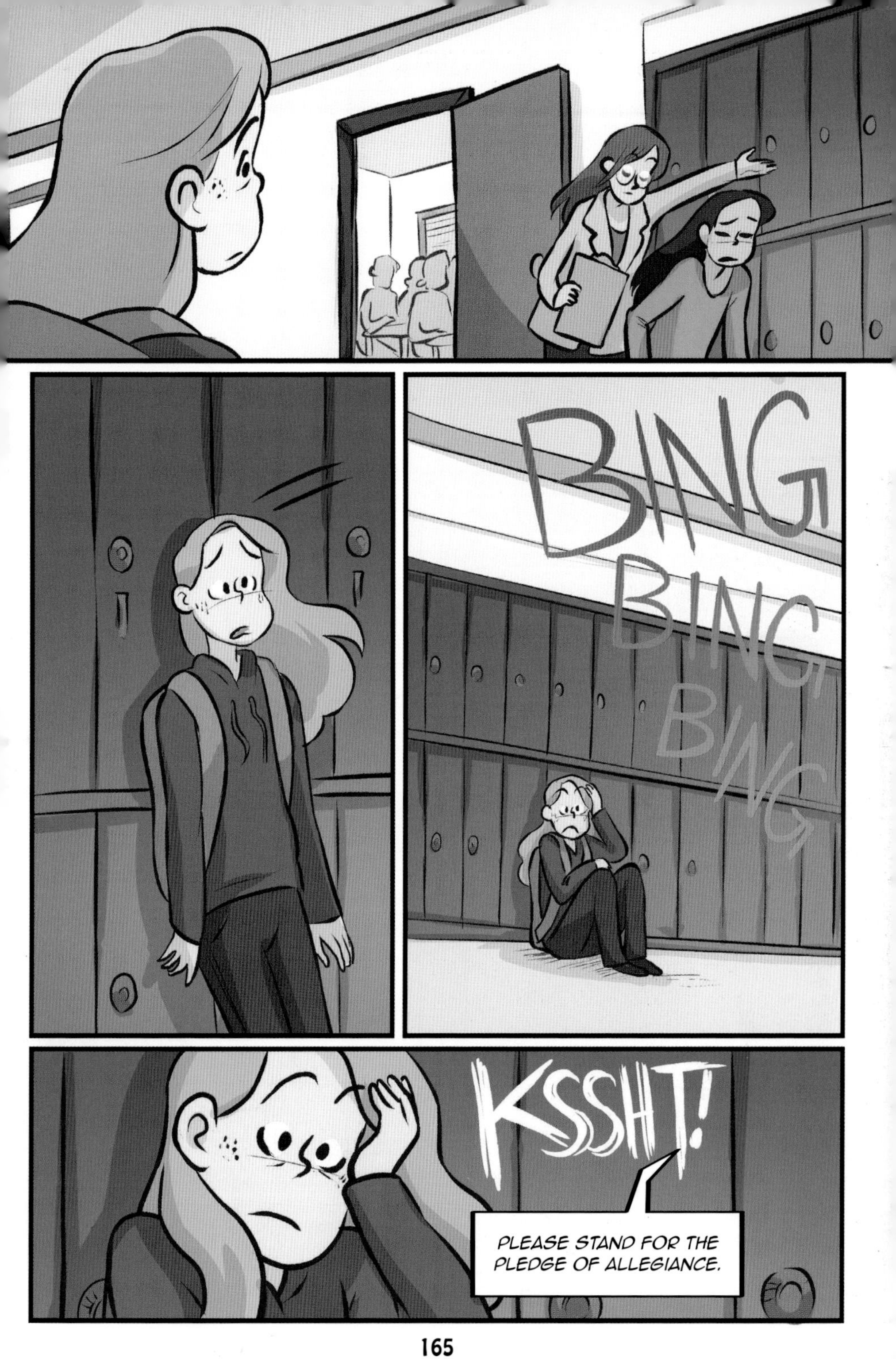
BING
BING
BING
BING
KSSHT!
PLEASE STAND FOR THE PLEDGE OF ALLEGIANCE.

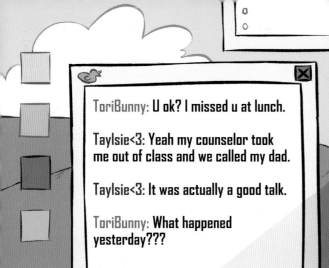

ToriBunny: U ok? I missed u at lunch.

Taylsie<3: Yeah my counselor took me out of class and we called my dad.

Taylsie<3: It was actually a good talk.

ToriBunny: What happened yesterday???

RYAN! I'M NOT DONE TALKING TO YOU.

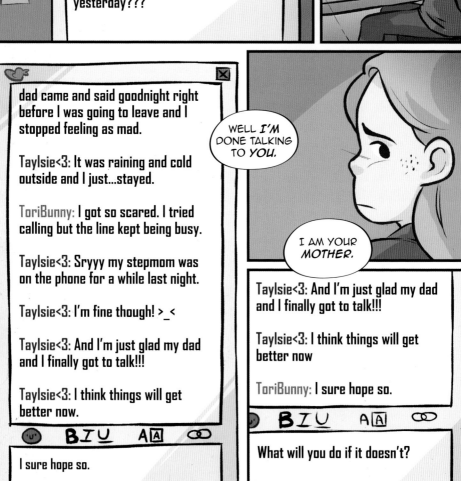

dad came and said goodnight right before I was going to leave and I stopped feeling as mad.

Taylsie<3: It was raining and cold outside and I just...stayed.

ToriBunny: I got so scared. I tried calling but the line kept being busy.

Taylsie<3: Sryyy my stepmom was on the phone for a while last night.

Taylsie<3: I'm fine though! >_<

Taylsie<3: And I'm just glad my dad and I finally got to talk!!!

Taylsie<3: I think things will get better now.

B *I* U    A A    ∞

I sure hope so.

WELL *I'M* DONE TALKING TO *YOU.*

I AM YOUR *MOTHER.*

Taylsie<3: And I'm just glad my dad and I finally got to talk!!!

Taylsie<3: I think things will get better now

ToriBunny: I sure hope so.

B *I* U    A A    ∞

What will you do if it doesn't?

166

I DON'T CARE.

"I CAN SEND YOU BACK,"
SAID THE WITCH. TALIA'S
HEART LEAPED WITH JOY.

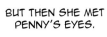
BUT THEN SHE MET
PENNY'S EYES.

A FEW MONTHS AGO, GOING HOME
HAD BEEN ALL SHE WANTED.

EVEN IF THE WITCH
COULD SEND HER BACK...
PENNY WAS FAMILY NOW.

HOW DID YOU
FIND US WAY OUT IN
THE WOODS?

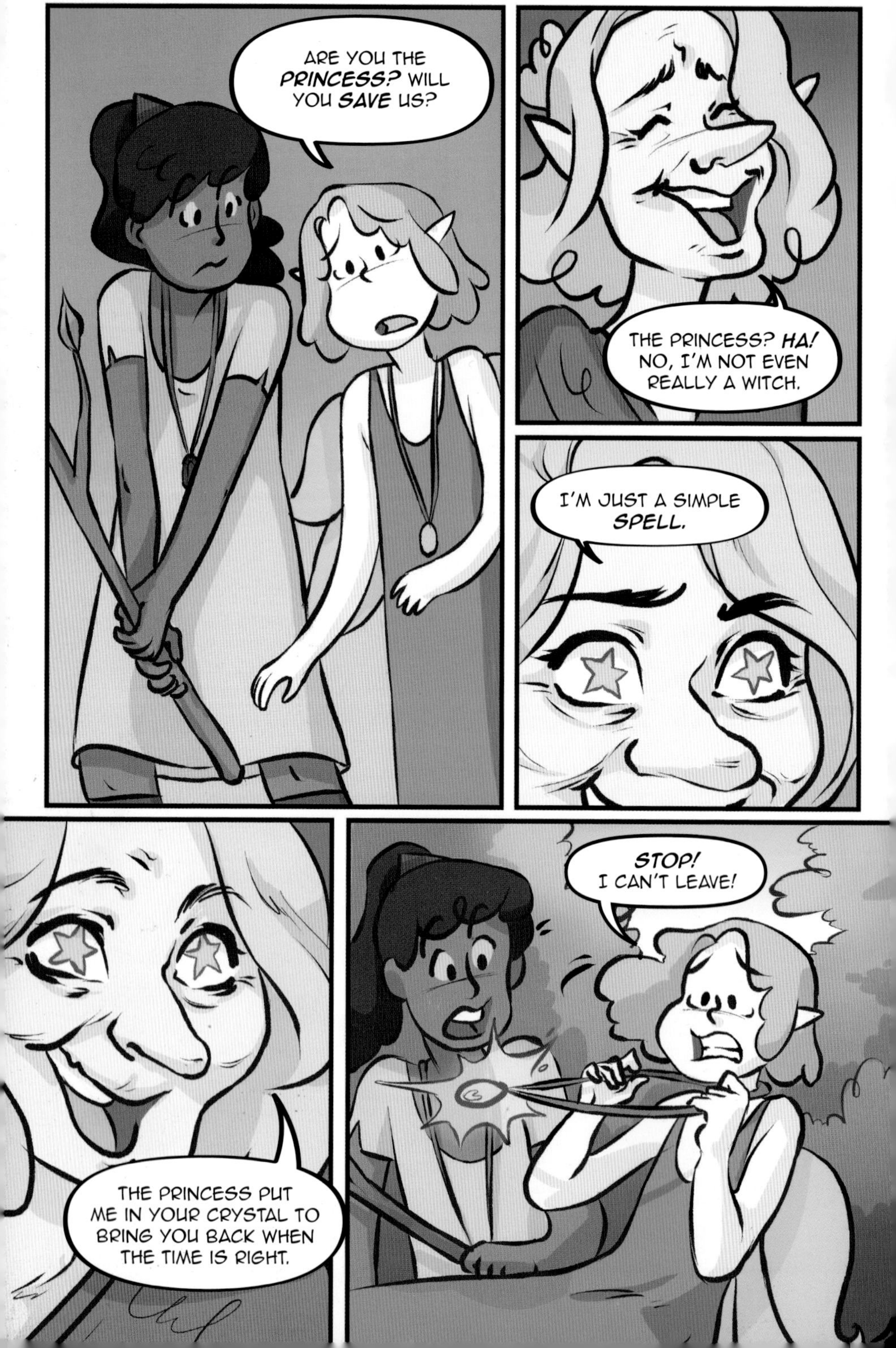
ARE YOU THE PRINCESS? WILL YOU SAVE US?
THE PRINCESS? HA! NO, I'M NOT EVEN REALLY A WITCH.
I'M JUST A SIMPLE SPELL.
THE PRINCESS PUT ME IN YOUR CRYSTAL TO BRING YOU BACK WHEN THE TIME IS RIGHT.
STOP! I CAN'T LEAVE!

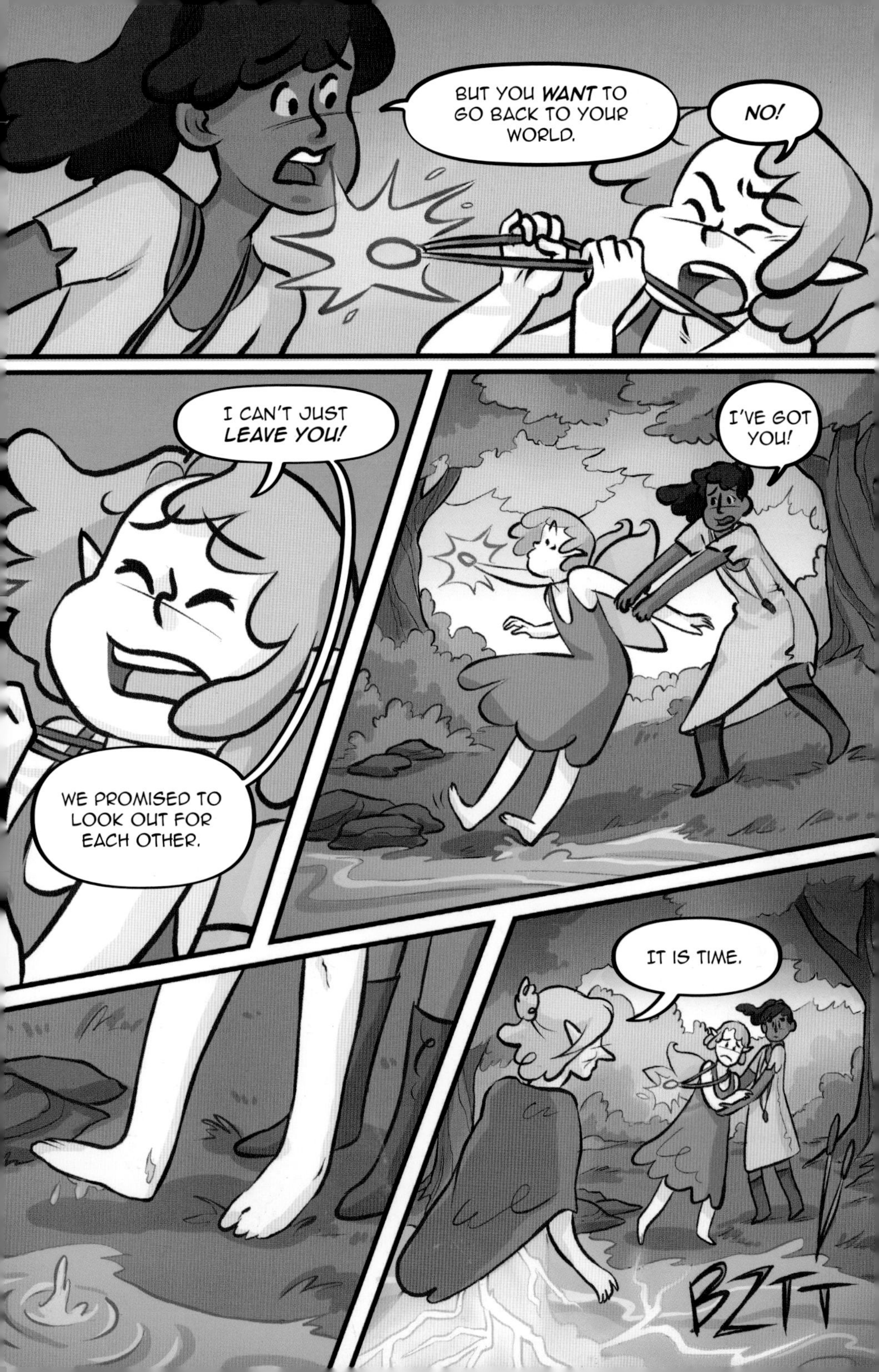
BUT YOU WANT TO GO BACK TO YOUR WORLD.
NO!
I CAN'T JUST LEAVE YOU!
WE PROMISED TO LOOK OUT FOR EACH OTHER.
I'VE GOT YOU!
IT IS TIME.
BZTT

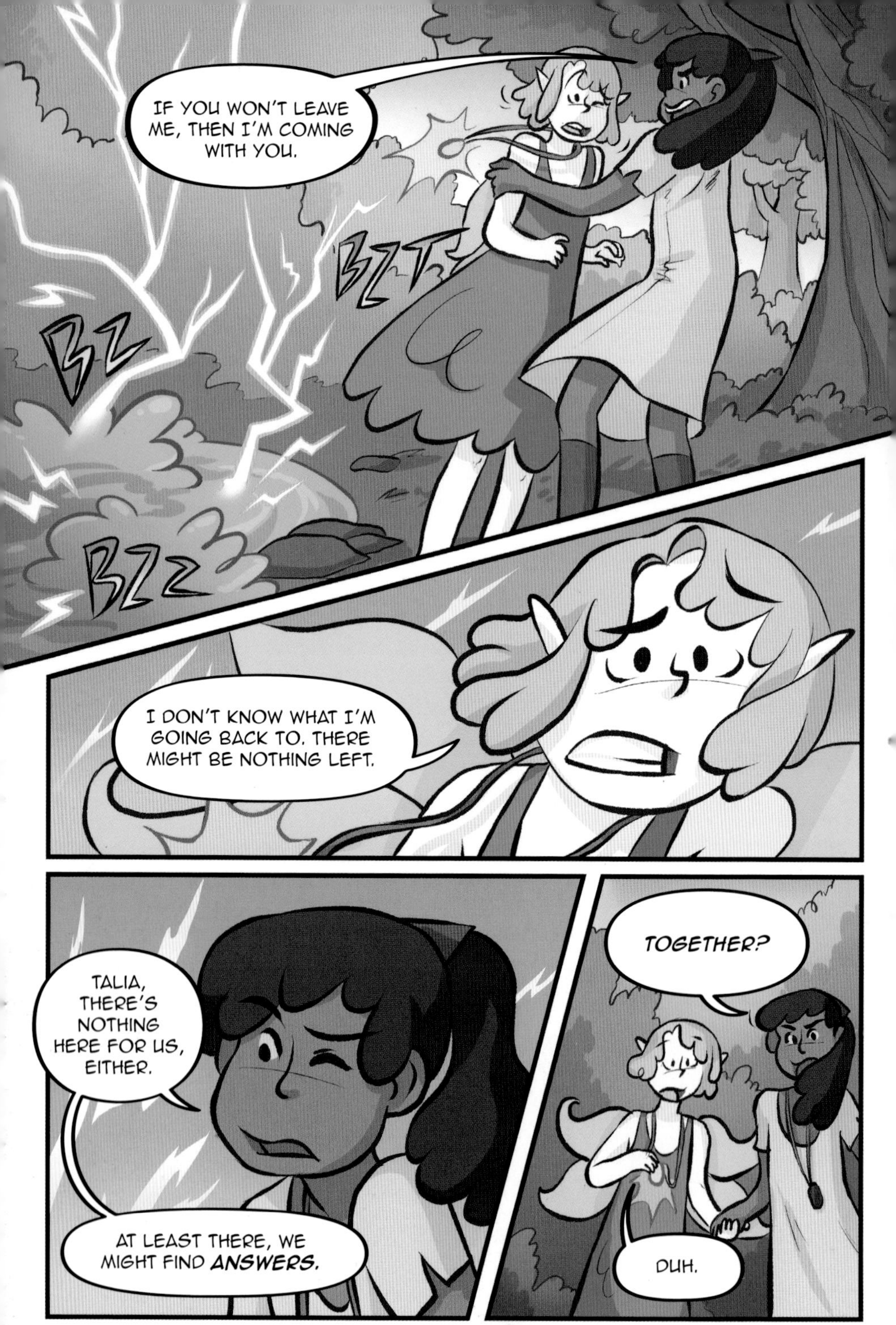
IF YOU WON'T LEAVE ME, THEN I'M COMING WITH YOU.
BZT
BZ
BZZ
I DON'T KNOW WHAT I'M GOING BACK TO. THERE MIGHT BE NOTHING LEFT.
TALIA, THERE'S NOTHING HERE FOR US, EITHER.
AT LEAST THERE, WE MIGHT FIND **ANSWERS**.
*TOGETHER?*
DUH.

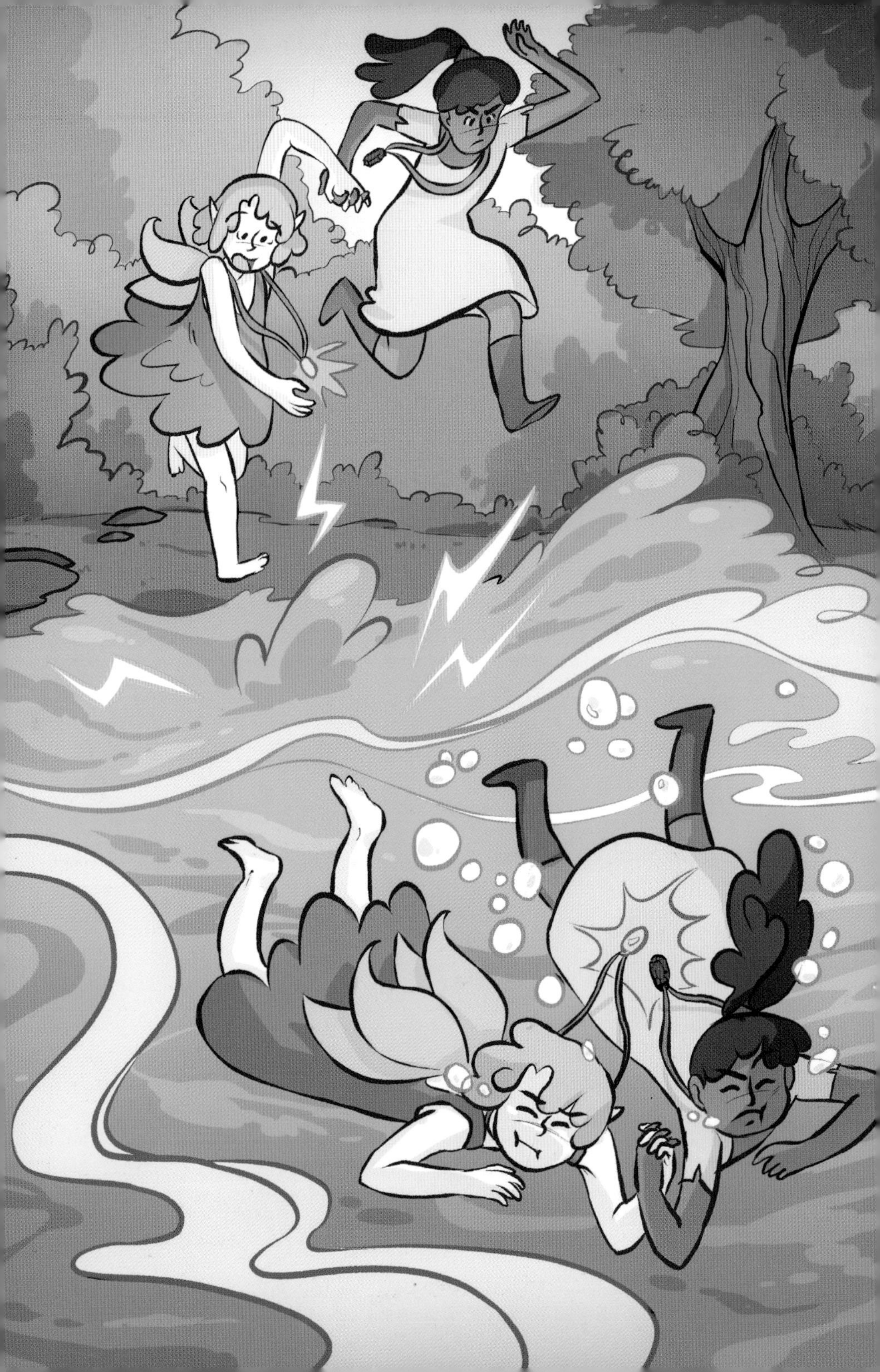

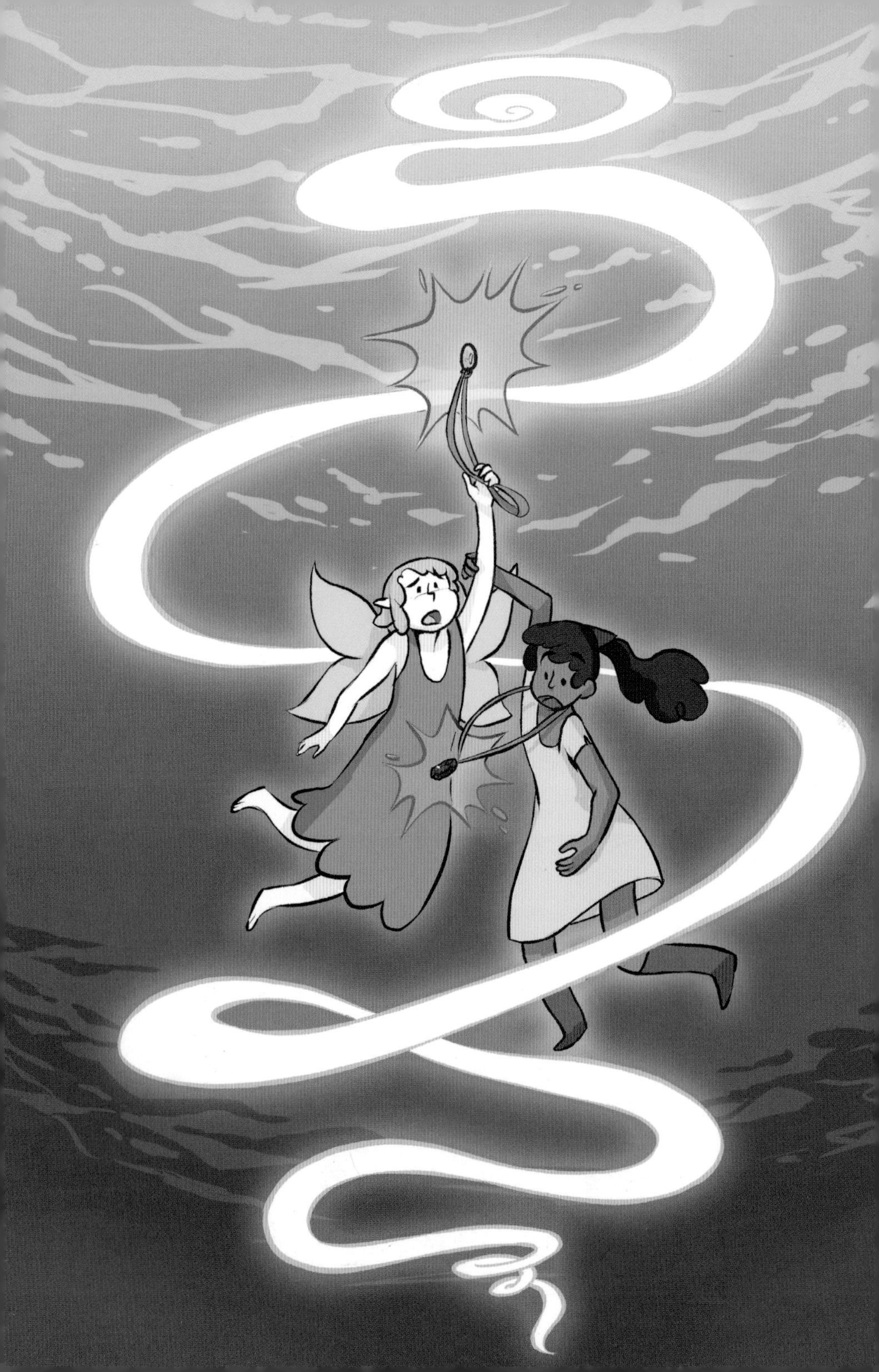

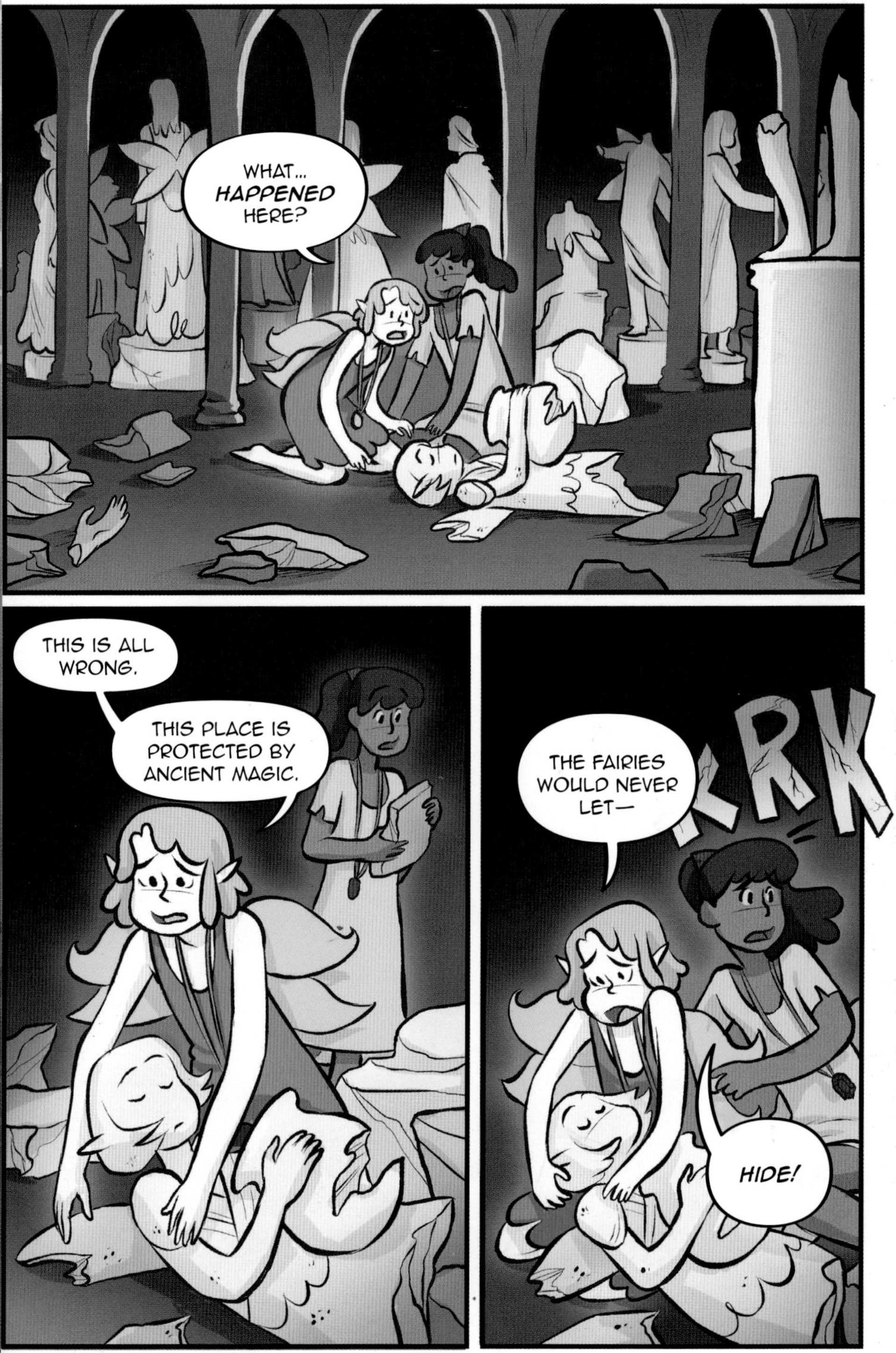
WHAT... *HAPPENED* HERE?
THIS IS ALL WRONG.
THIS PLACE IS PROTECTED BY ANCIENT MAGIC.
THE FAIRIES WOULD NEVER LET—
KRK
*HIDE!*

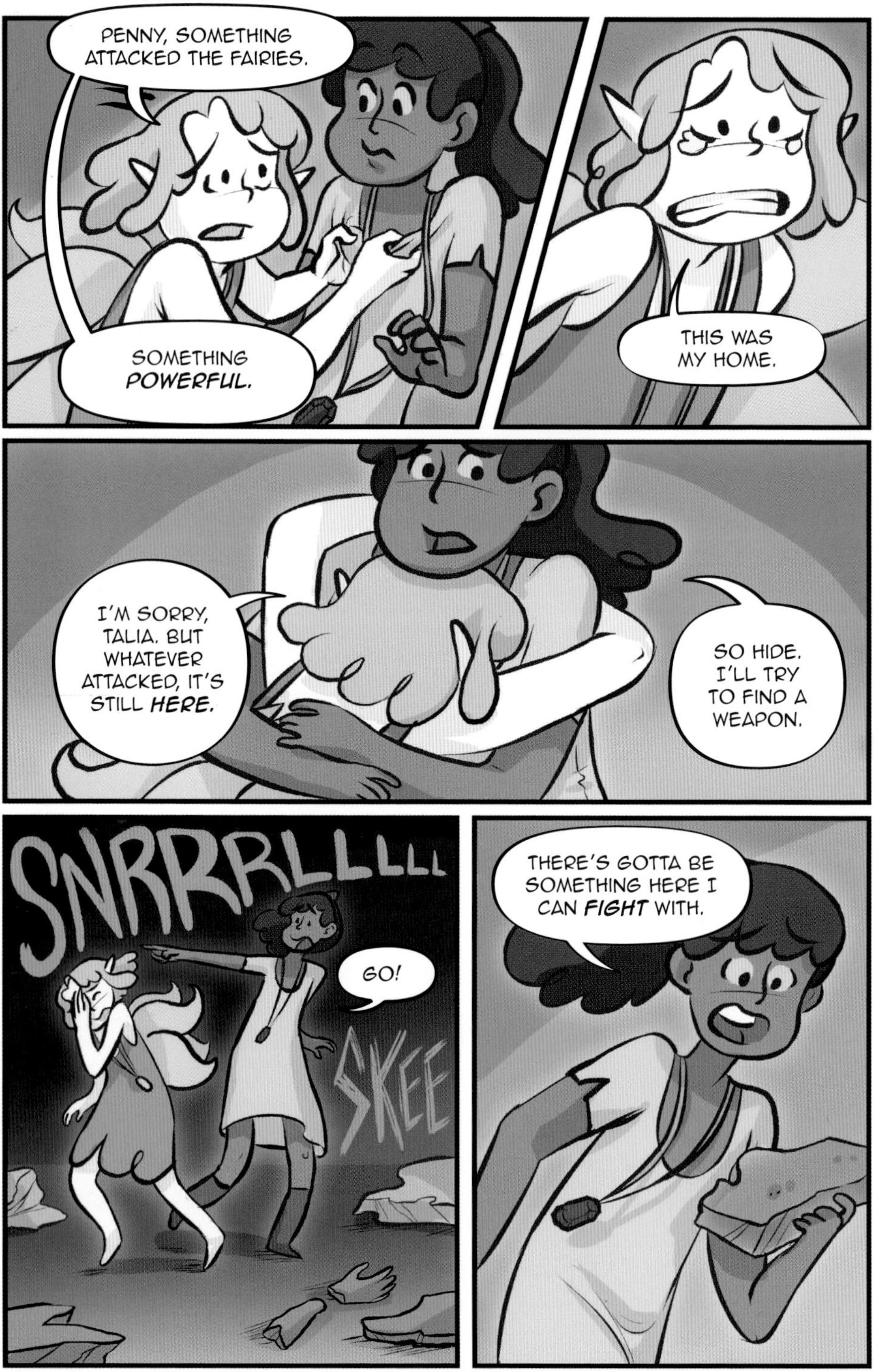
PENNY, SOMETHING ATTACKED THE FAIRIES.
SOMETHING POWERFUL.
THIS WAS MY HOME.
I'M SORRY, TALIA. BUT WHATEVER ATTACKED, IT'S STILL HERE.
SO HIDE. I'LL TRY TO FIND A WEAPON.
SNRRRLLLLL
GO!
SKEE
THERE'S GOTTA BE SOMETHING HERE I CAN FIGHT WITH.

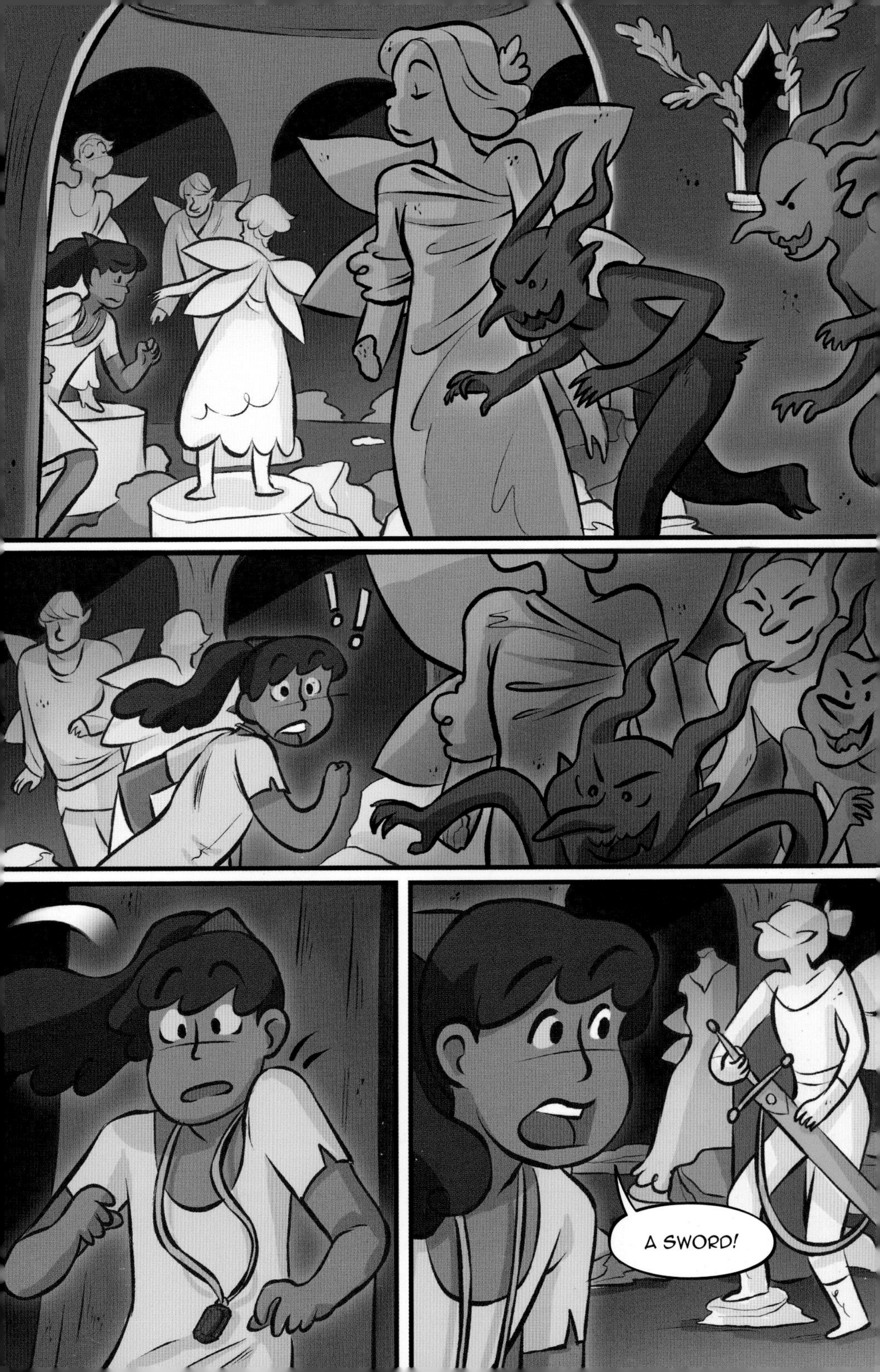

A SWORD!

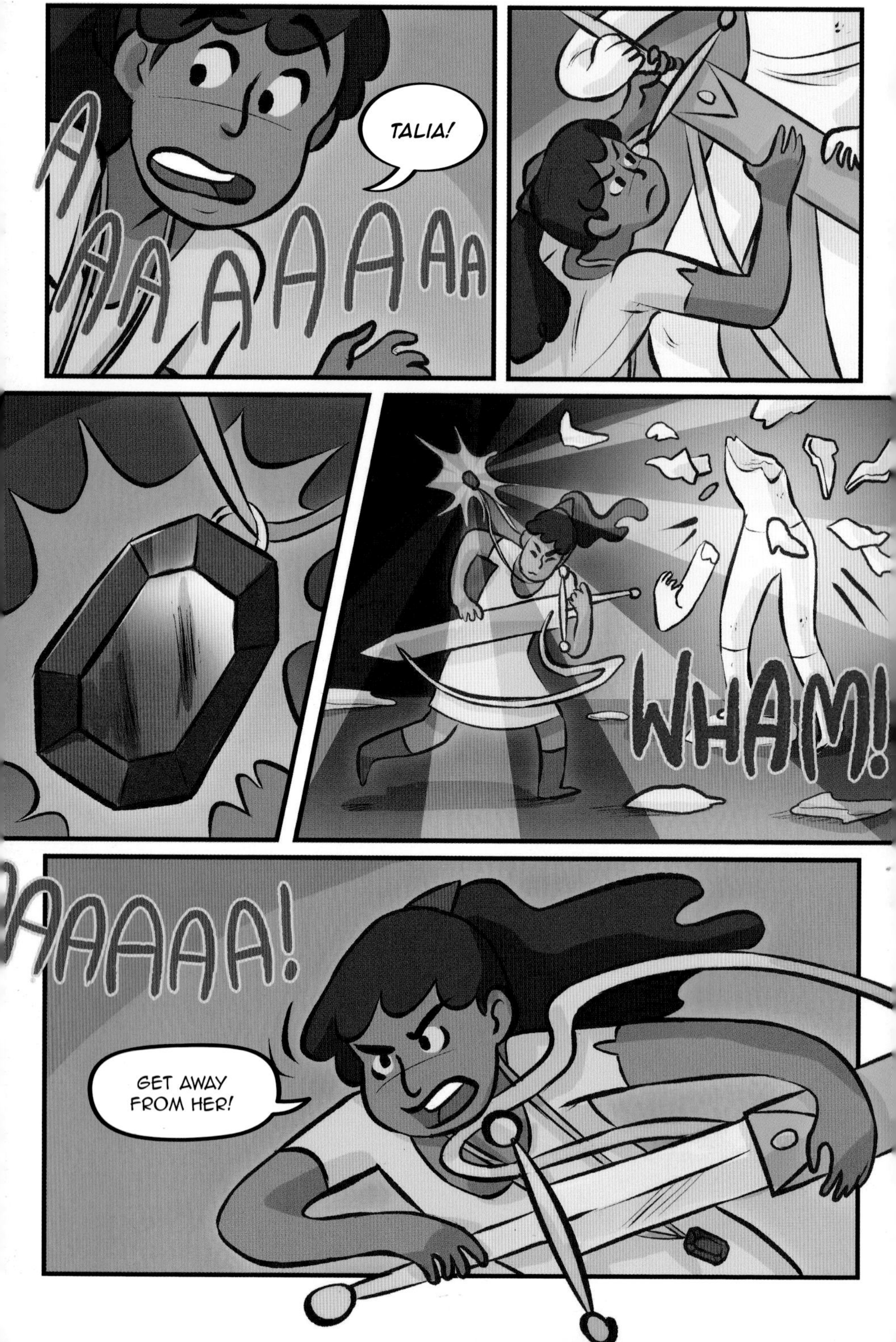
AAAAAAAAAA
TALIA!
WHAM!
AAAAAA!
GET AWAY FROM HER!

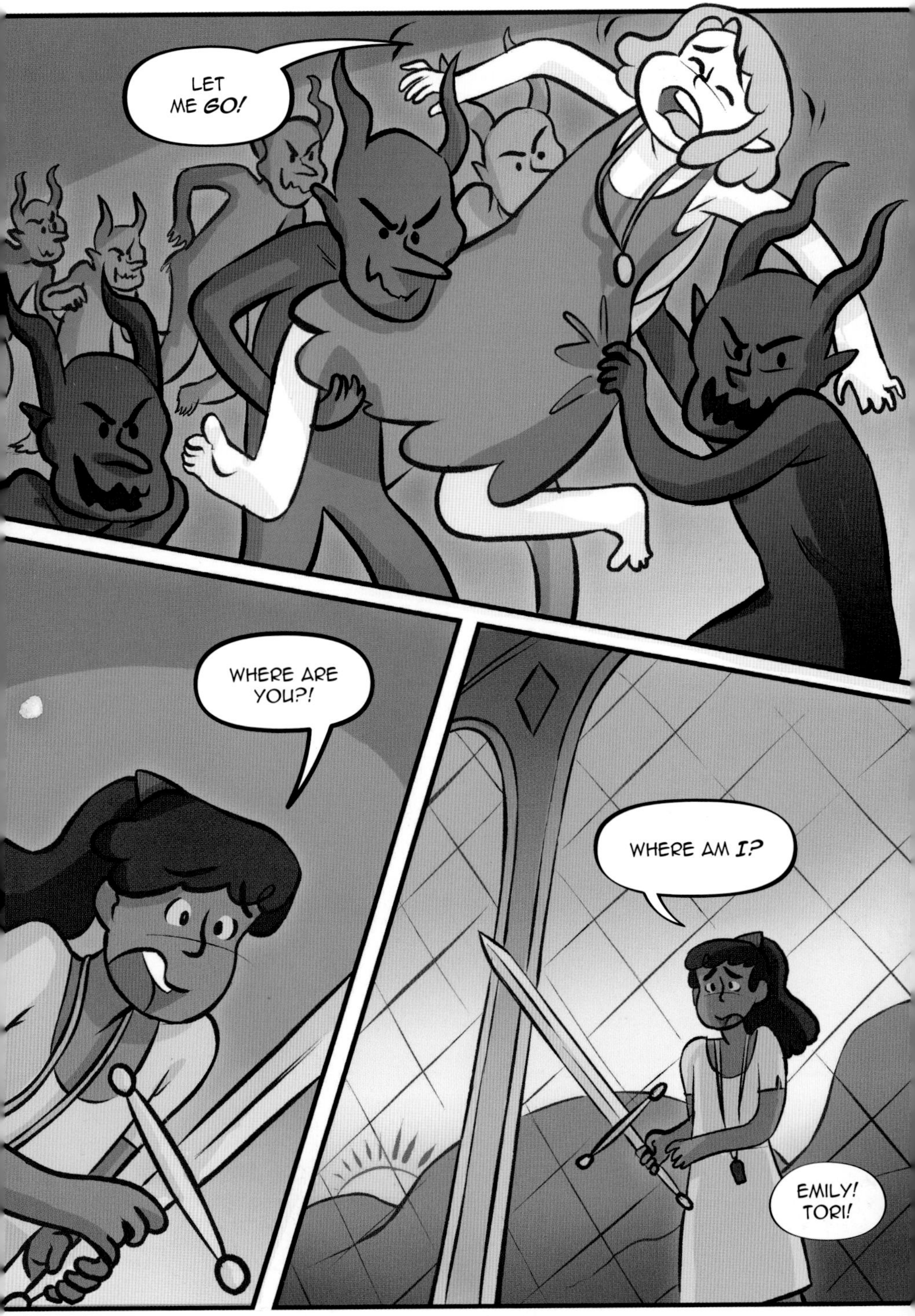
LET ME GO!
WHERE ARE YOU?!
WHERE AM I?
EMILY! TORI!

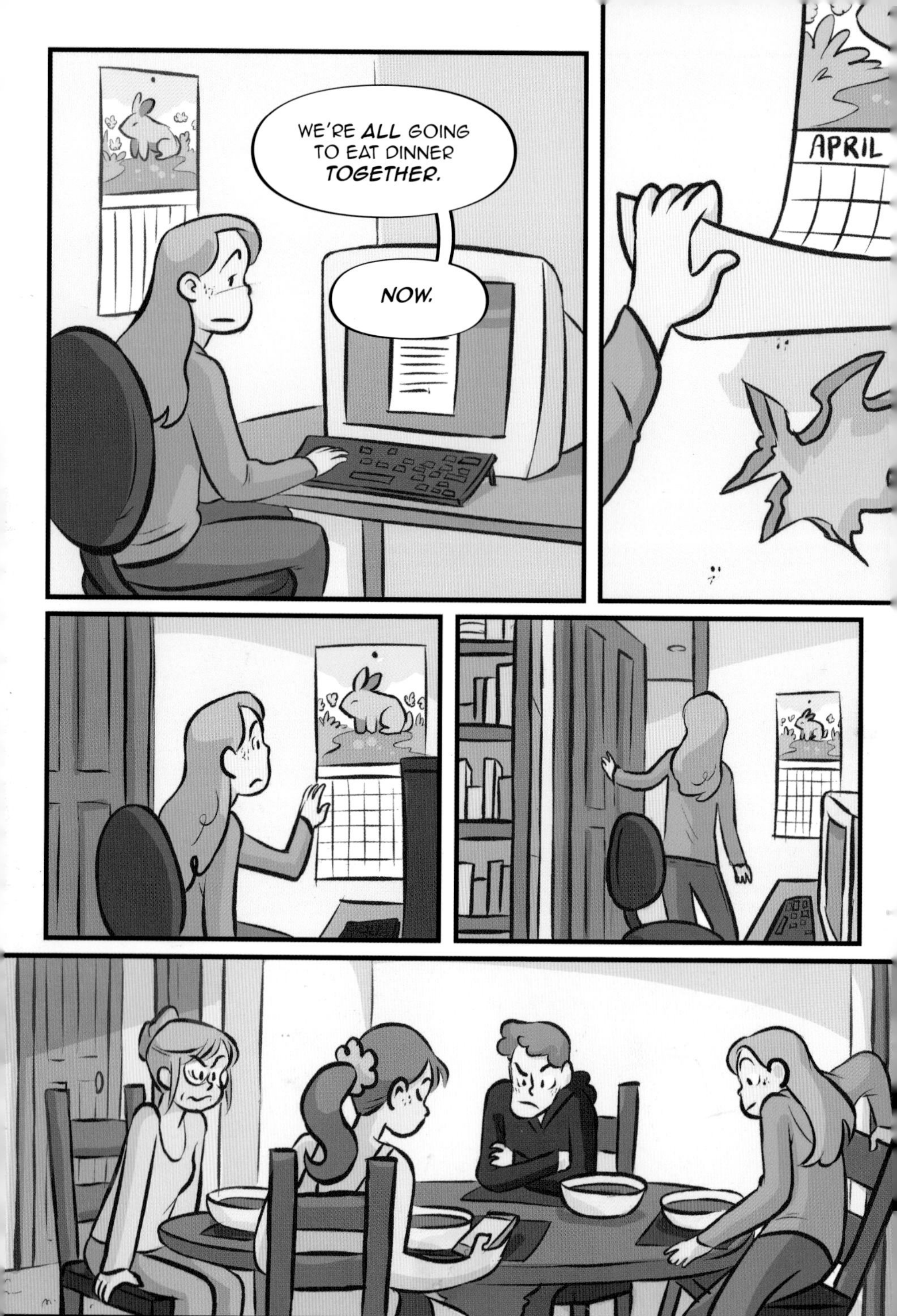
WE'RE ALL GOING TO EAT DINNER TOGETHER.
NOW.
APRIL

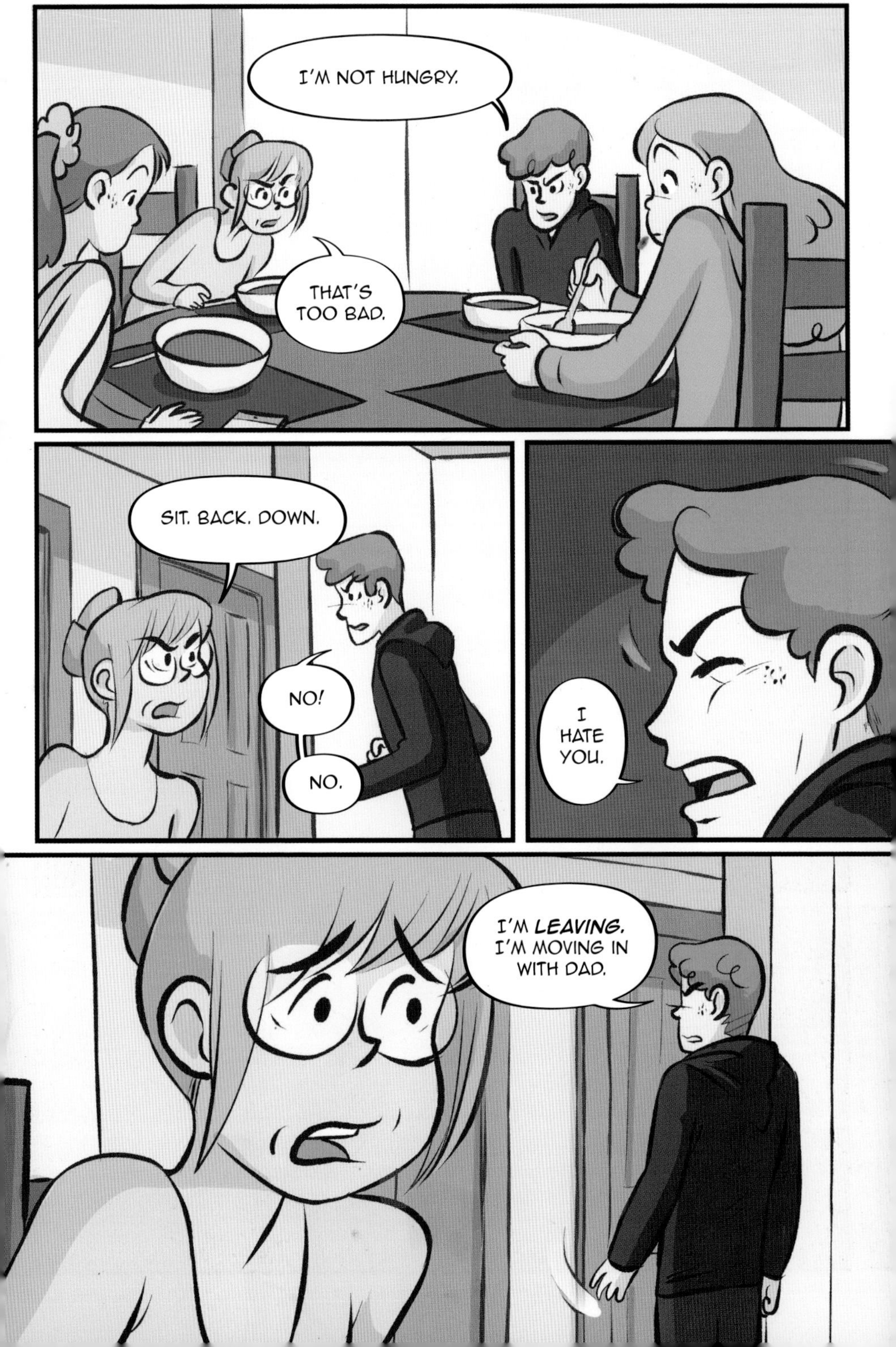
I'M NOT HUNGRY.
THAT'S TOO BAD.
SIT. BACK. DOWN.
NO!
NO.
I HATE YOU.
I'M *LEAVING.* I'M MOVING IN WITH DAD.

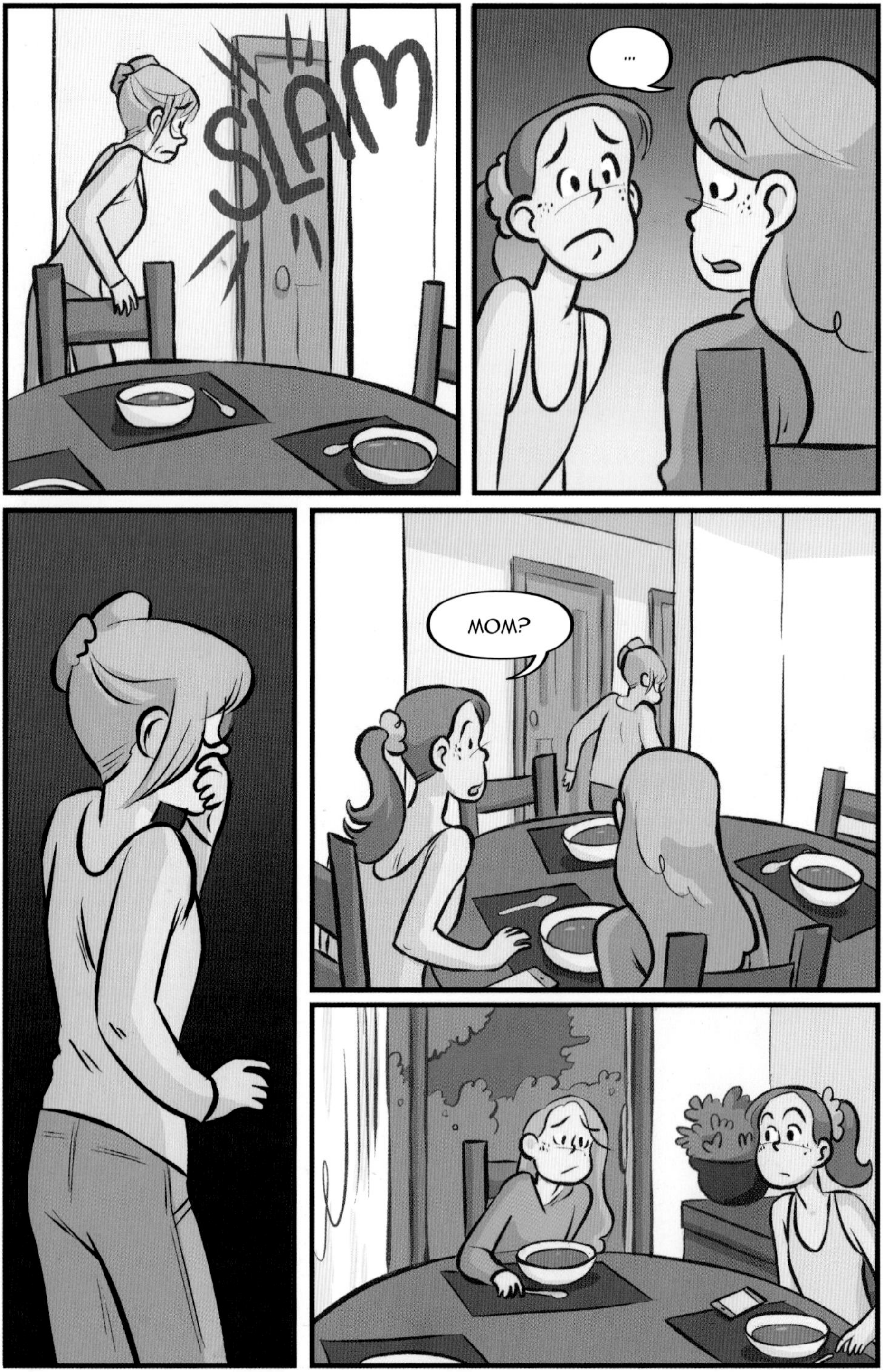
SLAM
...
MOM?

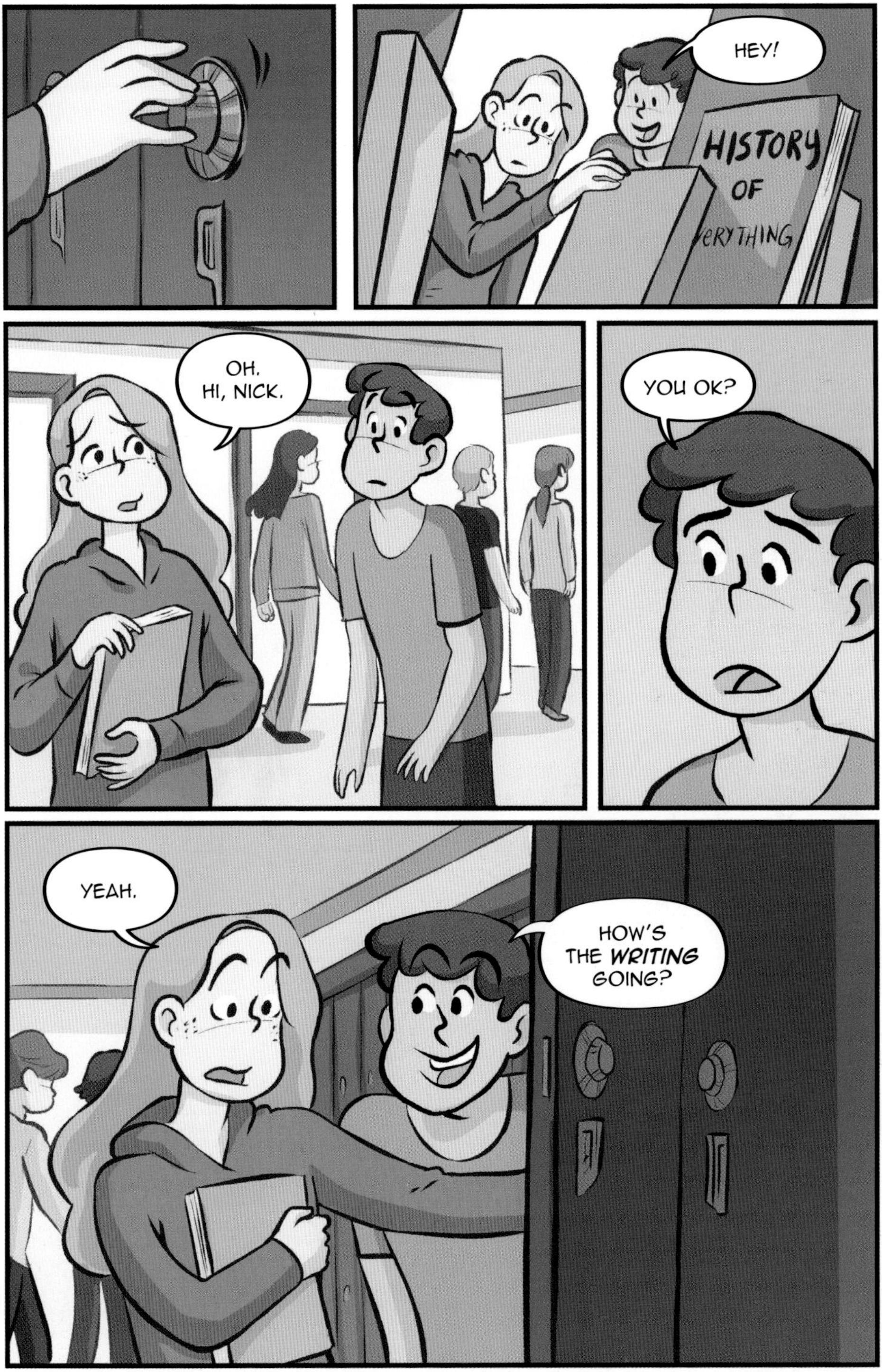
HEY!
HISTORY OF ERYTHING
OH. HI, NICK.
YOU OK?
YEAH.
HOW'S THE WRITING GOING?

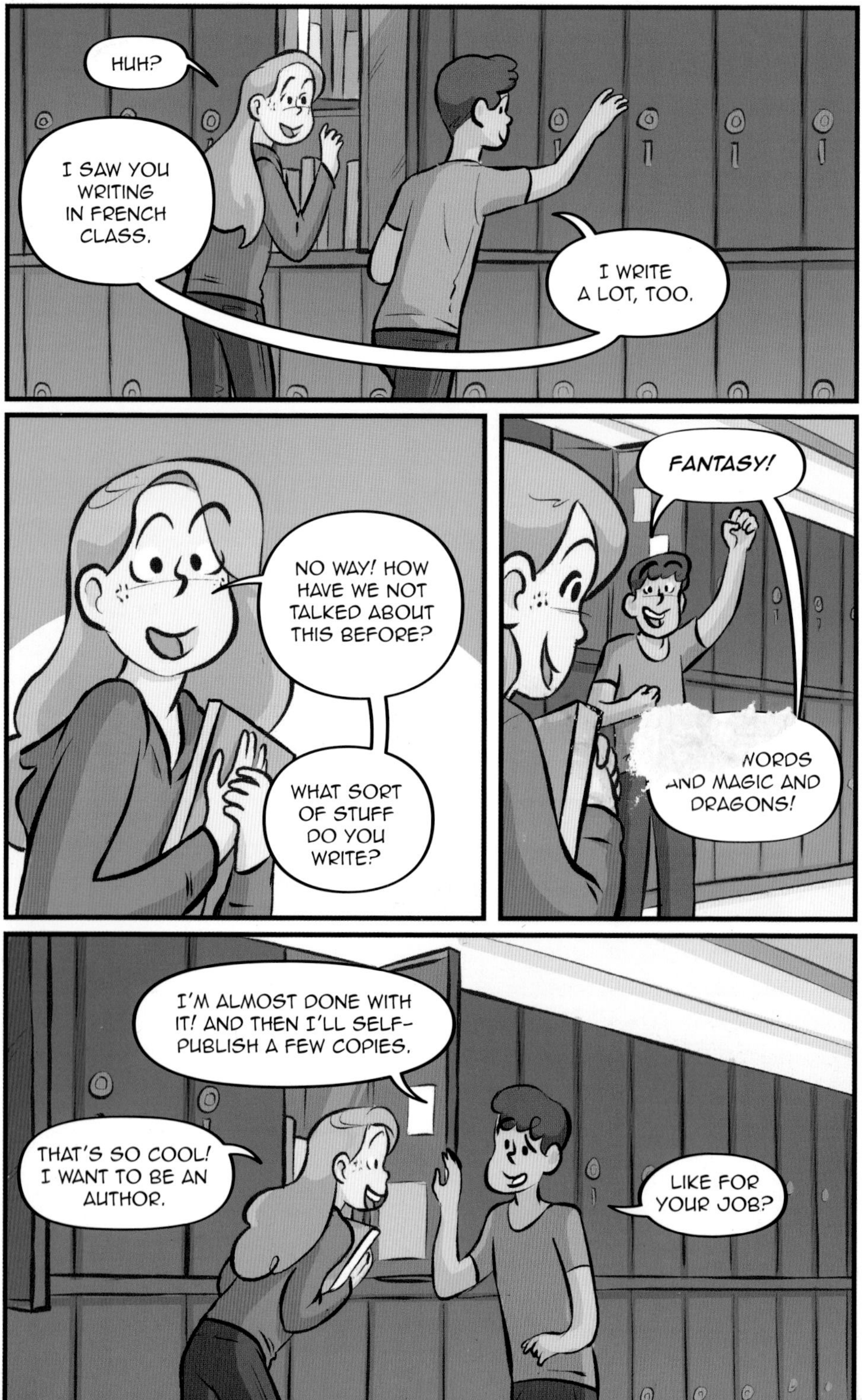
HUH?
I SAW YOU WRITING IN FRENCH CLASS.
I WRITE A LOT, TOO.
NO WAY! HOW HAVE WE NOT TALKED ABOUT THIS BEFORE?
WHAT SORT OF STUFF DO YOU WRITE?
FANTASY!
NORDS AND MAGIC AND DRAGONS!
I'M ALMOST DONE WITH IT! AND THEN I'LL SELF-PUBLISH A FEW COPIES.
THAT'S SO COOL! I WANT TO BE AN AUTHOR.
LIKE FOR YOUR JOB?

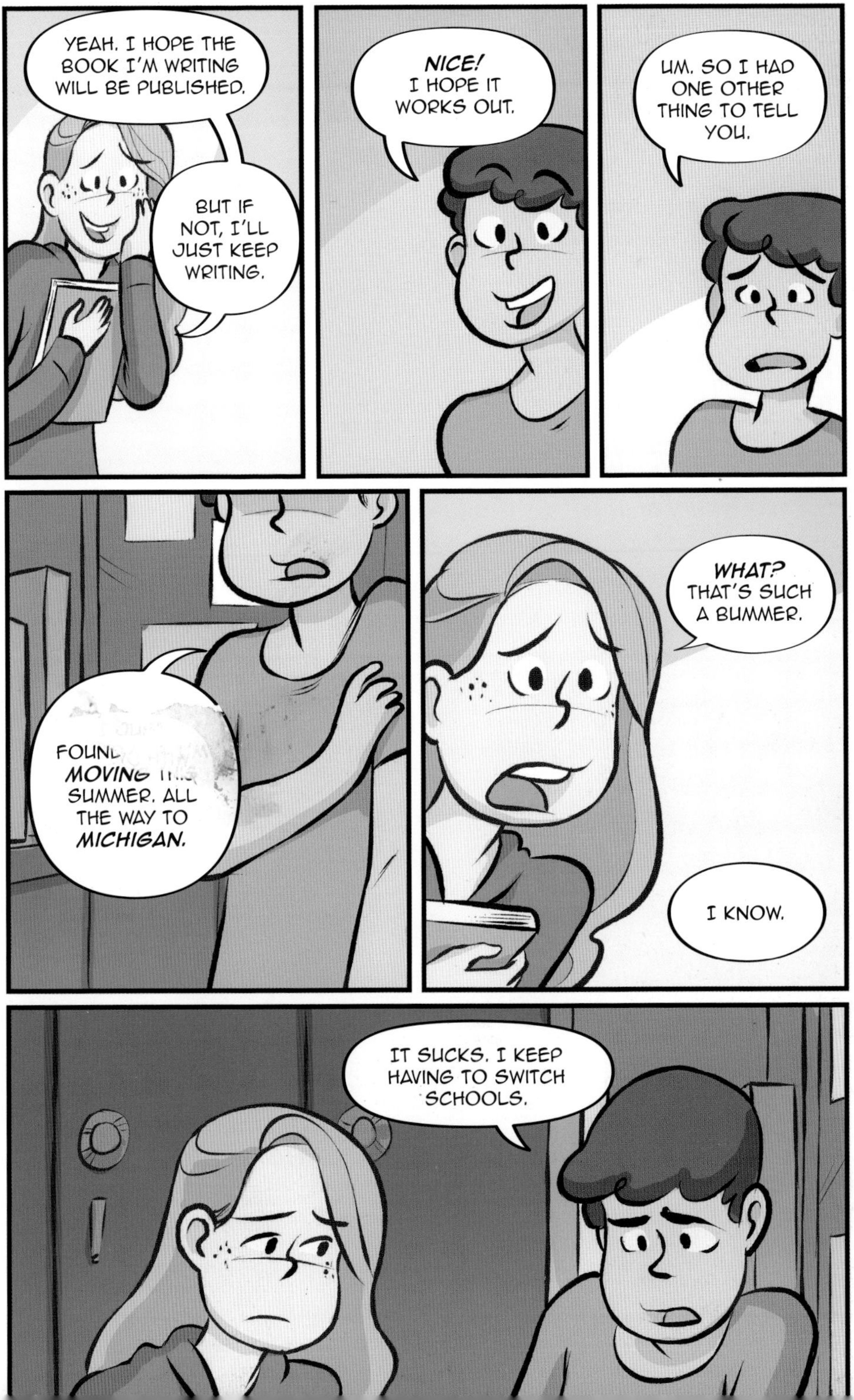
YEAH. I HOPE THE BOOK I'M WRITING WILL BE PUBLISHED.
BUT IF NOT, I'LL JUST KEEP WRITING.
*NICE!* I HOPE IT WORKS OUT.
UM. SO I HAD ONE OTHER THING TO TELL YOU.
FOUND *MOVING* SUMMER. ALL THE WAY TO *MICHIGAN.*
*WHAT?* THAT'S SUCH A BUMMER.
I KNOW.
IT SUCKS. I KEEP HAVING TO SWITCH SCHOOLS.

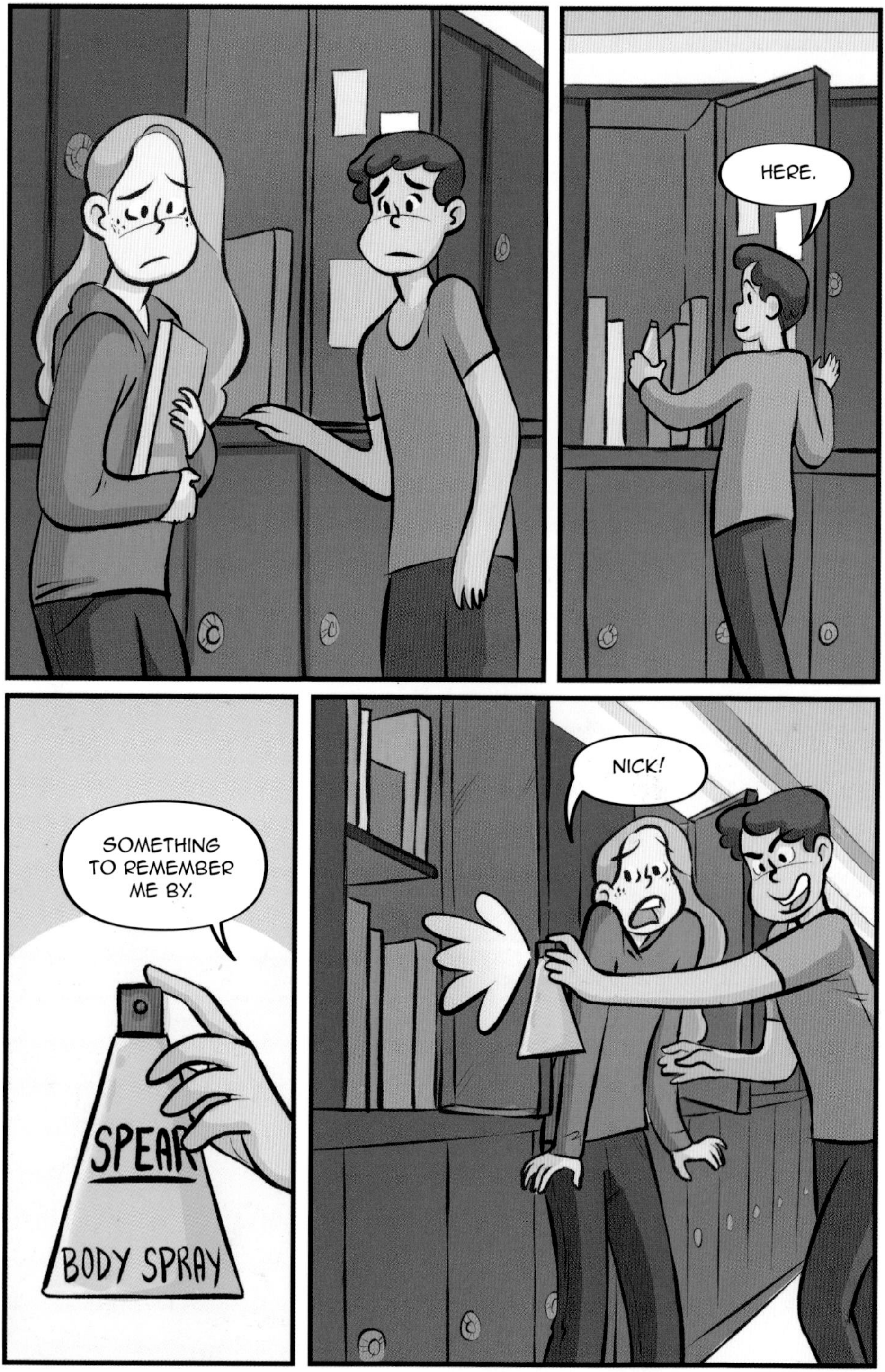
HERE.
SOMETHING TO REMEMBER ME BY.
SPEAR
BODY SPRAY
NICK!

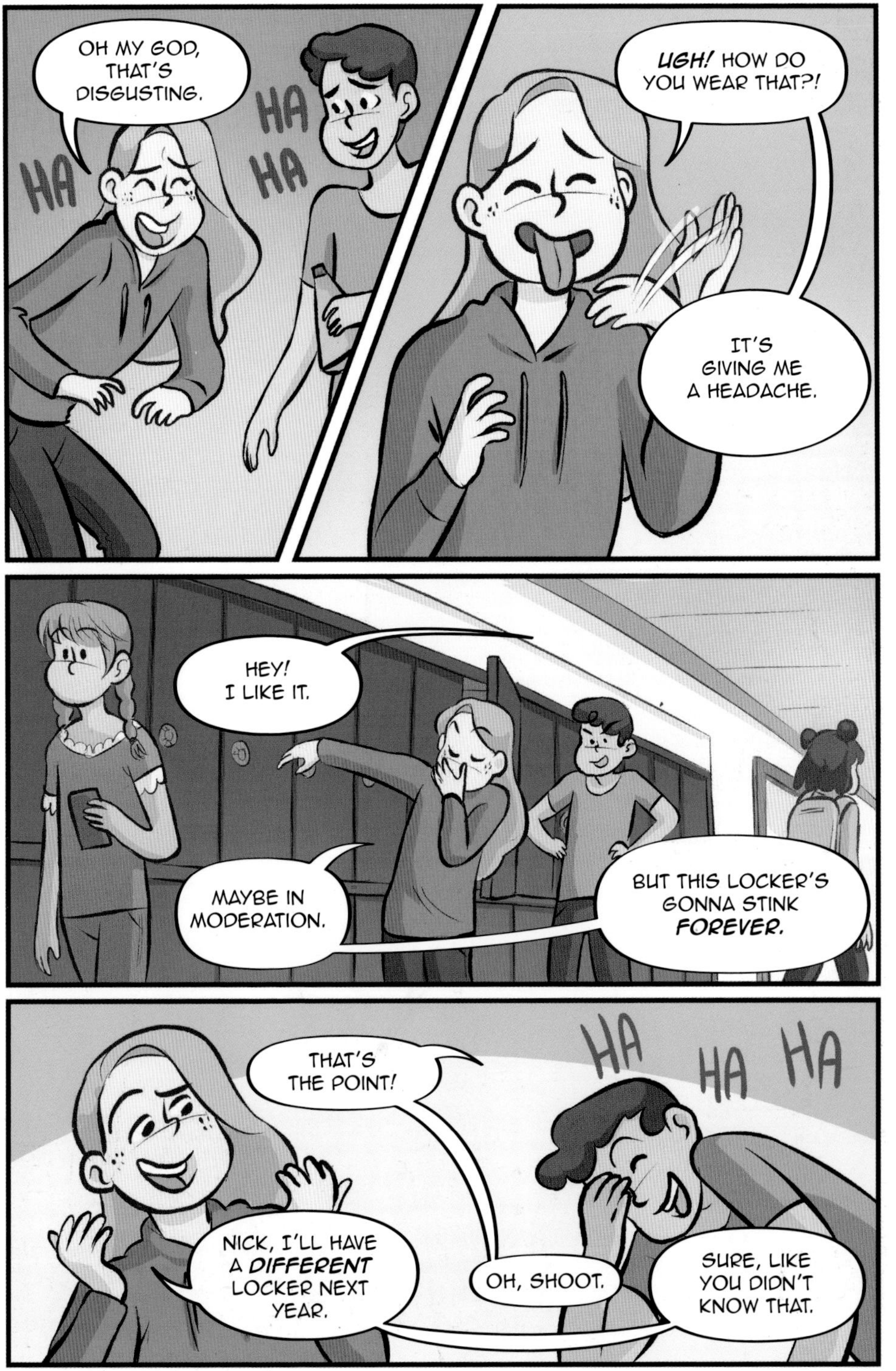
OH MY GOD, THAT'S DISGUSTING.
HA
HA HA
UGH! HOW DO YOU WEAR THAT?!
IT'S GIVING ME A HEADACHE.
HEY! I LIKE IT.
MAYBE IN MODERATION.
BUT THIS LOCKER'S GONNA STINK FOREVER.
HA HA HA
THAT'S THE POINT!
NICK, I'LL HAVE A DIFFERENT LOCKER NEXT YEAR.
OH, SHOOT.
SURE, LIKE YOU DIDN'T KNOW THAT.

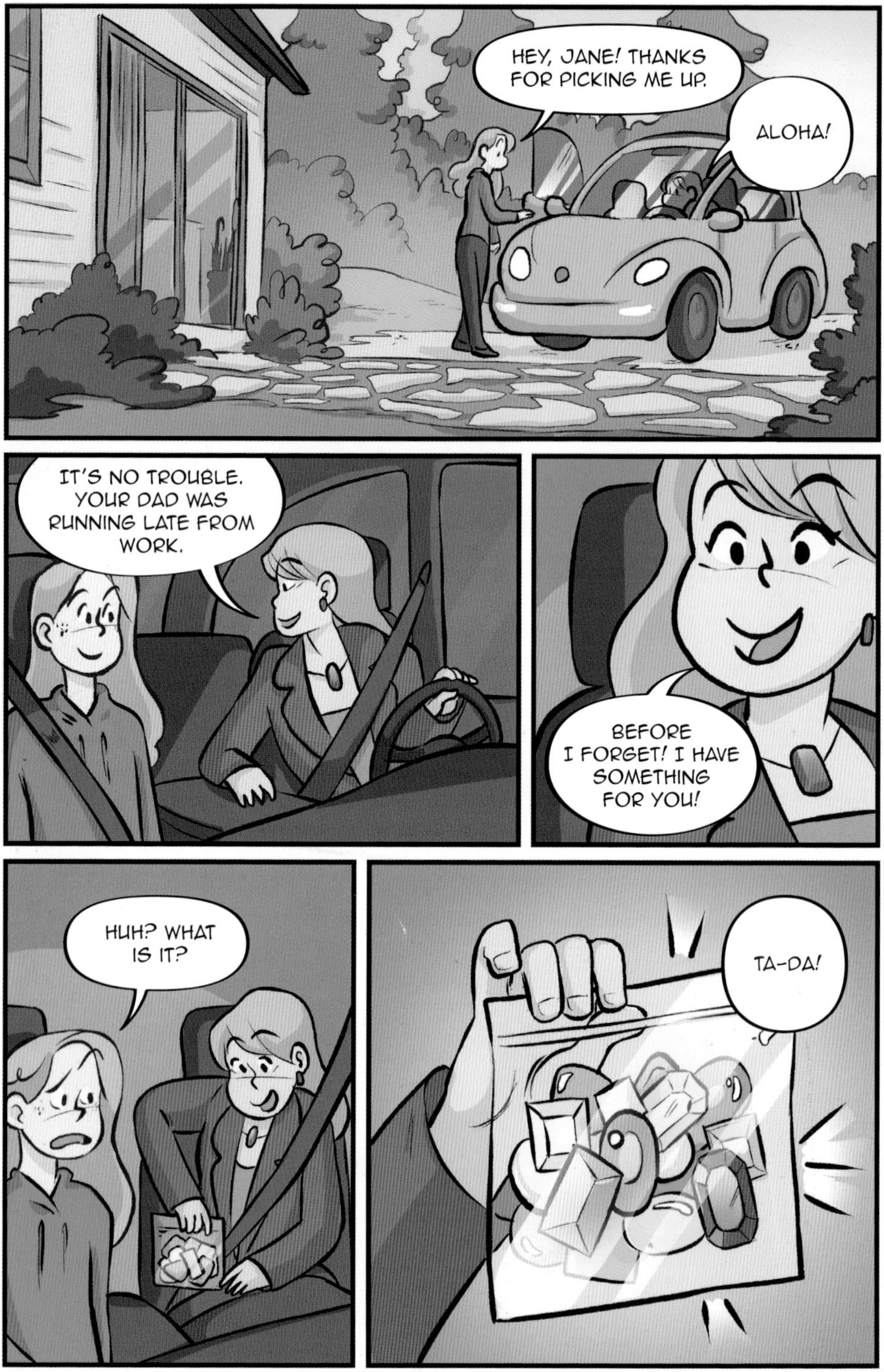
HEY, JANE! THANKS FOR PICKING ME UP.
ALOHA!
IT'S NO TROUBLE. YOUR DAD WAS RUNNING LATE FROM WORK.
BEFORE I FORGET! I HAVE SOMETHING FOR YOU!
HUH? WHAT IS IT?
TA-DA!

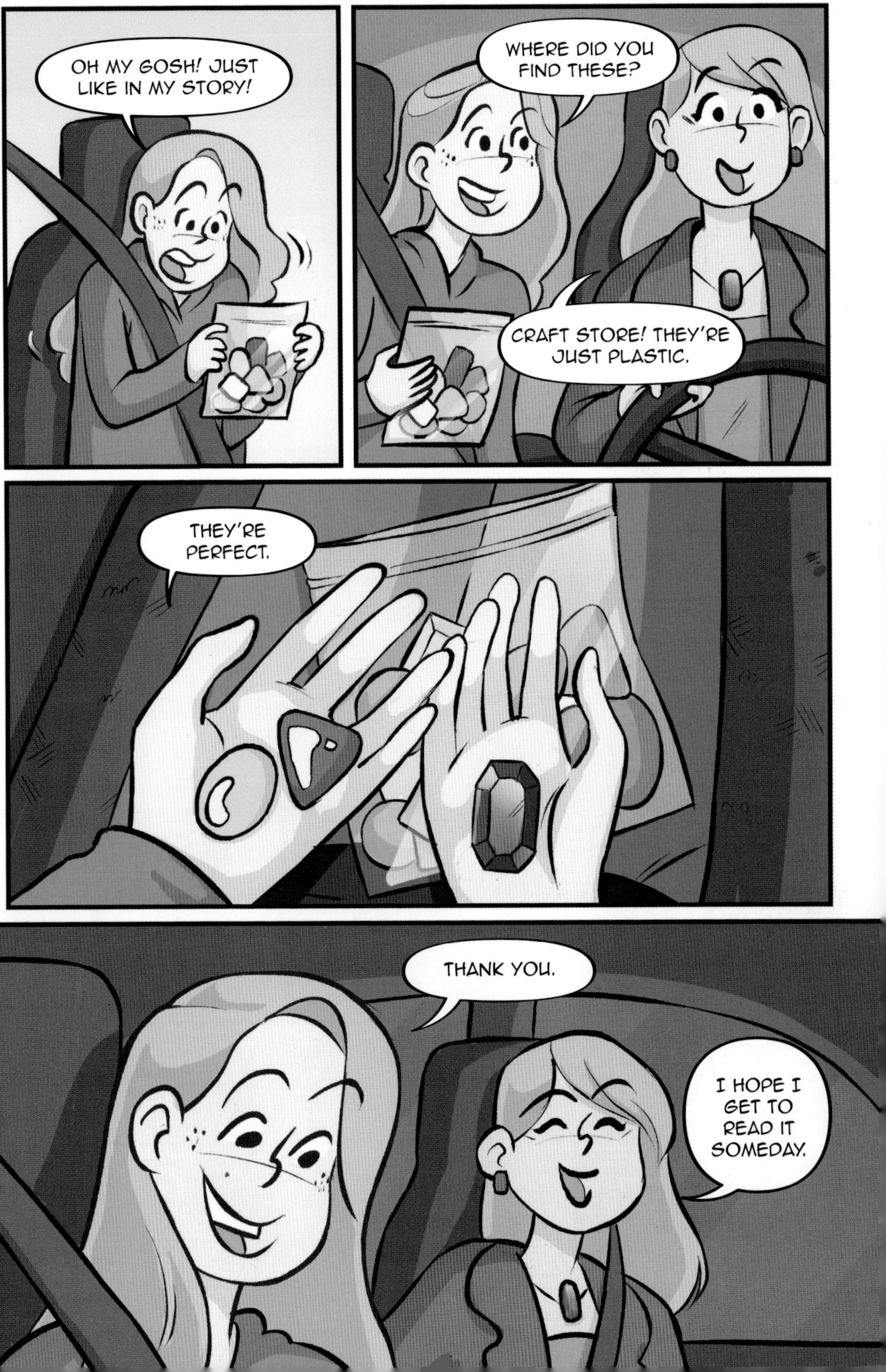
OH MY GOSH! JUST LIKE IN MY STORY!
WHERE DID YOU FIND THESE?
CRAFT STORE! THEY'RE JUST PLASTIC.
THEY'RE PERFECT.
THANK YOU.
I HOPE I GET TO READ IT SOMEDAY.

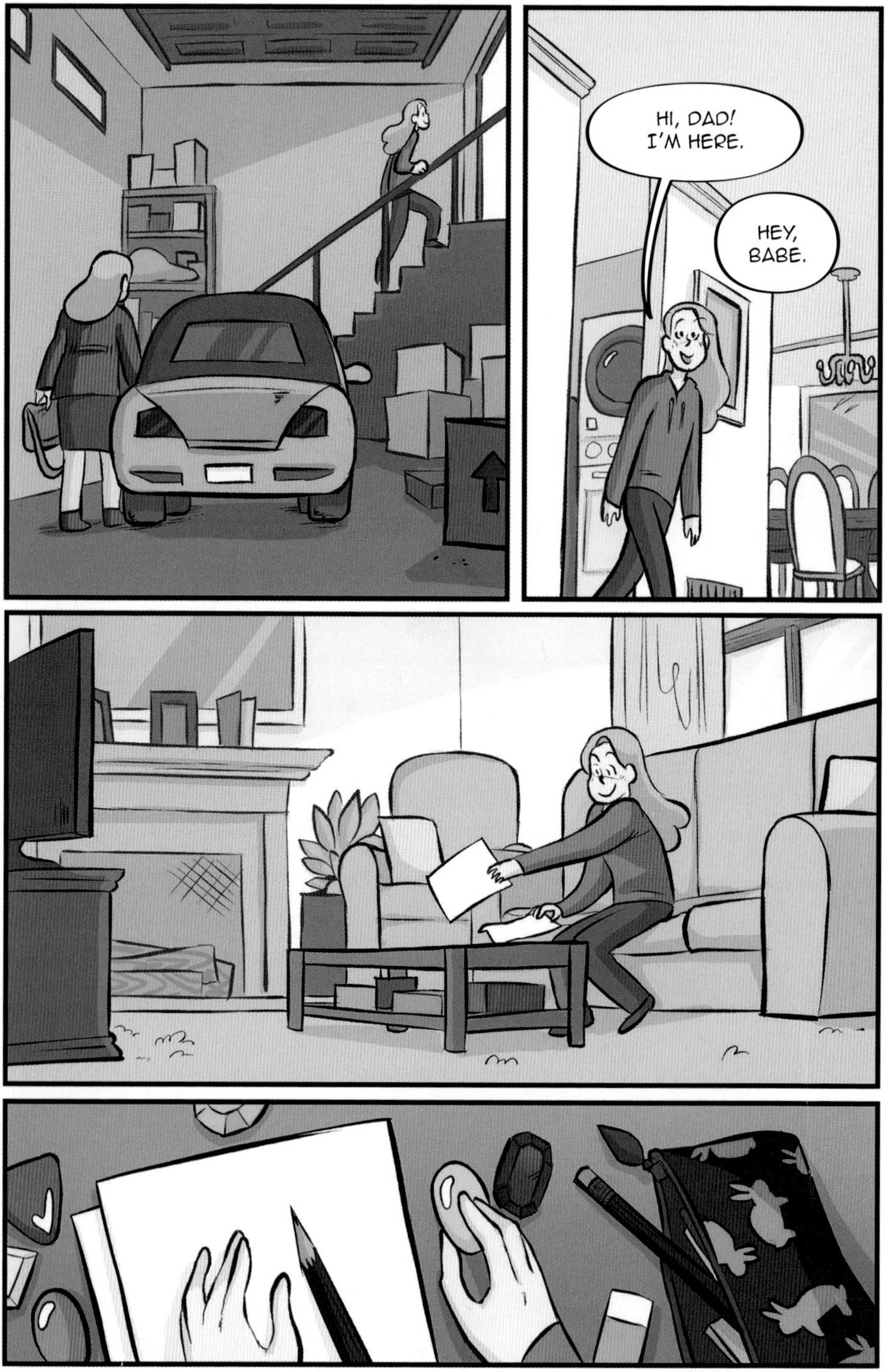
HI, DAD!
I'M HERE.
HEY,
BABE.

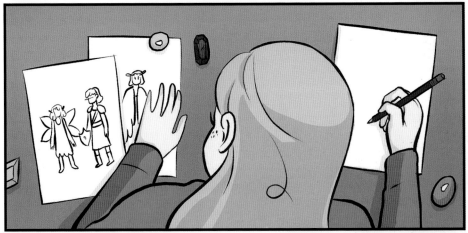

HUH! I ACTUALLY LIKE HOW THESE ARE TURNING OUT.

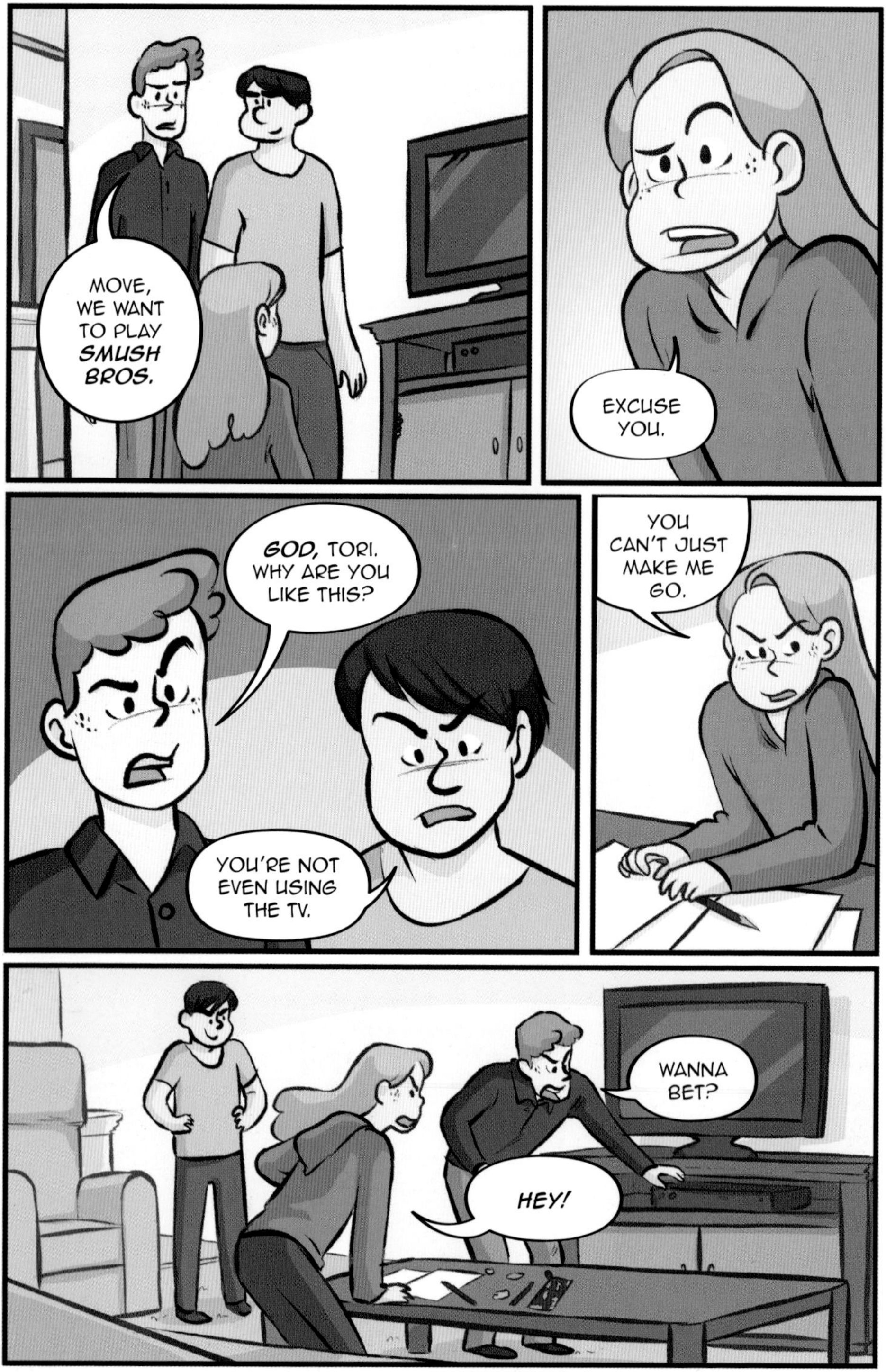
MOVE, WE WANT TO PLAY SMUSH BROS.
EXCUSE YOU.
GOD, TORI. WHY ARE YOU LIKE THIS?
YOU'RE NOT EVEN USING THE TV.
YOU CAN'T JUST MAKE ME GO.
WANNA BET?
HEY!

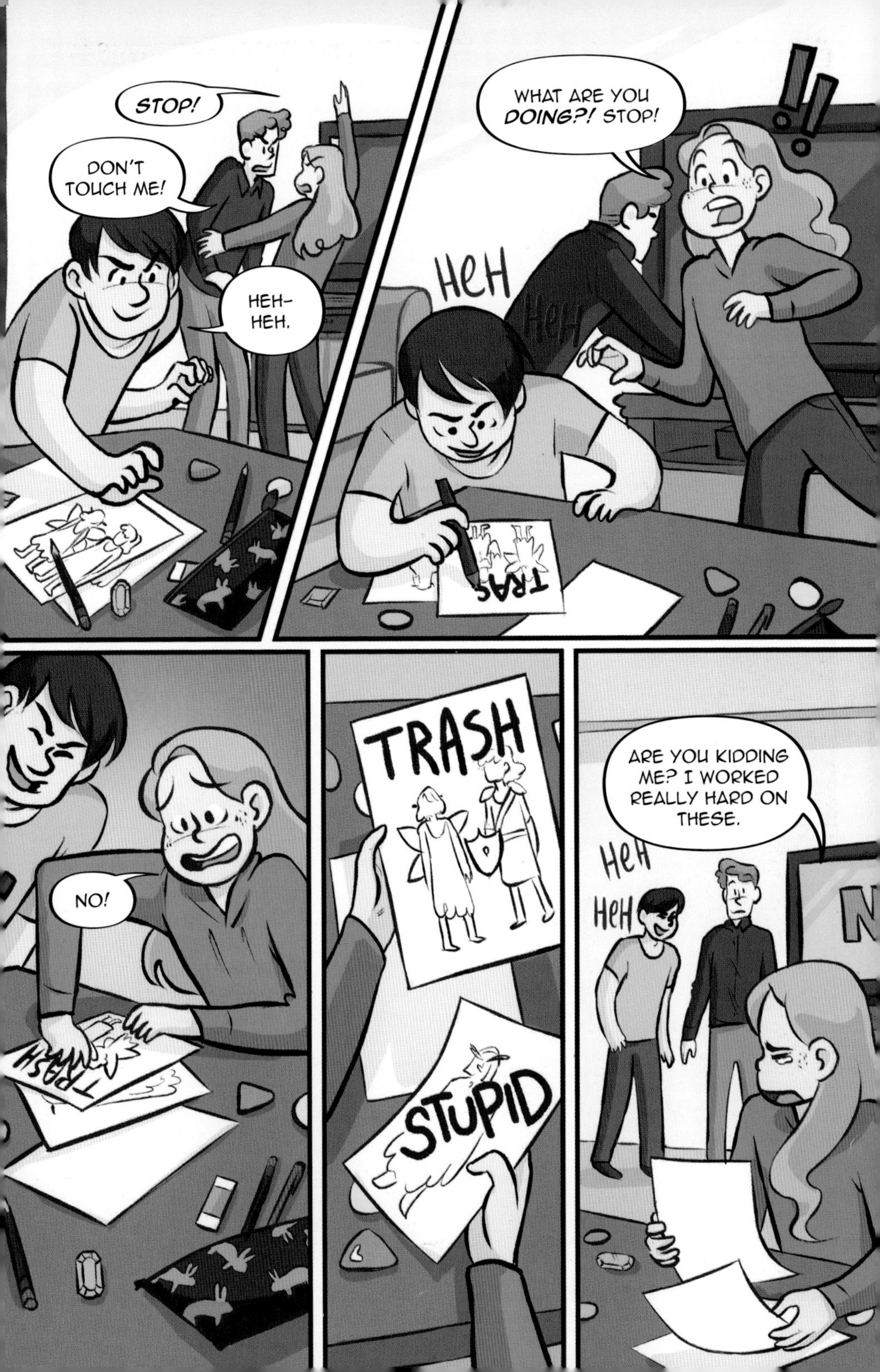
STOP!
DON'T TOUCH ME!
HEH-HEH.
WHAT ARE YOU DOING?! STOP!
HEH
HEH
TRAS
NO!
TRASH
TRASH
STUPID
ARE YOU KIDDING ME? I WORKED REALLY HARD ON THESE.
HEH
HEH

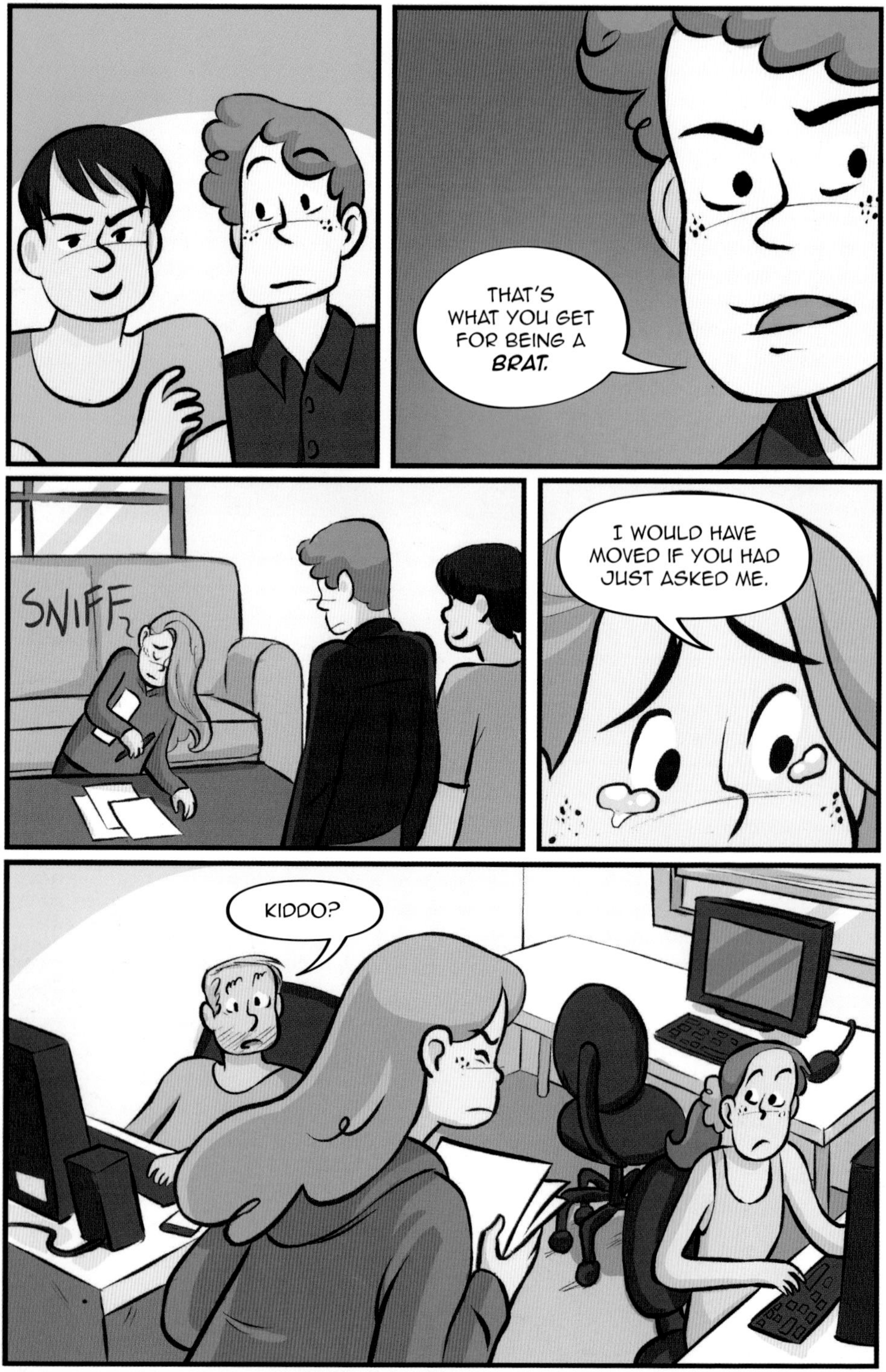
THAT'S WHAT YOU GET FOR BEING A BRAT.
SNIFF
I WOULD HAVE MOVED IF YOU HAD JUST ASKED ME.
KIDDO?

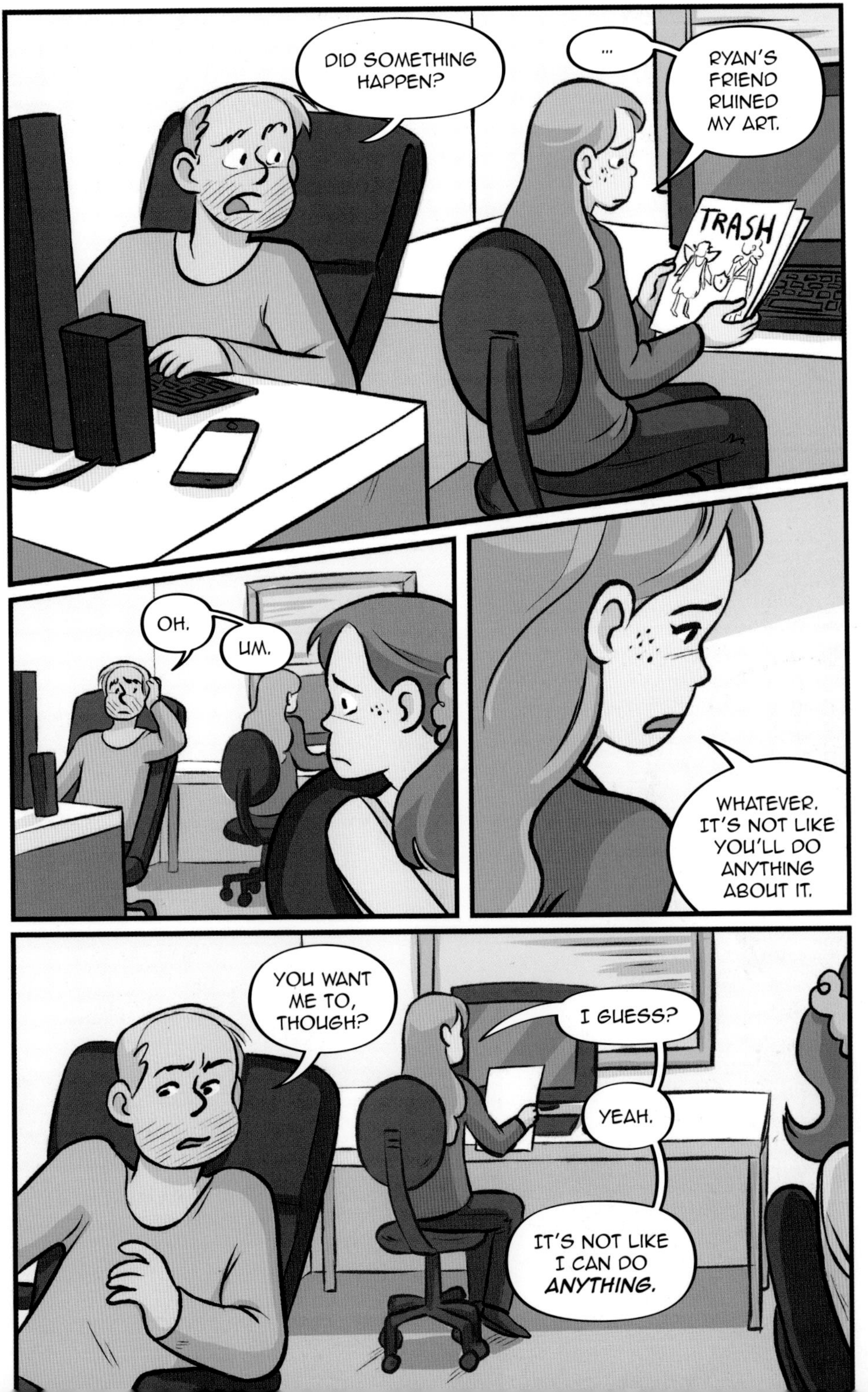
DID SOMETHING HAPPEN?
...
RYAN'S FRIEND RUINED MY ART.
TRASH
OH.
UM.
WHATEVER. IT'S NOT LIKE YOU'LL DO ANYTHING ABOUT IT.
YOU WANT ME TO, THOUGH?
I GUESS?
YEAH.
IT'S NOT LIKE I CAN DO *ANYTHING.*

...

FINE.

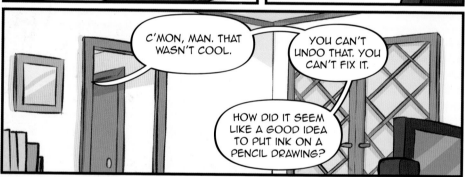

C'MON, MAN. THAT WASN'T COOL.

YOU CAN'T UNDO THAT. YOU CAN'T FIX IT.

HOW DID IT SEEM LIKE A GOOD IDEA TO PUT INK ON A PENCIL DRAWING?

YOU OK?

DAD?

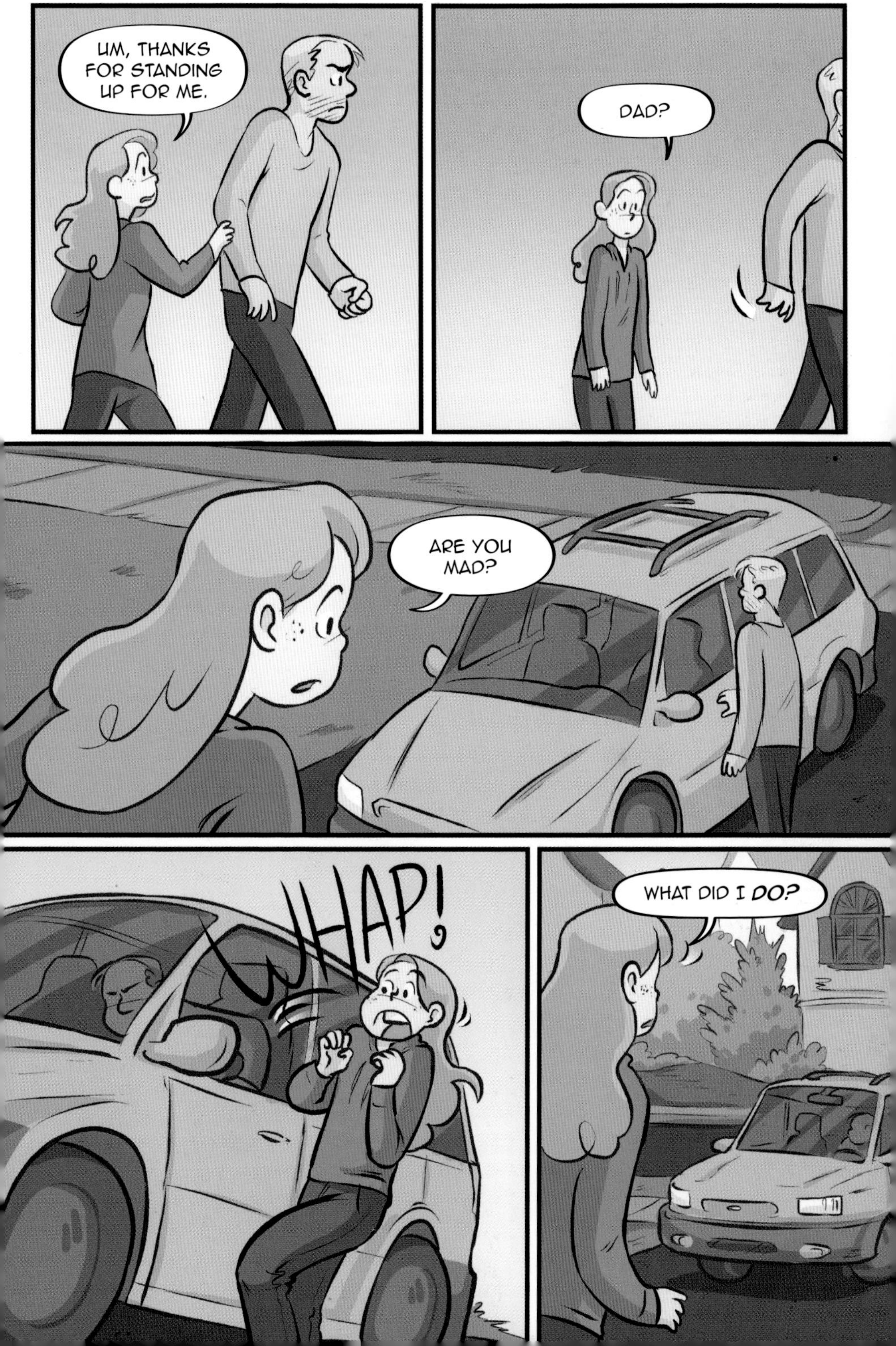
UM, THANKS FOR STANDING UP FOR ME.
DAD?
ARE YOU MAD?
WHAP!
WHAT DID I *DO?*

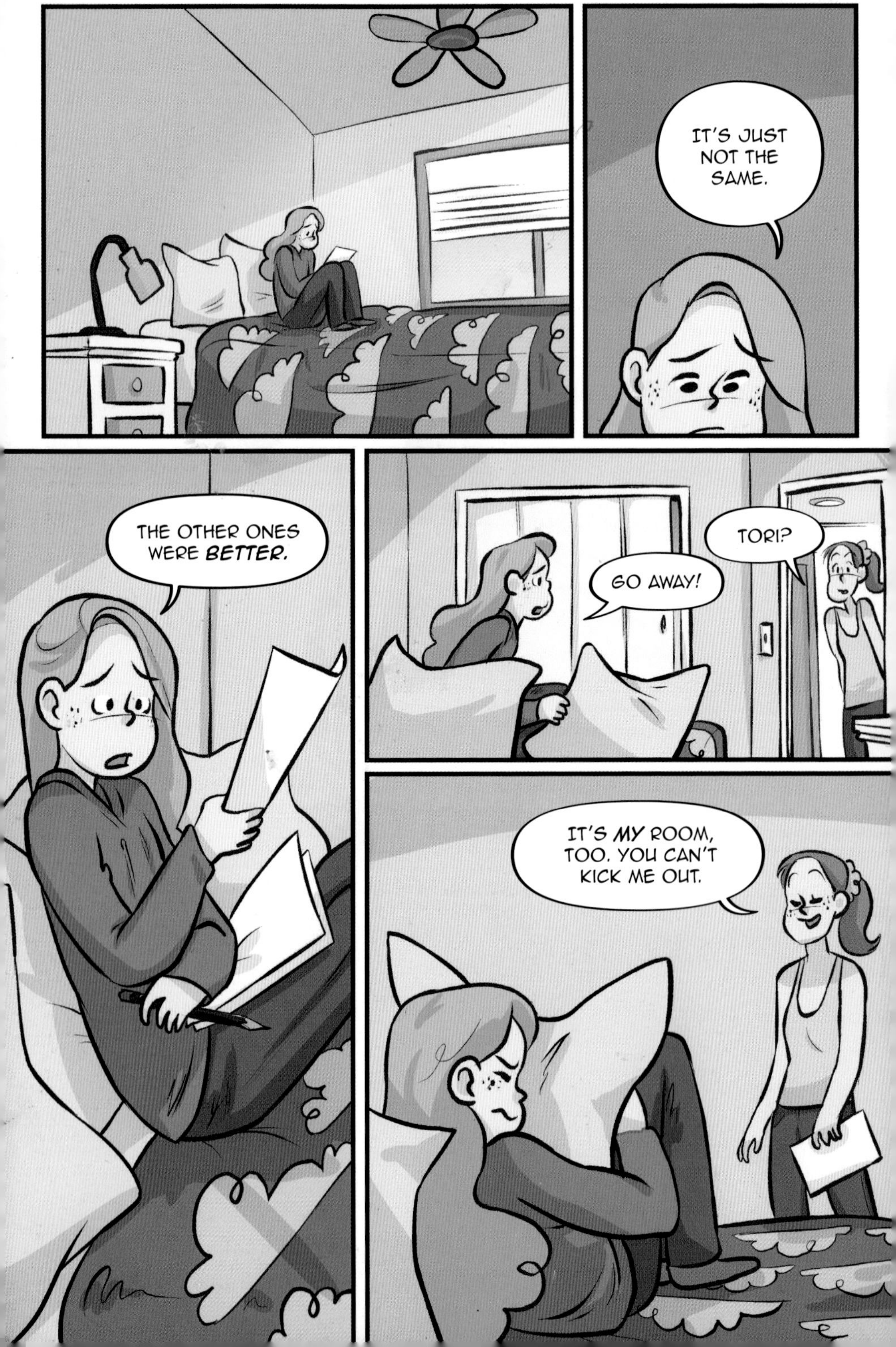
IT'S JUST NOT THE SAME.
THE OTHER ONES WERE **BETTER.**
TORI?
GO AWAY!
IT'S *MY* ROOM, TOO. YOU CAN'T KICK ME OUT.

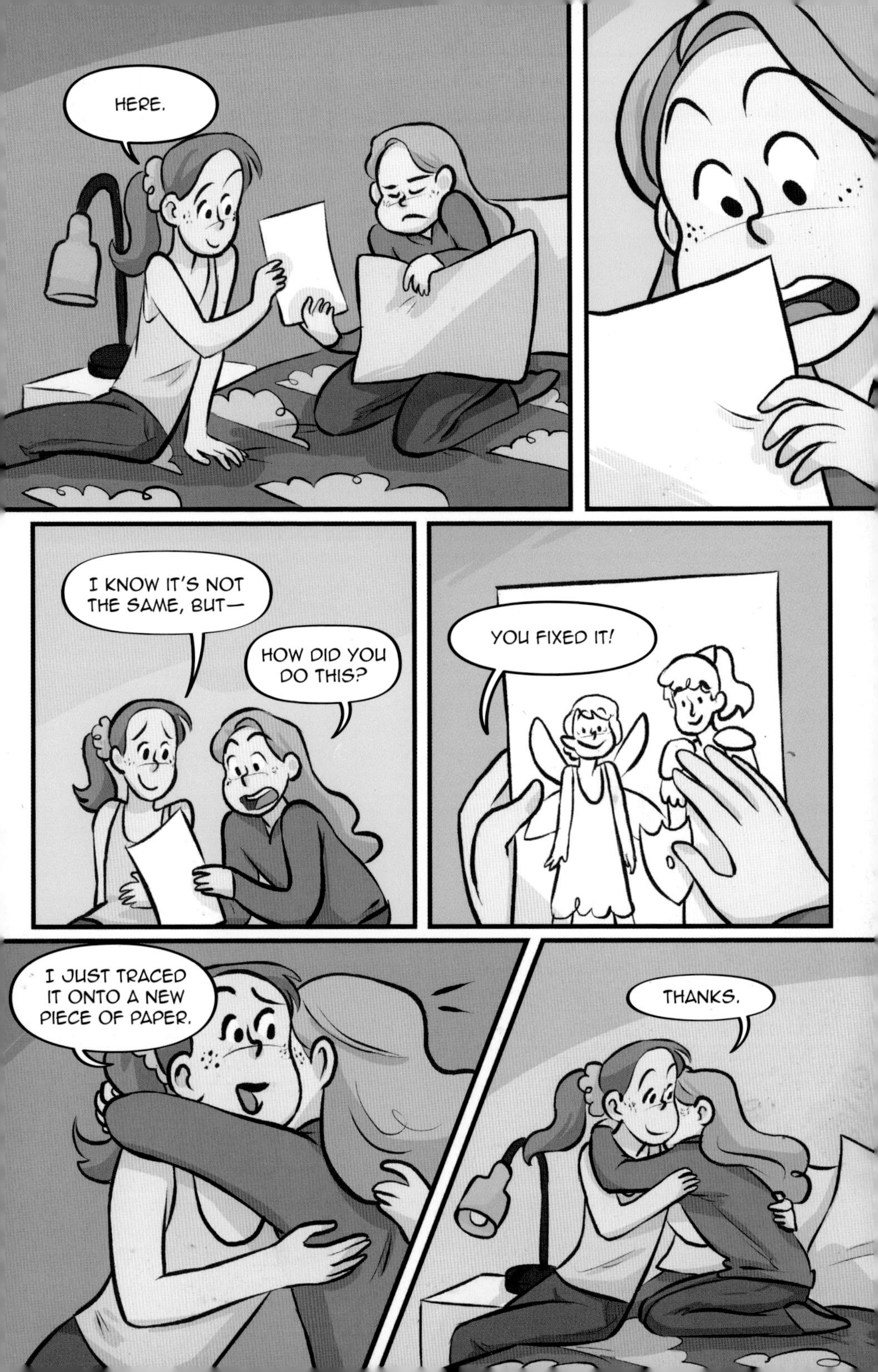
HERE.
I KNOW IT'S NOT THE SAME, BUT—
HOW DID YOU DO THIS?
YOU FIXED IT!
I JUST TRACED IT ONTO A NEW PIECE OF PAPER.
THANKS.

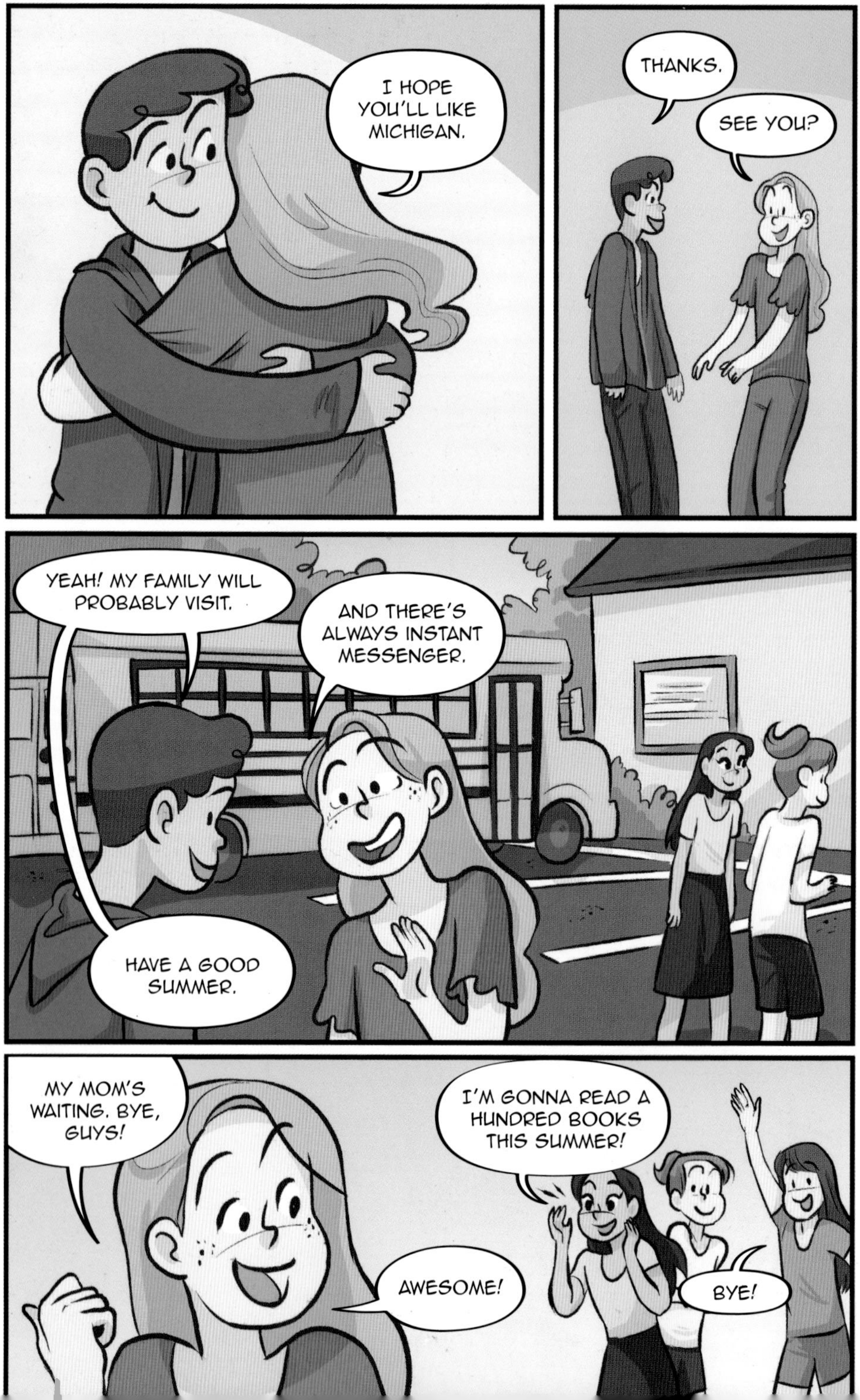
I HOPE YOU'LL LIKE MICHIGAN.
THANKS.
SEE YOU?
YEAH! MY FAMILY WILL PROBABLY VISIT.
AND THERE'S ALWAYS INSTANT MESSENGER.
HAVE A GOOD SUMMER.
MY MOM'S WAITING. BYE, GUYS!
I'M GONNA READ A HUNDRED BOOKS THIS SUMMER!
AWESOME!
BYE!

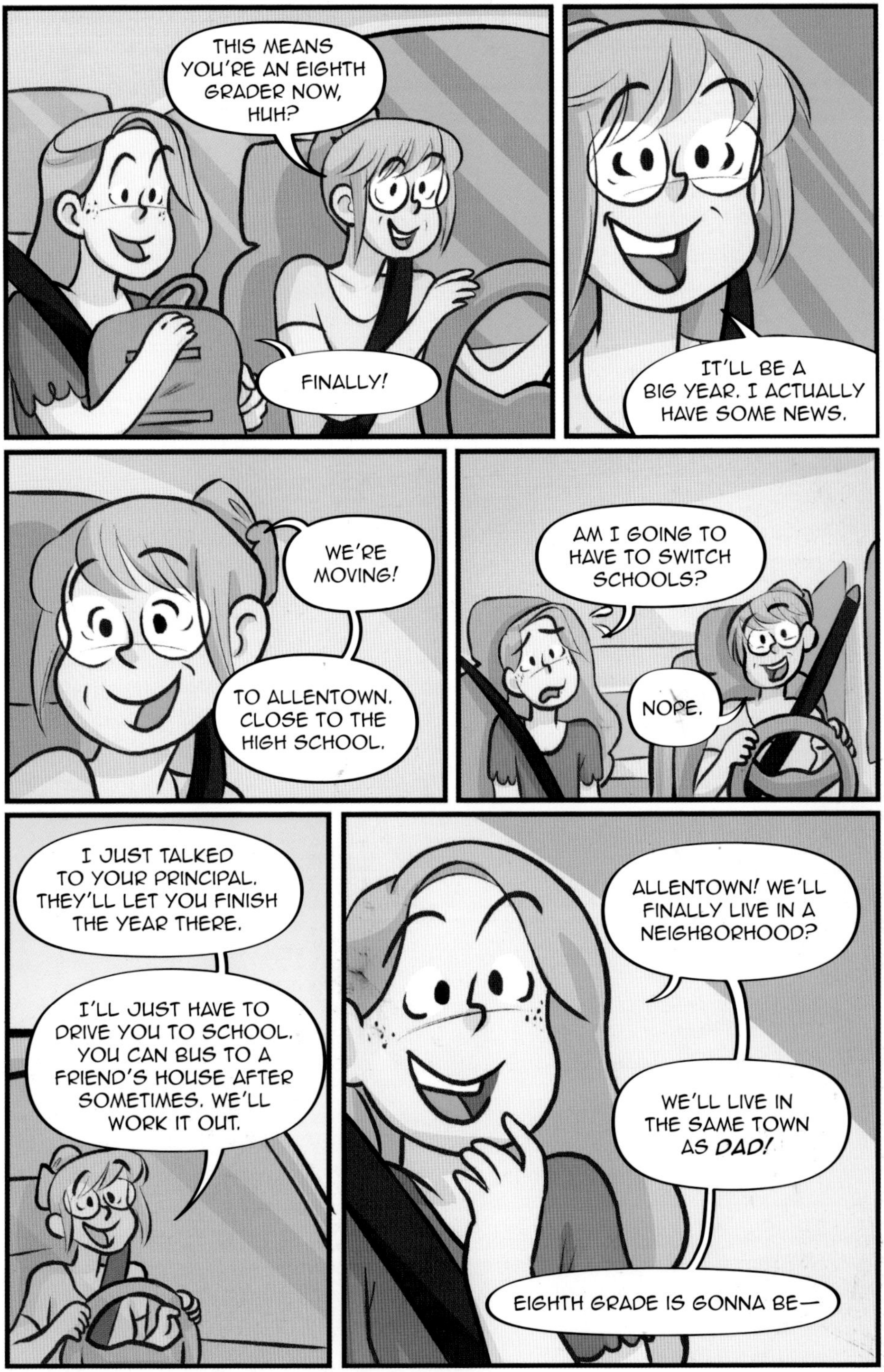
THIS MEANS YOU'RE AN EIGHTH GRADER NOW, HUH?
FINALLY!
IT'LL BE A BIG YEAR. I ACTUALLY HAVE SOME NEWS.
WE'RE MOVING!
TO ALLENTOWN. CLOSE TO THE HIGH SCHOOL.
AM I GOING TO HAVE TO SWITCH SCHOOLS?
NOPE.
I JUST TALKED TO YOUR PRINCIPAL. THEY'LL LET YOU FINISH THE YEAR THERE.
I'LL JUST HAVE TO DRIVE YOU TO SCHOOL. YOU CAN BUS TO A FRIEND'S HOUSE AFTER SOMETIMES. WE'LL WORK IT OUT.
ALLENTOWN! WE'LL FINALLY LIVE IN A NEIGHBORHOOD?
WE'LL LIVE IN THE SAME TOWN AS *DAD!*
EIGHTH GRADE IS GONNA BE—

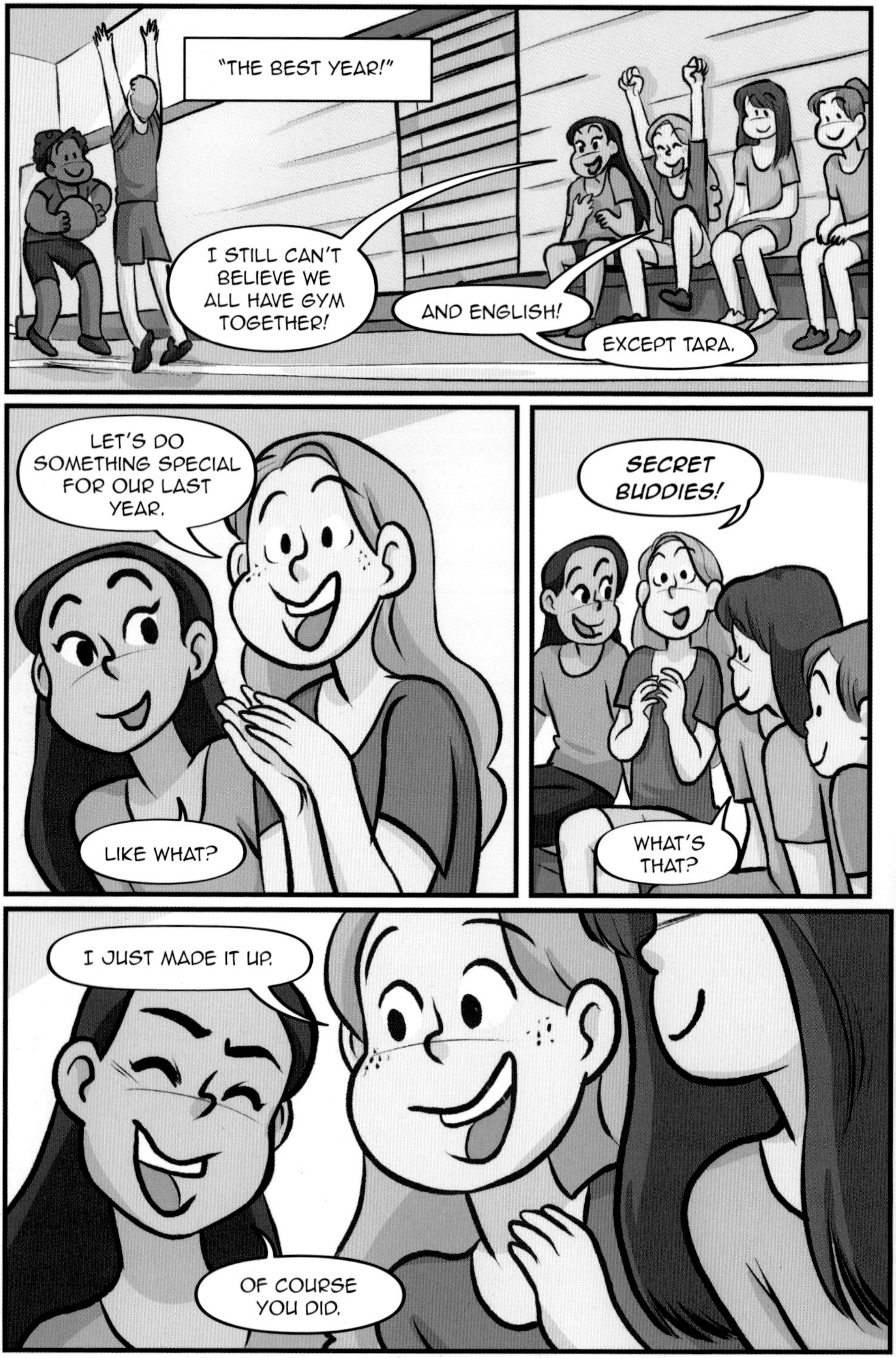
"THE BEST YEAR!"
I STILL CAN'T BELIEVE WE ALL HAVE GYM TOGETHER!
AND ENGLISH!
EXCEPT TARA.
LET'S DO SOMETHING SPECIAL FOR OUR LAST YEAR.
LIKE WHAT?
SECRET BUDDIES!
WHAT'S THAT?
I JUST MADE IT UP.
OF COURSE YOU DID.

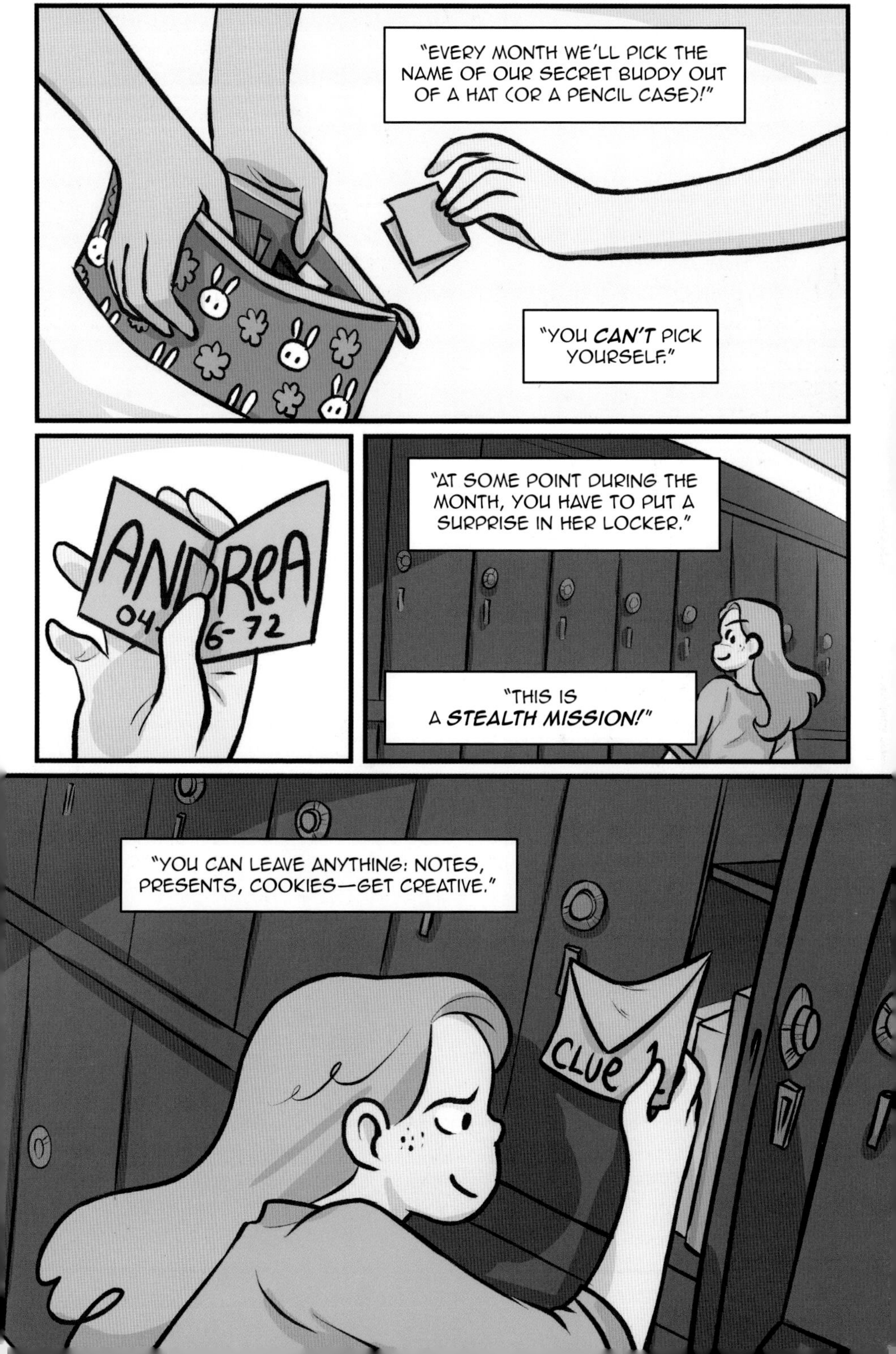
"EVERY MONTH WE'LL PICK THE NAME OF OUR SECRET BUDDY OUT OF A HAT (OR A PENCIL CASE)!"
"YOU *CAN'T* PICK YOURSELF."
ANDREA
04-
6-72
"AT SOME POINT DURING THE MONTH, YOU HAVE TO PUT A SURPRISE IN HER LOCKER."
"THIS IS A ***STEALTH MISSION!***"
"YOU CAN LEAVE ANYTHING: NOTES, PRESENTS, COOKIES—GET CREATIVE."
CLUE

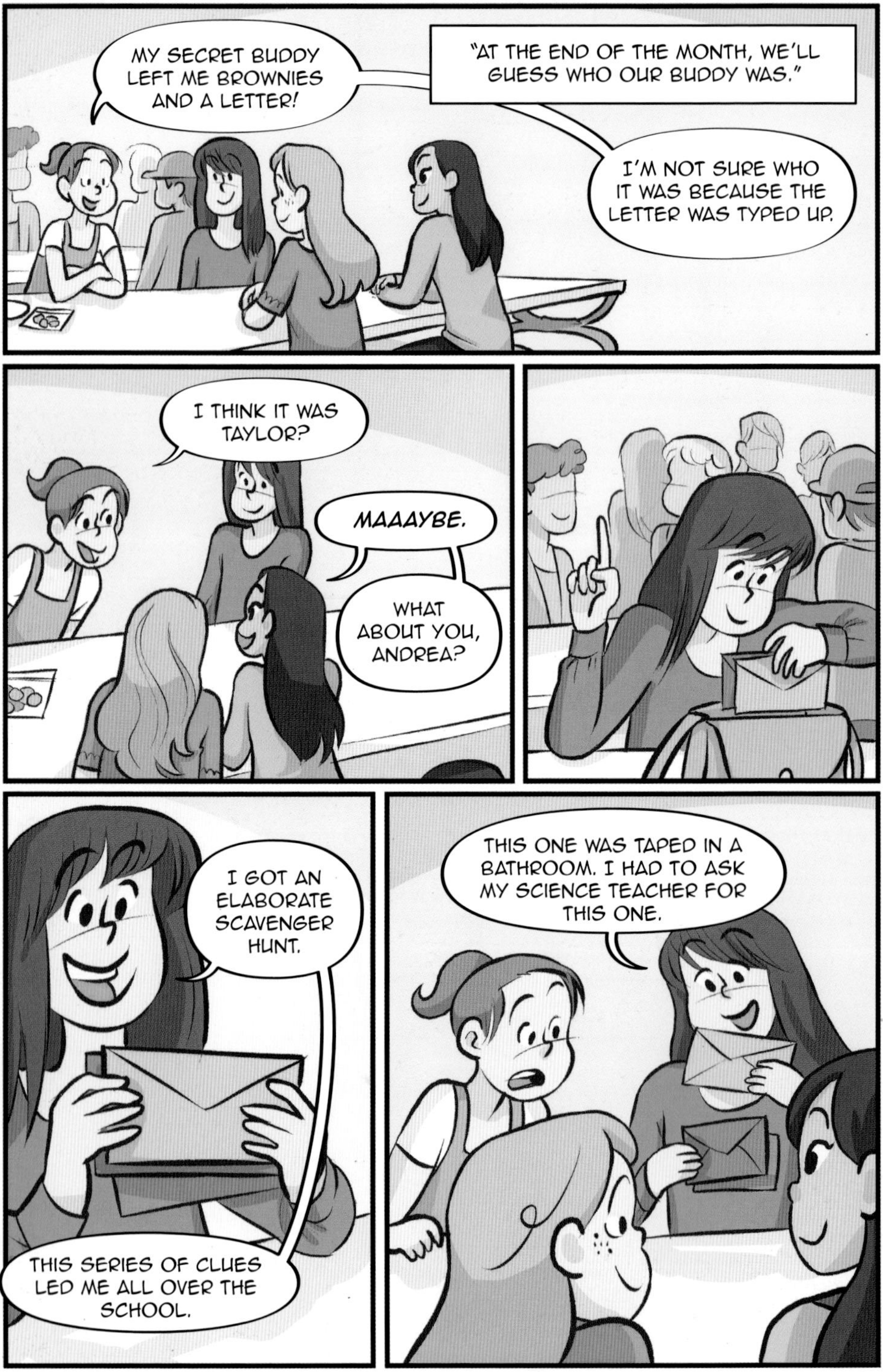
MY SECRET BUDDY LEFT ME BROWNIES AND A LETTER!
"AT THE END OF THE MONTH, WE'LL GUESS WHO OUR BUDDY WAS."
I'M NOT SURE WHO IT WAS BECAUSE THE LETTER WAS TYPED UP.
I THINK IT WAS TAYLOR?
MAAAYBE.
WHAT ABOUT YOU, ANDREA?
I GOT AN ELABORATE SCAVENGER HUNT.
THIS SERIES OF CLUES LED ME ALL OVER THE SCHOOL.
THIS ONE WAS TAPED IN A BATHROOM. I HAD TO ASK MY SCIENCE TEACHER FOR THIS ONE.

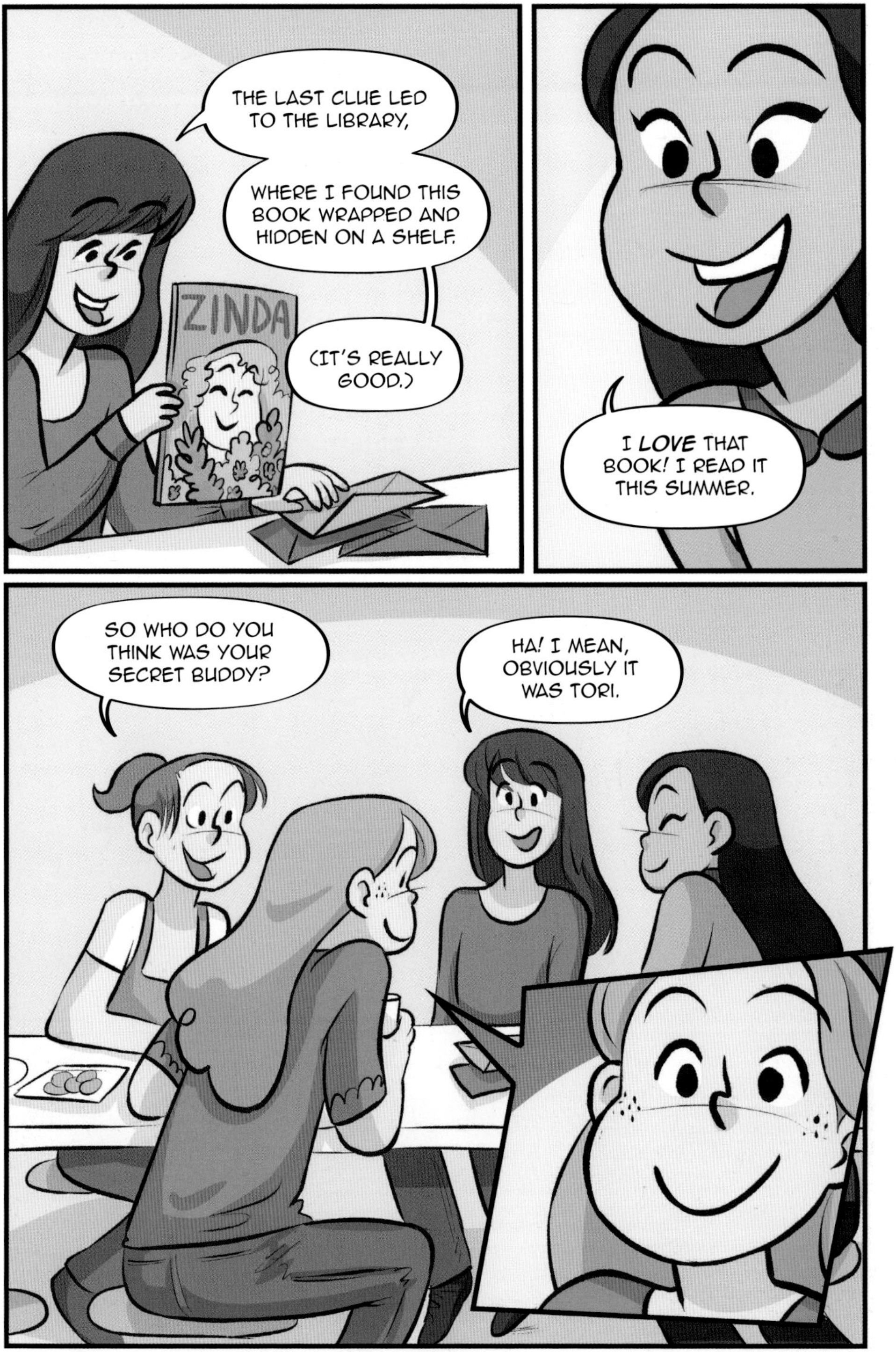
THE LAST CLUE LED TO THE LIBRARY,
WHERE I FOUND THIS BOOK WRAPPED AND HIDDEN ON A SHELF.
ZINDA
(IT'S REALLY GOOD.)
I LOVE THAT BOOK! I READ IT THIS SUMMER.
SO WHO DO YOU THINK WAS YOUR SECRET BUDDY?
HA! I MEAN, OBVIOUSLY IT WAS TORI.

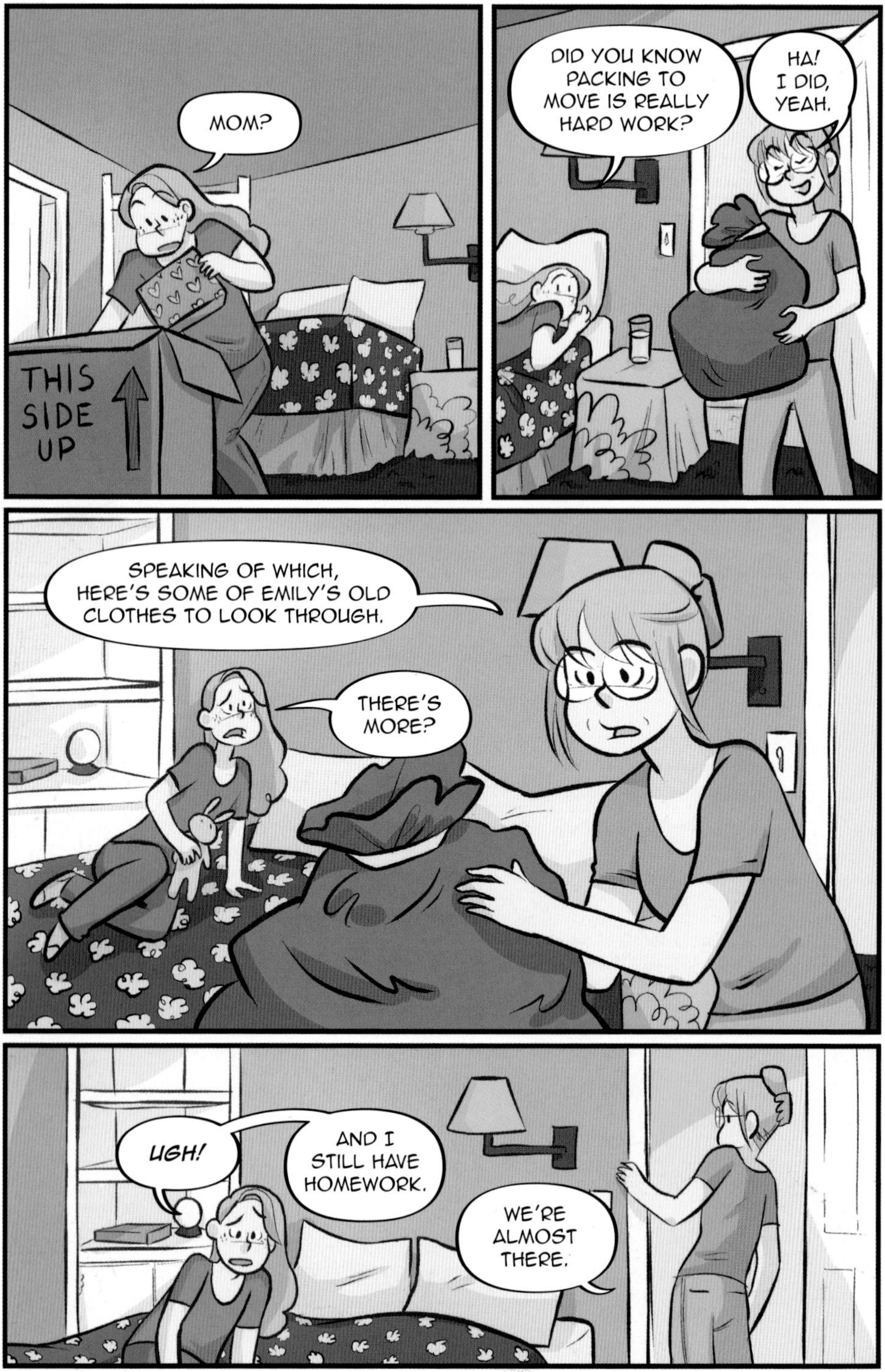
THIS SIDE UP
MOM?
DID YOU KNOW PACKING TO MOVE IS REALLY HARD WORK?
HA! I DID, YEAH.
SPEAKING OF WHICH, HERE'S SOME OF EMILY'S OLD CLOTHES TO LOOK THROUGH.
THERE'S MORE?
UGH!
AND I STILL HAVE HOMEWORK.
WE'RE ALMOST THERE.

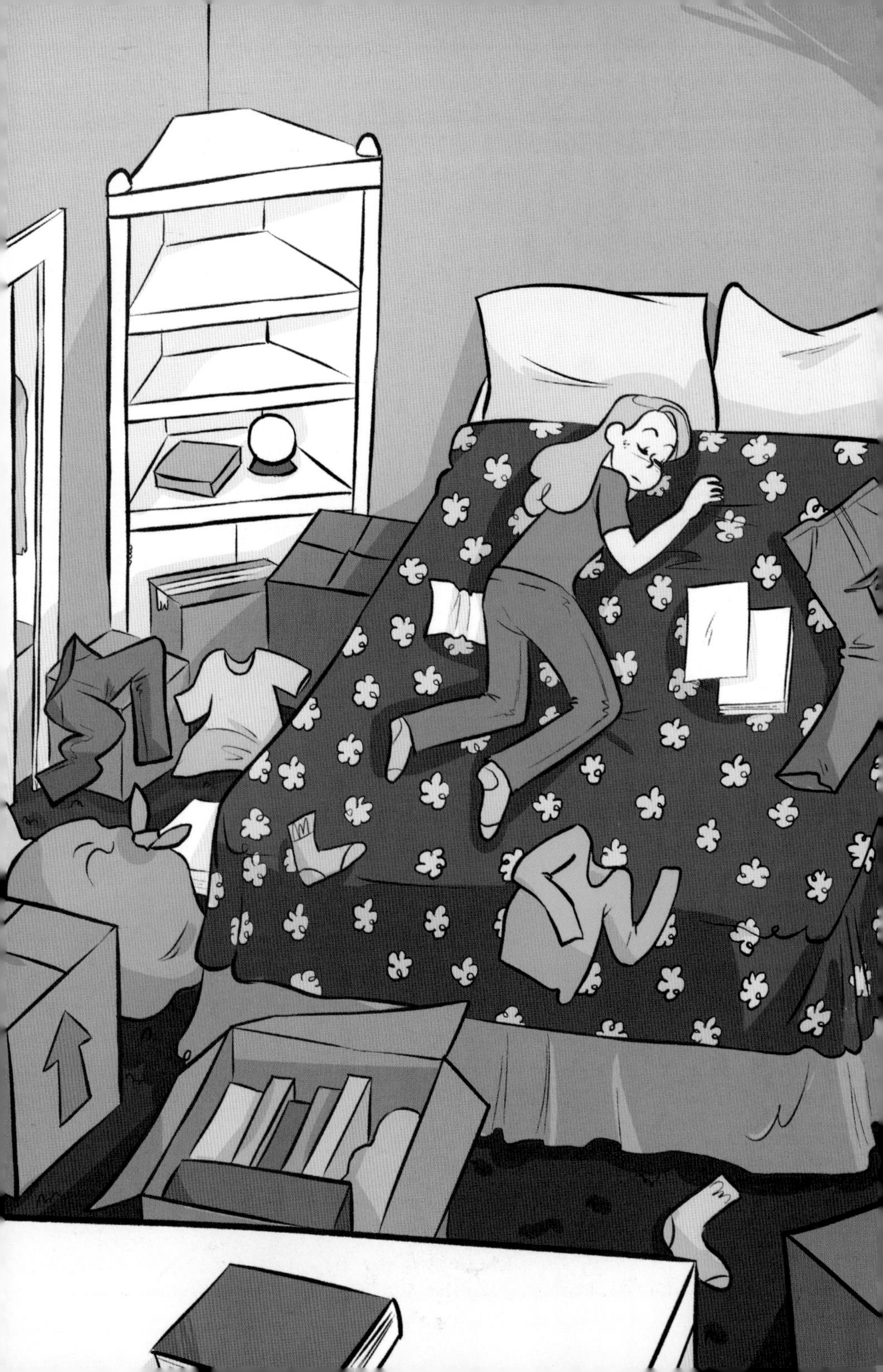

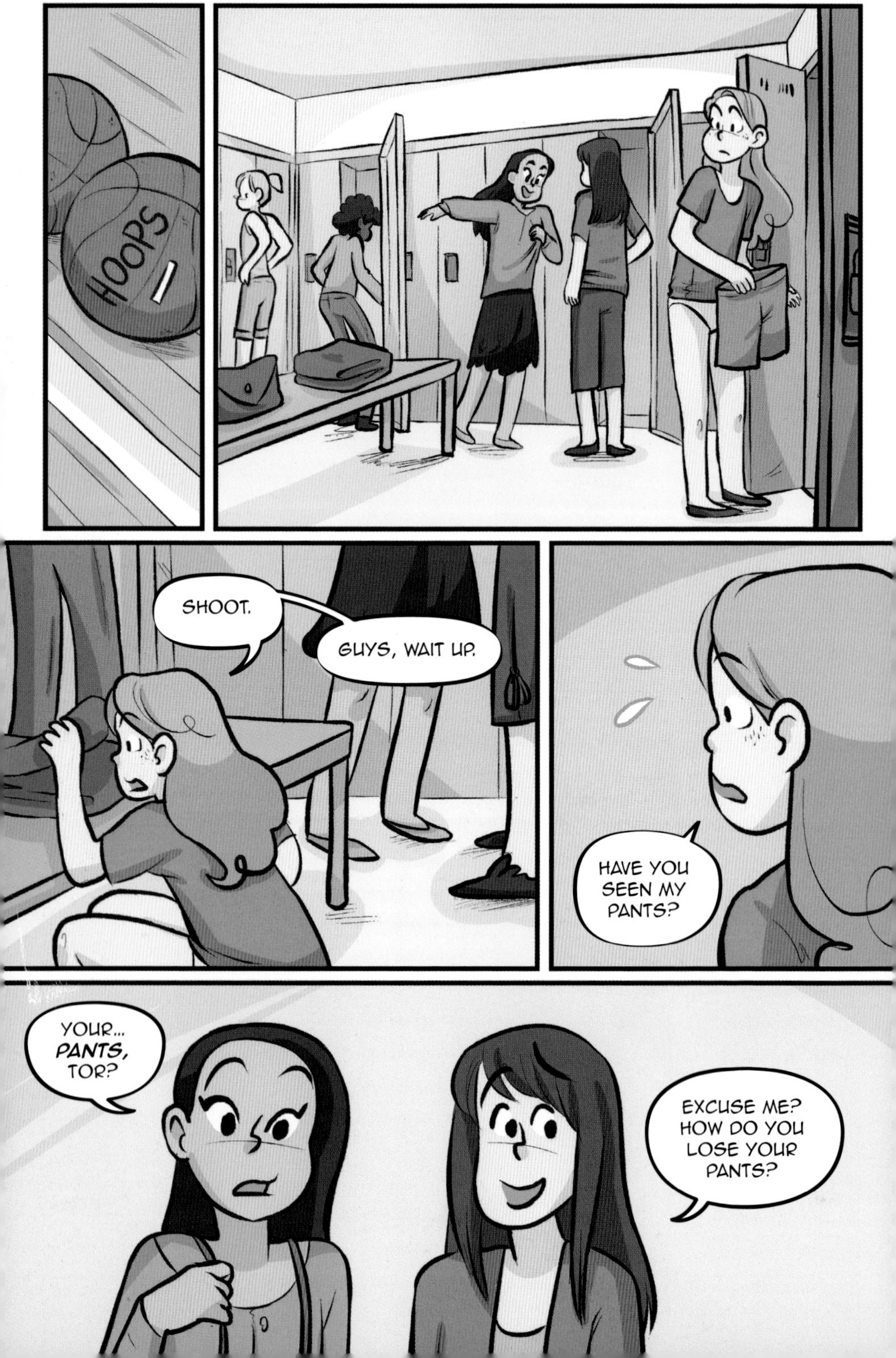
HOOPS
SHOOT.
GUYS, WAIT UP.
HAVE YOU SEEN MY PANTS?
YOUR... *PANTS,* TOR?
EXCUSE ME? HOW DO YOU LOSE YOUR PANTS?

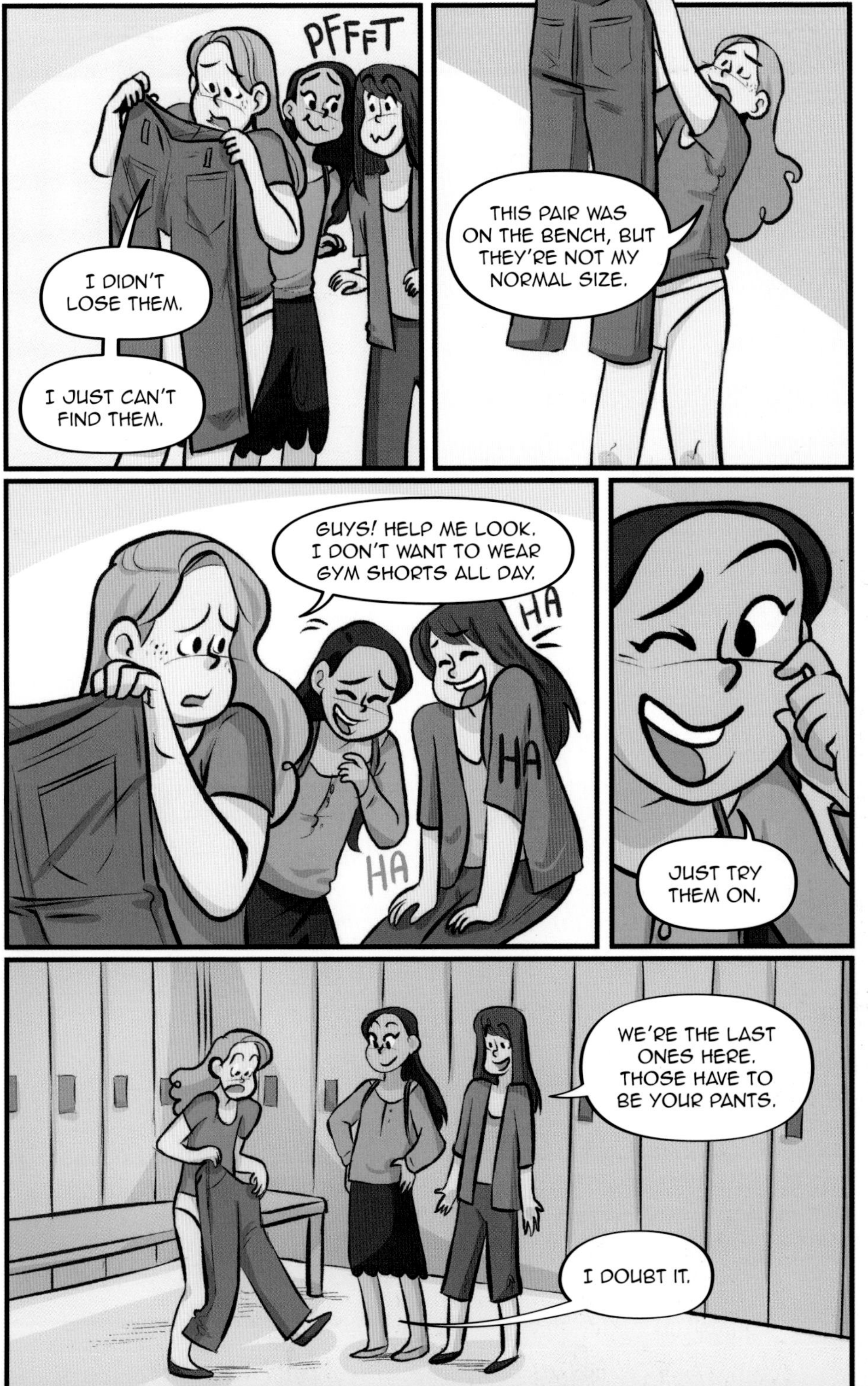
PFFFT
I DIDN'T LOSE THEM.
I JUST CAN'T FIND THEM.
THIS PAIR WAS ON THE BENCH, BUT THEY'RE NOT MY NORMAL SIZE.
GUYS! HELP ME LOOK. I DON'T WANT TO WEAR GYM SHORTS ALL DAY.
HA
HA
HA
JUST TRY THEM ON.
WE'RE THE LAST ONES HERE. THOSE HAVE TO BE YOUR PANTS.
I DOUBT IT.

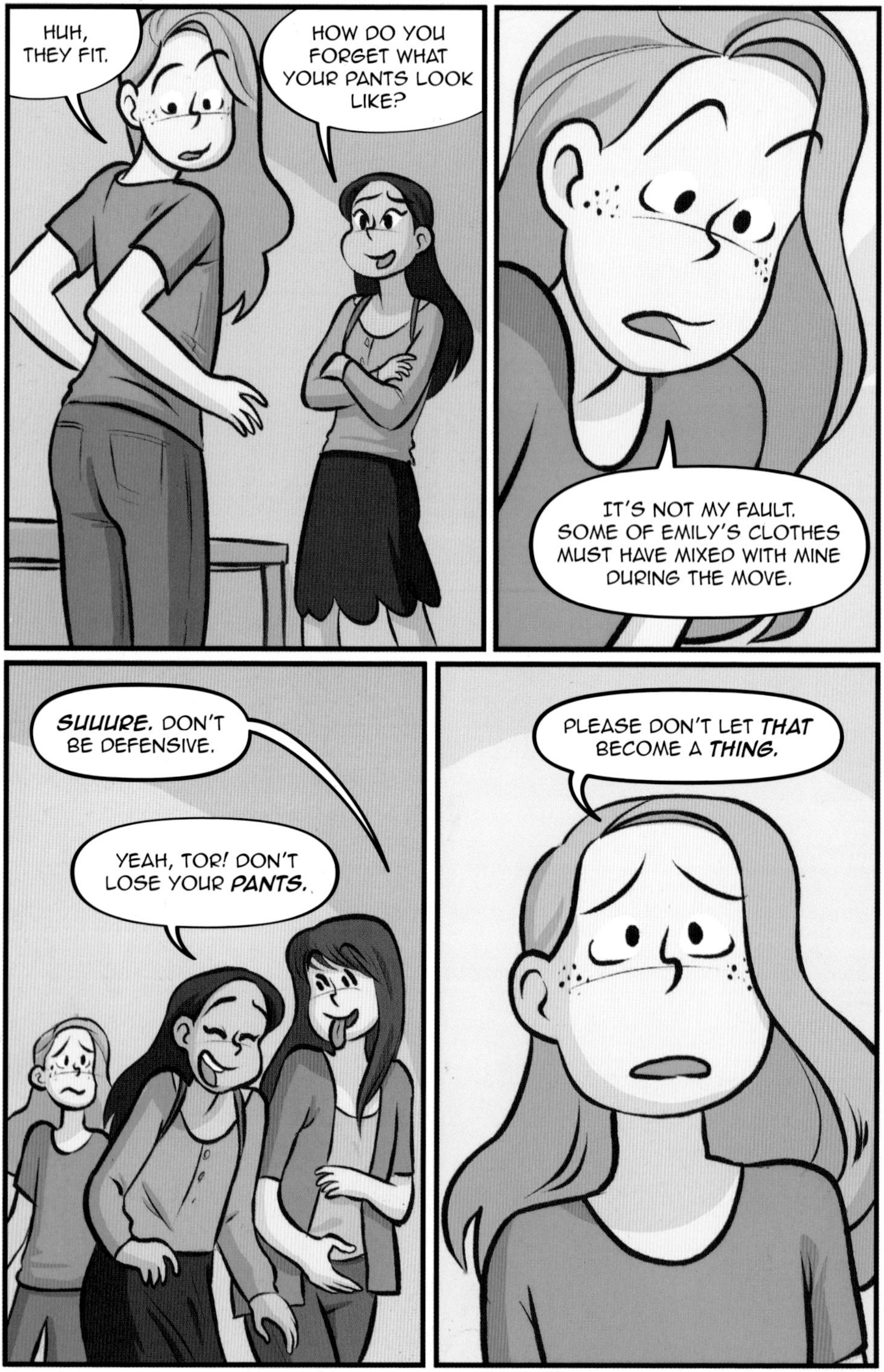
HUH, THEY FIT.
HOW DO YOU FORGET WHAT YOUR PANTS LOOK LIKE?
IT'S NOT MY FAULT. SOME OF EMILY'S CLOTHES MUST HAVE MIXED WITH MINE DURING THE MOVE.
*SUUURE.* DON'T BE DEFENSIVE.
YEAH, TOR! DON'T LOSE YOUR *PANTS.*
PLEASE DON'T LET *THAT* BECOME A *THING.*

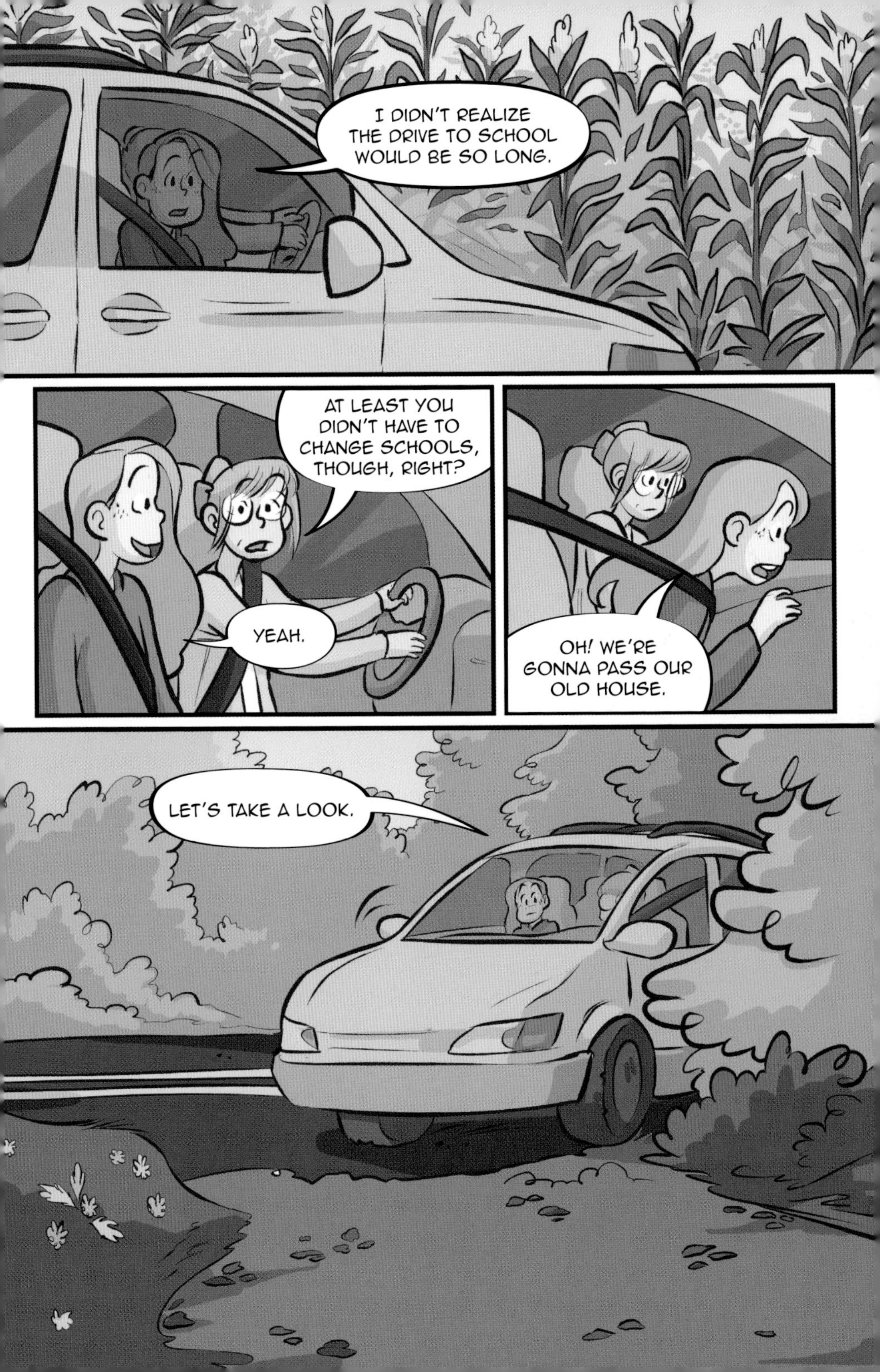
I DIDN'T REALIZE THE DRIVE TO SCHOOL WOULD BE SO LONG.
AT LEAST YOU DIDN'T HAVE TO CHANGE SCHOOLS, THOUGH, RIGHT?
YEAH.
OH! WE'RE GONNA PASS OUR OLD HOUSE.
LET'S TAKE A LOOK.

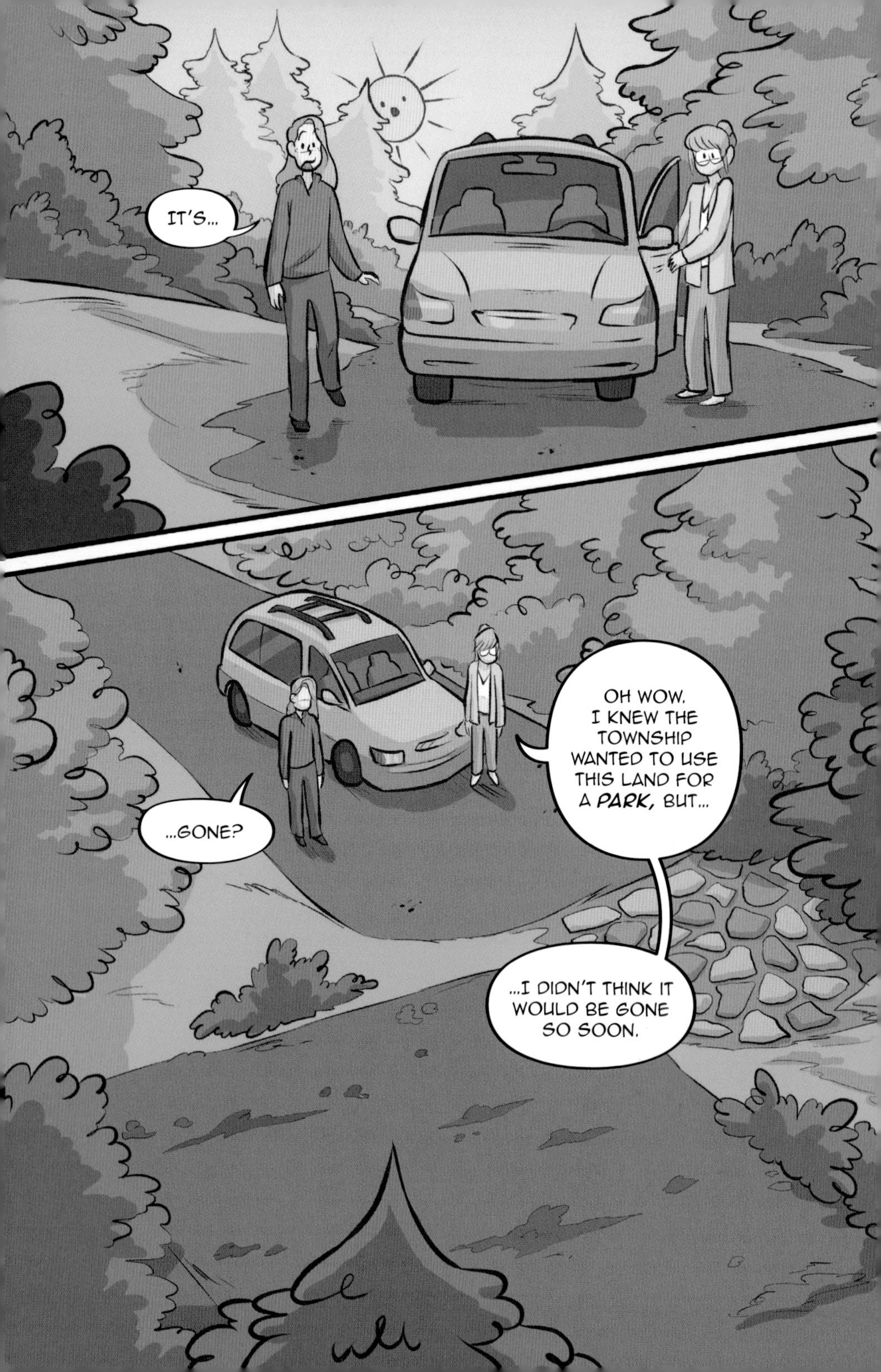
IT'S...
...GONE?
OH WOW. I KNEW THE TOWNSHIP WANTED TO USE THIS LAND FOR A *PARK,* BUT...
...I DIDN'T THINK IT WOULD BE GONE SO SOON.

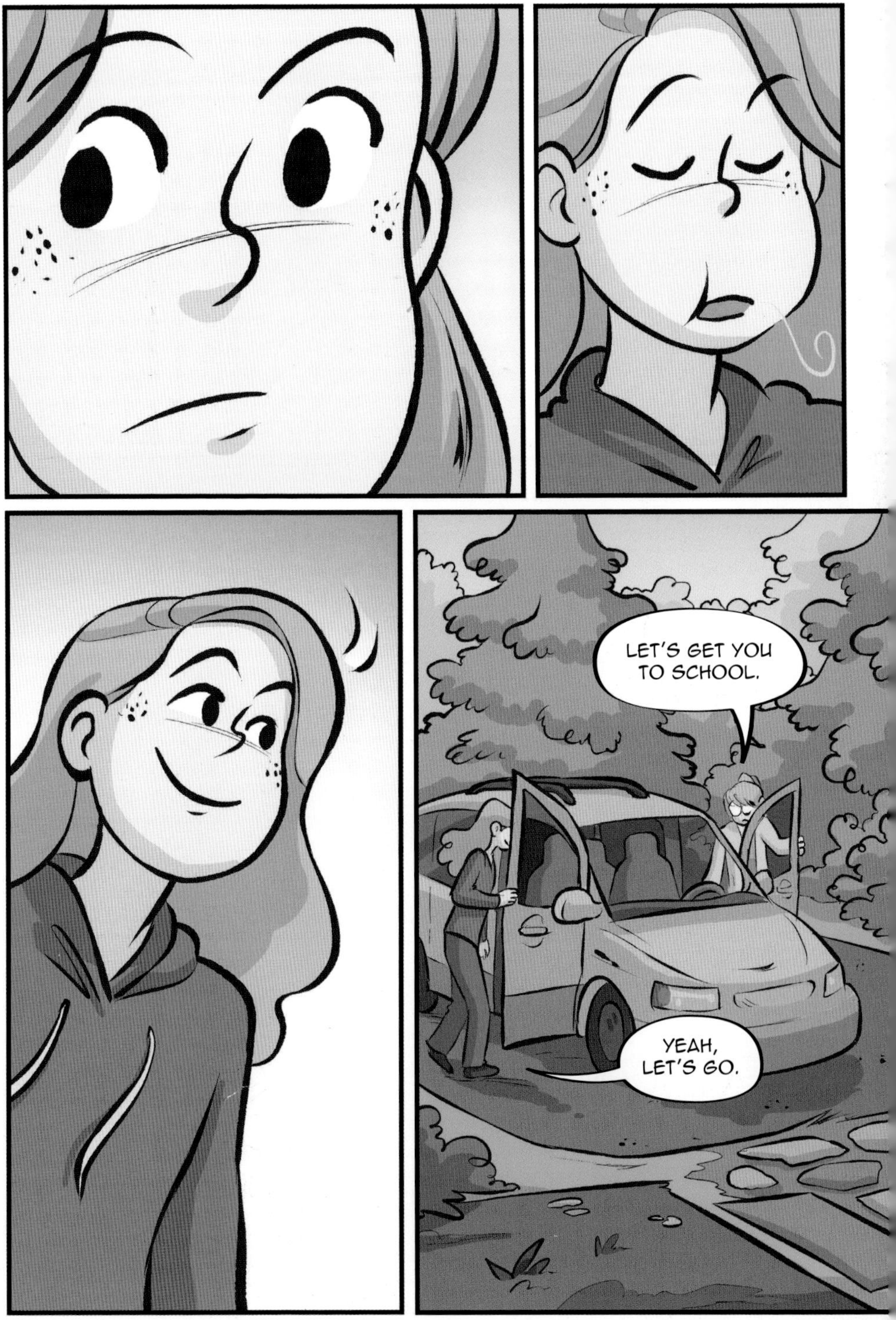
LET'S GET YOU TO SCHOOL.
YEAH, LET'S GO.

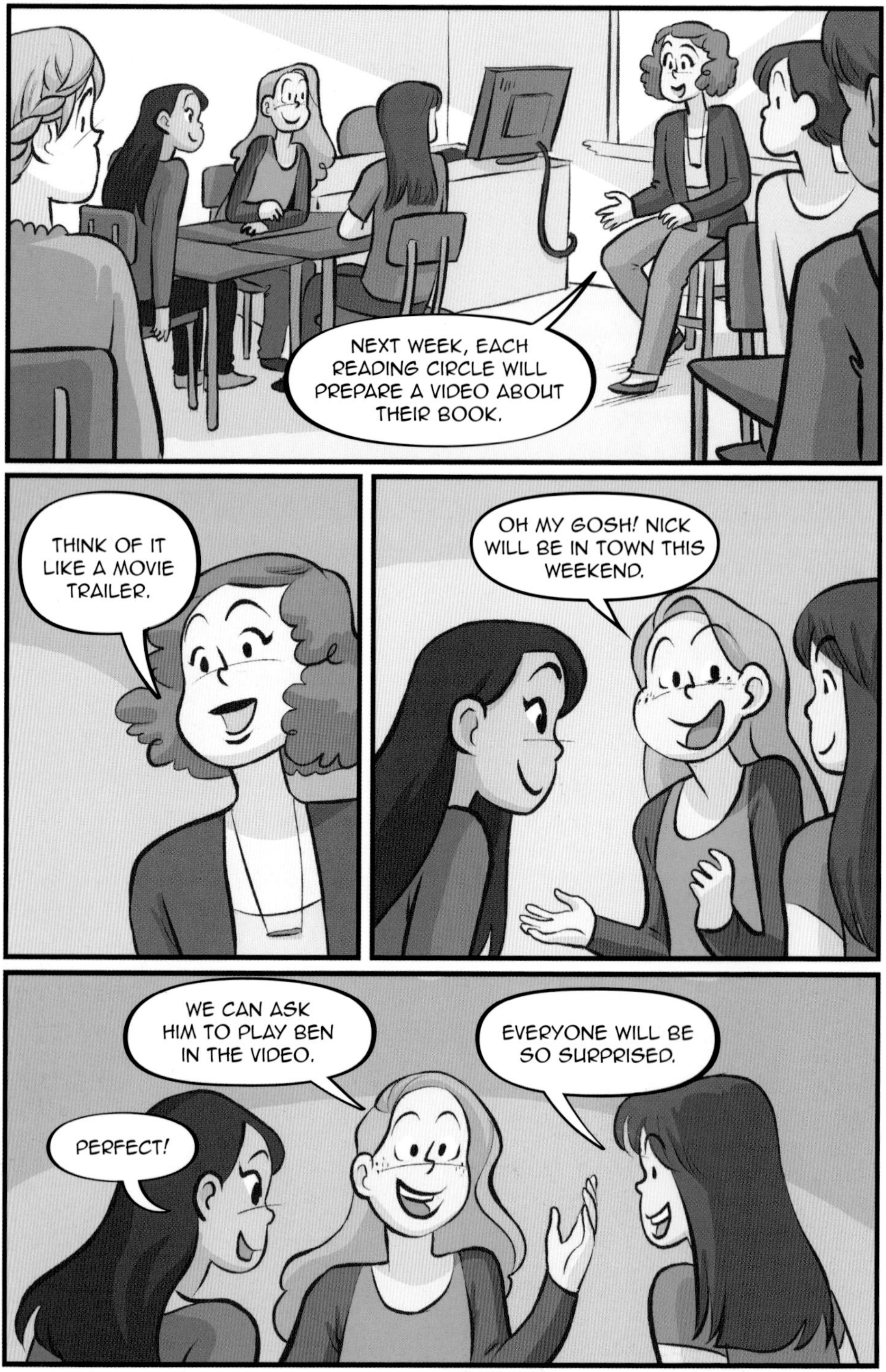
NEXT WEEK, EACH READING CIRCLE WILL PREPARE A VIDEO ABOUT THEIR BOOK.
THINK OF IT LIKE A MOVIE TRAILER.
OH MY GOSH! NICK WILL BE IN TOWN THIS WEEKEND.
WE CAN ASK HIM TO PLAY BEN IN THE VIDEO.
EVERYONE WILL BE SO SURPRISED.
PERFECT!

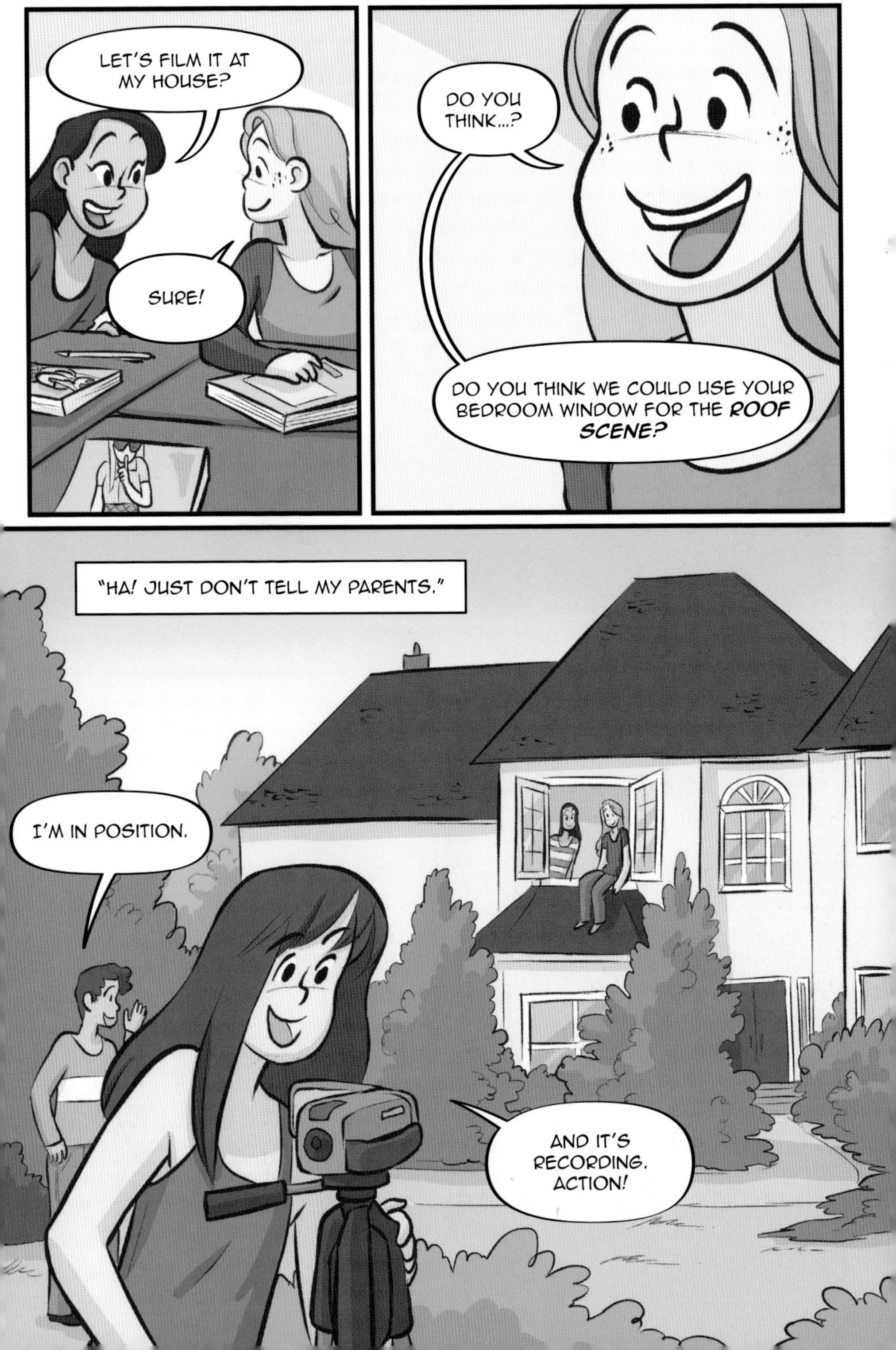
LET'S FILM IT AT MY HOUSE?
SURE!
DO YOU THINK...?
DO YOU THINK WE COULD USE YOUR BEDROOM WINDOW FOR THE *ROOF SCENE?*
"HA! JUST DON'T TELL MY PARENTS."
I'M IN POSITION.
AND IT'S RECORDING. ACTION!

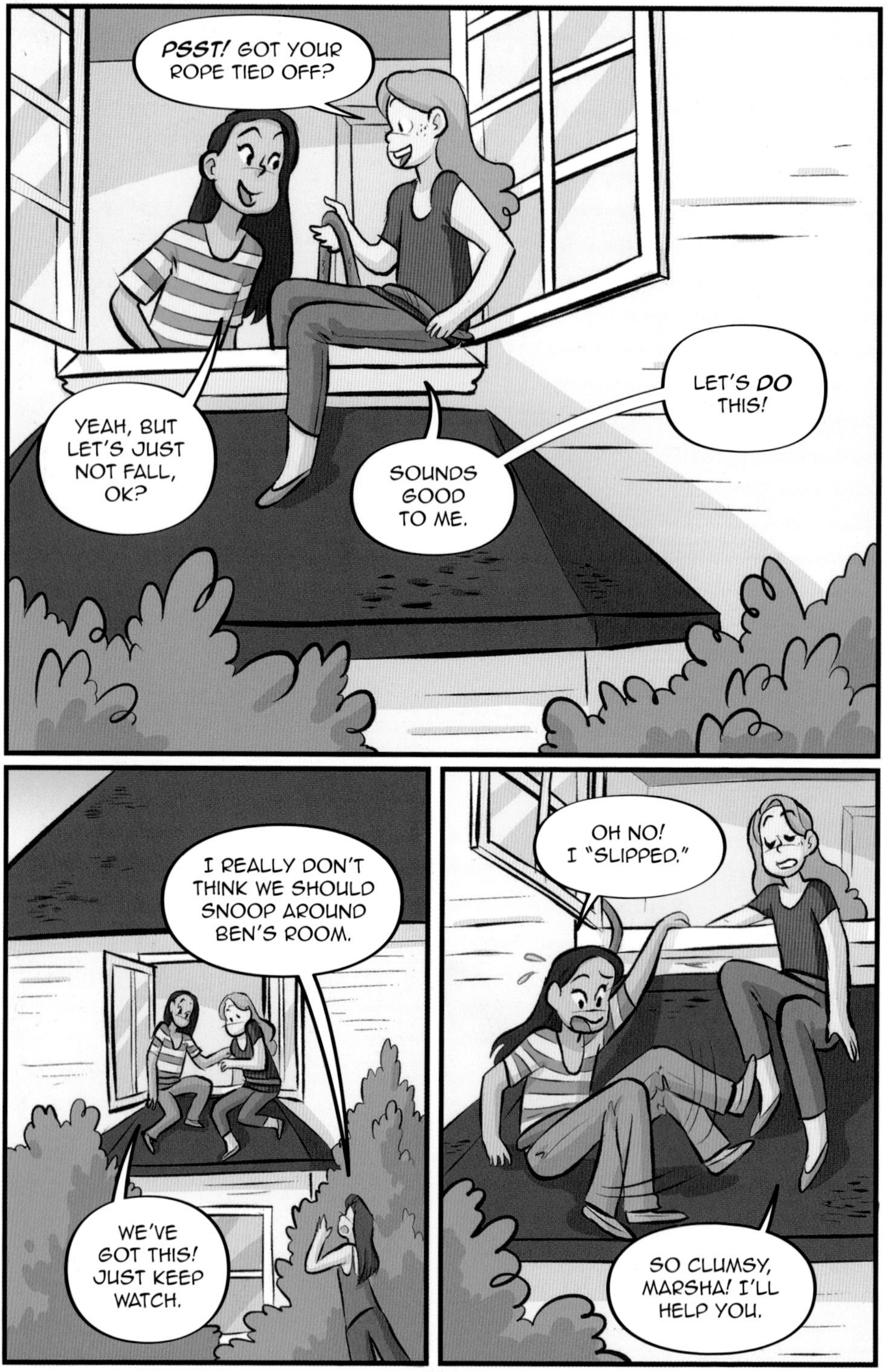
PSST! GOT YOUR ROPE TIED OFF?
YEAH, BUT LET'S JUST NOT FALL, OK?
SOUNDS GOOD TO ME.
LET'S DO THIS!
I REALLY DON'T THINK WE SHOULD SNOOP AROUND BEN'S ROOM.
WE'VE GOT THIS! JUST KEEP WATCH.
OH NO! I "SLIPPED."
SO CLUMSY, MARSHA! I'LL HELP YOU.

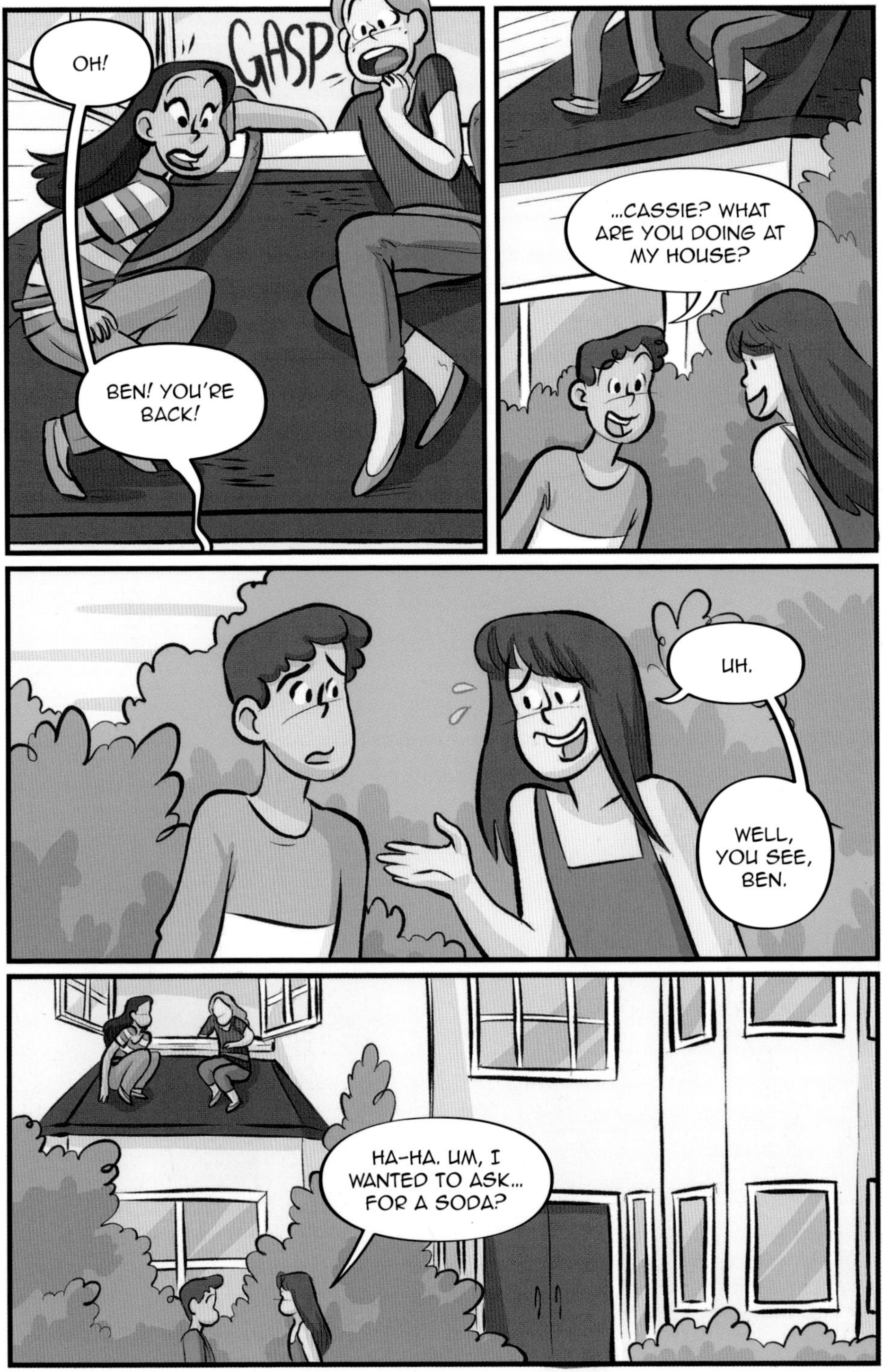
OH!
GASP
BEN! YOU'RE BACK!
...CASSIE? WHAT ARE YOU DOING AT MY HOUSE?
UH.
WELL, YOU SEE, BEN.
HA-HA. UM, I WANTED TO ASK... FOR A SODA?

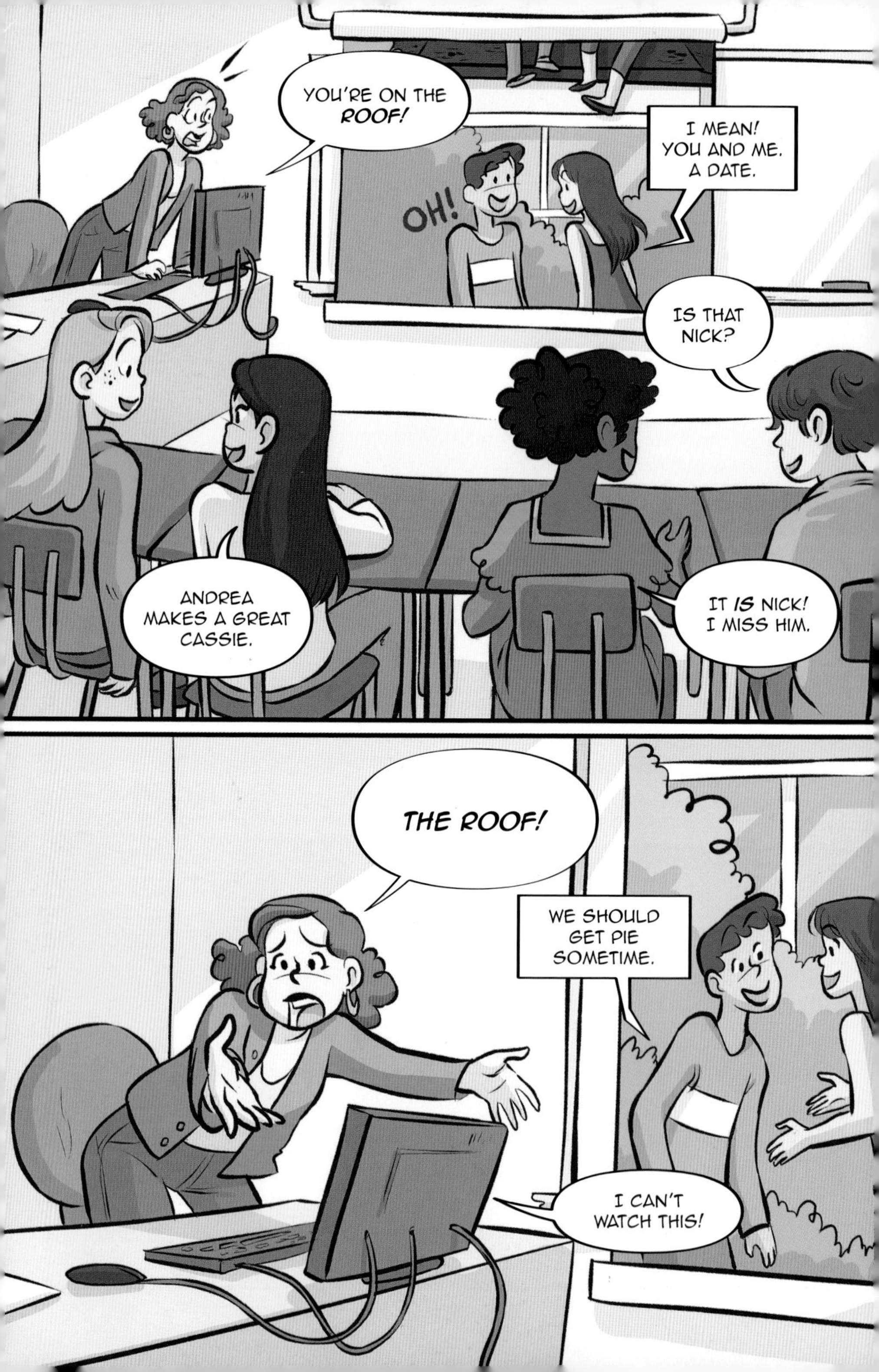
YOU'RE ON THE ROOF!
I MEAN! YOU AND ME. A DATE.
OH!
IS THAT NICK?
ANDREA MAKES A GREAT CASSIE.
IT IS NICK! I MISS HIM.
THE ROOF!
WE SHOULD GET PIE SOMETIME.
I CAN'T WATCH THIS!

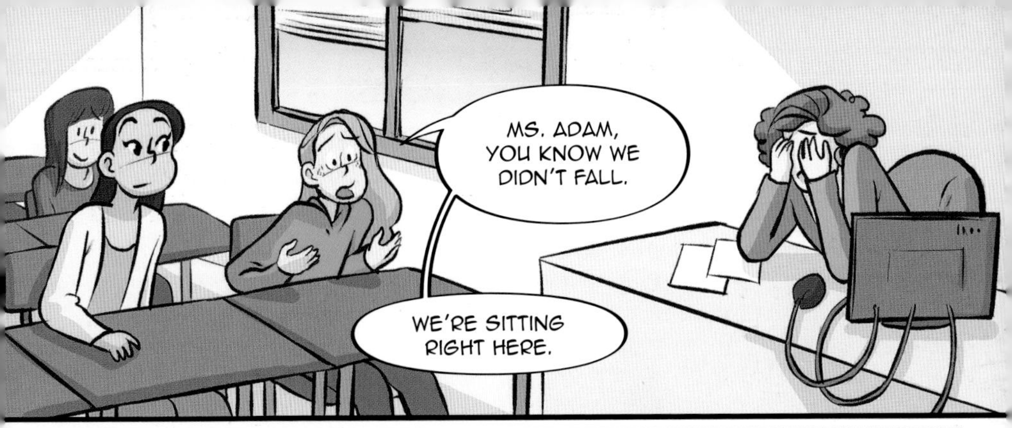
MS. ADAM, YOU KNOW WE DIDN'T FALL.
WE'RE SITTING RIGHT HERE.

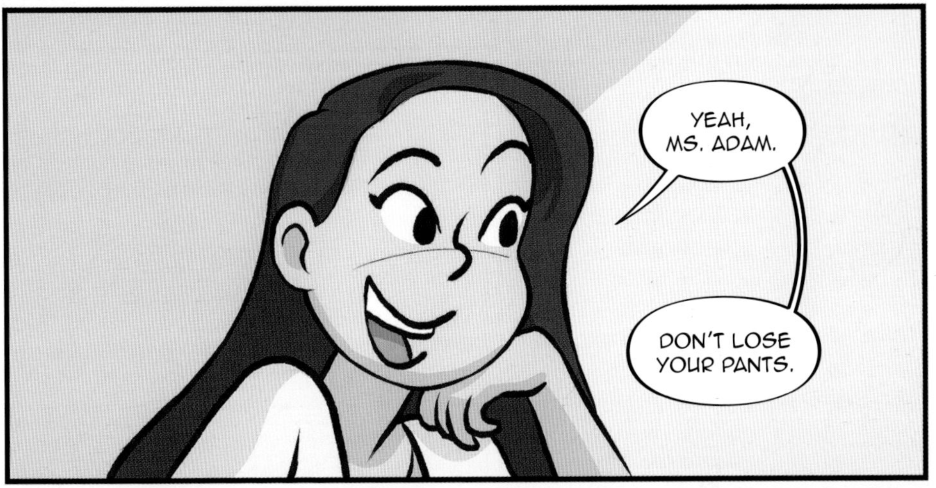
YEAH, MS. ADAM.
DON'T LOSE YOUR PANTS.

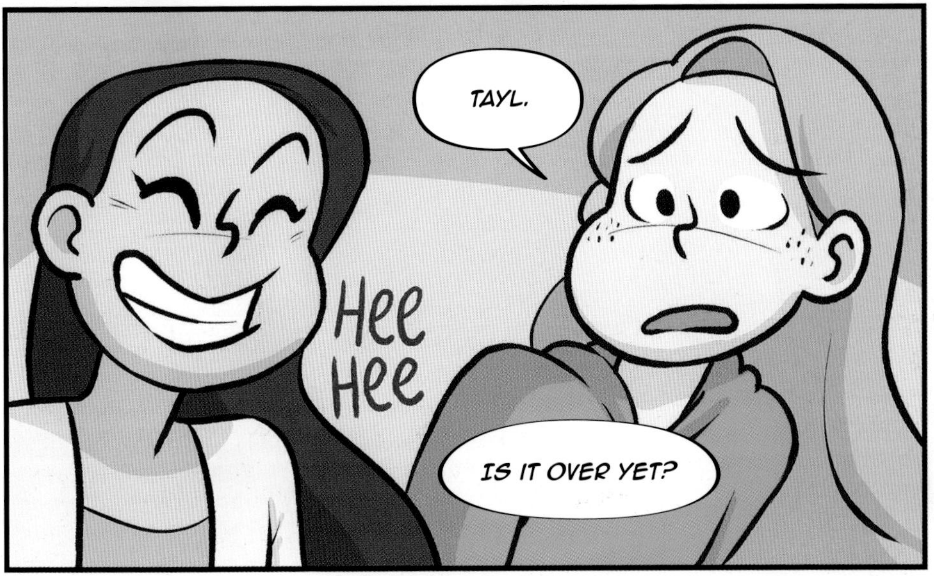
TAYL.
Hee Hee
IS IT OVER YET?

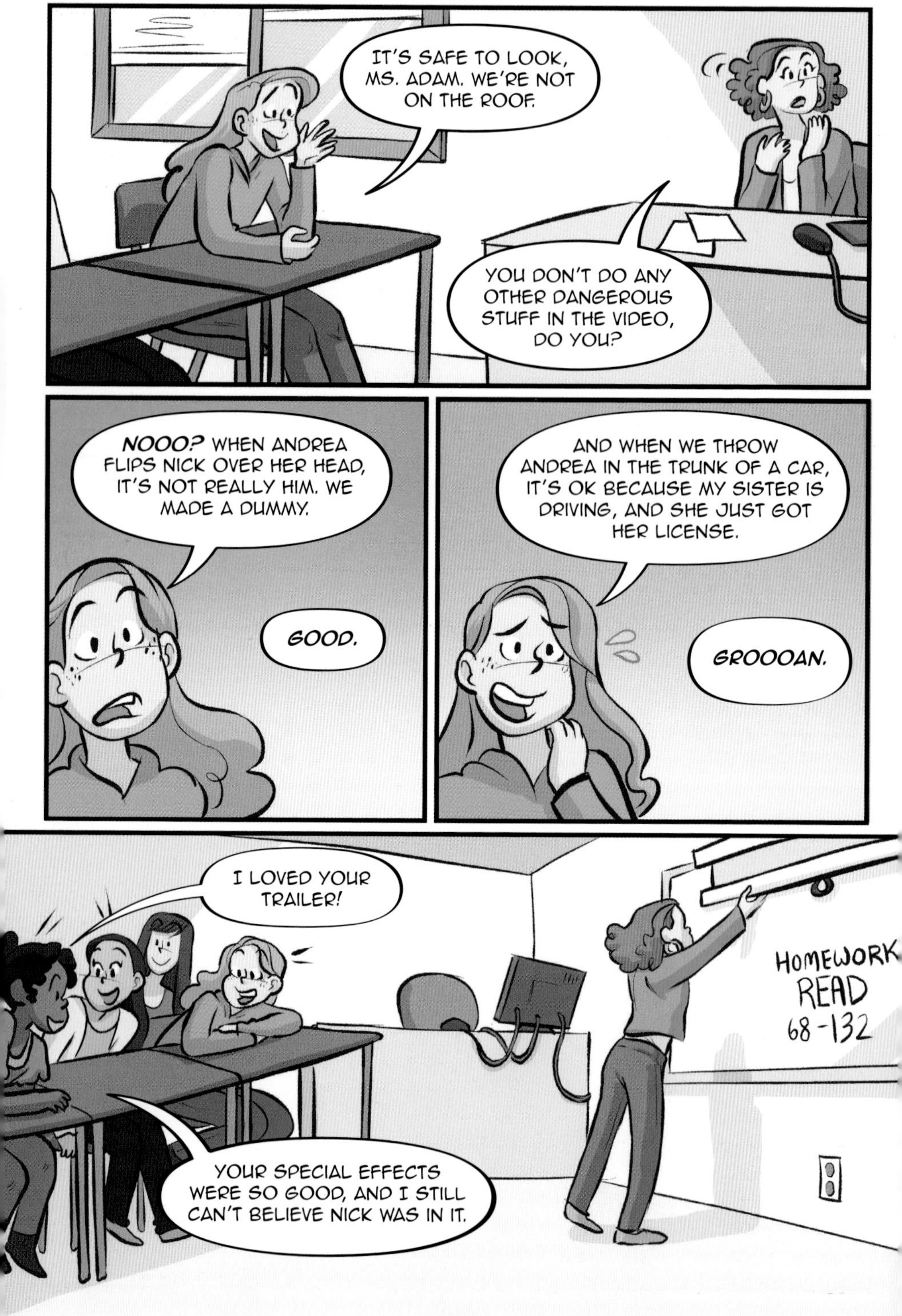
IT'S SAFE TO LOOK, MS. ADAM. WE'RE NOT ON THE ROOF.
YOU DON'T DO ANY OTHER DANGEROUS STUFF IN THE VIDEO, DO YOU?
NOOO? WHEN ANDREA FLIPS NICK OVER HER HEAD, IT'S NOT REALLY HIM. WE MADE A DUMMY.
GOOD.
AND WHEN WE THROW ANDREA IN THE TRUNK OF A CAR, IT'S OK BECAUSE MY SISTER IS DRIVING, AND SHE JUST GOT HER LICENSE.
GROOOAN.
I LOVED YOUR TRAILER!
HOMEWORK
READ
68-132
YOUR SPECIAL EFFECTS WERE SO GOOD, AND I STILL CAN'T BELIEVE NICK WAS IN IT.

OK! JUST ONE MORE THING BEFORE YOU CAN ALL GO HOME.

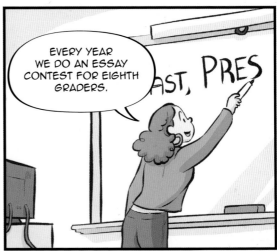

EVERY YEAR WE DO AN ESSAY CONTEST FOR EIGHTH GRADERS.

PICK PAST, PRESENT, OR FUTURE AS YOUR ESSAY TOPIC. WHOEVER WRITES THE BEST ESSAY FOR EACH TOPIC...

...GETS TO READ IT ALOUD AT GRADUATION.

GOOD LUCK.

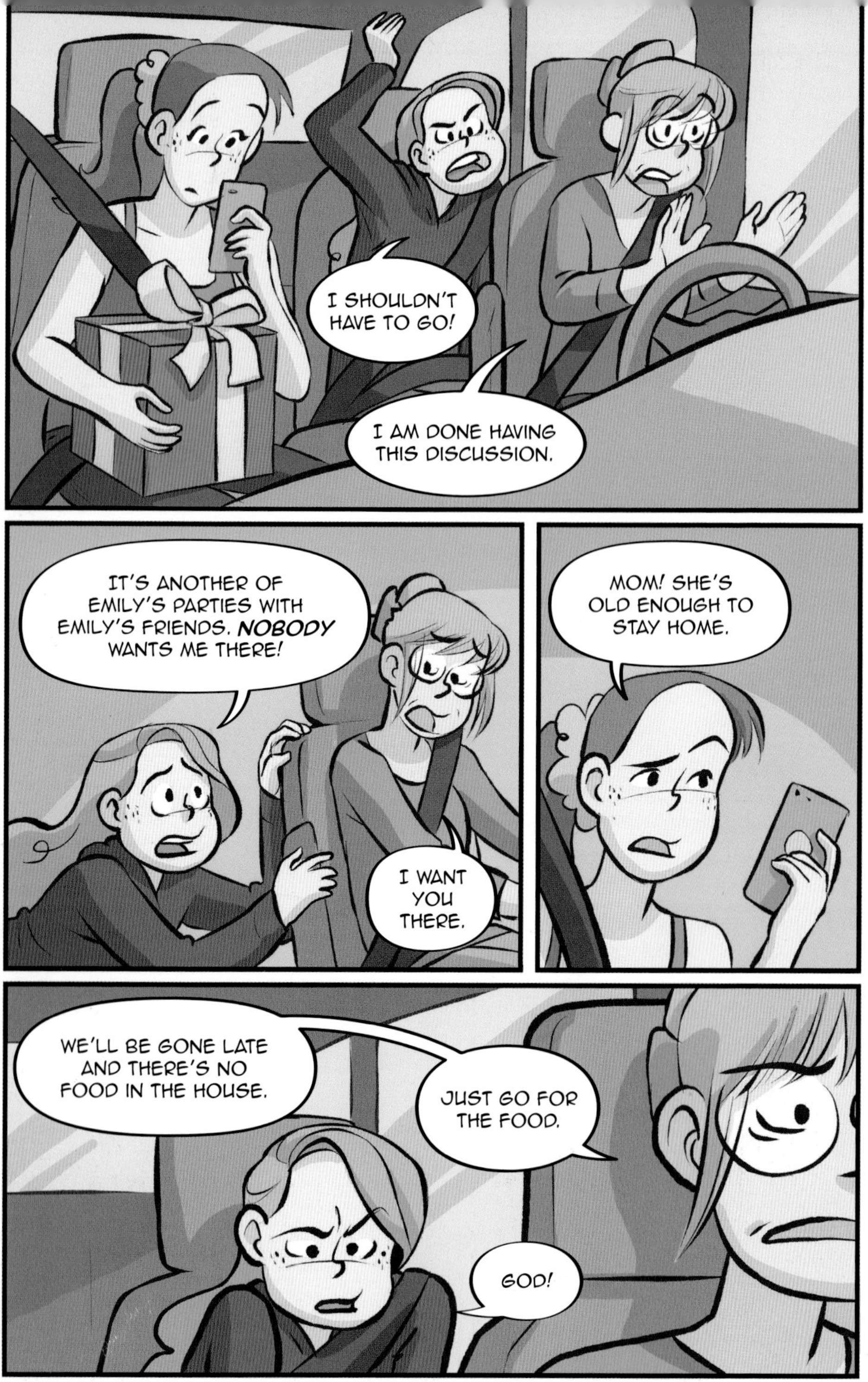
I SHOULDN'T HAVE TO GO!
I AM DONE HAVING THIS DISCUSSION.
IT'S ANOTHER OF EMILY'S PARTIES WITH EMILY'S FRIENDS. ***NOBODY*** WANTS ME THERE!
I WANT YOU THERE.
MOM! SHE'S OLD ENOUGH TO STAY HOME.
WE'LL BE GONE LATE AND THERE'S NO FOOD IN THE HOUSE.
JUST GO FOR THE FOOD.
GOD!

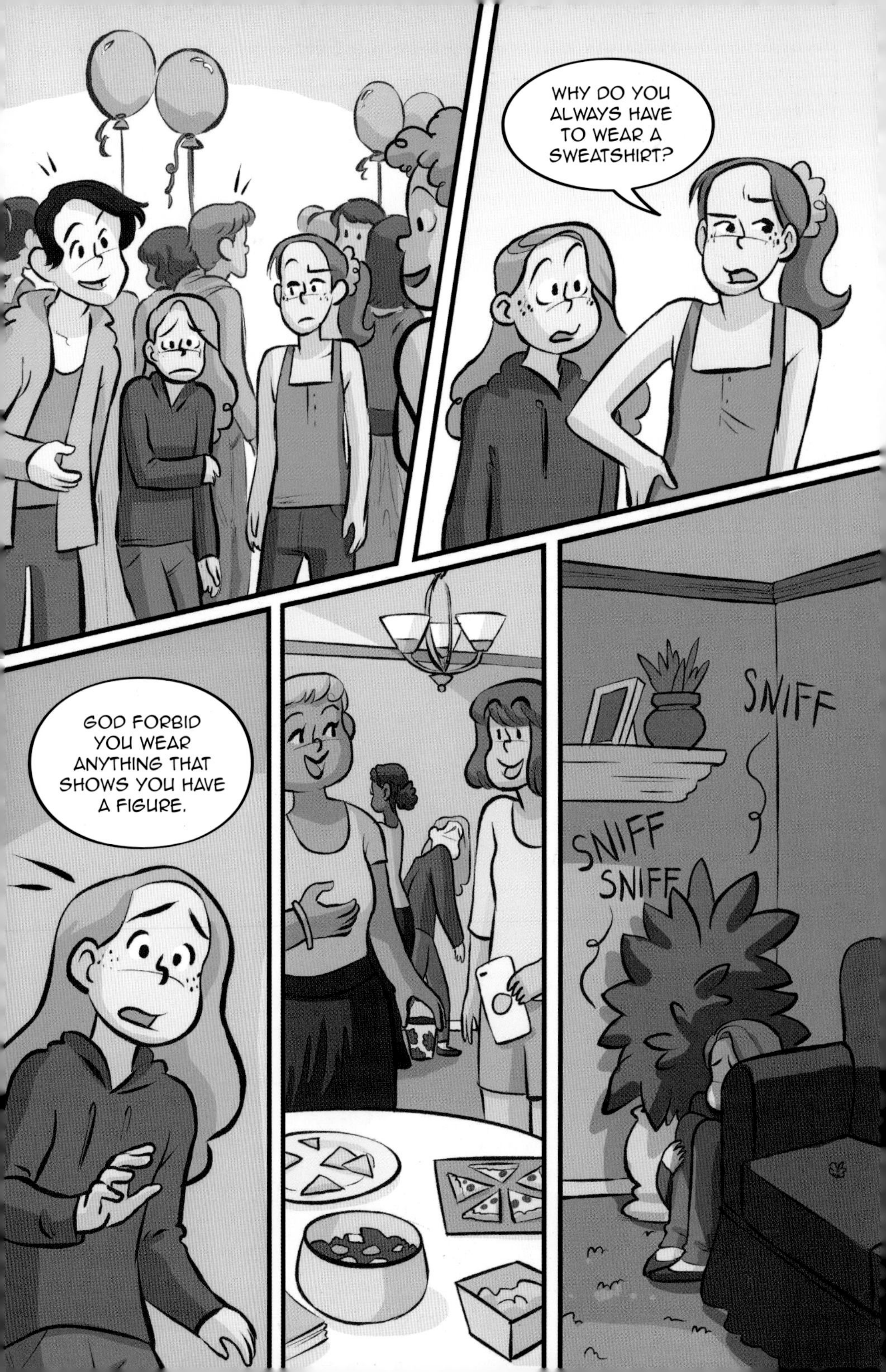
WHY DO YOU ALWAYS HAVE TO WEAR A SWEATSHIRT?
GOD FORBID YOU WEAR ANYTHING THAT SHOWS YOU HAVE A FIGURE.
SNIFF
SNIFF
SNIFF

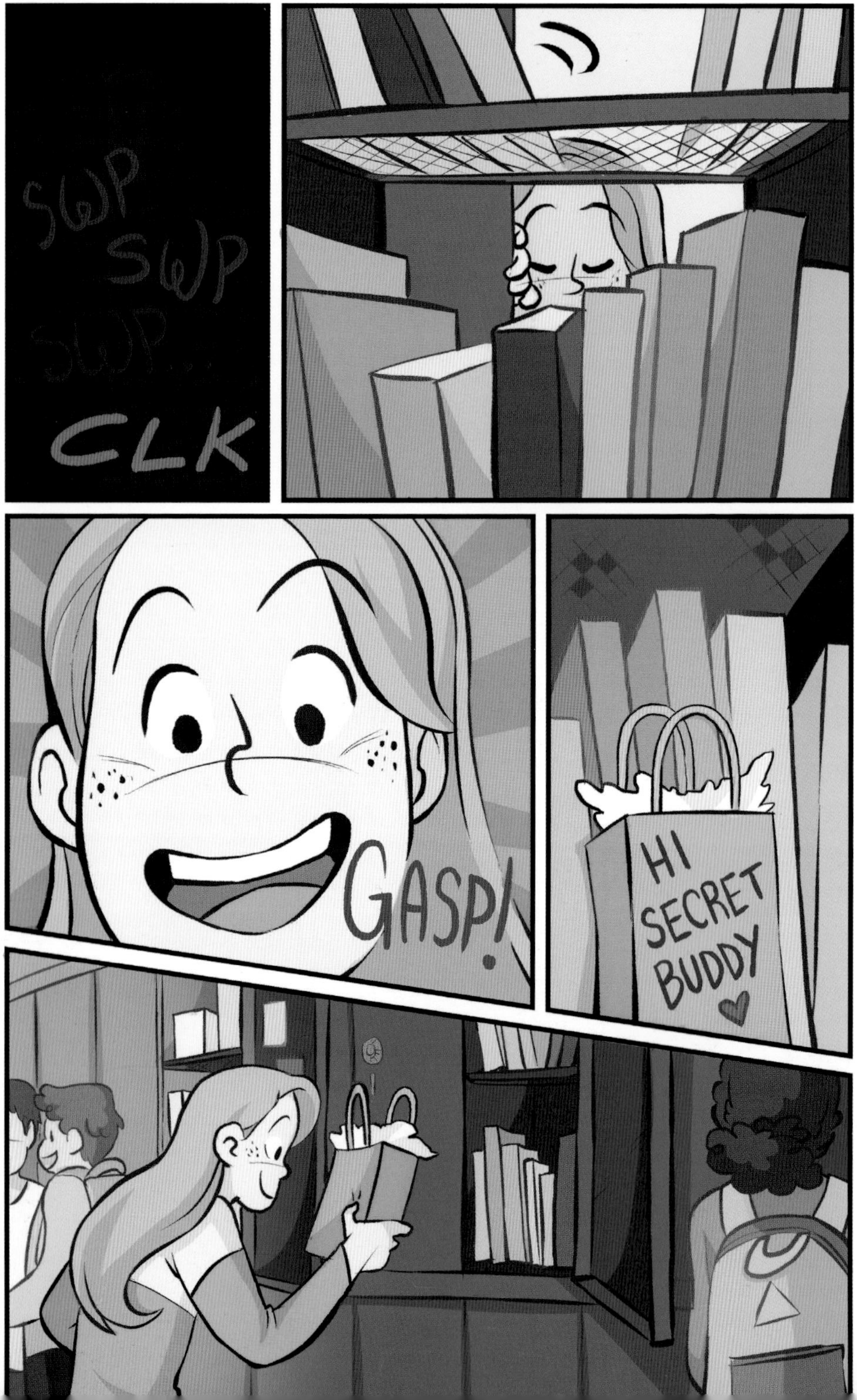
SWP
SWP
SWP...
CLK
GASP!
HI SECRET BUDDY

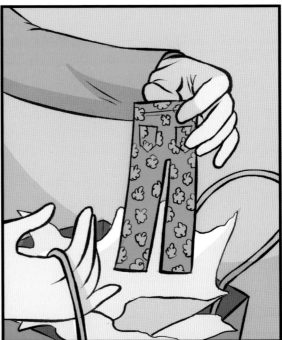

NOW YOU HAVE A BACKUP PAIR!

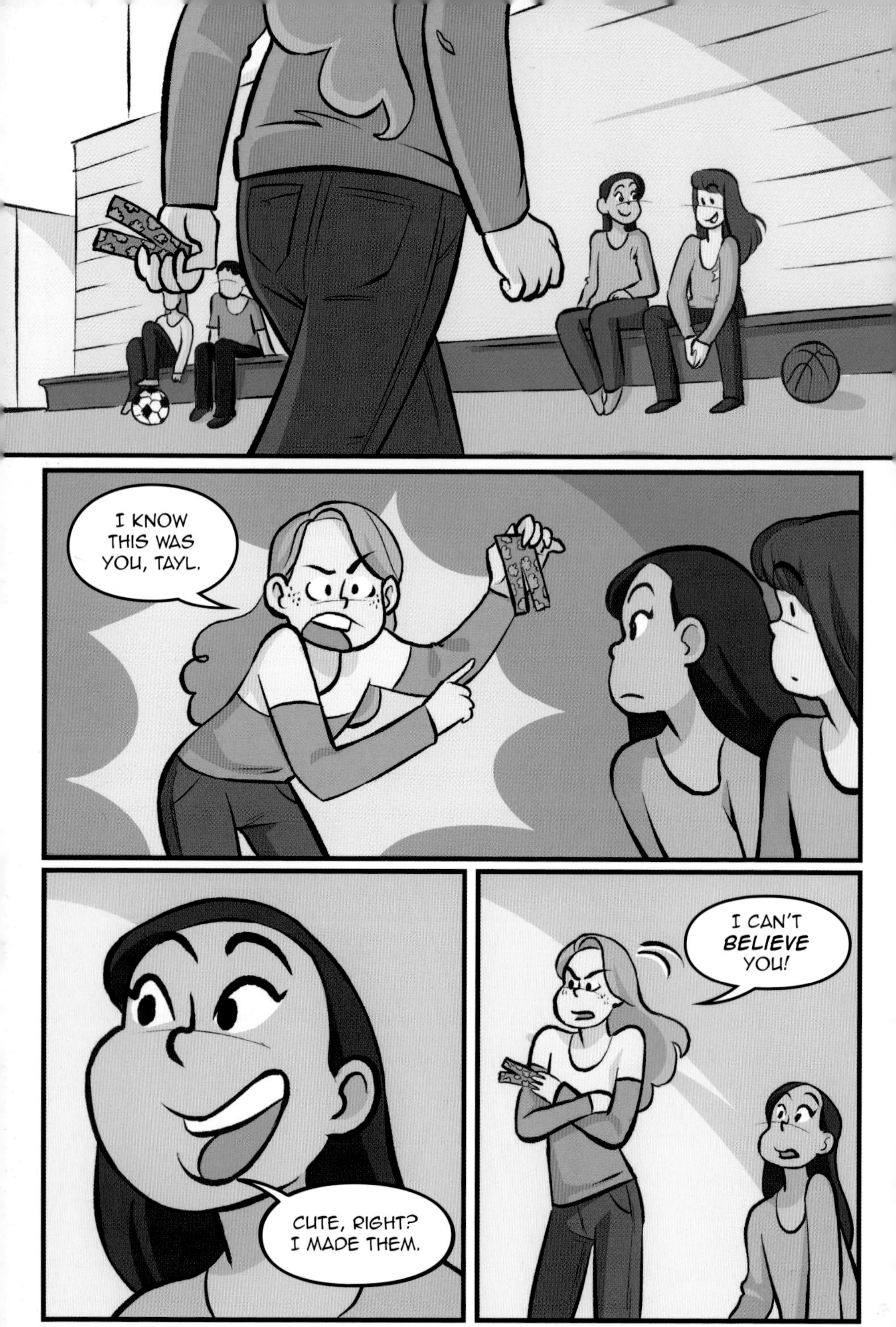

I KNOW THIS WAS YOU, TAYL.
CUTE, RIGHT? I MADE THEM.
I CAN'T *BELIEVE* YOU!

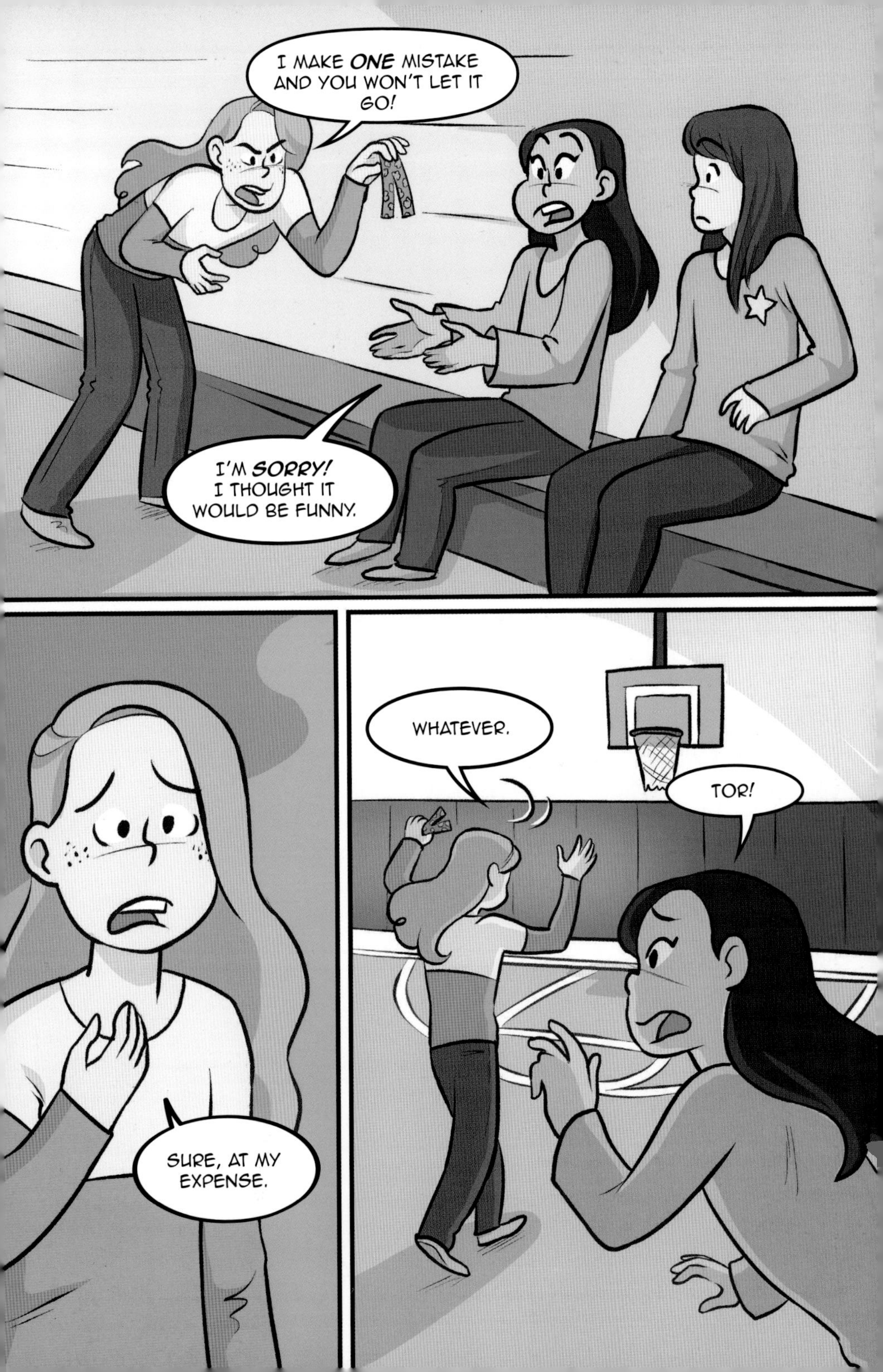
I MAKE ONE MISTAKE AND YOU WON'T LET IT GO!
I'M SORRY! I THOUGHT IT WOULD BE FUNNY.
SURE, AT MY EXPENSE.
WHATEVER.
TOR!

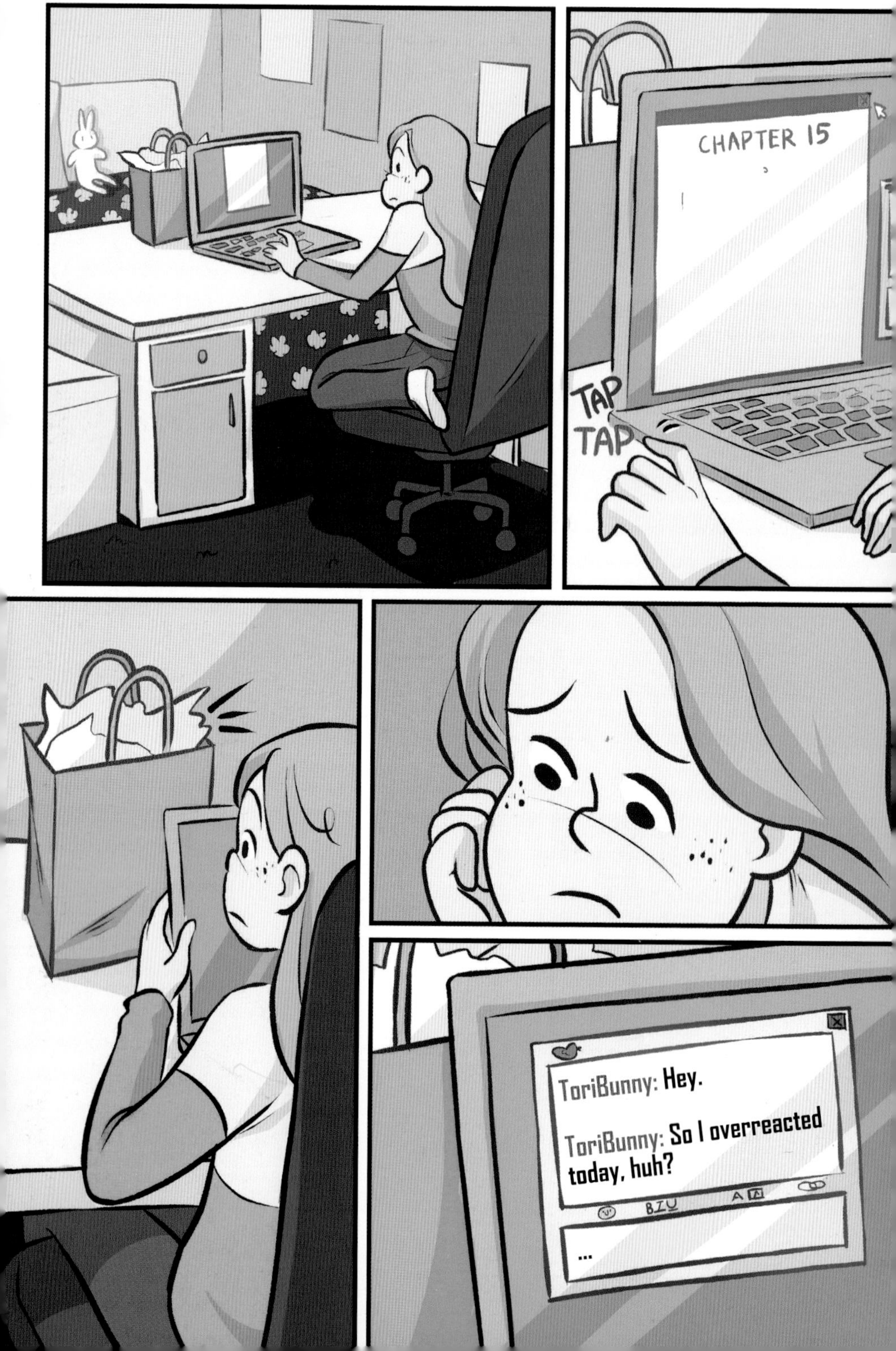
CHAPTER 15
TAP
TAP
ToriBunny: Hey.
ToriBunny: So I overreacted today, huh?
...

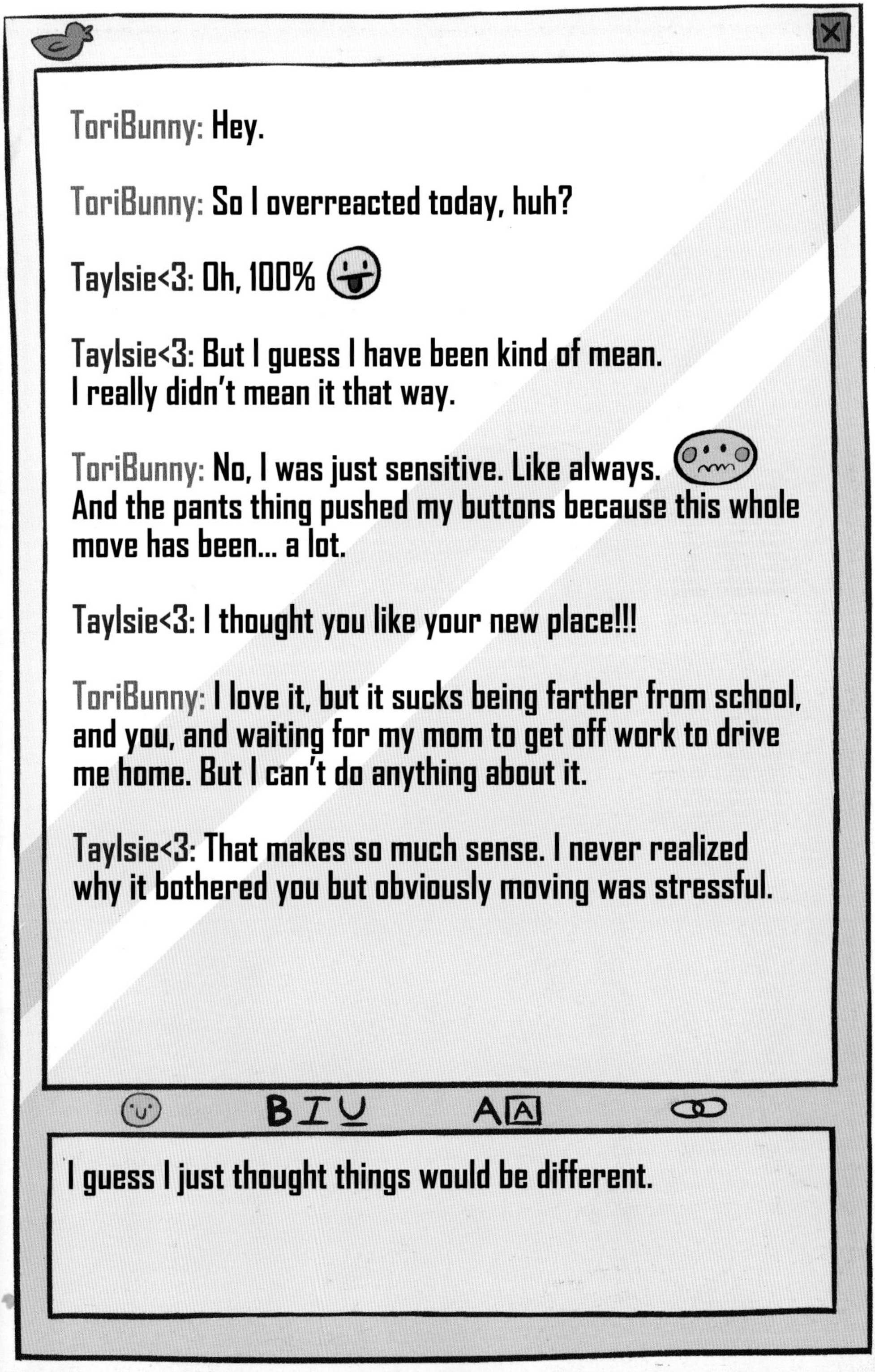
ToriBunny: Hey.
ToriBunny: So I overreacted today, huh?
Taylsie<3: Oh, 100%
Taylsie<3: But I guess I have been kind of mean. I really didn't mean it that way.
ToriBunny: No, I was just sensitive. Like always. And the pants thing pushed my buttons because this whole move has been... a lot.
Taylsie<3: I thought you like your new place!!!
ToriBunny: I love it, but it sucks being farther from school, and you, and waiting for my mom to get off work to drive me home. But I can't do anything about it.
Taylsie<3: That makes so much sense. I never realized why it bothered you but obviously moving was stressful.
BIU
AA
I guess I just thought things would be different.

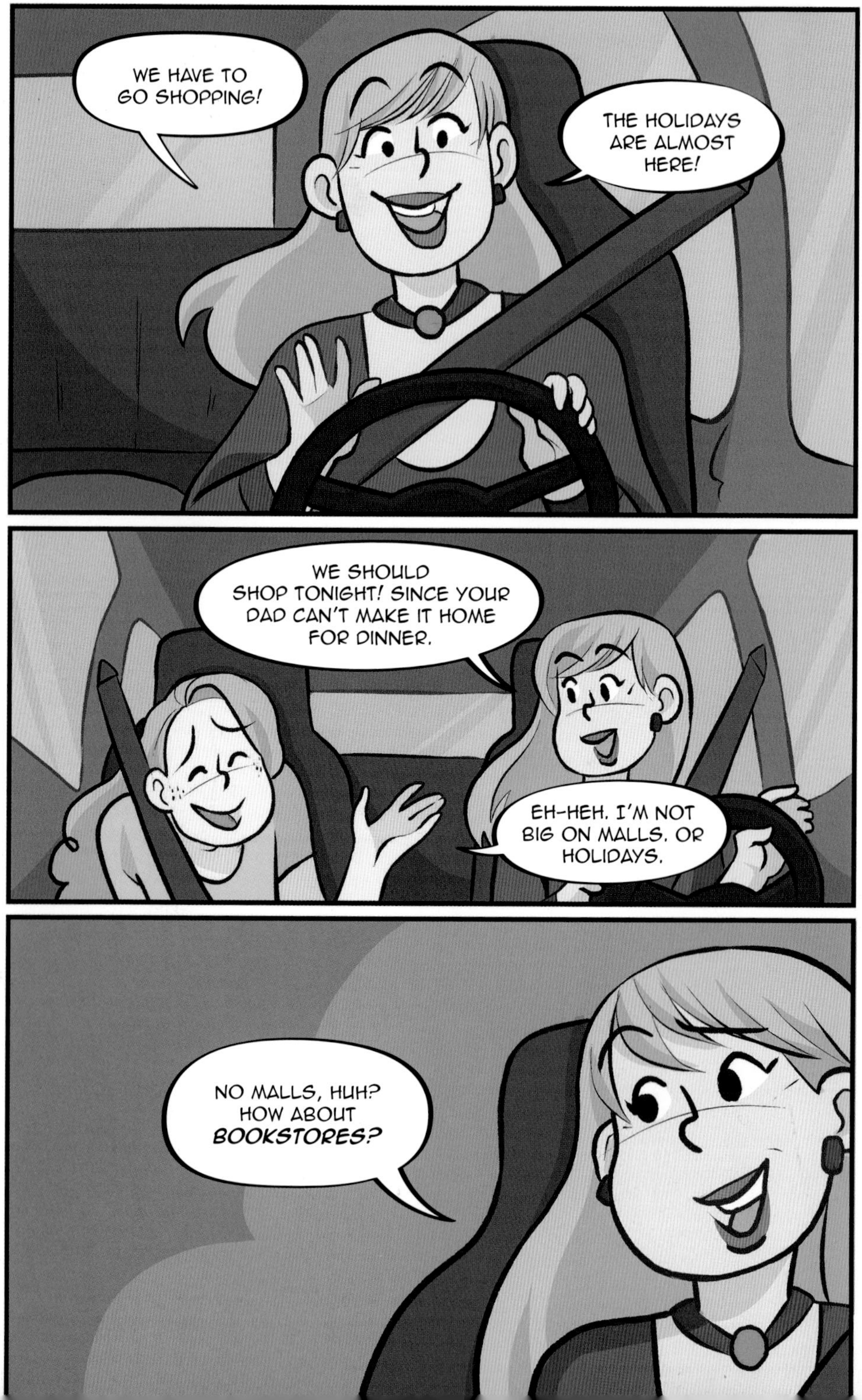
WE HAVE TO GO SHOPPING!
THE HOLIDAYS ARE ALMOST HERE!
WE SHOULD SHOP TONIGHT! SINCE YOUR DAD CAN'T MAKE IT HOME FOR DINNER.
EH-HEH. I'M NOT BIG ON MALLS. OR HOLIDAYS.
NO MALLS, HUH? HOW ABOUT *BOOKSTORES?*

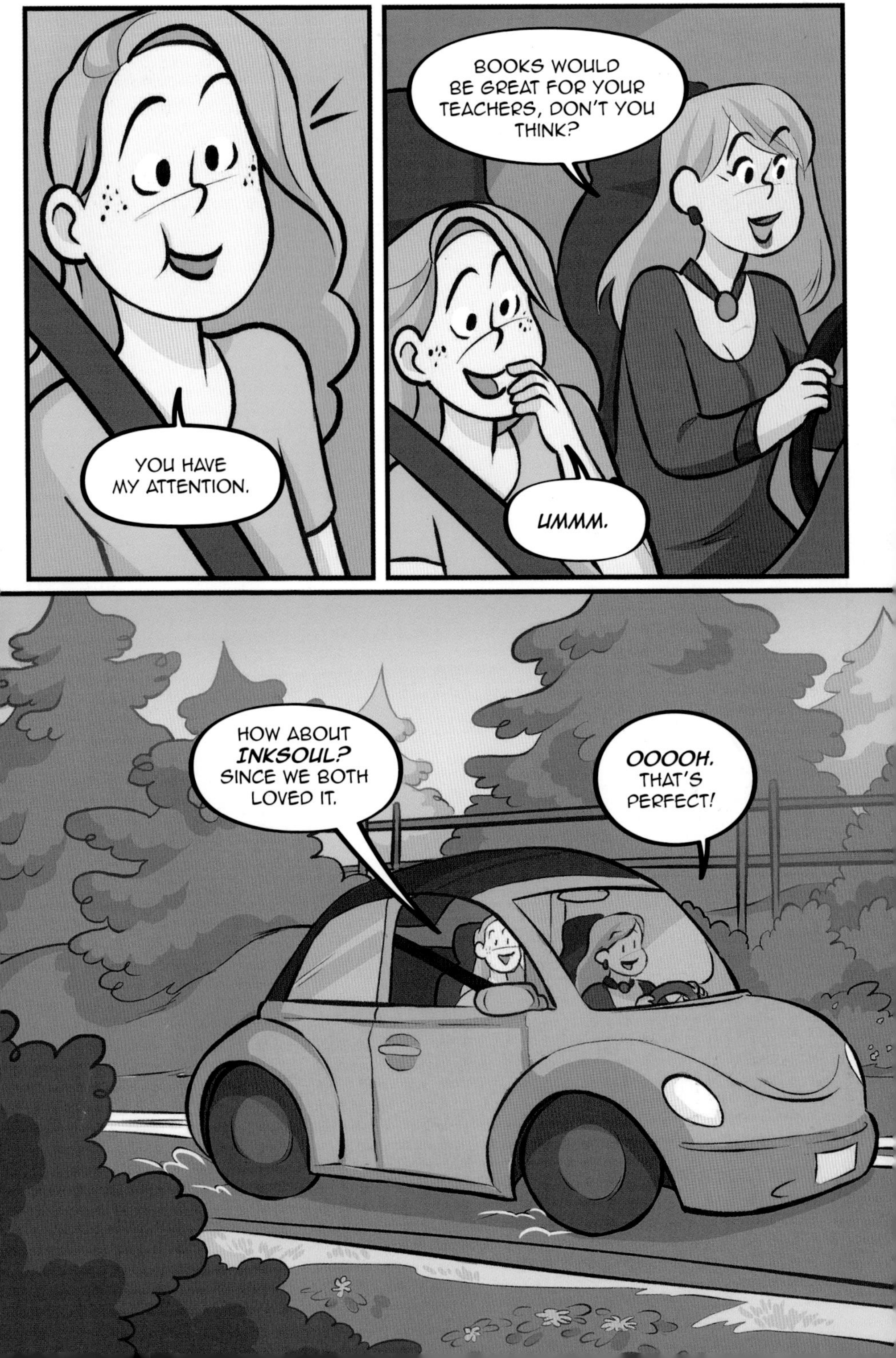
YOU HAVE MY ATTENTION.
BOOKS WOULD BE GREAT FOR YOUR TEACHERS, DON'T YOU THINK?
UMMM.
HOW ABOUT INKSOUL? SINCE WE BOTH LOVED IT.
OOOOH. THAT'S PERFECT!

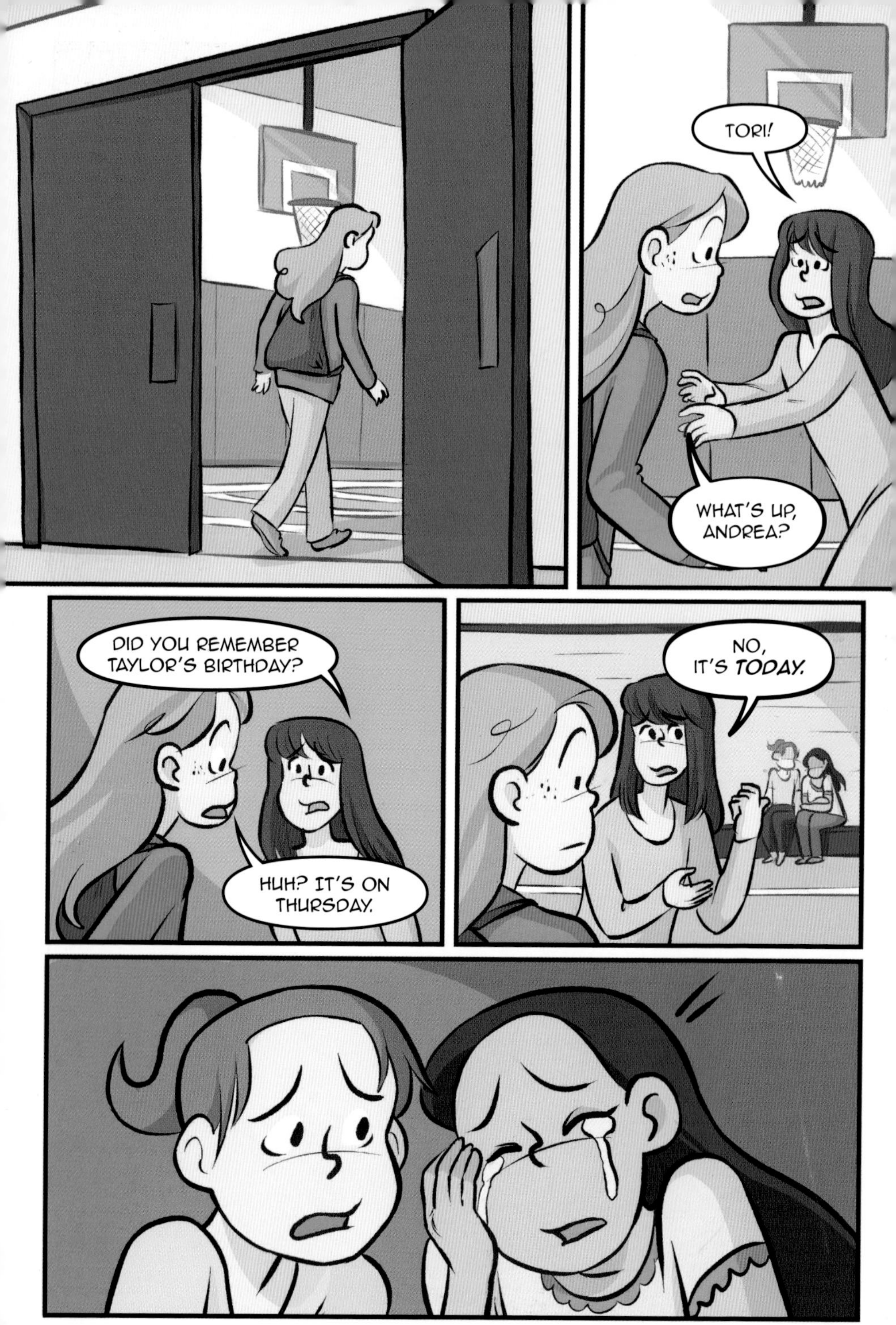
TORI!
WHAT'S UP, ANDREA?
DID YOU REMEMBER TAYLOR'S BIRTHDAY?
HUH? IT'S ON THURSDAY.
NO, IT'S *TODAY.*

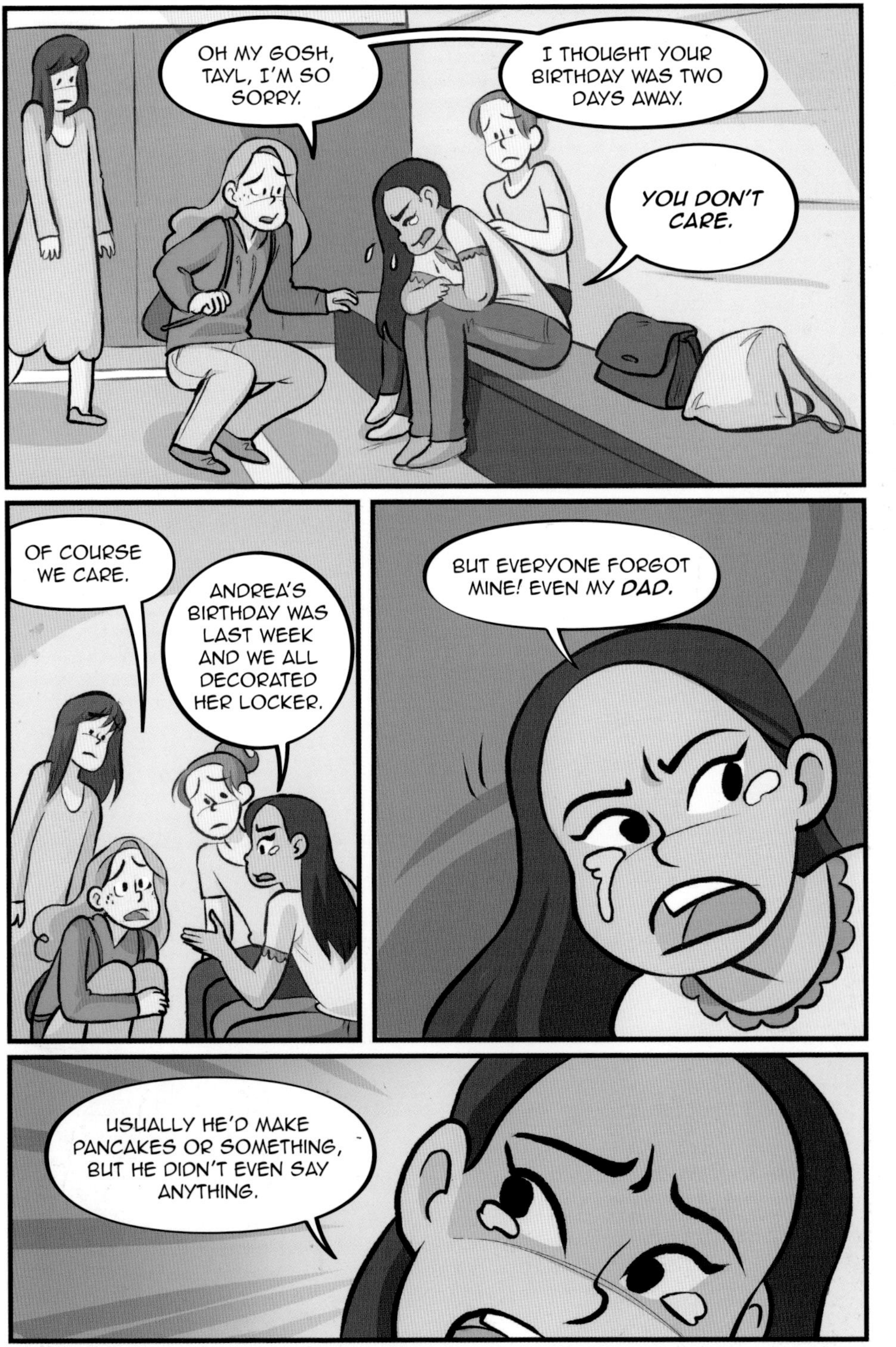
OH MY GOSH, TAYL, I'M SO SORRY.
I THOUGHT YOUR BIRTHDAY WAS TWO DAYS AWAY.
*YOU DON'T CARE.*
OF COURSE WE CARE.
ANDREA'S BIRTHDAY WAS LAST WEEK AND WE ALL DECORATED HER LOCKER.
BUT EVERYONE FORGOT MINE! EVEN MY *DAD.*
USUALLY HE'D MAKE PANCAKES OR SOMETHING, BUT HE DIDN'T EVEN SAY ANYTHING.

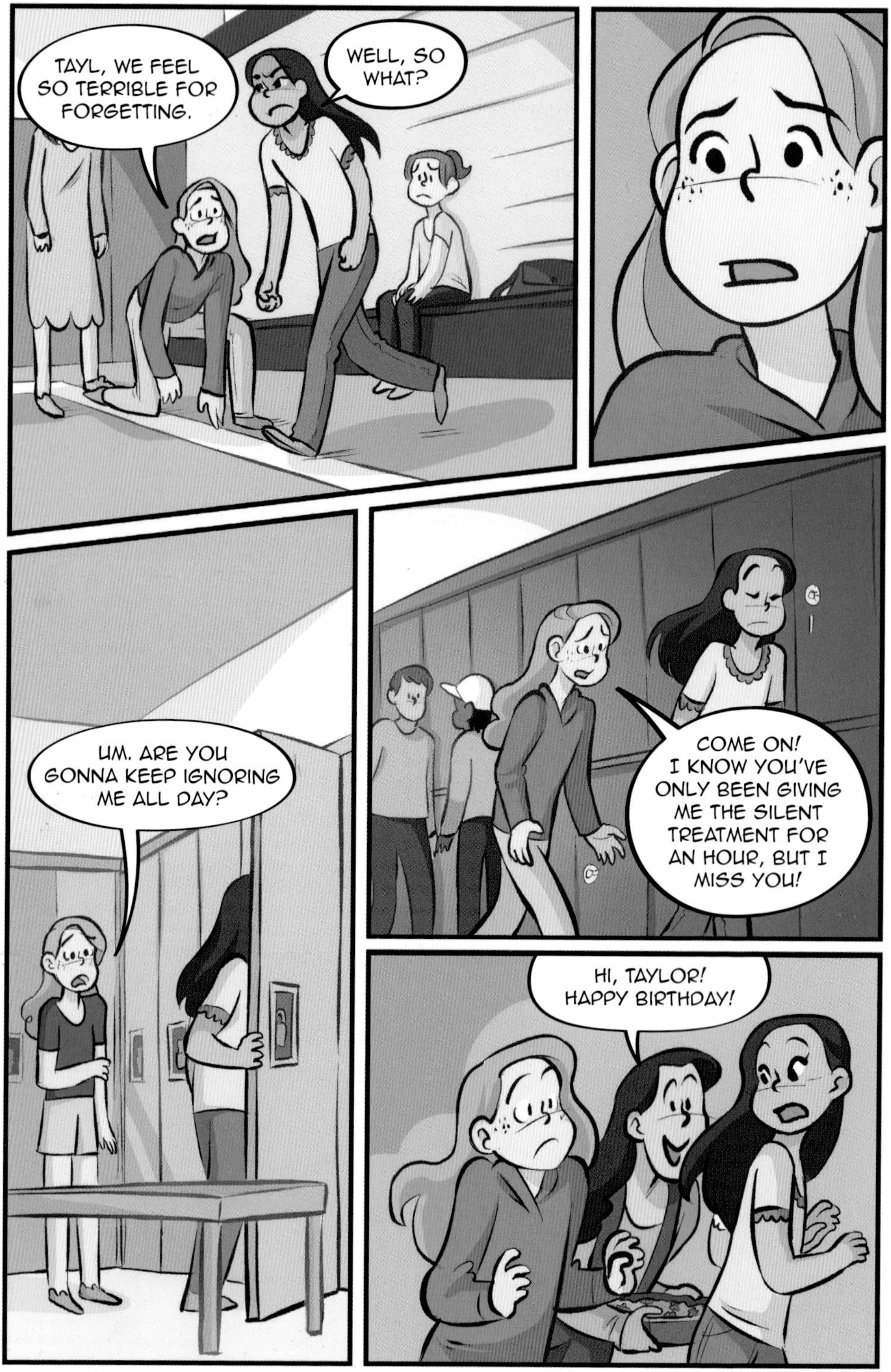
TAYL, WE FEEL SO TERRIBLE FOR FORGETTING.
WELL, SO WHAT?
UM. ARE YOU GONNA KEEP IGNORING ME ALL DAY?
COME ON! I KNOW YOU'VE ONLY BEEN GIVING ME THE SILENT TREATMENT FOR AN HOUR, BUT I MISS YOU!
HI, TAYLOR! HAPPY BIRTHDAY!

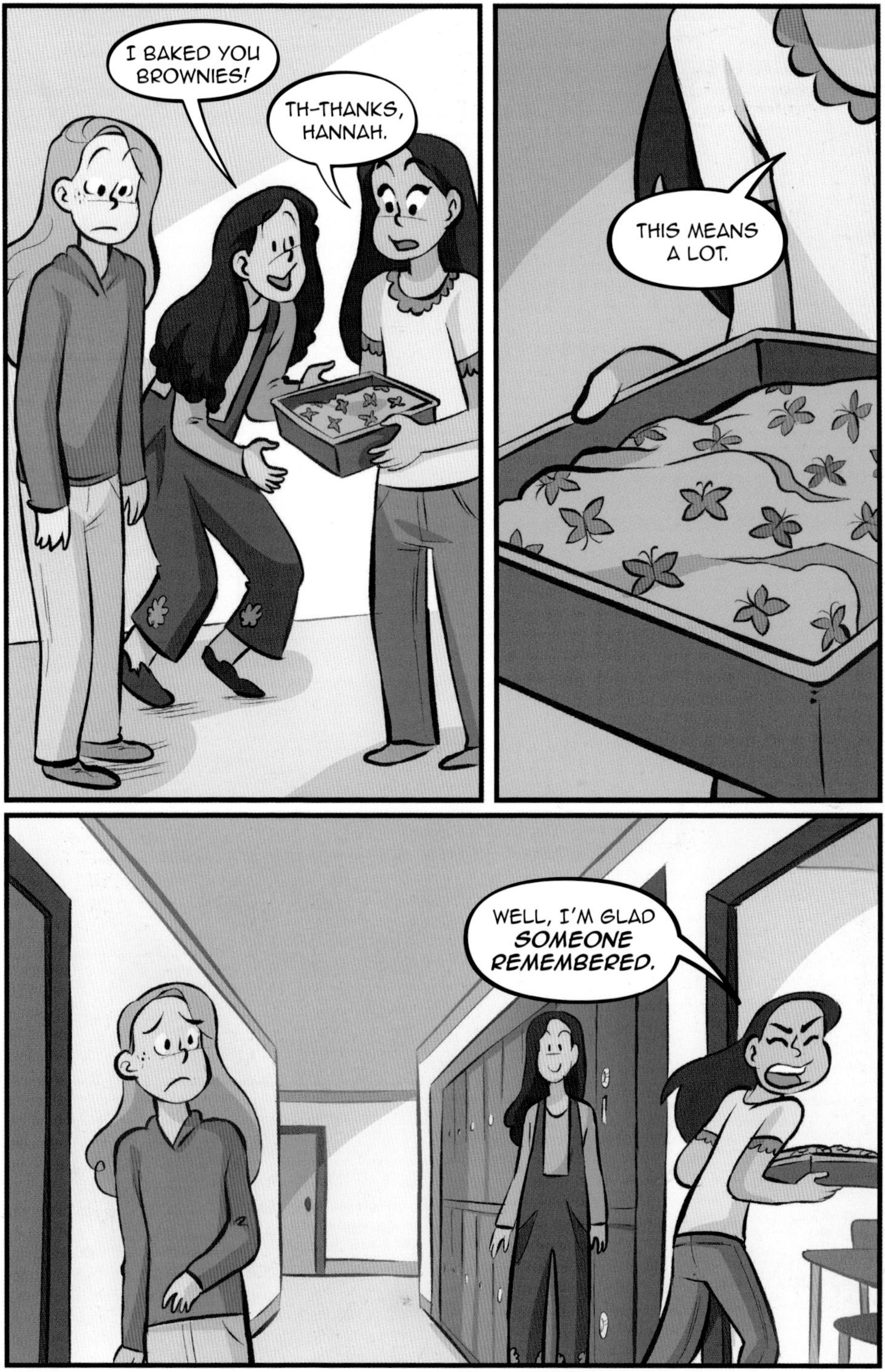
I BAKED YOU BROWNIES!
TH-THANKS, HANNAH.
THIS MEANS A LOT.
WELL, I'M GLAD *SOMEONE* REMEMBERED.

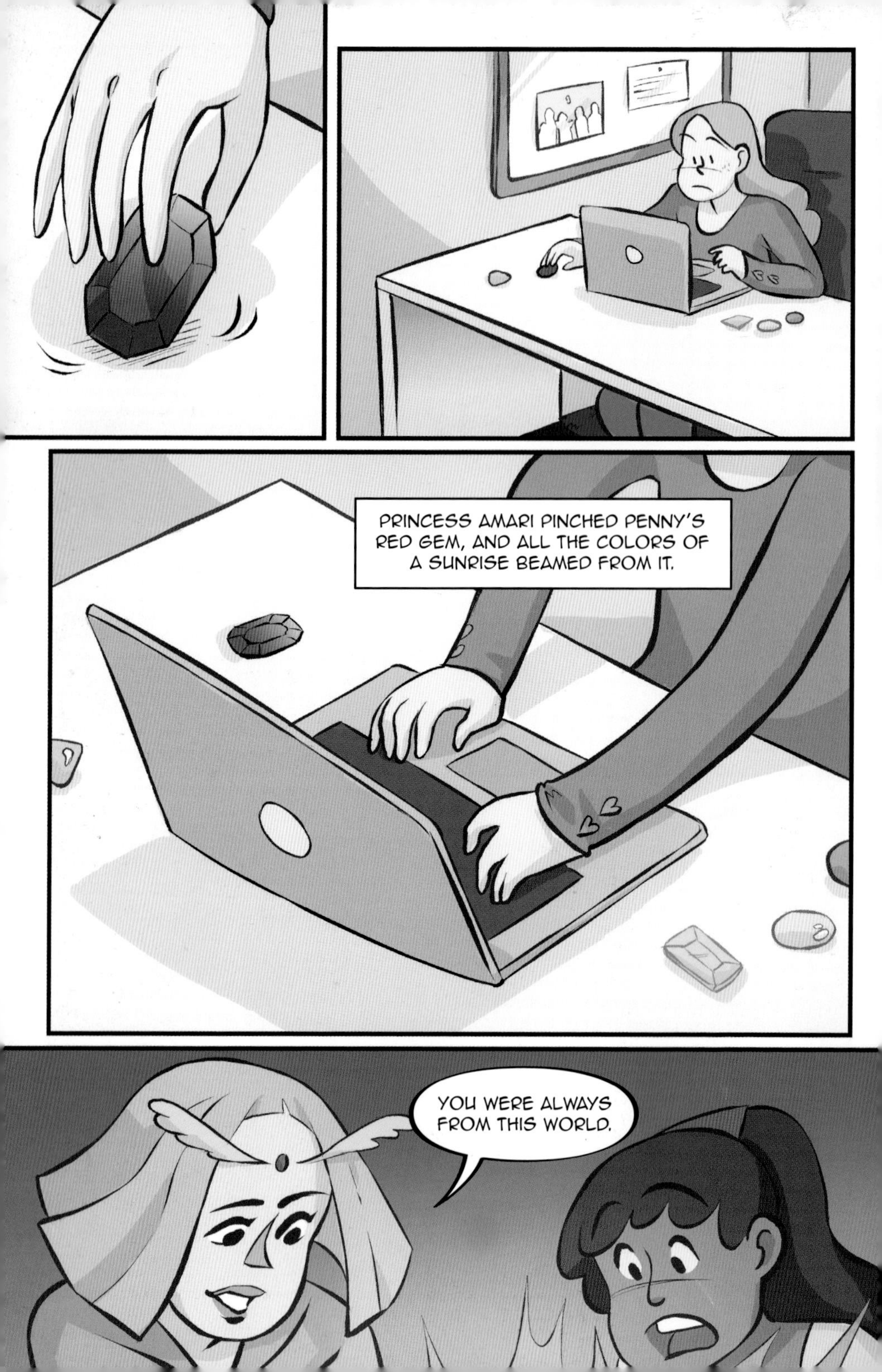
PRINCESS AMARI PINCHED PENNY'S RED GEM, AND ALL THE COLORS OF A SUNRISE BEAMED FROM IT.
YOU WERE ALWAYS FROM THIS WORLD.

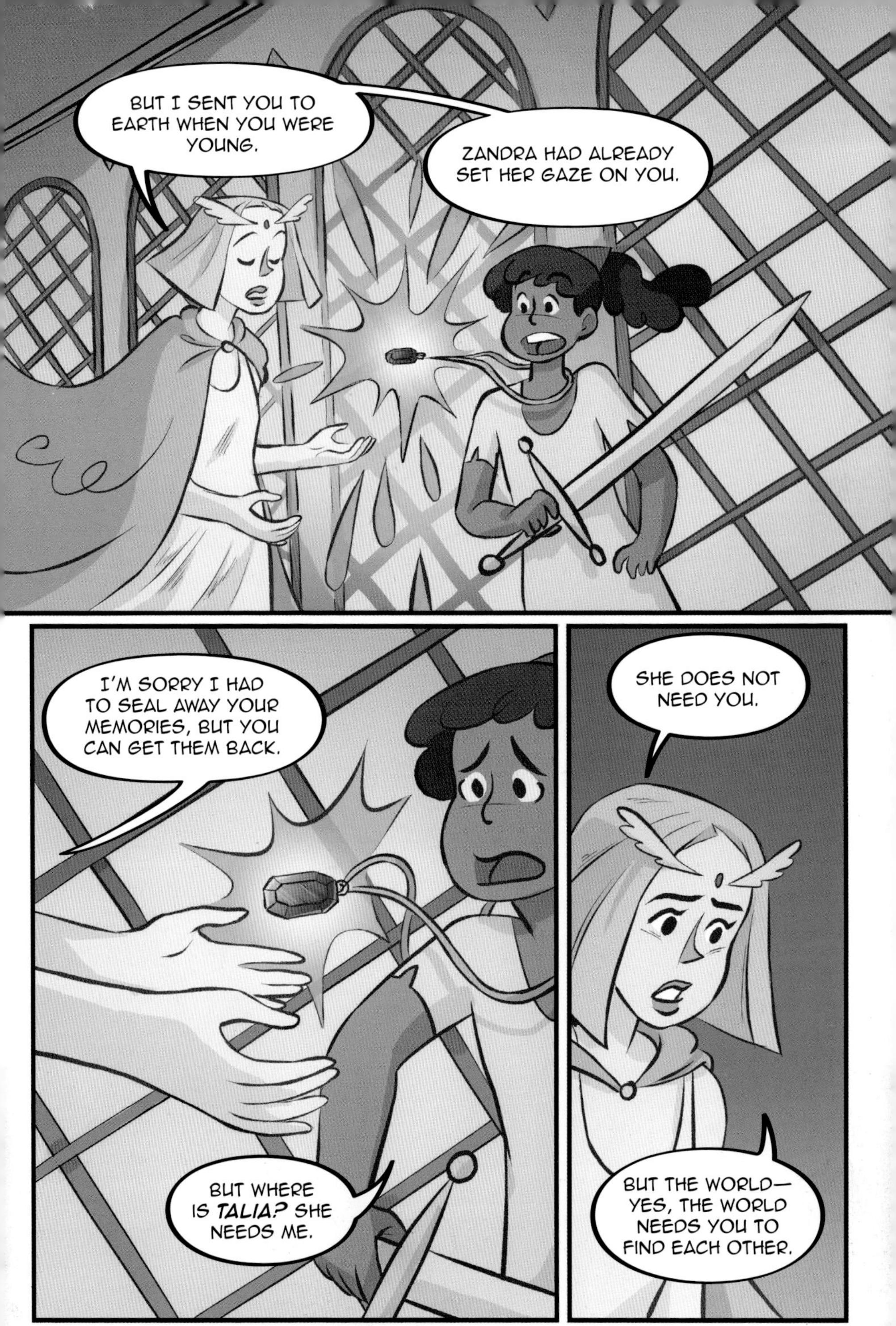
BUT I SENT YOU TO EARTH WHEN YOU WERE YOUNG.
ZANDRA HAD ALREADY SET HER GAZE ON YOU.
I'M SORRY I HAD TO SEAL AWAY YOUR MEMORIES, BUT YOU CAN GET THEM BACK.
BUT WHERE IS *TALIA?* SHE NEEDS ME.
SHE DOES NOT NEED YOU.
BUT THE WORLD— YES, THE WORLD NEEDS YOU TO FIND EACH OTHER.

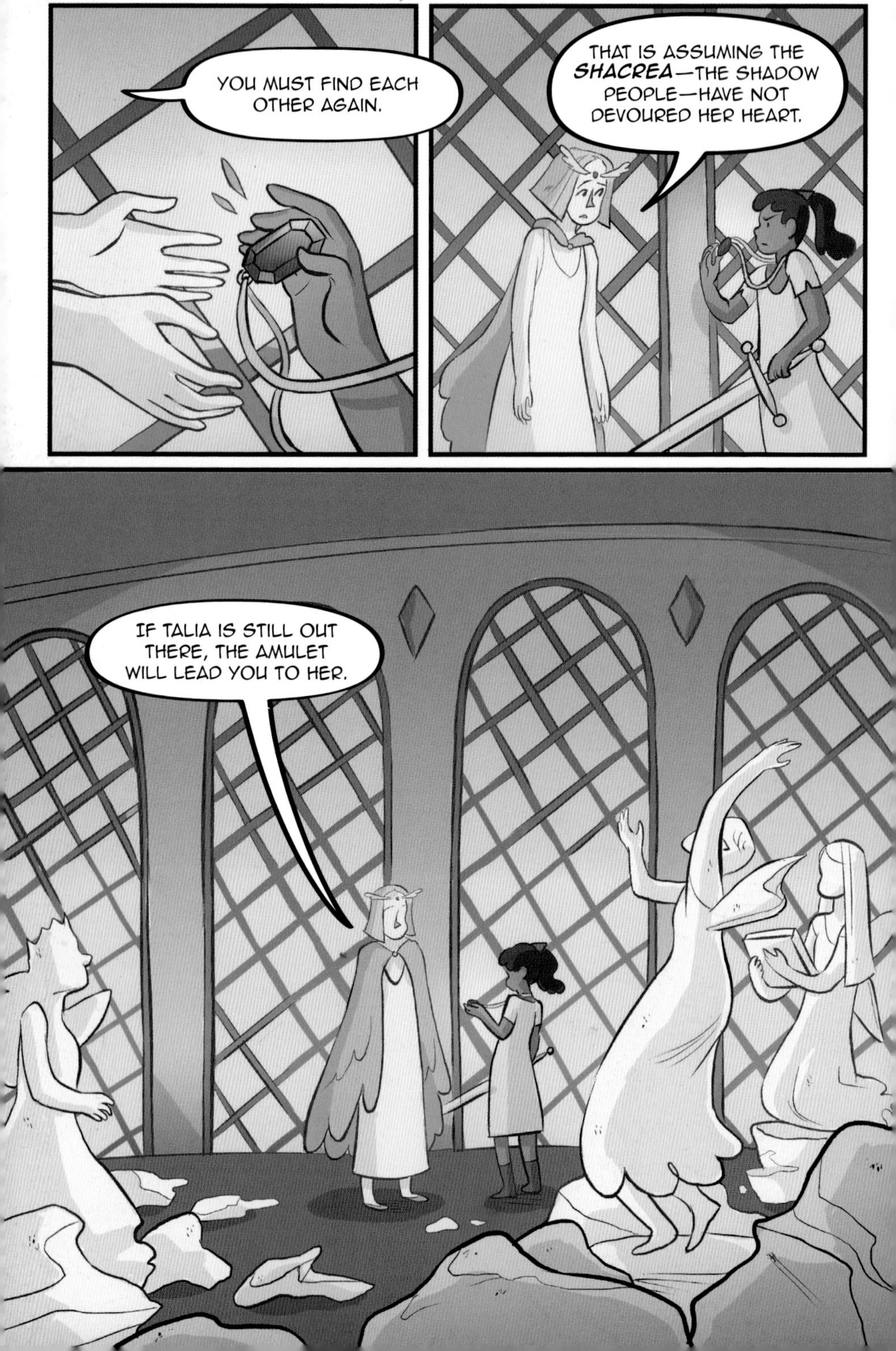
YOU MUST FIND EACH OTHER AGAIN.
THAT IS ASSUMING THE *SHACREA*—THE SHADOW PEOPLE—HAVE NOT DEVOURED HER HEART.
IF TALIA IS STILL OUT THERE, THE AMULET WILL LEAD YOU TO HER.

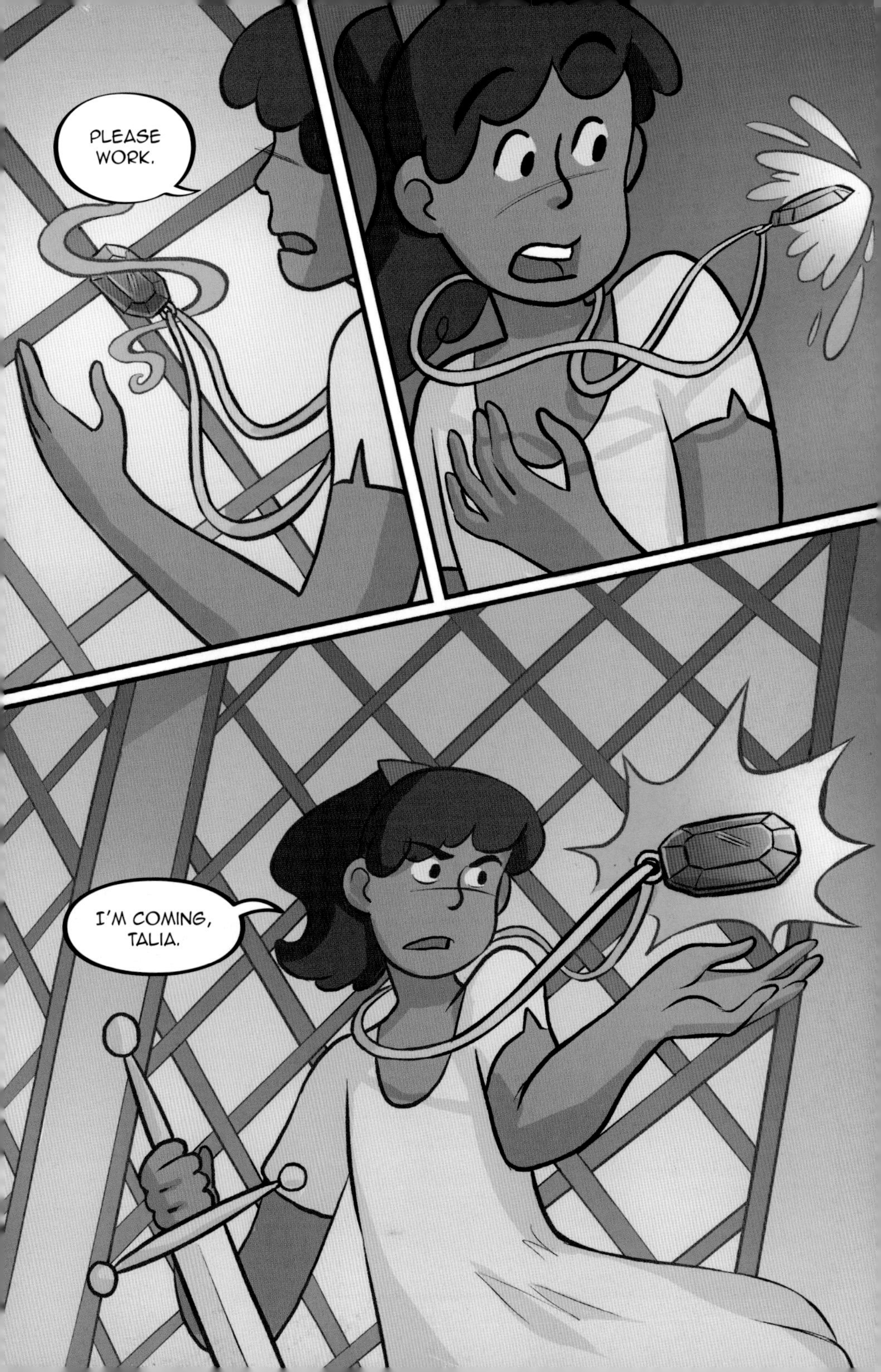
PLEASE WORK.
I'M COMING, TALIA.

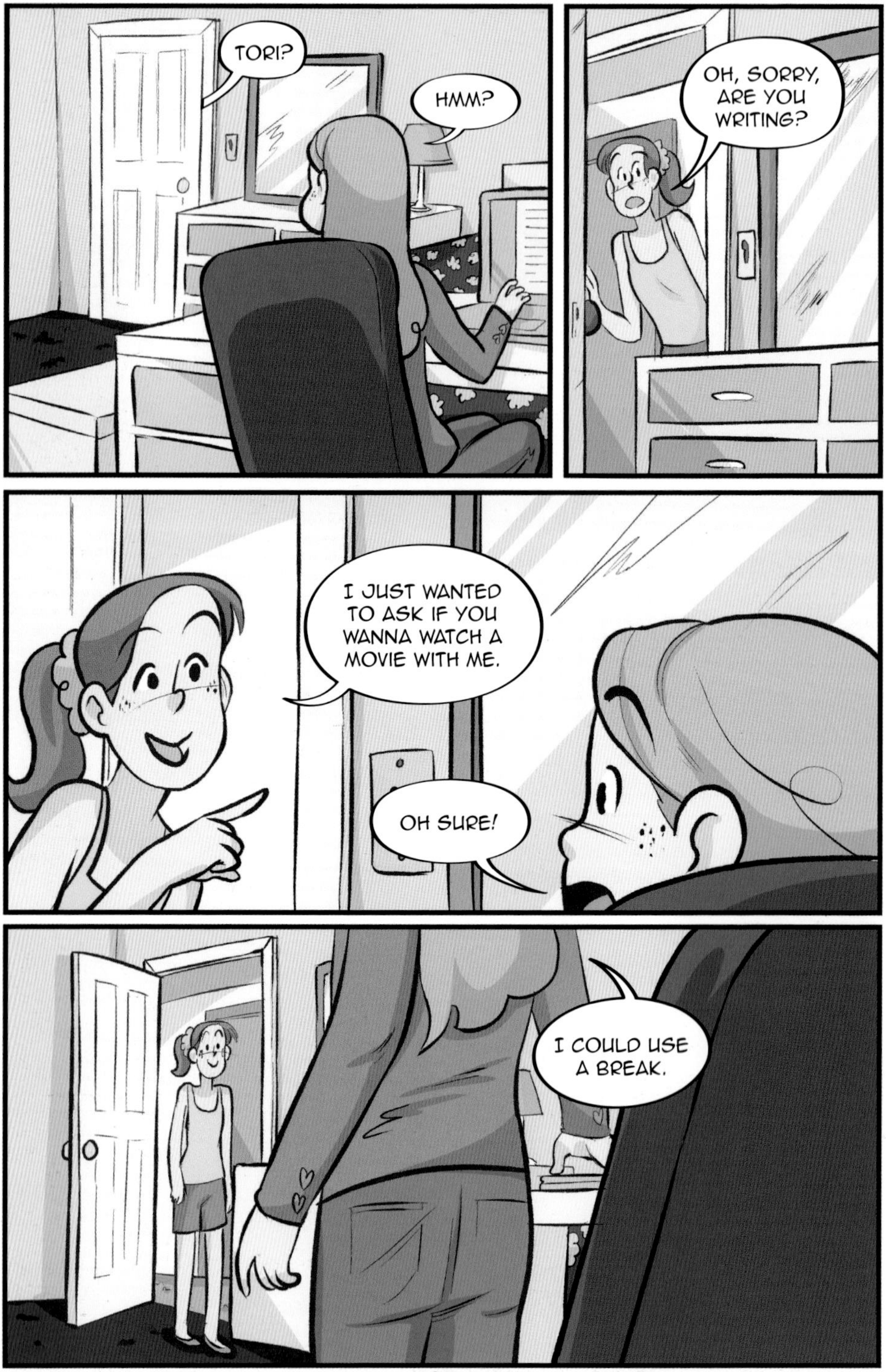
TORI?
HMM?
OH, SORRY, ARE YOU WRITING?
I JUST WANTED TO ASK IF YOU WANNA WATCH A MOVIE WITH ME.
OH SURE!
I COULD USE A BREAK.

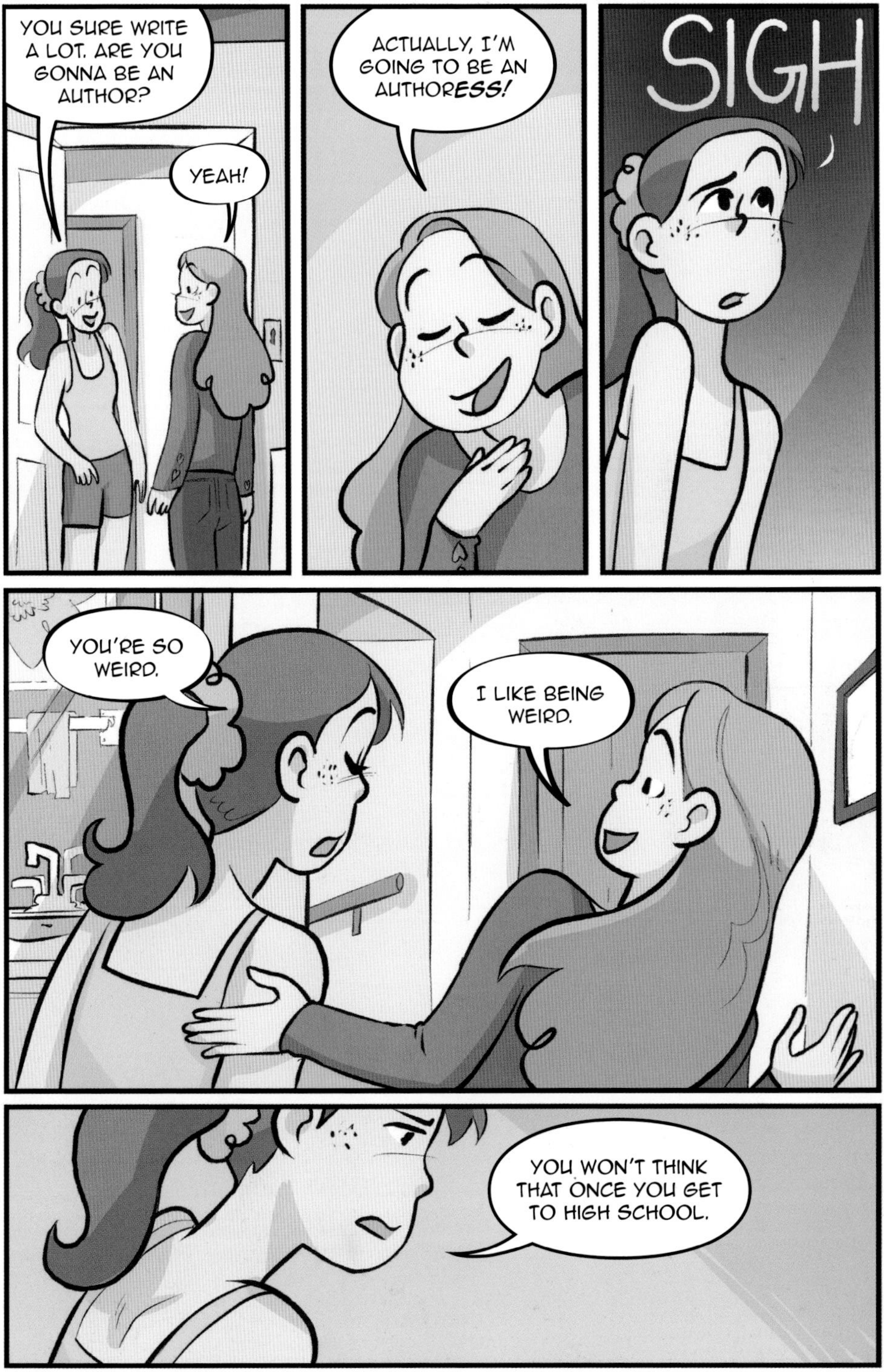
YOU SURE WRITE A LOT. ARE YOU GONNA BE AN AUTHOR?
YEAH!
ACTUALLY, I'M GOING TO BE AN AUTHOR***ESS!***
SIGH
YOU'RE SO WEIRD.
I LIKE BEING WEIRD.
YOU WON'T THINK THAT ONCE YOU GET TO HIGH SCHOOL.

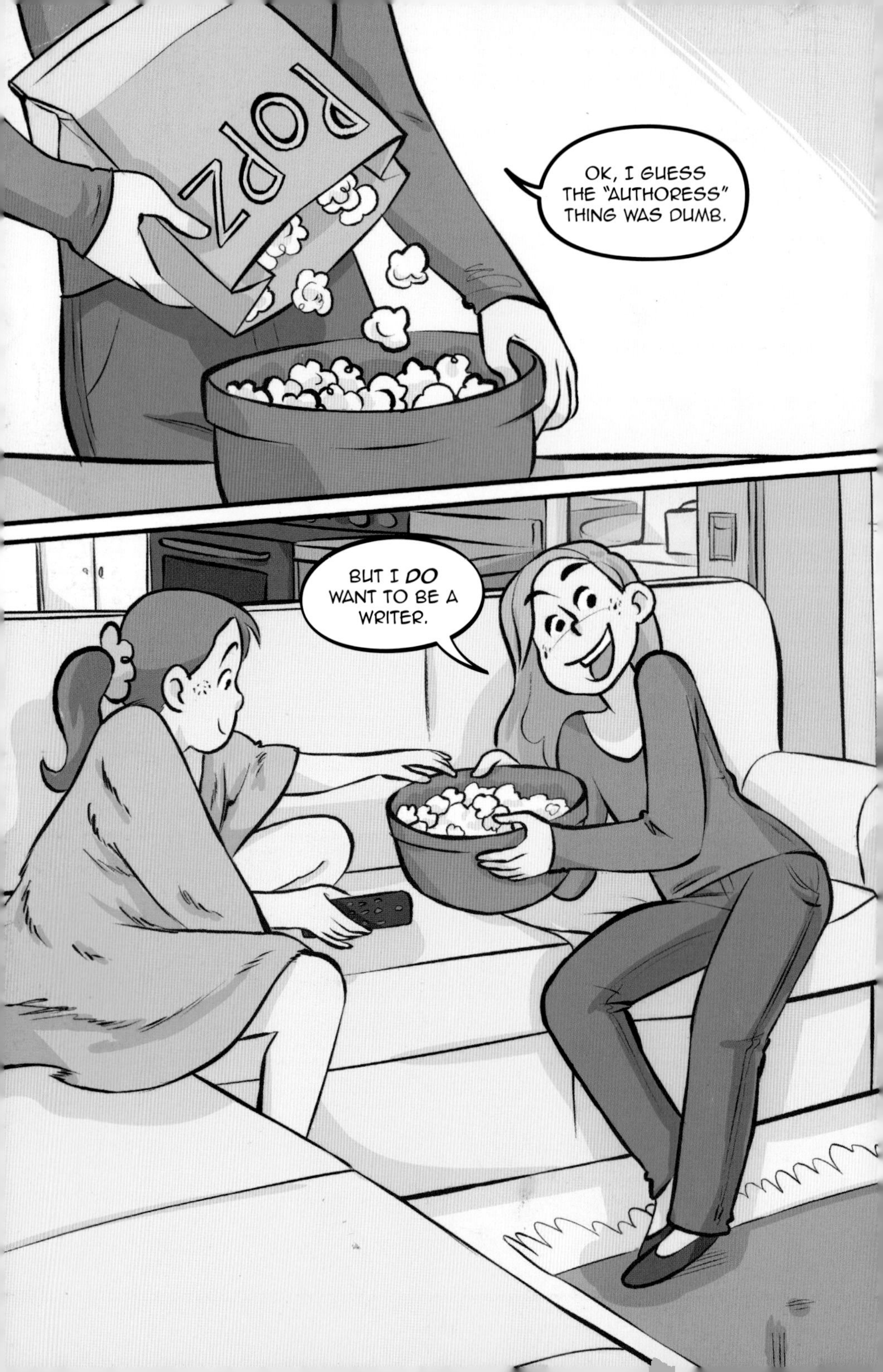
POPZ
OK, I GUESS THE "AUTHORESS" THING WAS DUMB.
BUT I *DO* WANT TO BE A WRITER.

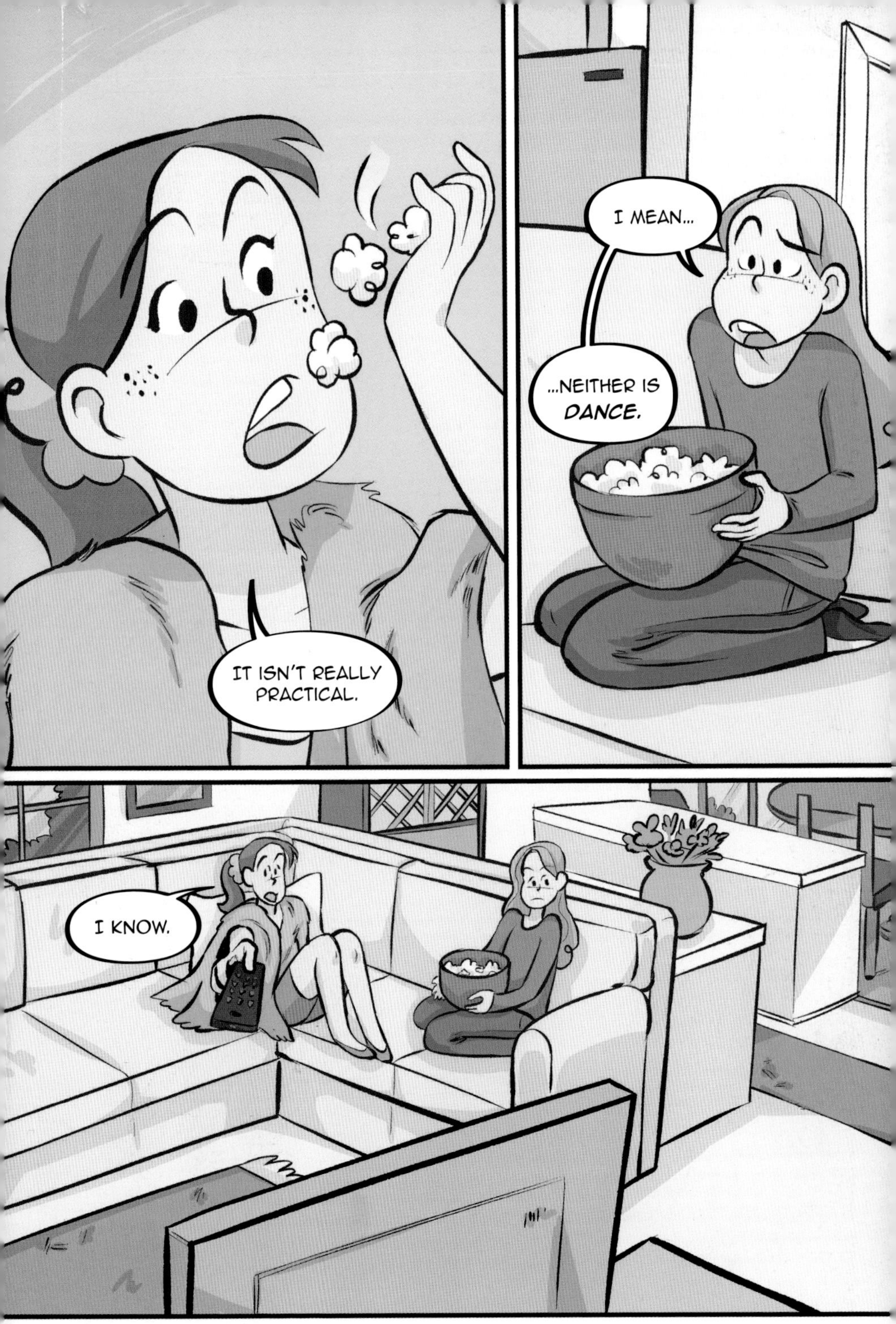
IT ISN'T REALLY PRACTICAL.
I MEAN...
...NEITHER IS DANCE.
I KNOW.

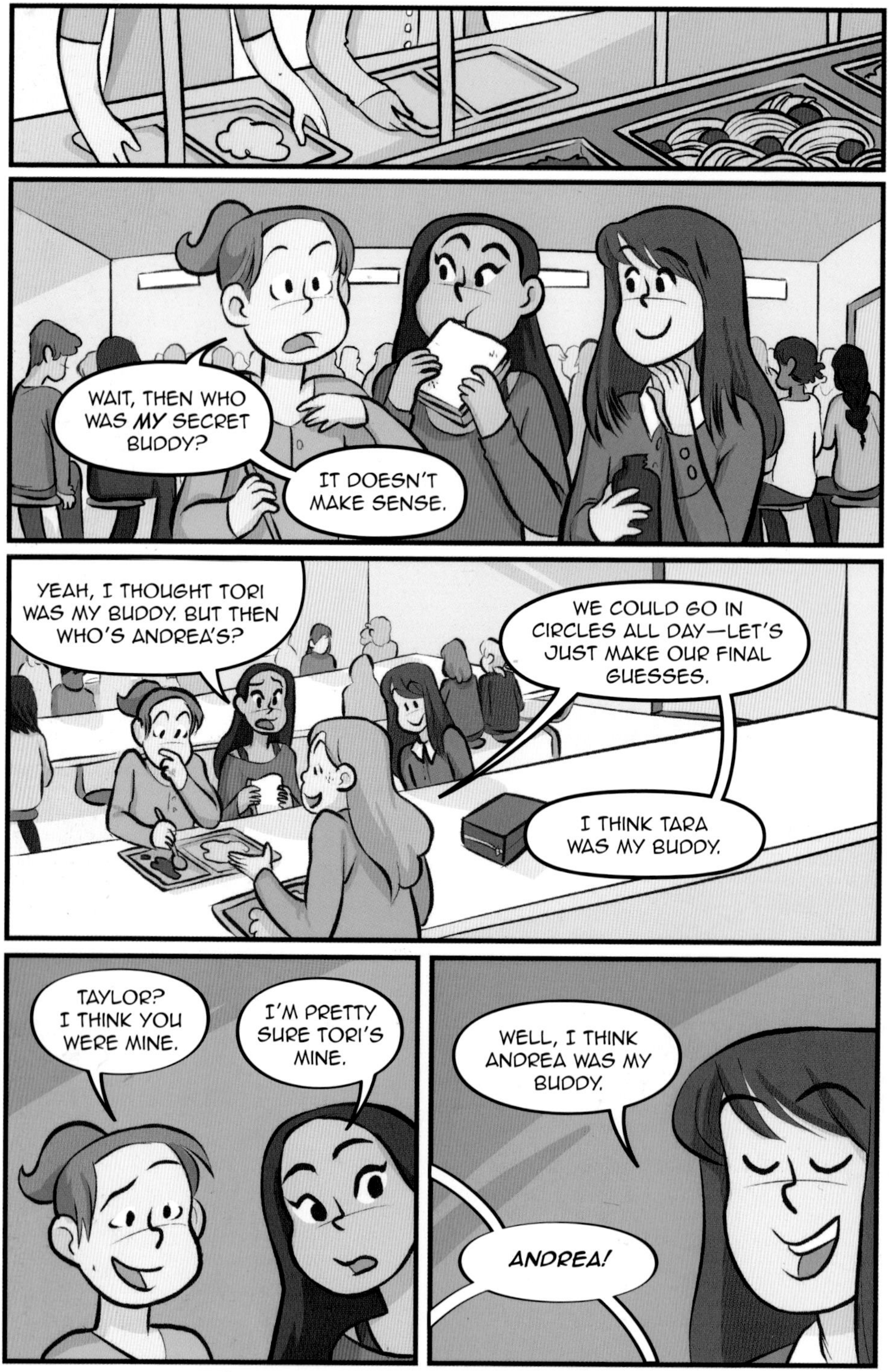
WAIT, THEN WHO WAS MY SECRET BUDDY?
IT DOESN'T MAKE SENSE.
YEAH, I THOUGHT TORI WAS MY BUDDY. BUT THEN WHO'S ANDREA'S?
WE COULD GO IN CIRCLES ALL DAY—LET'S JUST MAKE OUR FINAL GUESSES.
I THINK TARA WAS MY BUDDY.
TAYLOR? I THINK YOU WERE MINE.
I'M PRETTY SURE TORI'S MINE.
WELL, I THINK ANDREA WAS MY BUDDY.
ANDREA!

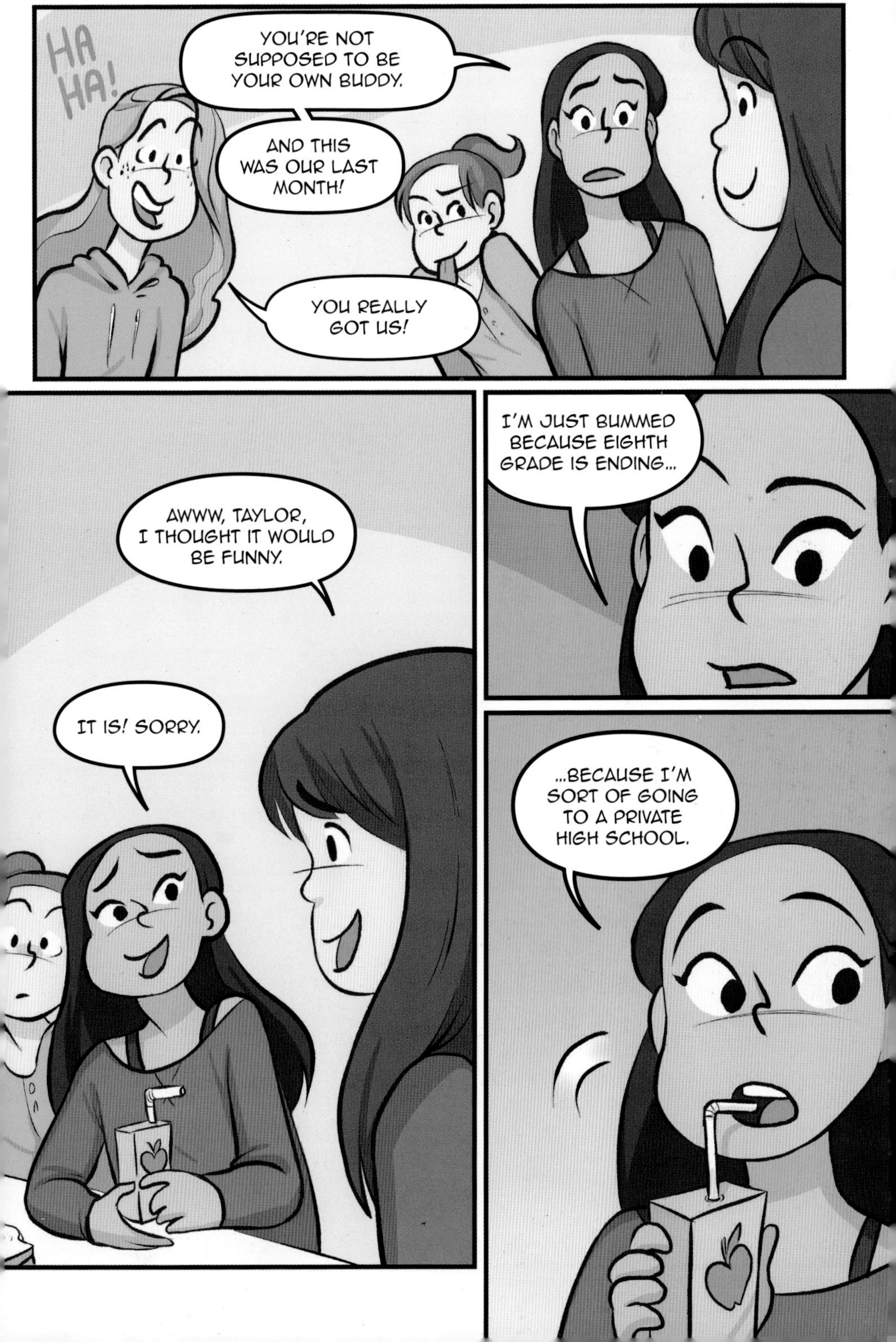
HA HA!
YOU'RE NOT SUPPOSED TO BE YOUR OWN BUDDY.
AND THIS WAS OUR LAST MONTH!
YOU REALLY GOT US!
AWWW, TAYLOR, I THOUGHT IT WOULD BE FUNNY.
IT IS! SORRY.
I'M JUST BUMMED BECAUSE EIGHTH GRADE IS ENDING...
...BECAUSE I'M SORT OF GOING TO A PRIVATE HIGH SCHOOL.

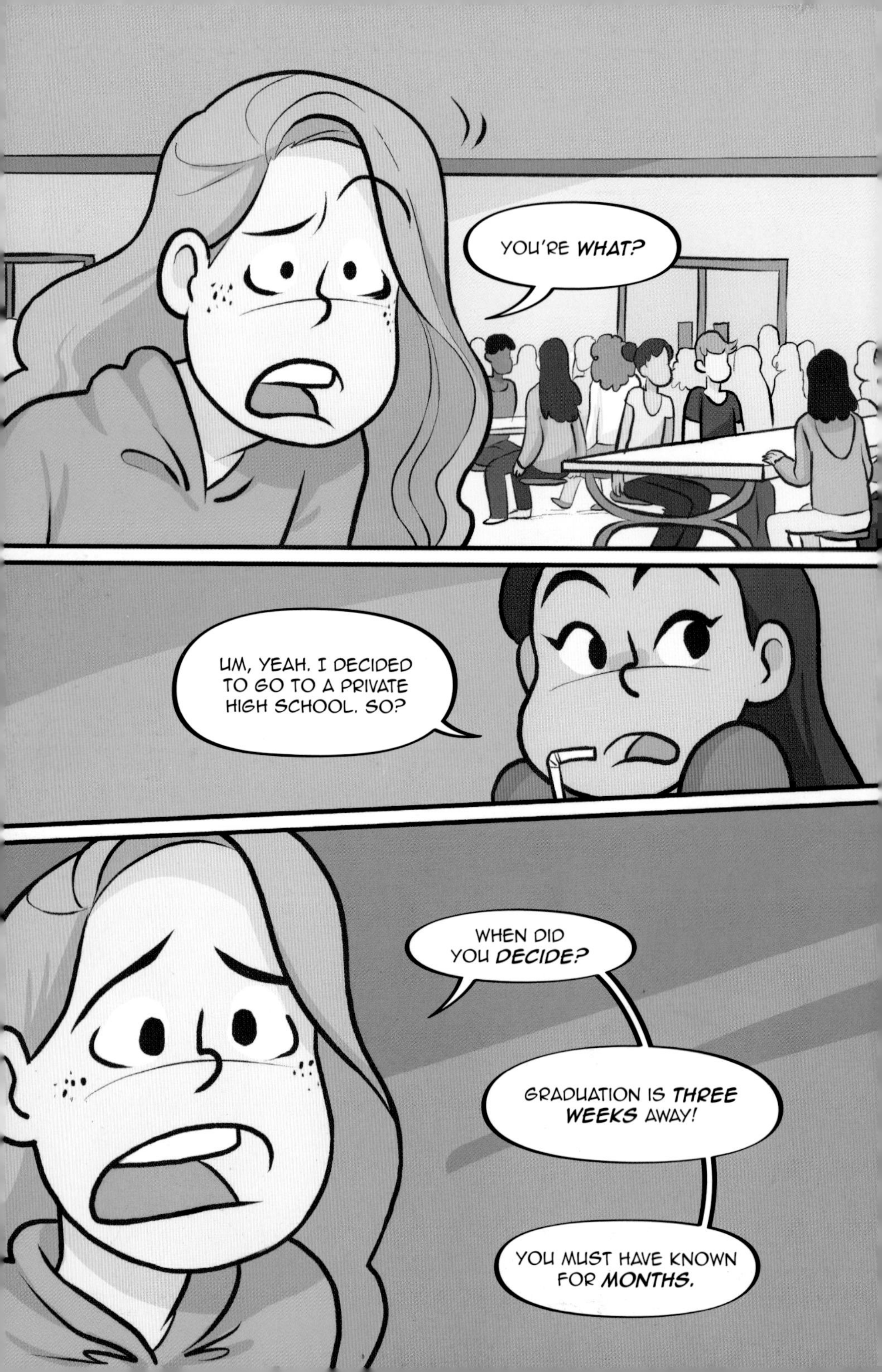
YOU'RE ***WHAT?***
UM, YEAH. I DECIDED TO GO TO A PRIVATE HIGH SCHOOL. SO?
WHEN DID YOU ***DECIDE?***
GRADUATION IS ***THREE WEEKS*** AWAY!
YOU MUST HAVE KNOWN FOR ***MONTHS.***

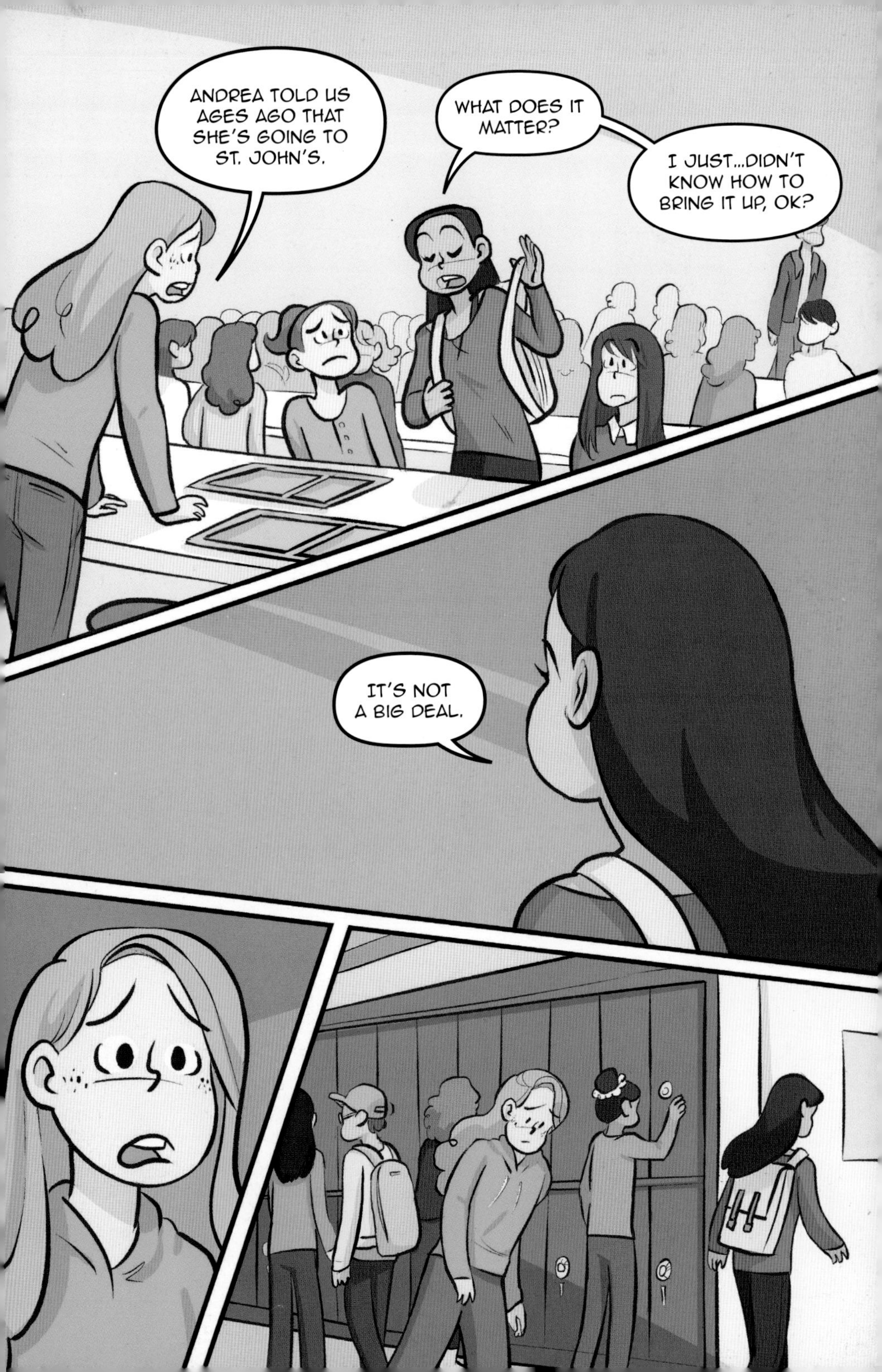
ANDREA TOLD US AGES AGO THAT SHE'S GOING TO ST. JOHN'S.
WHAT DOES IT MATTER?
I JUST...DIDN'T KNOW HOW TO BRING IT UP, OK?
IT'S NOT A BIG DEAL.

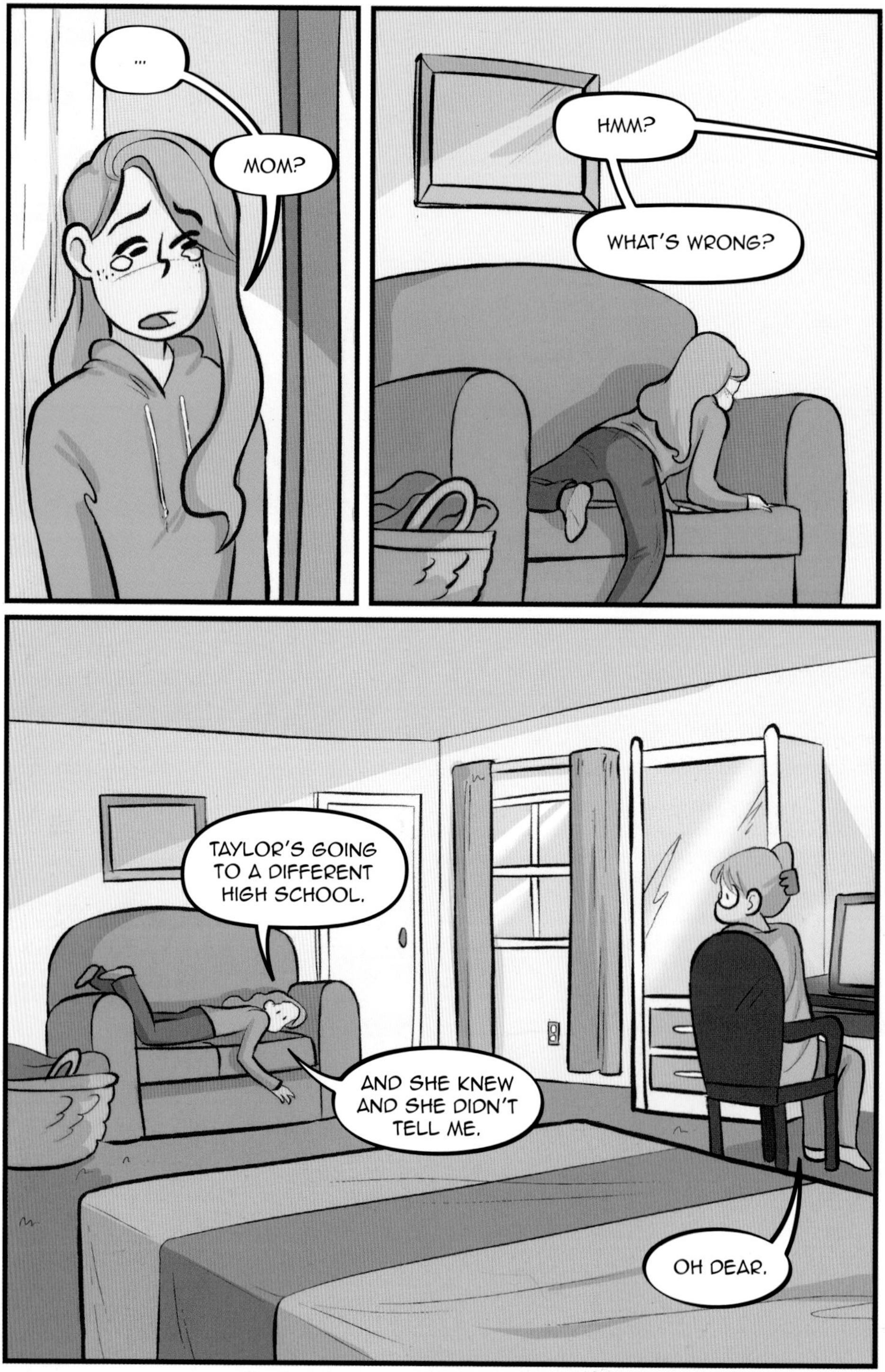
...
MOM?
HMM?
WHAT'S WRONG?
TAYLOR'S GOING TO A DIFFERENT HIGH SCHOOL.
AND SHE KNEW AND SHE DIDN'T TELL ME.
OH DEAR.

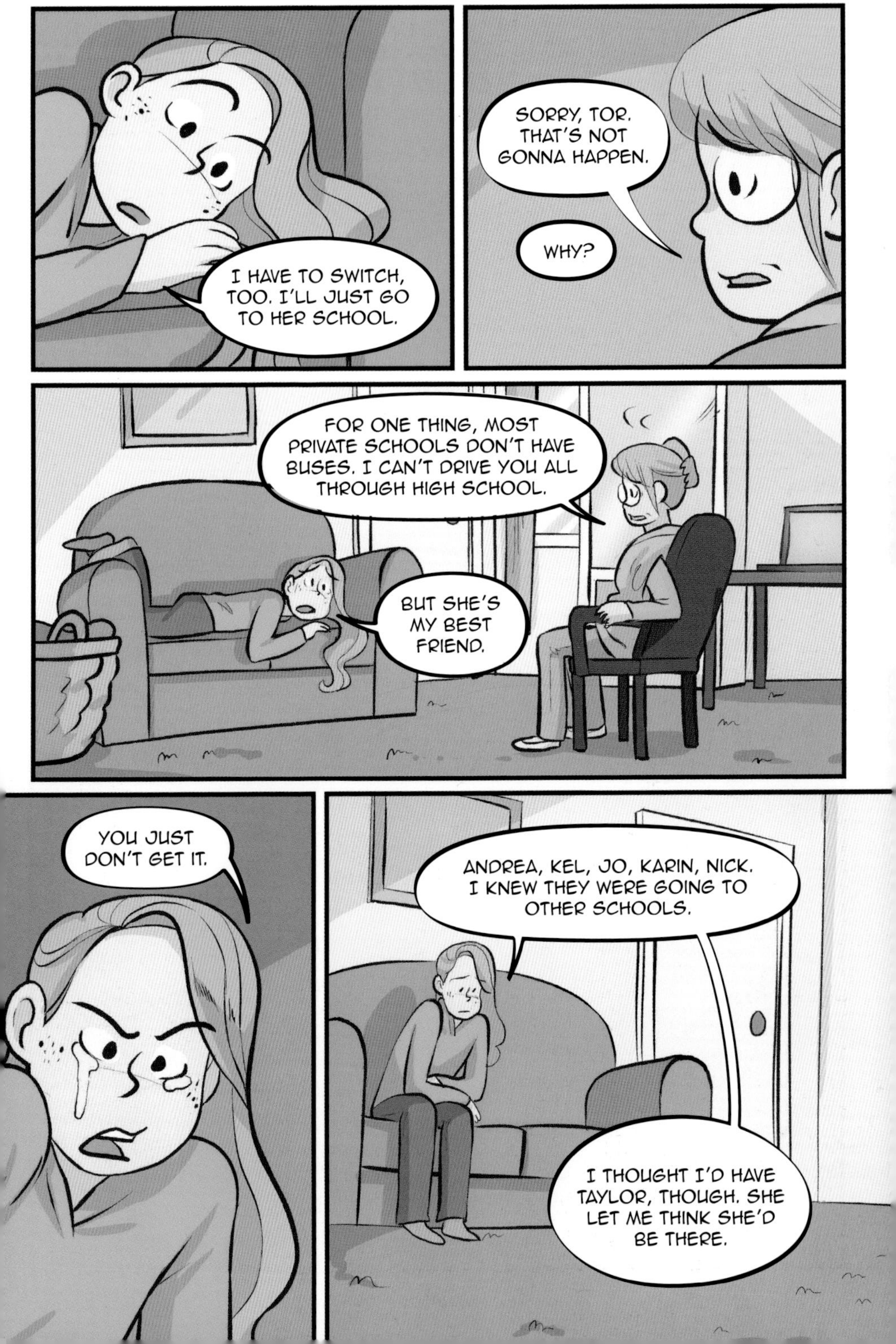
I HAVE TO SWITCH, TOO. I'LL JUST GO TO HER SCHOOL.
SORRY, TOR. THAT'S NOT GONNA HAPPEN.
WHY?
FOR ONE THING, MOST PRIVATE SCHOOLS DON'T HAVE BUSES. I CAN'T DRIVE YOU ALL THROUGH HIGH SCHOOL.
BUT SHE'S MY BEST FRIEND.
YOU JUST DON'T GET IT.
ANDREA, KEL, JO, KARIN, NICK. I KNEW THEY WERE GOING TO OTHER SCHOOLS.
I THOUGHT I'D HAVE TAYLOR, THOUGH. SHE LET ME THINK SHE'D BE THERE.

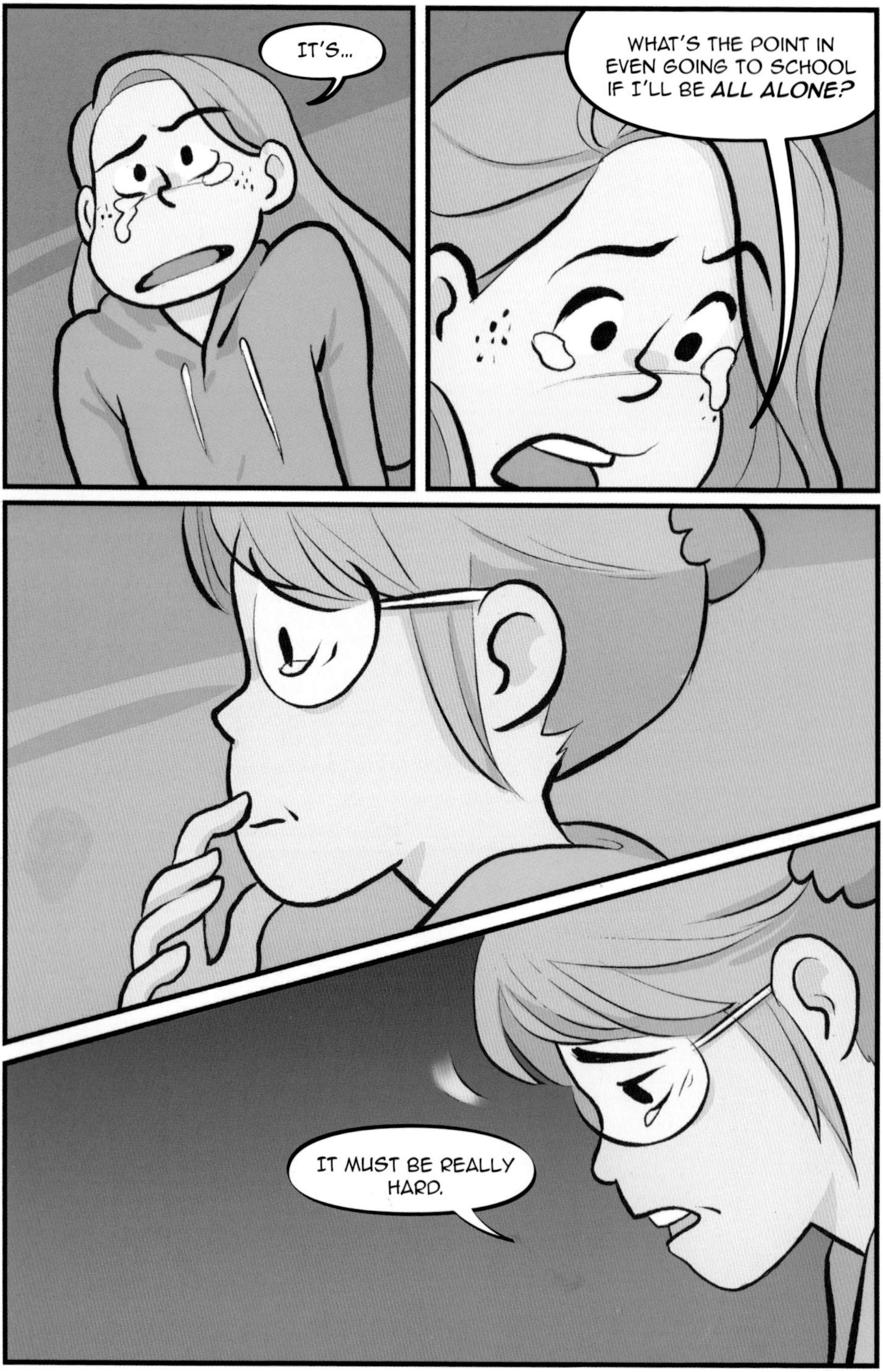
IT'S...
WHAT'S THE POINT IN EVEN GOING TO SCHOOL IF I'LL BE ***ALL ALONE?***
IT MUST BE REALLY HARD.

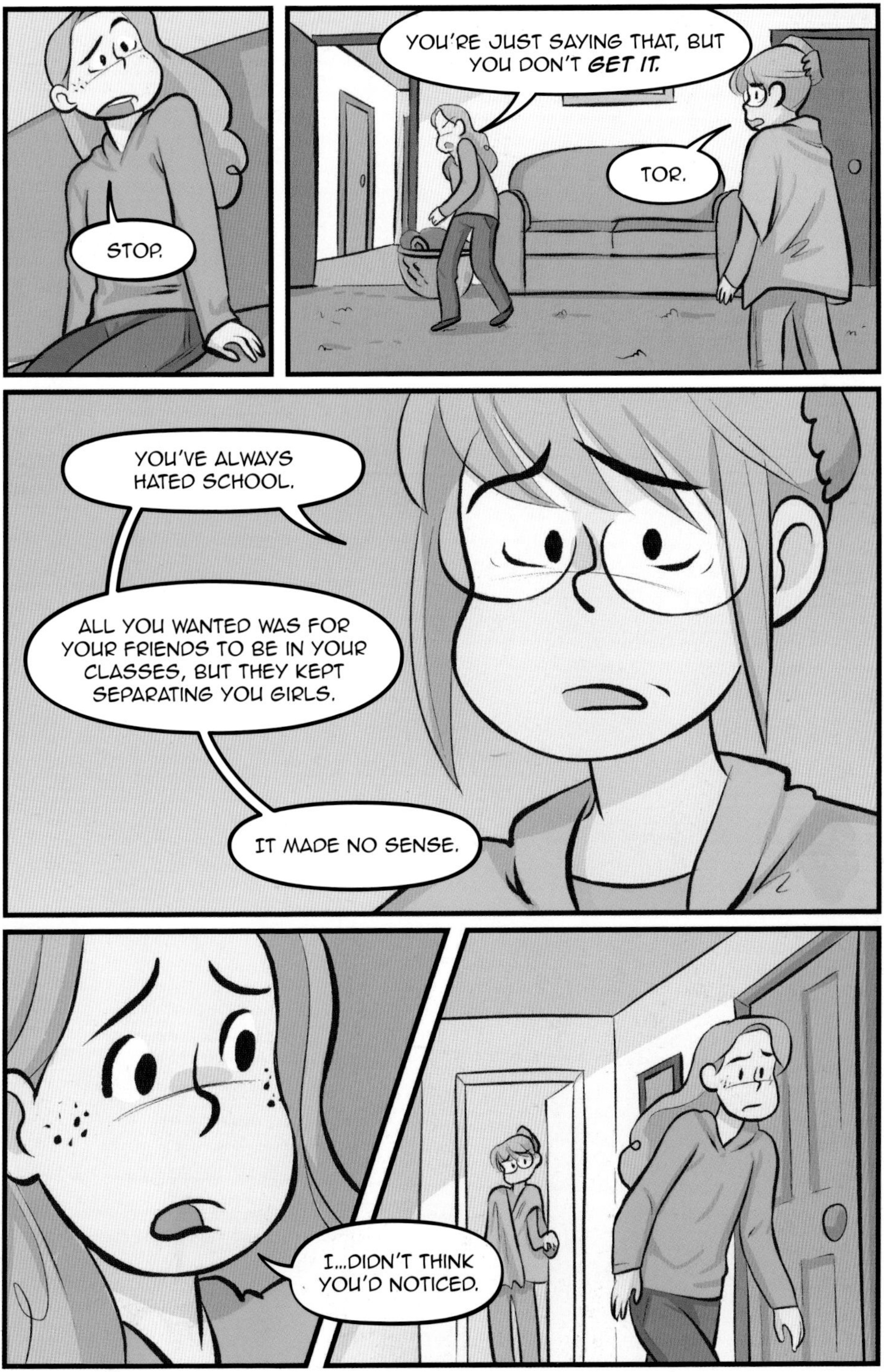
STOP.
YOU'RE JUST SAYING THAT, BUT YOU DON'T **GET IT.**
TOR.
YOU'VE ALWAYS HATED SCHOOL.
ALL YOU WANTED WAS FOR YOUR FRIENDS TO BE IN YOUR CLASSES, BUT THEY KEPT SEPARATING YOU GIRLS.
IT MADE NO SENSE.
I...DIDN'T THINK YOU'D NOTICED.

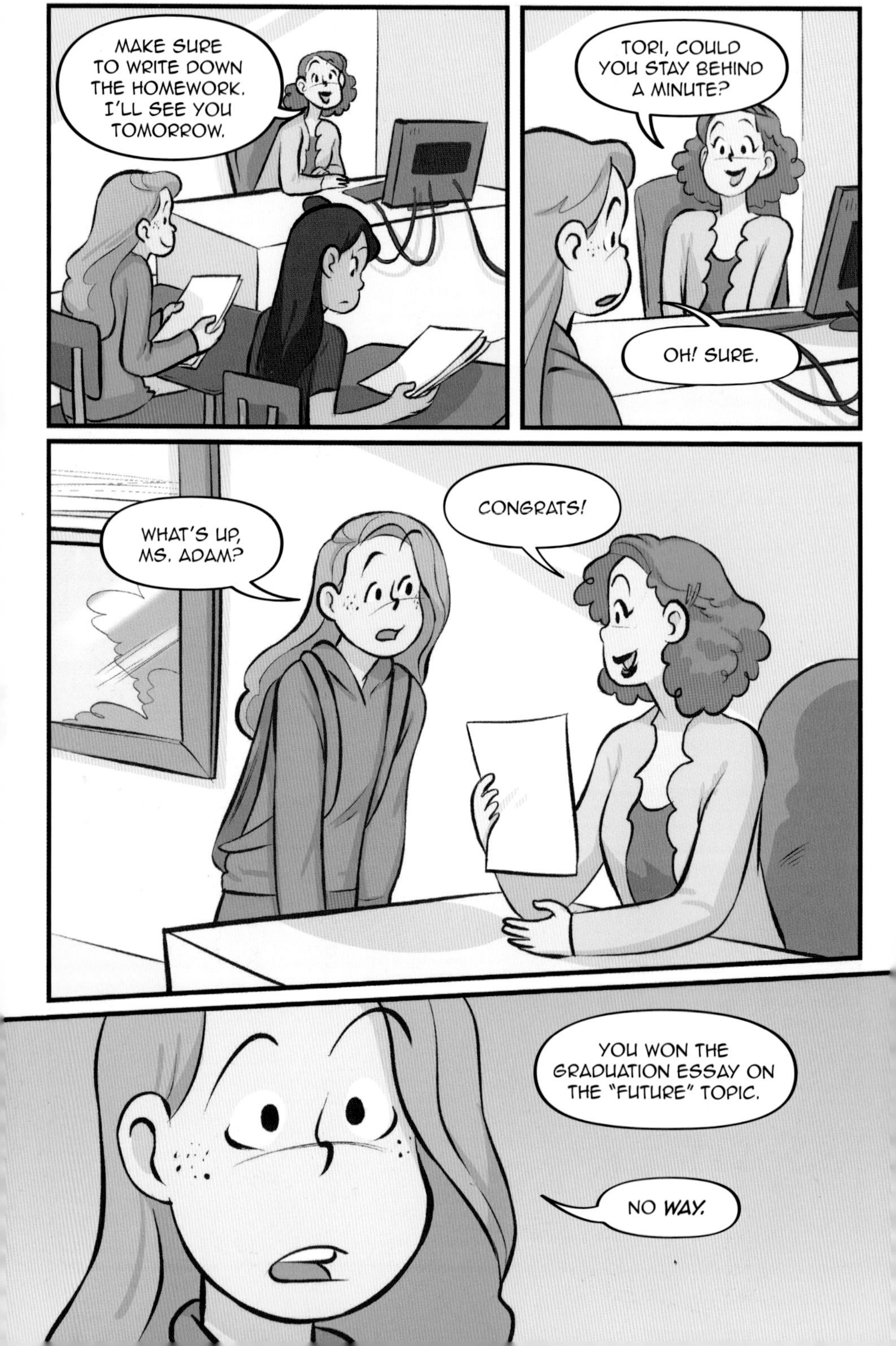
MAKE SURE TO WRITE DOWN THE HOMEWORK. I'LL SEE YOU TOMORROW.
TORI, COULD YOU STAY BEHIND A MINUTE?
OH! SURE.
WHAT'S UP, MS. ADAM?
CONGRATS!
YOU WON THE GRADUATION ESSAY ON THE "FUTURE" TOPIC.
NO *WAY.*

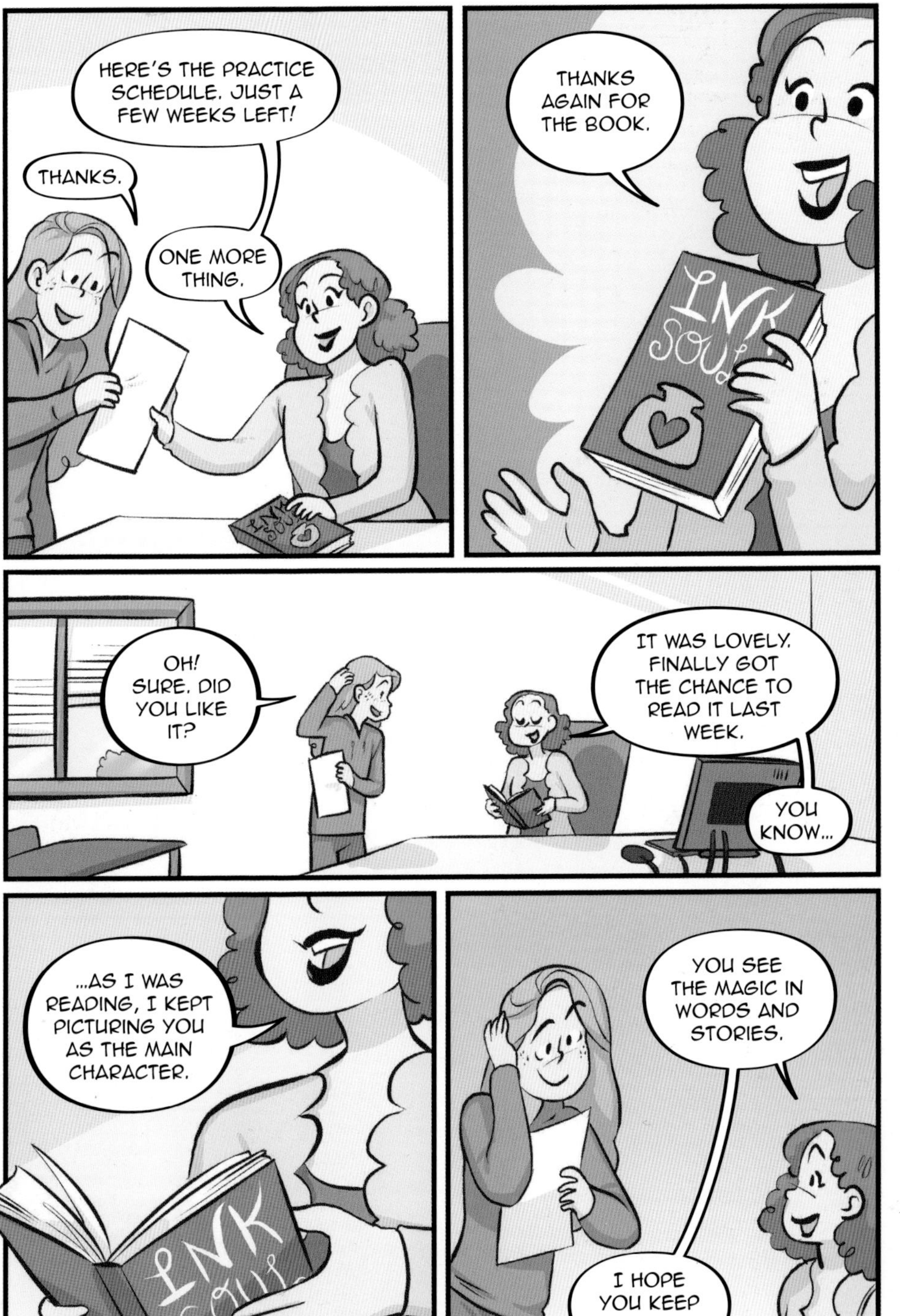
HERE'S THE PRACTICE SCHEDULE. JUST A FEW WEEKS LEFT!
THANKS.
ONE MORE THING.
THANKS AGAIN FOR THE BOOK.
INK SOUL
OH! SURE. DID YOU LIKE IT?
IT WAS LOVELY. FINALLY GOT THE CHANCE TO READ IT LAST WEEK.
YOU KNOW...
...AS I WAS READING, I KEPT PICTURING YOU AS THE MAIN CHARACTER.
YOU SEE THE MAGIC IN WORDS AND STORIES.
I HOPE YOU KEEP WRITING.

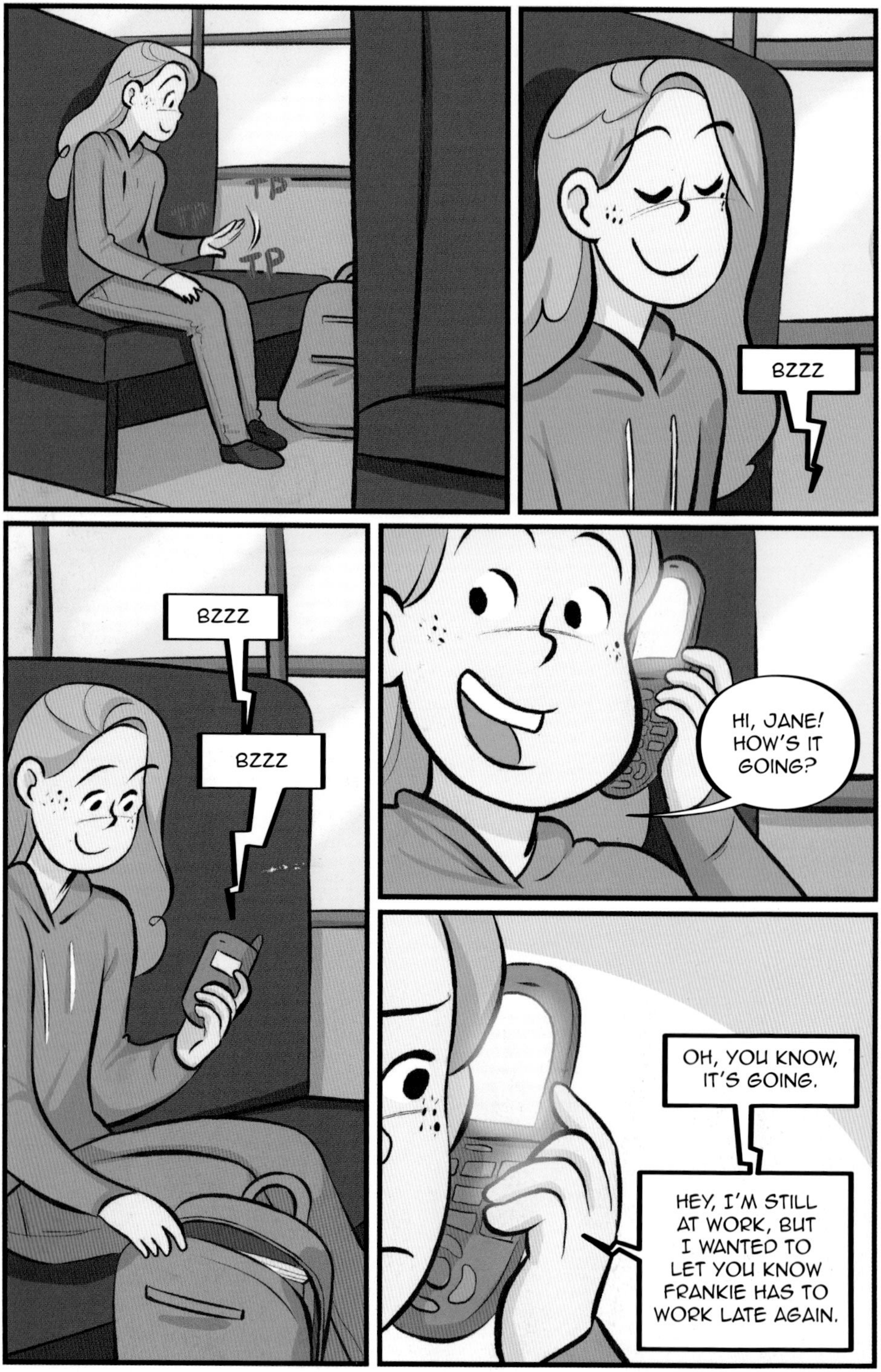
TP
TP
BZZZ
BZZZ
BZZZ
HI, JANE! HOW'S IT GOING?
OH, YOU KNOW, IT'S GOING.
HEY, I'M STILL AT WORK, BUT I WANTED TO LET YOU KNOW FRANKIE HAS TO WORK LATE AGAIN.

OK.

YOU CAN STILL COME OVER!

OR WE COULD GO OUT SHOPPING?

THAT'S OK. MAYBE NEXT TIME.

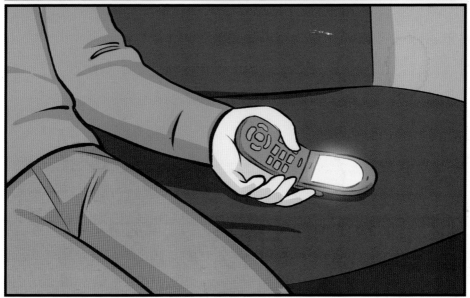

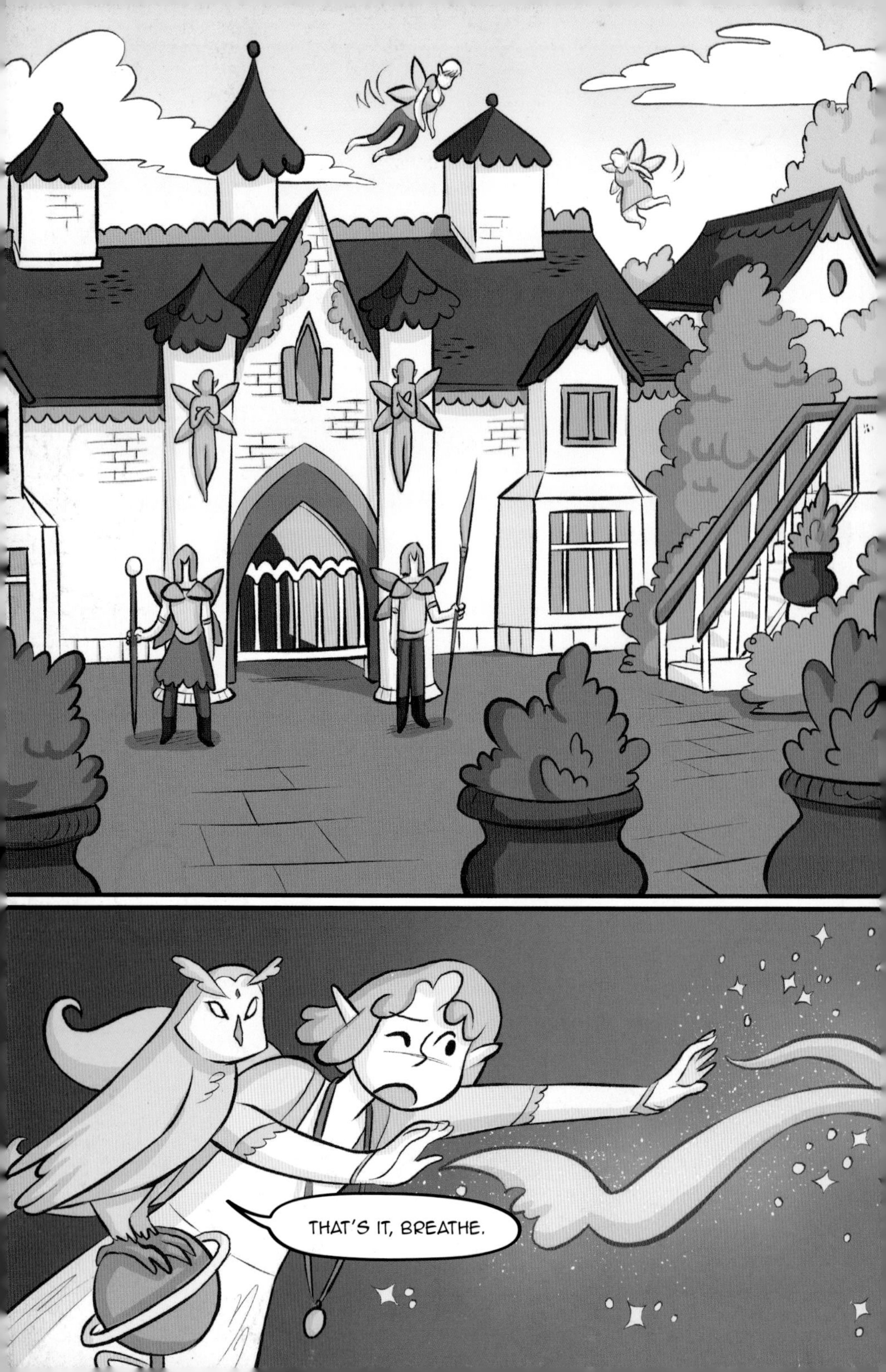
THAT'S IT, BREATHE.

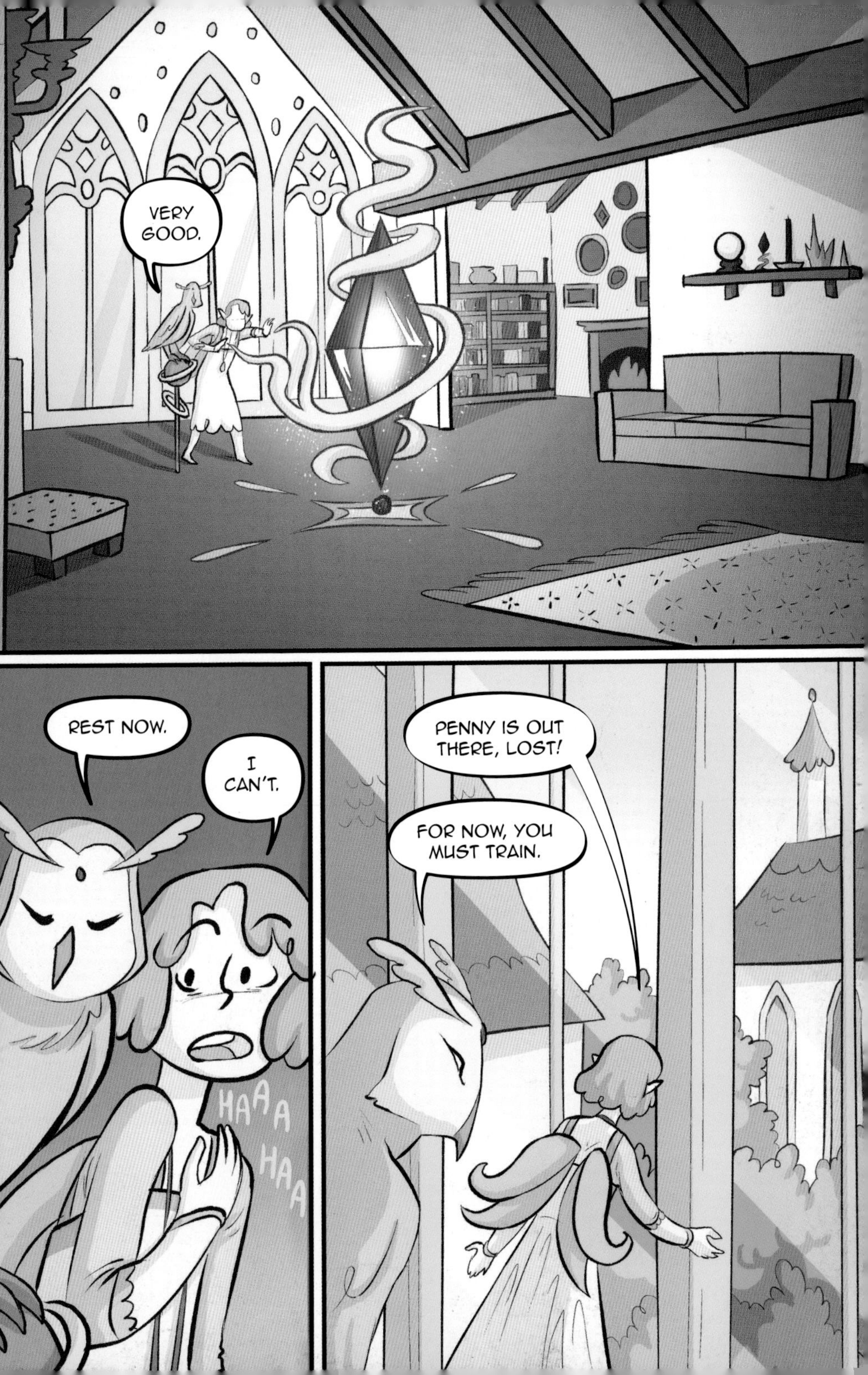
VERY GOOD.
REST NOW.
I CAN'T.
HAAA
HAAA
PENNY IS OUT THERE, LOST!
FOR NOW, YOU MUST TRAIN.

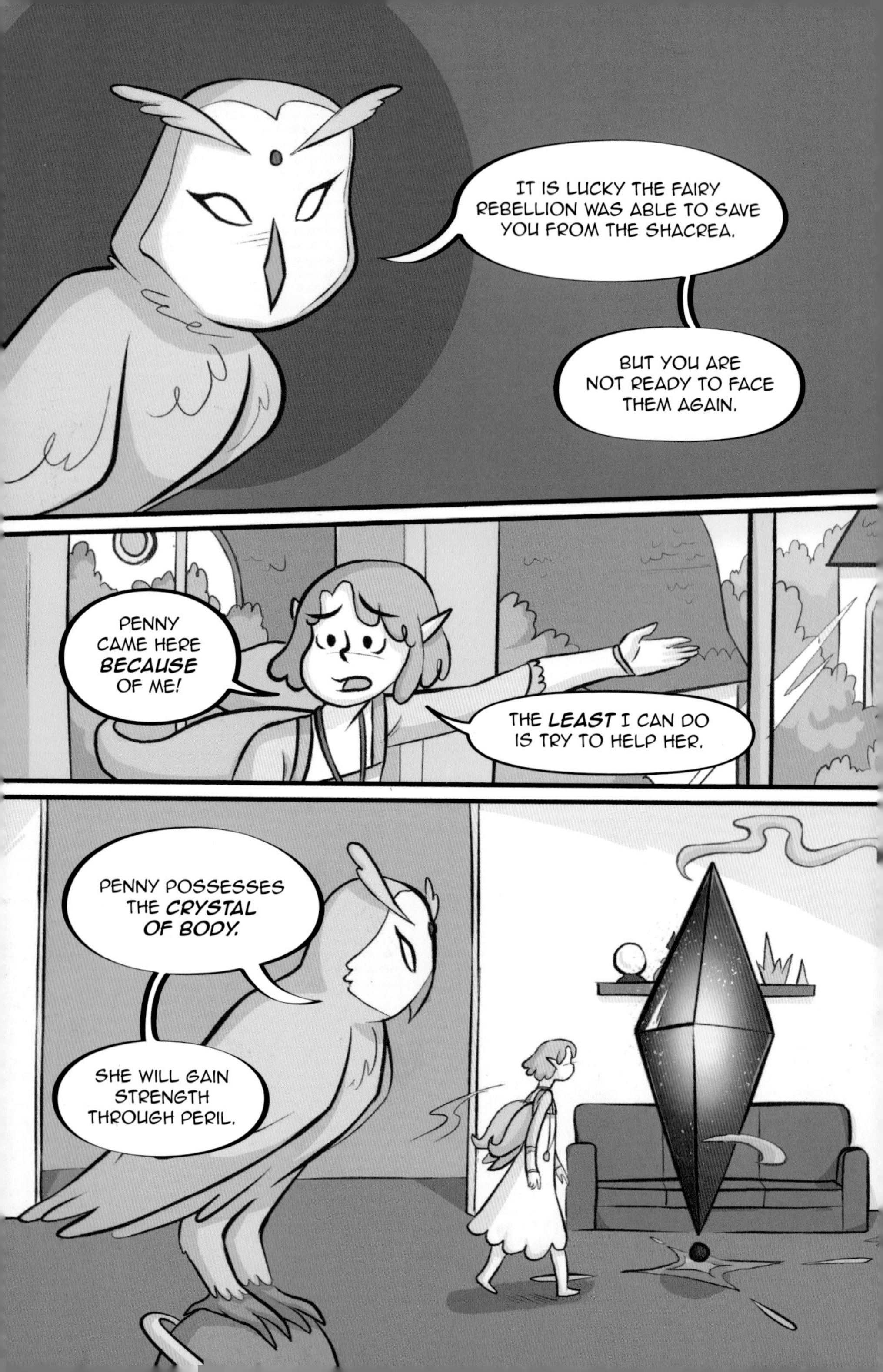
IT IS LUCKY THE FAIRY REBELLION WAS ABLE TO SAVE YOU FROM THE SHACREA.
BUT YOU ARE NOT READY TO FACE THEM AGAIN.
PENNY CAME HERE BECAUSE OF ME!
THE LEAST I CAN DO IS TRY TO HELP HER.
PENNY POSSESSES THE CRYSTAL OF BODY.
SHE WILL GAIN STRENGTH THROUGH PERIL.

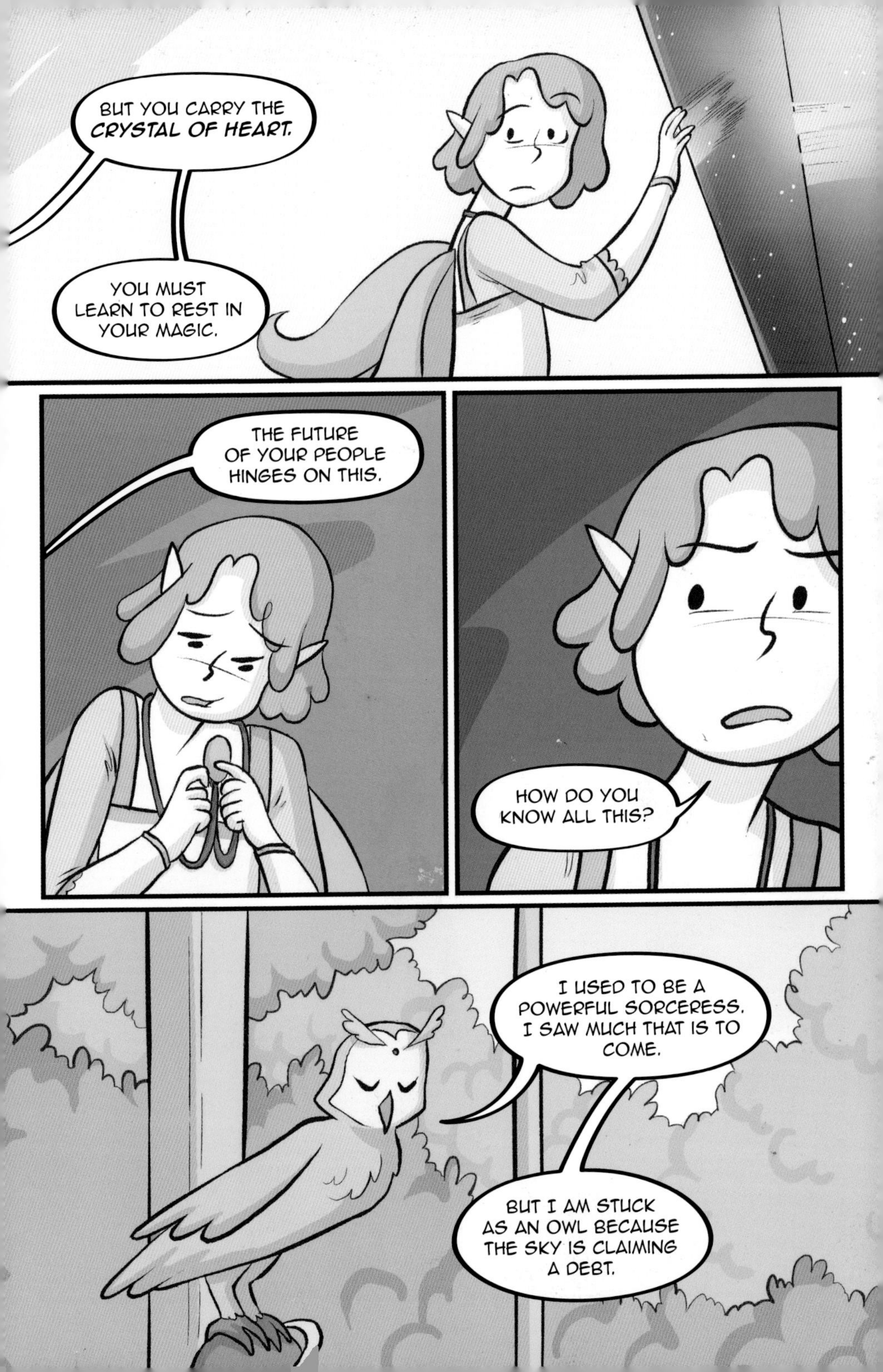
BUT YOU CARRY THE *CRYSTAL OF HEART.*
YOU MUST LEARN TO REST IN YOUR MAGIC.
THE FUTURE OF YOUR PEOPLE HINGES ON THIS.
HOW DO YOU KNOW ALL THIS?
I USED TO BE A POWERFUL SORCERESS. I SAW MUCH THAT IS TO COME.
BUT I AM STUCK AS AN OWL BECAUSE THE SKY IS CLAIMING A DEBT.

I WAS THE KEEPER OF THE THIRD CRYSTAL— *THE CRYSTAL OF MIND.*

THE SHACREA AMBUSHED ME.

THEY *STOLE* MY CRYSTAL, AND MOST OF MY MAGIC WITH IT, LONG AGO.

YOU AND PENNY MAY BE STRONG ENOUGH TO RECLAIM MY CRYSTAL *AFTER* YOU LEARN YOUR MAGIC.

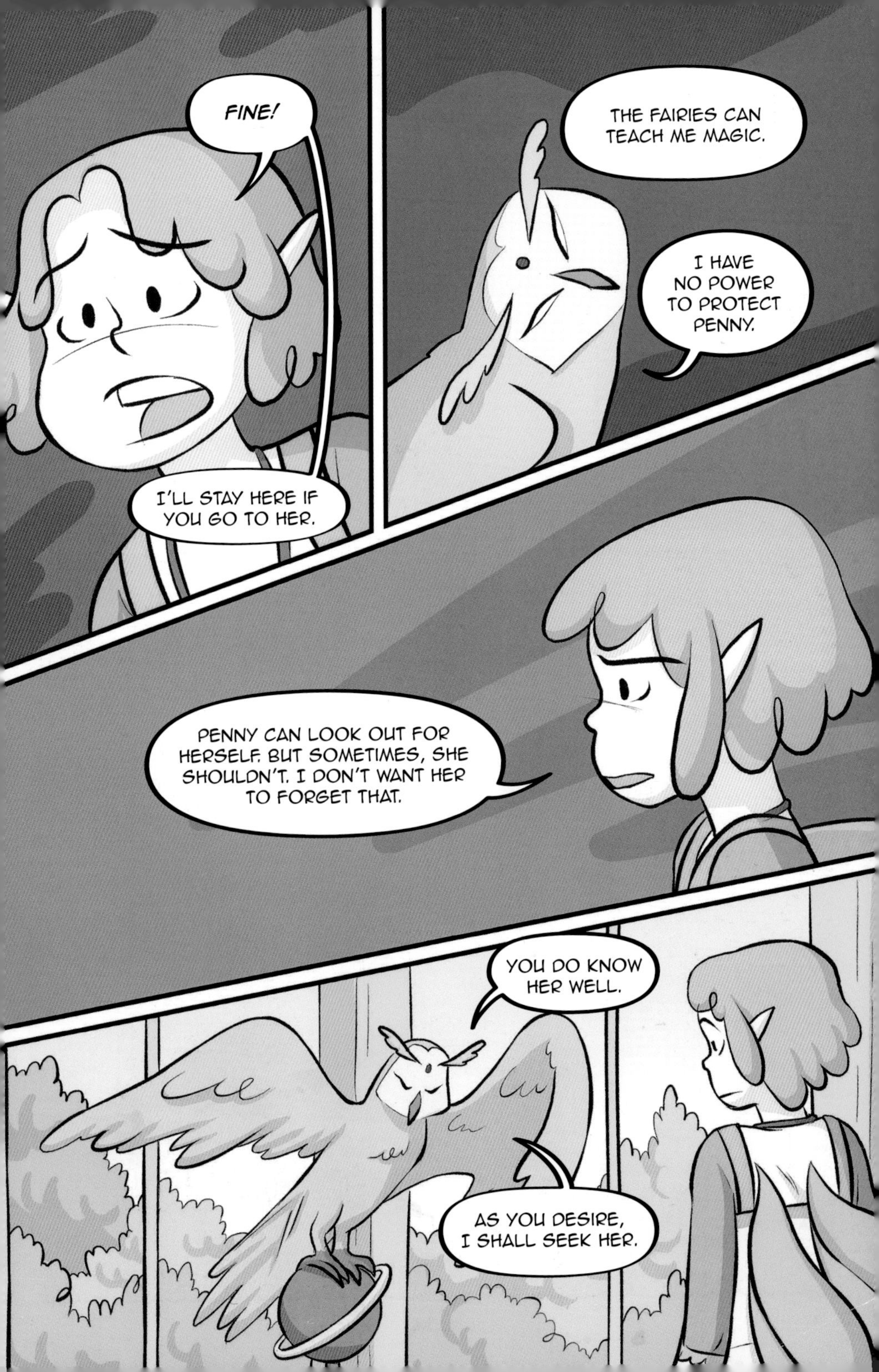
FINE!
I'LL STAY HERE IF YOU GO TO HER.
THE FAIRIES CAN TEACH ME MAGIC.
I HAVE NO POWER TO PROTECT PENNY.
PENNY CAN LOOK OUT FOR HERSELF. BUT SOMETIMES, SHE SHOULDN'T. I DON'T WANT HER TO FORGET THAT.
YOU DO KNOW HER WELL.
AS YOU DESIRE, I SHALL SEEK HER.

TORI SHARP WILL READ THE LAST ESSAY, ON THE TOPIC OF THE FUTURE.

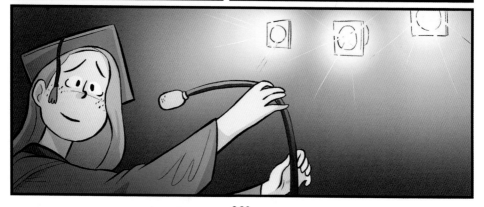

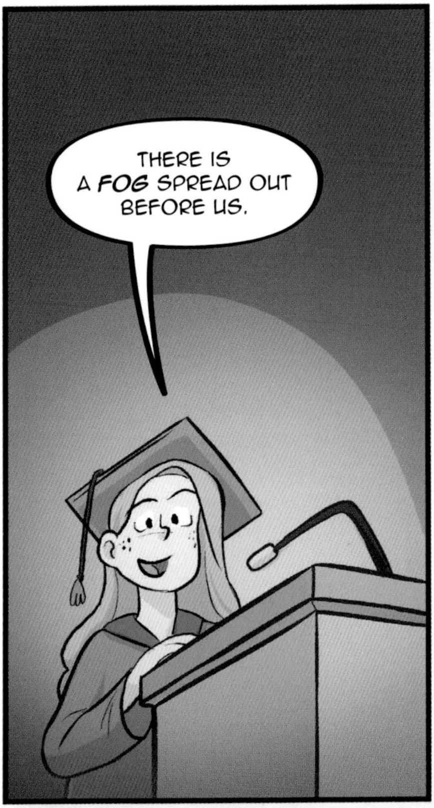
THERE IS A FOG SPREAD OUT BEFORE US.

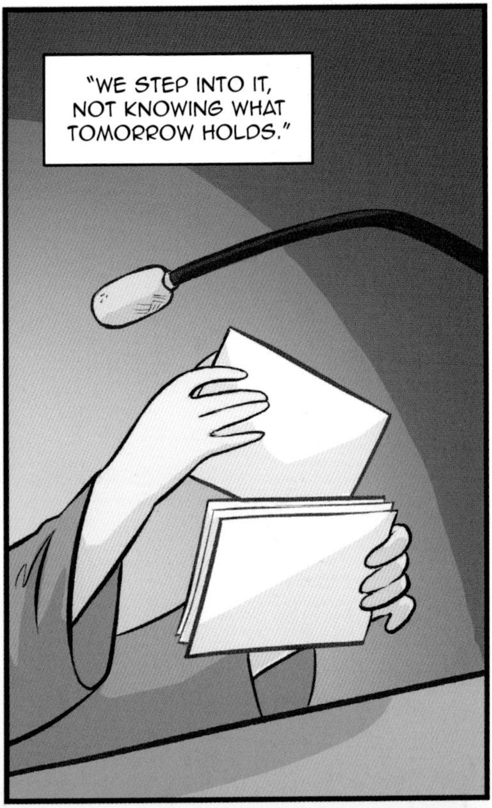
"WE STEP INTO IT, NOT KNOWING WHAT TOMORROW HOLDS."

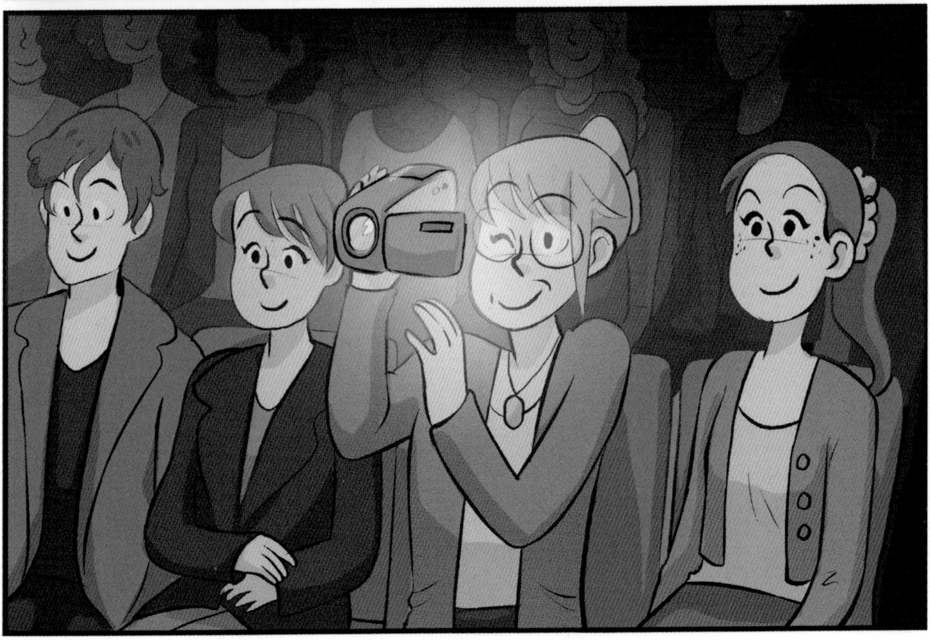

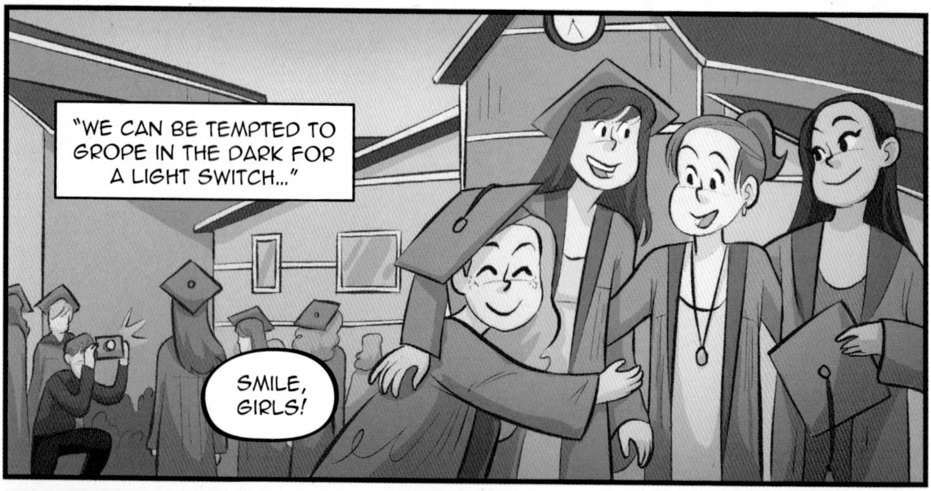
"WE CAN BE TEMPTED TO GROPE IN THE DARK FOR A LIGHT SWITCH..."
SMILE, GIRLS!

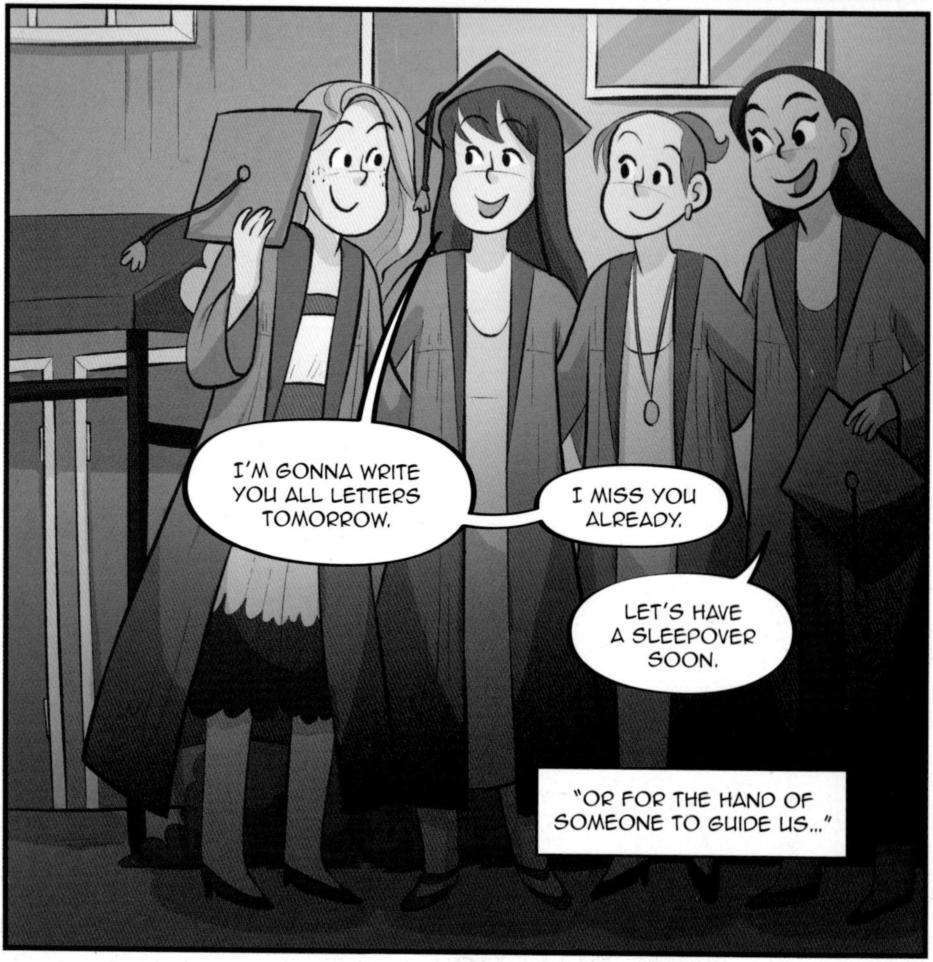
I'M GONNA WRITE YOU ALL LETTERS TOMORROW.
I MISS YOU ALREADY.
LET'S HAVE A SLEEPOVER SOON.
"OR FOR THE HAND OF SOMEONE TO GUIDE US..."

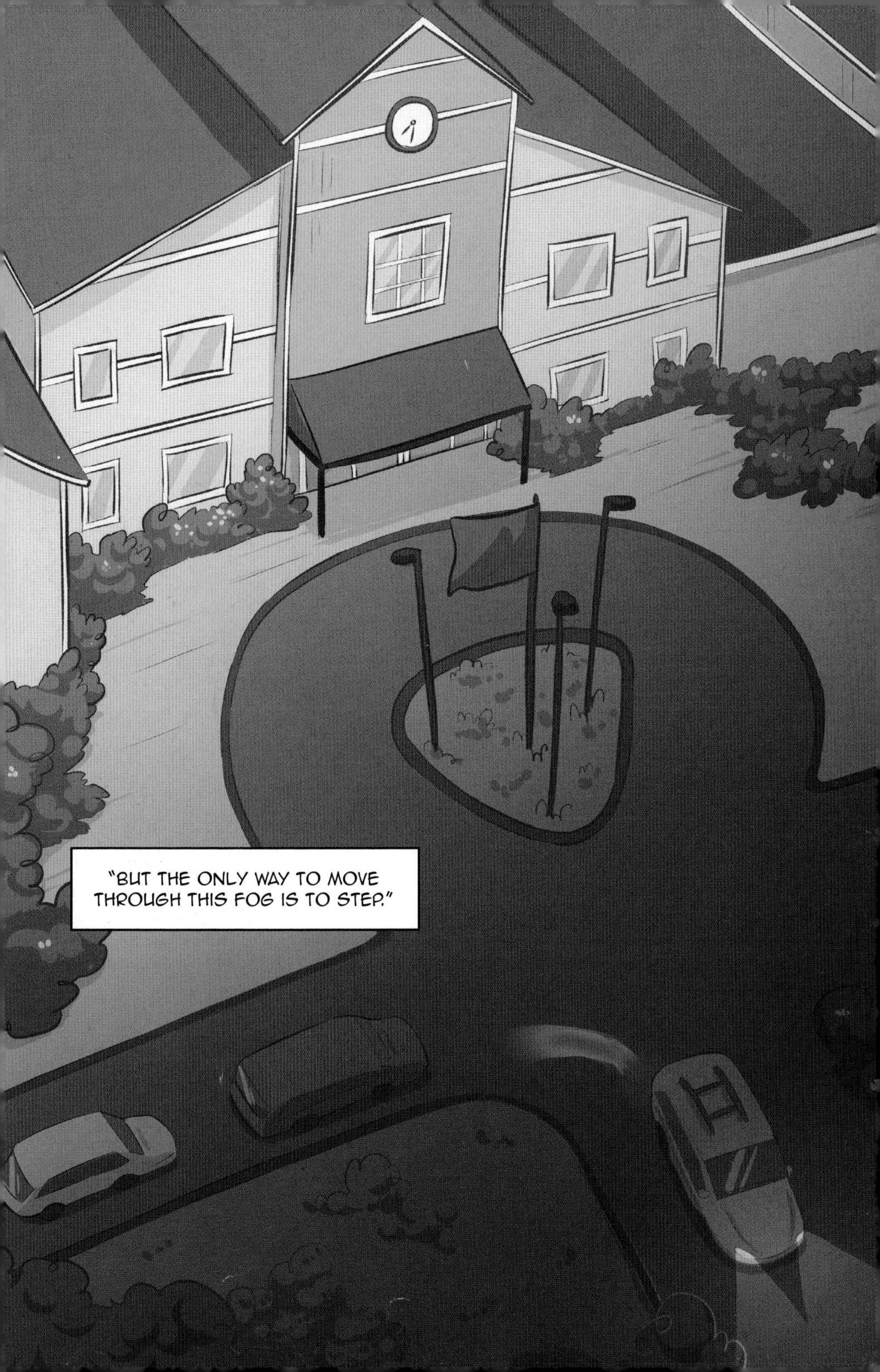
"BUT THE ONLY WAY TO MOVE THROUGH THIS FOG IS TO STEP."

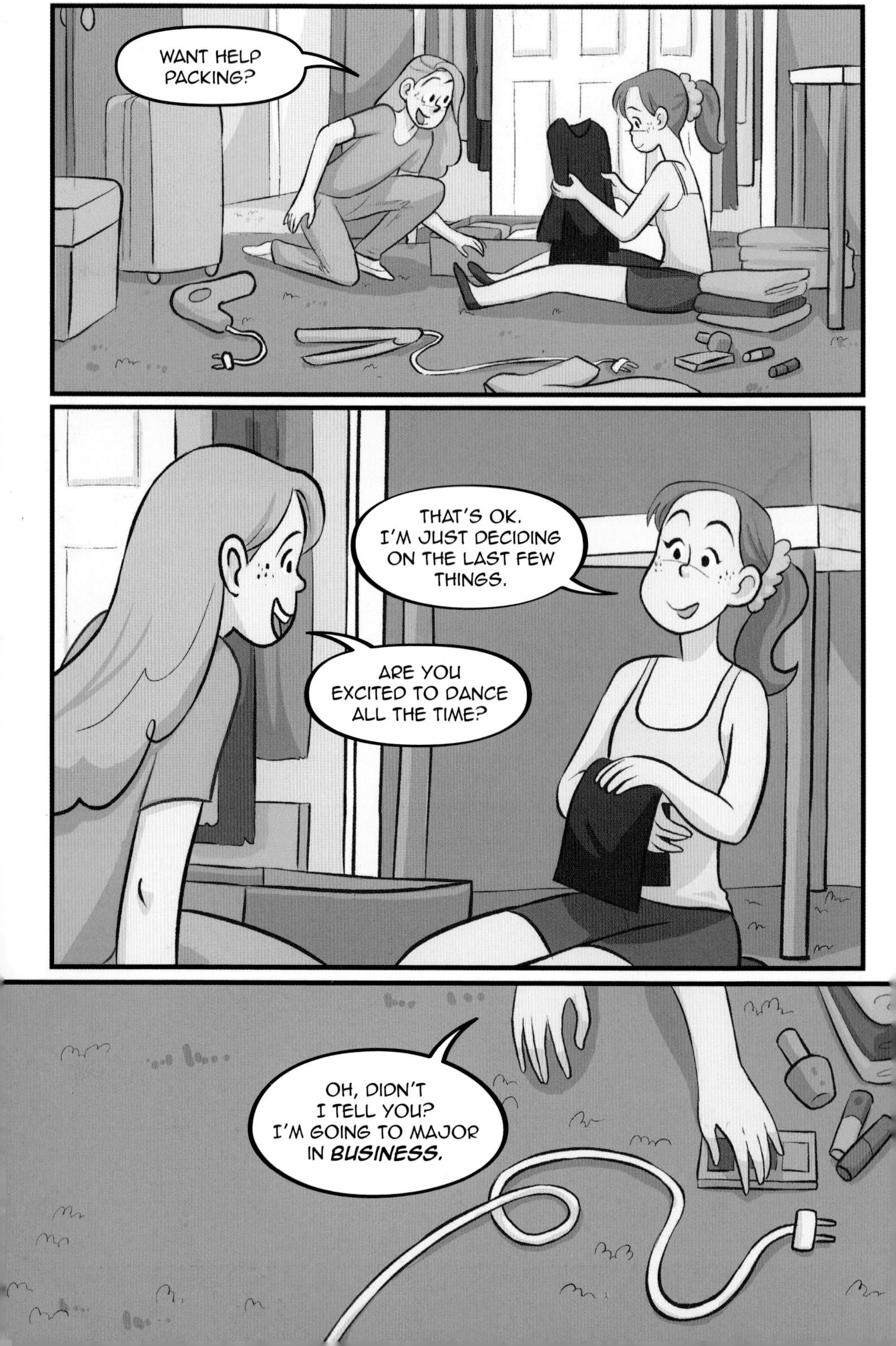
WANT HELP PACKING?
THAT'S OK. I'M JUST DECIDING ON THE LAST FEW THINGS.
ARE YOU EXCITED TO DANCE ALL THE TIME?
OH, DIDN'T I TELL YOU? I'M GOING TO MAJOR IN BUSINESS.

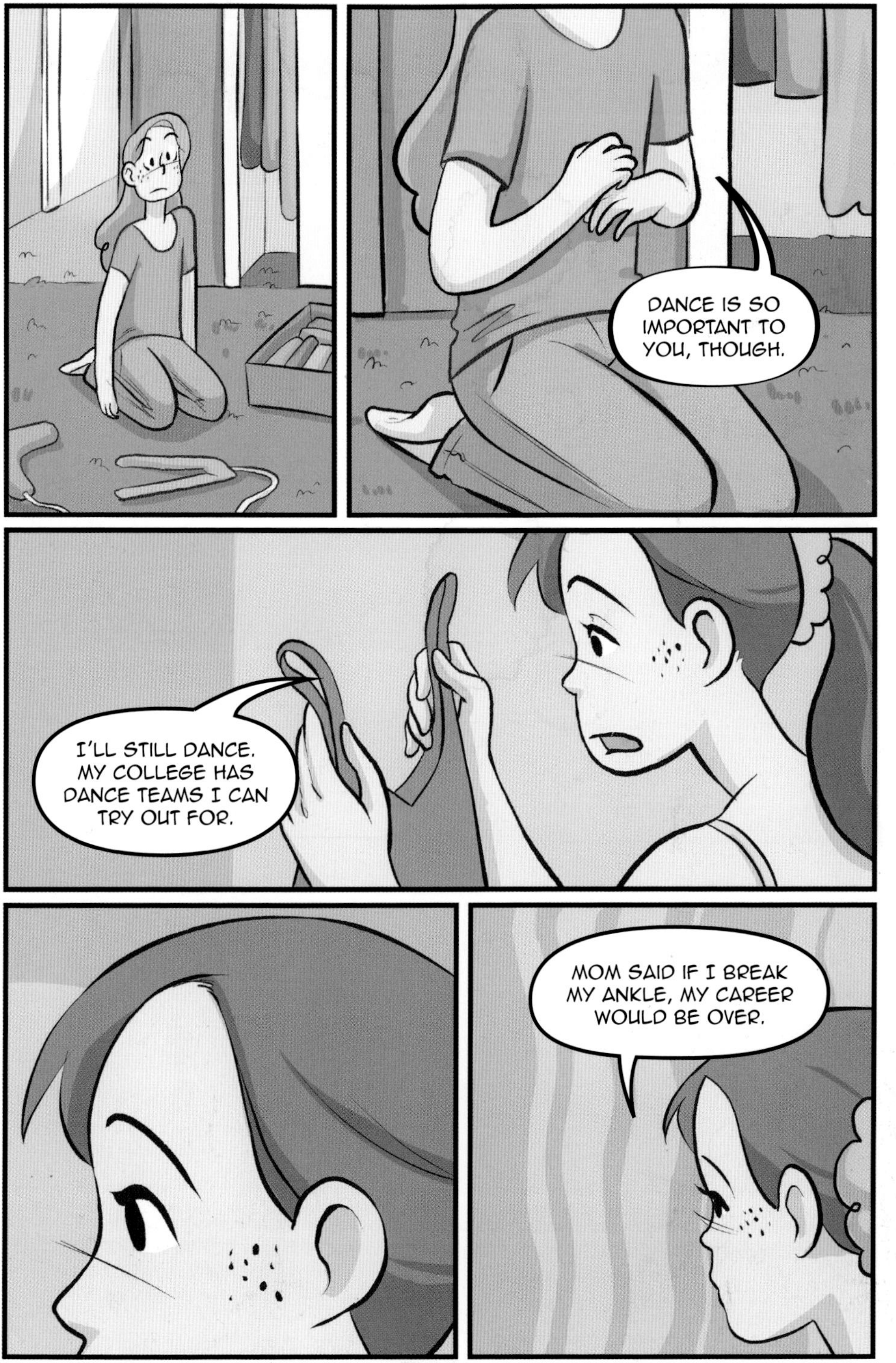
DANCE IS SO IMPORTANT TO YOU, THOUGH.
I'LL STILL DANCE. MY COLLEGE HAS DANCE TEAMS I CAN TRY OUT FOR.
MOM SAID IF I BREAK MY ANKLE, MY CAREER WOULD BE OVER.

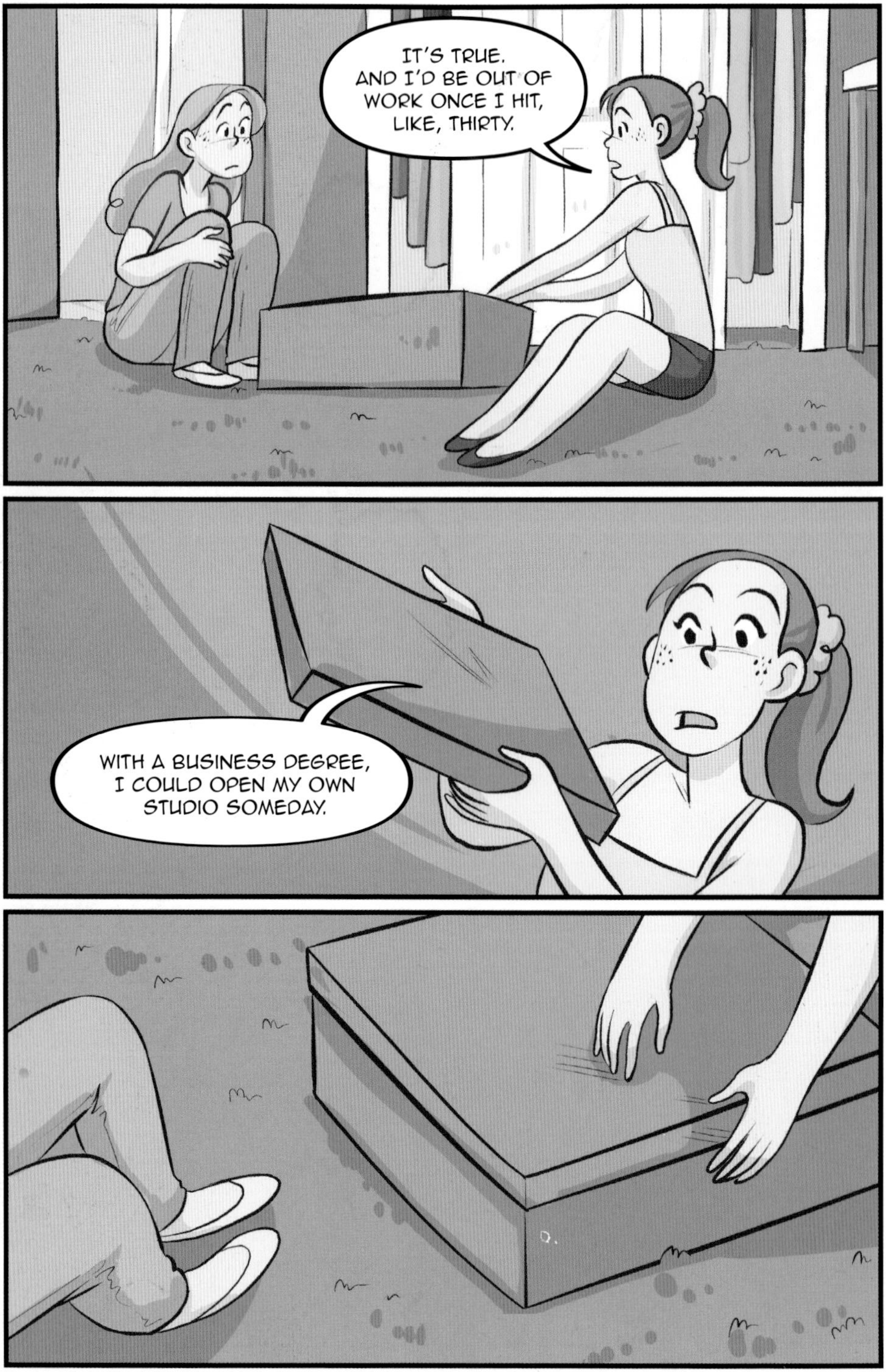
IT'S TRUE. AND I'D BE OUT OF WORK ONCE I HIT, LIKE, THIRTY.
WITH A BUSINESS DEGREE, I COULD OPEN MY OWN STUDIO SOMEDAY.

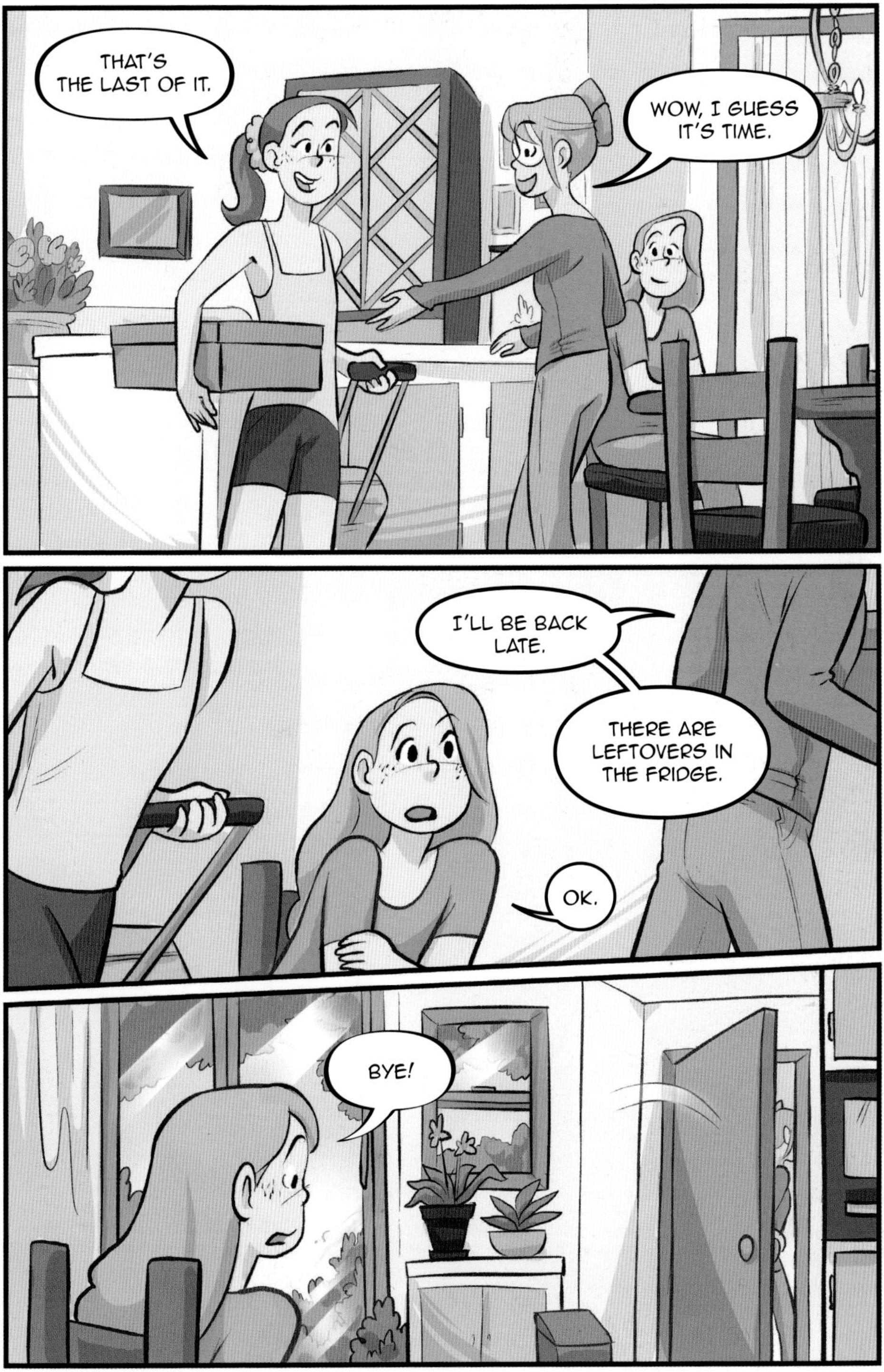
THAT'S THE LAST OF IT.
WOW, I GUESS IT'S TIME.
I'LL BE BACK LATE.
THERE ARE LEFTOVERS IN THE FRIDGE.
OK.
BYE!

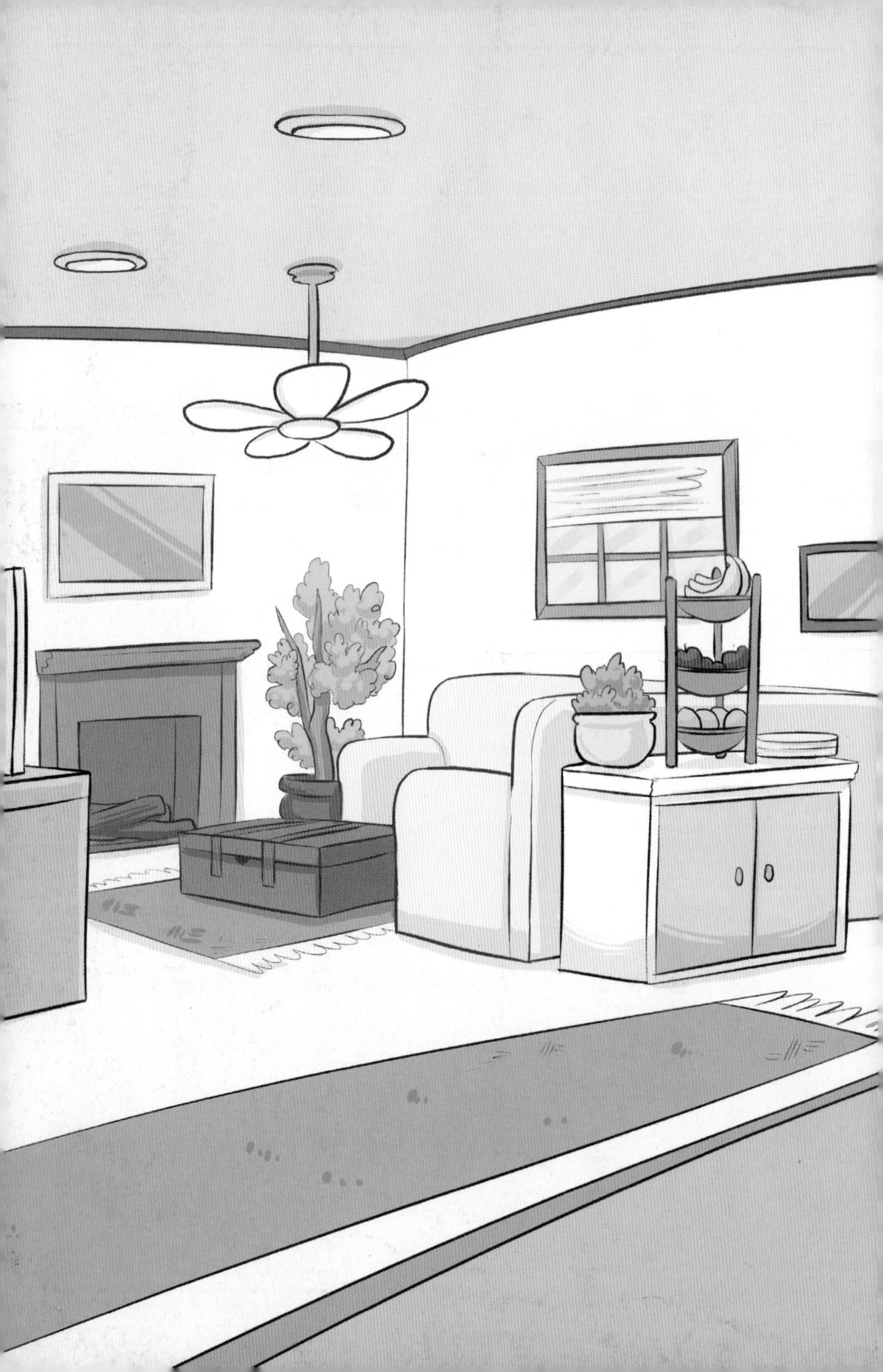

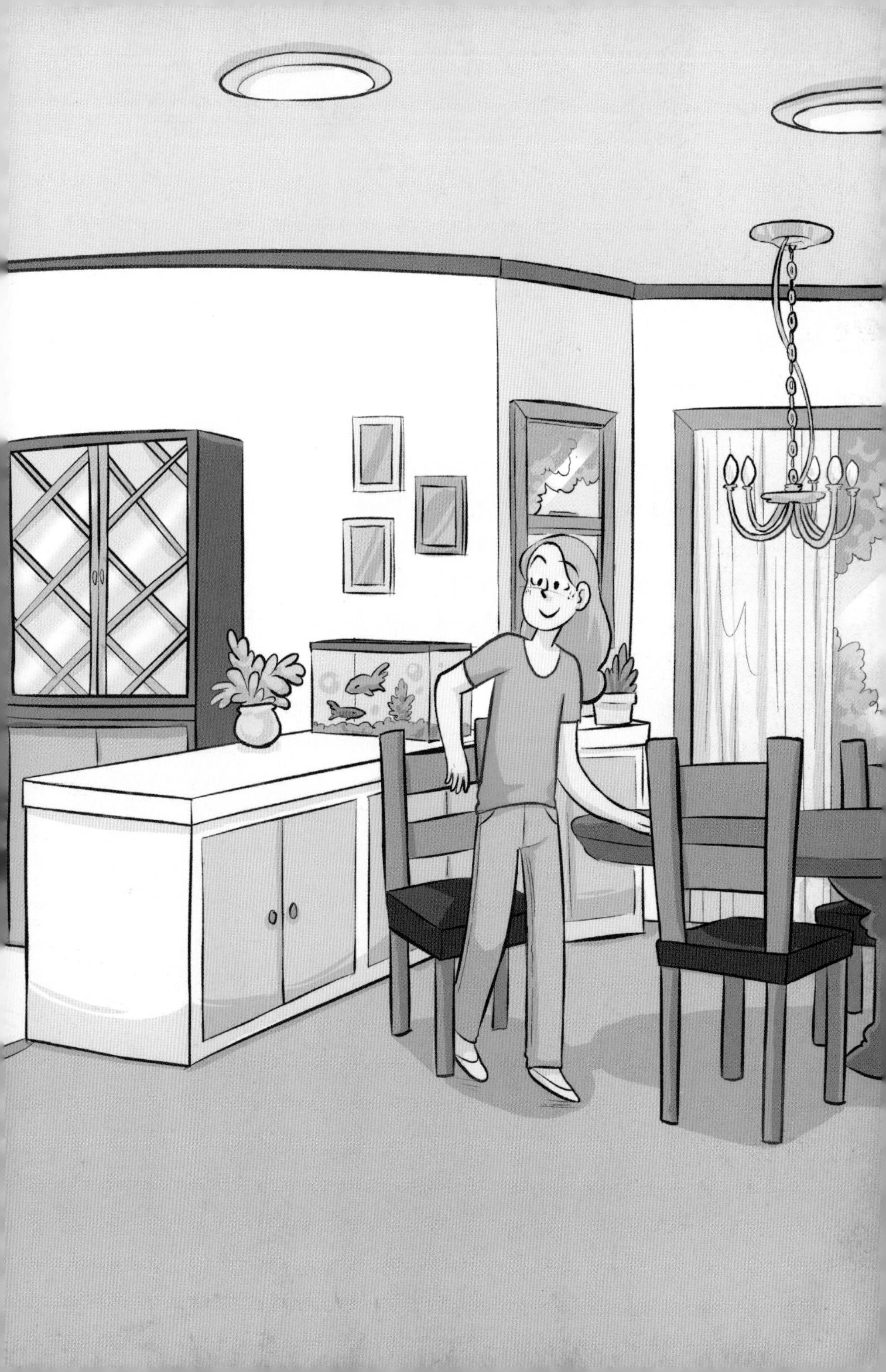

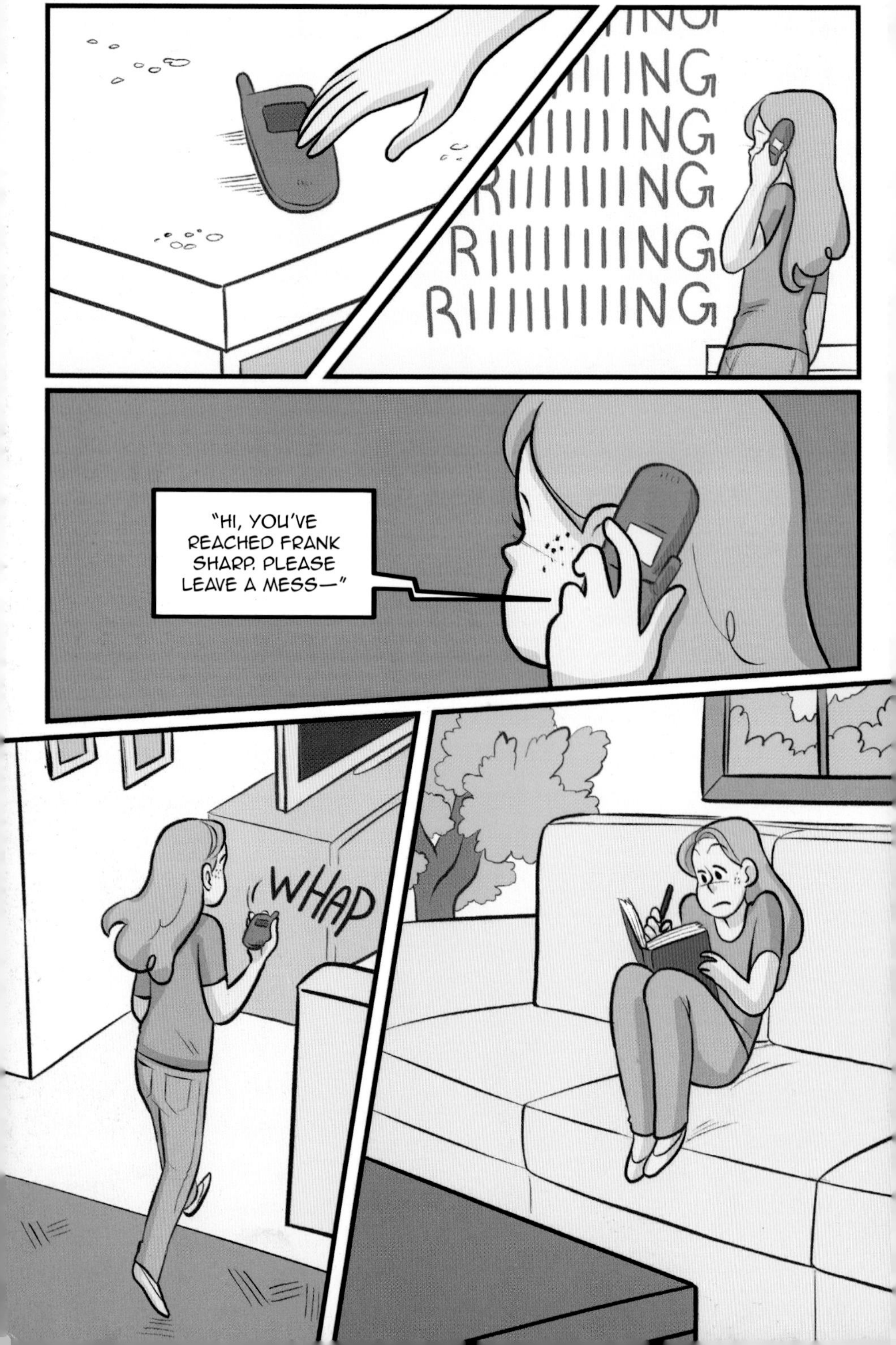
RIIIIING
RIIIIIING
RIIIIIIING
RIIIIIIIING
"HI, YOU'VE REACHED FRANK SHARP. PLEASE LEAVE A MESS—"
WHAP

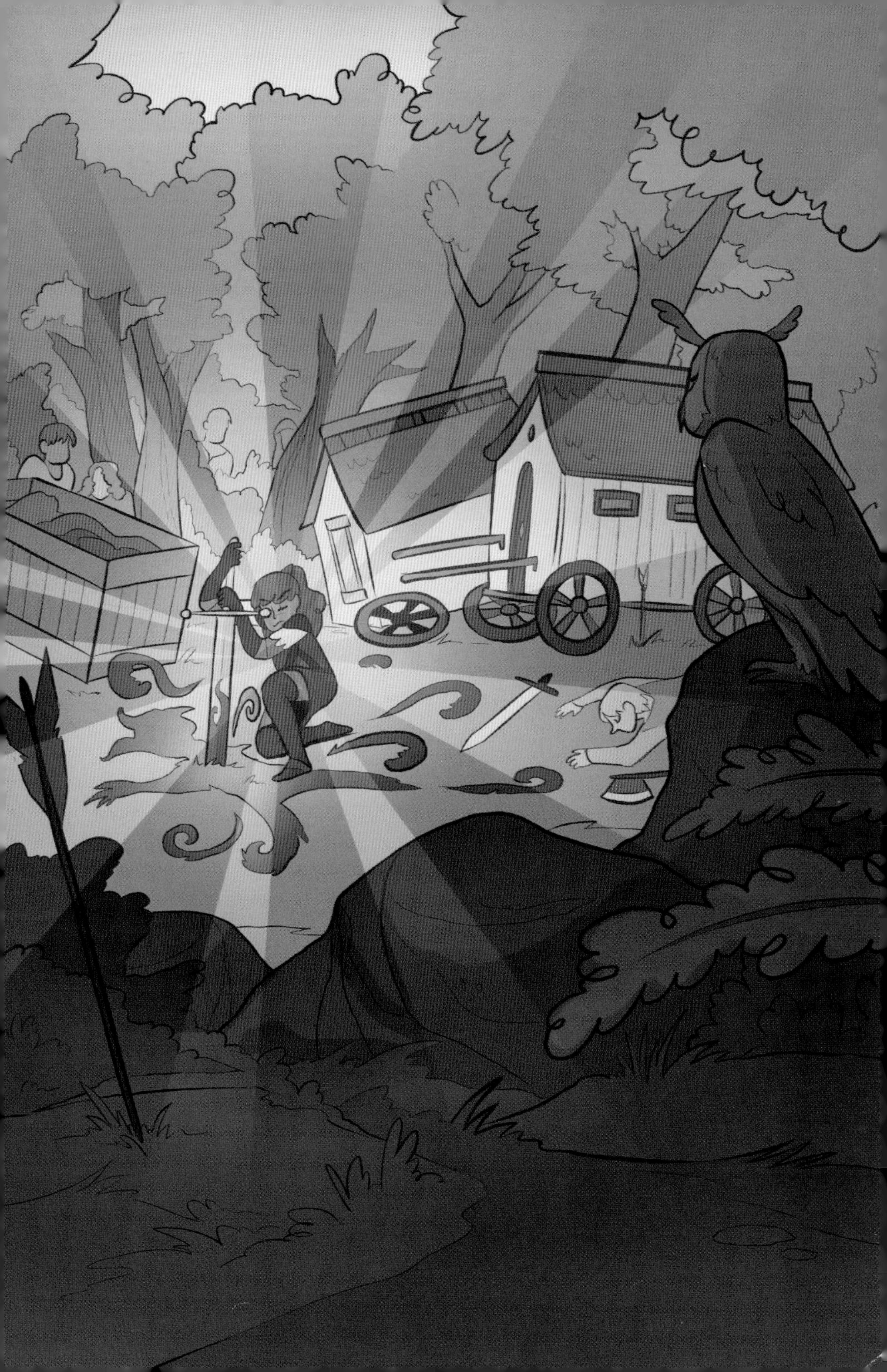

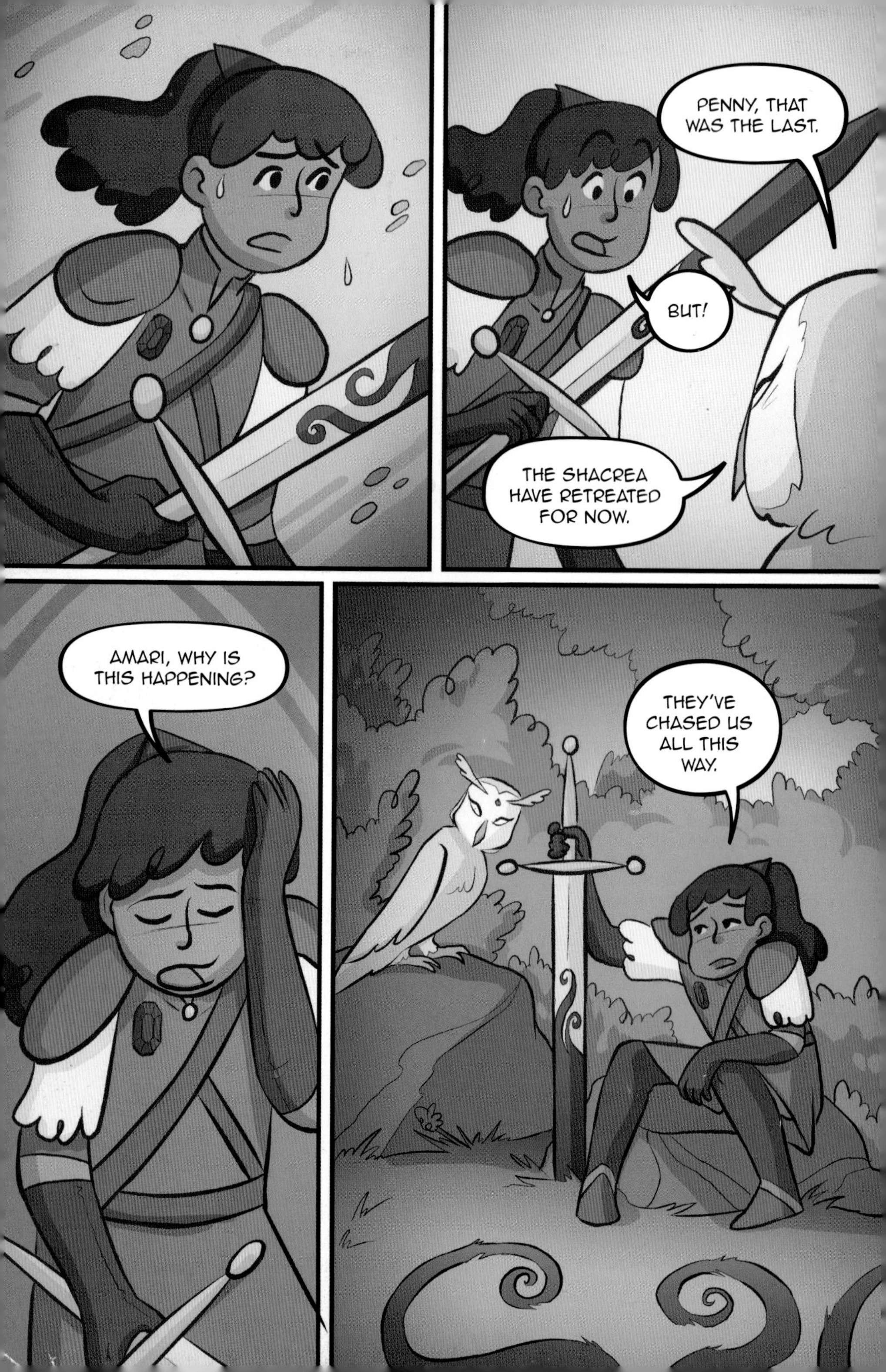
PENNY, THAT WAS THE LAST.
BUT!
THE SHACREA HAVE RETREATED FOR NOW.
AMARI, WHY IS THIS HAPPENING?
THEY'VE CHASED US ALL THIS WAY.

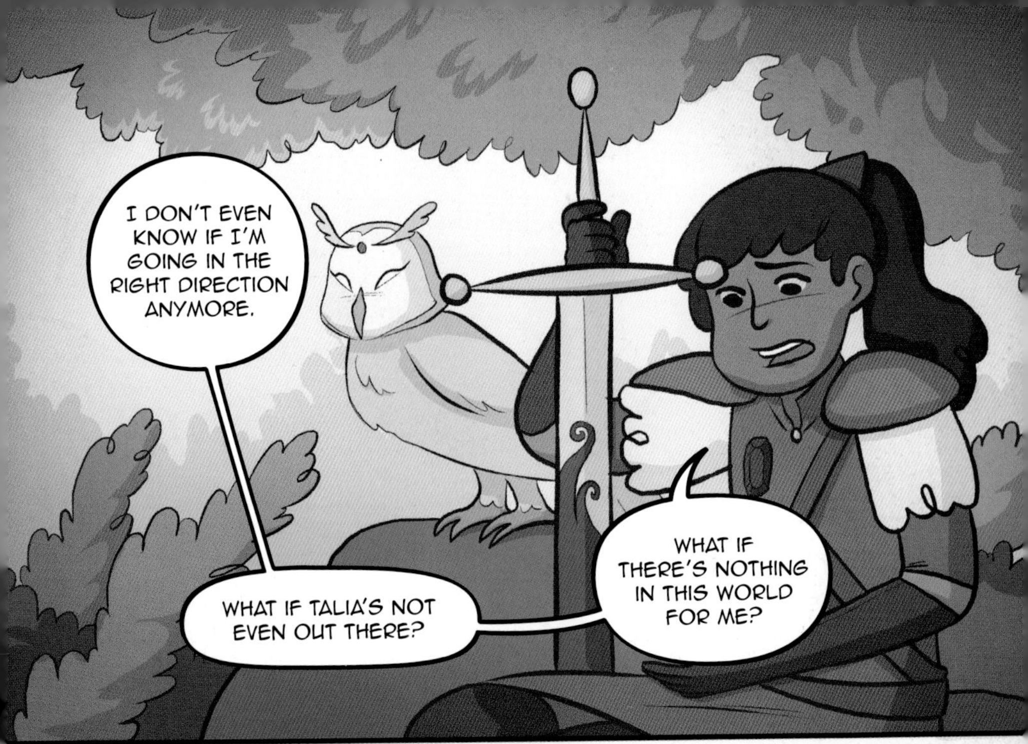
I DON'T EVEN KNOW IF I'M GOING IN THE RIGHT DIRECTION ANYMORE.
WHAT IF TALIA'S NOT EVEN OUT THERE?
WHAT IF THERE'S NOTHING IN THIS WORLD FOR ME?
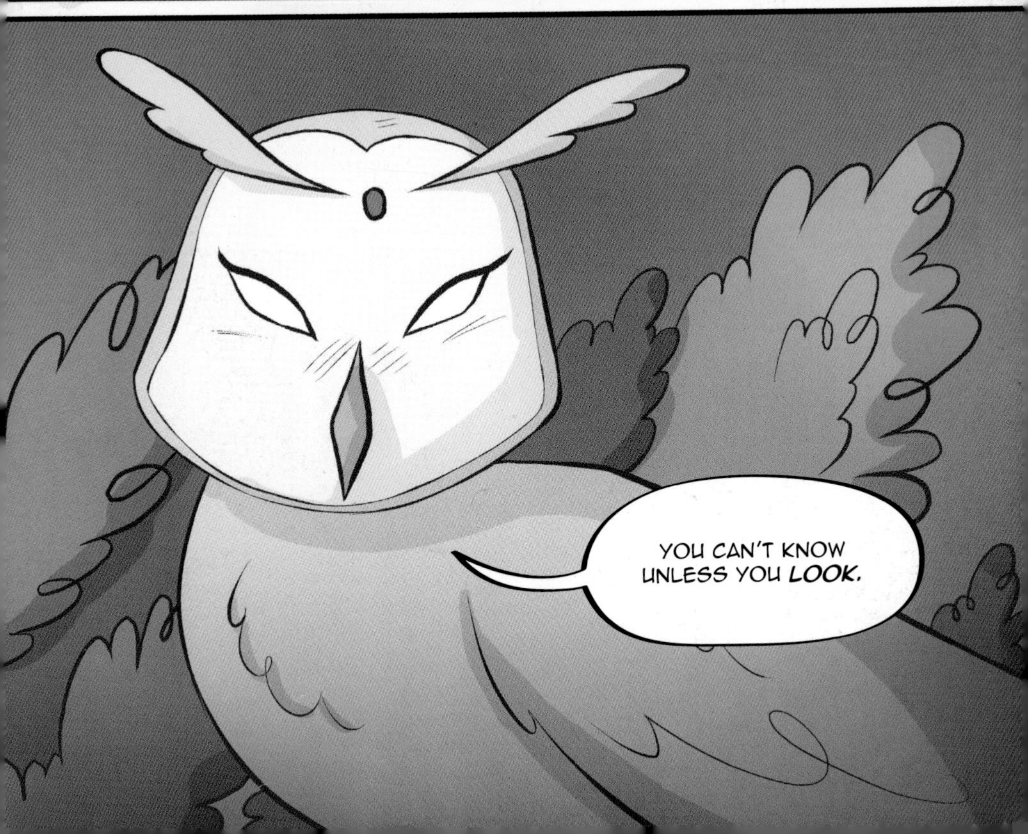
YOU CAN'T KNOW UNLESS YOU ***LOOK.***

RIIIIIIIN
RIIIIIIII
RIIIIIII
RIIIII
RII

HI, YOU'VE REACHED FRANK SHARP. PLEASE LEAVE A MESSAGE AFTER THE BEEP.

HEY, DAD. IT'S TORI.

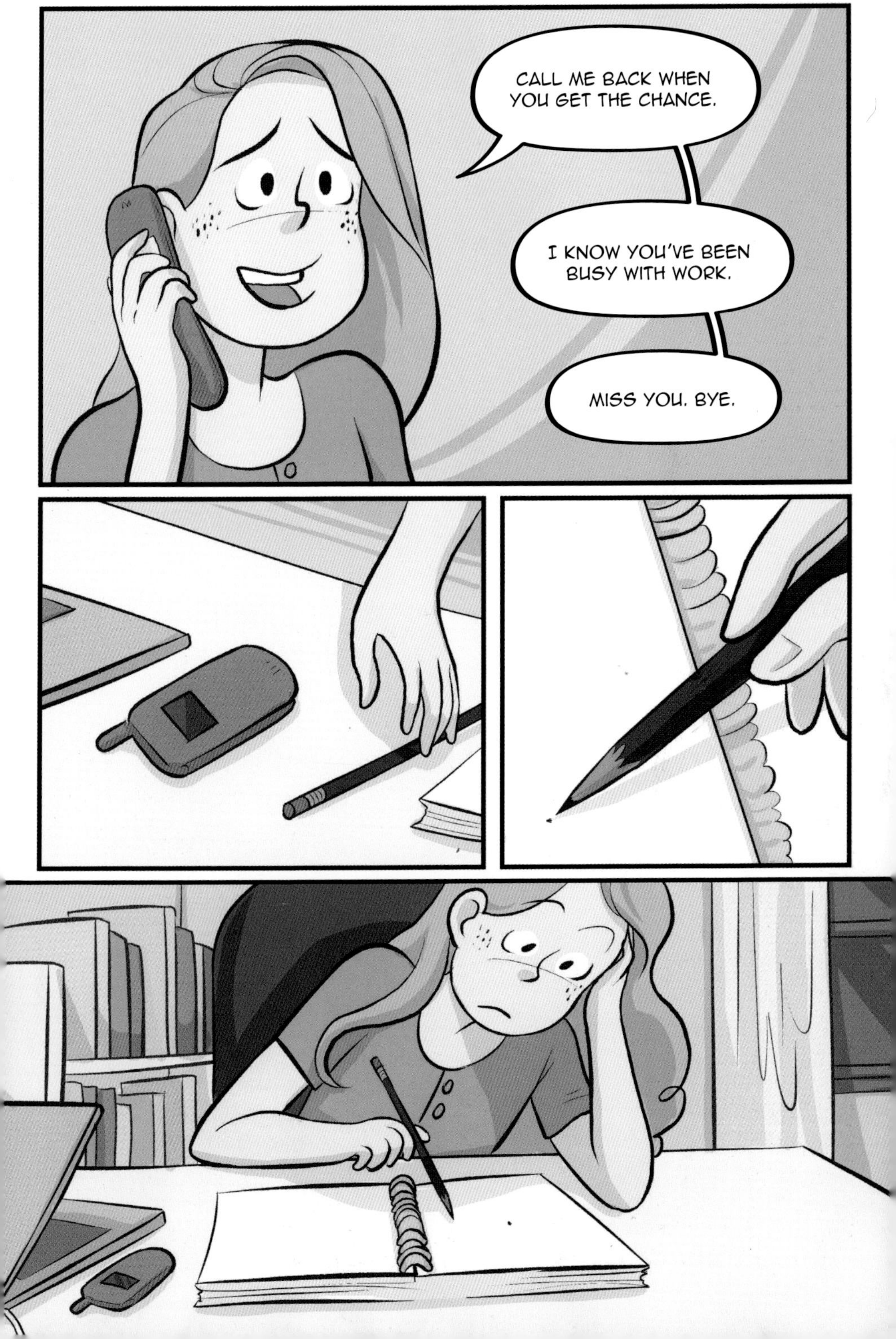
CALL ME BACK WHEN YOU GET THE CHANCE.
I KNOW YOU'VE BEEN BUSY WITH WORK.
MISS YOU. BYE.

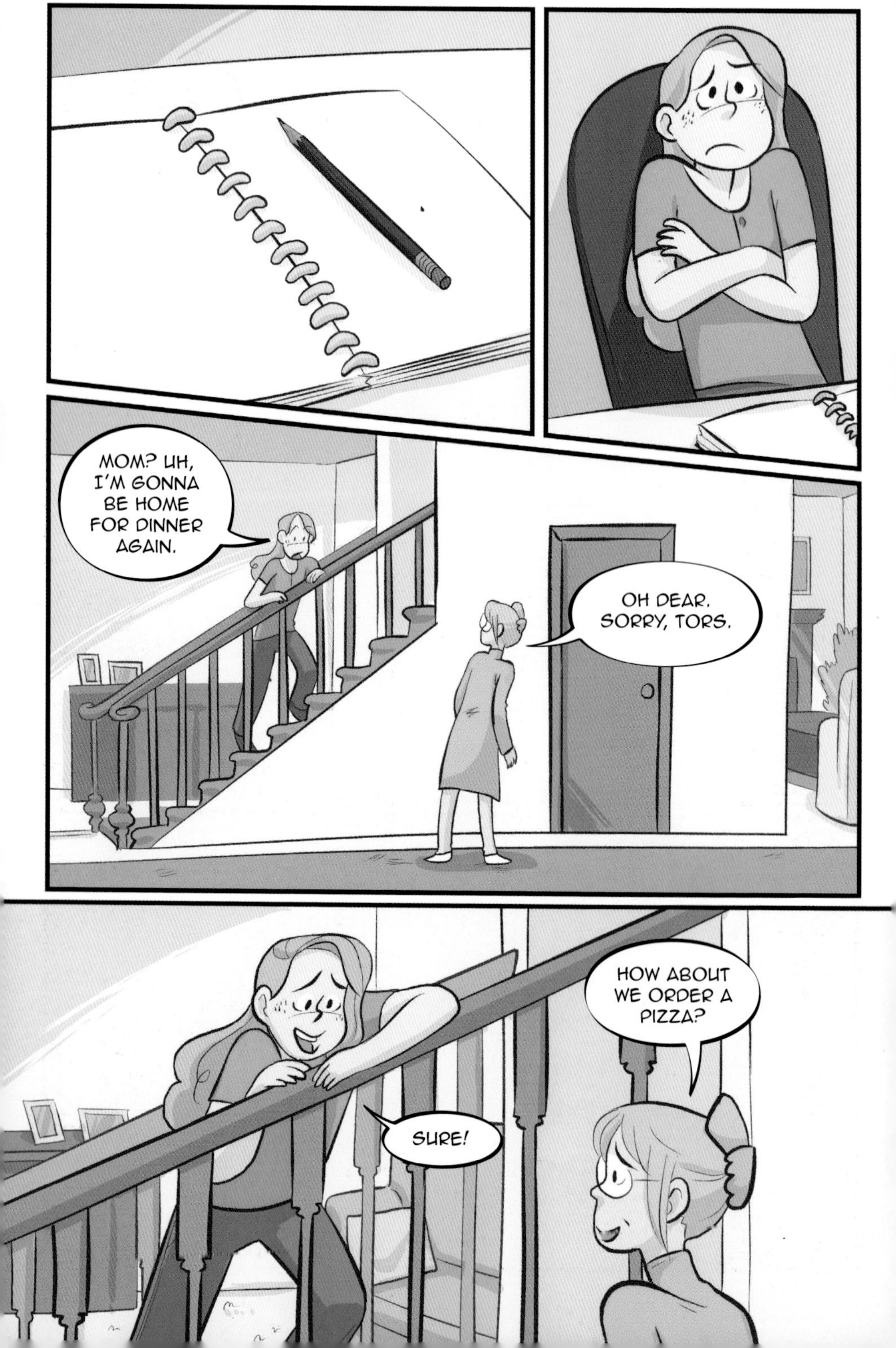
MOM? UH, I'M GONNA BE HOME FOR DINNER AGAIN.
OH DEAR. SORRY, TORS.
HOW ABOUT WE ORDER A PIZZA?
SURE!

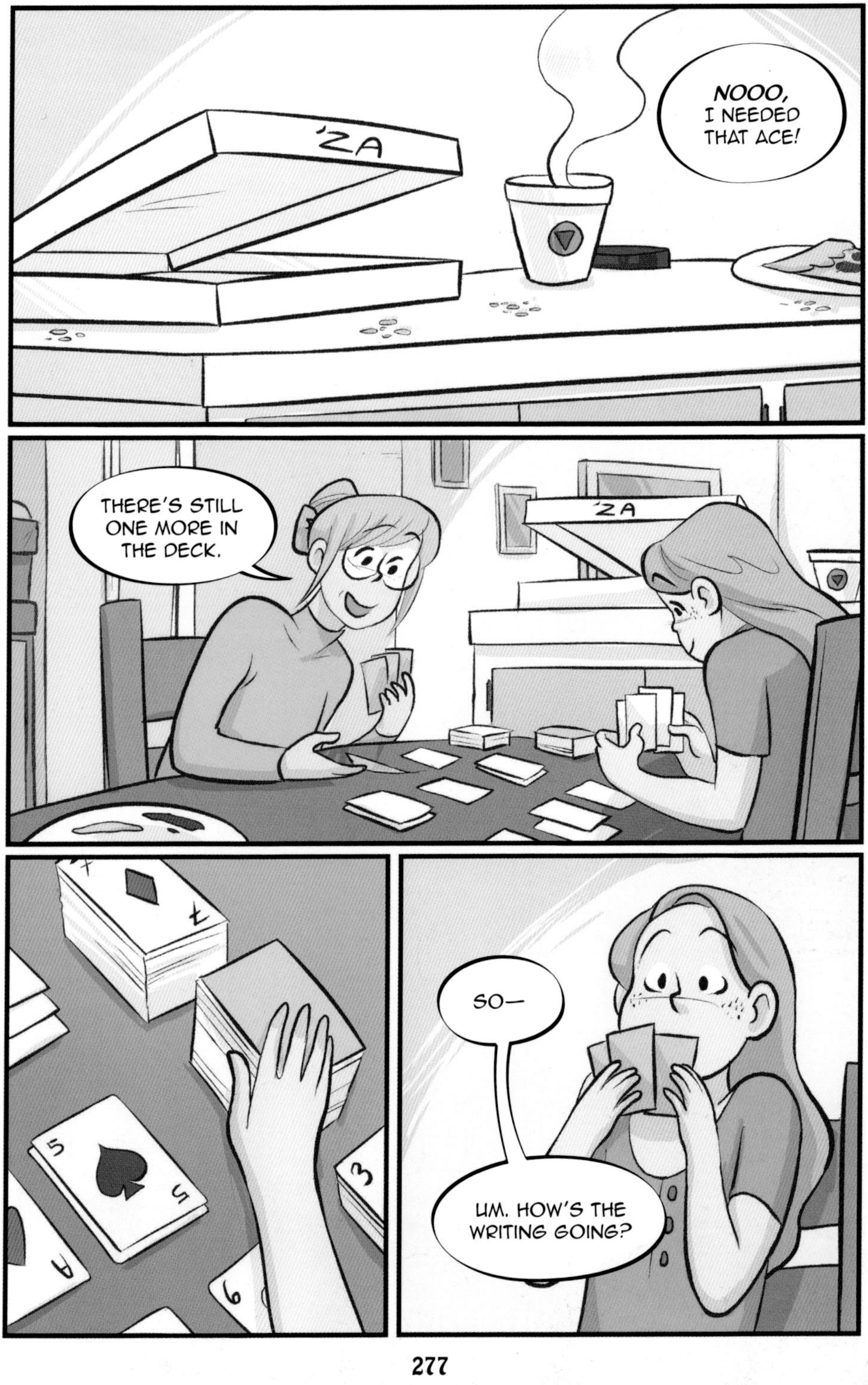
'ZA
NOOO, I NEEDED THAT ACE!
THERE'S STILL ONE MORE IN THE DECK.
'ZA
SO—
UM. HOW'S THE WRITING GOING?

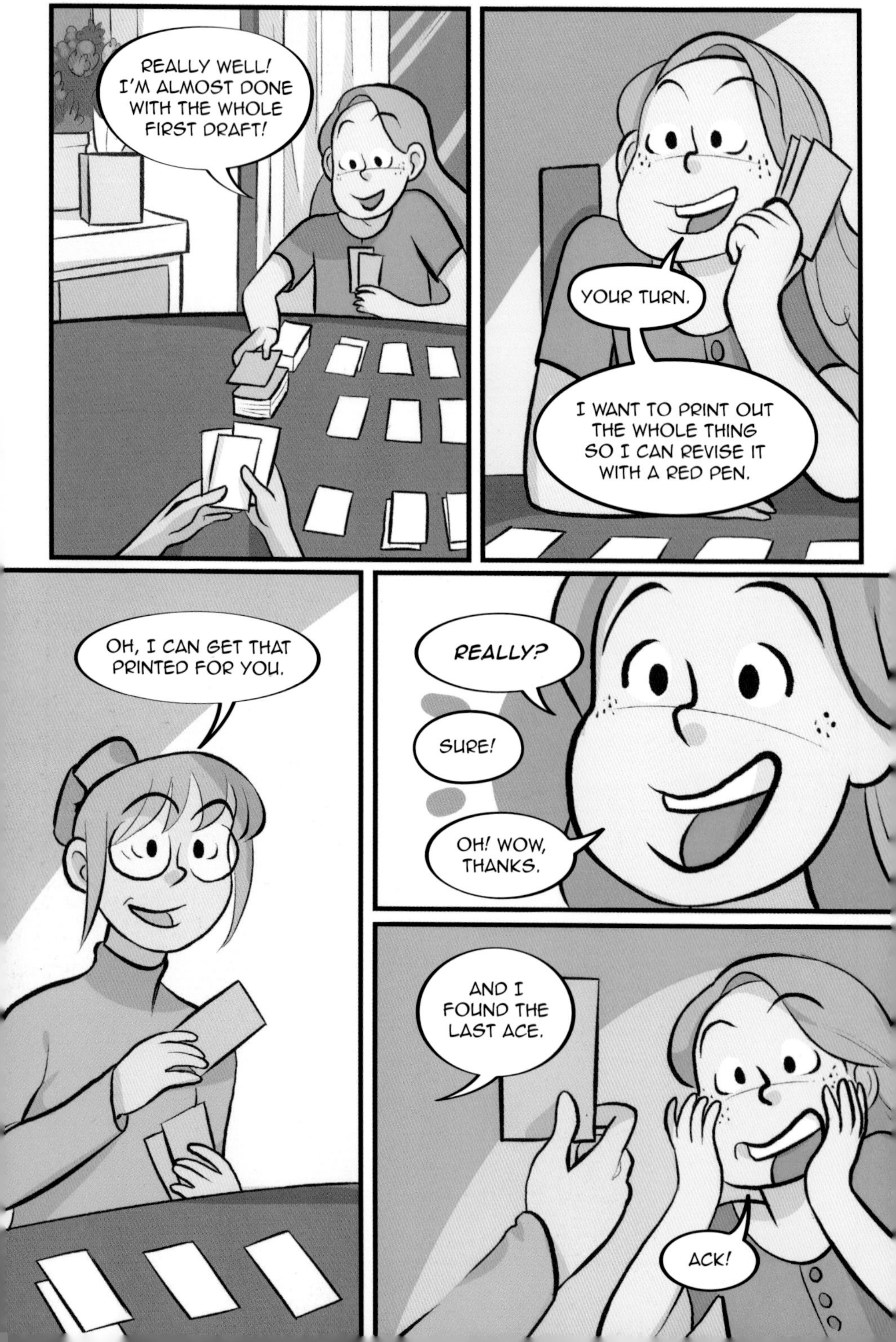
REALLY WELL! I'M ALMOST DONE WITH THE WHOLE FIRST DRAFT!
YOUR TURN.
I WANT TO PRINT OUT THE WHOLE THING SO I CAN REVISE IT WITH A RED PEN.
OH, I CAN GET THAT PRINTED FOR YOU.
*REALLY?*
SURE!
OH! WOW, THANKS.
AND I FOUND THE LAST ACE.
ACK!

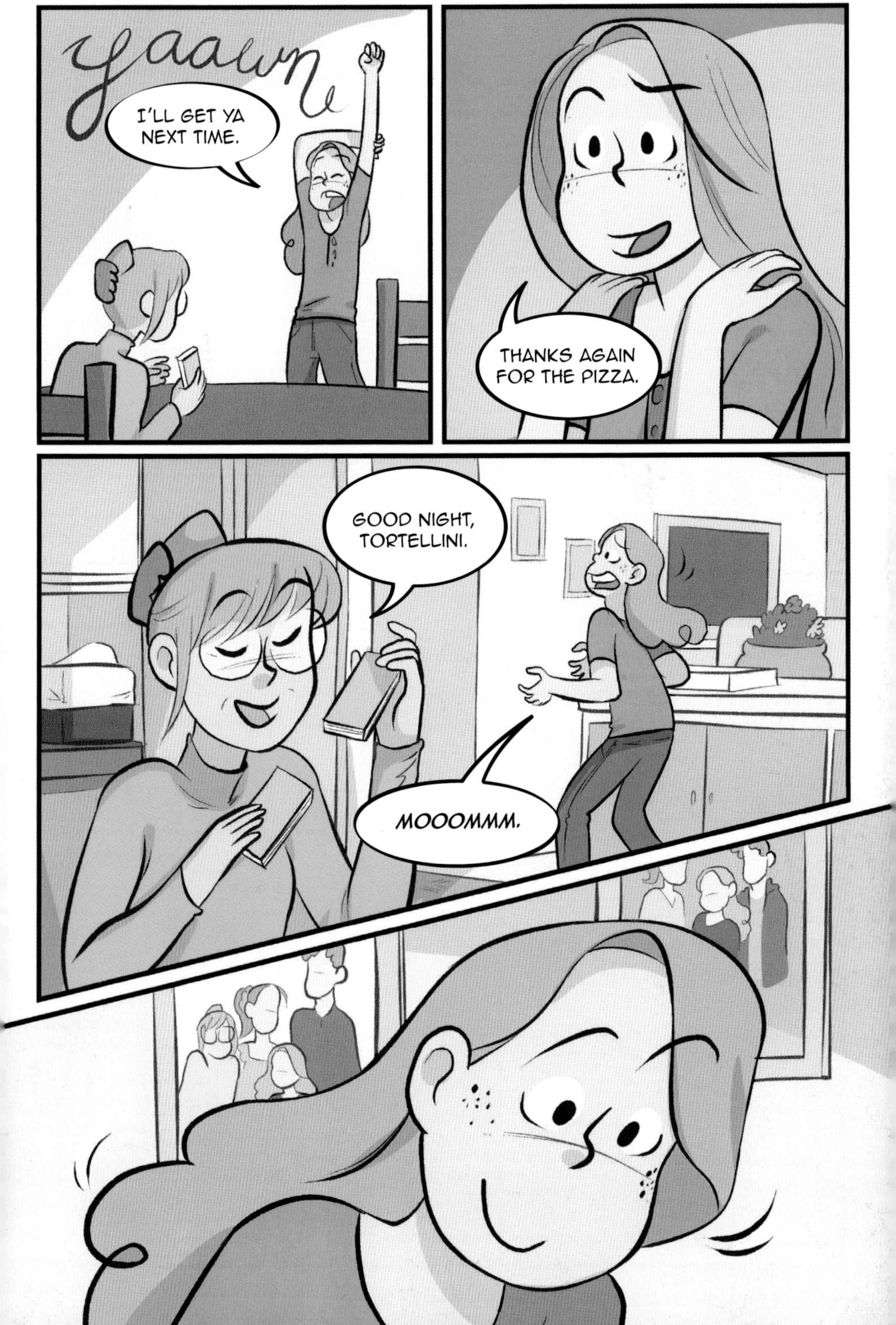

yaawn
I'LL GET YA NEXT TIME.
THANKS AGAIN FOR THE PIZZA.
GOOD NIGHT, TORTELLINI.
MOOOMMM.

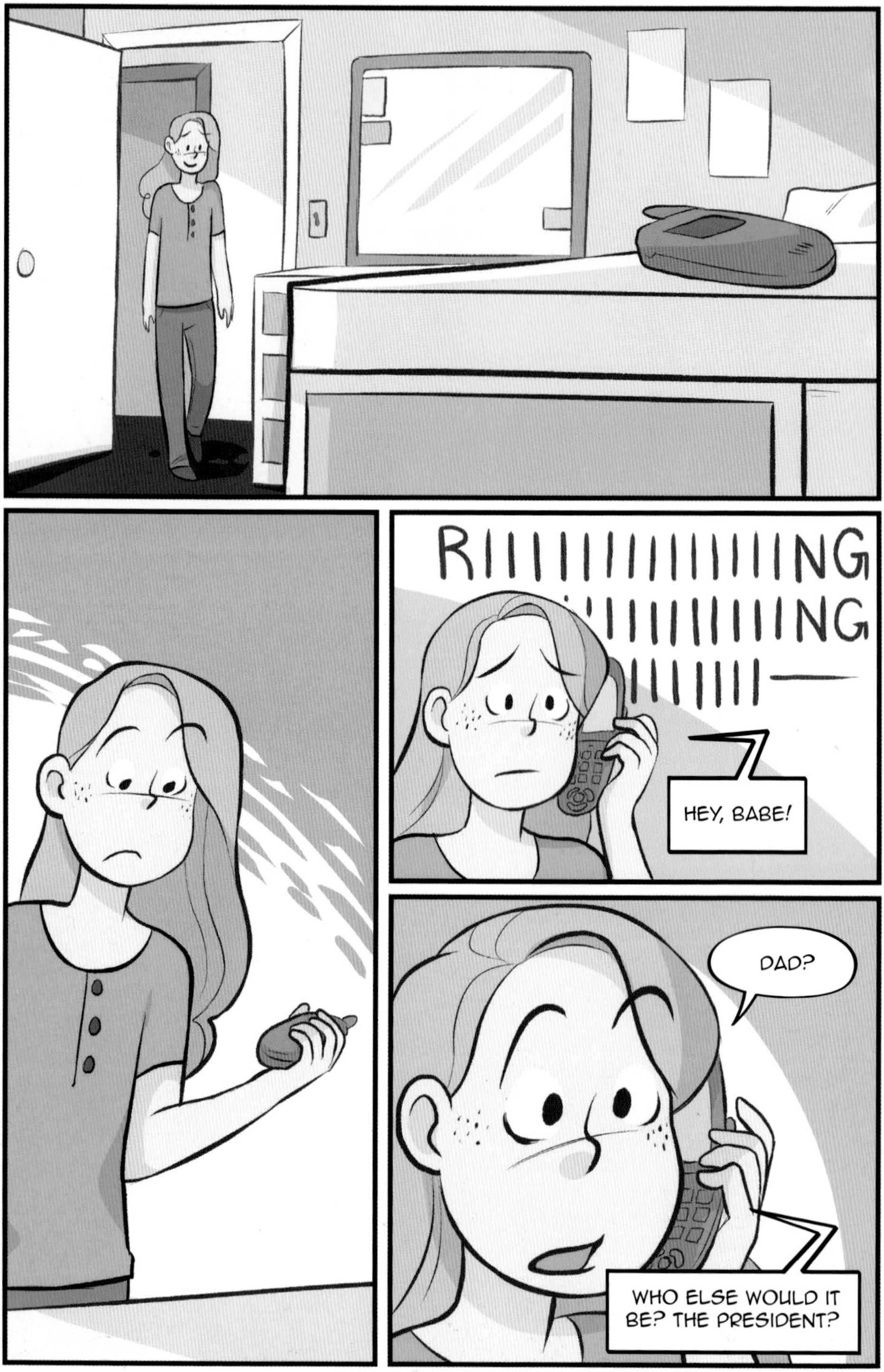
RIIIIIIIIIIIIING
IIIIIIIIIING
IIIIIII—
HEY, BABE!
DAD?
WHO ELSE WOULD IT BE? THE PRESIDENT?

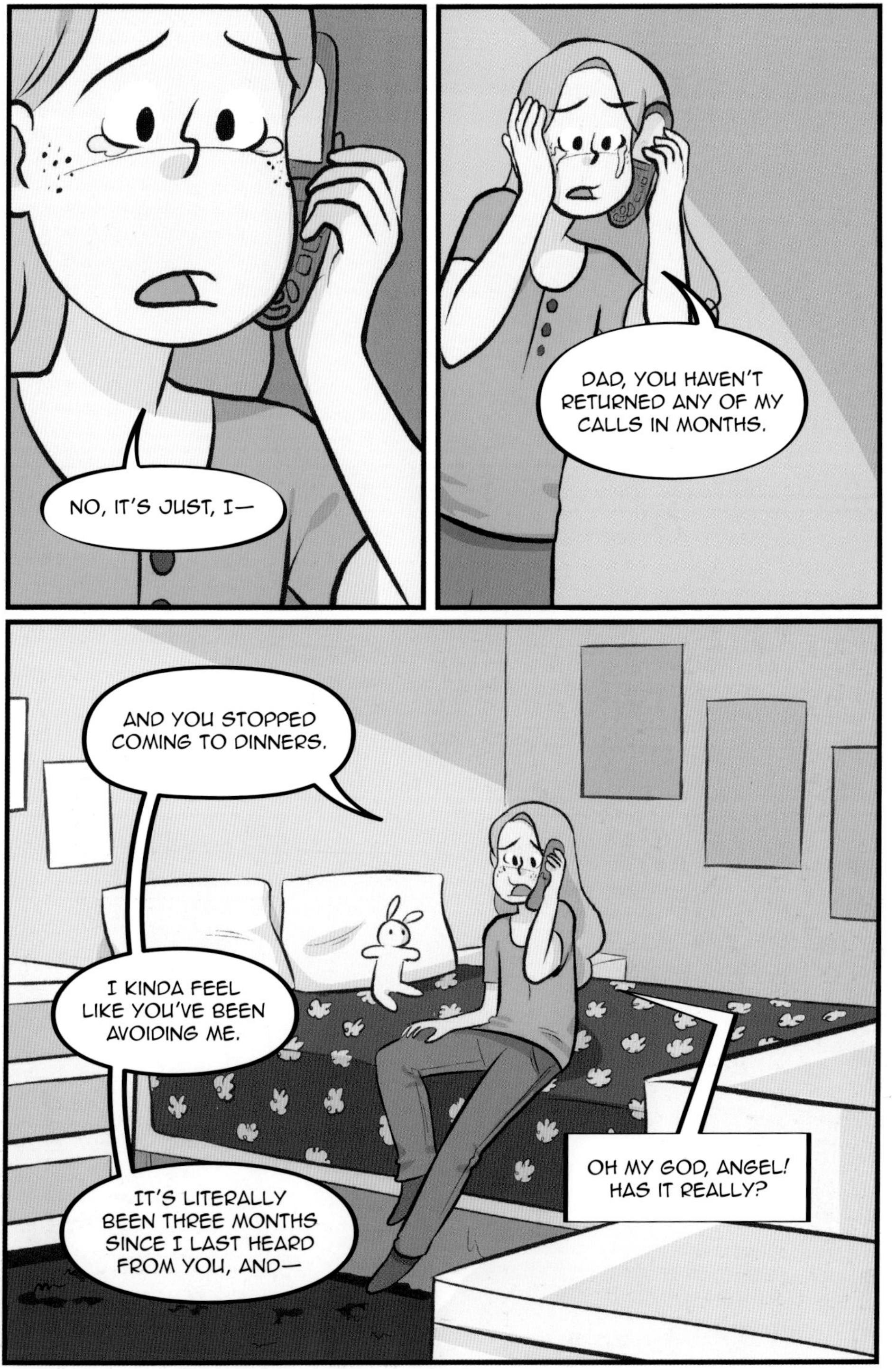
NO, IT'S JUST, I—
DAD, YOU HAVEN'T RETURNED ANY OF MY CALLS IN MONTHS.
AND YOU STOPPED COMING TO DINNERS.
I KINDA FEEL LIKE YOU'VE BEEN AVOIDING ME.
IT'S LITERALLY BEEN THREE MONTHS SINCE I LAST HEARD FROM YOU, AND—
OH MY GOD, ANGEL! HAS IT REALLY?

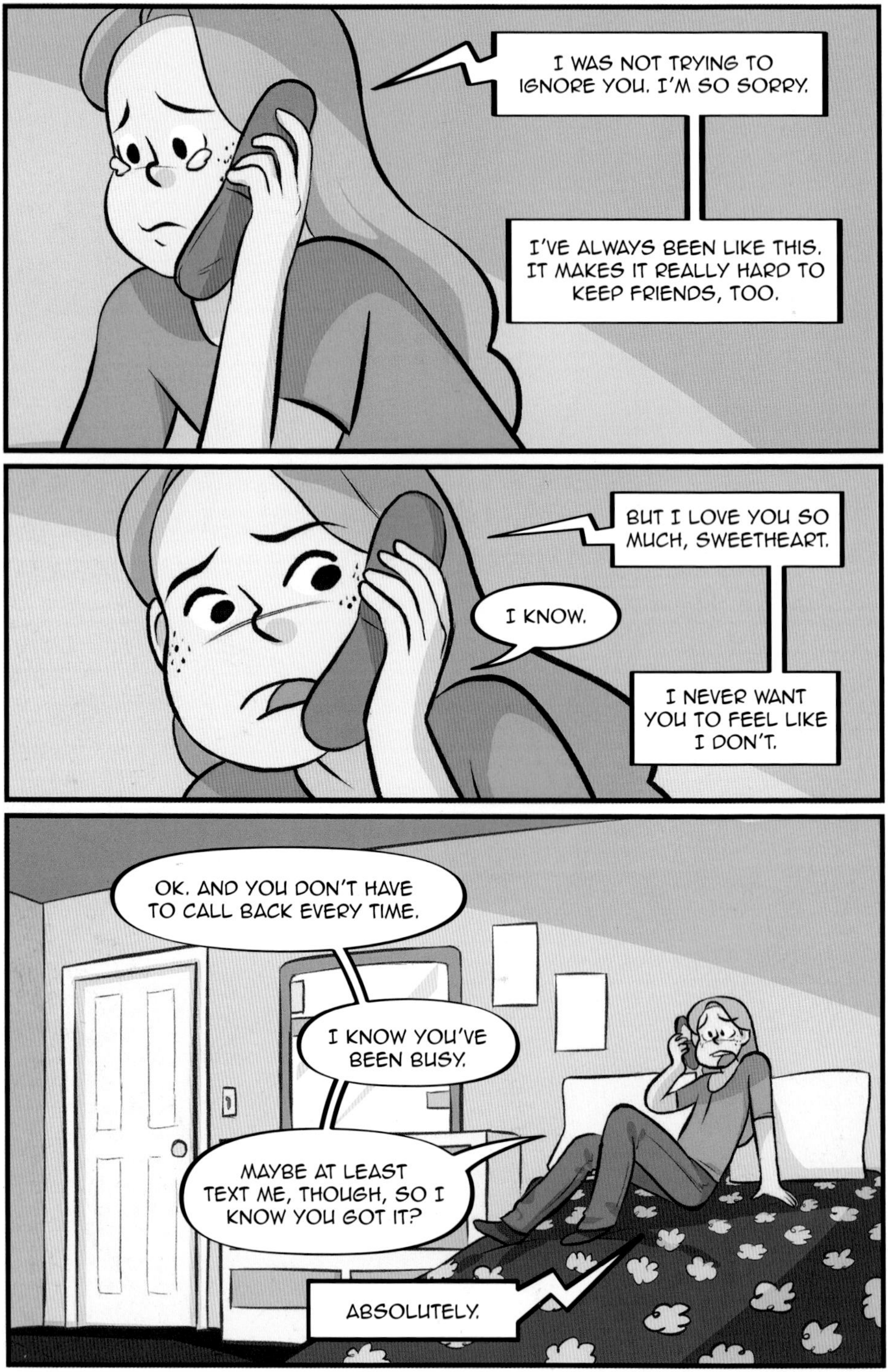
I WAS NOT TRYING TO IGNORE YOU. I'M SO SORRY.
I'VE ALWAYS BEEN LIKE THIS. IT MAKES IT REALLY HARD TO KEEP FRIENDS, TOO.
BUT I LOVE YOU SO MUCH, SWEETHEART.
I KNOW.
I NEVER WANT YOU TO FEEL LIKE I DON'T.
OK. AND YOU DON'T HAVE TO CALL BACK EVERY TIME.
I KNOW YOU'VE BEEN BUSY.
MAYBE AT LEAST TEXT ME, THOUGH, SO I KNOW YOU GOT IT?
ABSOLUTELY.

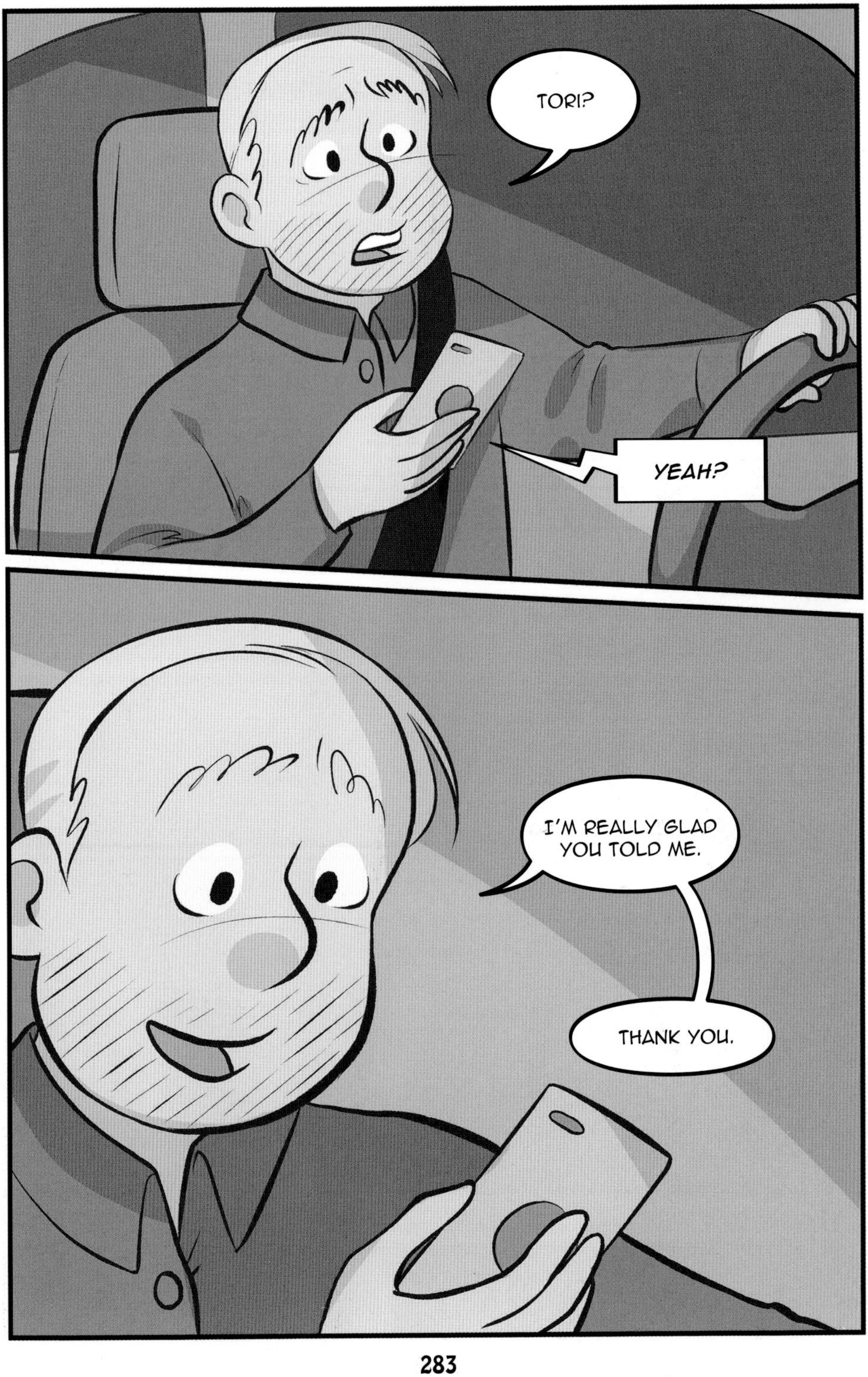
TORI?
YEAH?
I'M REALLY GLAD YOU TOLD ME.
THANK YOU.

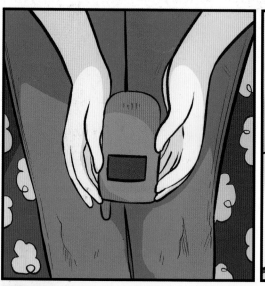

PHEW

HMM.

RIIIIIIIIIIIIING
RIIIIIIIIIIIIIING
RIIIIIIIIIIIIIING

HELLO?

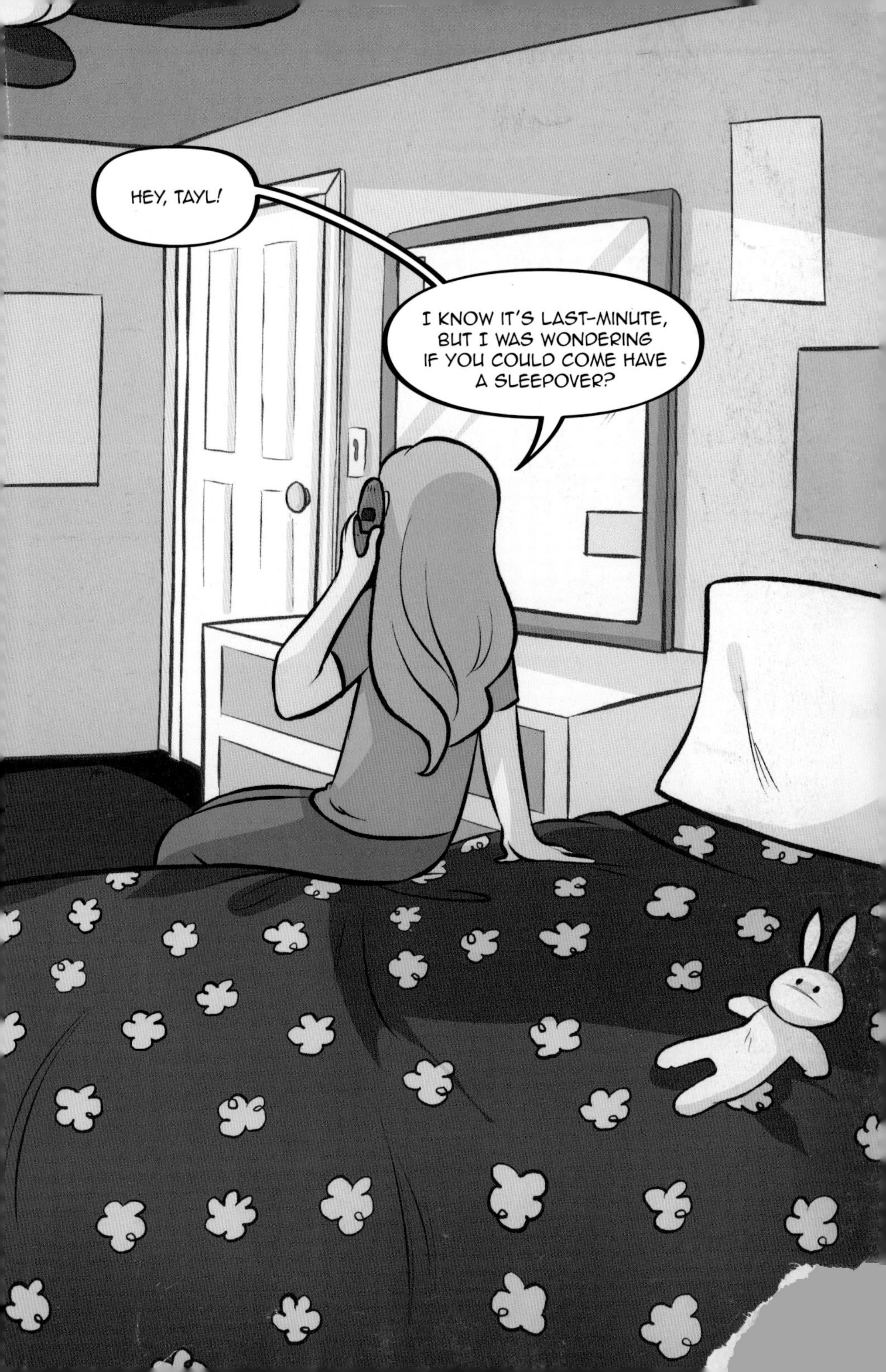
HEY, TAYL!
I KNOW IT'S LAST-MINUTE, BUT I WAS WONDERING IF YOU COULD COME HAVE A SLEEPOVER?

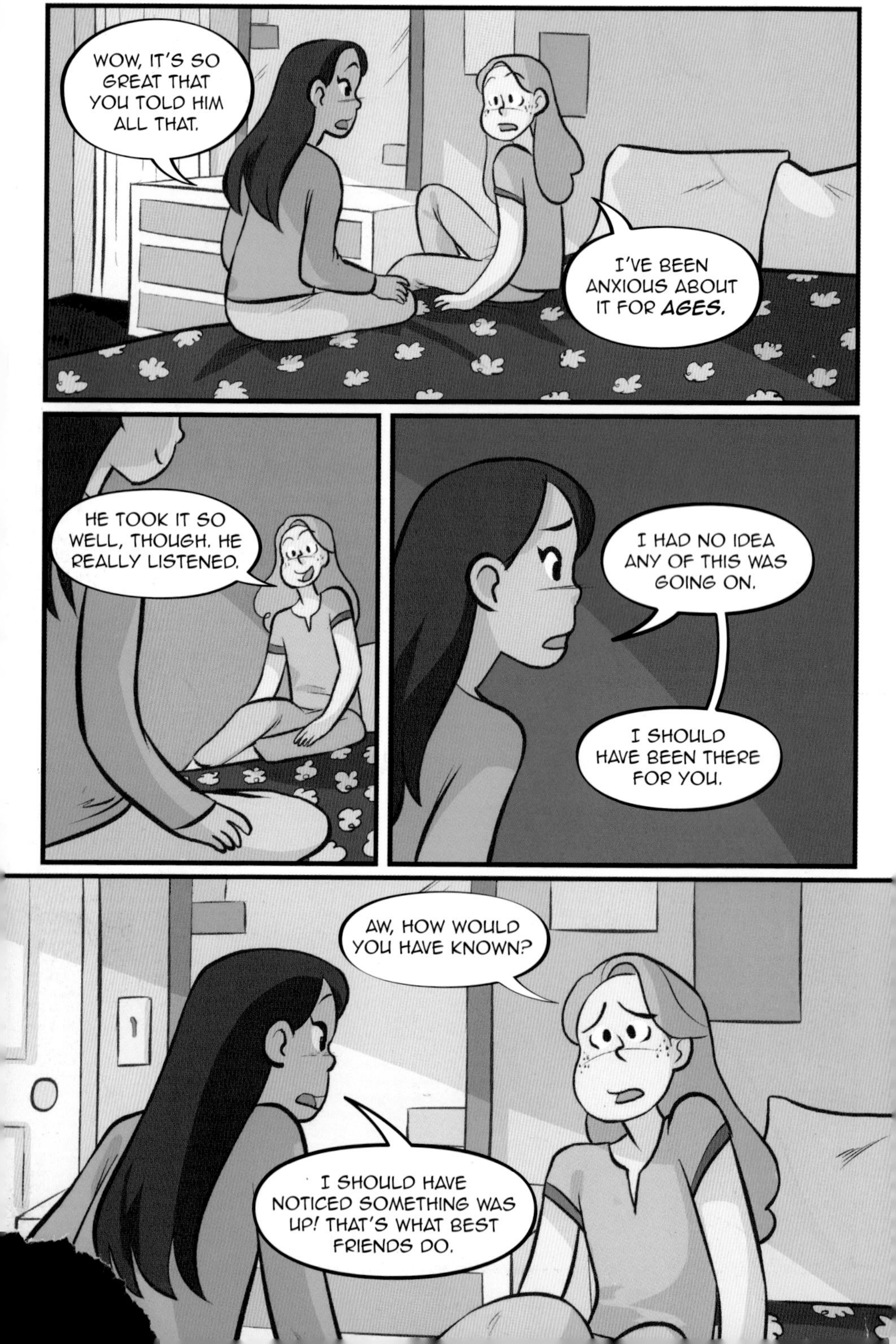
WOW, IT'S SO GREAT THAT YOU TOLD HIM ALL THAT.
I'VE BEEN ANXIOUS ABOUT IT FOR **AGES.**
HE TOOK IT SO WELL, THOUGH. HE REALLY LISTENED.
I HAD NO IDEA ANY OF THIS WAS GOING ON.
I SHOULD HAVE BEEN THERE FOR YOU.
AW, HOW WOULD YOU HAVE KNOWN?
I SHOULD HAVE NOTICED SOMETHING WAS UP! THAT'S WHAT BEST FRIENDS DO.

I MEAN... THINGS GOT SO WEIRD BETWEEN US THIS YEAR.

I WAS SUPER WEIRD ABOUT THE "PANTS" THING.

I STILL CAN'T BELIEVE I FORGOT YOUR BIRTHDAY.

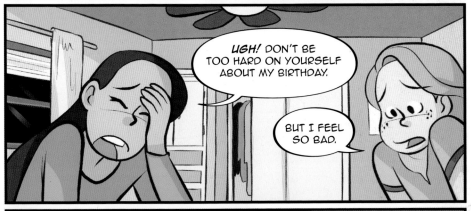

UGH! DON'T BE TOO HARD ON YOURSELF ABOUT MY BIRTHDAY.

BUT I FEEL SO BAD.

I SORT OF...*PURPOSELY* DIDN'T TELL ANYONE MY BIRTHDAY WAS COMING UP.

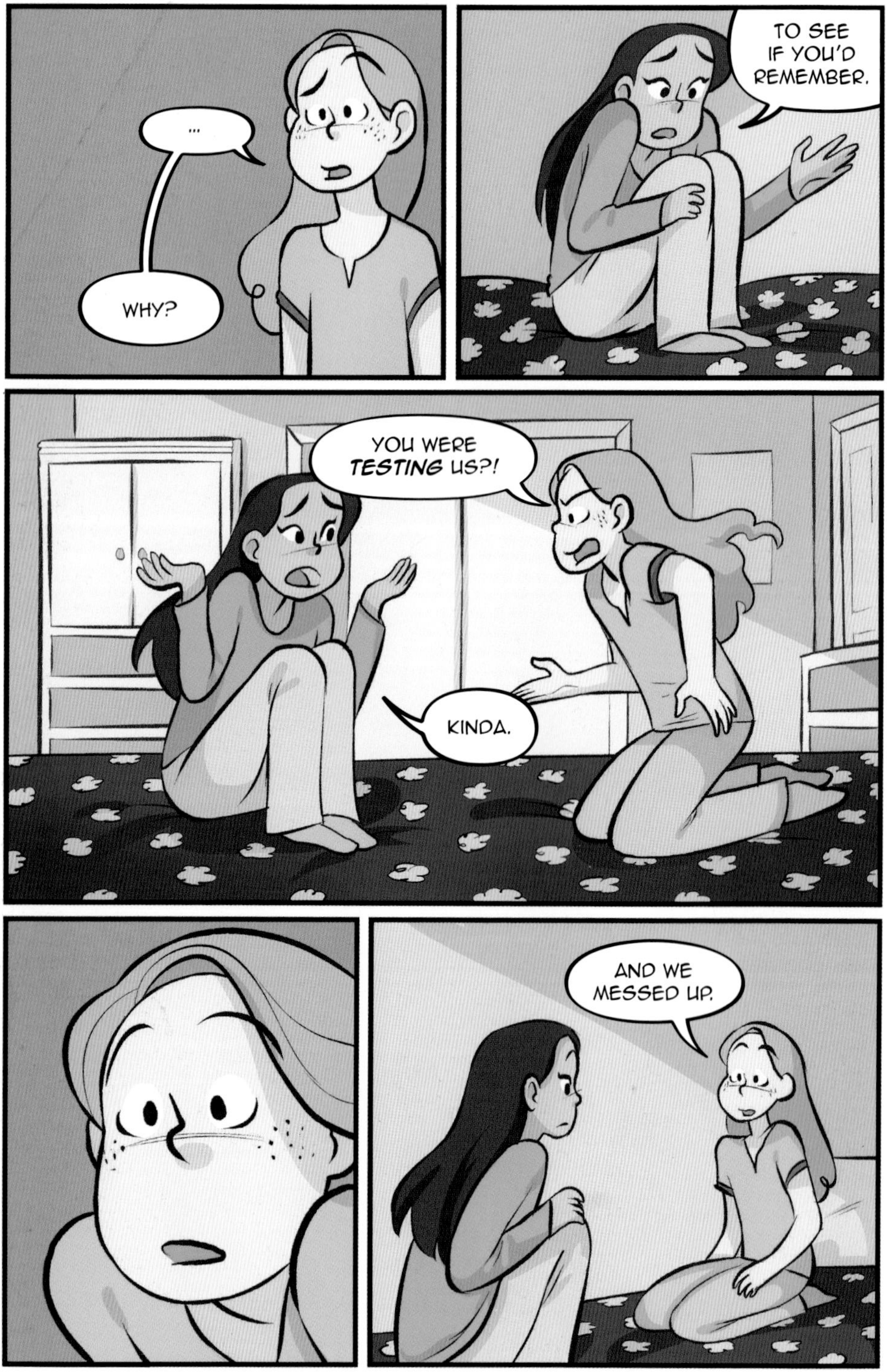
...
WHY?
TO SEE IF YOU'D REMEMBER.
YOU WERE *TESTING* US?!
KINDA.
AND WE MESSED UP.

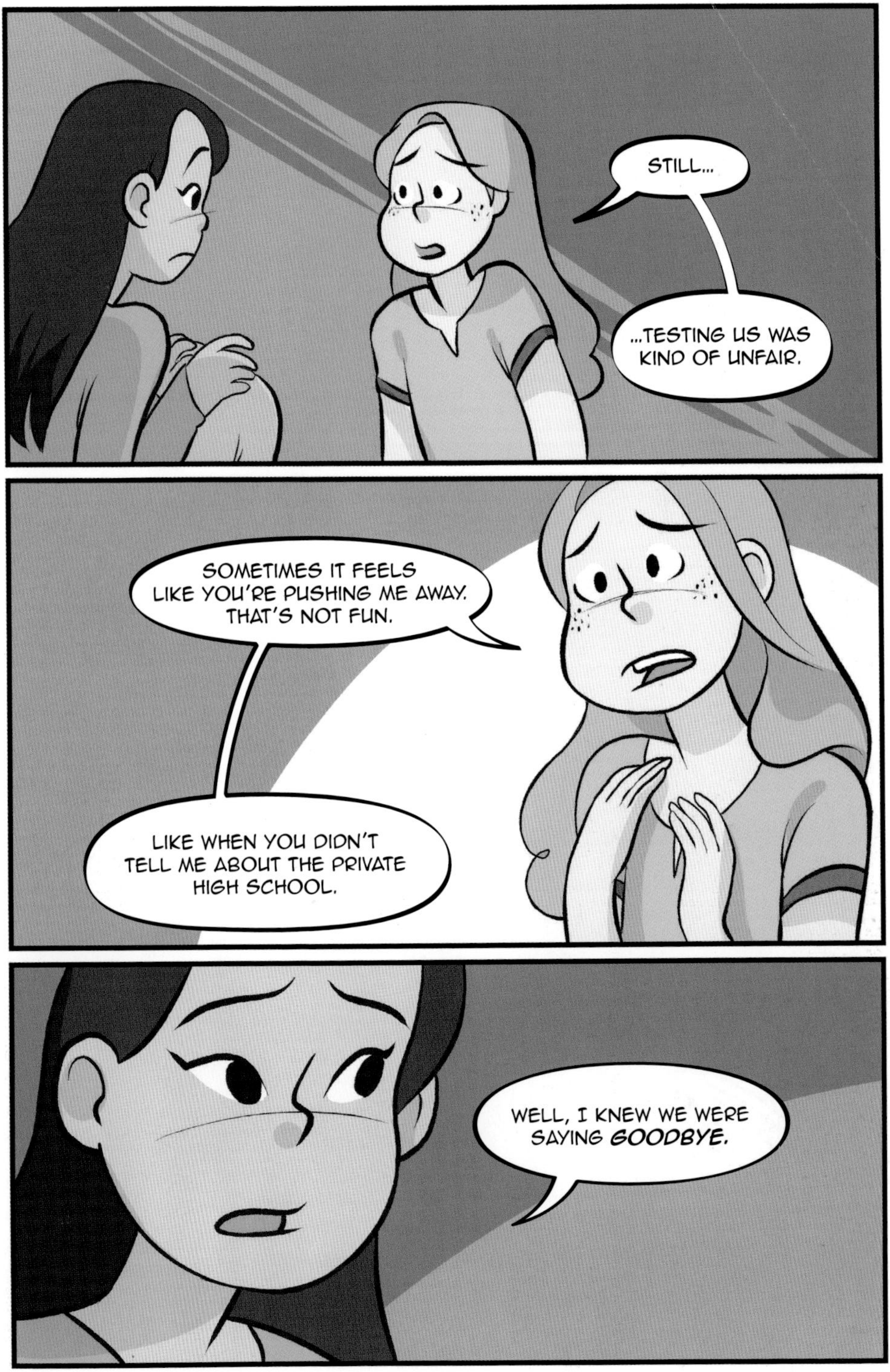
STILL...
...TESTING US WAS KIND OF UNFAIR.
SOMETIMES IT FEELS LIKE YOU'RE PUSHING ME AWAY. THAT'S NOT FUN.
LIKE WHEN YOU DIDN'T TELL ME ABOUT THE PRIVATE HIGH SCHOOL.
WELL, I KNEW WE WERE SAYING ***GOODBYE.***

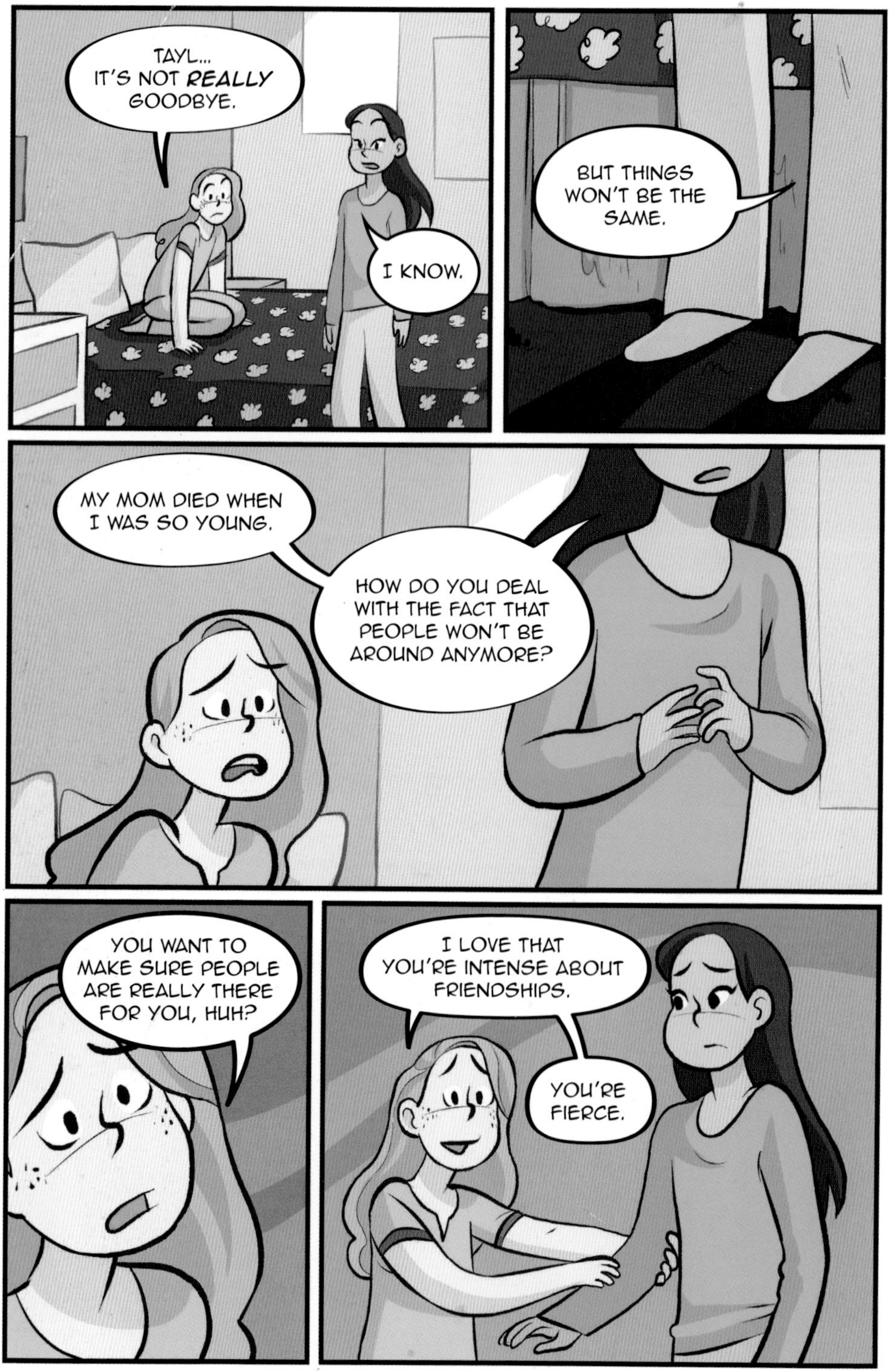
TAYL... IT'S NOT REALLY GOODBYE.
I KNOW.
BUT THINGS WON'T BE THE SAME.
MY MOM DIED WHEN I WAS SO YOUNG.
HOW DO YOU DEAL WITH THE FACT THAT PEOPLE WON'T BE AROUND ANYMORE?
YOU WANT TO MAKE SURE PEOPLE ARE REALLY THERE FOR YOU, HUH?
I LOVE THAT YOU'RE INTENSE ABOUT FRIENDSHIPS.
YOU'RE FIERCE.

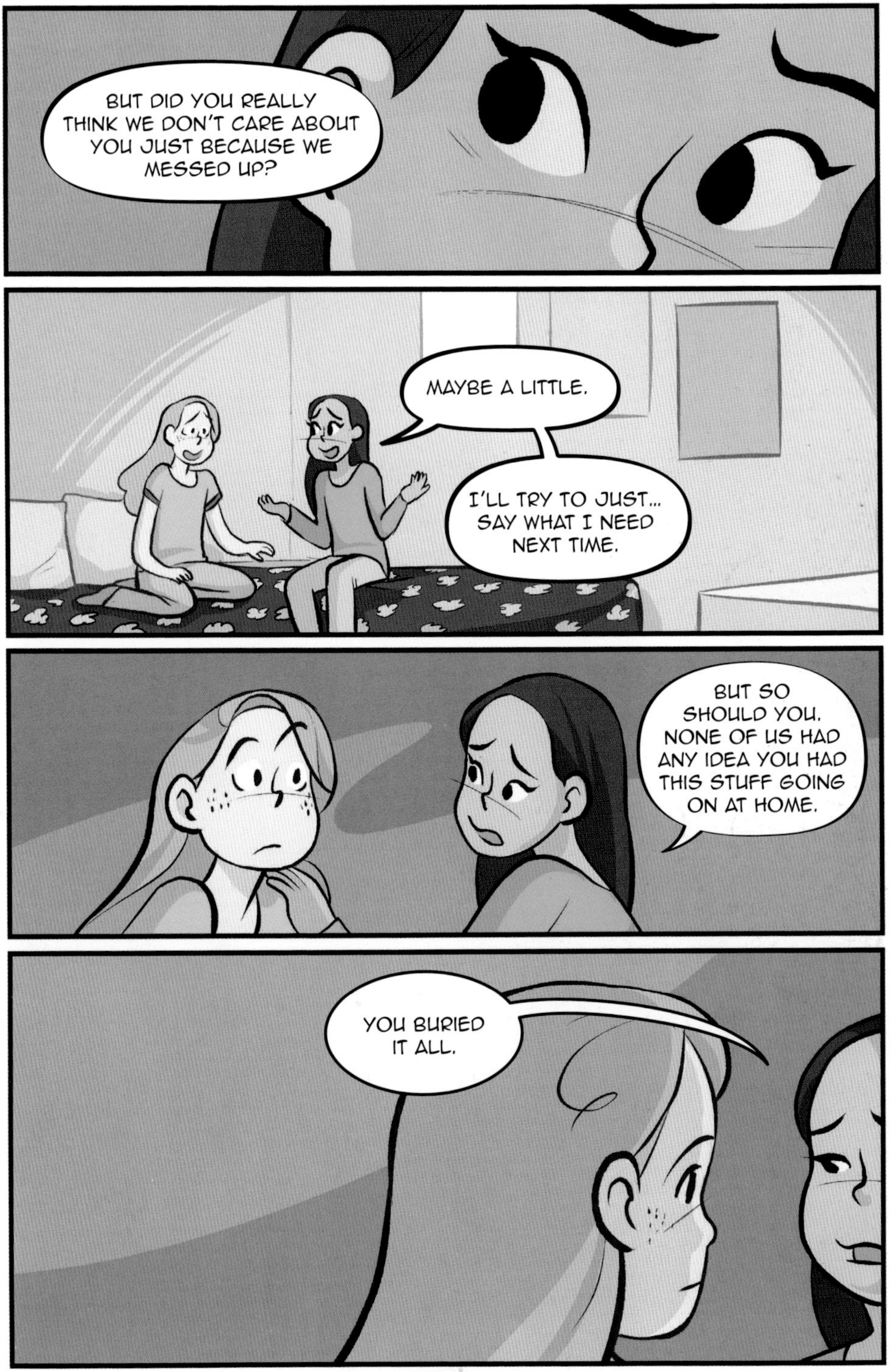
BUT DID YOU REALLY THINK WE DON'T CARE ABOUT YOU JUST BECAUSE WE MESSED UP?
MAYBE A LITTLE.
I'LL TRY TO JUST... SAY WHAT I NEED NEXT TIME.
BUT SO SHOULD YOU. NONE OF US HAD ANY IDEA YOU HAD THIS STUFF GOING ON AT HOME.
YOU BURIED IT ALL.

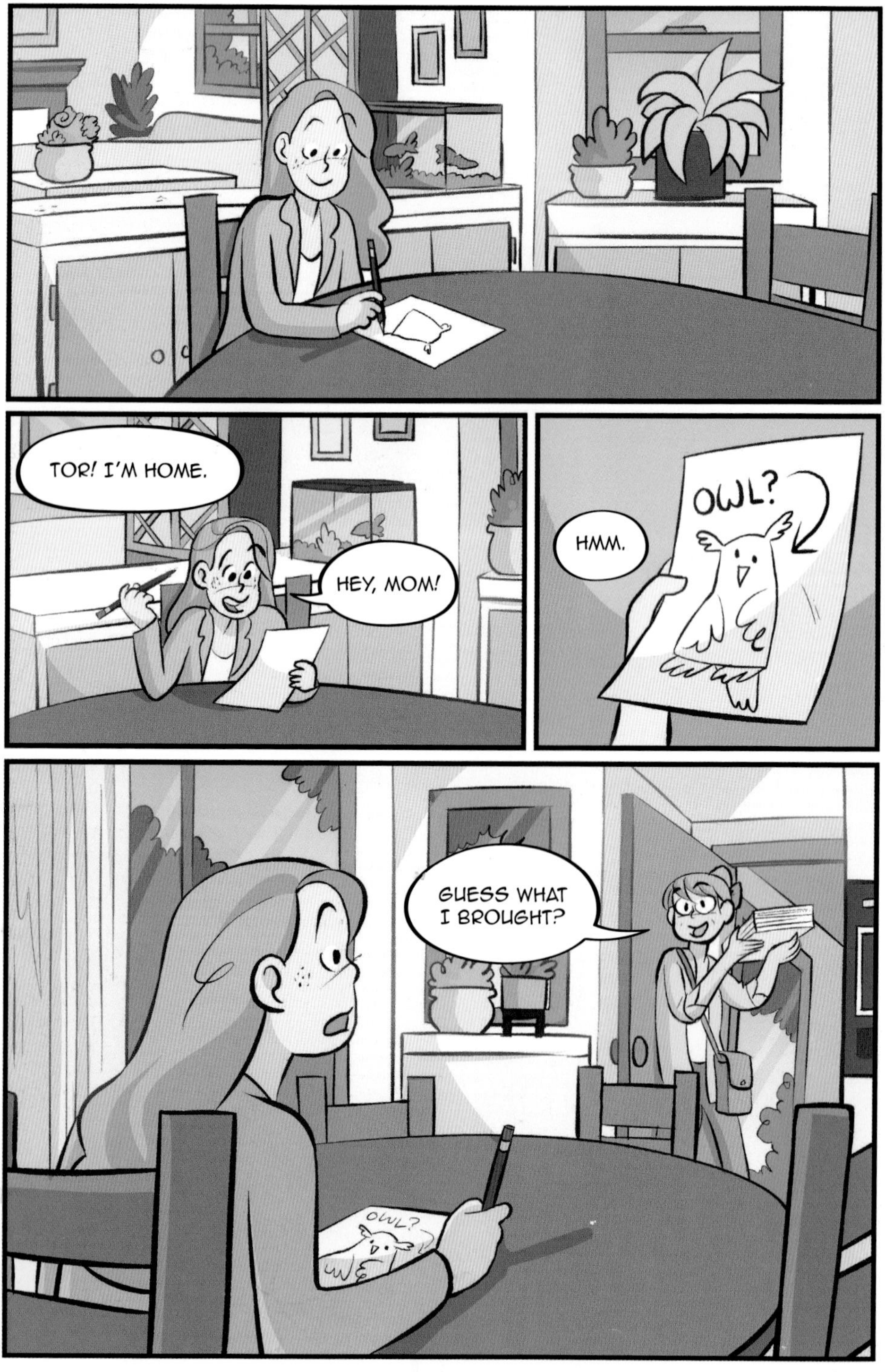
TOR! I'M HOME.
HEY, MOM!
OWL?
HMM.
GUESS WHAT I BROUGHT?
OWL?

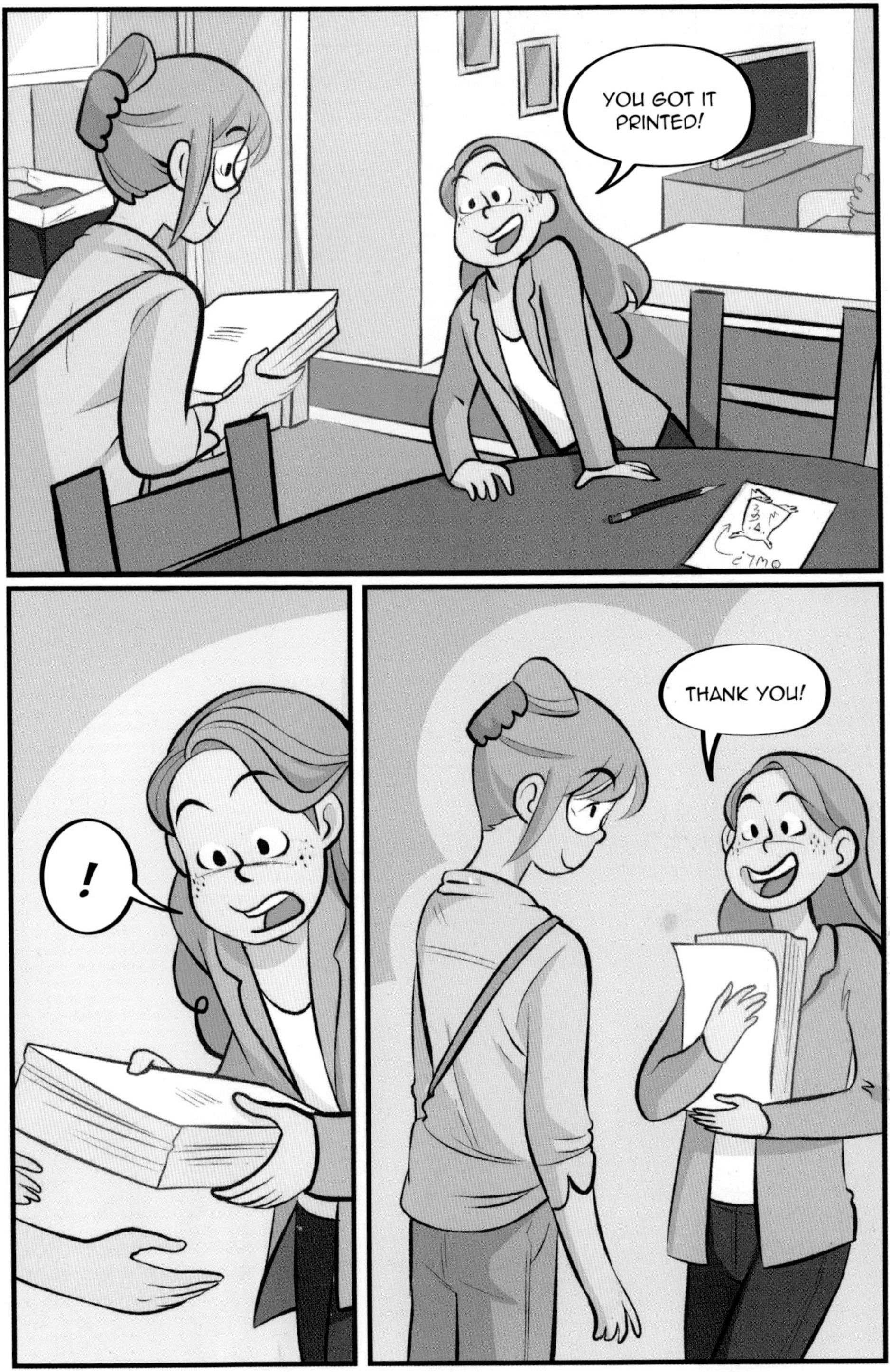
YOU GOT IT PRINTED!
!
THANK YOU!

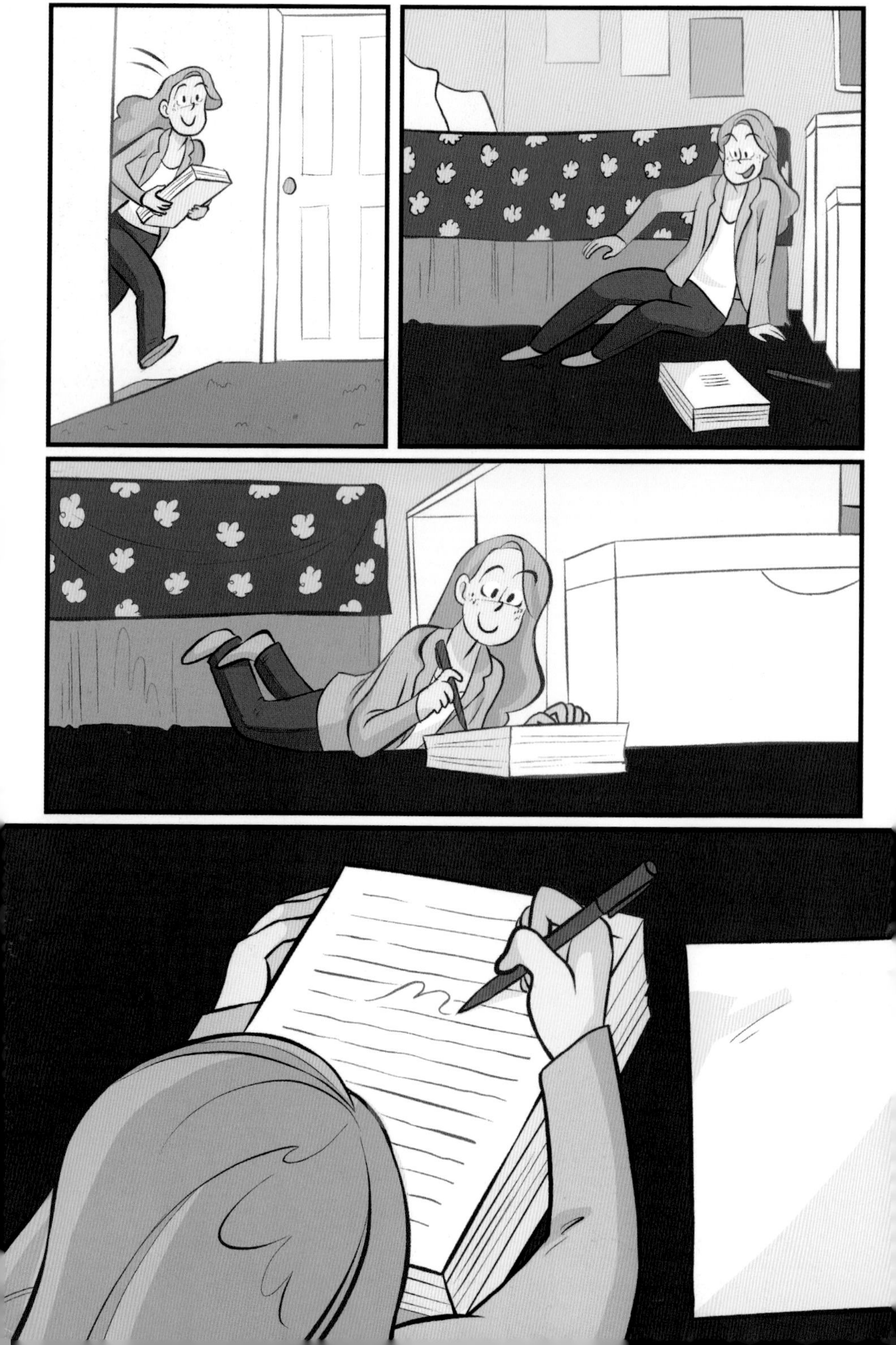

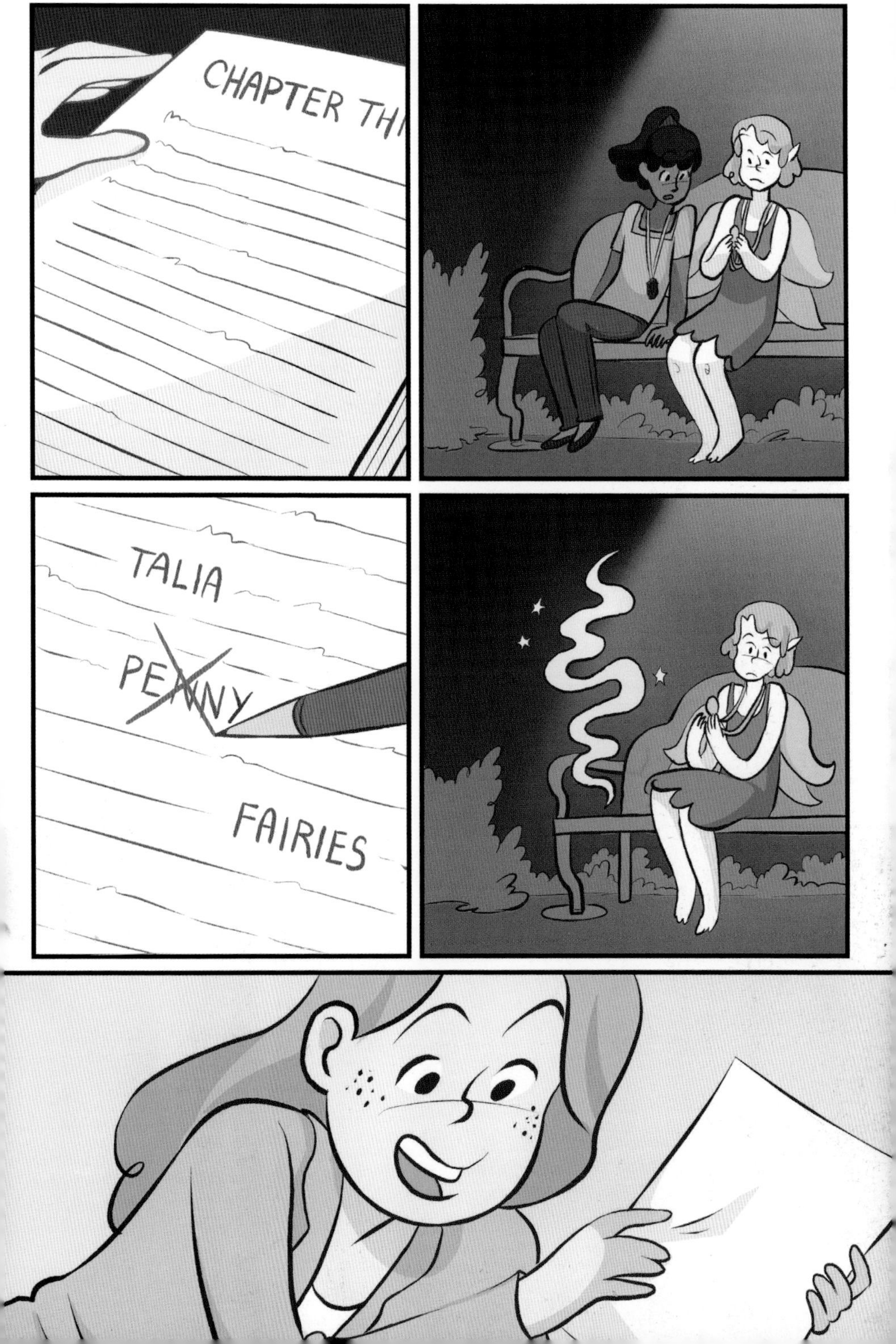

CHAPTER THI
TALIA
PENNY
FAIRIES

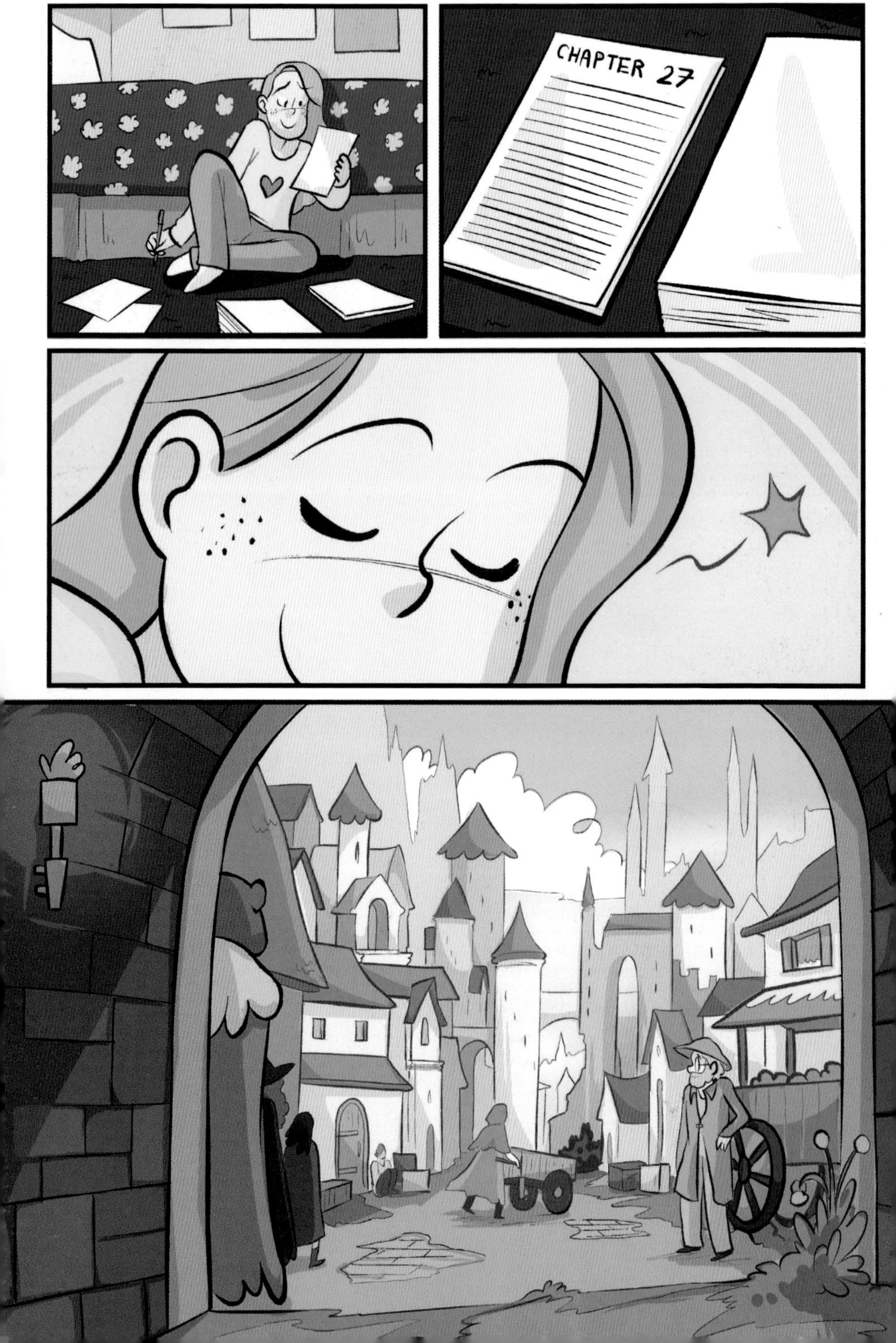
CHAPTER 27

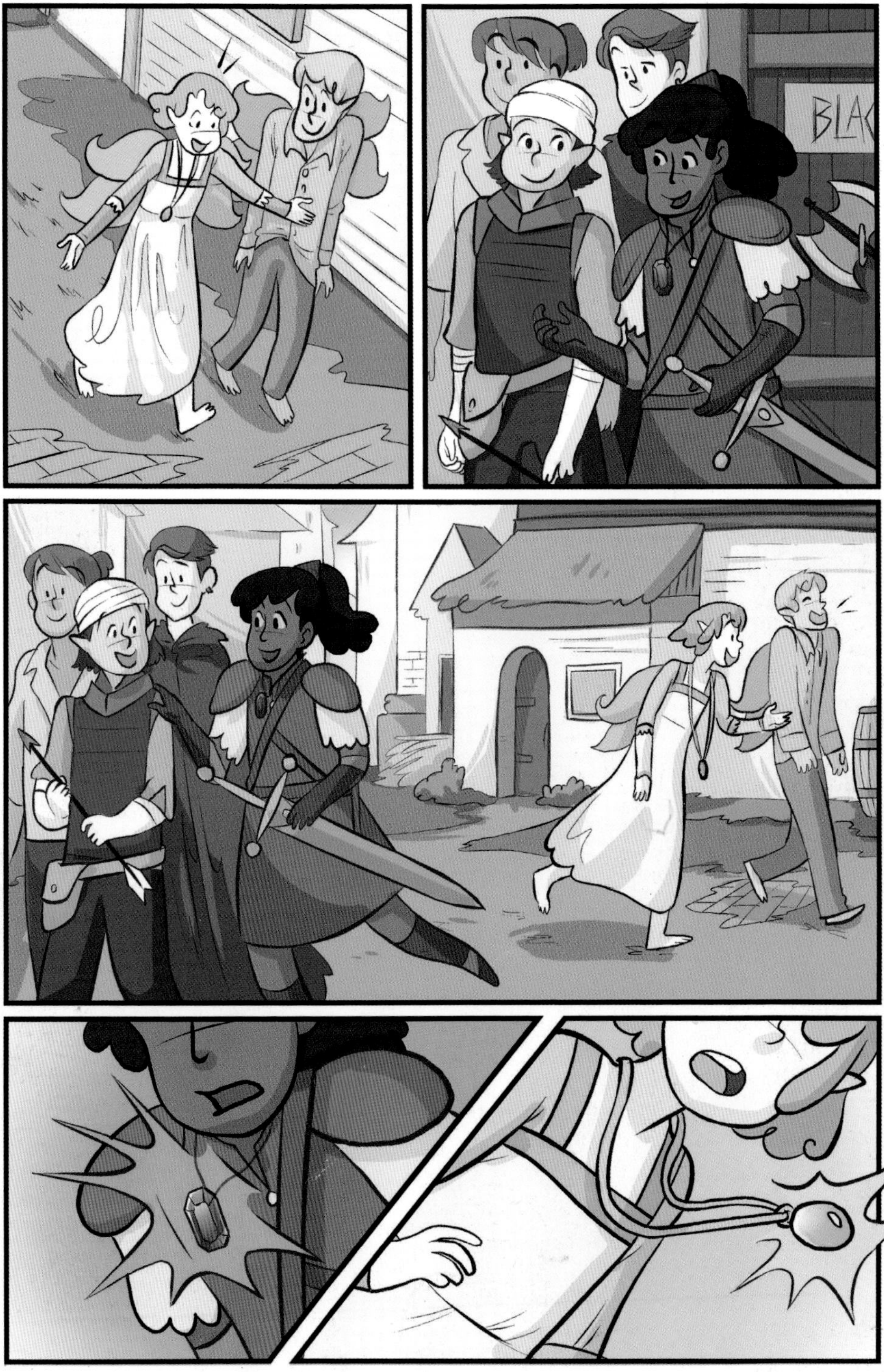
BLAC

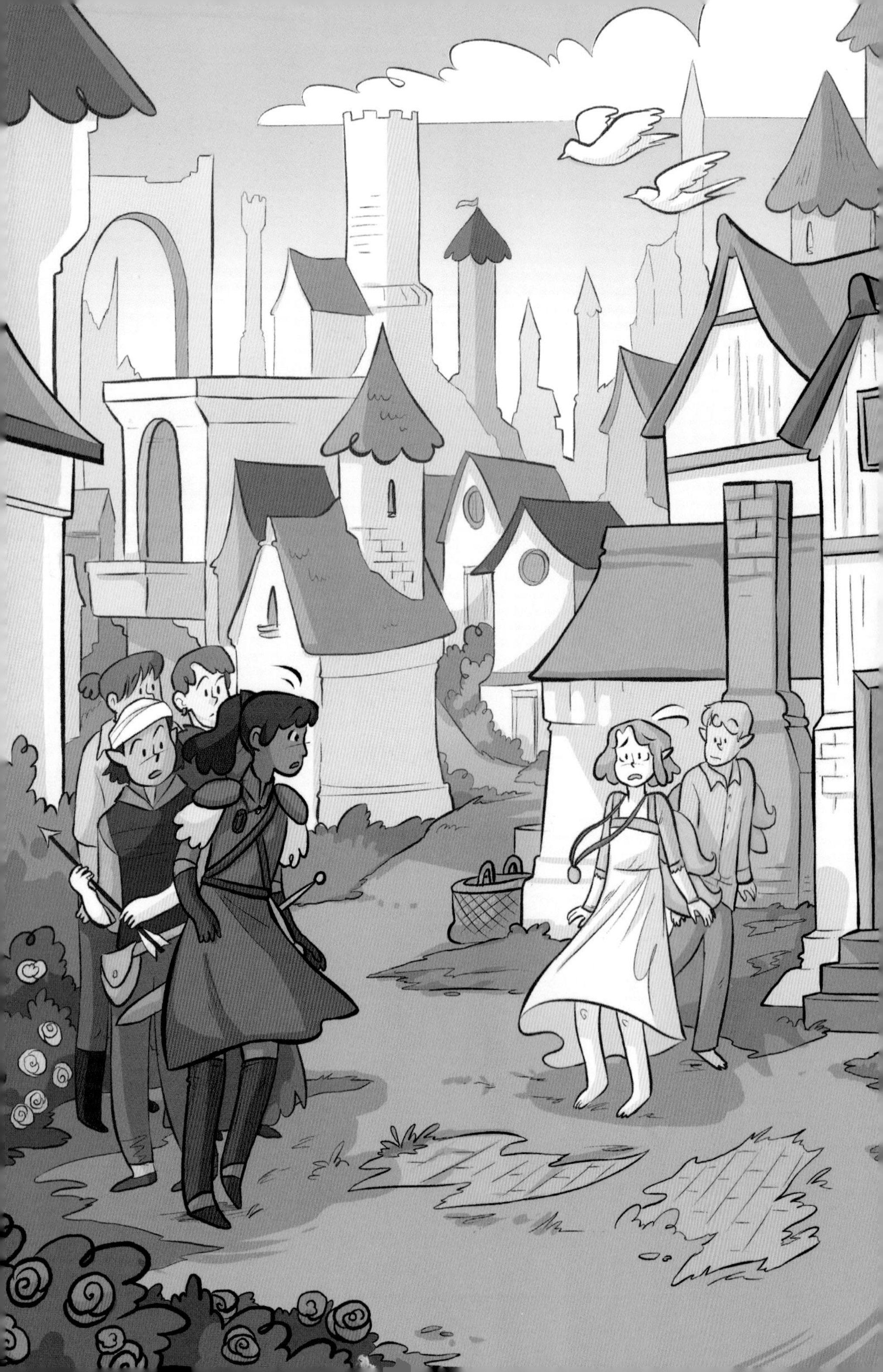

**W**RITING ABOUT YOUR LIFE IS A WILD, FUN, AND SCARY THING TO DO. This is a true story, which means it's a *story*. I tried to be as accurate as possible, but as the narrator, I got to decide how to tell it and which details to include. My family and friends will certainly remember these events differently.

This is a true story, but it's also about things that *aren't* real—what I imagined, hoped for, and wrote. I tried to be honest about what all of it *felt* like, but these events happened fifteen years ago, and I hope you'll forgive any inaccuracies. The only "lie" in these pages is how tidy my bedroom looks. I was more of a "messy artist" type of kid, but I didn't feel like drawing laundry and art supplies strewn across my floor in every panel. I am much tidier as an adult!

There are two events I could not have been present for but became family legends: the times my dad and Ryan broke holes in the walls of my mom's first house. I drew those how I *imagine* they must have happened. I remember Ryan trying to patch those holes with a can of plaster. I remember the blank sheet of paper he pinned over the hole and the outdated calendar covering my dad's footprint by the computer. What seemed like a big deal became trivial in the end. That house is gone now, so what do those holes matter? Sometimes the best way to erase a hole is to tear down the wall. Sometimes that's how you move forward.

Speaking of Ryan, I'd like to take a moment to brag about him: Ryan is one of the most supportive people about my art, and I love him very much. Growing up, we had a lot of reasons to dislike each other, but eventually we became friends. Now we play board games and talk about fantasy books. He's the coolest big brother!

I love my siblings, parents, and friends, and it's been a privilege to spend the past year drawing these stories about us. Since stories center on conflicts, a memoir tends to highlight the complexities and drama of personal relationships, skipping over most of the quiet, happy moments (since they would simply be less entertaining to read). A single book, no matter how thick, can't begin to capture a whole messy, complicated life or the nuances of a fractured family. Please think of this story as a single sentence in an even larger book. By the time I got the whole comic down on paper, I felt removed from my own story, as if I'd drawn someone else's life. Memory is funny like that; it changes all the time based on your new perceptions. Turning your childhood into a pile of cartoons changes how you remember it. So does growing up!

# CHARACTER DESIGN

To design the characters, I thought about what makes each of these people distinctive.

It was hardest to design Emily because she and I look so similar in real life! When we were teenagers, my friends would get us mixed up sometimes. My face is rounder (in the art and real life!), and I put her hair up, so you can't see that we have matching cowlicks. She resembles our dad, so I gave them both short tufts of hair on one side of their faces.

My dad's design came to me very quickly. I think he's secretly always been a cartoon.

I considered giving Ryan longer curls, since he wore his hair long in high school, but I ended up feeling like it looked too "flat" or exaggerated in this style of cartooning.

Taylor's hair was hard to get right because I wanted it to have some nice curves and movement but still look straight and glossy.

DAD & JANE

PENNY + TALIA

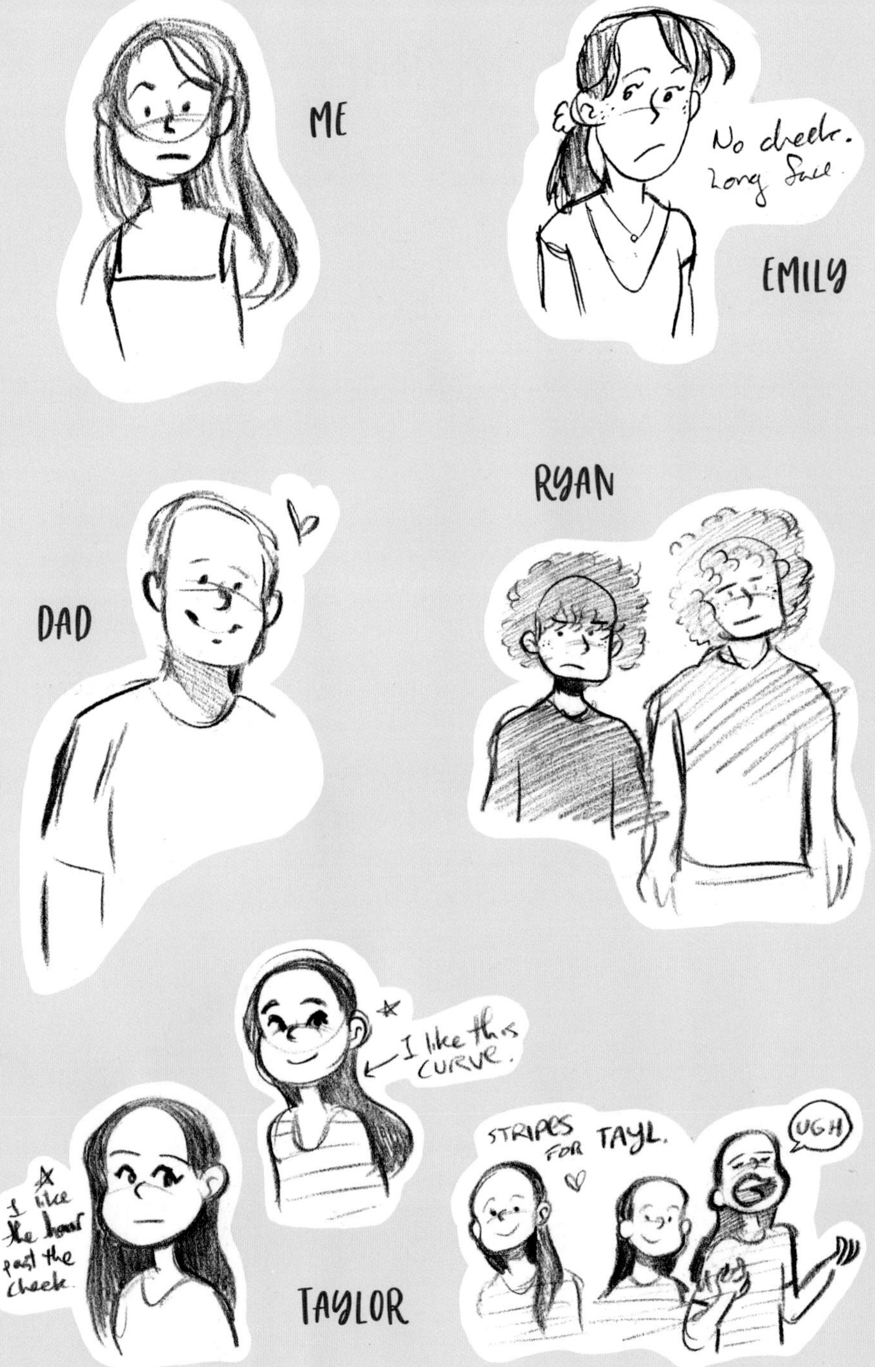

ME
No cheek. Long face.
EMILY
RYAN
DAD
I like this curve.
I like the hair past the cheek
TAYLOR
STRIPES FOR TAYL.
UGH

# MATERIALS

When I first start designing a character, I draw them again and again very quickly. I take what I like in each sketch and apply it to the next one while also trying new things until I land on a design that feels right. Little, tiny features—like the size of a character's ears and how thick their eyebrows are—can change a character design so much!

At first, I used a pad of newsprint paper and a tool called a china marker to draw the characters over and over and over, not spending too long on each sketch. China markers are also called grease pencils, apparently. I'm not sure which name is more common. Professors at the Savannah College of Art and Design—where I went to college—called them china markers because you can use them to write on hard, nonporous materials like porcelain…or china!

China markers aren't typical "markers." They're waxy like crayons, but very smooth and good for gesture drawing—quick sketches that capture (and often exaggerate) the energy of a pose or expression. I like these markers because, unlike pencils, they don't smudge much, and you can't erase; you have to keep moving forward and try again!

I also used ballpoint or felt-tip pens to do some messy, flowy sketches. Switching tools gives you a new kind of line quality, so it can help you notice different things about your designs and make you really think about the choices you're making while you draw. I love to doodle in pen.

Then, once I had a better idea of what the characters would look like, I did some tighter drawings in pencil and took notes about what was working in the designs. I also went "shopping" for them; I dressed them up in clothes they'd wear.

Finally, I did some clean digital drawings of the characters with a focus on each one's shape and color language.

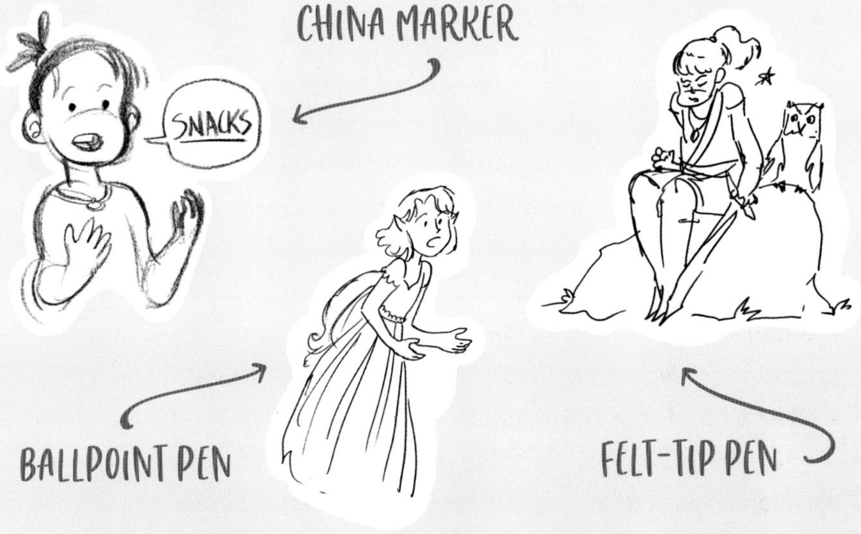
CHINA MARKER
SNACKS
BALLPOINT PEN
FELT-TIP PEN

Giving each character a basic shape gave me something to fall back on when I wasn't sure why they didn't look quite right in a panel. If Penny looked off, I tried to incorporate isosceles triangles, and if Ryan looked off, I tried to make his head shape and pose look more like trapezoids.

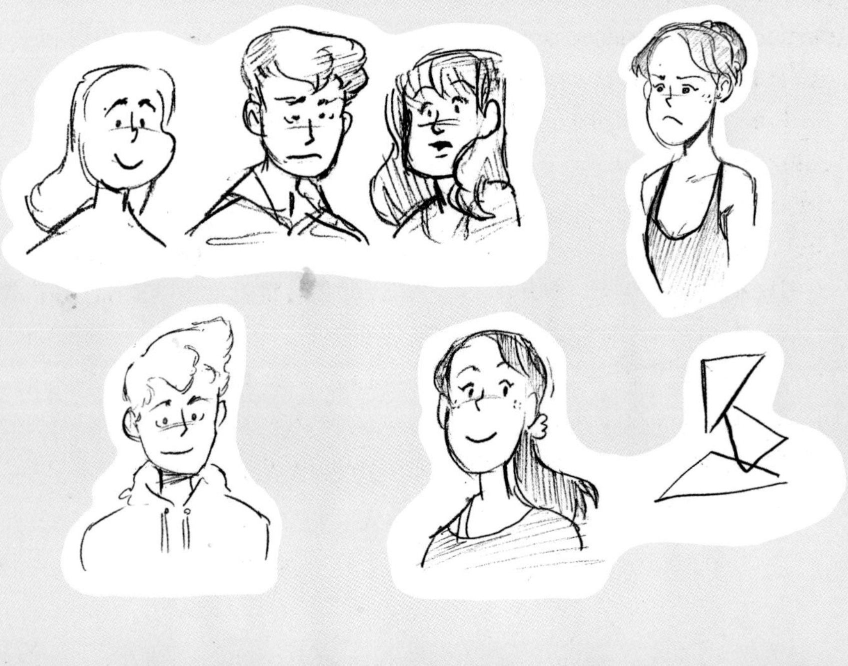

# PAGE PROCESS

Each page went through four phases: roughs, pencils, inks, and colors.

Roughs are quick, messy layouts. I try not to take more than 20-30 minutes roughing out a page, unless there's going to be an intricate background and I want to use reference photos.

My roughs are pretty detailed compared to what many artists do! Some comic artists do a "thumbnail" stage before the roughs that's even messier and squigglier, using stick figures to show where the characters are. Whatever works! I feel like my characters' body language and expressions are so important to the storytelling that I really need to see them during this stage.

Pencils are more refined than roughs, and inks are the final line art. Even though they're called "pencils" and "inks," I drew most of them digitally on my laptop, using a Wacom Intuos Pro medium drawing tablet and Clip Studio Paint Pro. The amazing thing about comics, though, is that you don't need special tools. You can draw comics with just paper and pencil, crayons or sidewalk chalk, or sticky notes. I used to draw comics on lined notebook paper on my music stand in band class!

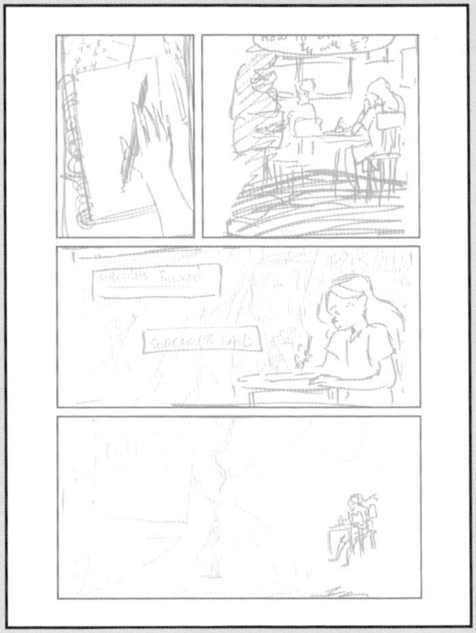

ROUGHS

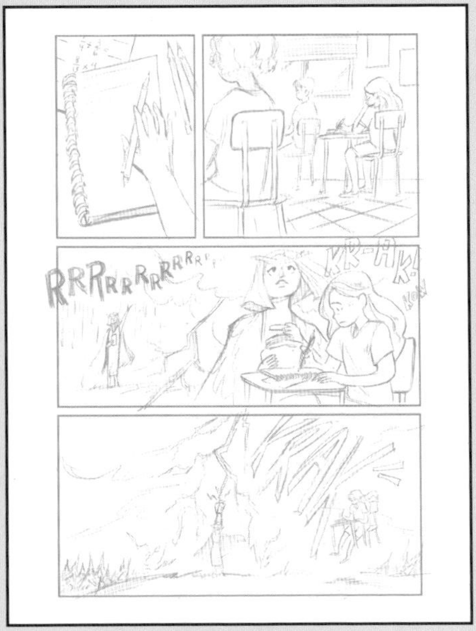
KR-AK!
KOW
KRAK

PENCILS

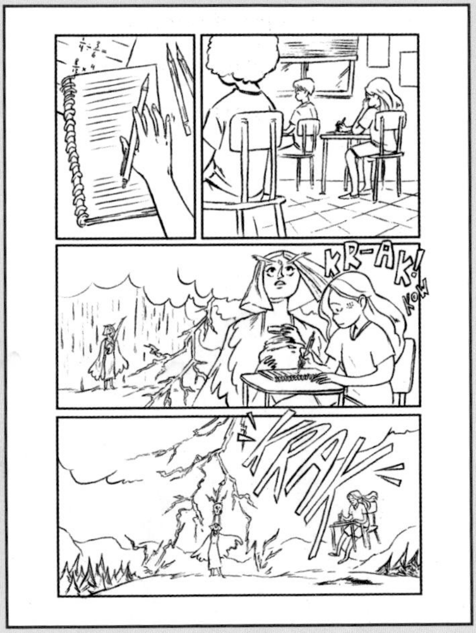
KR-AK!
KOW
KRAK

INKS

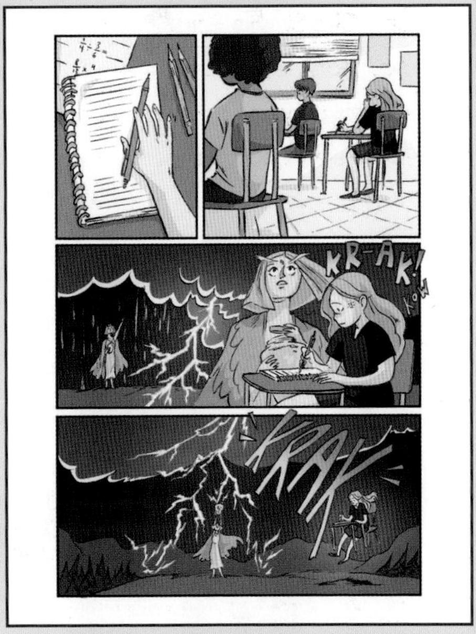
KR-AK!
KOW
KRAK

COLORS

# ACKNOWLEDGMENTS

This book simply wouldn't exist without my agent, Brent Taylor. Thank you for pushing me to write this memoir when I was tangled up in a few different story ideas. Thank you for your masterful pep talks and tireless dedication. You saw the spark in my messy first draft of *Just Pretend* and helped me see it, too. Sometimes you see the statue inside the marble before I've even started carving, like only the very best agents can.

Thank you to Andrea Colvin, my magnificent, brilliant editor, for helping me see straight into the heart of my own book. I feel lucky every day that you, specifically, acquired *Just Pretend*.

Thank you to the entire team at LBYR and to the colorists and letterers who lent their expertise to this comic and made it shine. Putting together a book like this takes a tremendous amount of work, and the fingerprints of so many people hide all over these pages.

Thank you to the many teachers who impacted me, among them Brad Nicklas, Ellen Jacko, Brian Ralph, John Larison, and Kit Seaton.

Many hugs to my critique partners and friends: Chelsea Crane, Hannah Golden, Gabrielle Stern, Ragon Dickard, Zach Turcich, Jeana Coppa, Carly Racklin, Sydnie Long, Rachel Lynn Solomon, Alec Marsh, and Karin de Weille.

A special thank you to Kel Lyle, my amazing friend and critique partner who patiently reads every scrap of writing I push at her (and who's always down to watch cartoons), and to Aimee Meester, a kindred spirit, for being my virtual coworker and Dungeon Master while I drew this book. I'm proud of you, too.

Thanks to Roseanne Wells, my mentor while I queried agents and worked on the proposal for *Just Pretend*, and to Jennifer De Chiara for the apprenticeship that followed. I have learned so much from both of you and the whole team at JDLA about the world of books and what makes good writing.

I owe enormous thanks to my friends and family members who encouraged me to tell this story. Thank you to my sister, one of the very first people I told when I decided to write a memoir, and to my dad, who knew I was a writer before I did.

Although I had many wonderful friends in middle school, this story—about writing and family—kept circling back to my friendship with Taylor. Thank you, Tayl, for being my first writing partner and for reminiscing with me for hours while I collected memories for this book. Here's to twenty more years of friendship and many more after that.

**TORI SHARP** is a Seattle-based author-illustrator and a swing and blues dancer with a BFA in sequential art from SCAD. You can find her online at noveltori.com and on Twitter @noveltori. This is her debut graphic novel.